DIARY BY E.B.B.

ELIZABETH BARRETT BARRETT
Oil attributed to Eliza Cliffe

"She has finished my picture, which, tho' it is not the *picture of me,* does her infinite credit."
Entry of 20 August 1831, p. 95

Diary by E.B.B.

The Unpublished Diary

of Elizabeth Barrett Barrett, 1831-1832

Edited with an Introduction and Notes by

PHILIP KELLEY

and

RONALD HUDSON

Including Psychoanalytical Observations by

ROBERT COLES, M.D.

Ohio University Press

Athens, Ohio

1969

Set by Browning Editorial Services, New York, N.Y.
Printed and bound by Kingsport Press, Inc., Kingsport, Tenn.

"A man's life is dyed the colour of his imagination."

M. Aurelius Antoninus

CONTENTS

Preface   xi

Introduction   xv

Editorial Approach and Apparatus

     Editorial Approach   xxvi

     Editorial Apparatus   xxx

Description and Provenance of the Manuscript

     Description   xxxiii

     Provenance   xxxiv

The Hope End Household   xxxv

"Psychoanalytical Observations on Elizabeth Barrett Barrett's Diary," by Robert Coles, M.D.   xxxix

Cue Titles   xlvi

Diary by E.B.B.   1

Textual Notes

     Manuscript Alterations   243

     Irregular Spellings   265

Appendix I: Letters   273

Appendix II: Poems   311

Appendix III: Hope End Sale Catalogue   323

Index   341

ILLUSTRATIONS

Elizabeth Barrett Barrett, 1831
   Oil attributed to Eliza Cliffe. Courtesy of the late
   Edward S. and Mrs. Moulton-Barrett   *frontispiece*
Hope End, 1831
   Water-colour by Arabella Barrett. Courtesy of
   Mrs. Violet M. Altham   *facing p.* xlviii
Facsimile of the Entry of 4 June 1831
   Courtesy of The Berg Collection   1
Ruby Cottage
   Date and artist unknown. Courtesy of Malvern Pub-
   lic Library   16
Turnpike on the Road to Ledbury
   Date and artist unknown. Courtesy of Malvern Pub-
   lic Library   16
View Taken from the Other Side of the Alpine Bridge,
   25 June 1831. Pencil sketch by Henrietta Barrett.
   Courtesy of Mrs. Violet M. Altham   17
Summer Cottage, 1831
   Pencil sketch by Henrietta Barrett. Courtesy of
   Mrs. Violet M. Altham   112
From the School Room Window, 1831
   Pencil sketch by Henrietta Barrett. Courtesy of
   Mrs. Violet M. Altham   113
View of the Upper Pond, 1831
   Pencil sketch by Henrietta Barrett. Courtesy of
   Mrs. Violet M. Altham   128
Hope End
   Two water-colours from Philip Ballard's sketch-book.
   Courtesy of Stephen Ballard, Esq.   129
New Year Card, 1827
   Ink sketch by Eliza Cliffe. Courtesy of The Berg
   Collection   200
Facsimile of the Entry of 8 January 1832
   Courtesy of The Berg Collection   201

MAPS

The Environs of Hope End, 1831
    Redrawn from the Ordnance Survey   *facing p.* 232
Plan of the Hope End Estate, 1831
    Courtesy of Stephen Ballard, Esq.   335

PREFACE

On 29 June 1961, exactly one hundred years after the death of Elizabeth Barrett Browning, I stood with Mr. and Mrs. Kenneth A. Moulton-Barrett in a dark, panelled solicitor's office in St. James's, London. On a table before us was a black deal coach-box, encrusted with a multiplicity of coloured wax seals. The box, containing Moulton-Barrett family papers that had been collected for nearly two centuries, was from the estate of Mr. Moulton-Barrett's father, the late Lt.-Col. Harry Peyton Moulton-Barrett—a nephew of the poetess. The exact nature of the papers was unknown.

For some time I had been seeking, for inclusion in a projected edition of the correspondence of the Brownings, the letters that E.B.B. had written to her father, advancing her reasons for her marriage, and seeking his forgiveness. I had seen evidence, in other family papers, that these letters had been sent to Lt.-Col. Moulton-Barrett in February 1924—and as I stood to one side, while the seals on the box were being broken, I was hoping that my search had at last ended. With formalities done, I made a cursory search of the box and was disappointed to find that these eagerly-sought letters were not in it.[1] However, my disappointment was lessened by the appearance of a manuscript, bound in a paper wrapper and annotated in the hand of Robert Browning—"Diary by E.B.B."; thus it is he who provides the title for this book.

Mr. Moulton-Barrett withdrew the collection from the solicitor's care and entrusted the box to me so that I could study its contents at leisure. For the next three months I was absorbed in compiling a checklist of the

1. To date, all efforts to locate these letters have resulted in failure. The box revealed an inventory, in the hand of Lt.-Col. Moulton-Barrett, with the cryptic entry: "2. Desk containing (destroyed) letters together with several sketches and obituary notice of EBB." There can be little doubt that these were the letters that E.B.B. wrote to her father. A desk, incorporating in its structure a concealed drawer, and believed by the family to be the one referred to, was sold at public auction in October 1945. Unfortunately, the transaction was done by proxy, without a search of the contents. The purchaser, a furniture dealer, cannot recall to whom it was resold.

The early history of the letters is of interest. In 1851, during the Brownings' first visit to England after their marriage, Robert wrote to Edward Moulton-Barrett in the hope of a reconciliation. He received in reply "a very violent and unsparing letter", and two packets enclosing E.B.B.'s letters, ". . . nine or ten of them." When "Pen" Browning died in 1912, his wife, Fannie, illegally took possession of these letters. In May 1913, she displayed them to Thomas J. Wise, and in his subsequent offer to purchase them, he mentioned ". . . 8 tiny letters, all but one still unopened. The one I saw was painful in the extreme." In June of the same year, the Moulton-Barretts, heirs

collection,[1] and in making and collating an initial transcript of the Diary, with the assistance of Ronald Hudson, who later agreed to become my co-editor.

But for this one example, E.B.B. is not known to have attempted to write a record of her daily life in diary form.[2] Originally the manuscript probably encompassed the twelve-month period June 1831 to the end of May 1832, but it was shortened appreciably when approximately sixty days were excised and presumably destroyed. Still, nearly 81,000 words remain that are unpremeditated, spontaneous expressions of E.B.B.'s thoughts and feelings at the moment of writing, set down with perfect candour and sincerity, in a rapid style that sparkles from time to time with wit and lucidity.

E.B.B.'s Diary is an invaluable and fascinating document, allowing us an unusual view of English country life in the early nineteenth century, and providing us with a wealth of biographical detail. She asks in it ". . . how could I write a diary without throwing down upon paper my thoughts, all my thoughts—the thoughts of my heart as well as of my head?" Consequently, here are revealed, more freely than anywhere else, her frustrations, conflicts, hopes and fears, and her relationship with her family and their social circle. The somewhat obsessive quality of her friendship with Hugh Stuart Boyd becomes apparent, in a way that augments and amplifies her published letters to him; the considerable range of her reading and study is underlined by comment and quotation; and the interest in politics, which was to become so marked in her later life, is clearly shown.

Although she wrote "My diary is not meant to be read by any person except myself," I think we have no need to feel guilt in forcing her to pay the price of literary fame by allowing us to share the privilege, granted by E.B.B. only to her sister Arabella, of being "let behind the scenes."

I would not be writing this Preface were it not for the deep and lasting debt I owe to Mrs. Mary M. Armstrong, co-founder and late director of

---

to their cousin's estate, requested the letters' return. They were placed in the care of a London solicitor until 1924, when by mutual family consent they were sent to Lt.-Col. Moulton-Barrett.

His acknowledgment of receipt, dated 20 February, stated: "The letters have been burned by me in the presence of a witness"—but why did he then trouble to list the "(destroyed) letters" in his inventory? Also his parlour-maid, in conversation with me, vividly recreated a scene. "One day I was serving the Colonel his soup, when a registered letter arrived. He opened the letter—so very angry he became. I remember his exclaiming, 'He cannot use them for his play! I shall tell him that they have been burnt!!!" Throughout his life, especially after being incensed by Besier's play *The Barretts of Wimpole Street*, Lt.-Col. Moulton-Barrett continued to perpetuate the story of their destruction. If he did eventually destroy them, he left no record.

1. Nearly 900 items were listed. The collection, of major Barrett Browning importance, is now in the Berg Collection, fully catalogued.

2. An early pocket diary for 1823 and various journals are in existence, but none of these can be classified as diaries in the ordinary sense.

the Armstrong Browning Library of Baylor University; she fostered and encouraged my interest in the Brownings, and I was inspired by the example of her energy and determination.

I owe a debt I cannot express in words to my mother, Mrs. Velma Prince Kelley, and to my brothers, Drs. W. D. and W. R. Kelley, for their continual encouragement, and for their ready and generous support.

Next I must attempt to record my great indebtedness to Edward R. Moulton-Barrett, Esq., who allowed me unrestricted access to family papers in his possession. It was very largely through his intervention that I met other members of his family, the late Lt.-Col. Edward F. Moulton-Barrett, the late Gp.-Capt. Edward S. Moulton-Barrett and Mrs. E. S. Moulton-Barrett, Mr. and Mrs. Kenneth A. Moulton-Barrett, Col. and Mrs. Ronald A. Moulton-Barrett, Miss Myrtle Moulton-Barrett, Mrs. Violet M. Altham, Miss Mary Altham, and the late Harry S. Altham, Esq. All these received me kindly, and gave me access to material in their possession; I am grateful for all their help and interest.

To Kenneth A. Moulton-Barrett and the late Edward S. Moulton-Barrett I owe much gratitude for their willingness to make the manuscript of the Diary available for my initial study and for their innumerable displays of hospitality, encouragement and friendship.

I wish to record my gratitude to the John Simon Guggenheim Memorial Foundation, whose award of a Fellowship enabled me to conduct my Browning research in England during 1962-63; to the Philosophical Society of America, whose grant enabled me to record source material by photo-duplication; to the late Sir John Murray, Gordon N. Ray, Cecil Y. Lang, Park Honan and the late John D. Gordan for their personal encouragement of my work on the Brownings; and to Marjorie M. Kelley, for assistance in the first phase of research.

Many others contributed in large or small degree to this book; space forbids more than a formal admission of gratitude and indebtedness. Ronald Hudson associates with me in offering special thanks to Miss Phyllis G. Mann of West Malvern, for her untiring response to many queries about local details and families—this book owes much to her enthusiasm and her deep interest in local history and genealogy. We also wish to acknowledge the many kindnesses of Mrs. Elizabeth Lloyd, particularly for permission to view Barton Court, and for information relating to the Bright and Peyton families. We also thank the Hon. Mrs. Hervey-Bathurst for permission to view Eastnor Castle, and for facts about the Somers-Cocks family; Lady Anne Montagu (then Lady Anne Holland-Martin) for permission to view Old Colwall, and for facts about the Martin family; Mr. and Mrs. Godfrey Harris for their permission to examine The Ruby (Ruby Cottage); Stephen

Diary by E.B.B.

Ballard, Esq., present owner of Hope End, for guiding us over the estate, and for details relating to it; Lord Biddulph, for directing our attention to John Biddulph's diaries; Miss Dorothy Hewlett, for reading the first transcript of the Diary, and for making valuable suggestions; Mr. N. H. Parker, Librarian of Malvern Public Library, for information about Miss Steers; Mr. A. J. D. Stonebridge and Mrs. Ann Saunders of the St. Marylebone Public Library, and Mr. J. F. W. Sherwood, Librarian of Hereford City Library, for considerable assistance with research material; Miss Hannah D. French, Research Librarian of Wellesley College, for facilitating our study of letters and books in the Wellesley collection; Neville Rogers, Professor Robert W. Carrubba, and the Rt. Hon. Quintin Hogg for valued assistance in identifying and translating some of the Greek and Latin; and particularly to the staff of the Reading Room of the British Museum, and to Dr. Lola L. Szladits of the Berg Collection of the New York Public Library, for their unvarying patience and helpfulness.

The manuscript of the Diary now rests in the Henry W. and Albert A. Berg Collection of the New York Public Library, and acknowledgment is given to the Trustees of the N.Y.P.L. for granting us unrestricted access to it.   We also record our debt to Wellesley College Library, the Henry E. Huntington Library, the Pierpont Morgan Library, and Stephen Ballard, Esq., for permission to draw on material in their collections; to the Trustees of the University of Illinois for permission to quote passages from *Letters of the Brownings to George Barrett*; to Edward R. Moulton-Barrett, Esq., Col. Ronald A. Moulton-Barrett, Miss Myrtle Moulton-Barrett, Mrs. Violet M. Altham and Richard J. L. Altham, Esq., for permission to quote from hitherto unpublished letters of E.B.B.

A final word of thanks and praise is due to Clifford E. Horton, who set the major part of this book, and coped cheerfully with a difficult format.

Permission to print the Diary of Elizabeth Barrett Barrett and other Browning copyright material has been granted by John Grey Murray, Esq., to whom grateful acknowledgment is made.

New York, December 1968   Philip Kelley

[xiv]

INTRODUCTION

Early in 1809, the young Edward Moulton-Barrett was busy negotiating the purchase of the Hope End estate in Herefordshire, three miles from the prosperous market town of Ledbury. On 12 May of that year, his wife Mary wrote to her mother:

> . . . With respect to Hope-End[1] we are just as when I last wrote— They have not agreed in the price—tho' the treaty is still on foot— and I still think will end to Edwards wishes he is delighted with the place— There are deer in the Park, & it is surrounded with fine hills covered with *wood*— A Stream runs through it—forming a Cascade— Nothing in short *Ever was* so picturesque & beautiful— there are 475 Acres— £27.<u>000</u> asked—Including house, *furniture, (which is old)* as it stands— Edward offers £24,000— I think they may meet half way, tho' it is at present the plan to *stand firm*— . . .[2]

An early letter written to E.B.B. by her father makes clear that the negotiations were still proceeding in September.[3] Neither the exact date of the sale, nor the final price paid, is known, but within a few months Edward (then twenty-four) was installed at Hope End with his wife (then twenty-eight) and their three children, E.B.B. (three), Edward (two) and Henrietta (not yet one). The wealthy young squire entered into ownership with enthusiasm, and at once set about enlarging and altering the house, allowing full rein to his far from conservative architectural notions.[4] Considerable inconvenience must have been endured, because as late as 1814 work was still in hand. On 3 March of that year, Mary Moulton-Barrett reported to her mother:

> . . . we have not any room but *this* to dine & sit in the library being painted. Some of the brass ballustrades are put up, & the Elegance of the hall, really reminds one of the Arabian nights tales. *I* think

---

1. "Hope" here meaning "a closed valley."

2. Unpublished letter; Collection of Edward R. Moulton-Barrett, Esq.

3. Unpublished letter to "My dear Puss" dated [5 September 1809]; Collection of Arthur A. Houghton, Jr.

4. The existing house, "a brick-built box with chimneys at the four corners, was built by Henry Lambert, out of money accumulated from the now unfamiliar craft of a dish turner" ("Elizabeth Barrett and Hope End," by Alfred Watkins, *Transactions of the Woolhope Naturalists' Field Club, 1924-1926*, Hereford, 1928).

it is beautiful & unique—— The Drawing Rooms, now, are the only
part of the house that exhibits *brick* walls *interior*. . . .[1]

By the following year, work seems to have been completed, because on
19 February 1815 Mary told her mother of a dinner party:

. . . there is no parallel for this Event in the records of Hope End for
the last 4 Years.   Lord Soñers, Mr Higgins, The Kearneys, The Commeline family . . . most lavish they all were of admiration of the house
& its furniture, which are indeed very *unique* & striking: I long for
you to see them . . .[1]

Edward had created a show-piece, later described as "a chef-d'œuvre,
unrivalled in this kingdom,"[2] some idea of which can be obtained from the
sketches published facing pages xlviii and 129.   George Moulton-Barrett,
writing to Robert Browning in 1889, told him:

. . . The architect was I believe Wyatt, but am not sure,——but that
Loudon at that time an eminent landscape Gardener laid out the
grounds, I am quite sure.   It had many admirers, & in summer time
was visited by sight seers from Malvern.   I remember one afternoon
going up the park homewards with others, meeting a young girl on a
pony coming from the house with a gentleman,——that young girl was
our present Queen, & the gentleman Sir John Conroy . . .[3]

More children were born; in all, E.B.B. had three sisters and eight brothers, but little Mary, the first of the children born at Hope End, died in
March 1814, a few months before her fourth birthday. They were given
to the use of nicknames, and in their early years the children called their
father "Puppy." E.B.B. acquired the name "Ba," which was to stay with
her all her life.[4]   Her brother Edward, the closest to her of all the family,
was "Bro"; Henrietta was "Addles" or "Daddles," though the name did
not stick to her for life; Charles John was "Storm" or "Stormie," through
having been born during a storm; Alfred was "Daisy" and Arabella Graham-
Clarke, the aunt who figures largely in the Diary, was "Bummy."

1. Unpublished letter to Mrs. Arabella Graham-Clarke (*née* Altham); Collection of Edward R.
Moulton-Barrett, Esq.

2. From the Sale Catalogue of Hope End, which contains a full description of the house and
grounds (see Appendix III, p. 327).

3. Unpublished letter dated 15 April 1889; Collection of Edward R. Moulton-Barrett, Esq.

4. She is not known ever to have explained the derivation of the name, but the popular theory
is that it originated in her references to herself as "Baba" (Baby); we do know, however, that the
name was pronounced with a long vowel sound, because it was rhymed with "spa" in one of the
many birthday odes addressed to her.

At Hope End, Edward Moulton-Barrett and his growing family enjoyed the peaceful seclusion afforded by the green acres and well-wooded hills surrounding the house. Their world was a small one, concerned with the seasonal needs of the estate, the relief of the poor, and the constant round of social pleasantry, with occasional extended visits further afield.

In the manner of his times, Edward ruled Hope End, but it would be a mistake to suppose that his subjects fretted under a heavy yoke. There is ample evidence that he joined whole-heartedly in their games, and the letters and birthday odes addressed to him by his children show that they were permitted a remarkable degree of familiarity. His occasional sternness in some directions was offset by great indulgence in others, and the letters of all his children in later life testify to a very happy childhood, and to a deep love of their father.

As his extant letters show, Edward was a deeply religious man, although for him religion seems to have been more a matter of endurance than joy. The family gathered daily to say prayers; the strictest observance of the Sabbath was expected; and the children were early imbued with the principle of total subservience to the Divine Will. Although the family attended services of the Church of England, Edward was by no means uncritical of the Established Church, and also participated in Baptist and Wesleyan-Methodist activities. His letters show that he was largely responsible for the antipathy toward "Popery" expressed in later life by E.B.B.

Elizabeth early showed her interest in reading and writing. In an autobiographical sketch written at the age of fourteen she recorded:

> . . . At four I first mounted Pegasus but at six I thought myself privileged to show off feats of horsemanship. In my sixth year for some lines on virtue which I had penned with great care I received from Papa a ten shilling note enclosed in a letter which was addrest to *the Poet Laureat of Hope End*; I mention this because I received much more pleasure from the word *Poet* than from the ten shilling note . . .[1]

From the same document we learn that, aged thirteen, she had "perused all modern authors who have any claim to superior merit and poetic excellence." She eagerly intruded on the lessons in Greek and Latin being given to "Bro," preparatory to his going to Charterhouse, by his tutor Mr. McSwiney, and wrote that, in her fourteenth year, she "read Homer in the original with delight inexpressible, together with Virgil." Her schoolroom translations and paraphrases of this period also indicate study of the works of Plato, Horace, Ovid, Xenophon, Bion, Anacreon and Claudian, amongst

1. "Glimpses into My Own Life and Literary Character," *HUP*, I, 3-28.

others. In 1817-18 she was occupied in writing and revising her first major work in verse, *The Battle of Marathon*, "an epic in four books," which through her father's indulgence appeared in print in 1820. In 1821, when she was only fifteen, two of her poems were accepted and published in *The New Monthly Magazine*, and this set an official seal on her vocation as a poet.

Writing in later life about her inclination toward poetry, E.B.B. said:

> . . . I wrote verse,—as I dare say many have done who never wrote any poems—very early—at eight years old or earlier—but what is less common, the early fancy turned into a will & remained with me—& from that day to this, poetry has been a distinct object with me—an object to read think & live for—& I could make you laugh . . . by the narrative of nascent odes epics & didactics crying aloud on obsolete Muses from childish lips.   The Greeks were my demi-gods, & haunted me out of Pope's Homer until I dreamt oftener of Agamemnon than of Moses the black poney. . . .[1]

In this same letter, E.B.B. said that at the age of fifteen she nearly died: a reference to the serious illness that she suffered in 1821-23. A letter from Dr. Carden of Worcester to Edward Moulton-Barrett in May 1821 makes it clear that E.B.B. and her sisters were all unwell at the same time. A regimen of cold shower baths was recommended for E.B.B., and "exercise in the open air . . . as much as possible."[2]   This Spartan treatment aggravated a spinal injury E.B.B. had met with in an accident with her pony, but that was not at this time suspected, and she began to suffer increasingly.   In the following month Dr. Coker, a nerve specialist, was consulted, and a letter from him gives details of E.B.B.'s case:

> . . . It began with pain in the head, which continued at intervals for seven weeks—   The pain then attacked various parts of the body, for a considerable period—and for the last month it has permanently seated itself on the right side . . .   The pain commences here is carried to the corresponding region of the back, up the side to the point of the right shoulder, and down the arm.   The suffering is agony— and the paroxysms continue from a quarter of an hour to an hour and upwards—accompanied by convulsive twitches of the muscles, in which the diaphragm is particularly concerned—   The attack seems gradually to approach its acmé, and then suddenly ceases— During its progress the mind is for the most part conscious of surrounding objects but towards its close, there is generally some, and

1. Letter to Richard Hengist Horne dated 5 October 1843, in PML; printed in *EBB/RHH*, I, 154-168.

2. Letter dated 8 May 1821; *B/GB*, pp. 342-343.

> occasionally very considerable confusion produced by it— There
> are generally three attacks in the day and none during the night. . . .
> I understand she has taken a variety of powerful medicines without
> any permanent benefit—Opium at one time relieved the spasms but
> it has ceased to have that effect . . . [1]

Her condition did not mend, and in July it was decided to move her to the
Spa Hotel, Gloucester, in order that she might be more easily attended by
the medical men than at Hope End. Improvement was slow; although she
was allowed to return home after almost a year of treatment, she was not
strong enough to walk from her room until February 1823. This illness
left its mark. Although E.B.B. writes in the Diary of running and riding,
her health was always erratic, she was soon tired, easily moved to tears,
and subject to fits of fainting and nervous hysteria.

Her enforced idleness at this time, and her always indifferent health
subsequently, turned her more and more to books and study, writing and
introspection. In later years, E.B.B. described her life at Hope End as:

> . . . a retirement scarcely broken to me except by books & my own
> thoughts . . . a retirement happy in many ways, although the very
> peace of it troubles the heart as it looks back. There I had my fits of
> Pope—& Byron—& Coleridge—and read Greek as hard under the
> trees as some of your Oxonians in the Bodleian—gathered visions
> from Plato & the dramatists—& eat [sic] & drank Greek & made my
> head ache with it. . . . [2]

Her love of seclusion grew, and no doubt engendered the marked reluctance
she later displayed whenever obliged to put aside her books and take part in
the social round of visits. She could not share the enjoyment of her sisters
in the formal entertainments of Lord Somers and his family at Eastnor
Castle; the dinners with the Biddulphs of Ledbury; the sipping of tea and
the polite small-talk with the Martins of Old Colwall, the Peytons of Barton
Court, or the Commelines of Redmarley D'Abitot. She did enjoy the company of Eliza Cliffe, of Mathon, but as she pointedly observed in the Diary
their relationship did not constitute friendship as E.B.B. chose to define it.

It was in 1826 that she published her second book, *An Essay on Mind,
with Other Poems*, which evoked a letter of praise from Uvedale Price of
Foxley, not far distant from Hope End. From this developed a correspondence that lasted until his death in 1829, in which they discussed the
classics, particularly from the technical standpoint of accent, metre and

---

1. Letter dated 24 June 1821; *B/GB*, pp. 343-346.
2. Letter to Richard Hengist Horne dated 5 October 1843, loc. cit.

pronunciation, and E.B.B. made detailed comments on the proof sheets of his *Essay on the Modern Pronunciation of the Greek and Latin Languages* (Oxford, 1827).[1]

The erudition of *An Essay on Mind* also earned the admiration of another local scholar, Hugh Stuart Boyd, who had published several books, including translations from the Greek, and who had been blind for more than fifteen years as a result of opthalmia. Early in 1827 he wrote to E.B.B. to praise her *Essay*; he also sent her copies of his works, solicited comment, and extended a warm invitation for her to call at his home in Malvern Wells, some five miles from Hope End. The known correspondence between them begins with E.B.B.'s second letter, dated 11 March 1827, carefully drafted and then copied out, in which she thanked him for his invitation, and said: "I very seldom have it in my power to leave home, & the first time I am able to do so, must visit some friends to whom I am under a long engagement."[2] She made a few critical remarks about some of his poems and translations, and sent him a copy of the January 1827 issue of the *Jewish Expositor*, containing some verses of hers. The foundation was now truly laid for an exchange of letters that slowly became deeper and less formal, and of increasing importance to both parties. H.S.B. repeated his invitations, and in November E.B.B. was forced to tell him that her father would not sanction the visit, taking the view that "as a *female*, and a *young* female," E.B.B. could not pay the first call "without overstepping the established observances of society."[3] With this, H.S.B. had to be content, and the flow of letters and comment continued, with him directing E.B.B.'s reading more and more to the Greek theologians.

On 13 March of the following year, while driving to the house of her cousin, Mrs. Trant, E.B.B. passed a lady and gentleman identified by Arabella and Henrietta as the Boyds. Too agitated to introduce herself, E.B.B. went into her cousin's but reappeared almost at once, and entered the adjacent house of Admiral Sir Charles Knowles. As E.B.B. later explained to H.S.B., she had learned that Lady Knowles was about to set out on a visit to Hope End, and had hurried to beg that it be deferred, on account of her mother's ill-health, but H.S.B. drew the conclusion that E.B.B. was making a social visit. The next morning she received from him a long letter, reproaching her for visiting the home of another man, while still refusing to enter his, and containing the veiled threat that he might soon yield to Mrs. Boyd's wish to leave Malvern.

1. Unpublished letter dated October 1826, at Huntington.

2. *EBB/HSB*, pp. 3-5; letter at Wellesley, draft in the Armstrong Browning Library, Baylor University.

3. Letter dated 3 November 1827; *EBB/HSB*, pp. 9-12.

As a result of this incident, E.B.B. renewed her application for paternal permission to visit H.S.B. This time she gained her object, and made her first visit on 16 April 1828. Writing to her grandmother, she gave this description of him:

> . . . My eccentric friend is a rather young looking man than otherwise, moderately tall, and slightly formed. His features are good— his face very pale, with an expression of placidity and mildness. He is totally blind—and from the quenched and deadened appearance of his eyes, hopelessly so!— His voice is very harmonious and gentle and low—and seems to have naturally a melancholy cadence and tone!—which is affecting when you look at his quenched and deadened eyes—totally and hopelessly blind. I did not see him smile once. . . .[1]

Unfortunately, no likeness of H.S.B., which would augment this word-picture, is known to exist. Even E.B.B.'s sketch, which she mentions drawing in the Diary, has not been found.

Paternal acquiescence having been finally obtained, other visits followed,[2] now to Woodland Lodge in Great Malvern, where H.S.B. had moved early in May on the expiry of his lease of Ruby Cottage. E.B.B.'s duties in the Hope End schoolroom, and her mother's ill-health, prevented the visits from being as frequent as either of them wished. Then fell the first of the blows that were to shatter this quiet happiness: on 7 October 1828 E.B.B.'s much-loved mother died, and thereafter nothing was the same. The visits to Malvern were interrupted, and despite H.S.B.'s protestations it was not until the summer of 1829 that E.B.B. could be persuaded to resume them. Their readings then continued, and the following year E.B.B. was allowed to accept an invitation to stay at Woodland Lodge, and spent an intensely happy visit of two and a half weeks there. A note by H.S.B. records that when she returned home on 7 October 1830 she had "read during her visit somewhat more than 2200 lines."[3]

In the enjoyment of this all-important friendship, E.B.B. was unaware that another blow was impending: the loss of her beloved Hope End, through the worsening of the financial difficulties besetting her father. After more than twenty years of litigation arising from the will of their grandfather, judgment had been given against Edward Moulton-Barrett and

---

1. Letter dated 17 March 1828; *HUP*, II, 87-93.

2. The second visit was paid on 16 May; this, together with the date of the first visit, was recorded by H.S.B. in his copy of *An Essay on Mind*, now at Wellesley.

3. Memorandum printed in "Some Unpublished Papers of Robert and Elizabeth Barrett Browning," ed. George S. Hellman, *Harper's Monthly Magazine*, March 1916, pp. 530-539.

his brother Samuel in 1824, and this had started the decline of Edward's prosperity. The problems attached to directing his Jamaican estates as an absentee landlord, and some injudicious business ventures, increased his difficulties. At the beginning of 1831 his creditors were pressing him, and the mortgagees foreclosed on Hope End. In February 1831 he was already aware that he would have to give up the estate, but did not wish his children to be worried prematurely. Writing from London to his brother on 15 February he said:

> . . . I expect soon to return into Herefordshire, altho it will be for a distressing object, the packing up of all my things for removing thence, God only knows where, but He knows best; I dread much the effect on my dear Children in tearing them away from all their most happy associations, again I say He who has inflicted the chastisement will so temper it, as to enable them to bear it. . . . Say nothing on the subject of removal to the girls. . . .[1]

Because of his protracted absences from Hope End while attempting to extricate himself from his financial dilemma, Edward asked his wife's sister, Arabella ("Bummy") Graham-Clarke, to stay there and care for his family. By this time, E.B.B. had already realized that all was not well, and hoped to be "let into all the mysteries" by her aunt, who joined the household early in May; in this she was disappointed, and reported to Boyd on 19 May:

> . . . She is, either from a promise to Papa or a judgment of her own, *hermetically sealed*—and all I can extract is—"How can you suspect *me* of having any information?". . .[2]

The years 1829-30 appear to have seen the high-water mark of E.B.B.'s friendship with H.S.B. The following spring he returned to Ruby Cottage, and the visits continued apparently unchanged, but by the time the Diary was started in June 1831, E.B.B. had convinced herself that his esteem for her was not as great as it had been, and was lamenting the increased infrequency of letters written to her in his own hand.

Thus, when the Diary commences E.B.B. is obsessed with two major threats to her security and happiness: the probable loss of Hope End, with its "serene green stilness,"[3] and thereby the rupture of her close and greatly valued association with H.S.B. These form the two principal and recurrent themes throughout the Diary.

1. Letter at Wellesley; this extract previously printed in *The Daily Gleaner*, Jamaica, 12 June 1938, and elsewhere.

2. *EBB/HSB*, p. 136.   3. Letter dated 6 December 1842; *EBB/MRM*, pp. 150-151.

Much additional light is thrown on the 1831-32 portion of the published letters from E.B.B. to Boyd, and it becomes even more a matter for regret that the other side of the correspondence has not been traced. One hundred and seventy of the letters from him to E.B.B. were included in the 1913 Browning Sale; they reappeared at Sotheby's on 14 December 1926, when they were bought and subsequently advertised for sale by G. H. Last, a dealer in Bromley, Kent, but he is no longer in business there, and the trail ceases at this point.

Apart from the insight into E.B.B.'s attitude to Boyd and the degree of importance she attached to his friendship, the Diary gives us a picture of daily life at Hope End, with its tea-cup storms and squabbles. E.B.B.'s only formal duty was that of instructing her brothers "Storm" and George in Greek, and we see how much leisure time she had, and the way in which she used it, in writing, studying or reading—reading that encompassed a wide range: poetry and multi-volumed novels sharing place with theological works, and Italian comedies giving light relief after Greek and Latin authors.

In the light of her subsequent history, it is of particular interest to read, in the entry of 26 August:

> . . . To whatever place we go [in the event of leaving Hope End], I will seclude myself there, & try to know nobody & like nobody,— but live with my books & writings & dear family. . . .

It is also of interest to learn her reason for discontinuing the Diary, after such a relatively short time, as she later explained it when writing to Richard Hengist Horne:

> . . . Once indeed, for one year, I kept a diary in detail & largely,—&, at the end of the twelve months, was in such a crisis of self-disgust that there was nothing for me but to leave off the diary. Did you ever try the effect of a diary upon your own mind? It is curious, especially where elastic spirits & fancies are at work upon a fixity of character & situation. . . .[1]

Shortly after the Diary was concluded, the break that E.B.B. had been dreading came, but it was H.S.B. who caused it. Being unable to ascertain Edward Moulton-Barrett's plans, he decided against renewing the lease of Ruby Cottage, and in May 1832 he moved to Bathampton. Edward's last efforts to avoid the loss of Hope End, by attempting to borrow money from his wife's family and elsewhere, failed, and the long-anticipated preparations for departure began.

1. Letter dated 5 October 1843, loc. cit.

Diary by E.B.B.

Writing to H.S.B. on 13 August, E.B.B. told him that men had been packing up furniture since the beginning of the month, and said:

> . . . Oh I do wish that all of this painful confusion were over! The noise of hammering, and of men walking up and down stairs, from morning till night—and dear Hope End looking so unlike the happy Hope End it used to be! I sometimes sit at the window and wonder if it is a dream. . . .[1]

On the morning of 23 August, E.B.B., the faithful "Bummy" and most of the family left Hope End and set out in a sad procession for Sidmouth, the father and two of the boys remaining to superintend the last of the packing. E.B.B. never returned; after her marriage, she was invited to visit Mrs. Martin, but wrote:

> . . . we could not go into Herefordshire, even if I were rational, which I am not; I could as soon open a coffin as do it: there's the truth. . . . if I went there, the thought of *one face* which never ceases to be present with me (and which I parted from for ever in my poor blind unconsciousness with a pettish word) would rise up, put down all the rest, and prevent my having one moment of ordinary calm intercourse with you, so don't ask me; set it down to mania or obstinacy, but I never *could* go into that neighbourhood, except to die, which I think sometimes I should like. . . .[2]

In December 1832, H.S.B. also went to Sidmouth, being disenchanted with Bathampton, and no doubt missing E.B.B.'s visits as much as she did. During the time they were together in Sidmouth, they met nearly every day, but their relationship never recaptured the intensity of the earlier years. E.B.B.'s outlook was more mature, she was making other friends, and she now began to see H.S.B.'s limitations, so that when he left Sidmouth in May 1834 there was none of the anguish that marked their earlier separation.

They were on visiting terms again in 1835 after E.B.B. and her family moved to London, where H.S.B. was then living, but E.B.B.'s health was undermined by the fogs and chills of London, and the visits became less and less frequent. In 1838 she was sent to Torquay, in the hope that the sea air would recruit her strength. She insisted on returning to London in 1841, as soon as she was able to travel after the loss by drowning of her dear "Bro," but there was no question of her health allowing the resumption

---

1. *EBB/HSB*, pp. 190-193.
2. Letter dated Tuesday [July-August 1855]; Kenyon, II, 206-208.

of the visits to H.S.B. Throughout this time, they had continued to correspond, and something of the old closeness returned in 1841-42, when E.B.B. again turned to the Greeks to while away the tedium of the sick-room, and H.S.B. was once more ready with comment and advice. It was not until 30 June 1846, however, shortly before E.B.B.'s marriage and departure for Italy, that she saw him again, when she:

> . . . stood at last, at the door of poor Mr. Boyd's dark little room, and saw him sitting—as if he had not moved these seven years—these seven heavy, changeful years. Seeing him, my heart was too full to speak at first, but I stooped and kissed his poor bent-down forehead, which he never lifts up . . .[1]

Only three letters are known to have been written to him by E.B.B. after her marriage, but she always spoke of him with affection, and was saddened by news of his paralytic stroke in 1848. Writing to Arabella about his illness, in a letter started on the day that H.S.B. died, she said "a great black shadow seems to have fallen down straight on me" and prayed "May God keep him in sunshine . . ."[2]

Three sonnets, "His Blindness," "His Death, 1848" and "Legacies," were her tribute to the memory of her old and valued friend. In a note printed with them, she said:

> . . . This excellent and learned man, enthusiastic for the good and the beautiful, and one of the most simple and upright of human beings, passed out of his long darkness through death in the summer of 1848; Dr. Adam Clarke's daughter and biographer, Mrs. Smith, (happier in this than the absent) fulfilling a doubly filial duty as she sate by the death-bed of her father's friend and hers. . . .[3]

1. Letter to Robert Browning [30 June 1846]; *EBB/RB*, II, 282-284.
2. Unpublished letter dated 10-11 May [1848], in the Berg Collection.
3. *Poems* (London, 1850), pp. 359-361.

EDITORIAL APPROACH AND APPARATUS

EDITORIAL APPROACH

Our primary aim in editing E.B.B.'s manuscript has been to present as faithful a reproduction as possible—a text from which other editors, biographers or critics might work as they wish. E.B.B.'s misspellings, punctuation, and other textual peculiarities reflect much of her personality and the state of mind under which she wrote. To have provided a "cleaned-up" text, neglecting the hundreds of textual alterations and many spelling irregularities, would have expedited our work considerably but it would have meant a loss. We feel that the text as presented here is no more difficult to follow than a letter from a personal friend, and certainly it retains much of her individuality that would otherwise have been lost to a reader of the Diary.

SPELLING

We have preserved all E.B.B.'s slips of the pen, together with all spelling errors and variant forms. Foreign words are given as she wrote them, with an exception in the case of a few Greek words. E.B.B. often copied the old forms of orthography used in the editions belonging to her or H.S.B.; in such cases, without altering her spelling, we have substituted for her ligatures the characters of the Greek alphabet now commonly used. She was frequently inaccurate in her use of accents, particularly in French words, but we have not supplied missing accents or altered incorrect ones.

Words that E.B.B. clearly separated (e.g., "pic nic") have been left as she gave them. If E.B.B. broke a word due to its falling at the end of a line, we have retained the hyphen only if it occurs in a word which she habitually hyphenated.

In cases where she has misspelled a proper name, her spelling is included in the Index, cross-referenced to the correct spelling, if the degree of error warrants this (e.g., Boardman/Bordman and Pindar/Pyndar). Where some clarification is needed (e.g., to indicate that Miss Hurd and Miss Heard are the same person) it is given in a footnote.

The editorial approach to her other spelling errors and variants posed problems. In many cases E.B.B. used spellings (e.g., "poney," "lightening," "pye") which, although not now the preferred forms, are recognized by the *Oxford English Dictionary*. As there are more than two hundred instances in the Diary of usages that are either wrong or no longer current, we rejected the frequent use of the obtrusive [sic] in conjunction with these. We only use this editorial emphasis to confirm unlikely errors (such as "Thurday" for "Thursday"), or where the sense of the text is not clear, due perhaps to a slip of the pen.

However, we felt that the reader was entitled to some assurance of editorial accuracy in transcribing, so the Textual Notes at the back of the book contain a list of spelling errors and variants for any reader who seeks confirmation, for example, that E.B.B. really did write "sory" and "dessimulation."

PUNCTUATION

In striving for fidelity to the source material, we have been hampered by E.B.B.'s style of punctuation, which could only be reproduced with total accuracy by means of facsimile. Her principal tool in punctuating was the dash, used either by itself or in conjunction with other punctuation marks; the dashes in her Diary vary from the merest elongation of a period to a continuous dash of over one and a half inches. In an attempt to convey her style and degrees of emphasis, while avoiding too much typographical complexity, we have employed dashes of three different lengths, viz. —, ——, ———. At first this does not make for easy reading, because the sentence division is not always obvious, but it gives such a clear picture of her scurrying pen trying to keep up with her rush of thoughts that any arbitrary tidying up of her punctuation would sacrifice much of her individual manner.

Both in letters and the Diary, E.B.B. habitually wrote the contraction of "would not" and similar forms with the apostrophe misplaced (i.e., "would'nt") or omitted ("cant"), and her usage has been preserved without further editorial comment.

Missing punctuation (e.g., the opening or closing set of quotation marks) has been added only where lack of it impairs quick understanding of the text; anything supplied in this way is enclosed in square brackets [ ].

One liberty we have taken is the omission of the repeated opening quotation marks that E.B.B. used at the beginning of each new line in a long passage of direct speech. As the printed line does not correspond to her written line in length, to retain the repetitious quotation marks where they fall in her text would be confusing; consequently, in passages of this kind we give only the opening and closing quotation marks, and record the omission in a footnote.

E.B.B. was also very liberal in her use of underscoring, and there are many instances of multiple underscores in the Diary. As this was an essential component of her literary style, we have retained it.

TRANSLATION OF FOREIGN WORDS AND PHRASES

In the Diary E.B.B. used words and phrases in Greek, Latin, French and Italian, and she also coined words by using Latin endings on English roots (e.g., "botherissime" and "bore-ibile"). Our policy has been:

1. to identify and translate all quotations, by means of footnotes.

2. to translate all Greek words and phrases, by means of footnotes (but a word appearing more than once has usually been translated only when first used).

3. for the remainder, to rely on judgment. Thus, we do not interrupt the text to give a footnote translating "indisposée" or "coûte qu'il coûte"; we have not translated phrases in general usage, such as "sine die" or "nota bene"; and we have not interpreted E.B.B.'s obvious pseudo-Latin constructions; but we have translated words like "dédommagée" and "vivida vis." Any arbitrary selection along these lines is open to criticism, and we apologize to those readers who may be annoyed by our sins of omission or commission in this manner.

USE OF FOOTNOTES

The personal nature of the writing in the Diary meant that references that E.B.B. would probably have made clearer in a letter were left oblique. From the outset, we realized that there was no middle way in editing the text: our choice had to be between few footnotes, or many, and we do not feel we need to apologize for choosing the many. However, to avoid any further increase in their number, we have adopted the following approach:

1. We have provided a list of the Hope End household with brief details (p. xxxv). Consequently, when these people appear in the text, there is no identifying footnote unless the reference requires some amplification.

2. Characters not dealt with in this manner are identified by footnote only at their first mention, unless subsequent references require clarification. While attempting to identify all living persons, in respect of ficitional characters we have used our judgment. Thus, we do have a footnote for Baron Munchausen, but not for Princess Scheherazade or Robinson Crusoe.

3. Books are identified in full only at their first mention. If subsequent references require the identification of a particular passage, a shortened form of the title is used.

This works to the disadvantage of a browsing reader, or of one wishing to check a name; to minimize inconvenience, heavier type is used in the Index to indicate the page where the principal explanatory note will be found.

TEXTUAL NOTES

Several hundred alterations were made by E.B.B. in the course of her writing of the Diary: some merely correcting spelling errors or deleting redundant words; some interpolating additional material with a caret; and others materially affecting the construction or sense of a passage. We have found it illuminating to compare the final text with her first thoughts, and for the reader who chooses to study the sequence of her writing, explanatory textual notes are provided at the end of the text, identified by page and line number.

Apart from these alterations, there are occasional obliterations, where the intention was not just to strike out a superfluous word or phrase, but to render the word(s) totally illegible. Despite this intention, the difference in density between the original ink and the obliterating ink, together with the ascenders and descenders left visible, do sometimes permit a degree of reconstruction. In some cases, it is only possible to identify isolated words, but these often indicate the general tenor of E.B.B.'s remarks, and in this event we include our deductions in the Textual Notes. In a few instances, we have been able to reconstruct a whole phrase, and this reconstruction is also given in the Textual Notes.

It is not possible to be sure when, or by whom, these obliterations were made, but it seems most likely that they occurred some considerable time after the original entries were written. Most of the passages so treated appear to relate to Boyd in some way, reflecting E.B.B.'s concern over the supposed diminution of his regard for her; her fears that he might hold

Diary by E.B.B.

Miss Mushet in higher esteem than E.B.B.; or her pain at the thought of the Boyds moving away from Malvern, and so rupturing the cherished days of quiet study at Ruby Cottage.

APPENDICES

As the Diary illuminates the letters E.B.B. wrote to Boyd, and as they in some measure amplify references made in the Diary, in Appendix I we give all the extant letters to H.S.B. written within the period covered by the Diary. With one exception they have all been previously published, but the texts given in the Appendix have been collated against the originals and E.B.B.'s misspellings and contractions have been restored; also, omitted passages have been reinstated, and their extent is shown by a marginal line. In several instances where the letters could not previously be dated with precision, E.B.B.'s references enable positive or conjectural dates to be assigned. We also include in Appendix I other relevant correspondence, such as letters from Edward Moulton-Barrett, either directly referred to by E.B.B., or relating to events mentioned by her.

In Appendix II we give the text of poems that E.B.B. mentions composing or publishing during the period of the Diary, together with one not cited directly, but which bears upon the painting of her portrait during the Diary.

In Appendix III we reprint the 1831 Sale Catalogue of Hope End. It contains a map of the estate, together with the fullest known description of the house and grounds; these help in clarifying some of E.B.B.'s references.

EDITORIAL APPARATUS

In order to present the text of the Diary with maximum clarity, we have:

1. Set the transcript of the manuscript in 12-point Italic type with line numbers in the outer margin,

2. Set editorial notes in 8-point Roman type, single column, at the foot of the page, and

3. Set textual notes in 10-point Roman and Italic type, double column, following the transcript, identified by page and line number.

In order to draw attention to alterations to or irregularities in the manuscript, and to make clear our own additions, we have used the following
editorial symbols in the text.

<   > :   light arrow brackets enclosing a word, phrase, or punctuation
          unit denote a manuscript alteration that we have been unable to
          decipher.

<$_\wedge$ > :   light arrow brackets enclosing a caret, in addition to the word or
          phrase, denote a straightforward interlineation, the caret being
          E.B.B.'s.

≪   ≫ :   double arrow brackets enclosing a word, phrase, or punctuation
          unit indicate an alteration not falling within either of the two
          previous categories, the nature of which is explained in the Text-
          ual Notes.

≪...≫ :   double arrow brackets enclosing three periods denote a deletion
          or obliteration, the nature of which is explained in the Textual
          Notes; where possible, we include an indication of the sense of
          the obliterated passage, or a reconstruction of it. Where the
          deleted matter occupies less than one line of the original manu-
          script, the symbol is placed directly in the text in the position
          occupied by the deletion. Where the passage deleted occupies
          more than one full line of the original, the symbol is placed on a
          line by itself, to convey the impression of a larger break.

⟨   ⟩ :   wide-angle brackets enclosing a word or part of a word denote
          a conjectural reading made necessary by some defect in the manu-
          script, such as a hole or missing corner, or an ink blot obscuring
          the text. This editorial addition is further emphasized by being
          printed in Roman typeface, in contrast to the Italic style used
          for E.B.B.'s text. In these cases the precise nature of the damage
          or irregularity is explained in the Textual Notes.

⟨...⟩ :   wide-angle brackets enclosing three periods show more extensive
          physical damage, caused by excision, where a conjectural reading
          is not possible. As the narrative is interrupted by these excisions,
          in some cases by several days, the symbol is placed on a line by
          itself, and a footnote states the extent of the excision.

[   ] :   square brackets are used to denote all editorial interjections in
          the text (with the exception of the conjectural readings dealt
          with above), including the clarification by expansion of some of

E.B.B.'s contractions, for example, M^{rs} C[liffe]. Again, emphasis is given to the editorial addition by the use of Roman typeface. (Square brackets are also used in the footnotes, in accordance with standard practice, to indicate additions to quoted material, or details given in identifying a book that do not appear on the title page of the edition cited.)

| : marginal line used in Appendix I indicates a passage omitted from a previous publication, now reinstated.

To prevent possible confusion it is worth stressing that, although we use ellipses in quoted matter in the Introduction and in footnotes, we nowhere use them in the body of the Diary, except when enclosed in brackets, as listed above. Consequently, any series of dots in the text of the Diary reproduces E.B.B.'s own punctuation.

DESCRIPTION AND PROVENANCE OF THE MANUSCRIPT

DESCRIPTION

The manuscript of the Diary is divided into two parts. The first, containing the entries for 1831, consists of 85 folded sheets (i.e., 340 pages) of quality paper, 11.5 x 18.4 cm., with a final page, 12.2 x 19.5 cm., the verso of which is marbled, predominantly in brown and blue. Five types of paper are used (although the watermark or embossed stamp does not appear in full on all sheets) and are summarized as follows:

Sheet	Description
1, 2, 4-10	Wove paper. Watermark: J LLOYD. Oval embossed stamp: [illegible name]	[crown]	.
3	Wove paper. No watermark. Octagonal embossed stamp: [indistinguishable device] |.
11-16	Wove paper. No watermark. Circular embossed stamp: [crown]	BATH	SUPERFINE	[garland: left-side of grain, right-side of flowers] |.
17-85	Wove paper. Lion's head embossed stamp: SUPER	BATH	.
Final Page	Laid paper. No watermark.

A study of this part of the diary shows that the sheets were subsequently sewn together, although only a small portion of the silk thread remained when the manuscript was found, and this has since been removed. The 341 pages are encased in a wrapper of manilla-paper originally 32 x 16.8 cm., but gummed to achieve a close fit; it is annotated in the hand of Robert Browning: "Diary by E.B.B." This portion of the diary is enclosed in a black silk slip case of contemporary date.

The second part of the Diary contains the entries for 1832, and is written in the central portion of a volume used by E.B.B. for making general notes on her reading. The volume originally contained 374 pages of inferior quality wove paper, 9.5 x 15.4 cm., watermarked: RUSE & TURNERS | 1825 |. The portion of this volume on which the Diary was written originally covered 144 pages of which 56 pages (i.e., 28 leaves) were subsequently wholly excised, and 18 pages excised in part. It is bound in russia, stamped in blind with a diamond design, and bears a brass clasp.

PROVENANCE

At some point in time the two sections of the Diary became separated. The first part was discovered and labelled by Robert Browning after E.B.B.'s death. Upon Browning's death it passed into the possession of their son, Robert Barrett Browning, and was one of the items withheld by his heirs, the Moulton-Barrett family, when the estate was dispersed by auction in May 1913.[1] It and other items retained by the family were lodged with a London solicitor until 1924, when by general family consent Lt.-Col. H.P. Moulton-Barrett took charge of them.

The second portion of the Diary was in Arabella's custody when she died in 1868, and it passed with other papers, including her own letters from E.B.B., to their brother George. In 1887 Browning expressed fears to George about the possible misuse of E.B.B.'s letters and papers after the two of them were dead. Consequently, it was almost certainly George who was responsible for the obliterations and excisions which mar the reading of the second part of the Diary. When George died in 1895, his papers passed to another brother, Henry, who died in the following year, leaving the collection to his eldest son, the Rev. Frank Morris Moulton-Barrett, who in turn bequeathed it to his brother Lt.-Col. Harry Peyton Moulton-Barrett.

Thus it was not until 1924, when Harry Peyton Moulton-Barrett took possession of the residue of the material from Robert Barrett Browning's estate, that the two halves of the Diary were reunited; the separation fortunately having preserved the first part from the censorship suffered by the second.

When Harry Peyton Moulton-Barrett died in 1937, his collection was dispersed, a great portion being sold at public auction. The remainder, including the two parts of the Diary, eventually became the joint property of Gp.-Capt. Edward S. Moulton-Barrett and Kenneth A. Moulton-Barrett, Esq., from whom, early in 1965, it was acquired by the Henry W. and Albert A. Berg Collection of the New York Public Library.

---

1. The value of the English portion of the estate was £22,064; this included the sum of £20,348 realized by the auction (after deduction of Sotheby's commission), and a payment of £1025 by Messrs. Smith, Elder & Co. for the copyright in the literary remains of Robert and Elizabeth Barrett Browning. The Italian part of the estate was valued at the equivalent of £28,440. Outstanding debts reduced the total value of the estate by some £21,000.

THE HOPE END HOUSEHOLD

Before starting the Diary, it will assist the reader to have a brief sketch of the members of E.B.B.'s family living at Hope End at this time, together with information about the indoor and outdoor staff mentioned in the Diary.

THE FAMILY

Edward Barrett
Moulton-Barrett

Born in Jamaica 28 May 1785, and baptized Edward Barrett Moulton. Was sent to England in 1792 with his younger brother Samuel and their elder sister Sarah (the "Pinkie" immortalized in paint by Sir Thomas Lawrence). In January 1798 the two boys assumed the additional surname Barrett, and in the same year were co-heirs to the extensive Jamaican estates of their grandfather, Edward Barrett of Cinnamon Hill. In May 1805 he married Mary Graham-Clarke, and the following year their first child was born. In 1809 he bought Hope End. He was elected Sheriff of the county in 1812, and again in 1814, and was an active supporter of the local Bible and Missionary Societies. Litigation arising from his grandfather's will went against him, and started the decline in his fortunes which eventually resulted in his having to sell Hope End. After his wife's death in 1828, he had to assume the whole burden of the upbringing of his children. On leaving Hope End in 1832, he took his family to Sidmouth, and then in 1835 they moved to London, finally settling at 50 Wimpole Street, which remained his home until his death on 17 April 1857.

E.B.B. married against his will and without his permission, and he never forgave her, neither reading the letters she sent him, nor replying, and he never saw her during her visits to London after her marriage. He also disinherited the other two children, Henrietta and Alfred, who married without his sanction.

Elizabeth Barrett
Moulton-Barrett
("Ba")

The eldest child, born 6 March 1806. Showed her interest in writing early in life, and published her first work, *The Battle of Marathon*, in 1820. She suffered a serious illness in 1821-23, and thereafter her health was always precarious. After the family moved to London in 1835, her health again declined, and in 1838 she was sent to Torquay. At her insistence, "Bro" was permitted to join her there, and when he was drowned in 1840, E.B.B. felt she was responsible for his death. She refused to remain in Torquay, and as soon as she was able to travel, rejoined her family in London, but remained in almost total seclusion. In 1845 Robert Browning started to write to her, and after some months secured permission to call on her. By the following year he had persuaded her that it was essential to her health for her to leave London. On 12 September 1846 they were married, and a week later left for Italy. Her only child was born in 1849. E.B.B. died in Florence on 29 June 1861, and was buried there.

Edward Barrett Moulton-Barrett ("Bro")

The eldest son, and second child, born 26 June 1807, to whom E.B.B. was especially attached. Attended Charterhouse 1820-26. As a result of E.B.B.'s pleas he was allowed to be her companion in Torquay, when she was sent there in 1838 on account of her health. His death there by drowning on 11 July 1840 prostrated E.B.B., and she was never able to speak of the tragedy in later years, even to Browning.

Henrietta Barrett Moulton-Barrett ("Addles" or "Daddles")

The second daughter, and third child, born 4 March 1809. In 1850 she married, without her father's approval, a distant cousin, William Surtees Cook, for which she was disinherited. She had three children, and died of cancer on 23 November 1860. Her death was a great blow to E.B.B. and may well have contributed to the general debility that led to E.B.B.'s death the following year.

Samuel Barrett Moulton-Barrett

The second son, and fifth child, born 13 January 1812. His death in Jamaica from fever, at the early age of 28, on 17 February 1840, was a blow still being mourned by the family when "Bro" died five months later.

Arabella Barrett Moulton-Barrett

The fourth daughter, and sixth child, born 4 July 1813. Remained unmarried, and cared faithfully for her father until his death in 1857. Devoted herself to Robert Browning and his son when they returned to London after E.B.B.'s death, and died in Browning's arms 11 June 1868.

Charles John Barrett Moulton-Barrett ("Storm" or "Stormie")

The third son, and seventh child, born during a storm on 28 December 1814. He was a life-long stutterer. After the death of his brother Sam, he became involved in the management of the family's estates in Jamaica, and spent most of the latter part of his life there. He married in Jamaica in 1865, and died there 21 January 1905.

George Goodin Barrett Moulton-Barrett	The fourth son, and eighth child, born 15 July 1817. He became a barrister of the Inner Temple, and served on the Oxford Circuit, but retired from active practice after inheriting part of his father's estate. He joined with his father in condemning E.B.B.'s marriage, and it was five years before he became reconciled to it, but after that time both E.B.B. and Browning corresponded with him until their respective deaths. George's letters to Browning give us much of our present knowledge about the family's days at Hope End. He died 11 August 1895, unmarried.
Henry Barrett Moulton-Barrett	The fifth son, and ninth child, born 27 July 1818. He did not marry until 1858, after his father's death. He died on 17 May 1896.
Alfred Price Barrett Moulton-Barrett ("Daisy")	The sixth son, and tenth child, born 20 May 1820. In 1855 he incurred paternal displeasure by marrying a distant cousin and was disinherited. He died in France on 24 May 1904.
Septimus James Barrett Moulton-Barrett ("Sette" or "Seppy")	The seventh son, and eleventh child, born 22 February 1822. Spent the latter part of his life in Jamaica, and died there on 17 March 1870.
Octavius Butler Barrett Moulton-Barrett ("Occy" or "Occyta")	The eighth son, and twelfth child, born 12 April 1824. He married twice, and died on 11 November 1910.
Arabella Sarah Graham-Clarke ("Bummy")	Born 27 June 1785, she was the fourth of the nine children of John and Arabella Graham-Clarke, her eldest sister Mary having been the wife of Edward Moulton-Barrett. She never married, and spent much of her time with her sister's family, particularly in the years 1831-32 and 1838-41. She died in Cheltenham on 30 December 1869.

INDOOR STAFF

Ann	E.B.B.'s maid.
Mary Robinson ("Minny")	Joined the household in 1817 as nurse to Arabella. She was later appointed housekeeper at Hope End, a position she maintained in all subsequent Moulton-Barrett residences. She was apparently held to be a considerable authority on children's ailments, and after the birth of E.B.B.'s son in 1849 there were many anxious enquiries directed to her, through Arabella and Henrietta. She died in the early 1860's at Arabella's London home, after a long illness.

OUTDOOR STAFF

Jack Cook	The son of Thomas Cook, one of the tenant-farmers; worked on the estate.
Daly	The gardener at Hope End.
Gent	Worked in the stables, and was often used to deliver messages for the family, or to drive one of the carriages.
John Lane	The groom/handyman, who lived in a cottage on the estate (no. 22 on the auctioneer's map, Appendix III, p. 335).
William Treherne ("Billy")	The son of John Treherne, tenant of one of the cottages on the estate (no. 29 on the auctioneer's map, Appendix III, p. 335). Billy was employed principally in the stables, and often drove E.B.B.'s carriage. He remained in the Moulton-Barretts' service for many years, finally becoming a baker in Camden Town.

PSYCHOANALYTICAL OBSERVATIONS
ON ELIZABETH BARRETT BARRETT'S DIARY

Freud's discoveries did not only come as a consequence of his work as a psychiatrist whose very sick and very troubled and very confusing patients eventually inspired books such as *Studies on Hysteria* and the great *Interpretation of Dreams*. Like Elizabeth Barrett Browning, and any number of other 19th century figures, he was a determined correspondent, particularly in the years that preceded his great break-through—his realization that dreams harken back to childhood experiences and can be quite rationally analysed, that repressed sexual conflict has a critical role in the life of the mind, that doctors receive from patients feelings once meant for (and likely as not, kept from) parents. In fact, we now know a lot of what was going through his mind as he made his psychoanalytic formulations. He had all along been writing to a close friend and fellow doctor, Wilhelm Fliess, who lived in Berlin. Again and again he shared his thoughts and feelings with Dr. Fliess, to the point that some analysts today become embarrassed —all that fervor, passion, despair. Scientists ought to have more restrained and orderly minds as they go about their business!

Clearly Freud needed a correspondent, needed someone to read his ideas and respond to them. He also needed to learn from himself, to write out his guesses and convictions and thus give them a form of permanence, an existence that can be welcomed or challenged by others. For that matter, in both *The Interpretation of Dreams* and *The Psychopathology of Everyday Life* he took pains to indicate his interest in explaining what goes on in minds like his own and those of people who have no symptoms. He could find a dream of his, a letter of his, as revelatory as the bizarre "associations" of a thoroughly disturbed patient. Put differently, he saw all of us, finally, more alike than not.

As for the artist or writer—men like Michelangelo, Leonardo da Vinci, Dostoyevsky—Freud made no claim to an understanding of their *genius*, their particularly inspired ability to instruct and arouse our minds and hearts. He did take an interest in the lives of great men, and was willing on more than one occasion to make a highly speculative generalization about a person he would never, could never, see and hear and question. Diaries, notebooks, letters had been left—or novels—and Freud looked at them as psychoanalytically interesting—but only that. He never intended that his way of putting things, his viewpoint, his chosen phrases be used to

Diary by E.B.B.

"explain" (or explain *away*) an artist's work, or sully and defame his name.

Of course, a major part of Freud's life was given over to a *search*, an effort to plumb the depths, to go deep, to uncover the hidden, to turn the obvious around so that the secret, the forbidden, the denied would come to light. Only later did he have time to see how powerfully we are influenced (yes, in our unconscious, too) by the world we live in, by customs, habits and conventions, by the time-bound, class-bound nature of our lives. It is foolish to call him "wrong" for emphasizing so long and so hard the psycho*pathology* of everyday life. Discoverers struggle against whatever darkness *they* face, something later generations tend to forget. In 1900 everyday life had all sorts of surfaces, many of them troubling indeed. But nothing "superficial" could quite satisfy Freud, or command his attention and his reverence. He had to ignore the obvious psychological importance of rituals or beliefs in order to explore the unobvious, in order to be the "conquistador" he later called himself. Freud pushed aside contemporary knowledge and made his own, only to hear it charged (and in a way, to find out himself) that there were indeed other worlds—the market-place, the public arena, with its books, cultivated styles, tastes and all too powerful symbols—than the one he had conquered, all of which did not embarrass, humiliate or even surprise him. It is some of his doctrinaire, religious-minded followers who can make him seem dated. They cling to his every word, his every theoretical statement, however tentative, speculative or purely clarifying its purpose. They want to stop the clock of history, to make dogma out of one man's brilliant effort to resolve and clarify the intellectual problems of *his* day. One can only say that we all have it in us to do that, to convert abstractions into real and enduring things, to attribute an unassailable substance or permanence to ideas, to fight for a chosen leader until the end of time.

I say all this here because I cannot avoid thinking what certain psychoanalysts might have done a few years back with Elizabeth Barrett Barrett's diary. There she was, at age twenty-five, very much isolated from the world, nervous, moody, excitable, fearfully attached to her father, and not in the best state of health by any means. For some reason in June of 1831 she started a diary, and for some reason in the spring of 1832 she abruptly stopped making further entries. No matter that she is not here to be questioned; the diary lets us know that the "facts" are obvious. She had a strong "super-ego," a conscience that curbed her, admonished her, lacerated her, and made her feel exceedingly timorous and shameful on occasion. Her "ego" was intact enough; she was, after all, a poet and in general a very intelligent, cultivated woman. She saw the world sensitively and in fact made sharp comments on the hypocrisy and foolishness of others.

(Again, her conscience did not let others off its hook any more than she herself was spared.) But what of her "id"? What did she do with all her "libido," her unconscious sexual and aggressive "drives"?

Well, to answer the kind of psychoanalyst who would put the question that way, she held all that energy *in check*, as any upper-class 19th century lady *ought* to have done. Obviously a vibrant even tempestuous person, she largely kept to herself. Amid all sorts of daily activities and in the presence of a large family she was in spirit very much alone. In 1831 her mother was dead and her father quite hard-pressed—not by poverty, but by the incredible burdens of wealth. Hope End, a magnificent estate in sight of the Malvern Hills, required more money than Mr. Edward Barrett could summon, and in 1832 the house had to be surrendered. In the last months Mr. Barrett spent little time there; he was desperately trying to straighten out and come on top of his financial difficulties, and London was the scene of his struggle. Elizabeth, the oldest child, always very close to her parents, and particularly a favorite of her father's, was in a sense orphaned.

The diary shows her loneliness, but also her almost defiant effort to know someone more than superficially, more than properly or conventionally or routinely. The diary gives a fascinating account of the day-to-day activities that kept the English gentry *going* in the early 19th century. Henry James has shown once and for all how significant and revealing customs and traditions can be; what happens in the living-room or the drawing-room can be as "revealing" and "profound" as anything that takes place in the bedroom, that temple of revelation which right now obsesses psychiatrists, not to mention a nondescript collection of American novelists, movie producers, television directors and playwrights. Elizabeth Barrett took in her fair share of luncheons, teas and walks, and into all of them she managed to put herself, her wishes and fears—rather in the fashion and tradition of lovers, or of the philosophers and psychiatrists who are engaged in today's eventfully described conversations, called "dialogues."

Well, who was the "self," the "person" who emerges in this short-lived, breezy, fitfully serious, occasionally frantic and passionate diary? Once her class is declared, her intellectual achievements and artistic promise (at twenty-five) recognized, we are left with her "mind," which somehow felt the need of a diary late one spring day and somehow—after a summer, a fall and a winter—allowed the diary to die. Of course, from the very start Miss Barrett had her doubts or misgivings—today called "ambivalence": "I wonder if I shall burn this sheet of paper like most others I have begun in the same way." Interestingly enough her hesitation was precisely the kind that psychoanalysts know so very well: "To write a diary, I have thought of very often at far and near distances of time: but how could I write a diary without throwing upon paper my thoughts, all my thoughts —the thoughts of my heart as well as of my head?—and then how could I bear to look on *them* after they were written?" How's that for a prelude to Freud's psychoanalytic method, some three-quarters of a century early? The woman who wrote those words knew already that "everyday life" has its "psychopathology." That is, she knew how devious yet revealing the mind can be—so that any sustained commitment to writing is inevitably self-revealing, and thus painful.

What matters is not that we find in these pages of hers all sorts of dramatic and satisfying "complexes" or "problems" or "neurotic trends." Frankly (and it may have taken us too long to do so) a good number of psychiatrists have at last given up pouncing on this or that fragment of behavior and making of it an awesome, clinical and categorical generalization. Yes, Dostoyevsky may have secretly, unwittingly yearned to do away with his father; Leonardo da Vinci surely did have quite enough "latent homosexuality"; and in this case, Miss Barrett's considerable "involvement" with her "beloved Papa," her "dear, dear Papa," stands clear. Yet, the really important thing (so we have come to think) is not the presence of violence and one or another passion, but the *use* a particular mind makes of its various urges, conflicts, difficulties, or whatever. In other words, if I am to say that Elizabeth Barrett had an "Oedipus complex," or more exactly, an "Electra complex," I am under an obligation to go on, in fact to show what in heaven's name made me single out this particular person for that rather common and unremarkable condition. To assert, then, that Elizabeth Barrett loved her father and feared him, and may ("deep down" or "way underneath") have wished for his death is to offer a commonplace.

More interesting is the part both Mr. Barrett and Hugh Stuart Boyd played in Miss Barrett's development as an observer and particularly a writer—the reason, after all, we find her thoughts, daily or otherwise, so valuable today. We know that in 1819 a father sent his thirteen-year-old daughter's poem to the printer. Fifty copies of *The Battle of Marathon* were made, and the father described it as a "great epic of eleven or twelve years old, in four books." They were very much companions, Mr. Barrett and Elizabeth. The world well knows what happened later, when Robert Browning came upon the scene, and the master of 50 Wimpole Street said no to him, no to the prospect that *any* of his children would marry. Meanwhile, Elizabeth spent years adoring, placating and appeasing her father before September 12, 1846, when she and another poet were married in the face of Mr. Barrett's angry refusal of sanction. I do not think it is stretching things to say she was encouraged by her father to have a mind that enjoyed wide freedom—so long as her body, her life as a woman, remained safely out of any suitor's reach. Under such circumstances she did not become a constricted, fearful, impossibly shy and suspicious woman. Protected enough from romances, she yet became a romantic, as a poet, letter writer, and briefly, a diarist.

Page after page of the diary shows just how alive, how yearning, how sensitive and alert was this strangely distant and gifted young woman. She reads voraciously in the classics, but she is very much aware of contemporary English politics. She attends church, reads the paper, reads Greek, writes, awaits anxiously her daily mail, and through it all reveals herself a very shrewd observer of people—and of herself. Certainly the woman who wrote the following words would not find Sigmund Freud's discoveries either surprising or shocking: "I dreamt last night,—for night dreams are as well worth recording as day dreams,—that I was re-writing the Warren-blacking lines,—and inserted in some part of them the following—'Fame o'er him flashed her meteor wing— | and *he*—he was a King.' What king I was writing of, is out of my head." And at another point she observes: "Arabel dreamt last night that *he* was dead, and that *I* was laughing! Foolish dream!—and more foolish I who could think of it in the storm!—" Her sense of irony may not have been "consciously" intended, but there can be no doubt that she would have been a very apt "analysand." When one of my patients calls a dream foolish, then goes on to point out its lingering presence in her thoughts, I know she only awaits another's permission to acknowledge the glimmers of her own mind's awareness.

If Elizabeth Barrett was pretty much able to sense a number of things going on in her psychological life, she probably did not—could not—stop and think about the strong and complicated "meaning" of her "relationship" with Hugh Stuart Boyd. Today, we can swoop down on a life such as hers and make our statements: she "transferred" her devotion from her father to Mr. Boyd, twenty-five years older, blind, highly educated and—rather like Mr. Barrett—able to be a literary companion. Much of this happened, moreover, when Elizabeth Barrett was quite without parents. Her mother died when she was twenty-two—three years before the diary began—and her father, as mentioned, spent increasing lengths of time away in London. She needed someone, even as she kept her distance from just anyone. Yes, there were brothers and sisters, and they come up again and again in the diary; but Elizabeth was the first-born child of devoted, possessive parents and apparently she was not about to consider the kind of strength and reassurance she had learned to expect from them as lost forever.

A major share of her diary is given over to Mr. Boyd, to her efforts to please him, to see him, to feel herself his good friend. I suppose it was all very "neurotic," the young lady sick with a variety of aches and pains, and her old, blind friend. There weren't even *other* friends. She is generally impatient with people, and with herself, too. She speaks of her boredom, her unwillingness to risk herself with people. Friendship is something very special—reserved it seems for Mr. Boyd almost alone. There are times when she can relax a little and glimpse the intensity of her feelings toward him, and there are even times when others seem able to twit her ever so gently on the matter: "Very soon after breakfast Eliza Cliffe came; but still sooner Bummy said to me laughingly, 'Are you going to see Mr. Boyd today?' And laughing was my answer—'Yes! If *you* will come too.' Then grave was her observation 'But you know you can go tomorrow.' 'Go tomorrow. Oh I think not.' (*Oh I wish I could!* was what my heart *assided*). 'Why certainly Mr. Boyd may not like your going quite so often.' How could I help saying 'If I thought Mr. Boyd did not like my going *very often*, I would not go at all.' "

There are moments when she is not so detached. She fears his silences, wonders how he will be at the next visit, and in general adjusts her mood to what she judges the success or failure of their precious friendship. Very simply—but also not so simply—she loved him, and he her. Nor is their love to be considered some bit of extravagant psychopathology. They shared ideas; they gave one another all sorts of information; they inspired one another. If psychiatrists have not yet come to the point that they can appreciate the dignity and worth of such a relationship, then there is indeed more for us to learn than even we appreciate—and the most arrogant psychiatrist will usually preface his remarks with a declaration of humility and an avowal of relative ignorance.

In point of fact Mr. Boyd was to Miss Barrett what Dr. Fliess was to Dr. Freud: a mind whose company made the world seem more hopeful, responsive and encouraging. The Elizabeth Barrett who sought after Mr. Boyd so persistently was trying hard to be a poet, a writer, a classical scholar, and thus a person apart from others. The Sigmund Freud who relied almost passionately—I put in "almost" where it is not necessary, and even misleading, out of my own shyness—on the correspondence with Dr. Fliess and on the "congresses," the walks and talks they had from time to time, was very much like Miss Barrett, a "loner," a person desperately trying to live with a particularly intense and gifted mind that needed at least one "other" person to receive ideas and feelings. Perhaps every writer is secretly speaking to someone; and every painter wants one other person to watch what he puts on canvas. I have had "creative" patients tell me that they can almost feel themselves talking as they work—silently and alone. Now, I am not trying to make yet another attempt to "explain" the writer or painter "at work." I am simply trying to suggest that a number of very significant men and women in the history of literature, the arts, and the sciences too, have at critical moments in their lives *turned to somebody*, and done so in a way that reveals not only neurosis (I suppose any time we get involved with another human being *that* can happen) but an effort to find—well, use whatever word is congenial: reassurance, support, sanction, the grace that comes when two people speak, when one person listens to another.

In a sense then, Elizabeth Barrett's diary can be "summarized" psychologically in a sentence or two, or be seen as one more example of how utterly, persistently (and wonderfully) elusive are the sources of the human mind's energies. In 1831, when there was no telephone to give a person's thoughts quick but strictly passing expression, Miss Barrett made her various moods and ideas submit to the permanence of a diary. (There were also, of course, letters.) She talked to herself, shunned many others, and found in Mr. Boyd reason enough to feel lonely but not alone. She also revealed how very much a large, intimate and well-to-do family can mean to a supposedly reserved or distant young woman. Freud, after all, mainly saw those Victorians who had fallen apart—at a time when the Victorian Age itself was coming to an end. We do not know enough about the very considerable strengths that characterized the family-life of some of the prudish or "repressed" people who lived in the 19th century. It is true that they didn't know what we know about atoms and molecules or the workings of the unconscious—so that to us they seem to have lived terribly in the dark, groping where we understand, faltering where we can see and cure. Yet, Freud himself came out of that century—he was born before Mrs. Robert Browning died—as did Wordsworth, Balzac and Tolstoy. It is hard to believe that a few psychoanalytic formulations, a few electron microscopes or space-capsules, make our life all that more knowing, all that different in its essentially comic, frivolous and importantly tragic nature.

To me the Elizabeth Barrett whose diary follows is best thought of as a *defiant writer*—self-centered and proud as anyone is who dares ask others to read, to listen, to pay heed. A social historian would find her diary a valuable introduction to a kind of living now almost gone. (Obviously there are remnants that persist, and not only in England.) And as for a psychiatrist, he has to take note of the tensions that crop up repeatedly in the young lady's written comments—but then go on to remind himself what she did with those tensions in the full course of her fifty-five years of life.

Cambridge, Massachusetts   Robert Coles, M.D.
January, 1968

CUE TITLES

B/GB	*Letters of the Brownings to George Barrett*, ed. Paul Landis (Urbana, Illinois, 1958)
Berg	Henry W. and Albert A. Berg Collection of the New York Public Library
EBB/HSB	*Elizabeth Barrett to Mr. Boyd*, ed. Barbara P. McCarthy (London, 1955)
EBB/RB	*The Letters of Robert Browning and Elizabeth Barrett Barrett, 1845-1846*, 2 vols. (London and New York, 1899)
EBB/RHH	*Letters of Elizabeth Barrett Browning Addressed to Richard Hengist Horne*, ed. S. R. Townshend Mayer, 2 vols. (London, 1877)
EBB/MRM	*Elizabeth Barrett to Miss Mitford*, ed. Betty Miller (London, 1954)
GNO	*Sancti Patris Nostri Gregorii Nazianzeni Theologi, Opera*, ed. Jacobus Billius, 2 vols. (Coloniæ, 1690)
Huntington	Henry E. Huntington Library, San Marino, California
HUP	*Elizabeth Barrett Browning. Hitherto Unpublished Poems and Stories*, ed. H. Buxton Forman, 2 vols. (Boston, 1914)
Kenyon	*The Letters of Elizabeth Barrett Browning*, ed. Frederic G. Kenyon, 2 vols. (London and New York, 1897)
LCL	*Loeb Classical Library* series:
-A	*Æschylus*, ed. E. Capps, T. E. Page, W. H. D. Rouse, 2 vols. (London & New York, 1922-26)
-C	*Cicero: Letters to Atticus*, trans. E. O. Winstedt, vol. III (London & New York, 1918)
-CL	*Claudian*, trans. Maurice Platnauer, 2 vols. (London & New York, 1922)
-E	*Euripides*, trans. Arthur S. Way, 4 vols. (London & New York, 1912)
-EP	*Epictetus: The Discourses as Reported by Arrian, The Manual, and Fragments*, trans. W. A. Oldfather, vol. II (London & New York, 1928)
-HE	*Herodotus*, trans. A. D. Godley, vol. III (London & New York, 1922)
-HO/O	*Horace: The Odes and Epodes*, trans. C. E. Bennett (London & Cambridge, Mass., 1960)
-HO/S	*Horace: Satires, Epistles and Ars Poetica*, trans. H. Rushton Fairclough (London & New York, 1961)

LCL-   *Loeb Classical Library* series (continued):

   -MA   *The Communings with Himself of Marcus Aurelius Antoninus, Emperor of Rome*, trans. C. R. Haines (London & New York, 1916)

   -P   *Plutarch's Moralia*, trans. Frank Cole Babbitt, vol. III (London & New York, 1931)

   -V   *Virgil*, trans. H. Rushton Fairclough, vol. I (London & New York, 1916)

PCC   *Patrologiæ Cursus Completus, . . . Series Græca*, ed. J. P. Migne, vols. LII & LXII (Paris, 1859-60)

PML   Pierpont Morgan Library, New York

RE   *The Reader's Encyclopedia*, ed. William Rose Benét, rev. edn. (New York, [1963])

SC   *The Browning Collections: Catalogue of Messrs. Sotheby, Wilkinson & Hodge* (London, 1913)

Weaver   "Twenty Unpublished Letters of Elizabeth Barrett to Hugh Stuart Boyd," ed. Bennett Weaver, *PMLA*, LXV (1950), 397-418

Wellesley   Wellesley College Library, Wellesley, Massachusetts

WG   The Wellesley *Gregory*, being the copy of vol. I of *GNO*, owned successively by Hugh Stuart Boyd and E.B.B., with marginal annotations by them both; it formed Lot 717 of the 1913 Browning Sale

HOPE END, 1831

Water-colour by Arabella Barrett

Saturday.
June 4th 1831. Hope End.

I wonder if I shall burn this sheet of paper
like most others I have begun in the same way.
To write a diary, I have thought of very often
at far & near distances of time: but how
could I write a diary without throwing upon
paper my thoughts, all my thoughts — the
thoughts of my heart as well as of my head? —
& then how could I bear to look on them
after they were written? Adam made physicians
necessary for the mind, as well as for the
body. And such a mind as I have
So very exacting & exclusive & eager &
headlong — & so very very often wrong! —
Well! but I will write — I must write —

ENTRY OF 4 JUNE 1831

Saturday.

June ≪4≫.*th* *1831. Hope End.*

    I wonder if I shall burn this sheet of paper ≪*like*≫ *most others I
have* ≪*begun*≫ *in the same way. To write a diary, I have thought of
very often at far & near distances of time: but how could I write a*   5
diary without throwing upon ≪. . .≫ *paper my thoughts, all my
thoughts—the thoughts of my heart as well as of my head?—&*
≪*then*≫ *how could I bear to look on <u>them</u> after they were written?
Adam made fig leaves necessary for the mind, as well as for the body.
And such <u>a</u> mind as I have!— So very exacting & exclusive & eager*   10
*& head long—<ᴧ&—<u>strong</u>—> & so very very often <u>wrong</u>! Well!
but I will write: I must write—& the oftener wrong I* ≪*know*≫ *myself to be, the less wrong I shall be in one thing—the less <u>vain</u> I shall
be!—*

    Eliza Cliffe rode here today with the Miss Cranes[1]*—singing*   15
*cranes! they sang like nightingales. We had luncheon with them; &
after they went, we had a thunderstorm to ourselves. Such a thunderstorm! I lay down on Minny's bed, & grew hot & cold for myself
& everybody near me, & many* ≪*bodies*≫ *not near me; viz for Papa
& Bro who were out,—*≪*& for*≫ *Mr. Boyd who is at Malvern where*   20
the storm was travelling.[2] *Arabel dreamt last night that <u>he</u> was dead,
& that <u>I</u> was laughing! Foolish dream!—& more foolish* ≪*I*≫ *who
could <think> of it in the storm!— After the storm had gone off,
the post came in. A letter expected from Mr. Boyd! A letter* ≪*received*≫ *from Mrs. Boyd!*[3] *"Mr. Boyd says that I was a true* ≪*pro-*   25
phetess about≫ *the verses, but that he would rather talk to me* ≪*on*≫
*that subject." Something of the kind. The verses are mine entitled
"Kings," & my prophecy was that he would not like them.*[4] *"He*

---

    1. Eliza Wilhelmina Cliffe (1810-48), later (1844) Giles, figures largely in the Diary. She
was the friend closest in age to E.B.B., but it will be seen from the entry of 4 October that,
by E.B.B.'s own definition, Eliza was regarded as an acquaintance rather than a friend. The
Miss Cranes were the daughters of Samuel Crane of Worcester, one of whom, Mary Brilliana
(d. 1901), later married Eliza's brother, the Rev. Allen Cliffe.

    2. In an unpublished letter to Arabella, dated 15-19 April [1848], E.B.B. wrote: "I *am*
afraid of only a few things in the world . . for instance, of thunder & lightning, ghosts, mus-
quitoes . . ." (Collection of Miss Myrtle and Col. R. A. Moulton-Barrett).

    3. Ann Boyd (? -1834), the daughter of Wilson Lowry the celebrated engraver, had
married H.S.B. in September 1805.

    4. Printed in *The Times*, 31 May 1831 (see Appendix II, p. 311). E.B.B.'s "prophecy"
was contained in a letter to H.S.B. (Monday [30 May 1831], *EBB/HSB*, pp. 138-139).

[1]

Diary by E.B.B.

w.^d rather talk to me on that subject." That means, he would rather
not write to me on that subject—or perhaps <ₐon> any other. I am
beginning to be wrong already—perhaps! He has often spoken to
me of his difficulties in getting some one to write for him—and yet
5 "he would rather not!!" Why should those words stick in my throat
like ≪...≫ Amen in Macbeth's?[1] There was a note too for Arabel
from Annie.[2] She has never answered my note—a note as affectionate as I could make it. No! not quite as affectionate; but very
affectionate. "Dearest Annie;" I said, "may we not be as we have
10 been"? No! we cannot. She has not written to say "Yes ≪...≫
—we can". If she were not Mr Boyd's daughter, should I love her as
I do still? In that case, my answer to that question w.^d be again "No!
I cannot." How very very very unkindly she has behaved to me! I
cannot bear to think of it: I wish she were not Mr Boyd's daughter;
15 for then some of my feelings would not clash in the painful way they
do now. Not that I wish to be at ease to dislike her. Oh no! I w.^d
not do that! But it is painful to be longing to <love> a person who
will not be loved, or to love a person who repays ≪your love≫ with
such coldness—such unkindness!— And then Mr Boyd likes me to
20 invite her here. How can I like it, except for his sake, when she acts
towards me as she does? I hope she may go to Sir John Gibbons's;[3]
for then I shall be in no difficulty about inviting her here. I would
invite her willingly, & have her here as long as she could be happy
here, even if this unkindness of hers were to <ₐbe> dashed,—cold
25 as it is, against the warmest pulses of my heart <ₐevery hour—>—
but Henrietta does not like her being here; & Bummy will not like it;
& I shall have a thousand difficulties as usual to contend with. Now
I must go to dress for dinner.

Annie ≪sends≫ her love to me in her note to Arabel, but says
30 afterwards that she wonders how I could publish such horrible verses,

1. *Macbeth* II.ii.31-33:

> But wherefore could I not pronounce 'Amen'?
> I had most need of blessing, and 'Amen'
> Stuck in my throat.

2. Ann Henrietta Boyd, later (1837) Hayes, H.S.B.'s daughter. At this time, there was a
certain coolness between her and E.B.B., due to the latter's "vexatious interference" in per-
suading H.S.B. to remain in Malvern after his lease of Woodland Lodge expired in May 1831.
Annie, with her mother's support, had advocated moving to Bath or Cheltenham (see *EBB/
HSB*, pp. 129-130).

3. Sir John Gibbons (1774-1844), 4th Baronet, of Stanwell Place, near Staines, Middlesex.

[2]

& that some of those on Warren's Blacking are as good.[1] *I am not angry at her saying so. But considering these words of hers, together with other words of hers,—Oh I feel how it is!— What is my sin? The ⟨having⟩ been ⟨anxious⟩, & appeared anxious for M.ʳ Boyd to remain near me. Could I ≪help≫ appearing so when I was so? Could I help being so? ≪Had I felt a less strong regard for him, I should≫ neither have been nor appeared: and now I should be bitterly regretting that they stayed ⟨ₐlonger⟩ in this neighbourhood. But I cannot regret it, as it is!— I do regret having printed those verses. M.ʳ Boyd does not like them: & I suspect that his regard for me is ⟨ₐdependant on his literary estimation of me, &⟩ not great enough, for me to afford the loss of any part of it. We shall see!— ≪& perhaps we shall feel!—≫*

Taylor[2] *told Papa today that Bro was the best speaker at the Reform dinner last Tuesday,*[3] *& that considering the youth of the speaker, he could not ⟨have⟩ expected so much from him. Papa seemed pleased as he ≪repeated≫ it to us. Dear Papa! dear Bro!—*

Sunday ≪5≫.ᵗʰ June.

I went to church with Bummy & Arabel in our wheelbarrow;[4] *& heard such singing—& such preaching. Alas for my ears & understanding! And alas for M.ʳˢ Peyton's*[5] *eyes, which were red ≪in≫*

---

1. The firm of Robert Warren advertised its shoe-blacking widely by means of puerile verses, e.g., the following, from the *Worcester Herald*, 26 June 1830:

> A NEW LIGHT.
> To highly polish Boots and Shoes,
> Warren's brilliant Blacking use,
> From well-known Mart, at 30, STRAND,
> The most renown'd in ev'ry land.
> Fam'd ROBERT WARREN always adds a grace
> To *understandings* of the human race.

Charles Dickens's first employment was with this firm.

2. Luke Taylor, keeper of the Feathers Hotel in Ledbury.

3. *Hereford Journal*, 8 June 1831: "On Tuesday the 31st ult. Mr. Hoskins . . . attended a Public Dinner . . . to celebrate his triumphant return to Parliament. Mr. Hoskins experienced a most flattering reception on his entrance into Ledbury, and a most numerous and respectable company, comprising upwards of 95 gentlemen, sat down to a splendid dinner. . . . The healths of the Chairman, Colonel Money, Captain Johnstone, Captain Adams, . . . E. Barrett, jun. Esq., . . . called forth able and eloquent addresses from those gentlemen, which were received with manifestations of approbation and pleasure from all present. . . ." Mr. Hoskins was a supporter of the Reform Bill.

4. A light, three-wheeled, open carriage, accommodating three passengers.

5. Eliza Peyton (1788-1861), wife of Nicholson Peyton, was the only surviving daughter of Mrs. Griffith of Barton Court.

consequence of the sermon.   How affected she must have been!
There seemed to me to be far more bathos than pathos in M.ʳ
Barnaby's[1] discourse: but it only lasted ten minutes, & so I forgive
≪him≫ my share of the weariness.

5   *No letters today.   I sent a note written last night, to M.ʳˢ Boyd,*
in which I send my love to Annie, & make no observations.   Arabel
sent a note to Annie reproaching her for unkindness to me; & would
not let me see it.   What will the effect be?   Nothing good I am afraid,
& I am afraid something bad.   If Annie does not answer it, Arabel

10   *<ₐsays she> will not go to see her on Thursday,—a day fixed for*
our going to Malvern.   Fudge! said M.ʳ Burchell![2]   Annie will not
answer it: & Arabel will go to see her.

      We were a part of M.ʳ Curzon's[3] congregation at the gate.   Able
sermon—but nothing eloquent—nothing to make me glow.   Met the

15   *Cliffes & Cranes at the gate.   Settled—that Eliza sh.ᵈ come here on*
Thursday to ride with us to Malvern, & bring a poney for Henrietta.
Henrietta & Bummy are going to hear Miss Steers[4] play.

      I read some of Chrysostom's commentary on the Ephesians.[5]   I
am getting tired of this commentary.   Such underground dark pas-

20   *sages before you get at anything worth standing to look at!   Very*
eloquent sometimes: but such a monotony & lengthiness!—— Sun-

1. The Rev. Thomas Barneby (1773?-1842), Rector of Edvin Loach and Tedstone Wafer, and Lecturer of Bromyard, in the Diocese of Hereford.

2. Otherwise Sir William Thornhill, in [Oliver Goldsmith's] *The Vicar of Wakefield: A Tale* (Salisbury, 1766), I, 104: ". . . I should have mentioned the very impolite behaviour of Mr. Burchell, who, during this discourse, sate with his face turned to the fire, and at the conclusion of every sentence would cry out *fudge*, an expression which displeased us all, and in some measure damped the rising spirit of the conversation."

3. The Hon. and Rev. George Henry Roper-Curzon (1798-1889), later (1842) 16th Baron Teynham. In 1828 he was ordained a Baptist Minister, and was appointed to Ledbury. In addition to the services in the chapel in Ledbury, he conducted meetings in a building by the Hope End south gate (described as "Chapel, or School House" in the Sale Catalogue; see Appendix III, p. 337). He left Ledbury shortly after the Barretts did, in 1832.

4. Frances Steers (1797-1860), of Well House, Malvern Wells. In an unpublished letter to Robert Browning, dated 7 April 1889, George Moulton-Barrett wrote: "With this I send, what seems to me a pretty drawing of Hope End. It was executed by a Miss Steers, who . . . was an artist at Malvern & gave lessons to my sister Henrietta in music & drawing. Afterwards I believe she became a member of the Society of Water colours." (Collection of Edward R. Moulton-Barrett, Esq.) Miss Steers did become a member of the New Water-colour Society (later the Royal Institute), and 59 of her pictures were included in their exhibitions between 1846 and 1860.

5. *PCC*, LXII, cols. 5-176. St. John Chrysostom (*c.* 345-407), Archbishop of Constantinople, one of the Fathers of the Christian Church, was one of the principal theological writers studied by E.B.B. with H.S.B.

*day is not a reading day with me.   Driving to church—driving back
again—driving to chapel—driving back again—& prayers three times
at home besides!   All that fills up the day—except the few interstices
between the intersections.   Mr Curzon told me that he saw Mr Boyd
on Friday evening & sate an hour & a half with him.*   5

Monday.   June ≪6≫.th
      *I have heard this morning that Kenrick¹ had another letter from
that Reid² on Thursday, & that instead of leaving off working on
Papa's ground, he has begun to weed the wheat.   No other particulars known yet.   Suppose we should go after all:—Oh I will not think   10
of it!   Papa's spirits are very good: & I am not presentimental—at
least I think not!   If we do go—why then I have more to suffer; that
is all!—& Annie will repent her <unkindness>—& Mr Boyd—what
will he do?   Will he be sory—very sorry?   Or will he only "regret"
it, as I do when I decline an invitation I dont care about?   But I ought   15
not to think so much of myself.   Poor Papa!   He is the person to be
thought of, & felt for!——*
      *No letters.   I wrote to Miss Knowles my congratulations on M^r
Knowles's marriage.³   Walked out with Bummy & Arabel.   Read.
Henrietta on the heath.   I have heard that Kenrick went today into   20
the garden!   I mentioned his hoeing the wheat to Bummy, who expressed herself "vexed at it."   She did however say that she knew
something was doing.   I wish I knew what it was!   A note came from
Eliza Cliffe enquiring about "our hopes & fears"; & Bummy being in
the room, I was obliged ≪or fancied≫ myself obliged to read part of   25
it.   Bummy angry—indignant at my allowing Eliza to mention the
subject to me!   I angry on the other hand.   I went into Bummy's
room afterwards to make friends.   Soon made.   Dear Bummy expressed her affection for me.   Was the expression of mine necessary?*

1. The mortgagees' agent had appointed William Kendrick, a local farmer, as Farm Bailiff at the end of March, to supervise the agricultural affairs at Hope End, pending the sale of the estate.

2. Of 170 Regent Street, London, the mortgagees' agent handling the sale of Hope End.

3. Charlotte Laura (1804-93) was the eldest daughter of Admiral Sir Charles and Lady Knowles. Entry 352 of the Marriage Register of St. George's, Hanover Square, London, records the marriage on 26 May 1831 of her eldest brother, Francis Charles, to Emma Pocock, the fourth daughter of Sir George Pocock, Bt. Sir Charles and his family had, until recently, lived at Malvern, and it was while calling on them that E.B.B. first saw H.S.B. (described in a letter to her grandmother, *HUP*, II, 87-93; see also page xx).

Diary by E.B.B.

No! it was not necessary <u>to be made</u>; but it was necessary for <u>me to</u>
<u>make it</u>.   Papa in good spirits, & playing at cricket with the boys.
He reports more commendation of Bro's speech.   I wish I had heard
it. Papa pleased—& I pleased, of course.

5 *Tuesday.   June ≪7≫.ᵗʰ*
   *   No letters again!   It is quite clear that the "something bad" has*
been the result of Arabel's letter to Annie.   Arabel <certainly> used
one of her own <feathers> ≪in writing≫ it—one way of calling her
a ≪goose≫!—   There will be no letter tomorrow: and I shall dread the
10 *interview on Thursday, not only on account of Annie, but Mͬ.ˢ Boyd.*
And as to Mͬ. Boyd, even <u>he</u> may blame me for letting Arabel
<ₐagain> turn up the green sod which had been turned down; tho'
there was not <ₐa> chance of its ever taking root.   I let Arabel do
it: because I could not <u>let</u> her <u>from</u> doing it.   Arabel loves me; &
15 *<u>would</u> shew that she ≪loves≫ me.   I wish she had not, in this instance.*
*   ≪Papa≫ has gone to the Newent Bible meeting:¹ & Bro & Sam,*
Stormy <Georgie> & Henry, to the Bosbury ≪fishing≫ brook.²
Bummy Henrietta Arabel & I dined at one; & then Bummy Arabel &
I went in the wheelbarrow to the Whyche.³   We walked thro' the
20 *rocky passage, & sate down on the Worcestershire side of the hill.*
Such a sight!   Such a <u>sea</u> of land: the sunshine throwing its light; &
the clouds, their shadows, upon it!   <u>Sublime</u> sight, I must still call
it!—   I looked along the Great Malvern road.   Shall I ever ≪travel≫
along it again? Not with the same feelings! & I <had> some sad ones

---

1. Newent: a market-town about 10 miles south of Hope End (map ref. N5) that contained a Wesleyan-Methodist meeting-place.

2. The River Leadon at Bosbury, 2 miles N.W. of Hope End (map ref. D3).

3. The Wyche was a pass, about 900 feet above sea-level, through the Malvern Hills south of the Worcestershire Beacon (map ref. C7). Several forms of spelling occur, but the modern usage is Wyche. It was a frequent excursion of E.B.B. and her family, on account of the view, despite the steepness of the road, which caused the carriage to overturn while descending from the summit on the occasion of her first visit to H.S.B. in 1828. A contemporary guidebook states: "The road from this place [Ledbury] to Great Malvern, over the Wytch, is not eligible for carriages in general, more especially such as are not accustomed to the country. But from the Wytch, which is a road cut through the rock, on the summit of the Malvern [Hills], the view is grand, extensive, and beautiful beyond description. On a clear day, with the naked eye, fifteen counties in England and Wales, four cities, and the shores of the Irish channel, besides innumerable towns and villages, and two beautiful rivers, are clearly distinguishable" (*Paterson's Roads; Being an Entirely Original and Accurate Description of all the Direct and Principal Cross Roads in England and Wales*, ed. Edward Mogg, 18th edn. augmented and improved, London, [1832?], p. 493).

in thinking so: tho' I would not have it otherwise.   I ran along the
walk to <u>see</u> if I could <u>see</u> Ruby Cottage.[1] *No! it was too far off.   We*
returned thro the Whyche: & I climbed the low hill, & Arabel the high
one; & Bummy sate below each of us.   I looked on each side of the
elevated place where I sate.   Herefordshire all hill & wood—undulating   5
& broken ground!—   Worcestershire throwing out ≪a≫ grand <ₐun-
broken> extent,—& more than Worcestershire, ≪to≫ the horizon!
One, prospect ≪attracting≫ the eye, by picturesqueness: the other
the mind,—by sublimity.   <u>My</u> mind seemed spread north south east
& west over the surface of those extended lands: and, to gather it up   10
again into its usual compass, was an effort.   If I had stayed there
another half hour, I should have made verses—or ≪shed≫ tears: and
if some circumstances had not happened, those tears w^d have had a
different character—they w^d have been <u>bitter</u> tears.   ≪ . . . As≫ it
is, Malvern is associated ≪still with≫ happiness: & I do like to feel   15
myself there.

   I dreamt last night,—for night dreams are as well worth recording
as day dreams,—that I was re-writing the Warren-blacking lines,—&
≪inserted≫ in some part of them the following—
            ≪Fame≫ o'er him flashed <her> meteor wing—   20
            And <u>he</u>—he was a King.
What ≪king≫ I was writing of, is out of my head.   They caught no
fish at Bosbury.   Read as usual.   ≪Papa walked eleven miles.≫

Wednesday.   June ≪8≫th

   No letters again.   The "something bad" is certain.   Arabel wrote   25
to Annie, enclosing a note to Miss Steers from Henrietta.   A good
pretext for writing! ≪for writing≫ her wonder at ≪the≫ silence, her
disappointment at it, & her intention of no more recurring to the

---

1. The house leased by H.S.B. when E.B.B. first visited him in 1828, and re-occupied by him in May 1831 (map ref. D8).   The nearby inn having been named after Admiral John Benbow (1653-1702), Ruby Cottage (now more correctly called The Ruby) was named after the only ship of his squadron to support him in action against the French in the West Indies in 1702, when the remaining five captains under his command mutinied.   The house, very little altered since the time of the Diary, stands in a small amount of ground adjacent to the main road between Malvern Wells and Great Malvern, with a short carriage drive linking the house to the road at two points.   The house stands on the eastern slope of the Malvern Hills, 500 feet above sea-level.   Behind it, the land rises steeply for more than 500 feet to the summit.   Some 300 feet up this slope is the footpath of which E.B.B. speaks, and which was frequently her mode of access to Ruby Cottage.

subject.   This is the best way.   Recurring to the subject can avail no-
thing: and five words explain everything—Annie does not love
<u>*me.*</u>   *I wish she were not Mr Boyd's daughter: and I almost wish that*
I were not going to Malvern tomorrow.   Oh no! not even <u>almost</u>!   I
5   *meant, "<I> almost <u>thought</u> I wished it"!   <Why should> I mind*
seeing Annie?   Why should I feel embarrassed?   What have I done
≪∧*to be embarassed about?≫   At any rate Mr Boyd will be glad to*
see me: & nothing, except his not being so, could make me less glad
to see <u>him</u>.

10   *Bro dined at the Bartons.*[1]   *Papa arrived at home, just before he*
did, from the Redmarley Bible meeting.[2]   *Papa's account of ≪the≫*
discussion between himself & Mr Jackson the Wesleyan Minister.[3]
≪*I said as little as I could; thro'≫ a recollection of past circumstances:*
but when Bummy expressed a general dislike towards the <u>Methodists</u>,
15   *it would have been something worse than cowardice in me, to have*
said nothing.   Read as usual.

Thursday June ≪9≫.th

Eliza Cliffe & two ponies arrived immediately after breakfast; &
we set off for Malvern at ≪about≫ half past ten: Henrietta & Eliza
20   *riding; Bummy Arabel & I in the wheelbarrow.   I was nervous about*
Annie & everybody at Ruby Cottage all the way there.   No use in it—
"thinks I to myself".   They drove ≪me≫ nearly to the gate, & then
≪*turning≫ back, left me to make my own debut.   I could scarcely*
stand <u>debout</u>.   Annie, espied in the garden, ≪walked≫ away on
25   *catching a glimpse of the carriage.   I was shewn into the drawing*
room— ["] sola cum sola"![4] *—& was, while I was <u>consternating</u> my-*

---

1. Barton Court, the home of Mrs. Griffith and the Peyton family (map ref. E6). It had
been purchased in 1792 by Mrs. Griffith's uncle, Henry Lambert, when he left Hope End after
a dispute with his son-in-law, Sir Henry Vane Tempest. He rebuilt and enlarged the house,
making the drawing-room the exact size of the one at Hope End, and decorating it in blue
and gold, in order to display the blue Persian carpet he had brought with him from Hope End.
The house, 1½ miles from Hope End, was on the road leading toward Malvern, and so would
be passed by E.B.B. each time she journeyed to the Wyche or to Ruby Cottage.

2. Redmarley D'Abitot: a village about 8 miles S.E. of Hope End containing a Wesleyan-
Methodist meeting-place (map ref. K6).

3. Richard Jackson, the Wesleyan-Methodist minister stationed in Ledbury for 1830-31
("The Stations of the Preachers for 1830-31," *Wesleyan-Methodist Magazine*, September
1830, pp. 611-622).

4. "Alone with myself." Possibly her phrase owes something to Cicero (*De Officiis*, III, i:
". . . nec minus solum, quam cum solus esset" — "never less lonely than when alone").

[8]

self, desired to go into Mrs Boyd's bedroom. She dressing. To my astonishment, she told me that Annie was going that day,—& <she> herself as her companion,—to Sir John Gibbons!! In the midst of our talking, into the room came Annie. Cool reception—on her part I mean. Very very cool manner! Mrs Boyd sent her in to Mr Boyd   5 to apprize him of my arrival; & in a few minutes, he was ready to see me. When I got into the room, I was at ease in one moment, & in a humour to forget all the worrying out of it.   With regard to my <$_\wedge$Warren Blacking> verses he told me, that he could not see the meaning of the <line> ending each verse?[1]—& my explanation   10 seemed to make darkness darker.   He said besides that there was <nothing> of my usual poetical manner in them: but that, as he was aware of the inequalities of the productions of people of talent, there was one thing which surprised him more than my having written them; tho' that had surprised him. I guessed the one thing to be,   15 my having published them. "No! you know, I am always blunt— I am very much surprised at the Times Newspaper having received them".   ≪He hoped that I had not blamed him for not writing to me! M^{rs} B had seemed so much occupied, lately!≫

We argued as to whether engraving <or> painting was the superior   20 art.   Agreed at last—that if we compared the engraver & the painter who ≪was a mere copyist≫, the engraver should stand first: but that the original painter ≪should stand≫ before the engraver. Talked of Reform.[2]   He led me to believe by his manner, that a letter he had just received from D^r A Clarke[3] contained an anti-reform opinion.   25

1. "And he—he was a king." (See Appendix II, p. 311.)

2. The burning political issue of the day. The outdated electoral machinery left the preponderance of voting power in the boroughs, and took no account of the growth of industrial areas such as Manchester and Birmingham; at this time, these two towns returned no members to Parliament, although Old Sarum, with only seven voters, still returned two. As far back as 1776, John Wilkes and John Cartwright had called for Parliamentary Reform, to give just and equal representation. Repeated attempts to introduce legislation had been blocked by those with vested interests in maintaining the status quo; (it had been calculated in 1793 that the Lords of the Treasury, 71 peers and 82 commoners between them controlled the nomination of 306 out of the 558 members of the Commons). The most recent Bill had been introduced in March 1831, and had been given a second reading by a majority of one, but the Government had been defeated on the third reading in April. The ensuing General Election had given further evidence of the popular will by returning Lord Grey's Administration with increased strength.

3. Adam Clarke (1762?-1832), Irish Wesleyan Minister and theological writer, a close friend of H.S.B. There was also a slight degree of consanguinity, as Clarke's grandmother was a Boyd.

Diary by E.B.B.

He then gave me the letter which contained an opinion warmly in favour of the bill.   I was pleased; and asked permission to show this letter which is a very able one, to Papa.   The rain came on; & as my party was thus detained at Great Malvern until six o'clock, I in the meanwhile, dined <u>superficially</u> with Mrs Boyd, that Mr Boyd might not be ≪detained≫ from his dinner by my being in the room.   After dinner, I went back again to him.   Talked of ≪Blomfield's≫ Septem apud Thebas,[1] which I have ordered from Worcester, to read with him.   Mrs Boyd's carriage, & our wheelbarrow at the door at the same time.   ≪ . . . She≫ is to remain away a week; & Mr Boyd asked me to ≪go≫ to see him in the interim.   Monday or Tuesday—cant you fix Monday?   ≪I≫ agreed to it.   Annie kissed me <u>affectionately</u> at parting; & when I asked her to let <u>us</u> hear sometimes from her, she said she would—that is, if I have time!—   We drove home at seven, in a pouring <u>rain</u>: Eliza dined & slept here.   Papa pleased with D^r A C's letter, shown to him after dinner.   ≪We talked a little; & I talked <u>boldly</u> about the Wesleyans.≫

Friday.   June ≪10≫.

As I heard last night that Bummy had agreed to visit Miss Steers again on Tuesday evening, I saw it was impossible to take the carriage to Malvern on Monday besides.   Therefore I wrote ＜four＞ lines in a ≪text≫ hand that Mr Boyd's servants might read ≪them≫ to him, saying that I could not be with him until Tuesday.   Enclosed D^r C's letter; & Bro left ＜my＞ packet, on his way to the Ely fishing.[2]

＜How unhappy＞ I seem on the brink of being!   While Eliza Bummy & I were sitting in the drawing room, talking ≪_∧& singing,≫ in came Lane.   He wished to speak with Bummy.   She went out; & I felt breathless—dreading to hear something past supporting.   In the meantime Arabel came into the room, & told us that a Gentleman a Lady & a little girl ≪had arrived≫ to see the house.   Bummy returned, & pretended to know nothing about it.   I ran up stairs,—& trembled until now.   I hear that Bummy has sent Lane up to Papa!   Those people are in the dining room.   I will pray now.   Will not ≪our≫ Father who is in Heaven, hear prayer for His Son's sake.   And

1. Charles James Blomfield ed. *Æschyli Septem Contra Thebas* (Cambridge, 1812).
2. Not identified. From the context, a small river or brook to the east of Malvern.

[10]

has he not often & often heard mine?   Yes!   & when I felt in more
certain sorrow than I do ≪at≫ this moment——

    I can take breath again.   The people are gone.   Their message
thro' Lane to Papa was, that they were sent by M.ʳ Reid to see the
house.   Papa's message to them was—that nobody belonging to M.ʳ   5
Reid was here to show them the house.   So they went away.   I hear
that their name is Brydges, & that they ≪ . . . ≫ have come from
Canonfrome¹ (how is the word spelt?)—& that their servant spoke
to ours of having seen Hope End advertised to be sold this month.²
How is it to be?   Are we really to go?   I am sick at heart about it;   10
but will hope on still.   Something may be doing, still.   Papa in bad
spirits at dinner.   Bro said something of my note to M.ʳ Boyd, which
made Papa ≪exclaim≫ "What! you were there yesterday—& ≪did≫
you write today—"?   So then ≪I≫ explained ≪how≫ he had
wished me to go to see him during M.ʳˢ Boyd's absence; & how I had   15
first agreed to go on Monday, & afterwards put it off.   No <objec-
tions> made.   ≪ . . . ≫ Papa is not in good spirits today.   ≪If they
dont go to Malvern on Monday, I must & will do so by myself.≫

Saturday.   June ≪11≫.

    Sam told me that Hope End is advertised in the Sun newspaper,   20
to be sold in August—no name, but a full description.³   ≪He≫ &
Bro heard it yesterday from Henry Trant!⁴   I begged him to ≪tell
nobody≫, & to let me tell Bummy.   <Ran> down stairs & found
Bummy in the drawing room by herself.   Told her.   She shed tears—
we both shed tears!   When will tears cease to be shed?   She seems to   25
fear the worst: but mentioned that Papa had written to Sam,⁵ who,
he says, is able to assist him.   If he is able, he is willing—if he is still

---

    1. Canon Frome: a village about 5 miles N.W. of Hope End. The family of Brydges had been prominent in the county for many years, but the particular members here mentioned have not been identified.

    2. The first local announcement of the impending sale of the estate by auction appeared in the *Hereford Journal*, 8 June 1831. Hope End was not mentioned by name, and no date was given for the sale.

    3. *The Sun*, London, 6 June 1831, announced the sale by auction "early in the month of August." The estate was not mentioned by name.

    4. The younger son of Mary Trant (*née* Barrett) of South Lodge, Malvern Wells, and a distant cousin of E.B.B.

    5. Samuel Barrett Moulton-Barrett (1787-1837), Edward Moulton-Barrett's younger brother, who was the co-heir to the extensive Jamaican estates of their maternal grandfather.

Diary by E.B.B.

Sam! So there may still be hope in that quarter. There is fear in every other. In every other? Can I not still look unto the <u>hill</u> from whence cometh my hope?[1] *That hope is a hope of spiritual blessing; but I have found & ≪known≫ it to be one of temporal comfort also!*

5 *Walked out with Bummy & Arabel, on the ≪bank≫ on the other side of the water. Strangers may soon walk there, with other feelings than mine. Bummy asked why I seemed grave. I <u>felt</u> grave. Read as I have often done lately, ≪not≫ for the pleasure of thinking: but for the comfort of <u>not</u> thinking. Papa in better spirits. How often I*

10 *thought of M.ʳ Boyd today! He is the only person in this neighbour-hood, whom it will affect my <u>happiness</u> to leave. I shall be very sorry to leave Eliza Cliffe ≪but not unhappy. Why did I scratch that out?———*[2] *Let me be honest, if I cant be wise!≫*

Sunday. June ≪12≫.ᵗʰ

15 *Went to church in the wheelbarrow with Henrietta,—Henry driving. Heard singing again!!! & a sermon from M.ʳ Deane*[3] *about Sisera's murder.*[4] *He wrote about it, Goddess & about it,*[5] *—until I was about going to sleep. If I had done so, I should have awakened just in time to hear what I went to sleep to avoid. ≪Over≫ & over*

20 *again the same thing; & no-thing <u>very</u> well worth hearing once!— There was however <u>some</u> good in the sermon. Eliza <rode> home with us, & walked down to the school*[6] *with Henrietta at half past two; while Bummy Arabel & I were wheeled in the wheelbarrow. Papa walked by our side. He <u>seems</u> in better spirits. A sermon from M.ʳ*

1. Cf. Psalms cxxi.1: "I will lift up mine eyes unto the hills, From whence cometh my help." In this context, E.B.B.'s misquotation, and the underscorings, may have been a deliberate play on the names of the two family estates, Cinnamon Hill in Jamaica, where her Uncle Sam was, and Hope End.

2. The original entry "but not unhappy" was deleted by E.B.B., then reinstated above the line.

3. The Rev. Thomas Dean, Curate of St. James's Church, Colwall, where the Barretts usually worshipped. In addition to his curacy, Mr. Dean ran a boarding school for 16 young gentlemen "who enjoy the advantages of careful Education, united with the domestic comforts and affectionate tenderness of their own home" (*Hereford Journal*, 5 January 1831).

4. Sisera, general of the Canaanites, whose murder is told in Judges iv.21: "Then Jael Heber's wife took a nail of the tent, and took an hammer in her hand, and went softly unto him, and smote the nail into his temples, and fastened it into the ground: for he was fast asleep and weary. So he died."

5. It seems that E.B.B. made some slip here, because her writing is quite clear, although the sense is not.

6. At the Hope End south gate (see fn. 3, p. 4).

[12]

Curzon on prayer. Good, very good,—but neither original, nor strik-ingly put! Mrs Cliffe & Mrs Best[1] were at the chapel. Mrs Best looks better than <u>Mrs Best</u> ever seemed to me, to look. What a sweet smile & countenance she has! Still water—but the sun shining on it! She ≪thought≫ of coming to see us on ≪Tuesday≫; but I told her of my engagement at Malvern, & begged her to put off her visit until Wednesday. I must positively go to Mr Boyd on Tuesday.

 Ever since hearing what I heard yesterday, I have been thinking— shall I ask Mr Boyd if he <u>will</u> endeavour to go where we go, in the case of our going at all? It w^d be a comfort to me to know if he would make the endeavour; & yet after my past "intrusions", I scarce-ly like asking. And yet (again) did he not tell me, that if I <u>had</u> left Hope End, he "would <_have> been happier at Cheltenham than at Malvern, for one reason—because at Cheltenham there was nothing to remind him of my going to see him". Must he not care a good deal for me, to feel <u>that</u>? And in the case of his caring <u>at all</u> for me, must he not wish, ≪for≫ his own sake, to ≪live≫ near me, wherever I am? I shall never get at any ≪certainty, by≫ this interrogative sys-tem. Hope says one thing; & ≪Fear≫, another, in reply!— If we do leave this dear place, what a consolation it w^d be to me, <u>not</u> to leave besides, the dearest & most valued friend I have in the world≪!!≫— But God's will be done in all things. I wish those words were as clearly written in my heart, as on ≪my≫ paper—in spite of my alledged illegibility!—— No letters today—except one from ≪Miss≫ Uniack to Bummy. Charlotte[2] so very weak that she cant walk with-out support; but well otherwise. Bummy thinks she will never be able to walk again. ≪ . . . ≫ Henrietta told Eliza that they intended not to go to Miss Steers's on Tuesday; so . . I shall go by myself to Malvern! After dinner Papa & we all walked hat-less out of the hall-door, & he led us among the shrubs, directing our attention, now to one, now to another. Is this "a good sign"? I dont know. He is not in good spirits; & I am not in great ones. Now I am going down to prayers! <bell> ringing!— Read nothing but the Bible today.

1. Elizabeth Cliffe (*née* Deane), the widow of the Rev. Allen Cliffe, and her eldest child, Mary Catherine, who had married Thomas Best in 1827.

2. Bummy's younger sister (1787-1834), wife of Richard Pierce Butler of Cloughgrenan, co. Carlow, Ireland. Miss Uniack is believed to have been her paid companion.

Diary by E.B.B.

Monday.   June ≪13≫.th

The gnats kept Arabel & me & half the house besides up half the night: witness my swelled finger—witness this <u>eccentric</u> writing.[1]   I will <u>gnat</u> ≪sleep≫ in that room again, until the weather changes.   I will go into the Bamboo room.   No letters on Monday, . . & if it had been Tuesday, I should have expected none.   M.ʳ Boyd cant write, & nobody else will.   M.ʳ Boyd cant write?   I wish he would try to write with a pencil.   Shall I ask him?   How I should like to receive from him an undictated letter!——   Henrietta on the heath.   Bummy Arabel & I went out to walk, & sate for a long time on the rock, where we were joined by Henrietta.   They have determined on not going to Miss Steers's.

Tuesday.   June ≪14≫.th

Henry drove me to Malvern, & Daisy filled as much as he could of the back seat in the wheelbarrow.   Papa in bad spirits at breakfast. After breakfast we were about to set off—when in consequence of Papa asking me to wait for something inaudible, I sent Henry in to the library, to ask what I was to wait for.   Bummy & Papa there. "What were they doing"? said Arabel.   "Crying"—replied Henry. I would not, could not wait.   If there is anything to hear, it <u>must</u> be something painful: & then I shall ("<u>un man</u> myself", I was going to say) unfit myself for talking to M.ʳ Boyd.   That was my "Thinks I to myself"—so we drove off.   I got to Ruby Cottage before twelve. Miss Hurd[2] was there,—≪ . . . ≫ & I was shown into the dining room, to wait ≪ . . . ≫ while she read some letters to M.ʳ Boyd.   Annoyed!— Took up Stewart's Resurrection,[3] with notes in M.ʳ Boyd's handwriting.   The poetry seems super-erogat<u>orily</u> written,—as far as words are concerned, but if it had been admirable, I was in a nil admiraris[4] humour.   Miss Hurd came to say that M.ʳ Boyd was ready for me. I dont like her.   Found him in the drawing room, where he spends

---

1. More erratic at this point than E.B.B.'s usual style.

2. E.B.B. means Miss Heard, about whom little is known beyond the details occurring in the Diary. In 1842, H.S.B. asked for E.B.B.'s help in obtaining reviews of a book Miss Heard was publishing (*The Shipwreck of the Dryad*; see *EBB/HSB*, pp. 252-253).

3. John Stewart, *The Resurrection: a Poem* (London, 1807).

4. "Marvel at nothing." (Horace: " 'Marvel at nothing'—that is perhaps the one and only thing, Numicius, that can make a man happy and keep him so," *LCL-HO/S*, pp. 286-287: "Epistles" I.vi, lines 1-2.)

[14]

part of every day "now that M^{rs}* Boyd is* ≪*absent*≫*". Two letters had been read to him: one from her, & one from M*^{r}* Barker;*[1] *& as he assured me they had been merely* <u>read</u>*, & the reader disfranchised immediately afterwards, I fell into a forgiving humour. He was not in good spirits. No more was his companion—I talked however as well as I could,—& read as well as I could besides, out of the Septem Apud Thebas, which I began today in his Porson's edition.*[2] *Read 78 lines. I do like reading* ≪*with*≫ *him. He was annoyed by my note; & because I had said in it that "perhaps I could not go to see him until the evening", he had fancied that I was to be engaged during the morning by visiting Miss Wall*[3] *at Gt Malvern in consequence of a request from Eliza Cliffe!!! Did* <u>my</u> *fancy ever take me so far . . . wrong?* <*Very often*>*! He said that he had felt "*<u>I</u> *w*^{d}* not have visited any one who had behaved about Miss Barrett, as Miss Wall has behaved about us". It is amusing to think that he could think so!— As if he were likely by* <u>any</u> *behaviour, to prove a regard equal* ≪*to*≫*, or greater* <*than*>*, the* <u>regard</u> *I feel towards him!— Impossible— at least as feelings & conduct go at present. Talked of M*^{r}* Curzon— Calvinism—Catholicism[—] Annie. A charge against Arabel with reference to the latter, warded off by me. Some* ≪*talking*≫ *of her coldness to me—attributed by M*^{r}* Boyd, to jealousy of Eliza. Fudge, said M*^{r}* Burchell.—— No love—no jealousy! Some* ≪*talking*≫ *of Annie abstractedly & Miss Wall's opinion of her!—& my opinion of her manners. Told him of the unending uncertainty about Hope End. He seemed interested in what I said—& "sorry"! Preached* <$_∧$*Chris- tian resignation &*> *philosophy to me; &* <u>wondered how I could show</u> *as little as I did at Woodland Lodge*[4] *when the subject of our leaving Hope End was agitated: He had been told that I had* ≪*shed*≫ <$_∧$*tears*> *& seemed much distressed. My tears did not fall then* <u>because I was about to leave Hope End;</u> *and that he should think so, brought them again into my eyes. M*^{rs}* Boyd will come back,* <u>probably</u>*, she said* <$_∧$*in her letter*> *at the end of this week. While we were reading the*

5

10

15

20

25

30

---

1. Edmund Henry Barker (1788-1839), classical scholar and friend of H.S.B. At one time, he formulated a plan to publish E.B.B.'s letters to H.S.B. (*EBB/HSB*, pp. 103 and 213).

2. [Richard Porson, ed.], *Æschyli Tragœdiœ Septem*, 2 vols. (Oxford, 1806).

3. Millicent Wall was a close friend of Eliza Cliffe and had been a witness at the marriage of Eliza's sister, Mrs. Best, in 1827.

4. H.S.B.'s previous house in Great Malvern, vacated in May 1831.

Diary by E.B.B.

*Seven Chiefs, he <observed> that tho' Plutarch preferred it to the
<other> Tragedies of Æschylus, he could not help believing it in-
ferior to the Agamemnon. "It is however very long since I read this
tragedy; & now I shall be able to judge better". The "now" made me*

5 *sigh. Is there any chance of his reading it thro' with me, <u>now</u>? I left
him at 20 minutes to six—too late to call on Mrs Trant.[1] Henry &
Daisy had been running & having luncheon on the hills. Got home in
time for dinner, & heard nothing about the conference. ≪Only that
more people had been here to see the place, & were sent away by*

10 *Bummy. Mericks from Ross≫[2]*

Wednesday, June ≪15≫

*Heard this morning that Papa yesterday discharged his women, &
told them that they might <work> for Kenrick but must not expect*

15 *him to pay them for it. They are all in the garden with Daly, Jack
Cook, & a man employed by Kenrick. I will never go there again;
unless we are to stay <u>really</u>. Sam has come into my room to say that
Papa has called Bro down stairs, & <is> still speaking with him.*

My hand & heart trembled as I wrote those last words: but nothing

20 *of the conference has transpired, except Bro's being sent to Ledbury.
What for, I dont know. "What for" is an unanswerable question just
now. Papa did not go out of the house until one; & talked a good
deal with Bummy in the library.*

The Cliffes & Mrs Best <passed> several hours here, in conse-

25 *quence of attraction & repulsion, from us & an anticipated thunderstorm. Mrs Best is going to send me a little tract of hers on Eden,
in ms.—& I am to say exactly what I think of it. I hope I may be
able to <u>say</u> civilly & conscientiously at the same time. Eliza told us,
when I asked her why she looked grave, that she had seen Hope End*

30 *advertised in the Worcester Herald: and I have since heard that the*

1. Mary Trant (*née* Barrett), the widow of James Trant, was a first cousin of E.B.B.'s paternal grandmother. At this time, she was living at South Lodge, approximately one mile south of Ruby Cottage, and E.B.B. would normally call there whenever she took the southern route, via Little Malvern, between Hope End and Ruby Cottage.

2. Dr. (in 1832, Sir) Samuel Rush Meyrick (1783-1848), the celebrated antiquary who superintended the arrangement of the collections of armour at the Tower of London and Windsor Castle. His seat was Goodrich Court, near Ross-on-Wye.

[16]

RUBY COTTAGE

TURNPIKE ON THE ROAD TO LEDBURY

VIEW TAKEN FROM THE OTHER SIDE OF THE ALPINE BRIDGE, 25 JUNE 1831

Pencil sketch by Henrietta Barrett

Hereford Journal has the same advertisement.[1] *Oh we shall certainly go.   There can be* [no] *doubt about it: and if some of my feelings were armed "in complete steel,"*[2] *I should bear it better.   I must fix my eyes upon it, & learn to bear the contemplation* <ᴧ*of it,*> *by God's teaching.   If M.ͬ Boyd were likely to follow us, the bearing*   5
would be a less hard task—but I must not lean too many of my hopes on that if.   I w.ᵈ rather trust to another if—for if he cared for me as I care for him, he could speak & act only in one way.   The Cliffes brought me The Seven Cheifs[3] *which M.ͬˢ Best had ordered from Worcester at my request; and I have been reading over again what I*   10
read with him yesterday, & writing in the margin such remarks of his as I could remember.   The last day's reading with him, must soon come, even if it be not past—but I cant bear to think that!—   He gave me yesterday ≪*his*≫ *letter from M.ͬ Barker,* <*to read*>.   *M.ͬ Barker intends "soon to have the pleasure of writing to Miss Barrett".*   15
Miss ≪*Barrett never*≫ *expected to hear from him again.*

*I did not go out to day.   I had another kind of exercise in crying, this evening!   * <ᴧ*I could not*> <*help thinking*> *of yesterday which certainly* ≪*does*≫ *not "look backward with a smile"*[4] *& of a thousand tomorrows which may not wear one.*   20

Miss Penelope Biddulp called here with a M.ͬ Bowers[5] *—a* ≪*vulgarissimus*≫ *who said "no thank you Miss" to me!—   Now I must go down to tea.   Papa's spirits were good at dinner today.*

1. The *Worcester Herald*, 11 June 1831, and the *Hereford Journal*, 8 June 1831, carried similarly worded notices of the sale, not mentioning Hope End by name, and not naming a specific date for the auction.

2. [John Milton, *Comus:*] *A Maske Presented at Ludlow Castle, 1634* (London, 1637), lines 419-420: " 'Tis chastity, my brother, chastity: | She that has that, is clad in compleat steel."

3. Presumably the 1824 Blomfield edition which formed Lot 313 of the 1913 Browning Sale.

4. [Edward Young], *The Complaint: or, Night-Thoughts on Life, Death, & Immortality. Night the Second. On Time, Death, Friendship* (London, 1742), p. 23:

> Whose *Yesterdays* look backwards with a Smile;
> Nor like the *Parthian* wound him as they fly;
> That common, but opprobrious Lot! Past Hours
> If not by Guilt, yet wound us by their Flight.

5. Penelope Biddulph was one of the daughters of John Biddulph, banker, magistrate, Governor of Guy's Hospital, and Treasurer of the Royal Geographical Society. He was one of the principal citizens of Ledbury.   Capt. Bowers of Boulsdon, a frequent guest of the Biddulphs, had recently returned to England after nine years in South America. In 1832 he was appointed Superintendent of the Seamen's Hospital Ship at Greenwich.

Diary by E.B.B.

Thursday. June 16<u>th</u>

    Papa was in very ≪good≫ spirits today at breakfast, most undoubt-edly.   He told Bro to put the clock half an hour more forward;[1] & this sent my hopes forward .. a little way. Would he think about

5   *altering the clock, if it were ≪likely≫ to strike so seldom before we are removed for ever from its sound?? I heard Stormy & Georgie read Homer & Xenophon—as usual,—tho' I have not yet commem-orated them here[2]—& I prepared a part of the first choral ode of the Seven Chiefs for M<u>r</u> Boyd. He seemed to wish me to "sound dread-*

10   *ful note of <u>preparation</u>"[3] before I read Æschylus with him in future; as in this way, the benefit to myself is likely to be greater. I looked also at the Greek verbs, which he ≪ ... ≫ wishes me to be more accurate about. ≪After≫ all, I am annoyed & discontented & dis-appointed by M<u>r</u> Boyd. He talked so <u>cooly</u> about our leaving Hope*

15   *End—seemed so little disturbed by it—& that little, more on my account, than his own. I can bear anything from anybody better than coldness from some people—and coldness, coldness, coldness, is ≪what I have to bear≫ from them. If they could communicate a portion of this frigidity to <u>me</u>, they would reconcile me to its exist-*

20   *ence. The society of that Miss Hurd is as much valued as mine— as much! <u>at least</u>, <u>as much</u>! and yet is it probable or possible that her friendship is like my friendship? Friendship!—the word makes me yearn for the time, the past time, when it was not familiar to my ear!——— Abused & vain word!—*

25   *Walked out with Bummy H & A half way down the road & round the walks till I was tired. Sate in the ice house & talked of the garden*

---

    1. This was the clock in the tower over the entrance to the courtyard at Hope End, which regulated the comings and goings of the whole estate. When the Moulton-Barretts left Hope End, they took the clock with them, and it was later installed in the Court-house of Brown's Town, Jamaica. One of E.B.B.'s early poems, about this clock ("Hark what deep tone pro-ceeds from yonder Tower"), appears in *HUP*, I, 87-88.

    2. In an unpublished letter of 27 March 1889, to Robert Browning (Collection of Ed-ward R. Moulton-Barrett, Esq.), George recalled these lessons: "I must add my brother Storm & I received from her all our early lessons in Greek, & that on our appearing in her room, she would at once lay aside her own books, her loved studies, & tolerate in her strong affection, with perhaps only a gentle reproach, our stupidity & ignorance."

    3. *Henry V*, IV, Prologue, 12-14:

> The armourers accomplishing the knights,
> With busy hammers closing rivets up,
> Give dreadful note of preparation.

[18]

& all the painful et cœtera. Papa in <good> spirits at dinner. The wholesale <u>stock</u> of the Biddulphs[1] called half an hour before dinner, but «was» not unpacked. Henrietta spoke to them at the door!—

On reading what I have written . . I am more than half ashamed of it. I have certainly <u>no reason</u> for accusing Miss Hurd of being as much liked <ᴧby Mʳ B> as I am; & «. . .» if I had the <u>reason,</u> I should be still without the <u>right.</u> And as to coldness—Mʳ Boyd «used not to be» cold to me! Had he been so, I should not have thought him so on Tuesday. The fact is—the greatest regard, <u>far</u> the greatest, is on my side:—or rather the fact is—my disposition is far too exclusive & exacting. Both those facts are <u>operative</u> facts. When will they cease to be so?— Read, as I do every day, seven chapters of Scripture. My heart & mind «are» not affected «by» this exercise as they should be—witness what I have written today. I would erase every line of it, could I «annihilate» the <u>feelings,</u> <ᴧtogether> with the description of them; but, since I cannot, let the description pass! That «Friendship» should fade away before my eyes, as Fame did in my poetical vision, is too painful! And that the "skeleton" of Friendship . . . but I am getting wrong again! Oh I never never should have begun this journal!— No one should write journals, who «is» not wiser, on a hundred points, than I am! & stronger, on a thousand!———

Friday. June 17ᵗʰ

Papa «was» in very «good» spirits at breakfast this morning; but when I observed it to Bummy, I saw plainly from her manner, that there was no happy cause for them. Hope is all in vain!— We shall leave this place!—& all that is dear, <u>in it,</u> & <u>near it!</u>— Where shall we go «. . .»? To Brighton? To the neighbourhood of London? Anywhere but in those suburbs!— Anywhere where there can be a chance of my having at some time, dear Mʳ Boyd's society. And yet is there any chance of <u>that,</u> anywhere, for me? Tais toi Jean

5

10

15

20

25

30

1. Mr. Biddulph recorded in his Diary (now in Hereford City Library) that he called at Hope End with three of his daughters. As the Biddulph establishment numbered four sons and five daughters, as well as Mrs. Biddulph, E.B.B. was guilty of a little exaggeration in describing this modest representation as "the wholesale stock of the Biddulphs."

Diary by E.B.B.

Jaques—[1]   Today's journal shall be no duplicate of yesterday's.

Did not go out all day.   Mrs Griffith called;[2] & groaned all the groans of Testy & Sensitive.[3]   Miss Peyton came with her; & what is still worse, I sate by Miss Peyton.[4]   How hard it is to make some peo-
5   ple talk!   ≪The≫ labouring & the progeny of the mountain!—   But I wont be <u>more</u> illnatured than usual.

After dinner, Papa unfortunately walked <u>after</u> me out of the room, because like "good Madam Blaize,"[5] I walked out <u>before</u> Papa.   The consequence of this was a critique on my down-at-heel shoes; & the
10   end of that, was, my being sent out of the drawing room to put on another pair.   So while Anne is mending the only pair I have in the world I am doing my best to write nonsense & catch cold without any.   I dreamt last night that I was staying at M^r. Boyd's house. ≪Almost≫ before the ≪<u>tail</u>≫ of the dream was out of sight,—&
15   certainly before my eyes were <u>quite</u> open, I said "Never again!"   I was too right.   Never, never again!—

Very busy today.   Reading Æschylus & learning the verb τυπτω!![6] This is being <u>et</u> Cæsar <u>et</u> nullus,[7] at once!——   But nobody ever was so ungrammatical in Greek <ᴀas I am,> since Greek was spoken or
20   written in any way.   Tea is ready; so I must go—or something be- sides the heels of my shoes will be found fault with.

---

1. This is taken to refer to the childhood incident recounted by Rousseau in his "Quatrième Promenade" (*Les Confessions de Jean-Jacques Rousseau, suivies des Rêveries du Promeneur Solitaire*, 2 vols., Geneva, 1782).   As a result of a prank of his young cousin, the tips of two of Rousseau's fingers were trapped and crushed in the rollers of his uncle's mill.   Rousseau gave a piercing cry, but his cousin, fearing to be punished, begged him to be silent; conquering his pain, Rousseau obeyed, and told his aunt and uncle that a large stone had fallen on his hand.

2. Charlotte Griffith (1762?-1837), the widow of Thomas Griffith, was at this time in nominal possession of the Barton Court estate, having inherited it from her uncle, Henry Lambert, but his will was disputed, and it was not until after her death that her heirs' owner- ship was confirmed.

3. A reference to [James Beresford's] *The Miseries of Human Life; or, the Groans of Samuel Sensitive and Timothy Testy. With a Few Supplementary Sighs from Mrs. Testy.* (London, 1806).

4. Charlotte [?] Peyton, sister of Nicholson Peyton, of Barton Court.

5. [Oliver Goldsmith], "An Elegy on that Glory of her Sex Mrs. Mary Blaize," *The Bee*, No. 4, 27 October 1759, p. 128, v. 5: "Her love was sought, I do aver, | By twenty beaus and more; | The king himself has follow'd her,— | *When she has walked before.*"

6. "To beat or smite." This verb was the grammarian's delight, and was frequently used in textbooks to illustrate the declension of the class of verbs ending in πτω.

7. "Both Cæsar and nobody."

Saturday.   June 1.8th.

   *Such a day! such a miserable day!—   After breakfast which past
as <breakfasts> usually do, I sate down in my arm chair to put the
verbs in* μι *in* me*.   Then Arabel announced Eliza Cliffe; then I ran
down stairs to bring her up stairs; then she began to paint at my pic-   5
ture—& then the door bell rang!   <Those> Brydges's come back
again to see the house!—   Oh to hear their feet walking all over it—
even up stairs—even to my very door!—   Arabel locked it, & burst
into tears!   And I—the tears which ran down my cheeks, seemed
scarcely to unparalyze me: I felt stone everywhere except <ᴧin> my   10
heart!   Well! they went away; & Arabel went out of the room; &
Eliza & I sate silent for about an hour.   Then Bummy came into the
room,—& tho' I tried to speak & seem as if I knew nothing, I could
not!—   Oh I could not!   She said that Papa was going to London
on Monday to settle everything, that there was no cause for uneasi-   15
ness, (said before & for Eliza Cliffe) & that Eliza must promise to
≪mention≫ nothing of this annoying visit, to ≪M^{rs}.≫ Cliffe.*

   *We went down to luncheon; & when Eliza had run up stairs (to
seem out of the way) to mix her colours, Bummy H A & I talked of
what had happened with melancholy voices.   Bummy told ≪us≫ that   20
Papa knew that it w^d. happen,—that it c^d. not be avoided,—≪ . . . ≫
that those London people had been enraged at the Meyricks having
been turned away the other day,—that the place must be seen until
the business is settled.   James[1] is to meet Papa in London.   [Uncle]
Sam has not noticed his letter!—   Is Sam still Sam?   What a wretched   25
day we have indeed had!   Every nerve in my body seems relaxed; &
the trembling has scarcely yet gone out of my knees.   But as Papa is
going to London, something may still be done.   This is the last effort!—   He was in tolerably good spirits at dinner.   I wish I had been
at Malvern today!   Eliza told me ≪ . . . ≫ that Miss Steers walks out   30
with M^r. Boyd whenever she can.   So he is not as considerate to her
as he once was to another person!!   He is not afraid of disgracing her
by his "slovenly appearance"!!*

   *Q[uer]y.   Will Papa be angry with Lane for showing the house to
those people?   He told him that if they wished to see it, they might*   35

---

1. James Altham Graham-Clarke (1791-1860), E.B.B.'s maternal uncle, and Bummy's
younger brother.

see it; but that ≪he would≫ not make himself a party to its being shown, by allowing any one belonging to him, to show it.   Lane certainly ought to have been passive.   Papa was annoyed at Eliza being here today: but he w.ᵈ not let Bummy send her away, for fear M.ʳˢ

5   Cliffe should hear of after circumstances, & <suspect> him of being ashamed of them.   ≪Wrote to Knibb[1] to propose an exchange of some useless books of mine.≫

Talked in the evening of my poem—that is, Papa talked to me about it.   He said of the essay on Mind[2] that the more he read it,

10   the more he liked it.   He advised me not to put "By the author of the Essay on Mind" on the title page of the 1.ˢᵗ edition of my next poem, —on account of my late intermeddling with living characters.   ≪If it comes to a 2.ᵈ edition I can do so.—   Lane was right in what he did.   Papa had given him other orders.≫

15   Sunday June 19.ᵗʰ

A far pleasanter day than yesterday.   We did not go to church,— because—I dont know what.   One could'nt,—& another would'nt, which was as effective.   Papa in good spirits.   Bummy told us that she had told him about our knowing of his going to London.   "And

20   what did they say," was his question.   "They were very glad of it"!— Now I was half sorry to hear of her having said that; and yet our present circumstances are certainly such as must make us glad even of his absence, if by being absent, ≪he≫ can in any way change those circumstances.   At any rate it is a last effort; ≪& sh.ᵈ be made!—≫

25   We walked down to the gate, & heard a substitute ≪for≫ M.ʳ Curzon.   Not a bad sermon; but such a delivery—& disfranchise- ment of ≪ₐhs≫.   It was enough to fill the ears of his congregation with a̲c̲h̆e̲s̲!   Yet it was not a bad sermon.   Read the Bible, & Horne on its critical study.[3]   I do not think enough of the love of God,

30   graciously as it has been manifested to me.   My thoughts are wan- dering ungrateful thoughts.   How strange it is, that I̲, who ≪can≫

---

1. James Knibb, Bookseller, 89 High-street, Worcester. He had been declared bankrupt on 6 May (*The Times*, 7 May 1831), and the business was currently under the control of official Assignees.

2. *An Essay on Mind, with Other Poems* (London, 1826).

3. Thomas Hartwell Horne, *An Introduction to the Critical Study and Knowledge of the Holy Scriptures*, 3 vols. (London, 1818-21).

feel so very gratefully towards those who benefit me partially, & often from interested motives, (as one human being must ≪benefit≫ an-other)——, that I, should be so cold & lacking in thanksgiving towards ≪Him≫ who has given me all!—— And how yet stranger, that in the midst of <professed thankgiving> unto ≪this≫ unweary benefactor, my mind should be turning towards ≪some who seem≫ weary of loving me & doing me good!—— Oh ≪Thou≫ who lovest for ever the being ≪Thou≫ hast once loved,—oh Thou who doest good unto the unthankful & unworthy!—teach me to love ≪Thee≫ better—teach me to think of Thee more!——

    Eliza & Mrs Best are going to Worcester tomorrow; & the former has promised to see Mr Knibb upon 'change, tho' in Worcester!—— [1] *She has taken a volume or two as samples!——*

    An intended-to-be-printed tract of M^{rs} B's, brought by Eliza yes-terday, I read regularly thro' today. "The Garden of Eden" may be useful; but it is not original nor is it well-written. [2] *As Papa said of it last night—"It is nothing particular."*

    Sent up stairs again, on account of a hole in my stocking. Mem— to show a fair pair of heels whenever I go into the drawing room in-stead of when I go out of it!—— ≪Shoes≫ & stockings have got me into scrapes lately; and yet I am not usually fundamentally untidy.

    Eliza had intended to visit Mrs Boyd on Tuesday; & Miss Steers; but the Worcester business moved an adjournment until Thursday. The last evening with dearest Papa!—— He in good spirits.

Monday—June 20th

    Papa's last breakfast with us until his return; therefore a sad one— He however in apparently good spirits; tho' not very good! After breakfast I began to chew the cud of such bitter thoughts; about Papa's going away, & about our going away,—that I was glad to be-gin to graze, instead, on the verbs in μι. I have learnt them & τυπτω, too perfectly for Georgie to puzzle me, as I begged him to try to do when he came to read Greek with me this morning. Felt rather

1. A play on "exchange". The Royal Exchange, Cornhill, in London, was commonly known as 'Change.

2. Although Mrs. Best published numerous works between 1831 and 1864, including several volumes of tracts on the Old and New Testaments, we have been unable to trace one with this specific title.

[23]

Diary by E.B.B.

triumphant—no! not <u>rather</u> triumphant,—afterwards. It certainly was disgraceful that I who can read Greek with some degree of fluency, should ≪have≫ been such & so long an ignoramus about the verbs. And besides, I have done what <u>M.ʳ Boyd wished</u>; & that is, of itself, a
5 *pleasant feeling.*

Sam called up at my window between three & four, to say that Papa had come down from the farm; so I went down stairs. But ·we sate in the drawing room (all but Bummy) while he dined in the dining room. What was the use of taking our crying faces in to him?
10 *He came to us & kissed us before he went. "May God bless you" he said! May God bless <u>him</u>—dearest dearest Papa—in all temporal & spiritual ≪blessing≫!*

Now that the parting is over, I am very glad he is gone. It is right, & it will be consolatory, to make every effort in this unhappy
15 *business; whatever the result may be. From Bummy's manner, I plainly see that he is not, & she is not, & we ought not to be, sanguine. But I am glad he is gone; & have now to long for him to come back!*

We had not dinner today. Bummy A H & I had tea instead, at
20 *six o'clock; and afterwards we walked backwards & forwards on the bank opposite ≪ . . . ≫ the drawing room windows. Such a lovely <u>green evening</u>! We sate down near the little island, & talked; & Bummy proposed that I sh.ᵈ go to Malvern tomorrow. Of course I agreed! & of course I am pleased to think of going. I am going im-*
25 *mediately after breakfast, & must be back to drink tea with them at six o clock,—& Bummy says that if I do not dine there I shall not go again. I hope M.ʳ Boyd will ask me to dine with him; & that M.ʳˢ Boyd may not be arrived; & that Miss Hurd may not be there!——— There are <u>three wishes</u>; & every one of them as foolish as the black*
30 *pudding!———¹*

Quære. Is it civil in me to go away tomorrow when Eliza is coming here?

Tuesday. June 21.ˢᵗ
≪Two of my wishes were≫ gained: but I must commencer par le
35 *commencement. Henry drove me to Malvern; & Daisy & Sette took*

---

1. A sausage made of blood, meal and suet.

[24]

their inside places with me & a packet of bread & cheese. We set off
at about half past ten—arrived at Mrs Trant's, where I got out. Talked
a little of Papa's going & our going; & Mrs Trant expressed herself hurt
by Bummys repelling manner when she asked some question on <u>the</u>
<u>subject.</u> <u>Hurt!</u> If you break stone into dust, you do not <u>hurt</u> it!—   5
I resolved on trying to persuade Mrs Trant to call on Mrs Boyd—did
all that I could—said all that I could—begged her for <u>my</u> sake—all
in vain!—   She "intended no incivility to Mrs Boyd"—"was a bad
visitor"—"did not give dinners"—& "could not bear saying <u>how do</u>
<u>you do</u> whenever she went out"—& besides "Mr Boyd could not   10
bear ≪a≫ noise"—& in short she would not go. I was & am pro-
voked about it; & think Mrs Trant . . what I have long thought her.
Sette & Daisy I left there; & was driven on to Mr Boyd's by Henry.
<u>Mrs Boyd not arrived</u>—≪Huzza≫!—— The servent introduced me
into the drawing room—"Miss Barrett is come Sir"— "Miss Barrett   15
—how did she come?" I think there was an expression of pleasure
in his countenance, tho' he did not know that I was by to see it. I
am sure he received me with pleasure. ≪We≫ had not talked for ten
minutes when that Miss Hurd was announced. "Miss H wishes to
know Sir if she is to wait, or to go back on the donkey". "<Ask>   20
Miss H to go into the next room".   So of course as the conference
was to be <u>secret,</u> <u>I</u> begged to go into the next room; & Mr Boyd
<agreed>, observing that he wished me to bring Barker's <Lexicon>[1]
out of it. I went away very quickly, & shut the door, & sate down,
thinking little enough of Barker's Lexicon. In five minutes or less,   25
Miss H desired me to "<u>please to go</u> in to Mr Boyd!" Vulgar girl!—
And yet——! ≪Of≫ course I regretted to Mr Boyd that I should
be the cause of his sending ≪Miss≫ H away. "She can come another
day," was his only answer!—   I wonder <$_{\wedge}$on> how many days she
comes, & on how many other days he w.^{d} <u>like</u> her to come!—   Well   30
—but we began to read the Seven Chiefs out of Blomfield's edition;
& were very happy. Presently Miss Steers called, & was admitted.
She brought back my poem which Mr Boyd had lent her, of which
she said that she could not say all she thought, on account of my
presence. In a few minutes she got up to go—she w.^{d} not disturb   35

---

1. Edmund Henry Barker and George Dunbar, *A Greek and English Lexicon, for the Use
of Schools and Colleges* (London, 1831).

[25]

us any more: but Mr Boyd begged her to stay a little longer. M.^r B's
begging annoyed me rather. ≪Soon≫ annoyed—you know; I sh^d
say, if writing for any ≪other≫ person's eyes but mine: as it is,—
"soon annoyed—I know". Mr Boyd attacked me & made Miss Steers
5   *attack me on the subject of science ≪standing≫ higher in the scale*
of intellect than poetry. We disputed amicably tho' animatedly.
Miss Steers ended by being inconsistent, & agreeing with my poem &
me, on the subject of a poet deriving more exalted enjoyment from
nature than the painter or man of science. Mr Boyd called it "abso-
10 *lute nonsense."[1]   After talking a little more on French poetry, Miss*
≪Steers≫ not only got up to ≪go≫, but did positively go. And when
she was gone, Mr Boyd said—"I hope you did not think that I wished
Miss Steers to stay for my own sake. I was quite disinterested about
it—" & then he went on to say that he had fancied it would please
15 *her to talk ≪longer≫ with me. So that annoyance vanished away:*
and for the thousand & first time I <owned> myself (to myself) a
fool. He asked me to have luncheon: and I asked him to have dinner.
"Not while you are here". "But I am going to stay later". Upon
this he asked me to dine with him; & upon that, I agreed to do so.
20 *We read until four; & then went into his room, & dined very com-*
fortably. And after dinner I tried to puzzle his memory in the oration
on Eutropius,[2] by ≪reading≫ two words here & there dodgingly.
Puzzling him was out of the question; but cheating him was not; so I
turned to another part of the book & read two words there!— He
25 *thought & thought; & then I laughed, & betrayed myself. Then I*

1. She had previously argued this point with H.S.B. in her letter to him of 1 May 1828 (*EBB/HSB*, pp. 35-41), referring to p. 73 of her *Essay on Mind*: "Surely poets *do* see more in nature than artists do! Surely you cannot disagree with me in this! . . . the poet . . . looks *thro'* nature that he may look *beyond* nature!" She expressed this in lines 1022-29 of the *Essay* (ed. cit., pp. 73-74):

> The artist lingers in the moon-lit glade,
> And light and shade, with him, are—light and shade.
> The philosophic chymist wandering there,
> Dreams of the soil and nature of the air.
> The rustic marks the young herbs' fresh'ning hue,
> And only thinks—his scythe may soon pass through!
> None "muse on nature with a Poet's eye,"
> None read, but Poets, Nature's poetry!

2. St. John Chrysostom, "In Eutropium Eunuchum, Patritum et Consulem," pronounced at St. Sophia's, Constantinople, A.D. 399 (*PCC*, LII, cols. 389-396). A translation was included in H.S.B.'s *Select Passages of the Writings of St. Chrysostom, St. Gregory Nazianzen, and St. Basil* (London, 1806).

examined him in Lucan:[1] *& there he was not so omnipotent. After this, «we» adjourned to the drawing room, & I read the newspaper to him for a few minutes before & after the carriage came. I left him at <∧past> six—— A happy day!——*

Think of those boys having had nothing to eat all day—of their leaving their cheese & bread & Mrs Trant's,—& getting nothing instead of it!—— But they were only hungry—not ill!—— We arrived at home at seven; & found tea <∧in> waiting. Nobody angry in spite of somebody deserving it. After tea, I walked out a little with Bummy Henrietta & Arabel; & talked of Mr Boyd—& tired myself not with talking but walking. Thoroughly tired when I went to bed. Mrs Boyd is not to return until the end of this week—& Mr Boyd has sent to Worcester for a drum. Two pieces of information omitted in the proper place for them. Mr Boyd seemed interested in what I said of Hope End, & Papa going to London. He asked me if there was any chance of Hope End being let to Papa, & of our living there even in the case of its becoming another person's purchase. «As he was hearing» my answer, I looked to see if he seemed sorry, but his countenance said nothing decidedly.

I «mentioned» the possibility of Henry walking out with him while "I might amuse myself by reading". "And you stay here! Oh no! I w^d not do that." "Indeed I «would» not mind it." "But I w^d mind it." I liked that answer. Certainly I had a pleasant day. I found a parcel on my return directed by Papa <∧to me.> Opened it in a fright. Six pairs of black silk stockings «...» sent by him from Cheltenham; & one line in pencil from him, to say that he intended to sleep there & proceed to London on the next day. My own dear kind Papa!—— How very very kind to think of me & my pedestals at such a time!—— How I ought to love him!—ought!—how I do!————

«Eliza did not come today. I took my sketch of Mr Boyd with me, & half spoilt it, instead of improving it.»

Wednesday. June 22.

Very soon after breakfast Eliza Cliffe came; but still sooner Bummy said to me laughingly "Are you going to see Mr Boyd today?" And

---

1. Marcus Annaeus Lucanus (A.D. 39-65), whose only extant major work is *Pharsalia*, treating of the civil war between Cæsar and Pompey.

Diary by E.B.B.

*laughing was my answer—"Yes! if you will come too." Then grave
was her observation "But you know you can go tomorrow". "Go tomorrow. ≪Oh≫ I think not." (Oh I wish I could! was what my
heart <u>assided</u> [sic]). "Why certainly Mr Boyd <may> not like your*
5   *going quite so often". How c.^d I help saying "If I thought Mr Boyd
did not like my going <u>very often</u>, I w.^d not go at all".*

    *Eliza arrived; & Bummy ran up stairs to give me pre-warning
that in the case of any <u>horrible</u> visitors arriving, I was to keep quiet &
say nothing before her. Eliza says that Knibb will give me books to*
10   *the amount of only £2—10 in exchange for those I wish to part with.
I wish so much to part with them, & wish so much <u>more</u> to get Heyne's
Pindar[1] &c that I w.^d close with his proposal. But everybody thinks
me a goose for <u>giving away</u> my books (as they call it); & Eliza insists
on trying another bookseller at Worcester, which she is to do next*
15   *Saturday per carrier. Well! she may do it!—but I <u>must</u> have Heyne's
Pindar—coute qu'il coute!!—so if Deighton[2] <u>wont</u>, Knibb <u>shall</u>, for
EBB <u>will</u>—*

    *Eliza painted me & dined with us at one, & ≪drank≫ tea with us
≪at≫ six, & afterwards we went down the carriage road with her, I*
20   *riding her poney at a slow pace. I rode round to the old gate, & then
dismounting, she rode on, & we walked home. A lovely calm soft
evening!—*

    *I wrote a guarded note to Mrs Best expressive of my <u>interest</u> in
her nothing-particular tract. And I wrote a few lines to Mr Boyd en-*
25   *closing Paganinis criticism—or rather a criticism on Paganini cut out
of the newspaper[3]—for Eliza to take with her & read. Eliza is to
call there while Mrs Cliffe calls on Mrs Selwyn.[4] When Bummy heard
this, she said—"Really <u>all</u> the young ladies in the neighbourhood seem
to me to be in the habit of going to see that poor man". I did not*
30   *say anything, but thought something.*

    *This was an idle day with me—respecting study. Mrs Peyton
called here & stayed a short eternity, which seemed to me anything
but short. In the midst of her visit, I heard Minny was come, & ran
up to see her. Dear Minny is looking thin, & began to cry when I*

1. Christian Gottlob Heyne, ed. *Pindari Carmina* (Göttingen, 1773).
2. Henry Deighton, Bookseller, of 53 High-street, Worcester.
3. For the letter, see Appendix I, p. 273.
4. The wife of Congreve Selwyn, surgeon; he was in charge of the Dispensary in Ledbury.

[28]

*kissed her.   But her low spirits seem more on our account than her
father's, who is much better than she expected or could have expected
to find him.   Mrs Cliffe wishes us to spend a long day at Mathon next
week.¹   The petition was ordered to be laid on the table² —that is,
Bummy evaded it for the present by saying that we w^d think of it, &
wait to hear from Papa.   I w^d a thousand times rather go to Mathon
than to the Bartons; & Mrs Peyton was teazing us kindly about going
to drink tea there.   How they have beseeched us about tea.*

<u>*Te veniente die, te decedente canebant!*</u>*—³*

Thursday June 23^d

*At breakfast this morning, Bummy proposed that I sh^d go to see
Mr Boyd in the evening.   But I would not do it—Eliza Cliffe was to
go!—   Henrietta exclaimed "≪This≫ is the first time I ever heard Ba
refuse to go to see Mr Boyd".   "Ah!" but Bummy ≪responded≫—
"remember the <u>reason</u>!"—   I wonder if she will propose my going
tomorrow.   If she does, I <u>will</u> <u>go</u>!——— And I w^d not go tomorrow or any day if I did not believe in my heart that he really does
like to have me with him.   Read as usual . . and wrote a long letter to
Papa.   A long & cheerful letter without one allusion to <u>the</u> subject.
At about six B H A & I went out to take a ≪ . . . walk≫.   We walked
up coome hill⁴ & sate down nearly at the ≪summit≫, & tried our
fate ≪by≫ daisies—"il aime—<un> peu—beaucoup—point du
tout"!—   ≪And there≫ are the degrees of my philosophy—un peu*

5

10

15

20

1. We have not traced any reference by E.B.B. to the home of the Cliffes more specific
than this general reference to Mathon. Mrs. Cliffe's husband, in his will dated 1809, described
himself as being "of the Shipend House, Mathon," which in the 18th century had been the
richest and most important house in the vicinity, but his obituary notices in 1812 described
him as being of Mathon House, Mathon, and newspaper references at the time of the Diary
continued to associate the Cliffes with both houses. Shipend House was shown on older
maps, but those contemporary with the Diary showed only Mathon House, in virtually the
same location. This leads us to believe that early in the 19th century the family house was
altered and renamed Mathon House, but we cannot be positive about this. The Cliffes'
association with Mathon terminated in the 1870's, and present descendants of the family to
whom we have spoken were unable to provide any additional information about the Cliffes'
house at Mathon.
     The drive from Hope End to Mathon House was approximately 3½ miles, over inferior
road surfaces (map ref. C6).
     2. The parliamentary phrase for indefinite postponement.
     3. A play on IV, 466 of Virgil's *Georgics*: "Te veniente die, te decedente canebat." Using
the assonance of *tea* and *te*, and by making the verb plural, E.B.B. here conveys the jibe "of
tea they sang, at the coming of the day and at its passing."
     4. Coombe Hill, some 450 feet high, about ¾ mile north of Hope End (map ref. D5).

[29]

Diary by E.B.B.

—*beaucoup*—*point du tout!!!*   Bummy mentioned the Malvern subject again; proposed that I sh.^d go there tomorrow, & that Gent sh^d drive me.   I am to go!—.   We drank tea at eight o'clock, & Bro read the debates to us afterwards.[1]   I ≪irrepressibly≫ sleepy; & they,
5   —the debates, not the company,—inexpressibly dull.   How much happier I am in having a seat in my arm chair, than one in the House of Lords.   How they are brawling & quarrelling just now, about nothing, _for_ something: at once aristocratically & _cacistically_.[2]

Friday June 24.
10   Gent drove me to Malvern, where we arrived I sh.^d think very soon after eleven.   I was shown into the dining room, & therefore of course took it into my head that Miss Heard[3] was there.   Of course <∧con-sequently> out of humour.   She was not however there; & I was admitted into the drawing room & Mr Boyd's presence, before five
15   minutes had past.   He said that it was very kind in me to come so often, but that he hoped I had not inconvenienced myself.   How I do hate those set phrases.   _I_ inconvenience myself by going _there_!— Well!   we sate down & began to talk about Paganini,—& Mr Boyd thanked me for sending him the extract which Miss H had read to him
20   yesterday, & which had very much interested him.   Then we adjourn-ed to Mr Boyd's own room & read Æschylus.   At two o'clock I was asked whether I would have any luncheon—& how long I would stay. "_No_" to the first question: to the second a little hesitation.   I had ordered ≪the≫ carriage at a late hour,—but there was no necessity
25   for my staying until a late hour—I could easily have the carriage at the door earlier.   "At what hour have you ordered the carriage?"   "At seven—but you know, if you do not like my staying—"   "If you dont go until seven, will it not be very late for you to be on the road?" How impatient & surprised I felt; & how moderately I answered—
30   "There is no reason why I sh.^d not go before, if you dont like my stay-

1. The debate in the House of Lords on 21 June, following the Speech from the Throne on the opening of Parliament that day by the King.   In debating the customary Address to the King, the issue of Reform was a major topic, and some acrimonious personal exchanges passed between certain of Their Lordships.   A report of the debate occupied 13 columns in *The Times,* 22 June 1831.

2. From kakistocracy: the government of a state by its worst citizens (*Oxford English Dictionary*).

3. This is the same person as the Miss Hurd previously mentioned.

ing." "*I was thinking only of your being late on the road, when I said what I did: you know very well whether I <like> your staying or not*". *The smile which spoke at the same ≪moment≫, satisfied me— but still two years ago when so much used to be said about "moon light nights", nothing was ever said about* <u>lateness</u>. *Quantum muta-* 5
tus!—[1] *We dined together at half past three; & afterwards went into the drawing room, & talked miscellaneously of novels & Romances— of how many thousands I had read in my life; & of his surprise at hearing me say so. He recollects* <u>Modern Philosophers</u>[2] *coming out. Another work on the same subject entitled "The Young Philosopher" (by* 10
a M.ʳ Walker, he thought)[3] *came out at the same time: and he considered it superior to M.ʳˢ Hamilton's. He spoke of a German novel called the Family of Haldon, which he read & liked extremely, in his youth.*[4] *I was provoked to hear of his having advised Eliza Cliffe to read Tom Jones.*[5] *If M.ʳˢ Cliffe hears of it, she will like the adviser* 15
none the better. I wish he had not done it; & I said <ₐto him> ≪what≫ I have written here. Afterwards we returned to M.ʳ Boyd's own room, & read Æschylus again. We read the scene after the first chorus of the Seven Chiefs, & both of us abused it.[6] *I had abused it before reading it with him; & ≪he≫, from ≪indistant≫ recollections,* 20
≪had≫ taken it's part; ≪but≫ by this co-reading our opinions became united. While I was reading, I observed the closing of eyes & imperfect attention—what he calls "his heaviness" coming on. I may be wrong; but I cant help thinking that if he were <u>much</u> *interested, he w.ᵈ not suffer in this way. I thought so yesterday, till my voice abso-* 25
lutely <u>trembled</u>. *I may be wrong. When the reading was over, we*

---

1. "How changed." (Virgil: "how changed from that Hector who returns after donning the spoils of Achilles," *LCL-V*, I, 312-313: "Aeneid," II, lines 274-275.)

2. [Elizabeth Hamilton], *Memoirs of Modern Philosophers*, 3 vols. (Bath, 1800). [Purporting to be edited by Geoffrey Jarvis.]

3. His memory was at fault; the author was Charlotte Smith. *The Young Philosopher: A Novel*, 4 vols. (London, 1798).

4. August Heinrich Julius Lafontaine, *Die Familie von Halden*, 2 vols. (Berlin, 1797). The preface to the first English edition (London, 1799) said of Lafontaine: ". . . he is called the German Fielding. He is a Saxon Clergyman, and was lately presented to a living by the King of Prussia, who at the same time sent him a handsome letter, informing him that he was indebted for his promotion to the pleasure which his Majesty and the Queen had received from perusing his works."

5. Henry Fielding, *The History of Tom Jones, A Foundling*, 6 vols. (London, 1749).

6. Beginning "You, I ask, insufferable creatures that ye are!" (*LCL-A*, I, 334, lines 182 ff.)

talked of the Knowles's.   He scarcely liked (evidently!) my having
written any congratulation to them.   He told me that Lady Knowles[1]
had misrepresented me in one thing.   He had <doubted> my essay
on mind ≪having≫ been my own unassisted composition,—& Lady
5 *Knowles had said "wait till you see her",—& had written in a letter,*
which is preserved in the box with my letters, that my "conversation
was brilliant & witty".   "Now" M.ʳ Boyd ≪continued≫ "as far at least
as I have observed, tho' some of your letters have a good deal of wit,
you are not lavish of it in your conversation".   He is certainly ≪right≫
10 *in that observation.   Why should I blame him for being disappointed*
in me?—& why should I,—observing & knowing what I do observe
& know,—seek farther for a cause of ≪his≫ colder manner & conduct,
than <ₐthe simple circumstance of> his being disappointed in me?—
But then should he have expressed such warmth of regard, if <he
15 *felt> only literary estimation or admiration?   ≪I wonder where he*
has put my letter box.   It is invisible!≫

  We talked, in conclusion, of Annie & injudiciousness, until the
carriage came, & a little while afterwards.   I went away at seven, at
past seven o'clock,—& got home at eight.   Just in time for tea.—
20 *Heard as I came thro' our gate of M.ʳˢ Martin's return.   Henrietta*
doubtful whether she should or should not be pleased.   I not doubt-
ful at all—Not pleased!   Had tea & talking; & I w.ᵈ have gone to
sleep if I could,—at least two hours before I was in bed.   Sam had
been at Mathon, & brought back a letter from Eaton the bookseller[2]
25 *to Eliza Cliffe, about my books.   He must see them before he de-*
cides upon them.   If he has not ≪the≫ books which I require, why
sh.ᵈ he either see ≪them≫ or decide upon them?   He shant.   M.ʳˢ
Boyd is to return today at nine.   I feel misanthropically this eve-
ning, ≪on account of some things which past this morn.ᵍ≫

30 *Saturday June ≪25≫.ᵗʰ*

  Bummy said at breakfast, that driving to Malvern always ≪seems≫
to do me good.   I hope they will try that panacea upon me again
soon—

  Read Æschylus—the part I read yesterday,—& wrote down all

1. Charlotte, wife of Admiral Sir Charles Knowles, and sister of Capt. John Johnstone
of Mainstone Court, near Ledbury.

2. T. Eaton & Sons, trading in College-street, Worcester.

that I c.^d remember of Mr Boyd's sayings upon it. Heard the boys read Greek as usual; & <examined> them in τυπτω not as usual. That they sh.^d know no more of the verbs than they do, is ≪my≫ disgrace not theirs.

Dined at one. No going out on account of the rain. On opening my drawer I saw the ms of Thoughts versus Words, & a Thought struck me that I w.^d address & send it to Mr Boyd.[1] Bummy came into the room while I was writing, & I showed it to her. She seemed amused & pleased—I hope somebody else will be in statu illo. I wanted to finish <ʌthe transcription> before Sunday morning came, therefore I finished in the drawing room, while they were reading the paper loud out. On the last page I have written a few lines from ≪myself unallegorically≫ to Mr Boyd. Will he answer them? How long ago is it since ≪he≫ answered a letter of mine?—

No letter from Papa or anybody. If there had been good news, w.^d he not have sent it?

≪A note of enquiry from Mrs Martin. I answered the enquiry.≫

Sunday. June 26th.

Dearest Bro's birthday.[2] Not kept but thought of. As the clouds looked as if they would rain, we would not put ourselves in the way of them by going to church. ≪Bro read prayers.≫ Mr Watts[3] called at one o'clock, & Eliza rode up to the door at the same moment. Was she to come in or not?—a message sent up to Minny. Mrs Best's baby has the measles—& Sette & Occyta have not had them. We admitted her. She ≪brought≫ me Heyne's Pindar[4] as a present. How kind of her: & how yet more foolish in me to have said a word before her about that book. She brought Bummy a present, in the shape of an original drawing of hers—a lion springing upon an antelope. Beautifully executed, & well designed—but the design seems to me rather deficient in spirit & animation. We dined & <walked> down to the gate. Mr Curzon preached upon faith, very ably but too loudly & energetically, as my headache testified. When we went up

1. E.B.B.'s letter is printed in Appendix I, p. 275.
2. His 24th. As it fell on a Sunday, celebration was deferred until the following day.
3. The Rev. James Watts, Vicar of Ledbury since 1810.
4. Presumably the three-volume 1824 edition which formed Lot 986 of the 1913 Browning Sale.

Diary by E.B.B.

afterwards to speak to him, & ask him about Papa, he said "I have seen M.ʳ Barrett several times. He looks very well & is in good spirits. <ᴧWhen I saw him last, on Friday,> ≪he≫ desired me to tell you that he was going down to Eastbourne, & that you must not expect
5   to hear from him until Tuesday". I felt the blood fly to my heart like a hot arrow. Going to Eastbourne? Then we are going from Hope End—there is no hope!— Going to Eastbourne. Close to Hastings, where M.ʳ Boyd w.ᵈ <ᴧhave> probably been by this time, had I not brought forward my "vexatious opposition"! Going to
10   Eastbourne!——

      Well! I recovered myself, & talked on. M.ʳ Curzon is not to preach here again for four Sundays. Shall ≪we≫ ever hear him preach here again? He said "God bless you" at parting. He <thinks> that we shall not!—and I think so too!—

15   As Bummy H A & I walked home, & sate down upon the pillar at the water side of the house, we talked of Eastbourne & Hope End. It is plain ≪that≫ Bummy has little hope. ≪Has she any?≫—

      Bro read prayers. Afterwards he read Lord John Russell's speech on Reform,[1] in the midst of which, I who am interested in reform &
20   admire Lord John Russell, fell fast asleep. My politics were not strong enough to keep my eyes open. However I slept only over the calculation of populations. I am not of a <u>calculating</u> disposition, in any sense of the word. I ≪sent≫ my packet to M.ʳ Boyd. No advertisement in the Gloucester paper today.

25   A letter from M.ʳˢ Boyd enclosing a note to Eliza & me, from Annie. Mine cool enough. But that she sh.ᵈ have written at all, is more than I expected. M.ʳˢ Boyd was prompter, most <probably>. She is not to return until October, & then with the two younger Miss Gs.[2] <u>Then</u> I shall be here no longer.

30   Monday June 27. ≪ . . . ≫

      After breakfast, I was surprised in my room by Eliza running up

1. On moving the reading of the Reform Bill in the House of Commons on 24 June. A six-column report of the speech appeared in *The Times*, 25 June 1831. Lord John Russell (1792-1878), 3rd son of the 6th Duke of Bedford, was Paymaster-General in Lord Grey's Administration. He had been advocating reform since 1819, and Grey had selected him to pilot the Bill through the Commons. He later (1846) became Prime Minister.

2. Emily and Charlotte, the younger two of the three unmarried daughters of Sir John Gibbons.

stairs ≪ . . . ≫ & kissing me vehemently, with an exclamation—"The advertisement is withdrawn from the Worcester paper."[1]   Is that all?   Her manner had excited me into hope about something.   That is nothing.   Papa went down to Eastbourne on Friday or Saturday. There is no hope.   I obliged her not to go back in the rain but to stay   5 & dine with us at one.   After dinner she rode out ≪with≫ Arabel, & promised to return to drink tea here; a promise which the weather prevented her from keeping.   Storm of thunder lightening & rain. I in my usual heroics on such occasions.   Lay down on Minny's ≪bed.≫   Crashing thunder.   ≪Thought≫ of M.ʳ Boyd who, when I   10 told him of my boldness during thunderstorms, admitted his own ditto,—& ≪ . . . ≫ owned even that he lies down on his bed, as I do.

At about eight Arabel returned, escorted by M.ʳˢ C[liffe]'s servent. In the evening, writing instructions for Bro respecting my books, which he is to obey tomorrow.   Very kind of him to go <ₐto Wor-   15 cester> on purpose.   ≪His birthday both kept & thought of!—— M.ʳ & M.ʳˢ Martin came & drank tea with us.≫   I <read> ≪Pindar's≫ first Olympic today—& thought of tomorrow—tomorrow's fatal decisive letter.   ≪Will it not, must it not be decisive?——≫

Tuesday June 28ᵗʰ.   20
    ≪Bro rode to Worcester.   I wrote a note to M.ʳˢ Boyd.≫
    Bummy H & I drove immediately after breakfast to call upon M.ʳˢ Martin who lent me the <two> last Edinburgh Reviews,[2] & Lamartine's poems.[3]   I have admired two of them already.   No conversation about us.   Then we went to the Bartons.   M.ʳˢ Peyton   25 invisible.   I wish M.ʳˢ Griffith had been inaudible.   My attention distracted both morally & physically, by the thoughts of Papa's letter & by the sight of the thunderclouds.   However, the latter broke away. What will the former <do>?   We came home.   No letter.   The boy did not go until 12 & ≪had≫ not returned.   We had dinner.   Still no   30 letter.   Struck three!   Still no letter.—   How my heart is beating inwardly, as it always does, when I am agitated!

1. The first announcement, which did not mention the estate by name, appeared in only two issues of the *Worcester Herald*, those of 11 and 18 June 1831.

2. The issues of March and June 1831.

3. Alphonse Marie Louis de Lamartine (1790-1869).   The quotation used by E.B.B. on 23 July (p. 64) indicates that the volume here mentioned was *Méditations Poétiques* (Paris, 1820).

Diary by E.B.B.

Well.   The boy came & brought no letters of any kind.   Papa has not written as he said he w^d*   Are we to attribute this omission to a favorable or unfavorable ≪cause≫?   Bummy says the former—but I—I will not throw myself again into the agonies of hope.*

5   *Bro returned from Worcester rather late than otherwise, & says of Eaton, that he will say nothing of my books till he sees them.   How provoking that Bro sh*^{d}*. have left his catalogue*[1] *at M*^{rs} *Trant's!*

A battle fierce between Henry & Georgie.   I dreadfully fright-ened.   But I wont make my being hysterical, ≪historical≫.

10   *Read the second Olympic today.*

I wonder M^r*. Boyd did not write about my Thought on Thoughts—*

Wednesday ≪ . . . ≫ June 29.

Distracted (in both senses of the word) by looking for stray books, & packing up a full box of inutilities, to be sent p^r*. coach to*
15   *M*^{r}*. Eaton.   ≪When≫ the letter-time came—no letters came!— Yes!   one from M*^{rs} *Boyd, containing a message!!!   from M*^{r}*. Boyd, who likes the talent, & nothing else, of my "Thoughts," & wishes me to write something cutting biting shining on the anti-reformers for the Times newspaper.   I have tossed her letter into my drawer—*
20   *prestissimo—agitato!!   I suppose he means to neglect me altogether, never to write to me <*$_\wedge$*again!—> & expects that I should show my gratitude!   by continuing to write as I have written, & ≪feel≫ as I have felt!——   Well!—I feel bitterly —— as I have felt—for some time at least.   He has not written to me once since the 16*th
25   *of May; and this is the 29*th *of June.   I may be <exacting> & irritable & inconsiderate & passionate—but I cannot feel satisfied or feel that I ought to feel satisfied.   I wish I had ≪half≫ the regard which I retain for him, impressed on this paper, that I might erase it thus* ▬▬▬ *.   ≪M*^{rs}*≫ Boyd may throw difficulties in the*
30   *way of his writing.   She may ≪ . . . ≫ be busy & be out of the way, & he out of the humour for ≪it—≫   But if he wished it—oh if he really & indeed wished it, there could be no lasting obstacle—none!!*

1. The *Worcester Herald*, 5 February 1831, advertised Eaton's Catalogue "CONTAINING History, Antiquities, Voyages, Travels, Biography, Arts, Sciences, &c. Also, Works in the Greek, Latin, French, Italian, and other Languages; together with a Supplement of English Divinity . . ."

How was it during the first year & a half of our intercourse? Did he ever even delay writing, then?

Well! It is better far better that I should go ≪away≫; better in everyway, & perhaps for everybody. Better for me, I dare say. I am not of a cold nature, & cannot bear to be treated coldly. When cold 5
water is thrown upon hot iron, the iron hisses. I wish ≪that≫ water w^d make my iron as cold as itself. Perhaps it may—in time.

M^{rs} B thinks that because I did not notice her proposal about coming here, I did not wish her to come. Judging of me by herself!!— I will ≪ . . . ≫ to-morrow ≪ . . . ≫ write down my meaning in a man- 10
ner which anybody may be able to read—& direct it to Mrs B. R[uby] C[ottage]. M[alvern] W[ells]!

I have <sent> to Mrs Trant's for Eaton's Catalogue— ≪Select-ing≫ the books will amuse me, & make me forget some of my thoughts. They are, I fear, sour as well as bitter. 15

B H A & I walked out on the hill opposite the drawing room windows. <Kenrick's> people are all working in front of the house. I shall soon wish that I was away—away. Read Pindar's 3^d Olympic.

The catalogue arrived in the evening. It did amuse me, looking over it, & marking the eligible books. 20

Thursday June 30.
Met Billy Trehern in my dressing gown. Had a ≪fright≫ & a run in consequence!—

Wrote to Mrs Boyd & sent the letter. Wrote to Annie & did not send the letter. I shall send it tomorrow. I told Mrs B. to tell M^r 25
Boyd of Papa's message; but it will not affect him. Oh no!——

No letters today. What can be the reason? Bummy says she looks on the bright side. I look for it, but cannot do more. What miserable suspence we have suffered on this subject,—& no out-let from it, even now! My lord & My God! Unto ≪Thee≫ do I com- 30
mit my earthly as my eternal happiness!—

Mrs Martin called here just before dinner. I should think from her manner that her mind had a great deal of repose about it—I do not mean insensibility—not a smooth sea, not a rough sea, but an undulating sea. I wish I resembled her. 35

But some circumstances & some people make my mind & feelings foam all over. Can I throw chains upon them, as Xerxes did upon

Diary by E.B.B.

the ≪ocean≫.[1]   Yes! as Xerxes did—ineffectually!———

Bro & Sam are engaged ≪in≫ the Colwall green cricket match this evening; & the minor boys are to accompany them.   Good fun to them!—   Now I must go & read Pindar.

5   As Bummy ≪ . . . ≫ A ≪&≫ I were sitting on the pillar, up the road came an Irishwoman in distress.   Her daughter was lying at the gate apparently dying.

We went down (I on the poney) to investigate the case.   The poor girl very ill—allowed to sleep in the schoolroom.   Much controversy
10   pro & con imposture.   No imposture ≪ . . . ≫, in my opinion.

I <u>cantered</u> up the road & up the hill, without holding the pummel. The poney carried me swiftly; <but> more swiftly <∧did> my mem-ory <∧carry me back> to the far days when I used to ride, with the halo of happy reveries about my mind & heart.   I enjoyed this riding
15   today, in spite of everything.   Tired.   Bro & Sam did not return until I was in bed.

Friday July 1ˢᵗ

After breakfast Henrietta came up stairs to propose to me that we should drive to Allen's the overseer[2] about the Irishwoman.   As
20   Bummy wished me to go, I went.   At the gate however we found the poor girl better, but <u>indisposed</u> about the <overseer>; therefore in-stead of driving to Allan's, we drove to the Whyche.   Before we arrived quite at the usual resting point, I proposed climbing the hill with Henrietta.   So we commenced operations & Bummy suspended
25   ≪the≫ same; she being left as garrison to ≪our≫ wheelbarrow.   I climbed the hill quickly enough, but with so much fatigue!—   At the summit there was the sight of the tops of Mʳ Boyd's chimneys; & I sate down & looked at them.   I sate down & looked at them. I could not do any more.   I could not run down the hill as I wished
30   to do—because tho' <u>facilis descensus</u>,[3] how was I to get up again?

1. Herodotus, in Bk. VII, 34-35 of *The Histories*, described the destruction of Xerxes' bridge across the Hellespont, during his invasion of Greece in 480 B.C.: ". . . no sooner had the strait been bridged than a great storm swept down and brake and scattered all that work. When Xerxes heard of that, he was very angry, and gave command that the Hellespont be scourged with three hundred lashes, and a pair of fetters be thrown into the sea; . . ." (*LCL-HE*, III, 346-349).

2. "An officer (appointed annually) to perform various administrative duties mainly con-nected with the relief of the poor," (*Oxford English Dictionary*).

3. "Easy is the descent" (to Avernus: Virgil, *Aeneid*, VI, line 126).

[38]

My feelings today were not as pleasant as they were, when I was
≪near≫ this spot, nearly a month ago.   Not so pleasant in any way!
Whose fault is that? Partly the fault of circumstances, & partly——!!
Henrietta & I slid down Bummy's side of the hill, & drove home.   I
was so tired & exhausted, that attempting to stand when I got out of   5
the carriage, was a vain attempt.   Bro carried me to the sofa; & I soon
got better—indeed well enough, for Bummy to propose our drinking
tea with the Martins.[1]   I did not feel equal to it: but <ₐas> she
wished it, <ₐI agreed!—>   Henrietta & Sam walked; B, A, & I in
the wheelbarrow.   Bro had preceded us, in consequence of an invita-   10
tion to shoot rabbits.   On the way, Bummy said to me that she had a
proposal to make for tomorrow which I was sure to like; but that be-
fore she made it, I must promise one thing.   I was about to promise,
when Mrs Cliffe's carriage appeared.   Mrs C. Mrs Best & Fanny!![2]
M^{rs} C appeared to me, out of humour; but whether about our going   15
to the Martins, or about our ≪putting≫ her upon quarantine,[3] depo-
nent saith not.   I asked after Eliza—"Eliza is at Malvern where she
has spent the whole day!!!"

I wonder where she has been.   At Mr Boyds?——   Perhaps she
may have been painting with Miss Steers! — —   20

After Mrs Cliffe had past, I, imagining that B's proposal might
regard Mr Boyd in some way, was anxious for her to re-mention it.
She did not.   Arabel even asked her what it was.   She had forgotten
all about it. For forgotten, read changed her mind. <Had tea> with
the Martins. I & Mr Martin discussed about Ld Byron. <The> Bid-   25
dulphs called while we were there. I annoyed—felt so. B annoyed
—looked so.   Mrs Martin proposed that I sh^d drive to Malvern with
her on Tuesday.   Tuesday a long <way> off; but better on Tuesday
than not on Tuesday.   And yet why sh^d I wish so much to be with a
person, who certainly does not wish so much to be with me.   Why   30
sh^d I take pleasure in lacerating myself, & kissing the rod?—— Tais
toi![4] again.   Got home & to bed—at last!   Intolerably tired!   So

---

1. James Martin (1778-1870), a member of the banking family, and his wife Julia (*née*
Vignoles, 1793?-1867?), who lived at Old Colwall, adjacent to the Hope End estate (map ref.
E5). Despite references to Mrs. Martin and herself as "oil and water," E.B.B. kept up a cor-
respondence with the Martins until her death.

2. Mrs. Best's infant daughter.   3. Because of the measles (see p. 33).

4. See fn. 1, p. 20.

Diary by E.B.B.

tired as to lie awake instead of sleeping,—& to dream when I did sleep, of my teeth tumbling out.

 Arabel told me today that there is to be an auction at the farm on Monday, of all Papa's crops. And that papers are printed & hung up
5 at the farm & at Ledbury, to that effect.[1] Henrietta & Bummy do not know it,—& I swore Arabel to silence, for fear of distressing them. No letter from Papa today; & Bummy rather elated about <u>that</u>? Is there any reason why I should be elated about anything?

≪Saturday≫. July 2ᵈ
10 Got up this morning, tired thro' & thro'. The dreams I had last night about my <teeth>, were ineffectual in refreshing me altogether. While Stormy & Georgie were reading Greek with me, a cry from Henry called my attention to his figure suspended by the hands from the roof of the dairy. I called out to him to take care; & the boys, to
15 take courage. I was in a fright; & they, in a rage. I sent them down to carry the ladder to him, for which he was asking them. Stormie got upon the roof, & dragged him up, poor fellow, by the arms. How frightened I was!

 But how yet more frightened, when the horse's hoofs in the yard
20 announced the arrival of the post. No letters!!! How very extra-ordinary!— Oh if I knew when & how this uncertainty is to end . . . . I might be yet more uncomfortable perhaps than I am. Well! I shall know soon! Bummy has not said one word about her "proposal" for today. I think, tired as I am, I could go to Malvern;
25 if there, she meant to go. No letter from Malvern again today. It wᵈ be well for me if I could think of some things <ₐ & persons,> as little as I am thought of. I must go & read Pindar. I have not read a line of him, these two days.

 Did not read Pindar after all—but read.
30 I wonder why Eaton does not write. Impatient. Henrietta's protegèes[2] transferred from our gate to a lodging near the wyche on the poney. ≪Maddox[3] came.≫

1. The sale was announced in *Berrow's Worcester Journal*, 23 and 30 June 1831. The notice also appeared in the *Hereford Journal*, 29 June 1831. The crops comprised 160 acres of grass, 26 acres of wheat, 12 acres of peas and 4 acres of beans.

2. The Irishwoman and her invalid daughter.

3. Mary Maddox, who acted as dressmaker and seamstress for the Barretts. She was the subject of a poem ascribed to E.B.B., published in *HUP*, I, 128.

[40]

Sunday July 3.^{d}

H A & I drove to church, where we heard Mr Deane preach a sleepy kind of sermon. Mrs Martin there. She asked me to drive with her to Eastnor[1] on Tuesday, in the case of Mr Martin not accompanying her ≪...≫, on Monday. I w.^{d} rather have gone to Malvern, but it is right for me, & indeed it will be a satisfaction to me, to visit poor Lady Margaret.[2] Has she not felt for me? And can I not feel for her? <Too> well!——

Eliza was at church, & quite inclined to go home with us. But I thought of the letter, the expected letter; & begged her not to come here until Wednesday. It appears that Mrs Cliffe is not offended——

How hot & cold I grew as we approached the house! Is it possible? No letter!——

B & H drove to church. Arabel & I walked to chapel. A man, some heads shorter than I am, preached;[3] and if his voice had been in proportion to his size, I should not have had the headache. Vox, et prœterea nihil.[4] The sermon was very weak & bad. Its matter must however have been thought excellent by the preacher; for he repeated it again & again. The doctrine was scriptural—so I ought perhaps to have been better satisfied than I happened to be.

B & H did not get home until seven—& then we had prayers.

Settled. That I am to go with Maddox tomorrow morning early, & be left at Ruby Cottage.

Read the bible of course; but thought the bible, far less than I should do. I have left off praying for the specific object of remaining at Hope End. I pray now only that God may direct our going forth or our staying in: for the Giver of all Good must, surely, know better than I, what it is good to give. Thy will—Oh Lord!——

---

1. Eastnor Castle, the seat of Earl Somers, about 3 miles S.E. of Hope End (map ref. H5). It was a modern structure after the style of Edward I, begun in 1814 to designs by Smirke.

2. Lady Margaret Maria Cocks (1792-1849), daughter of the 1st Earl Somers. E.B.B.'s epithet derives from the death of Lady Margaret's mother, the Rt. Hon. Margaret, Countess Somers, on 19 February 1831.

3. This was the Rev. E. Elliott, who normally preached in Gloucester. On this occasion he filled Mr. Curzon's place while the latter preached at Uley (*The Baptist Magazine*, September 1831, p. 397).

4. "Voice, and nothing else." (Plutarch: "A man plucked a nightingale and finding almost no meat, said 'It's all voice ye are, and nought else' " *LCL-P*, III, 399, "Sayings of Spartans" 233A.)

Diary by E.B.B.

*Monday July 4*th.

Dearest Arabel's birthday. She is 18; and an interesting intelligent amiable feeling girl. I should love her even if she were not my sister; & even if she did not love me.

5   As Bummy <told> me to go into her room before I went away, I undrew her bed curtains before she was awake. I wondered what she c^d have to say to me, & was perfectly provoked when she asked me to promise not to mention at Ruby Cottage, anything of our un-happy business. I promised that I would not, if the subject were not
10   mentioned to <u>me</u>.

How I do hate & abhor this reserve, so foreign to my nature, so contrary to my professions, to be forced upon me! What is the use of a friend, if my heart is to ≪ . . . lock . . . ≫ itself against him? "No confidence,"—as Mr Boyd once said to me—["]no friendships".
15   I cd have cried with mortification: but there is enough to cry about, without this!—   Maddox & I drove away at seven, after my having had a partial breakfast in the nursery. Arrived at Ruby Cottage at 8. Mrs Boyd in ≪bed≫. Mr Boyd up,—but he had gone back again into his bed room. So I desired that my name sh^d be unnamed for the
20   present: & when the dining room door ≪was≫ shut upon me, out of the window I jumped. My hat I left behind, & ran up thro' the grove to the hill where I let my hair blow about & my feet walk about ad libitum. But I was not there long. I ran back again; & then came a message from Mrs Boyd who wished to see me. I went into her bed
25   room & sate down upon the bed, & talked. Presently Mr Boyd wanted to see me, which I gladly heard. Found him at breakfast. He is suf-fering from a painful boil on his <upper> lip. "I wish" he said, "that I c^d get rid of my ≪boil≫, as well as Bently did, of his"—[1] He talked of the difference between moral & physical pain,—& pre-
30   ferred as I have ≪ . . . ≫ heard him do before, suffering the former to the latter. The fact is, he is singularly constituted,—for the enjoy-ment of intense pleasure, rather than for a sensibility to intense pain. In general,   Chords that vibrate sweetest pleasure,
              Thrill the deepest notes of woe—

---

1. A punning allusion to the celebrated feud in 1697-99 between Richard Bentley and Charles Boyle (later Earl of Cork and Orrery), regarding the authenticity of the *Epistles of Phalaris.*

but his chords are not so strung.[1]   He asked <me> if I had heard
from Papa; «and» said little more on the subject.   His anxiety about
it, can scarcely be very great.

   After I had been down stairs to breakfast with Mrs Boyd, I came
up again & began to read Æschylus.   We read the 2.^d chorus; & I felt   5
happy while I was reading it.   A kind of happiness which cannot now
last long!—   Certainly, which may not!   My voice trembled once,
as I thought so!—   I wish I were constituted «like» Mr Boyd.

   We talked about Euripides & Sophocles & Æschylus; & I observed
that Euripides was the more pathetic writer.   He w.^d not allow that   10
Euripides can produce more pathetic passages than some in the Œdipus
Colonœus: & dwelt upon the pathos of one sentence in the Persœ—
where Atossa <exclaims to> the messenger, "Tell me of those who
are not dead".[2]   He accused Euripides of verbiage—but owned «to
a» personal prejudice against him, on account of his conduct to   15
Æschylus.   We talked comparatively about Homer Æschylus & Shakespeare: and positively about Æschylus's Prometheus—   Praises of
<the> speech in the Medea.[3]   After dinner, we had some politics;
and indeed before dinner.   Than I examined his memory in the
chorus's of the «Agamemnon», in Casandra's three speeches,[4] & in   20
Gregory's orations on Cœsarius & Basil.[5]   Then we talked about a
fourth edition of his Select Passages,[6] which I urged him to put in
motion.   No! he w.^d not—he c.^d not—nobody w.^d take the trouble
of being his «amanuensis» without being paid for it: & to anyone

1. Robert Burns, "On Sensibility" (1786), v.4:

> Dearly bought the hidden treasure
> Finer feelings can bestow;
> Chords that vibrate sweetest pleasure
> Thrill the deepest notes of woe.

   2. *LCL-A*, I, 135, lines 293-295: "Compose thyself, and even though thou groanest at our loss, yet unfold the sum of our disaster and speak out! Who is there that is *not* dead?"

   3. Beginning: "O children, children," (*LCL-E*, IV, 364-367, lines 1021-80).

   4. *LCL-A*, II, 100-113, lines 1178-97, 1214-41, 1256-94.

   5. Orations 10 and 20 (*GNO*, I, 160-176 and 316-373).   The notes made by E.B.B. on the flyleaf of *WG* included the comment: "Peroration of the funeral Oration on Cæsarius— I am uncertain whether this be not the finest passage, I have read in Gregory."

   6. His book of *Select Passages of the Writings of St. Chrysostom, St. Gregory Nazianzen, and St. Basil* was first published in 1806.   A fourth edition never appeared, although in the Preface of *An Essay on the Greek Article; to which is Added, an Essay on the Atonement*, 2nd edn. (London, 1835) Boyd said: "In the beginning of 1834, I was employed in preparing a new and much enlarged edition of my *Select Passages* ..."

who was paid, he could not commit the task of correcting the press,
<without> his own attention being strictly directed to every sheet;
which w^d <fatigue> & make him nervous. I ≪longed to beg him to
trust me≫ with the employment; but I was ≪too≫ afraid that he w^d
5   *say something I might dislike hearing: So I observed first—"I sh^d*
think that you might easily find somebody who would <correct> the
proof sheets for you." "Easily! You dont know how difficult it w^d
be.   My sister corrected the proof sheets of ≪the≫ first edition of
my Select passages: and attention was not paid to them.   You see
10   *even my own sister did not like the drudgery".*

    I took courage & begged him to employ me, & assured <ᴧhim>
of my liking & wishing for the employment. "Ah! I am well aware
that ≪you≫ would do it for me sooner than any body else would.
But I ≪should≫ not like you to drudge for me.   And suppose you
15   *should be ill—" "Ill! I am not going to anticipate being ill. Do let*
me manage it for you.   I should like it so very much!"   "But we
must <see> first ≪whether≫ you leave Hope End or not".   I said
that ≪whether≫ I left Hope End or not, the sheets might be sent to
me—& I said more—& he said more—& I think it will end by my
20   *doing what I wish to do.*

    My dear friend Mr Boyd!—— If he knew how much it gratifies me
to assist him in any way (≪I wish . . .≫ I c^d do so in every way) all
his 'drudgeries' w^d ≪ . . . devolve≫ upon me.   ≪It≫ pleased me to
hear him acknowledge that I would do more for him than other people
25   *would!   And is not that true? I think so.*

    I left Malvern somewhere between 7 & 8, ≪&≫ got home to the
relics of tea.   Bummy ————— at my being away so long.   Bro
D[itt]o.   Well!   I may not pass many more such long days with M^r
Boyd—perhaps not any more.   ≪But≫ I cannot bear to think that
30   *—I will not bear it—I will not think it.*

    Mrs Boyd & Miss Steers had intended driving here today; & I had
some difficulties & delicatus about putting them off until Wednesday
or Thursday.   After all nobody at home, is satisfied.   Neither am I,
quite.   I w^d rather that they did not come just now.

35   *The auction of the crops, at the farm today.   I am glad it is over.*
Oh if there is no chance of our staying here altogether; & I believe
there is little chance: and if Mr Boyd were not at Malvern, I would
yearn to be ≪away≫ from the sight & hearing of all that we see &

[44]

*hear every day.   But it is God's will!——   And I have in spite of
everything, felt happy several times today!——*

*M͔ͬˢ Boyd called me Miss Barrett.   She used to call me Ba.   Quære
why?   Another Quære——Why should I care?   Certainly I dont care
very much for M͔ͬˢ Boyd.   M͔ͬ Boyd (backed by M͔ͬˢ B's reported
opinion) <ₐstill> maintains, that jealousy <of> Eliza Cliffe, is the
occult cause of Annie's late conduct to me.   Fudge again; said M͔ͬ
Burchell.*

*Bummy proposes my proposing to M͔ͬˢ Martin, when she is driving
me to Eastnor tomorrow, to call on Miss Baker at the Pindars.[1]   How
provoking it will be, in the case of our not going to Eastnor, if Bummy
proposes my calling on the Pindars instead of<ₐmy> going to Malvern!——*

Tuesday.   July 5ᵗʰ

*I was up <a> little after seven this morning.   So ≪were≫ the
clouds; and to make them more decisive, the rain is down; ≪& . . .≫
there seems no chance of my driving out with M͔ͬˢ Martin.   Surely
a letter, a decisive letter will come today! or else surely Papa will
come!——   If it does—or if he does—what will be the consequence?
Nothing good, I fear, humanly speaking: but everything good, I know,
by my knowledge of the providence of God.   I have prayed for good
—I have asked for <fish>, & shall receive no serpent.[2]*

*<The> rain went off; & M͔ͬˢ Martin arrived before the letters.
So I was forced to go without them.   As she had heard of my visit to
<Ruby> Cottage yesterday, she did not propose my going there; &
we went past the house to Grt Malvern.   I never thought it possible
that I c͔ͩ be made to do such a thing.   But as we <returned>, I c͔ͩ
refrain no longer, & begged to be allowed to go & see M͔ͬ Boyd for
two minutes.   Allowed.   She was "just thinking of proposing it".
As we drove up to the door, there was M͔ͬ Boyd walking!   I walked
into the house, & he after me; & we talked for not one minute.   I ran*

5

10

15

20

25

30

---

1. The Rev. Reginald Pyndar (1755?-1831), Rector of Madresfield since 1793, and a local
magistrate, cousin of the 1st Earl Beauchamp, lived with his family at Upper Hall, near Ledbury (map ref. G4). Miss Harriet Baker is believed to have been his niece from Worcester. In
an unpublished, undated letter to Henrietta, c. 1827, E.B.B. described her as "a particular
friend" of Lady Margaret Cocks, of an "age a good deal past 'the certain age'!" (Collection
of the late H. S. Altham, Esq.).

2. Matt. vii.10: "Or if he ask a fish, will he give him a serpent?"

Diary by E.B.B.

up to Mrs Boyd who was dressing. *Talked not one minute. Then
⟨went⟩ into M^r. Boyd's sitting room, & talked to him there, not one
minute. Then Exit. Cool—cool—cool. Warm—warm—warm!!—
As ⟨I⟩ came away without hearing of the letters, & as my writing
5 about them, by ⟨this day's⟩ post, is out of the question,—Mrs Boyd
agreed not to come here until Thursday. I am glad of it. We drove
home.   Mrs Martin has agreable conversation, & is a feeling excellent
person; but she has not vivida vis[1] enough about her, to please me
altogether.   She left me at our ⟨nearest⟩ gate,—& I walked to the
10 house as quickly as my trembling feet & heart would let me.   Henrietta met me in front of the house. "Any letters." "Yes! but no
good!!   He says he has ⟨waited⟩ for some good, but has none to
tell us". I got into the drawing room—& got the letter. Yes! There
is no good, but it is written in good spirits. Thank God for that!—
15 I could scarcely read it, I trembled so much.*

Wednesday.   July 6th.
*   Eliza Cliffe arrived; & brought a note from Eaton in which he
agrees to allow £3 for the books exchanged.   It is ⟨less⟩ ⟨∧than⟩
their value,—but it is more than their value to me,—they being to
20 me valueless: therefore I will close with him.   There is a strong opposition of prudent people against me; but I will close with him.
    By Bummy's desire, I left Eliza at 12 o'clock, & let Gent drive me
to Eastnor.   Was shewn into the dining room, to wait for Lady Margaret. A coldness & desolateness about the room; an exactness about
25 the posture of the chairs,—which made me think that no one inhabited it, or sate down on them.   I could not; but walked about, &
looked out of the window, & worked myself up into an agitation in
the fear of Lady Margaret's.   However, it was not so. She ⟨came⟩
into the room with a chearful countenance & unagitated manner. She
30 received me affectionately—said that she had given orders to be denied to everybody except Mrs Martin & me—& seemed particularly
glad to see me. "So much," she said, "has occurred to each of us,
since we parted." Yes! So much!—— She enquired immediately
with respect to our present situation—"Are you stationary at Hope
35 End?"—   "But I fear you are likely to leave it?" She told me that*

---

1. "Vital force."

[46]

she had heard of Papa's intention of going to Brighton; & that both
Lord Somers¹ & herself very much wished ≪it . . .≫ on account of
≪Brighton's≫ being near Reigate where they intend residing two
months ≪in≫ every year.² Lord Somers wished that we ≪would≫
pass some time at Reigate. ≪That≫ was kind: & I laid my hand on   5
Lady Margaret's hand, & said so. But I told her my prejudice against
noisy, rattling, brick-dusty Brighton; & ≪. . .≫ my love of silence &
quietness & a sight of the green trees & fields out of the window.

  For an hour I sate with her, & when she had asked me to visit her
once more before she went away on Saturday week, I said good bye.   10
How much pleasanter it w^d* have been to have driven home immediate-*
ly, instead of calling upon Miss Baker at M^r* Pindars! But Bummy had*
desired me to do it—so I did it. After all Miss Baker had gone the
day before. I was obliged to get out ≪&≫ call on M^{rs}* Pindar, which*
*was a double bore!— ≪I≫ did <*ₐ*not> stay longer than five min-*   15
utes,—& ≪got≫ home faster than was safe. ≪Three≫ o'clock—
dinner over; & Eliza & Arabel out of doors sketching. Eliza painted
at my mouth till she spoilt it,—& then had tea,—& then went home.
I tired, too tired to be agreable,—all the evening.

  <I> wrote this morning one line to M^{rs}* Boyd, to say that Papa's*   20
letter contained no obstacle to our receiving her.

Thursday ≪July≫ 7.
  Up at a little after seven, & writing to Eaton. I have sent him a
list of the books which I wish him to send me immediately. Wrote
also a few lines (a very few) to M^r* Boyd, to tell him what ≪he≫ asked*   25
me to write about: i e Lady Margaret's opinion of the House of lords'
intended doings about the bill. What an awkward sentence, that is,—
but I am scribbling against time—& tune ≪ergo≫. Prepared some of
the seven chiefs, & heard Storm & George read Greek—in which I
was interupted by M^{rs}* Boyd's arrival. Miss Steers she left behind*   30
vis a vis the great ash.³ When I had talked to M^{rs}* Boyd a little while,*
M^{rs}* Cliffe M*^{rs}* Best Eliza & little Fanny <arrived>, on their way to*

---

1. Lady Margaret's father, John Somers Cocks (1760-1841), 1st Earl Somers.

2. The Priory, Lord Somers's other seat, was at Reigate.

3. "In the deer park, which is not very extensive, is an ash, said to be one of the largest in Great Britain" (account of Hope End, from *A Description of Malvern* . . . [by Mary Southall], Malvern, 1822, p. 212).

Diary by E.B.B.

call at the Bartons.   Fanny is a pretty ⟨inte⟩resting-looking bam-
bina,—but as to writing a poem on her, as M.ʳˢ Best begged me to do
——excuse me there.   I never can write when I dont feel; & my
feelings are not apt to rise extempore in consequence of an hour's
visiting.   Everybody dined with us at one o'clock—except poor Miss
Steers who was constant ≪to≫ the ash.   We sent her down some
strawberries; and after the ash was painted in oils, Henrietta sate with
her on the bank, while she was sketching the house.   I longed to be
παρεδρος,¹ —but I could not leave M.ʳˢ Boyd.   And M.ʳˢ Boyd, tho'
goodnatured & kind in her manner,—is certainly nothing more.   She
is a very trying person to spend a day with!   Empty minded, & without real sensibility—which extends to the tastes as well as to the
feelings—frivolous & flippant.   What a woman to be M.ʳ Boyd's
wife!—   But she is his wife; & therefore I w.ᵈ not be inattentive to
her on any account.   So I fidgetted about with her, from one subject
to another, & from one place to another—from the drawing room
to the front of the house—from the front of the house to the drawing room.   Oh how tired I was!—
    ≪Miss≫ Steers came into the house a few minutes before they
both left it finally.   She sate on the sofa by me; & we talked of Lamartine.   She is not, I think, a clever woman of nature's making; but
she seems to have refined tastes, & a cultivated mind.—   There is a
little effort now & then to seem to have more—
    They went away at six; and the clouds which looked fearfully like
a thunderstorm, went away soon after them.   Not after them, I
hope!—   ⟨Bummy⟩ had a letter from Papa today.   I suspected the
black seal² at dinnertime; but she did not tell us until ≪after≫ every
body had gone, that the seal was his, & that he could not fix the time
of his return—that on Friday he had an engagement—& that he w.ᵈ
write to Henrietta before he saw us.   So he is coming!—   So there is
indeed no hope.   God's will—the wisest will—be done!
    Eliza gave me a note to give to M.ʳˢ Boyd directed to M.ʳ Boyd.
What did she write to him about, I wonder!   I sent ≪a≫ note from
⟨myself⟩.   Which will he read first?—   There is no use in asking

    1. "Sitting beside."
    2. He was still in mourning for his mother, Elizabeth Moulton, who had died in London
on 29 December 1830.

[48]

questions on this subject.   It is <u>unquestionable</u>, that he ≪prefers≫ me
to Eliza Cliffe.

Friday.   ≪July≫ 8.

Henrietta <u>à la Henriette</u> about going to call on Mrs Martin to apologize for not have [sic] noticed her invitation for yesterday evening.   5
Set off at last: and in about ten minutes afterwards, M.^r & Mrs Martin
arrived here.   An express sent ≪over≫ the hill for Henrietta, which
missed her—but she came nevertheless.   Mrs Martin urgent upon us
all to drink tea there this evening, & meet the Miss Biddulphs.   Henrietta Bro & Sam agreed: Bummy & I demurred.   I was afraid lest the   10
demurring might produce a recurring . . to the point: but Bummy
assured me in an asside that she w.^d not go.   So it was agreed that
she & A & I sh.^d go to the Wyche instead.   Nature & the Biddulphs
are a contrast, & I never could doubt about preferring the former.

(No letters.)   ≪Bummy wrote to Papa to dissuade him from   15
coming.≫

Arabel walked down to Mrs Barker's;[1] & Henrietta occupied her
place in the wheelbarrow, until we had conveyed her safely to the
Colwall first gate.[2]   In the meantime it began to rain, which made
Henrietta à la Henriette again.   She w.^d go & she w.^d not go.   I was   20
angry & I was not angry.   I was certainly provoked.   She went at
last.   B & I returned to Arabel at Mrs Barker's & dried our wet
exteriors by Milly's extempore fire.   The rain went off, & so did we,
to the Whyche.   Bummy sate in the carriage with the newspaper, on
this side of it, while Arabel & I walked along the terrace on the other.   25
We walked to the spot immediately above Ruby Cottage, & in five
minutes, if I had descended, I should have ≪been≫ <u>in</u> Ruby Cottage.

1. She lived in a cottage by the south gate of Hope End (no. 15 on the auctioneer's map,
Appendix III, p. 335), and acted as gate-keeper. In a juvenile poem E.B.B. described her thus:

> And Madam Barker with the sallow cheek
> The lanky shape and with the long thin neck
> Sweet Madam Barker!

("A Journal of the Adventures of our Journey from Hope End to Worthing, written in the
carriage June—1819." Autograph ms. at Wellesley.)

2. i.e., the entrance to Old Colwall, the home of James and Julia Martin since shortly
after their marriage in 1819, a substantial and commodious house, "built for posterity" in
Mr. Martin's words. It was the nearest house to Hope End, the distance between the two
being slightly less than ¾ mile, although they were hidden from each other's view by the
intervening hill. By road, however, the distance was 1½ miles (map ref. E5). The house
stands today largely unchanged from when E.B.B. visited it.

Diary by E.B.B.

And in less than five minutes, I w^{d}*. have descended, if I had not thought of Bummy & the late evening.   If I had not thought of them, w*^{d}*. M*^{r}*. Boyd have been glad?—   W*^{d}*. he indeed have been glad?*
I enjoyed this walking, & the ≪odours≫ of the fresh evening, &
5 *the ＜sights＞ of the superb expanse & majestic hills, very much indeed. We were not at home until 9 oclock; & Henrietta was not, until ten. Bro & Sam arrived at the same time; so we had prayers, & went to bed directly.*

Saturday.   ≪July≫ 9th*.*
10 *Read Pindar's 4*th*. Olympic before breakfast—read & digested it. After breakfast, heard the boys read Homer & Zenophon; and at twelve, drove with Bummy & Arabel to M*^{rs}*. Cliffe's.   We ＜rounded＞ it by the Bartons, & called there, & had to wait for M*^{rs}*. Griffith's & Miss Peyton's out fitting, & for the opening of the window shutters;*
15 *& after all, could not get away without leaving behind us a promise of drinking tea there next monday.   At least so Bummy thought, for she made the promise.   Twenty necessities w*^{d}*. not have torn it from me.   N.B. A Bull!!*
Talking of bulls, as we proceeded on our road to Mathon, we met
20 *one, coming to meet us in a narrow lane, ≪&≫ with a bellow.   Out of the carriage we all three jumped, & took refuge in a field close by. But one gate seemed to me by no means a satisfactory go-between for us & our enemy; so I climbed a very high railing with a rather deep ditch at the ＜ₐother＞ side—which, if I had not been frightened*
25 *out of my senses, I could by no means have done.   At last a man came to our rescue & drove away the bull; & we got miraculously safe thro' the frying sun, ＜over＞ the earthquaking roads, to Mathon. M*^{rs}*. Cliffe was at dinner at two, & we joined her by invitation.   After-wards I went into Eliza's room—indeed into every room in the house*
30 *—indeed into every room not in the house, for I visited the hermitage. ≪...≫ Then I lay down on the sofa & rested my body & mind with the Literary Souvenir, ≪while≫ ＜omnes＞ præter me*[1] *went out to walk.   Miss Landon's contributions are not superior,*[2] *—& I could see*

---

1. "All except me."
2. Letitia Elizabeth Landon, later Maclean, contributed three poems, "The Maiden Astrologer," "Robert Burns and his Highland Mary" and "The Violet" to *The Literary Souvenir* (London, 1831).

[50]

nothing else in the book which was very much so. We had tea,—&
at seven Mrs Cliffe w.^d save me a shaking, by driving me to our gate in
her carriage. And besides she <_∧w.^d.> ≪lend≫ me the first two vols
of the mysteries of Udolpho[1] before she had finished them herself—
a <kind> of generosity which quite dazzled my weak moral sense. I   5
have read the mysteries; but am anxious to read them again—being a
worshipper of Mrs Radcliffe. Bummy drove Mrs Cliffe's carriage a
part of the way; ≪so≫, she escaped a part of the shaking. Parted at
the gate with the kind Mathon people; & found at home the Colwall
ones. Henrietta had been driven by Mrs Martin to call on the Bid-   10
dulphs, & had persuaded her to drink tea at Hope End. Mr Martin
there too—playing cricket. Sate on the hay a little while,—& then
went in to tea the second!

  No letter today. I scarcely expected one, ≪but did expect≫ one.
I believe Bummy's letter urged <him> not to remove his family until   15
the last, & urged him not to return home <_∧now.> If ≪that had≫
weight with him, we may have no letter again tomorrow. I hope we
may not. And yet if there is no hope & can be no hope (—and
whence are we to gather it?—) it w^d be better for us to leave this
fatally dear place at once—to go at once!— It w.^d be better for all   20
but me—and better for me, for every reason but one reason. ≪ . . . ≫

  The Martins stayed until twelve. I dont know how it is. They
have not the key of my mind. They are superior & feeling people;
and yet I can neither think nor feel aloud when <they> are present.
Read more than a chapter of the Mysteries, between the acts of pull-   25
ing off my stockings & going to sleep.

Sunday July 10.th

  Uncomfortable night between the rush light & dark thoughts. This
morning I refused to go to church, because, if I went, somebody w.^d be
obliged either to walk or stay at home; neither of which, they might   30
like. I am in a fever about the letters—and ≪the≫ <_∧fever> must
last some time longer, as it is now only five minutes past twelve, & I
have no spurs for ≪Time≫. If a letter comes, I wish Eliza w.^d not
come!—

---

  1. Ann Radcliffe, *The Mysteries of Udolpho, A Romance; Interspersed with some Pieces*
of Poetry, 4 vols. (London, 1794).

[51]

Diary by E.B.B.

Neither a letter nor Eliza came; but a thunderstorm! ≪ . . . ≫
However the thunder grumbled courteously at a distance until we
had done dinner,—& then it lightened until five oclock.   Minny
<u>protected</u> Bummy & Arabel in the library,—& I lay down on Minny's
5 bed <u>meo more</u>.[1]   No going to church or chapel of course.

A letter from Mrs Boyd who tells me that whenever the weather
has been good, Mr Boyd <ₐhas> ≪said≫ "Well, I think Miss Barrett
might have come on such a fine day."   I was there last Monday &
Tuesday; Mrs Boyd was here on Thursday: therefore only on Friday
10 & Saturday, was there a possibility of my going when I did not go.
I am pleased, very much pleased, ≪by≫ his seeming to wish to see
me.   Mr Spowers,[2] Mrs Boyd says, is coming on Tuesday—(provoking Mr Spowers!) & Mr Boyd would like me to come on Monday if
I ≪could≫,—if not early on Tuesday.   He <u>must</u> like me to be with
15 him, I think.

Now we are going to the Bartons to drink tea tomorrow evening,
—& if I sh.^d not be able to have the carriage tomorrow morning—
why then I must wait until Tuesday.

Arabel felt Bummy's pulse for me on the subject.   Decidedly un-
20 favorable.   "Nasty Boyds"! she said—but Arabel did not tell me
<u>that</u>, or I sh.^d have been sulky instead of goodhumoured.   I ≪w.^d≫
have said no word more about it—w.^d have staid at home tomorrow,
—& set off the next morning!   ≪But≫ in my blissful ignorance,
while B was curling her hair, I asked her why she objected to my
25 going,—elicited that she was afraid of my being late, & making her
so, at the Bartons; promised to behave ≪ₐpunctually≫;—& got leave
of absence.   I am going tomorrow morning at <u>8</u>, & am to leave Ruby
Cottage at half past <u>3</u>.

"Nasty Boyds"!   Arabel said she was not in her <u>particularly best</u>
30 humour at the time,—but what an expression!   Why sh.^d she dislike
them?—at least <u>Mr Boyd</u>, whom she never saw, & has heard nothing
≪ . . . ≫ but good of?—

---

1. "According to my custom."

2. On p. x of *The Agamemnon of Æschylus: A Tragedy* (London, 1823), Boyd referred
to "my learned and much esteemed friend, Mr. Spowers of Hampstead, . . . I embrace this opportunity of acknowledging and recording the obligations which I am under to Mr. Spowers,
as the instructor of my youth, and my initiator in those studies which have been the amusement of my riper years." Mr. Spowers died in 1841, at the age of 77.

I am very glad Papa did not write by this post.   Now, he cant write (i e. we cant get his letter) until Tuesday, & cant come until ≪Wednesday≫.   And as his coming would be his dispairing, I am anxious for him not to come.   Prayers—& read the bible,—& wrote about the <∧Biblical> MSS. of course.   But on the whole, & thro' the thunderstorm, an idle day.   5

Monday.   July 11.

Up at six, intending to go at eight.

Went however, at half past eight—& not my fault.   Breakfasted by myself, & found M[rs] *Boyd breakfasting, & had from her, details*   10 *about ≪the≫ thunderstorm, & influenza & Miss Marshall & M*[r] *Biscoe*[1] *& a thousand other things not worth remembering.   I went up to M*[r] *Boyd, & fancied he was glad to see me.   I really believe he was.   When we had talked we read the seven chiefs, and when we had read we talked, and when we had talked, I assisted him in learning*   15 *some passages in the Prometheus.   Happy day!—   He said once "is it really your opinion that you will leave this house"?   "Yes:["] I answered—"it is indeed".   "And will you go away then next month—"?   I thought there was in his voice an expression of dejec-tion. The tears came fast into my eyes!—   I wish he may miss me . .*   20 *a little.   He showed me a letter from the German booksellers, in which Wolf's folio Homer is stated to be either out of print or so rare as to have escaped the exertions of their correspondents.*[2] *My feel-ing on reading ≪this≫, was pleasurable.   I w*[d] *rather that he had not given me the book; yet I am glad he thought of giving it to me.   I went*   25 *away at half past three.   Called for a minute at M*[rs] *Trants, & found her at dinner with Sam & Henry.   She begged me to spend a day with her as I do with M*[r] *Boyd.   What ≪an idea≫!—what a misapprehen-sion of ideas!   On cross questioning, I found out that she preferred my ≪going≫ to her by myself—in other words, without Bummy!*   30 *Selfish woman!—   Is her want of courtesy towards my friends, to*

1. Miss Marshall has not been identified. Mr. Biscoe was Annie Boyd's suitor, possibly the Rev. William Biscoe (1805-77), recently appointed Rector of Donnington, near Ledbury, who was unmarried at this time. Alternatively, he may have been Joseph Biscoe, whose marriage was mentioned by E.B.B. in a letter [30 May 1834] to H.S.B. (*EBB/HSB*, pp. 202-205).

2. Friedrich Augustus Wolf, ed. *Homeri et Homeridarum Opera et Reliquiæ* (Lipsiæ, 1806). H.S.B. presented this edition to E.B.B. on 16 July.

Diary by E.B.B.

≪be≫ *remunerated by my superabundant courtesy towards her? For nothing but courtesy could force me to spend a day with her.*

I got to the Bartons at half past four, before their dinner, & was obliged to dine & talk until tea.   Everybody was emptied out of Hope End into Barton court, at six—and <u>our children</u> seemed to enjoy themselves very much.   Dear little things!—   How tired I was, & unwell this evening.   As, on our return, I was sitting by myself in ≪our≫ bedroom, I heard what I used to hear in the summer of 1828, & only <u>then</u>—the <u>deathwatch</u>.[1]   I grew sick & pale, & dizzy—& slept miserably all night—solely I believe from the strong unaccountable impression produced on me, by ≪this≫ circumstance.   I have mentioned it to nobody, & dont much like mentioning it ≪here≫. There never was a more foolishly weakly superstitious being than I am.

Tuesday.   July 12.

Went ≪into≫ the library to try to rationalize my mind about the deathwatch,—by reading the Cyclopædia.   Feel very unwell today, & nervous.   Read the mysteries of Udolpho—by way of <quieting> my imagination?   & heard the boys read Homer & Zenophon—& read some of Hugo Victor's & Lamartine's poetry—his last song of Childe Harold.[2]   Miss Steers kindly sent a packet of French poetry to Mr Boyd's for me yesterday.   ≪Le≫ dernier chant wants the Byronic character (—an inevitable want for a French composition—) and is not quite equal ≪even to≫ Lamartine.   No letter!!—

Wednesday.   July 13.

Much better day,—in spite of the violent rain last night which agitated me ≪teeth≫ & all!—   Arabel & I got out of bed & ran to Minny (little dears!) and I was in a thunder-&-lightening fright; & my ≪teeth≫ did what my tongue does sometimes—<u>chattered</u>.   Dreaming over Udolpho.   My impression is that M.[rs] Radcliffe's spell-word is "Tremble" not "Weep".   She is not great in pathos.

1. "There are several circumstances which are considered, as signs of approaching death. If a dog howls, or a death-watch ticks, or a looking glass is broken, the approaching death of some person in the family, where the circumstance occurs, is supposed to be signified. . . ." (*Popular Superstitions*, Philadelphia, [1830?], p. 60). E.B.B.'s mother died on 7 October 1828, and E.B.B. obviously believed that the loss was heralded during that summer by the death-watch beetle.

2. Alphonse Marie Louis de Lamartine, *Le Dernier Chant du Pèlerinage d'Harold* (Paris, 1825).

[54]

*Wrote a part of a letter to Papa. None from him. Grumbled & had
my hair curled, & went to Colwall with Bro, to meet as I understood
only Lord Somers & Lady Margaret. Found there M^{rs} G Jones*[1] *& Miss
Biddulph, & Col: Drummond & Mrs Drumond.*[2] *Provoked— But I
can wear sackcloth, (sometimes), without making faces—so I made   5
none on this occasion. Mrs Jones & Miss Biddulph are ≪unassuming≫
& apparently amiable, & not silly; but their faces & manners & conversation want expression. "Stirring up with a long pole" would be as
useful ≪with≫ regard to them, as to the ≪wild≫ beasts late of Exeter
Change.*[3] *Col: Drummond "thinks himself an Adonis" according to   10
the general opinion. As long as he does not think ≪himself≫ <$_\wedge$a>
Solon, I wont complain. A goose may plume herself; & so may he, . . .
on his externals. Mrs Drummond talks like thunder. Lady Margaret
sate next me after dinner, & we had some interesting conversation,
about German & Italian. I ≪confessed≫ that if ever I learnt German,   15
it sh^d be more for the sake of reading the Sorrows of Werter*[4] *than
Klopstock's Messiah.*[5] *So it sh^d. We got home at half past ten; &c——*

Thursday July 14.
    *At breakfast, <my> parcel of books from Eaton came up the
road. Fresh from the carrier. Unpacked it eagerly, & read the title   20
pages of Barnes's Euripides*[,] *Marcus Antoninus, Callimachus, the
Anthologia, Epictetus*[,] *Isocrates, & Da Vinci's Painting.*[6] *The last I*

---

1. The mother-in-law of Mr. Biddulph's daughter Augusta Eleanor.

2. Members of the local social circle, who lived at Underdown, ½ mile from Ledbury (map ref. H4).

3. The menagerie was removed from Exeter 'Change in 1828, prior to the demolition of the building during the widening of the Strand in 1830. Until then, ". . . the sight-lover had to pay half-a-crown to see a few animals confined in small dens and cages . . . the walls painted with exotic scenery, in order to favour the illusion; . . . The roar of the lions and tigers of Exeter 'Change could be distinctly heard in the street, and often frightened horses in the roadway" (Walter Thornbury and Edward Walford, *Old and New London* . . . , 6 vols., London, 1873-78, III, 116).

4. [Johann Wolfgang von Goethe], *Die Leiden des jungen Werthers* (Leipzig, 1774).

5. [Gottlieb Friedrich Klopstock], *Der Messias: ein Heldengedicht* [first three cantos], (Halle, 1749).

6. Most of these books appeared in the 1913 Browning Sale: Lot 661, *Euripidis Tragoediæ XX*, . . . ex edit. J. Barnes, 6 vols. (Oxford, 1812); Lot 338, *Marci Antonini Imperatoris De Rebus Suis* . . . studio T. Gatakeri (1697); Lot 540, *Callimachi Cyreni Hymni et Epigrammata* (Glasgow, 1755); Lot 654, *Epicteti Manuale*, illustravit J. Simpson (London, 1758); Lot 785, *Isocratis Orationes et Epistolæ*, cum latina interpretatione H. Wolfii (1613). The Rivinus *Anthologia*, later offered to H.S.B. by E.B.B. (see p. 113), was not catalogued. Da Vinci's *A Treatise on Painting* E.B.B. subsequently exchanged (see p. 60).

had sent for, for Eliza Cliffe; but the externals are so <shabby> that
I have a mind to send it back again.   Finished my dream about Udol-
pho;—& began Destiny, a novel by the author of the Inheritance,[1]
which Miss Peyton lent me.   I liked the Inheritance so much that my
5 *desires respecting this book were "all alive".   I forgot to say that I*
dont like the conclusion of the Mysteries.   It is "long drawn out" &
not "in linked sweetness".[2] *Read some of the Alcestis.   Mr Boyd*
wished me to read it; & I wished ≪so≫ too.
  ≪No letter!——— Sent mine to Papa!——≫

10 *Friday.   July 15.*
  Wrote to Mr Boyd.   Glad of it—for I received afterwards a note
from him announcing the arrival of Wolf's Homer! and desiring me to
go for it. ≪He≫ seems disappointed about the ≪ . . . ≫ paper, &
about ≪there≫ being in this edition only 6 books.   In the envelope
15 *Mrs Boyd advises me to come soon.   If the book had been a fine one*
she says, I might have appeared to come ≪on account≫ of the book:
but as it is not, ≪I shall appear to go≫, on account of the giver.   Ah!
if it were on account only of the book!— —.   I will go tomorrow,
if I can.   Mr Boyd's note is not — — what his note would have been
20 *3 years ago.   He certainly does not care much for me! not as I care*
for him!
  Read the second volume of Destiny, & a little of the Alcestis.
  Mrs Cliffe & Eliza drank tea with us; & so did Mr Martin; & so did
Reynolds & Tom Peyton[3] *who had been invited to cricket.   Agreed*
25 *—that ≪B H≫ A Bro & Sam sh.^d dine tomorrow at Mr Martins, &*
drink tea at Mrs Cliffes.   I rescued my expedition to Malvern, with dif-
ficulty: at least it was rescued for me,—for I urged them to take the

---

1. [Susan Edmondstone Ferrier], *The Inheritance*, 3 vols. (London, 1824); *Destiny: or, the Chief's Daughter*, 3 vols. (Edinburgh, 1831).

2. *Poems of Mr. John Milton, both English and Latin, Compos'd at several times* (London, 1645), "L'Allegro," p. 36:

> Married to immortal verse
> Such as the meeting soul may pierce
> In notes, with many a winding bout
> Of lincked sweetnes long drawn out,
> With wanton heed, and giddy cunning,
> The melting voice through mazes running;
> Untwisting all the chains that ty
> The hidden soul of harmony.

3. Reynolds Peyton (1815-61) and Thomas Griffith Peyton (1816-87), the two eldest of the Peyton boys.

carriage & let me prorogue until Monday.   We drove to Mrs Martin's
this morning, & sate there more than an hour—until Mrs Hanford[1]
& my patience had gone away.   Mrs Martin is an intelligent & feeling
≪woman≫; but I dont know how it is.   She & I dont ≪amalgamate≫.

No letter from Papa today!——   Whenever I hear "there is no   5
letter", I take breath.   It is a respite.

Mrs Biddulph & Mrs Phillips[2] & Miss Biddulph called here.   I
caught in the hall, when I was going up stairs to put on respectable
shoes without ventilators.   But I dare say they care as little about my
feet, as I do about their heads.   10

Saturday July 16th.

Clouds but no rain.   ≪Dreamt last night≫ of all the passengers
of a West India vessel,—except two rescued by Bro,—being drowned.
I hope <u>that</u> does not indicate a drowning for me in my way to or
from Malvern today.   Read a little of the Alcestis before I got out of   15
bed,—I think I shall like it.

Went to Malvern, & called <_∧at the Barton door, about Destiny;
&> on Mrs Trant on my way to Mr Boyd's.   She asked me when I
≪meant≫ to spend a day with her.   I said I did not know, & <u>she</u>
said —— nothing.   Silence is eloquent; & silence on this occasion   20
did not I think, speak on the courteous side of the question—of
which I was glad.   Found Mrs Boyd in the drawing room; & was soon
released ≪to≫ Mr Boyd.   Before <he> admitted me, I heard him say
"You did not show it to her?   You did not say anything about it?"
About the book of course.   ≪Well! I was received into his room!——≫   25
He asked me if I chose to look at ≪the≫ book there, <or> wait until
I got home.   "<u>There</u>", my answer was.   So he sent me back into the
drawing room, for Mrs Boyd to show me the sight.   Bad paper!!   Only
six books!!   Twelve books—and the most splendid paper & type.   He
had wished to take me by surprise; & the surprise was complete.   It is   30
the most magnificent Greek book I ever looked upon;[3] &, what is better & more valuable; has τη φιλτατη[4] written on one of the first pages,

1. Of Woolashill Hall, about 14 miles east of Hope End.

2. Mrs. Biddulph's sister-in-law.

3. Wolf's *Homer*, ed. cit. Volume I, with an inscription by E.B.B. recording the gift, formed Lot 755 of the 1913 Browning Sale.

4. "For the nearest and dearest."

Diary by E.B.B.

in his own hand.   I shall often look on & $<_\wedge$ think of$>$ that writing, when the heart that dictated it, kind & gentle as are its feelings, shall not be dwelling on the thought of my thoughts!—

I went back into M.ʳ Boyd's room, & expressed, how imperfectly!
5 *—what I thought & felt of his present to me.   We then read the seven chiefs,—$\ll$ . . . $\gg$ Yes! but he first asked if we had heard from Papa, & spoke a little about Hope End.   Will he be very sorry, if I go away?   I am afraid of answering that question.   I wish I were more sure of his regard.   And I wish that he had not made me so costly a*
10 *present!—   How little & yet how much is necessary to please me!—*

$\ll$His$\gg$ sister & a Miss Nelly something[1] is coming to stay at Ruby Cottage.   The young lady is 16; & was, when she was 6, a clever child. $\ll$Her father$\gg$ had amused himself by teaching her the Greek character[s], & had made her read the Hecuba thro', without of course, her
15 *understanding a word.   M.ʳ Boyd does not think that she understands Greek.   I hope that she — — I hope he wont prefer her society to mine.   I hope Miss Boyd will like me.   I will take pains to please M.ʳ Boyd's sister.*

He asked me to talk to M.ʳ Spowers at dinner: "on his account,
20 *he thought I ought to do it."   I promised to do my best; and as I went out of the room, he $\ll$said$\gg$ that I must remember what I had promised, & that he w.ᵈ ask M.ʳˢ Boyd if I had been "naughty or good".   I in a panic of course.   Found M.ʳ Spowers solo in the drawing room. Exit I in a fuss, went to M.ʳˢ Boyd's room, down stairs—no M.ʳˢ Boyd*
25 *—returned perforce to M.ʳ Spowers.   Talked to him of M.ʳ Boyd— my best introduction.   Down to dinner.   I impelled myself to talk, $<$whether$>$ I had anything to say or not—to talk about the country, & the newspaper, & the raven, & $\ll$Joanna Baillie$\gg$[2] & Lord Byron. So that $\ll$when$\gg$ I had to answer M.ʳ Boyd's "naughty or good", I*
30 *could say "good".   M.ʳ Spowers is a sensible man; & gentlemanly & goodnatured.   Before dinner, M.ʳ Boyd had walked out with him up & down the garden.   M.ʳ Boyd $<$said$>$ a good deal about leaving me —& begged me to believe that it was not his wish to do so,—$\ll$that$\gg$*

---

1. Eleanor Page Bordman (1815?-78), later (1848) Jago, daughter of the Rev. James Bordman, Curate of Ickham, Kent. The friendship which sprang up between Miss Bordman and E.B.B. was to persist until the latter's death.

2. Joanna Baillie (1762-1851), poetess and dramatist, whose house at Hampstead was the centre of a distinguished literary circle. Mr. Spowers also lived at Hampstead.

he went only on account of his health. It was certainly right for him to go. But could he not have asked me to go with him? He evidently dislikes my walking with him. What is the reason? Shall I ask? No!—

While we were at dinner M.ʳ Wood[1] called, to tell ≪him≫ that a celebrated preacher M.ʳ ＜James＞, is to preach on Tuesday, at the anniversary of the chapel.[2] M.ʳ Boyd wishes me to go, & to write or speak to Eliza Cliffe about it, & to make her use her influence with Miss Wall—that every body may go.

After dinner we had a little more of the Seven Chiefs; & I heard him recite some of the Prometheus; & then we talked; and at half past 7 I went away. As I was taking leave of him, he ≪asked≫ me to tell M.ʳ Spowers to ＜take＞ the newspaper & read it to him. Is it possible that I sh.ᵈ have forgotten this message until I got to South Lodge? Very near going back again,—but it w.ᵈ have seemed ridiculous.

Found, on arriving at home, that there was no letter; & that ≪nobody≫ except Bro & Sam had gone to the Cliffes, on account, not so much of the rain as the clouds. *So I understand it. Made them all stare at my book—& promise to hear M.ʳ James preach on Tuesday. Not very well.*

Sunday. July 17ᵗʰ

Not well—& as an ergo, did not go either to church or chapel. M.ʳˢ Cliffe & Eliza came & I displayed my Homer to them,—& settled about Tuesday. They will go, & take me. *Not sure that I like it. If I go in M.ʳˢ Cliffe's carriage, I may not see M.ʳ Boyd. I* must *see him, if I go at all!—— No letter!— I wrote about the Biblical MSS. Afterwards wrote to M.ʳ Boyd about my forgetting to give his message to M.ʳ Spowers—& also about the Homer.[3] I told him that tho' I wished he had not given me so costly a present, I was "pleased,—*

---

1. The Rev. John Wood, Minister of the Chapel in the Connexion of the Countess of Huntingdon, Malvern. This chapel "lately erected in the village of Great Malvern, was solemnly set apart for divine worship, on Wednesday, the 18th of July [1827], . . ." (*The Evangelical Register*, August 1827, pp. 224-225).

2. *Berrow's Worcester Journal*, 14 July 1831:

> The FOURTH ANNIVERSARY of the OPENING of the late COUNTESS OF HUNTINGDON'S CHAPEL, MALVERN, will be held on TUESDAY, the 19th inst. when TWO SERMONS will be Preached by the Rev. JOHN ANGELL JAMES, of Birmingham.

3. For the letter, see Appendix I, p. 279.

Diary by E.B.B.

≪in≫ *associating the most beautiful book I ever saw, with the kindest & most valued friend I ever had". Said a great many words besides, but not one word* <∧*that*> *I did not feel—more than feel.*

Monday. July 18th

5   *Bro went to Worcester, & I entrusted him with a commission, about exchanging Da Vinci for Reynold's Lectures.[1]   He went at 8, with Mr. Martin.   At breakfast time we heard a speaking in low voices between Bummy & Lane at the door.   Something wrong,—but I wd. not be grave before my time.   It wd. not have been before my time.*

10 *After breakfast Bummy told us that Reid had come, & requested to look at the house.   We all four got out of it as soon as we could, & walked down to Mrs. Barker's—& stayed there until Minny brought us word that the coast was clear.   Such a trembling, I had in my feet—& within me.   The suspension of the advertisements is nothing*

15 *favorable, after all our strawcatching hopes.   Well! it will be well!— Bummy wrote to Papa, to tell him,—& she let me write one page of the letter, in which I told him about my Homer.   I sent too my note to Mr. Boyd.   At four, she fancied that it would do me good to drive out; & as she could not go herself on account of wishing to write*

20 *letters, she sent both H & A with me.   We drove to the Wyche— & tied the poney to the turnpike gate; & then ≪walked≫ along the Worcestershire side walk.   When we had reached the point immediately above Ruby Cottage, I sate down meditating a descent.   But Henrietta remonstrated, & talked of fatigue & Bummy & Mrs. Martin*

25 *& "what oclock ≪is it≫", until my resolution to walk backwards instead of forwards was almost taken.   At ≪the≫ instant that I was wondering whether I might ≪. . .≫ see Mr. Boyd walking out, Henrietta imagined "There he is",—and Arabel ≪confirmed≫ that there he positively was.   "I ≪know≫ the way to the walk ≪which he has*

30 *taken—≫—   Come & I will show you."   So down the hill, she bounded; & after her, I bounded; & Henrietta, after me.   Down the hill—down the perpendicular—steeper & steeper—into the wood —steeper than ≪steeper≫!   I ran because I could not walk, from one tree to another, half laughing & half crying & half scolding Arabel.*

---

1. [Sir Joshua Reynolds], *Seven Discourses Delivered in the Royal Academy by the President* (London, 1778).

[60]

*For I was half inclined to imagine that she was taking me in; & had no
more seen M.ʳ Boyd than I was likely to see him. At last we arrived
at the entrance of Essington's gardens:[1] & Arabel declared that he &
M.ʳ Spowers were walking within them. But I had suddenly grown
modest,—& declared that I would not investigate the point any* 5
*further. I fancied that the gardens were private, & that M.ʳ Boyd
might — — in short I shyed. But as I was turning, a clear view
was caught of him & his companion,—so I changed my mind, & went
to meet him. Met him—<I said> "Henrietta & Arabel are with me".
And then they said that they would go & find a donkey; & then M.ʳ* 10
*Boyd offered me his arm, & we walked up & down the pleasant shady
walk, until the ≪donkey . . .≫ arrived. Talked about Homer & Virgil,
& M.ᵉˢˢʳˢ James & Collyer,[2] et cœterœs & a. Donkey came—& I was
obliged to go. <Arrived safely> at the Wyche, & from thence home
at 20 minutes to 8—talking of our adventures—of M.ʳ Boyd—and* 15
*of his not shaking hands with Henrietta when she held out hers &
said "Good morning M.ʳ Boyd." How should <he> know about her
holding out her hand?—*

*He had <ₐnot> received my note when I met him; of which I
was glad.* 20

Tuesday July 19.

*At a quarter to ten, Bummy & I were down at M.ʳˢ Barkers, close
to M.ʳˢ Cliffe's carriage. Eliza & Henrietta & Arabel followed us in
the wheelbarrow—& we got to the chapel just in time. M.ʳˢ Boyd
took me into her pew. As soon as ever I saw the preacher,[3] I* 25
*≪thought≫ he was not <eloquent>,—as soon as ever I heard him,
I was sure of it. A most excellent sermon; but not the sermon of
"the first preacher in England," according to M.ʳ Boyd. I should
have been much pleased, if I had not expected to be very much
pleased: as it was, I was pleased.* 30

1. "Essington's Hotel has a pleasure ground, with a number of pretty walks attached to it, and commands a fine view over the country" (*A Guide to Malvern; with Observations on the Air and Waters . . .* , Malvern, [1840?], p. 37).

2. As Mr. James was "a celebrated preacher" (see entry of 16 July), it seems probable from the context that the Mr. Collyer discussed here was the Rev. William Bengo Collyer (1782-1854), a renowned Congregationalist minister, and author of several series of popular lectures on scriptural subjects.

3. The Rev. John Angell James (see fn. 2, p. 59).

Diary by E.B.B.

When it was all over, I began to meditate the subject I was med-
itating, before it began—"how am I to manage a visit to Ruby Cot-
tage?" Mrs Cliffe & Eliza were going to pay visits at Great Malvern
—& Bummy H & A to see the library.   Therefore I could have no
5 *carriage. Mrs Boyd was going to walk home with Mr Spowers.   There-*
fore I decided in walking with her.   There was a little remonstrance
on the side of my party—about the possibility of my being tired;
but nothing vehement.   I walked & was tired—what with the walk
& what with the wind.   Mrs Boyd placed me on the sofa, & would
10 *have bolstered & pillowed me if I had been passive.   She is a good*
natured woman.   After five or ten minutes, I began meo more to
fidget, & wonder why Mr Boyd did not send for me.   After a quarter
of an hour or half an hour, I could have cried—in thinking that I had
<exposed> myself to all this fatigue willingly, & that he seemed to
15 *have no will or wish to fatigue himself by talking to me until the car-*
riage came.   I could have cried!——   At last Mrs Boyd who was reading
the newspaper close to me, (just as if I had gone there to see her read
it), observed "Are you not going to Mr Boyd?"   "Why he is not ready:
is he?"   "Yes to be sure he is! & waiting for you."   And so he was.
20 *A mistake had kept <u>me</u> down stairs, & him in an expectation for half*
an hour or more.   How provoked I was.   ≪He≫ did not shake hands
with me when I went first into his room.   Forgot it, I suppose!!——
He put his hat before his face, & talked—first of Henrietta, ≪whom≫
he did not know was with me yesterday until "a third voice" said
25 *"Good morning Mr Boyd".   He understood that Arabel & I had left*
her on the Wyche: and as to ≪ . . . ≫ her ≪offering≫ to shake hands
with him, he was ignorant of <u>that</u> until Mr Spowers told him of it.
Then he talked of my note ≪—≫ yesterday's note.   "I had said too
much—it was not necessary for me to say so much about ≪the≫
30 *book—but of course he felt gratified & obliged by the sentiments I*
expressed." 'Gratified & <u>obliged</u>!'—— Well!———

We talked about the book, which he advised me to have half bound
<u>in russia</u>—not in <u>vellum</u>.   ≪It <u>shall</u> . . . be≫ russia.   Even the binding
shall remind me of the giver.   ≪ . . . ≫

35 δεχομαι φιλον γε δωρον <_∧εκ> φιλης ≪ . . . ≫ χερος[1]
That line from the Alcestis, w^d be a good motto for the first page:

1. "I take them—precious gift from precious hand" (*LCL-E*, IV, 436-437, line 376).

[62]

but no—I wont have it <there>. After a little talking of M.ʳ James
& my disappointment about his eloquence & my satisfaction ≪about≫
his scriptural knowledge, Eliza Cliffe came in & announced the car-
riages!— Obliged to go. Was not with him a quarter of an hour,—
& tired to death for it. Oh so tired. Got home,—but could scarcely 5
get thro' dinner—& then to ≪oblige≫ Bummy, off to M.ʳˢ Martin's.
There I sate in the armchair more dead than alive,—certainly more
disagreable than agreable—until tea-time. The tea was a <collation>
for the cricketers & sinecure visitors; & it was hardly over, before I
fainted fairly away. They dragged me out of the room, & packed me 10
up on the sofa. I got better soon, & sate quietly till Miss Peyton went
≪home≫; & she had the mercy to take me away with her <ₐ& leave
me at Hope End.> To bed of course—but Lady Macbeth's dreams
were nothing to mine. ≪ . . . ≫

There was a letter from Papa today.[1] Henrietta was later than I, 15
in coming from Malvern,—& it fell into my hands first. They were
trembling ones. But they need not have trembled. Not one word
on the subject. Dearest Papa is well, & in apparent good spirits.
Thank God thank God for this best news!———

Wednesday. July 20. 20
How the days of this month are coming to a close,—quickly
quickly; & probably much of our happiness with them. ≪Next≫
month—oh!—next month!— My fatigue has not quite gone off,
—so I have determined on not going to M.ʳˢ Cliffe's,—& they have
all gone without me. I liked my solitude, even <tho'> I had no one 25
to say so to—& in spite of La Bruyère, & Cowper!—[2] ≪Nearly≫
finished the Alcestis. I will finish it tomorrow, before breakfast.

Thursday July 21—

——— — — —.

1. Addressed to Henrietta (see Appendix I, p. 280).
2. Jean de la Bruyère (1645-96) and William Cowper (1731-1800). E.B.B.'s comment
springs from their remarks on solitude: "All men's misfortunes proceed from their aversion
to being alone" (*La Bruyère: Characters*, trans. Henri van Laun, London, 1963, p. 199);
"The slavish dread of solitude that breeds | Reflection and remorse," (Cowper, *The Task*,
London, 1785, Bk. I, lines 488-489).

Diary by E.B.B.

Friday July 22.

 I could not write in my diary yesterday. A new sorrow: a letter from Papa to Bummy communicating to us the death of dear Mary, Sam's beloved wife, wh^{ch} took place on the 3^d of last month in
5 *Jamaica.*[1] *Lovely, loving, & beloved she was! She loved me—I am sure she did: and I loved her—how could I help it? Does it not appear, as if all those who have loved, or been loved by me, are to be separated from me? The Lord's will—the Lord's will be done. But I am human, & very sad at heart. Yet if ≪He≫ is my shepherd, will*
10 *he not ＜make me lie＞ down, still, ≪on≫ the green pastures—either on the pastures of earth ≪or≫ Heaven? Let me not think now of ≪myself≫. Poor Sam! I have prayed for him. Comfort him Only comforter— Support him Only staff— preserve him Only Lord!—*
 I have written to Papa today. It was an effort, but a necessary
15 *one. Oh dear dear Mary—was our parting the very very last? How many tears I shed that day!—and then there was a hand ≪here≫, to wipe ＜tears＞ away!—*[2] *I will not write anymore.*

Saturday July 23.

  Compagnons de l'exil, quoi! vous pleurez ma mort!
20   *Vous pleurez! et deja dans la coupe sacrèe*
   J'ai bu l'oubli des maux, et mon ame enivrèe
    Entre au celeste port.[3]
 Those lines of Lamartine's may be applied to her—
 I have heard the boys read Greek today,—& feel more tranquil.
25 *Nay! I have read myself, a good part of the Enchiridion of Epictetus, —but I read the Bible before—& it was that ≪that≫ did me the good. Epictetus's philosophy never could make a philosopher in*

---

 1. *Berrow's Worcester Journal,* 28 July 1831: "DIED.—On the 3d of June, in Jamaica, aged 28, Mary Clementina, the wife of Samuel Barrett Moulton Barrett, Esq."

 2. i.e., E.B.B.'s mother's.

 3. The final lines of verse 4 of "Le Chrétien Mourant," the 21st of Lamartine's *Méditations Poétiques* (Paris, 1820), translated as:

    Companions of my exile, mourn you this?
    How! weep my death? when, from the sacred bowl,
    I drink oblivion, and my ravish'd soul
     Is ent'ring into bliss!

(J. C., *Solitude, and other Poems, with Translations from . . . Lamartine, and from Metastasio,* London [1830?], p. 115.)

sorrow: it approaches indeed wonderfully near to Christianity, but not near enough to catch the warmth, with the light.   "Think", he says, "that thy pitcher is a pitcher; & when it breaks thou wilt be calm: think that those whom ≪thou≫ lovest, are ≪human,≫ & when they die, thou wilt be calm."[1]   *Cold philosophy! weak philosophy!* _∧*vain*   5
philosophy!>   Thou wilt <u>not</u> be calm.   <u>Thou</u> art human too!—

I had a letter from M^{rs}*. Boyd today, & wrote two or three lines to her this morning, telling her the reason of my not being at the Malvern Bible meeting & at Ruby Cottage last Thursday as I had intended. She wishes me to spend next Monday or Tuesday <at> Malvern.   If*   10
Thursday's letter had not come, how happy I sh^d *have been in doing ≪so≫!   Miss Boyd*[2] *is to arrive on Wednesday; & Miss Gibbons*[3] *on Tuesday.   No more happy quiet days with M*^r*. Boyd!—*

Sunday July 24.

The month is coming to a close.   Next month!—   They are all   15
gone to church.   I did not feel happy enough to mix with the many who are going there; and M^r*. Dean's preaching is not worth disturbing one's feelings, that it may be listened to.   But I may as well have listened to it, as have read D*^r*. Wheatley's Essays on Cowper Newton Heber &c*[4]*—& far better.   D*^r*. Wheatly disbelieves in the <u>total</u> corrup-*   20
*tion of human nature, & in the <*_∧*regenerating> influence of divine grace; and yet M*^{rs}*. Martin admires & lent me his book,—& I have nearly read it thro'!!   <*_∧*which> I believe ≪ . . . ≫ is neither to her credit nor to mine.   Paul called himself the <u>chief of sinners</u>.*[5]   *D*^r*. Wheatly w*^d *call <u>that</u> an <u>orientalism</u>.   Let him call it what he will.*   25

1. *LCL-EP*, II, 486-487: "If you are fond of a jug, say, 'I am fond of a jug'; for when it is broken you will not be disturbed.   If you kiss your own child or wife, say to yourself that you are kissing a human being; for when it dies you will not be disturbed."

2. H.S.B.'s only sister, about whom nothing has been ascertained beyond the details contained in this Diary.

3. One of the daughters of Sir John Gibbons, Bt., of Stanwell.   As E.B.B. refers to her always as Miss Gibbons, without Christian name or initial, the usage of the period indicates that she was Eliza, the eldest of the three unmarried daughters.   In an unpublished letter to her sisters [1 October 1830] E.B.B. described Miss Gibbons as "a pleasing, Ladylike girl" (Collection of the late H.S. Altham, Esq.).

4. *Essays on the Lives of Cowper, Newton, and Heber; or, an Examination of the Evidence of the Course of Nature being Interrupted by the Divine Government* (London, 1830). Although Dr. Richard Whately (1787-1863), Archbishop of Dublin, was a prolific theological writer, E.B.B. erred in crediting him with responsibility for these essays; the British Museum *Catalogue* ascribes authorship to John Philips Potter (1793-1861).

5. I Tim. i.15.

Diary by E.B.B.

We _are_ sinful, deeply sinful, sorrowful creatures; & if Thou Oh Lord
most merciful holy & true, dost not wipe away our sins & our tears,
oh Lord Who <ᴧunder Heaven,> ≪will≫ cease to sin & weep? Speaking & feeling for myself,—the dye of _my_ sin, & the stain of _my_ tears,
5 will last for ever!——— Not all great ocean's waters could wash out
that, which one drop of the blood of ≪Christ _can_≫ wash out— Yea!
hath washed out!———

    I had a letter from Papa today. Its subjects are exclusively
religious.

10 Monday. July 25.
    I finished Epictetus, & began Marcus Antoninus.
    I was urged to go out in the carriage, & agreed to it; & I was after-
wards asked by Bummy to call ≪at the≫ Bartons ≪ . . . ≫; _not to get
out but to make an enquiry about_ M.ʳˢ <Peyton>. _Agreed to that._
15 At our gate she proposed driving to drink tea with the Cliffes. Did
not agree to _that_. Went on to the Bartons, & there we were entreated
to <ᴧget out &> have tea. _I_ answered decidedly that we could not.
Bummy ≪answered≫ in a manner that made both me & M.ʳˢ Griffith
feel convinced of her wish to do so. She pushed me _visibly_,—& at
20 last said positively, that we w.ᵈ return after our drive & _drink tea with_
them. The tears were in my eyes while M.ʳˢ Griffith was ≪entreat-
ing≫, but they fairly & foolishly started from them when we had
driven from the door. And then tho' I did not say much & not _one_
word of reproach, & tho' I yielded the point, Bummy's manner was
25 so _very_ unkind! I told her that I had ≪ . . . ≫ refused going <ᴧeven>
to M.ʳ Boyd's. "_That_" appeared to her "of no consequence". Well!
we returned & had tea—made a more agreable Barton tea-drinking
than usual, by Miss Glasco's[1] conversation; And after all, on our way
home & when we arrived at home, there was nothing for me but grav-
30 ity & coldness & silence. After I had yielded—after I had said so
little—& after that little had been extorted from me by natural, recently wounded feelings!—Oh it went to my heart. I ran up stairs,
& suffered tears to do me good. And then I sate down to write a
note to M.ʳˢ Boyd in answer to her proposal about my going there

---

1. Miss Glasco was a member of the Barton Court household, probably in the office of
companion to Mrs. Peyton or Mrs. Griffith, or as governess for the Peyton children. Bro
referred in a letter to playing chess with her, as far back as 1821.

today or tomorrow. <If> Mr. Boyd shd *hear of my having been to the Bartons, he will not think any excuse I can send him, reasonable enough* ≪not≫ *to be unkind. Henrietta came up stairs while I was thinking so; and she strongly advised me to go to Malvern tomorrow.*

We went down stairs together. No smile, no word for _me_!—— 5
≪*I had a hearty cry afterwards*≫.

Tuesday. July 26th.

This morning, at breakfast before Bummy came down, Henrietta & Arabel & Bro tried my persuadibleness by begging me to go to Malvern. It yielded—& partly, of course, because the feeling within, 10 *about Mr. Boyd, took their side of the question. When Bummy came down, Bro said something indicative of my intention. "What"! she* ≪cried≫ "*is Ba going to Malvern today. Then I hope, Ba, you have forgotten the impropriety of drinking tea with Mrs Griffith yester-day.*" 15

I might have answered that if it had **not** *been for drinking tea with Mrs Griffith yesterday, I* ≪wd.≫ *not have been persuaded to think of going to Mr Boyd's today—but my only answer was, — — bursting into tears. Nothing more was said; & I wiped them away as fast as my nature wd. let me. Foolish to cry—but I was nervous & weak &* 20 *unwell,—& really could not help it.*

The first thing I did after breakfast, was to counter order the carriage whch. Henrietta had ordered: and the next thing, to run up into my room & cry. I sent my note to Mrs Boyd. ≪Out of spirits≫ *all day, & B—out of humour. We climbed the hill to pick mushrooms* 25 *in the eveng.; & then her manner to me became kind again, &* _I_ *became happy—or* happier—*again.*

No letters. I finished <the first> *book of Marcus Antoninus, & began the second. He is disagreably corrupt,—& Gataker's readings are placed in the notes instead of in the text.*[1] 30

One of the advantages which Antoninus derived from his brother Severus, was, το πιστευτικον περι του υπο των φιλων φιλεισθαι.[2] *I wish Severus had been* my *brother. But perhaps after all I shd. have been a duller pupil than Antoninus was.*

---

1. E.B.B. was using a 1697 4to edition (*SC*, Item 338).
2. "Confidence in the love of friends" (*LCL-MA*, pp. 10-11, Bk. I, 14).

Diary by E.B.B.

In my note to Mrs Boyd today, I proposed deferring my visit
<^to Malvern> until next week; as Mr Boyd & Miss Boyd might like
to be undisturbed on her first arrival. <u>Will</u> he like to be undisturbed
by <u>me</u>?

5   A low-spirited day. I could not help thinking bitterly <&> sadly
of the dear days for ever gone ≪ . . . ≫,—& of ≪those≫ dearer beings
gone with the days! The Lord's will—the ≪Lord's≫ will be done.

Wednesday. July 27th.
Dear Bummy & I are quite good friends now! Could we ever be
10   otherwise? Not in heart. This is Henry's birthday, & a holiday;[1] &
it ought to be ≪a very≫ studious day with me—but I am without
energies this morning. I have however finished the second book of
Marcus Antoninus, & begun the third. ≪Heard from Mrs Boyd who
proposed my going to Malvern on <u>Saturday</u>.≫

15   Thursday. July 28th.
Finished the third book of Marcus Antoninus. <I am getting>
on. Found in the first part of it, the <u>picturesque</u> <u>passage</u> ≪which≫
Sir Uvedale Price in his Dialogue made Mr Payne <u>Knight</u> quote;[2] &
which he probably <u>did</u> quote, <either> in writing or conversation.
20   Weak & unwell all day; at least feeling actually weak, and as if I <u>could</u>
be unwell—a common feeling with me, & not an agreable one. A
letter from Annie to me; written in her usual manner, both as to
kindness & levity. <She has> quick perceptions; and it is to be
lamented that she has . . . associated so much more with one of her
25   parents than with the other. But I am glad very glad to hear from

---

1. His 13th.

2. The passage (commencing: "Id quoque observandum est") occurs in Section II of Bk. III. Sir Uvedale Price (1747-1829) drew from it in *A Dialogue on the Distinct Characters of the Picturesque and the Beautiful* (Hereford, 1801), pp. 191-192. Mr. Hamilton (not Mr. Knight, as stated by E.B.B.) said: "you will be surprized to hear what a powerful ally I have met with, . . . no less a one than Marcus Verus Aurelius Antoninus, Emperor and Philosopher! The passage is in his third book; he there describes such a loaf as this, with a comment not very unlike your's, and afterwards mentions several other objects, which, together with the circumstances attending them, we should call picturesque; such as the bursting of figs when over-ripe; the appearance of olives when just approaching to decay; the heads of corn bent downwards; the over-hanging brows of a lion; the foam of a wild boar; all of which, he observes (together with many other things of the same kind), though far from beautiful to the eye, yet, if considered distinctly, and as they follow the course of nature, have an ornamental and alluring effect."

*her; to know or to guess that I am forgiven. Bummy had a letter
from Papa!! Arabel says it <u>was</u> a letter from him. She went into
her own room afterwards, & without mentioning having received it,
to one person! Something bad!!—*

*I was relieved by her consenting to call at Colwall with Henrietta. 5
They will bring the carriage back: and then I <u>am</u>, volens or not, to
take a drive. My very heart is shaken. I have no heart for driving—
but I will go, as they wish it. Ann & I were covering ≪some≫ of my
≪dumb Greeks≫ with cartridge paper. How well they look—and
<how> unwell I am!— 10*

*Henrietta Arabel & I drove out—up the rough road <to Brand>
Lodge,[1] round the rough road to the Whyche,—home. Tired—&
the stars!!—[2] Met Minny coming out of Bummy's room. There
<u>must</u> be "some thing bad".*

*Before Arabel came to bed, I was reverie-ing about Papa coming 15
home immediately, & our going away almost as soon. But after
Arabel came to bed, she turned my reverie from black to brown, by
telling me that Bummy had mentioned to herself & Henrietta, having
received the letter; & had assured them that it related in no way to
our business, & was silent as to Papa's return. So I went to sleep 20
quietly, & dreamt of ≪a unicorn≫.*

Friday. July 29th

*A hard day at Greek & philosophy. Began & finished the 4th
book of Antoninus. He repeats him⟨se⟩lf a good deal, & his style
is not flowing or harmonious: but there is ≪an elevation≫ in his 25
thoughts & an energy in their expression, which I very much admire.
How I do wish that Gataker's system of reform[3] had been <u>applied</u>
i.e. introduced into the text. As it is, to refer constantly to the <u>notes</u>
when you wish to understand the text, is like dipping this pen into*

---

1. The principal route from Hope End to the Wyche was via Colwall Green. A more
circuitous drive could be taken by way of the Chances Pitch turnpike, and thence to the
road running along the western slope of the hills; this road joined the main road just below
the Wyche. Brand Lodge was about ¾ mile from the junction of the turnpike and this
secondary road (map ref. E7).

2. We believe this to be a slip of the pen. E.B.B. did not often drive after dark, and
as her room was at the top of the house, "stairs" seems a more probable word to associate
with her tiredness.

3. As set forth in his *De Novi Instrumenti Stylo Dissertatio* (London, 1648).

ink every time you wish to make a single stroke, which by the way I am obliged to do—or like being forced to look at the sun before you can see any object by its light.

Some thunder & lightening today—not very severe; but sufficient-
5 *ly so, to prove what ≪they≫ might be.   No letter.*

Besides the 4th book of Antoninus, I prepared a part of the Seven chiefs for Mr Boyd tomorrow.   Not very much tired after all; and tranquil & comfortable in my mind.   Thank God for that.

Saturday.   July 30.
10 *Set off ≪for≫ Malvern at a quarter to nine, with Ann who wished to visit her mother; & William [Treherne] in an official capacity.   I had my breakfast at home, & found Mrs Boyd at hers.   She met me at the door, & after a few considerate words in the dining room, she took me vol, nol, into the breakfast room.   There I was introduced*
15 *to Miss Boyd & Miss Boadman, & shook hands with Miss Gibbons. Miss Boyd is old fashioned in dress manner & <u>countenance</u>.   She has not Mr Boyd's.   Miss Boadman is pleasing & even pretty, ≪ . . . ≫ & has a voice & manner even more pleasing than her face.   She went up stairs to tell Mr Boyd of my being there, & I was admitted into his*
20 *room almost immediately.   "Is that Porsonia?"[1]   But how annoyed I was when he desired me to sit only a minute with ≪him≫, & then to return to the majority.   I pleaded conscience & inclination.   He insisted, on the ground that I should otherwise make him appear self- ish—that he had promised to give me up to his sister & Miss Boadman,*
25 *for the greater part of the day—that I could not doubt its being a sacrifice on his part.   I did not know what to doubt.   There is ≪no≫ doubt of my having been in an irritation—not to say, an indignation. However I was obstinate as to remaining until the hair dresser came; & then I went away quite <u>nol</u>.   He told me to talk more to his sister*
30 *& Miss Boadman, than to Miss Gibbons.   Of course, as he wished it.*

Well!   I did talk to Miss Boadman & to Miss Boyd as much as I could, <u>until past luncheon time</u>—for until then, I did not get back to Mr Boyd.   I could not help saying "I did not think that you meant to admit me again today".   "How can you say so?" &c &c &c —— ——

1. H.S.B.'s name for E.B.B., presumably derived from that of the classical scholar Richard Porson (1759-1808).

[70]

Stayed with him until dinner. Dined & discussed the ≪Socinian≫,
Bible-society question[1] <with> Miss Gibbons—& had, in my own
opinion, not merely the best <u>side</u> but the <u>best of the</u> argument. If
the Bible Society excludes the Socinians, it must be consistent & ex-
clude all those who are not spiritual christians. Returned to M.ʳ Boyd,   5
& sate with him until he proposed walking a little in front of the
house, as he had not been out all yesterday. It is a shame that he
sh.ᵈ be allowed to remain in the house, from the want of a person
to walk with him. Once more I begged him to let me ≪do so≫.
No! ≪Now his≫ objections could not effect my ≪being his≫ com-   10
panion in ≪the≫ garden; as <u>there</u>, there can be no ≪carriages or≫
horses! But I did <u>not</u> like proposing it. <u>He</u> w.ᵈ have done so, had
<u>he wished</u> it!—— Before he went, I begged him to let me know of
his return; & I sate meantime talking to Miss Boyd & Miss Boadman
in the drawing room. We talked of French & Italian & English &   15
German Literature—of much that I knew something ≪. . .≫ about;
& much that I knew nothing about. In a quarter of an hour, M.ʳ
Boyd's voice said "Ann" at the door. "She is not here" ≪answered≫
Miss Boyd. In five minutes more the same voice said —— what
Miss Boyd thought was, "Ann" again; & she answered again as before.   20
Nothing more from the voice! I sate & sate & talked & talked &
thought & thought, until I was boiling over. Half an hour longer
before they went down to tea, & <ˏbefore> I was sent for into M.ʳ
Boyd's room!! I determined to let myself be in a passion; but to say
nothing <ˏpassionately.> However M.ʳ Boyd began to tell me that   25
the second supposed "Ann" was "Porsonia"; ≪. . .≫ that he had
walked to the door a third time, but had <soliloquized> "I will not
be selfish" & had returned to his room without speaking. "I knew
how much my sister & Miss Boadman would like to talk to you". I
could ≪restrain≫ myself no longer—≪&≫ overflowed—<ˏgently>   30

1. The Socinians, following the doctrine of Lelio and Fausto Sozzini set forth in the
Confession of Rakow (1605), held that Christ was not the Son of God, but a prophet of
God's word. At a meeting of The Bible Society in Exeter Hall, London, on 4 May 1831, one
faction, led by a Lieut. Gordon, sought to exclude from membership all unbelievers in the
doctrine of the Holy Trinity. His view was that The Bible Society was pre-eminently a
Christian institution, and that the Socinians, by their denial of the Holy Trinity, could not
be members of such an institution. "After a long discussion, during which the tumult was
great beyond all description and precedent," his proposal was put to the vote, but was not
carried (*The Evangelical Magazine and Missionary Chronicle*, June 1831, p. 249 and pp.
255-257).

Diary by E.B.B.

≪with— . . .≫ *"you seem to have thought a great deal about what they like—but very little about what I like!" M.ʳ Boyd exculpated himself, and said that his feeling was "If I can be disinterested, she ought to be so also".*

5   *He was very kind in his manner to me today; & spoke in an anxious manner of our unhappy business. He said "Well! it is not certain", with respect to my going away; as if the no-certainty were a relief to him. Well: if it is certain—if I do go away—nobody will be left behind who cares for him more than I ≪care≫. <ₐMore!!!>*

10 *He reproached me for not having come to spend a few days with him —"You might have thought that this might possibly be the last opportunity you w.ᵈ have, of staying with me—at least while I am here." Does not that expression seem to look forward to a removal consequent upon ours. Oh! I hoped & hope so!——*

15   *No Greek reading today.*

   He seems to like Miss Boadman very much. So do I; but I hope he will not learn to like her society better than mine. I hope — —

— —

   What a narrow heart I must have.

20   *Miss Boadman kissed me when I went away. Curtseying in the morning, & embracing in the evening!— ≪But I never dislike such a general principle. It is the principle of warm hearts & unsuspicious heads.≫*

   I went away at past eight, & got home at past nine. A little grum-
25 *bling indirectly, about lateness; but nothing which demands grumbling ≪in return≫. No letters.*

Sunday July 31.

   Hotter than hot—but went to Church in despite of the sun. Went to church? Yes! & to Chapel—& heard a preacher, who reversed an
30 *ancient precept, <ₐinto>—Si vis me ridere, dolendum est tibi.[1] So much melancholy never before created so much mirth!— I am very sorry I went to hear him; <for> the frame of mind into which he*

---

1. The entry of 7 August suggests that the preacher was Mr. Davis, substituting for Mr. Curzon. The "ancient precept"—"si vis me flere, dolendum est | primum ipsi tibi"—is from Horace's *De Arte Poetica*, lines 102-103 (*LCL-HO/S*, pp. 458-459: "If you would have me weep, you must first feel grief yourself"). The "reversed" version substitutes "laugh" for "weep."

[72]

threw me more than once, was unchristian & to be repented ≪of≫.
Oh that the frame of a Christian's mind should be dependant on the
countenance or the manner or the language of him who preaches &
prays! This is not as it should be!— ≪I≫ thought he meant ≪liter-
ally≫ to obey the Apostolic precept—Pray without ceasing.[1] *My*   5
knees never were so tired before!—

We had prayers in the Evening, as usual.

*M*ʳˢ *Cliffe & Eliza came here today; but no letter did. It is my*
impression that something unpleasant & nearly if not quite decisive,
was contained in Papa's last letter to Bummy.   10

*Monday. August 1*ˢᵗ

This day—this month! How ≪&≫ where will this month end,
to us?——

Tho' Henrietta & Arabel set me a good example by going to the
heath on district business,[2] *at half past five in the morning, it was*   15
all in vain—I fell asleep & did not wake until eight oclock—just
in time to read a chapter on early rising (the 1 cap of the 5 lib of
M Antoninus) before breakfast. Will Eliza Cliffe come today? She
*said she w*ᵈ. *Shall we go to Malvern today? It is half arranged that*
we shall: & it was with this object, that H & A ≪ . . . ≫ settled the   20
district business so early. But Bummy seems to me—not to them,
disinclined to go. And at any rate I may be detained ≪at≫ home on
*account of no-conveyance— "≪I≫ must not be selfish", as M*ʳ
Boyd said,—& thrust myself into a party, in a manner which ≪may≫
inconvenience them.   25

*I have written a note to M*ʳˢ *Martin to ask her to lend me Boiardo's*
Orlando,[3] *—which Miss Boyd asked me to lend her. I wonder what*
the answer will be. I hope, the book. I shall like to be able to oblige
Miss Boyd. I shall like her to like me.

*M*ʳˢ *Martin not at home.*   30

*≪M*ʳˢ *C & Eliza came to say "We can not come."≫*

Vexatious work à la Henriette about "who shall go to Gt Malvern"?

1. I Thess. v.17.

2. i.e., Wesleyan-Methodist District business, at Wellington Heath, 1 mile S.W. of Hope
End (map ref. F4).

3. Count Matteo Maria Boiardo (1434-94), whose unfinished poem *Orlando Innamorato*
was first published in 1495.

Diary by E.B.B.

Gained my point at <last>.   H A & B went, & I stayed at home.
They did not return until past nine; & I meanwhile was hard at work
at Antoninus.   Finished his 5th book—read 7 chap: in the Bible, &
then went out to walk in the dark.   Frightened by a man with a coat.
5   ≪Jumped≫ in at the drawing room window.

≪Tuesday≫.   August 2.^d
   A note from Mrs Martin.   No Orlando—but a present in preparation for me.   She has got another copy of ≪ . . . Moore's≫ Life of L.^d
Byron,[1] —& therefore when the other is "in a presentable state" I am
10   to be presented with it.   Very kind of her.   A large packet from London of bombazeens silks &c—& a catalogue inside, in Papa's writing.
Surely if he were coming immediately he w.^d not write—but Bummy
& Minny dont say "surely".   They have some certain knowledge I
feel ≪ . . . ≫ certain, of something unpleasant.
15   The boys, save Stormy, & the girls, save nobody, to <Colwal> this
eveng. to play cricket & drink tea.   I wish a little shyness & obstinacy
c.^d have kept me at home with the only saved person.   Bummy in low
spirits—nay, H & A apart,—with tears in her eyes, all the evening.
Something wrong.
20   Mr Martin showed us his drawings & read us some of his journal in
& out of Africa,—so that we were amused.   How very very odd it is,
that Mrs Martin, who, I think, likes me, & I, who, I am sure, like M.^{rs}
Martin, should be oil & water together.   Some want of conformity &
sympathy, I suppose!   Got home late—at past 11.
25   ≪I read half the≫ 6th book of Antoninus today—so I cant say,
after all, perdidi diem.[2]

Wednesday.   August 3.^d
   Read very little of Antoninus, before Eliza came.   Painted at the
picture, which never will be like me until I change my nose mouth &
30   eyes.   ≪Yes≫!   Mrs Griffith (who called here today with Miss Glasco
& Miss Peyton to be congratulated on the new Peyton[3]) declared that

   1. Thomas Moore, *Letters and Journals of Lord Byron: with Notices of his Life*, 2 vols.
(London, 1830).
   2. The Roman Emperor Flavius Sabinus Vespasianus Titus, having let a day pass without
bestowing a present, exclaimed, "I have lost a day."
   3. Nicholson Julius Peyton (1831-1915), the 5th son and 9th child of the Peytons.

the eyes & the forehead are "*extrame* like." *In which case, I must be
extrame wrong.   Miss Glasco is an agreable, very agreable woman;
agreable without effort: but, as to her interesting me, or anybody
else, that is out of the question.   Mind—I like her.*

Eliza stayed until quite the eveng.: long past eight.   I amused her   5
*in the morning by telling the story of the White cat and the man with
the nose.*[1]   *I thought or dreamt that my vanity had fallen to cinders:
but it must indeed be easily redivivus*[2] *if I could be pleased by Eliza
& Arabel telling me that my ≪storytelling≫ was "admirable".   And
yet such was actually & deplorably the case.   Am I more difficult to*   10
be reformed than the House of Commons?   The Ayes have it!—

*Eliza has seen Hope End advertised by name in the Worcester
paper.*[3]   *I w.ᵈ & c.ᵈ ask no particulars.   I was so afraid of her telling
me on what day it is to be sold.   To be sold!—   How like a dream!
But from this dream we shall not wake.   No letter.*   15

*Settled.   I am to go to Malvern tomorrow.   When this was sug-
gested Bummy advised me to do so—"Your Papa may be <ₐat>
home, you do not know when".   Does she know when?   I am sick
of thinking.   But I will go.   No last opportunity of being with my
dear friend, shall be lost "for want of thought.["]*   20

*<Bro> & Sam went with M.ʳ Martin, who breakfasted here, to
the Hereford assizes.*[4]   *≪M.ʳ Martin≫ had tea here, on their return.
Poor Eliza "abhorred"—, but for what reason, deponent saith not.
I argued that this was the highest compliment which c.ᵈ be paid <ₐto>
any individual.   That the person who professed to abhor her, should*   25

---

1. Although E.B.B. appears to refer to a single story, we have been unable to find any story combining these two elements. If, as we believe, she told two stories, they can be tentatively identified as:

    a) "The White Cat," derived from "La Chatte Blanche," one of the *Contes Nouveaux* of Marie Catherine, Comtesse d'Aulnoy (1650?-1705), and

    b) [Charles Lamb], *Prince Dorus: or, Flattery Put Out of Countenance. A Poetical Version of an Ancient Tale* (London, 1811). Stanza 8 predicts: "From your unhappy nuptials shall be born | A Prince, whose Nose shall be thy subjects' scorn."

2. "Revived."

3. Sale notices revealing the name of the estate first appeared locally in the *Hereford Journal*, 27 July 1831; the *Worcester Herald*, 30 July 1831; the *Gloucester Journal*, 30 July 1831; and *Berrow's Worcester Journal*, 4 August 1831. A London paper, *The Sun*, carried the advertisement on 30 July 1831. The auction was to be conducted in London on 25 August.

4. The opening day of the Assizes. The *Hereford Journal*, 10 August 1831, recorded that of the 25 prisoners found guilty, 20, including one woman, were sentenced to death.

Diary by E.B.B.

be unable (willing he must be, in his own defence) to find out one
cause for the abhorrence.

Thursday, August 4.

5 *Ordered the carriage at a quarter past 8,—& it was not ready*
until a quarter past 9.   I in a passion of course.   But as soon as it
began to flow, it began to ebb.

Got to Malvern at ten, & found M.ʳˢ Boyd & company at break-
fast; & ≪after≫ a consultation in M.ʳˢ Boyd's ≪bedroom≫ on the
case, Biscoe versus Boyd, was admitted into M.ʳ Boyd's room.   M.ʳˢ B
10 *showed me M.ʳ Biscoe's two last letters to Annie.   One of them had*
as a motto, a quotation from a poem of mine—

> *Unless you can dream, that his faith is fast,*
> *Thro' months & years of roving—*
> *Unless you can die when the dream is past—*
15 > *Ah no! this is not loving.*[1]

It ≪...≫ certainly is not loving, in Annie Boyd; who calls his letter,
≪...≫ expressive of the most passionate attachment, & ≪utmost≫
distress of mind, "another stupid letter".   I never could understand
how a delicate woman can even tolerate the attentions of a man
20 *whom she does not love: ≪or≫ <ₐhow a kind hearted woman can>*
<wound> the feelings of a man whom she does love.

M.ʳ Boyd received me, as if he were not displeased to do so,—&
enquired with an apparent interest about Hope End &c.   Presently
he desired the servant to beg Miss Boyd to read the paper to him,
25 *whenever it came.   Would he have had the paper read to him, when*
he could have talked to me,—at one time?   "Yes! Change!—"

I was desired, as soon as the paper came, to go & talk to Miss
Boadman—to go down stairs into the ≪breakfast≫ room, & talk to
her.   I c.ᵈ not do it—immediately.   I went for a few minutes into
30 *the drawingroom, to recover the newspaper!— <Down> stairs; &*
sent up again by M.ʳˢ Boyd with Miss Boadman.   <ₐWe talked—as
desired!—>   She told me that M.ʳ Boyd had heard her read a little
of the Greek new Testament, ≪as≫ her father had taught her a little
Greek—very little,—≪which≫ she had neglected ≪...≫.   M.ʳ Boyd
35 *had told me before, that he had written some verses upon her, at her*

---

1. For the poem, see Appendix II, p. 313.

<u>request</u>: that he mentioned them to me, because they might possibly be shown to me,—& that I might think him inconsistent in writing upon a person whom he had known for so short a time,—after his professed intention of writing no more.   As to his <u>inconsistency</u>— that is not the word I should think of applying. ≪ . . . ≫   The verses were <u>not</u> shown to me.

More than half an hour passed over the newspaper; & then I was readmitted into M.ʳ Boyd's room.   I felt very unwilling to read Greek. I fancied that he proposed it as if it were a self infliction; ≪originating≫ <u>from a feeling of general benevolence inclusive of me.</u>   I assured him that I did not wish to read.   When I did read, my voice faltered in spite of my resolution.   I am <a fool>.

Went down to dinner, feeling wretchedly out of spirits, out of a talking & laughing condition.   I could not do more than smile, even when M.ʳ Boyd's message ≪was so≫ gravely delivered to his sister. "M.ʳ Boyd wishes to know if Melindore ever took sallts; if he did, whether they were Epsom or Cheltenham salts."   Melindore is the hero of Miss Boyds folio romance, which she keeps profoundly secret.[1]   Her reply—"Tell my brother, that I never answer impertinent questions."   After dinner, when we were in the drawing room,—I could <u>not</u> talk; & the tears were in my eyes ≪oftener≫ than once. M.ʳ Boyd's voice first called for M.ʳˢ Boyd; then for Miss Boyd: not at all for me.   After nearly 3 quarters of an hour, M.ʳˢ Boyd advised me to go in to him.   I went.   Heard him repeat some passages from Æschylus, which he was not clear ≪ . . . ≫ about.   I could not help it. The tears rolled down my cheeks.   They should not injure <u>him</u>—not even by blistering his book: so they were wiped away very quickly. Perhaps this was the last time of our being together!—

<Talking about Annie> & Eliza Cliffe—jealousy & insincerity.   I would not, & will not, attribute one to one, & the other to the other. He wished that I had never been intimate with Eliza. (She cares more for me than <u>he</u> does!) ≪ . . . He≫ told me that he was not aware of any single fault I had; & that Miss Boadman's disposition (it was paying her, he said, a great compliment) ≪seemed≫ to resemble mine, more than the disposition of any person with whom he was acquainted. <I> observed "I thought you had found out my faults long ago—

1. To the best of our belief, Miss Boyd's novel was never published.

*particularly after my having been so cross about the Terence".[1]
"Cross≪!≫ you were not cross"—and then he repented <∧vivâ
voce> having ever made the application to me, which I had considered
in such a light.*

5   *There is no use in it. Of one thing I am convinced; that if, from
any change of circumstance, ≪one of≫ his visitors were forced to
return home immediately,—≪he≫ would feel more sorrow,—than
if I were to leave his neighbourhood for ever. And this is the weight
of human friendship! Ashes! ≪Dust≫ is too heavy!—*

10   *I wish I had not gone today. I will not go again soon. I said
something to him, about depriving his sister of his society: & he
begged me not to consider her. He would always be "happy to see
me"— I have scarcely patience to write all these details. They
make me sick—& mad———*

15   *Left Ruby Cottage in the rain. Not a happy day. Oh no!—*

*I forgot to mention the remarks which were made on Arabel's no-
visit the other ≪evening≫. M.ʳ Boyd observed that "if we remained
at Hope End, & if I were to die, it was clear to him that my family w.ᵈ
break off all intercourse with his." If I were to die!— <Not> an*
20 *improbable case; but supposed so coldly!———*

*Got home at 8. While I was away, they had been showing my
Wolf's Homer to M.ʳ & M.ʳˢ Martin. Black thinking before sound
sleeping, in my room tonight. No letter.*

Friday. August 5.

25   *Finished & sealed a letter to poor beloved Sam[2] before breakfast;
& yet not up early. May it find <∧him lying> by the still waters of
the peace of God; & on the green pastures of his love!— I pray for
him everyday.*

The darkness of yesterday's fancies has still left a cloud over
30 *my mind, today. It seems to me that I am reconciled, quite reconciled, to the prospect of leaving Hope End. I can bear any thing
but "an altered eye". How profound Gray was, in selecting that*

---

1. See *EBB/HSB*, p. 140. E.B.B. was greatly upset when H.S.B. sent for the Terence he
had used at school, which he had given her in 1829.

2. This letter to her recently bereaved uncle has not been traced; doubtless it was despatched by the same Packet as her father's letter to his brother dated the previous day (see
Appendix I, p. 281).

[78]

epithet!—[1]   I read the other half of Antoninus's sixth book,—&
half his seventh, besides.   What a creature I am—to spend my time
in this way, between philosophy & folly.   Antoninus w^d not be well
pleased, if he could know whom he has for a reader!—

I wrote yesterday "I will not go to Malvern again soon".   Is it
credible that I should be really & actually anxious about going <u>to-
morrow</u>?   Henrietta wishes to ≪visit≫ Maddox about her pelisse;
& Bro threw up a shilling—, 'heads or tails', to decide upon her
companions, after Bummy.   Is it credible that I should have looked
"blank" when my saying "tails", excluded <u>me</u>?   And yet they say
I did; ≪ . . . ≫ <u>non incredula odi</u>.[2]

No letters!—& no further memorabilia.

≪Except that Eliza≫ Cliffe sent me a parcel of new walking shoes,
a print of Paganini bespoken by Bummy; & a promise of the Last
man,[3] which is far from being the last book I am anxious about seeing.   Mrs Martin is to send it to me tomorrow; & I must finish the 7th
book of Antoninus before it comes.

Eliza is really an amiable girl,—& very fond of me.   ≪ . . . ≫
Which quality is most valuable in my eyes?   I have an oath in Heaven
to be altogether sincere in ≪this≫ journal of mine,—therefore—the
<u>latter</u> quality.   I am always apt, too apt, ≪irrepressibly≫ apt, to feel
with an old poet—

　　　　If she be not fair to <u>me</u>,
　　　　What care I, how fair she be?—[4]

Narrow, narrow heart!——   It is this that makes me so ———— about
somebody else————

---

1. [Thomas Gray], *An Ode on a Distant Prospect of Eton College* (London, 1747), p. 7:
　　　　The Stings of Falshood Those shall try,
　　　　And hard Unkindness' alter'd Eye,
　　　　That mocks the Tear it forc'd to flow;

2. Cf. Horace, *De Arte Poetica*, l.188: "quodcumque ostendis mihi sic, incredulus odi"
LCL-HO/S, pp. 466-467: "whatever you thus show me, I discredit and abhor").

3. [Mary Wollstonecraft Shelley], *The Last Man*, 3 vols. (London, 1826).

4. George Wither, *Fair Virtue the Mistress of Philarete*, A New Edition, reprinted from
the Edition of 1622 (London, 1818).   Sonnet IV, v.1, p. 120:
　　　　Be she fairer than the Day,
　　　　Or the flowery meads in May;
　　　　　If she be not so to me,
　　　　　What care I how fair she be!

The original publication (*Fidelia*, London, 1615) contained a different version of the final
couplet.   A copy of the 1818 edition formed Lot 1219 of the 1913 Browning Sale.

Diary by E.B.B.

Saturday August 6.

    Well! I am really to go with Bummy & Henrietta to Malvern; &
this afternoon!—— I shall make myself miserable all the time, I dare
say; & yet I am pleased at the thoughts of going. Bro & Sam have
5 *ridden to call upon M.ʳ Allen Cliffe,[1] who is "too proud" not to be*
called upon ≪...≫, before he calls here. How I hate this punctili-
ousness of mind which can only exist in a petty mind. Trees may be
cut into peacocks, when they stand in a small inclosure: but who w.ᵈ
think of cutting into peacocks, the trees of America's vast forests?——
10 *Who am I, who w.ᵈ be severe upon littleness in character? Have I not*
just been measuring my own?
    I had time to finish reading the 7.ᵗʰ book of Marcus Antoninus,
before we went to Malvern, which we did not do until four 'oclock.
Called at M.ʳˢ Trant's gate; Henrietta at her door,——& while Bummy
15 *& I ≪were≫ keeping the poney quiet, down the hill, came Dominick*
& Henry.[2] Dominick full of his reported title, & of having given
Miss Emma Pocock to M.ʳ Knowles,[3] & of her being very handsome
& ≪27≫ & the youngest of four sisters,——& of our going back to tea,
& of his having a great deal to say to us. I laughed with him & at
20 *him; & then we drove on. ≪M.ʳ≫ Boyd walking in front of the house.*
I preceded the carriage to beg him to go into the house while it past.
He ≪said≫ with a smile, an apparently pleased smile, that he did not
expect to hear my voice tonight. M.ʳˢ Boyd was out; so when I had
opened the opposite gate for Bummy & Henrietta, I followed M.ʳ Boyd
25 *into his room. "<As> they are all out, shall we sit in the drawing*
room; & will you go & shut the window."? But he heard Miss
Gibbons' voice, & changed his mind, & did not change his room. We
talked a little about reform, & Miss Boadman's illness, & mine; &
then I was asked if I had brought my book—, my Æschylus? No!
30 *I did not think that, at that time in the evening, he would like me to*
read Greek to him. I "might have brought it, at any rate—he would
<ₐhave> liked it". So I proposed reading, & did read, out of his

    1. Eliza's brother, the Rev. Allen Robert Cliffe (1806-97), Curate of Coddington, who
had recently graduated from Trinity College, Dublin.

    2. The two sons of Mary Trant (*née* Barrett), distant cousins of E.B.B. Dominick had
unsuccessfully contested the Parliamentary election at Shaftesbury in May 1831, standing
with his friend Francis Charles Knowles. We are unable to explain the reference which follows to "his *reported* title."

    3. At their marriage on 26 May. See fn. 3, p. 5.

folio Æschylus; but we did not read much. He could not have liked hearing me, _much_. Kind in his manner. Some talking of the Hope End business.

Bummy & Henrietta called on Mrs Boyd when they called for me; & of this I was glad. It was past seven when we left Ruby Cottage. 5
A happier visit than my last! Oh I would give anything if I could _know_—not think, not guess—but _know_, what the feeling is there, with respect to me. I _know_ my own exclusive & exacting disposition; but not to that only — ——— —.! —— Tais toi Jean Jaques! ——

On arriving at home, we found Sam who had not been very well, 10
very well; Bro not yet returned from Cliffes; & Arabel in preparation & expectation. Had tea & <went> to bed. Uncommon & memorable occurences!—

No last Man arrived; & after ≪ . . . ≫ Mrs Martin's ≪_affidavit_≫! An _acceleravit_ w.^{d} have been more to the purpose. 15

Sunday. August 7.th

Bro gave me a note from Eliza Cliffe, to say . . nothing! She feels very warmly & kindly: but she does not write well. Better than vicê versâ. As it is, there is certainly no vice in the case.

Went to Church with Bummy & Arabel; not with Henrietta— 20
because a carriage <that holds> only three, wont hold four—which is remarkable. When we returned, Henrietta wanted to know if there was any news—   None in Mr Dean's sermon certainly! The rain spared us a re-infliction of Mr Davis, at the gate.[1]

Maddox came from Ledbury this morning; & she has been talking 25
to me in my room for the last two hours. I love her for the sake of past & present. She is a dear feeling creature!—& _that_, I always thought & felt!— But now I must occupy a little more time more profitably, than even in talking with her—or writing here.

Mr Boyd said yesterday that from the four words "Good morning 30
Mr Boyd", which he once heard Henrietta say, he thinks her voice agreable & _clear & distinct_. "The best voice of the three"—alluding to Arabel's & mine!

My voice pleased him ≪once≫. Well!—there is no use <$_\wedge$in> thinking of it any more!— 35

---

1. The preacher of the previous Sunday, substituting for Mr. Curzon.

Diary by E.B.B.

Maddox is going in our carriage to Malvern tomorrow. Shall I go with her? If I had not gone yesterday, I would: & if Henrietta had not opposed it (very gently tho') <ₐI wᵈ:>: & if I <were not> <u>unknowing</u> on one subject, I would. ≪...≫ But as it is, I think—
5 *no! I will not do so.*

Monday. August 8.
    In spite of my "No I will not do so", when I got up this morning, & found Maddox 'going going' I took an irrepressible fancy to be "gone" with her. But will Bummy like it? I agitated, o'connellized,[1]
10 *about, in my flannel dressing-gown,—& at last decided on feeling her pulsations on the subject. If she is against it, I wont go: & in that case ≪my≫ staying wont be my fault. If this shᵈ be the last or almost the last opportunity—how painful the thought would be, that I should myself myself [sic] have thrown it away. Went into*
15 *Bummy's room—"Bummy! shall you think me very mad if I go to Malvern today". The answer decided me. <u>No! I did not do so.</u>*
    <I> have had such a hard day's work today, that I am quite exhausted & can scarcely write. I have written a letter to Papa, read the first vol: of the Last man, which Mʳˢ Martin has sent me at last,
20 *—& read the <u>whole</u> of the 8ᵗʰ book of Marcus Antoninus,—& prepared some of the Seven Chiefs for Mʳ Boyd,—besides hearing Storm & George read out of Homer & Zenophon. I feel nervous all over— <tingling> in my hands & feet—& cant write a word more.*

Tuesday August 9.
25 *I believe I was more tired last night than was good for me; certainly more so than was good for my diary which I had to bring to an untimely end, without noticing Bummy & Henrietta & ≪Arabel≫ drinking tea at the Martins; & Bro & ≪Sam≫ dittoing it at the Trants. I was left to my soliloquies—, & my Antoninus, & my Last Man.*
30 *This morning I sent off my letter to Papa. None from him. One from Miss Price,[2] in which she alludes for the first time & in a mournful manner, to our prospect of leaving Hope End. Dominick arrived*

---

1. Derived from Daniel O'Connell (1775-1847), energetic House of Commons agitator and champion of the Irish Catholics.
2. Miss Caroline Price (1783?-1853), of Foxley, the only daughter of the late Sir Uvedale Price, Bt.

[82]

to dine & sleep; an unprompted honor— Arabel was so goodnatured as to walk to Colwall <∧before breakfast> for Mrs Shelley's second volume,¹ —& I have read it thro'. And I have read besides the whole of Marcus Antoninus's 9th book. He becomes easy to me, as I become familiar with ≪him≫; & this, I am ≪becoming by≫ degrees, tho' he _is_ an emperor & a philosopher.

I did not like Mrs Shelley's first volume at all, & fancied that all her genius had exhaled in Frankenstein.² But <∧in> the second volume, Richard's himself again!³ There is a great deal of power & originality about it—and yet I devoutly wish that the book had been unread as far as I am concerned. It has dessolated me! I wish I had the 3^d volume! There are two wishes—like what most of my wishes are!—

Shall I go to Malvern tomorrow? If I can. And I think I can.

Henrietta & Bummy walked to the Bartons today, & asked Miss Glasco to come to us this evening. The rain seems to me to have come instead. Henrietta at the window— Tea. 𝄞_____
No fal_setto_ I hope!—⁴

Wednesday. August 10

Went to Malvern, tho' Bummy, when I proposed it last night, opposed it. In consequence of the opposition I withdrew my motion; after which, she herself brought it on again; & I went. But _after_ breakfast, ≪& the≫ lateness out-of-humoured me.

I forgot to say that Dominick arrived yesterday, with a shirt or two —to pay what we imagined w^d be a morning visit; but which turns out to be several morning & eveng visits joined together. He asked me to bring back his newspaper & letters from Malvern. Accordingly I called on Mrs Trant—did not stay long. Got to Mr Boyd's about 12, & was received by M^{rs} B who took me into the ≪breakfast≫ room to

---

1. Of _The Last Man_.

2. _Frankenstein; or, the Modern Prometheus_, 3 vols. (London, 1818).

3. E.B.B. must mean Raymond, the hero, who is believed lost in battle against the Turks at the end of volume one. The opening of volume two discloses that he is not dead, but a prisoner; his release is secured after some months of hardship and he returns to the war to win fresh laurels, but is ultimately killed.

4. This is one of E.B.B.'s more obscure word plays, which may be more obvious to some readers than it is to us. Henrietta was probably using the window seat while tea was served, which could have led to the alliterative link between "tea" and the musical note "ti"; hence fal_setto_, suggesting a play on "false" and "sit".

Diary by E.B.B.

consult over the Biscoe versus Boyd case. Poor M.ʳ Biscoe. From my heart & heart's heart I pity him. He devotedly loves one who does not, & never will, love _him_. Well!—these things are to be borne. If they are not, they will destroy: & then they need not be borne.

5 <Wisely> said, Marcus Antoninus![1] Annie observes in her letter to M.ʳˢ Boyd, that there are many people whom she c.ᵈ like as well as M.ʳ Biscoe, & some whom she c.ᵈ like better!!!!!——

M.ʳˢ Boyd soon took me into M.ʳ Boyd's room, where Miss Boyd was sitting. He said "I had just been thinking of you". Miss Boyd

10 & I were turned out, & then I was re-admitted, & sate with him until dinner-time. I read some of the seven chiefs—the <description> of Amphiarus, which is very fine:[2] & we talked. He sighed when I was speaking of Hope End: but people will sigh sometimes without sorrow. I may be wrong. If I am, I wish I knew it. Went down to

15 dinner, which was considered "very long" in coming. At dinner something was said of ——. I am ashamed of writing down my own feelings & the causes of them.

After dinner, M.ʳ Boyd was discovered walking in front of the house; & M.ʳˢ Boyd asked me if I had ever done so with him. No!—

20 Will you go & do so now? "No. I think M.ʳ Boyd does not like it." "_I_ will go & try?" observed M.ʳˢ Boyd. "Shall I do so?" asked Miss Gibbons who never stirred. But M.ʳˢ Boyd stirred. She went out —& walked backwards & forwards with M.ʳ Boyd for half an hour, before the windows. I fancied at first, that she might mean to ask

25 him whether or not _I_ sh.ᵈ walk with him? ≪If≫ she did, his answer was like mine—"No".

Could I help saying, _no_? Has he not proved to me that he disliked my walking with him? If I had gone out, either he might have been forced to do what he disliked; or I should have been sent back to the

30 drawing room to explain what I ≪did≫ not understand myself about this distaste which seems exclusively to regard _me_. Painful it was to me to say "I <think> M.ʳ Boyd does not like it." But what c.ᵈ I do!? The tears are in my eyes as I am writing. Oh that people sh.ᵈ be so kind—& so unkind!— He came in, & called at the door for Miss

35 Boyd, who went up stairs & stayed there about a quarter of an hour.

1. Bk. VII, 33.
2. Beginning: "Sixth I will name a warrior passing wise, a seer most valiant in combat, even mighty Amphiaraüs" (_LCL-A_, I, 368-371, lines 568-596).

*When she returned, M*ʳˢ *B asked if she had brought a message for me,
respecting my going up stairs, "On the contrary, my brother sent me
down that I might ≪have≫ the pleasure of Miss Barrett's company".
So there I sate for half an hour; for more than an hour; until M*ʳˢ *Boyd
suggested that if I did not go to see M*ʳ *Boyd now, I ≪w*ᵈ*≫ not do so
at all, as it was seven! Miss Steers was there, & we ≪had been≫ talking of Keats & ≪Shelley, &≫ Coleridge's Ancient Mariner*[1]*—& M*ʳˢ
*Boyd had been confessing that she had lost all her taste for poetry.
Lost! ≪Did she ever possess≫ it? Can any one* <u>lose</u> *≪his≫ taste for
poetry? Can any one lose his life, & yet live?—*   5 ... 10

*<When> I went into M*ʳ *Boyd's room, I c*ᵈ *not help being grave
& silent.   Before we had begun to talk, Miss Boyd came in & offered
to remain in the room "if you are not going to study."   M*ʳ *Boyd was
silent, & did not seem to like it.   "If you ≪object≫, to my staying,
brother, why dont you say so?"   "You must ask Miss Barrett's permission" said M*ʳ *Boyd.   I stammered out something inaudible—M*ʳ
*Boyd was silent—, & after an awkward pause of five minutes, she
retreated.   Silent still!—   At last I said—I could not help it—"I am
sorry that you w*ᵈ *not let me come up stairs before"—   And then
came the assurance that he had never intended me to stay away; & an
observation coldly enough <made>, that I was "fanciful".   Tears
again.   They* <u>would</u> *come.*   15 ... 20

*We talked, & talked chearfully,—but I went away sadly.   My
spirits are broken, by strokes of pain from every side; & I am become
morbidly & foolishly sensitive.   ≪The≫ <ancient> Athenians delighted in the* τι καινον.[2]   *If some modern ones, do the same, should
I wonder?*   25

*Well! we shall go <*ᴧ*away> soon; & in the meantime I will* <u>not</u>
go as frequently as I have done, to Malvern.   I am not the τι καινον.
*I am not the favorite at this present time.   And yet whose regard has
been professed & proved as mine?   <There is> no use in all this.*   30

*On my return, I found a parcel from M*ʳˢ *Martin <containing>
Moore's Life of Byron, handsomely bound.*[3]   *A kind & valuable*

---

1. "The Rime of the Ancyent Marinere, in Seven Parts," pp. 5-51 of *Lyrical Ballads, with a Few Other Poems* [by Williams Wordsworth and Samuel Taylor Coleridge], (Bristol, 1798).

2. "That which is new."

3. This copy of the Paris, 1830 edition, with an inscription by E.B.B. recording its presentation by Mrs. Martin, formed Lot 536 of the 1913 Browning Sale.

Diary by E.B.B.

present.   Oh I <wish>, I do wish that I had not left home this morning!——

Thursday. August 11.

*   What a weight there is on my heart today.   It is like lead, only*
5 *colder.   I wish I had not gone yesterday, where I did.   I wish Miss Boyd had stayed in the room, when she proposed staying: I wish I had commanded myself sufficiently to avoid making that foolish observation!   I wish I had <u>never</u> gone to Malvern!   <Vain>wishes, all of them!——*

10 *   I wrote a note to Mrs Martin, to thank her for ≪her≫ kind present; & I hope she may send back the 3^d vol of the Last Man, by my messenger.   If she had read as many books <as> I have, she must have been at least six hundred years old by this time.   No answer! Mrs Martin was out—& so was I.*

15 *   On Wednesday before breakfast, I read the beginning of Antoninus's 10th book, & I went on with it today, but not to the end. My energies felt dead within me: & how could I do anything without them?   Nothing but reading the 3^d vol: of Mrs Shelley, which I despatched in two hours[1] —(which <u>did</u> come at last!!—) No going out*
20 *today.   Marcus Antoninus after Mrs Shelly, & drinking tea after Marcus.   Not a letter!——*

Friday August 12.

*   A hard day's work . . I finished the 10th & read the 11 & 12 books of my emperor.   Done with him.——   I wish I were as good a philos-*
25 *opher as he is, or was: but I wonder if he practised what he thought, as little as I do, what I read.   If he had been a poet; I know I sh^d have canonized him.   Why not?   Bolidori reports Petrarch to have been received into the number of the elect, there to receive the reward of his belli versi:[2] and Antoninus's w^d have been <u>belli</u> too.   They w^d*
30 *have been inharmonious enough, I dare say; but very <energetic> & original & full of picturesque imagery.   Well! there is no use in contending against destiny.   He was not a poet: & I am not a philosopher!——*

---

1. No wonder Mrs. Martin's reading speed did not match E.B.B.'s—the third volume contained 352 pages.

2. Bolidori has not been identified among the biographers of Petrarch, but E.B.B.'s autograph is quite clear.

[86]

Miss Glasco called here today,—& we walked back with her to ≪the gate≫ which ushers you in to the green path parallel with our road. She said "Where shall we meet next? Recollect where we parted." She goes to Cheltenham tomorrow, & remains three weeks away. 5

An agreable, a very agreable woman—and a kind amiable warmhearted woman besides. Bummy Henrietta & I were met, on our returning hatless, by Lane who brought an open letter from ≪Papa≫ to Bro, sent by Bro to Bummy. She dared not ≪read≫ it before us—. I could see that very well. Bro met us in our tribulation . . 10 *He was riding down the road ≪on≫ his way to a ≪pic nic≫ party on the Malvern hills—the Webbs the instigators.[1] So to Bro, Bummy applied—"What am I to do with ≪this≫ letter?" "Read it—all of you read it—there is nothing in it." Nothing in it? Then we may breathe. Yes! there was nothing,—except ≪an order≫ for the dis-* 15 *charge of those workmen who could get situations. Nothing besides.*

I did not go out again. I felt too unwell for it: but I finished Antoninus: & then I began & nearly finished the Messeniennes by Casimir De la vigne.[2] He is an energetic poet for a frenchman; but <does> not bring with him the certificate of his baptism in Helicon.[3] No 20 *No!—I would not take a poetical oath by him. I would not rank him ≪among≫ the Θεοι—but the παρεδροι!—[4] So much for Casimir.*

Unwell, very unwell all the evening! A strange nervous depressed feeling, as if I were both soulless & boneless!— 25

Saturday August ≪13≫.

Miss Glasco told me yesterday that Eliza Cliffe was to be here this morning, so I suppose she will. Henrietta is going to Malvern in the evening—, & something was said of my going too, tho' I really really actually feel "Nolo"— But in case of the possibility of it, I 30 *prepared <ₐbefore breakfast,> some of the Seven Chiefs for M.ʳ Boyd.*

---

1. It is not clear whether the reference is to the family of Thomas Webb, banker and magistrate, of Ledbury, or to that of Richard Webb, of Donnington Court, 3 miles from Ledbury.

2. Casimir Jean François Delavigne, *Trois Messéniennes. Elégies sur les Malheurs de la France* (Paris, 1818).

3. The springs of Helicon in Bœotia, sacred to the Muses, were held to give inspiration.

4. Θεοί: "the gods"; πάρεδροι: "those sitting near."

Diary by E.B.B.

Bummy said yesterday that she w.^d not go.   Now if <u>she</u> does not, <u>I</u> will: not so much because I desire it, as because my not seeming to desire it, might seem strange to everybody here.   It almost seems strange to myself!   And yet w.^d it not be stranger if—?—   There
5   *is not any use in writing of it.   Feeling about it, is bad enough!—*

How depressed <I> felt yesterday evening.   How I hung upon the past, as if my life as well as happiness were in it!   How I thought of those words <u>"You will never find another person who will love you as I love you"</u>—   And how I felt that to hear again the sound
10   *of those beloved, those ever ever beloved lips, I w.^d barter all other sounds & sights—that I w.^d in joy & gratitude lay down before her my tastes & feelings each & all, in sacrifice for ≪the≫ love, the exceeding love <ₐwhich> I never, in truth, can find again.   Have I not tried ≪this≫, & know ≪this≫ & felt ≪this≫: & do I not feel*
15   <u>now</u>, *bitterly, dessolately, that <ₐhuman> love like her's, I never can find again!—*[1]   *Let <u>Thy</u> love oh Lord Jesus, ≪. . . be poured≫ as balm & oil into ≪my≫ heart which is stricken for the loss of human love.   Surely "greater love hath no <u>man</u>"*[2] *than ≪<u>Thine</u>≫!—   And surely Thou wilt give ≪Thy≫ beloved sleep!*[3]   *W.^d that my heart*
20   *could sleep from some thoughts—& not dream!—*

Eliza Cliffe came, & I sate for my picture.   <The> paint is beginning to crack from redundancy.   In fact my features are now literally beginning to stand out from the canvass.   I shall soon be a companion for the Roman Emperors, for Marcus Antoninus himself, in <u>bas</u>-relievo.
25   *Such pro & conning & à la Henrietting about "who will go to Malvern"? & "shall we go to Malvern at all?"   I am really wonderful. I began to feel a wish—yes!—actually a wish—to go.   No going at last; & when it was decided I was glad; not merely that it was decided, but that it was decided <u>so</u>.   H A & I in the carriage, Eliza riding, to*
30   *Warm's well.*[4]   *Washed our faces & wet our hair,—& then, I on Eliza's poney, we mounted the hill.   "Round we went" & then "down we went"; for a black cloud in the distance frightened everybody but*

1. E.B.B. was, of course, speaking of her mother.   2. John xv.13.

3. Psalms cxxvii.2. This text later inspired E.B.B.'s poem, "The Sleep," printed in *The Seraphim and Other Poems* (London, 1838), pp. 283-286.

4. *Letters on Malvern Descriptive and Historical* (Worcester, [N.D.]), p. 35: "On the Western side of the [Hangman's] Hill is a Spring, called Walms Well; which is much esteemed in the neighbourhood for its beneficial effects; especially in cutaneous disorders" (map ref. F7).

[88]

me.   So ≪...≫ "home we went".   But oh how exquisite the hills looked, stretching forward before us, in the midst of that expansive & sunlit scenery!— Eliza parted from us, at our gate.   I was unwell this morning, but well this evening.   How some thoughts will hang about me!—

Sunday.   August 14.

Everybody except me, went to church.   I stayed at home, & felt wretchedly unwell all the time, & read ≪the≫ Bishop of Salisburys (Jewel's) Apologia Ecclesiæ Anglicanæ.[1]   I got thro' more than half of it; lying now in my <armchair> & now on the bed, & now smelling aromatic ≪vinegar≫.   The soul must be a weak being after all, that it cant animate one's body without aromatic ≪vinegar≫; and my soul has life & energy enough about it, as souls go.   Jewel writes very well, very eloquently, very nervously.   I like him very much.   I bought this little book before I could read it, when I was eleven or twelve years old.   I have read ≪some≫ of it, here & there, since then: but never so much as I have read today.   I wish I could write Latin as well as ≪Jewel≫!—

Eliza Cliffe came up stairs & found me inbedded.   I transplanted myself immediately into my sitting room,—& then, up came M.rs Cliffe, who looked at the picture ≪&≫ by asking a hundred questions about my opinion of it, put my conscience in jeopardy.   We went to chapel, & hoped to find M.r Curzon.   In vain!   A young man preached "indifferently well".[2]   I am in doubt up to this moment whether he or the sun made me ≪feel≫ sleepy.   As Bummy Arabel & I were driving home we ≪made≫ a sejour[3] among the cows for some time; & while they were studying the picturesque, my thoughts went away where they liked.   I forgot to say that the preacher put a note direct-ed to Miss Barrett, into M.rs Cliffe's hand.   The note was from M.r Curzon, & proposed dining with us on Wednesday or Thursday.   Then I ≪will≫ <ᴧgo> to Malvern on Tuesday.   I felt better, far better, this evening.

1. [John Jewel, Bishop of Salisbury], *Apologia Ecclesiæ Anglicanæ* (London, 1562). E.B.B.'s copy of the 1692 edition formed Lot 790 of the 1913 Browning Sale.

2. *Henry V* II.i.53: "I have an humour to knock you indifferently well."

3. "Sojourn."

[89]

Diary by E.B.B.

Monday August 15.

    Henrietta asked me yesterday if I would go to Malvern today. No! Tomorrow, it will be nearly a week, since I was there. How heroic I am,—& vindictive too!—

5   *I wrote this morning, a note to M.ʳ Curzon; a letter to Miss Price, & a letter to Annie!— I am in doubt whether to begin to read <u>Cebes</u>[1] or Callimachus.[2] Philosophy w.ᵈ do me more good than poetry, just now, I think. ≪. . . Had≫ I always studied philosophy exclusively of poetry, <ₐI wonder> if I should have been differently & more happily constituted in some respects. I am afraid—<u>no</u>. I am afraid I resemble the student of Ossuna, mentioned in Don Quixote, who even if he had been educated at Salamanca, would have been nevertheless <u>mad</u>.[3] Well! tomorrow may—oh may tomorrow, remove one mad symptom. It is too painful.*

15   *Solved my doubts, & read half Cebes's dialogue before I went to bed. It is rather a pleasing than a profound performance,—& on this account as well as on <account> of the extreme facility of the Greek, it can bear fast reading. ≪. . . Nearly≫ the easiest Greek I ever read!—*

20   *Tuesday. August 16.*

    The rain, the provoking rain, prevented my going to Malvern as soon as I intended: but I went after breakfast & after doubting whether I sh.ᵈ go at all. Met M.ʳˢ Boyd on the stairs, & was detained by her in the drawing room for a little while, after which, I was dismissed into

25   *M.ʳ Boyd's room. He had expected me yesterday, & <ₐw.ᵈ have> expected me today, if he had not heard that it rained. I like to hear of his expecting me!— He asked if I had any good news to tell him. Good news!— He said something about the 25ᵗʰ of August, as if that were the day fixed <ₐon> for the sale by auction.[4] I would not*

30   *enquire—I w.ᵈ not satisfy myself ≪if≫ it were. I will not know anything about it!— We read some of the Seven Chiefs—very little! M.ʳ*

1. Cebes of Cyzicus, 2nd century philosopher and contemporary of M. Aurelius Antoninus, known for his *Tabula*.

2. Callimachus of Cyrene (*c.* 305-*c.* 240 B.C.), cataloguer of the Library at Alexandria. E.B.B. later refers to reading his *Hymns.*

3. *Don Quixote*, Pt. II, Chap. 1.

4. That was the day appointed.

*Boyd proposed that we sh.^d read in future what he is familiar with,—
as my voice is not always audible to him—that we sh.^d read Gregory's
poems & Basil &c.   ≪I≫ am sorry: but as he likes it, let it be so—
Farewell to the Seven Chiefs—<χαιροιτε> λοιπον ημιτ ῾Ηρωες:¹ I
sh.^d have liked to have finished the play with him, which I suppose   5
I c.^d not have done, at any rate!——— He said "We can read Basil
<ᴧtogether> you know, if everything is happily settled". If!!———
We shall never read Basil together!—*

*Mr Boyd wishes to learn forty more lines out of the Prometheus:
& in search of them, I read to him nearly the whole of the last scenes   10
of the Prometheus.   I quite love the Prometheus.   It is an exquisite
creation: & besides,—I was so happy when I read the first scenes of
that play!*

*We talked about the Heaven & Earth in Colossians & Ephesians,
considered by him to refer to the Jews & Gentiles, by an Hebrew   15
≪idiom≫.   He made me feel clear about it,—& then he said—"≪I
want≫ you to do something for me—something to please me".   This
was, to state my convictions on the subject to Miss Gibbons, while
Miss Boyd was reading the paper to him!   Paper again!   I went out
to do as he desired—& did it.   Before the paper was quite read, he   20
thought what I had thought long ago, that he might as well hear it,
after I was gone.   So he had me back again—& we talked till dinner-
time—thro' such a thunderstorm!!—   If I had been anywhere else
I sh.^d have been in heroics!   Flashing lightening & crashing thunder!
<ᴧTo add to the sublimity of the scene> ≪I took my metal comb   25
out & let my hair "stream like a meteor".!≫²*

*We had dinner, & afterwards I went back to Mr Boyd, without
waiting for an embassador.   A discussion about a ≪trickery≫ note
which he & Miss Bordman had sent to Miss Gibbons,—as from her
man of the mountains.   I said I w.^d know in a moment whether the   30
<composition> were his or not.   He showed ≪it≫ to me, & I said
wrong.   I said it was his.   But I thought all the time that the style*

---

1. "Farewell to the remaining half of the Heroes."

2. *Odes by Mr. Gray* (Strawberry Hill, 1757), p. 14, Ode II [later called "The Bard"],
I.2:

> With haggard eyes the Poet stood;
> (Loose his beard, and hoary hair
> Stream'd, like a meteor, to the troubled air)
> And with a Master's hand, and Prophet's fire,
> Struck the deep sorrows of his lyre.

Diary by E.B.B.

was <ₐa> _disguised style;_ tho' the beginning of the first sentence
appeared to me <ₐin> his manner of writing.

I asked how long his sister intended to remain with him. He did
not know. I think he likes Miss Bordman as much as he dislikes
5 Miss Gibbons. ≪...≫ _I_ like Miss Bordman too, & I sh.ᵈ <like>
her better still, if it were not for—...! When _I_ go away, _I_ shall not
be missed!—

"I wish it would rain furiously all the evening". "Why?" "Because
then you c.ᵈ not go home". I was pleased by that answer; & wish!—
10 Got home in the dark, & found that poor Bro was gone to bed with
an attack of headache & feverishness. Talking. I was goose enough
to tell Bummy about Miss Boyd's secession from M.ʳ Boyd's room, on
my last visit to him: & she was severe enough to call his conduct "ungentlemanly & disgusting." I was lighted up into a passion of course!!
15 But there was no serious breach of the peace. I cannot imagine the
quia of Bummy's evident aversion to my dear friend, & everything &
body connected with him—

He told me to consult M.ʳ Curzon about the passage in Coloss: &
in the case of <its being> given in his favor, to write to him about it.

20 _Wednesday August 17.ᵗʰ_

I left my Seven chiefs at M.ʳ Boyd's yesterday. Now there are
sundry notes in it, which I sh.ᵈ prefer the readers there, not reading;
therefore my first precaution this morng. was to send for it. I ≪sent≫
at the same time my ≪...≫ Neapolitan _vocabolario_[1] for Miss Boyd,
—& Miss Steers's books.

≪Finished Cebes; & began Theophrastus.[2]≫

Clouds—& an imitation of ≪yesterday's≫ thunderstorm; and fortunately for my nerves, Virgil to Homer![3] M.ʳ Curzon came ≪at≫
three, & when I went down stairs to see him, I found M.ʳˢ Martin in
30 the drawingroom—, M.ʳ Martin at the window! A little talking. When
we went in to dinner, they sate down near us—& were _not_ very
agreable. M.ʳ Martin dumb & deaf to M.ʳ Curzon. M.ʳˢ Martin ≪rather

1. Lot 1194 of the 1913 Browning Sale: _Vocabolario Italiano-Latina et Latino-Italiano_,
2 vols. (Napoli, 1818), a gift to E.B.B. from her father.

2. Theophrastus of Eresus (_c._ 371-287 B.C.). His major works were two botanical trea-
tises, but later entries indicate that E.B.B. was reading his _Ethical Characters_.

3. In her letter to H.S.B. of 3 March 1828, E.B.B. said of critics who compare Virgil and
Homer "they may as well compare the mouse with the mountain!" (_EBB/HSB_, p. 22).

[92]

icy to≫ me!   At least I fancied it, & did'nt care!—   Talking to M.ʳ
Curzon all the evening.   He wont admit M.ʳ Boyd's interpretation of
Colossions—so I suppose I am not to write.   I sighed as I wrote that;
& not because I cannot send M.ʳ Curzon's receipt in full, of the inter-
pretation.   5

        A note from M.ʳˢ Boyd, with ≪my≫ Seven chiefs.   A note too,
from Miss Steers, with Keats & Shelley.   ≪Poets≫ wont do me much
good just now,—I believe,—& yet,—I am glad to have them.

        A great deal of conversation, with M.ʳ Curzon, altogether religious.
He sleeps here, to our surprise!—   No letter.   10

Thursday August 18.

        I finished Keats's Lamia, Isabella, Eve of St Agnes & Hyperion,[1]
before breakfast.   The three first disapointed me.   The extracts I had
seen of them, ≪were≫ undeniably the finest things in them.   But
there is some surprising poetry—poetry of wonderful grandeur, in   15
the Hyperion.   The effect of the appearance of Hyperion, among the
<ruined> Titans, is surpassingly fine.[2]   Poor poor Keats.   His name
shall be in my "≪Poets≫ Record.["][3]   Like his own Saturn, he was
dethroned from ≪the seat≫ <which> his genius claimed: and in the
≪ₐradiance≫ of his own Hyperion, will he appear to posterity—in   20
                          "splendour, like the morn,
            Pervading all the <beetling> gloomy steeps
            All the sad spaces of oblivion."[4]

        I talked to M.ʳ Curzon until three, when we dined.   Afterwards
he went away;—& we went out.   Gathering mushrooms.   I am glad   25
we were so employed.   It gave me an excuse for rambling away by
myself, & letting my mind roll itself out, as ≪the≫ chart of a sad
voyager.   I knew, poetry w.ᵈ do me no good just now.   I knew right.
My spirits are very very cloudy!   ≪ . . . ≫ I wish one wish!——
Vain,—as if I wished a thousand!—   No letters today!—but a parcel   30
from Worcester, containing a little edition of Reynolds's Lectures for

    1. John Keats, Lamia, Isabella, The Eve of St. Agnes, and Other Poems (London, 1820).

    2. At the conclusion of Bk. II of "Hyperion."

    3. Wellesley has three manuscript versions of this early poem, one of which was published
in Anthony Munday and Other Essays, by Eustace Conway (New York, 1927). Keats is not
mentioned—perhaps E.B.B. contemplated a further revision.

    4. Lines 357-359.

Diary by E.B.B.

Eliza Cliffe,[1] *&* <∧*Holwell's*> ≪*Dionysius*≫.[2] *I looked over some of Dionysius: a good part of his letter to Gnaius Pompeius,*[3] *which defends his criticism on Plato; while they were playing chess. I dont think that I shall sit down seriously to Dionysius, before I have fin-*
5 *ished Theophrastus, & read Isocrates's Panegyricus. Bro is better today, but not well.*

Friday. August 19.
      While we were at breakfast two men came ≪up≫ to the house, & rang the front door bell. I knew very well what their business was,
10 *tho' Bummy talked about* <*lion*>-*hunters from Malvern. As we went out of the diningroom, Lane past her, & said something in a low voice. I was therefore prepared for what followed. We ≪had to≫ go up stairs, that the lower part of the house might be seen by these gentlemen—one of them dark & foreign-looking, the other*
15 *apparently an agent. I have heard no other particulars,—not even their names. I wrote to my dear dear Papa today, & made an allusion which was scarcely an allusion, to his present distress—begging him to let none of his anxious feelings rest on* us *who loved him more than we loved anything else, & felt that we* must *be happy when*
20 *we* <*shall* ∧*be*> *all together once ≪again≫— It seemed to me better to say this, that he might not suffer the additional pain of fancying us unprepared for the stroke which he knew to be impending.*
      No letters.
25 *I finished the Endymion*[4] *today. I do not admire it as a fine poem; but I do admire many passages of it, as being very fine poetry. As a whole, it is cumbrous & ≪unwieldy≫. You dont know where to put it. Your imagination is confused by it: & your feelings uninterested. And yet a poet wrote it. When I had done with Keats, I*
30 *took up Theophrastus. Theophrastus has a great deal of vivacity, &*

---

1. This suggests that E.B.B. bought for Eliza the 12mo edition of the *Discourses*, which formed volume 20 of *The British Prose Writers* (London, 1820).

2. William Holwell, ed. *Selecti Dionysii Halicarnassensis de Priscis Scriptoribus Tractatus* (London, 1766). E.B.B.'s copy of the 1778 edition formed Lot 625 of the 1913 Browning Sale.

3. Ed. cit., pp. 105-127 of the Latin text, and pp. 171-189 of the Greek text.

4. John Keats, *Endymion: a Poetic Romance* (London, 1818).

power of portraiture about him; & ≪uplifts≫ that veil of distance
≪ . . . veiling≫ the old Greeks with ≪∧such sublime≫ mistiness; &
shows you how they used to spit & take physic & wear nailed shoes
tout ≪comme≫ un autre.   In short he makes you ≪a≫ valet de
chambre (to whom no man is a hero) to the ancient heroes!   This is   5
amusing enough: but I am not in a humour for it!—   Theophrastus
does me no good just now: ≪& as≫ I cant laugh with him, I shall be
glad when I have done hearing him laugh.

   This evening B H & A <went> out to walk; & I was their attend-
ant cavalry.   The poney carried me beautifully, past M.ʳ Hailes;¹ &   10
there was some delightful cantering as we came back.   I ventured
to ≪carry≫ Isocrates down to tea, that I might read while they played
chess.   As Bro remonstrated, I wont do so any more.   I read the
opening of the Panegyricus.   It is lengthy; but the cadence of the
sentences, has a full & beautiful harmony, ≪& does≫ not at all re-   15
semble the cadence in that treatise addressed to Demonicus, which
some attribute to Isocrates.²   I think I shall admire the style at least,
of the genuine Isocrates.

Saturday August <20>

   I had intended to finish today, Theophrastus's Ethic characters;   20
but ≪Eliza≫ Cliffe's arrival after breakfast, put all my good resolu-
tions to the route,—as the Dutch have lately done the Belgians.³
Eliza has not been Dutchlike & slow.   She has finished my picture,
which, tho' it is not the picture of me, does her infinite credit: con-
sidering her deficiency not merely in instruction, but experience.⁴   25
≪The white≫ gown is changed into grey,—& the red background
into green,—& the hair from black, into something nearer ≪ . . . ≫

   1. Mr. Berrington Hailes had land immediately to the east of Hope End (see auctioneer's map, Appendix III, p. 335).

   2. *Isocratis ad Demonicum Parænesis*; modern opinion tends to accept the authenticity of its attribution.

   3. *The Times*, 10 August 1831: "The invasion of the Dutch upon Belgium has taken place at four points . . . The attack has been made at all points by surprise. The Belgian troops, none of which were prepared, were forced to fall back, after having sustained the attack as long as they were able. These engagements have been very bloody. . . ." Belgium had only just gained independence from Holland. A cessation of the war was speedily brought about when France sent 50,000 troops to the aid of Belgium.

   4. For E.B.B.'s verses "To E.W.C. Painting my Picture," see Appendix II, p. 314.

Diary by E.B.B.

its "proper hue",—& the lips from scarlet into a human rosiness: so that altogether, Eliza & I are to be congratulated.   Before tea, we went out to ride, & rode all round by the farm & <Petty> France.[1] My estomac &c none the better for it; & I went to bed by myself, at ten o'clock.   Never mind.   I enjoyed my ride.   And there is no kind of enjoyment which one can have on this side of the grave, ≪without≫ paying its price in pain—no flower that one can pick, without nettling one's fingers!   Is not this an unthankful thought of mine?   Oh yes!   There are heaps of flowers, which my hand, even <u>mine</u>, has picked, & in joy! tho' they are now lying afar, lost, & withered—

 I forgot to say, that I did read a little of Theophrastus, before breakfast this morning—& that I gave Reynolds's ≪Discourses≫ to Eliza Cliffe.   No letters.   Dear Bro convalescent.—

Sunday.   August 21

 All gone to Church, except me; and I am going . . . . to finish Jewel.

 M.ʳˢ Cliffe & Eliza came to have luncheon during our dinner.   M.ʳˢ Cliffe investigated the picture, & pronounced it to be extremely like. It is not <u>likely</u> at any rate.   She took me down to the gate in the back seat of <u>her</u> carriage, Bummy driving,—& we had the satisfaction of seeing M.ʳ Curzon's congregation augmented by several of the Colwall people—<u>not</u> by M.ʳˢ Martin.   His ≪text≫ was from Amos "Can two walk together, unless they are agreed?"[2]   The first part very good,— the latter part straggling, & heavy besides.

 A note from M.ʳˢ Boyd, to say ≪that≫ somebody has formed an attachment for Annie, & that, in consequence, somebody's Mama, wishes her to be sent home.[3]   I was foolish enough, to make a report of ≪this≫ note to Bummy: & now, more items are put down to poor Annie's flirtibility.

 I am very much afraid that she will trifle away her ultimate happiness.   May it be otherwise!   M.ʳˢ Boyd says "I have not told M.ʳ or Miss Boyd of the reason of her returning sooner".   M.ʳ or Miss Boyd! An extroardinary [sic] manner of introducing M.ʳ Boyd's name: & an

1. A smallholding about ¾ mile S.E. of Hope End (map ref. F5).
2. Amos iii.3.
3. As Annie was staying at Stanwell, the seat of Sir John Gibbons, the inference is that Lady Gibbons was attempting to nip in the bud any romantic attachment between Annie and one of the unmarried Gibbons boys,—either Richard (then 24) or Joseph (18).

extraordinary silence to preserve towards the father of her child!——

I cant help being pained by M.ʳ Boyd not writing to me, & not sending even a message in M.ʳˢ Boyd's note. Probably he did <ₐnot> know about her writing; but then he might have thought of writing himself —— he might have been anxious to see me, when soon he may be able to see me no more. I ≪dare≫ not trust myself to dwell on these points. One thing is too <clear>.

This week may decide, perhaps must decide, everything. If I can go to Malvern tomorrow, I will go. Only a little more strength of mind—a little more power of self controul,—& it will all be over. God give me strength & power!—— I have not felt at all well today, with an occasional pressure at the heart, & sickness.

Better, however, now: & I must try to keep so.

No letter from Papa: at least none that I know of.

Finished Jewel, & admire Jewel, & ≪will≫ read some parts of Jewel again, if I live much longer. He is very eloquent & energetic & learned; & well worth reading. His references to the councils, ≪are≫ tedious & heavy . . to me.

Monday August 22.ᵈ

It must have been nearly nine when I set off for Malvern where I arrived as M.ʳˢ Boyd was breakfasting. So M.ʳ Boyd is going to scold me about something! But he wont be very severe; for M.ʳˢ Boyd told me that he ≪exclaimed≫ "Good creature"! when he heard of my having come. "A good kind creature" he called me, when we met. His manner very kind—"Have you any good news for me?" No, still—no, always! The scold was about my not having shewn him, my "disquisitions on Plato", which M.ʳ Davidson read in ms five years ago.[1] M.ʳ Davidson is dreaming. "Have you brought your seven chiefs?" Why what a question! We read some of Gregory's poems —53 lines of his poem on Nemesius[2]—the opening lines: and the concluding lines of the second long poem—on Christ:[3] & then we read merely the Greek of a passage in the ≪ . . . ≫ poem <ₐnext> to

5

10

15

20

25

30

---

1. Although E.B.B. wrote various critical comments on her readings of Plato, the manuscript referred to here cannot be identified. The Mr. Davidson E.B.B. speaks of is believed to have been the Rev. John Davison, Prebendary of Worcester, and Rector of Upton-on-Severn.

2. "Ad Nemesium" (*GNO*, II, 140-146).

3. "De Testamentis, et Adventu Christi" (*GNO*, II, 173-174).

Diary by E.B.B.

my favorite poem; & then M.ʳ Boyd gave me Meleager's ode to spring,
to read, while he "stretched his legs" in the garden. Very very happy!
—Meleager's ode is beautiful ≪tho'≫ monotonous: but the monotony is much less felt in the concluding lines. Nota Bene Ba! Buy
5   Wakefield's Bion, & Moschus & Meleager.[1]

M.ʳ Wood disagreed with Miss Gibbons & agreed with M.ʳ Boyd about
the passage in Colossions. So M.ʳ Boyd told me. He 'cant ≪abide≫"
Miss Gibbons—thinks her "nauseous"—that is, he <thinks> her vanity & deviations nauseous. She seems a goodnatured person, ≪&≫
10   in her conversation, ≪ . . . ≫ a religious person: but the spirit of man
cannot search the spirit of man. After dinner, I was over-asked into
playing on the guitar & singing— I sang Kathleen,[2] very badly, in
my own ≪opinion≫. When I got again into M.ʳ Boyd's room, he
told me that he had heard today what he had often heard about—
15   that he had been standing at the open window while I ≪sang≫, &
≪thought . . . that≫ my voice was sweet tho' low!— If I had known
his "whereabouts" my singing w.ᵈ have come to an end—or at least,
to a trembling. An exhortation to practise!——— I am glad he
liked my singing. He seemed to like it, certainly! We talked — —
20   I cant recollect all we talked about,—but we talked very pleasantly
& on pleasant subjects. So M.ʳˢ Boyd thinks that there is no use in
his asking my opinion of any composition of his own, as I "cannot
be impartial".!! When he reported this, I answered nothing. What
could I answer?—

25   I begged him to be less reserved to M.ʳ Curzon than he has been,
with regard to his religious opinions; & he half promised me that he
would. I hope the promise may be binding. Why should M.ʳ Curzon
"stand in doubt of him", as M.ʳ Curzon seems to do?

I told him that altho' M.ʳ C did stand in doubt of him, yet that he
30   liked his society extremely. "Then", he observed, "M.ʳ Curzon is
inconsistent. According to his own views he sh.ᵈ not like the society
of any man not decidedly & clearly religious". My answer made him
laugh. "But M.ʳ Curzon ranks you with anchovy <sauce>"! He
asked me to read the <Epistle> to the Romans, with a humble &

---

1. Gilbert Wakefield, ed. βιωνος και Μοσχου τα Λειψανα (London, 1795). Although
Meleager is not mentioned on the title page, this edition contains an Idyll of his.

2. Probably *Kathleen O More, an Irish Ballad* (Dublin, [1830]).

*attentive mind,—& proposed doing the same himself,—that we might
afterwards compare notes, on calvinism & arminianism.*[1] *I have agreed
to do so. "I should like very much," he added "to read it <u>with</u> you,
critically". Should <u>I</u> not like it? Yes indeed! But there may be no
opportunity for <u>that</u>!— †*[2]

*I left his room at twenty minutes to eight: & neither of us imag-
ined it to be so late. How happy I was today. Indeed I do him great
injustice very often,—& believe at this moment that he has a true
friendship & regard for me. But because I have a fault in one way,
I am apt to accuse him of one in another.*

"Miss Bordman says that it is ≪*a shame*≫ *for me to pocket you
in this manner." "It w*ᵈ *be a shame if you did'nt"— He gave me
Dawes's miscellanea critica,* ≪*that I might*≫ *ferrett out for him, Kidds
notes on the digamma.*[3] *Will this be the last employment of the
kind, which he will give me?*

*One thing gave me pain. He told me that in the case of my leaving
Hope End,* <*which*> ≪*. . .*≫ *he hoped (said emphatically) w*ᵈ *not be
the case, perhaps it w*ᵈ *be better <u>for</u> him to have back those books*
≪*that*≫ *I have in my care.— And not a word of his going where we
go!————*

Well: everything ≪*must*≫ *be borne. I was going to quote Marcus
Antoninus: but what good can <u>he</u> do in this case————*

*Got home, & heard of the Cards & Walls having been here in the
course of the day.*[4] *Their conduct* <ᴧ*when*> *here, was more heartless than their* <ᴧ*heartlessness in*> *coming! Miss Wall* ≪*has*≫ *no
finely tuned & feminine feelings: & why should we expect the sound
of the organ from the jews harp. Everything "after its kind"! — —*

≪*I called at M*ʳˢ *Trant's for five-minutes—*≫

---

1. The doctrine of Jacobus Arminius (1560-1609) was largely an expression of reaction
against the tenets of Calvin (1509-64). The Arminians insisted that real free-will in man was
compatible with Divine Sovereignty; that Christ died for all men and not only for the elect;
and that the theory of predestination was unbiblical.

2. No positive explanation of E.B.B.'s use of the dagger throughout the Diary can be
offered. Similar marks appear in *WG* and obviously relate to passages studied; it seems
likely that the dagger denoted some supplementary entry in another journal, containing
general notes on her reading.

3. Richard Dawes, *Miscellanea Critica*, with Notes by Thomas Kidd, (Cambridge, 1817).

4. To inspect the house, with no serious intention—"a party of pleasure" to use E.B.B.'s
words. Miss Wall was Eliza's friend, and her family held the manor of Cradley, Herefordshire. Dr. Henry Card, Vicar of Great Malvern, was a friend of H.S.B.

Diary by E.B.B.

*The moon was shining exquisitely, one star by its side, before I
left the open air.*

Tuesday August 23ᵈ

Today was as unhappy as yesterday was happy.   Wheels will turn
5 *round.   My first doing, was writing a long note to Mʳ Boyd, to tell*
≪him≫ about Dominick's desire to consult him "≪ₐupon≫ the Greek
historians", & to beg him to be philosophical, if not historical, &
receive his visit; & to tell him besides of Miss Wall's amiable conduct
with regard to us.¹   Heard Georgie's Xenophon,—& read a letter
10 *from Miss Price.   Had dinner—afterwards Bro said to me "Ba: here is*
a note for you to read.["]   From Papa!— It was to procure ≪Bro's≫
& my signature to some testamentary document of my dear dearest
Granny²—& it spoke besides of our dearest Papa having had himself
a violent attack of cholera.   He is in consequence weak & low, & is
15 *going out of town for two days, that change of air may recruit him.*
The note altogether made us all melancholy; & nobody thought until
past three, that the document might be of consequence & should be
returned by this day's post.³   Then, when it was thought of, what a
bustle there was!   Bro & I drove off to Mʳ Deane's, as hard as horse
20 *cᵈ go!   What might not depend on our being in time!— And Sam*
was in readiness at Mʳ Deane's to gallop off with the packet, as soon
as the signatures were ≪affixed≫.   He did gallop, & just ≪gained≫
the coach!—just as it was going to descend the Eastnor hill!   Thank
God!   upon that packet, much may depend.   Bro & I arrived at
25 *home safely; I very much tired with the mental & physical agitation.*
Hysterics kept off, however.   Bro to the Martins, to dine!   When we
had ascertained the safety of the packet, I wrote to tell him of it, that
his anxieties might not "dam up ≪his≫ flow of ≪ . . . ≫ soul."⁴
At six oclock, a large party arrived to see the house.   Henrietta A

---

1. For the letter, see Appendix I, p. 283.

2. E.B.B.'s grandmother, who had died the previous December, left her £4,000 (letter
from Edward Moulton-Barrett to his brother Samuel, dated 15 February 1831, in the collection at Wellesley).

3. At that time, the London mail left Ledbury at 4 p.m. (*Hints of Ledbury* . . . Ledbury,
1831, p. 43).

4. Cf. "The Feast of Reason and the Flow of Soul," from *The First Satire of the Second
Book of Horace, Imitated* . . . [Alexander Pope], (London, 1733), p. 17, line 128.

[100]

& I ran up into my ≪ . . . ≫ room, & lay on the bed.   Nothing but curiosity brought them; ≪yet we≫ must be patient.   Very soon, *this* kind of pain will come to an end.   My pains are διαδοχοι.[1]

My parcel to M.ʳ Boyd, containing my letter to him & Keats's poems for Miss Boyd, ≪was≫ not sent in the confusion, until seven oclock.   A letter was brought back, forwarded from Annie!   Nothing in it.

I was falling into a fever <about> M.ʳ Boyd's not noticing my letter, when I found that M.ʳˢ Boyd's message was, "If any answer is required, I will write tomorrow".   So most probably, indeed most certainly, <she> had not read my letter to him.   Glad, more than glad, to get to bed—& be tranquil.   What a bustling thundering wretched day I have had.   May God bless & preserve our beloved Papa<!—>   Anything but anxiety on *his* account!—

Wednesday August 24.

I read a little of Theophrastus,—not much,—for a letter arrived from Malvern, & I had to write to M.ʳˢ Boyd as well as to my friend. He wrote to me, but not many lines; kind ones, however.   He calls the Walls' conduct, "brutal & unfeeling," but vindicates D.ʳ Card who was *asked* to accompany them.   In my answer I told him what ≪*I*≫ thought of D.ʳ Card!—& think!—[2]

He says that he felt ≪ . . . ≫ on reading my letter how unworthy <he> was of the regard which I feel for him—   Perhaps unworthy in one way.

I copied some music this evening, & did nothing else worth com-memorizing.

Thursday August 25.

If this *should* be the day fixed on for the sale,—& I very much suspect—but I wont think or hear any certainty about it.   The <feel-ing> has weighed on my brain & heart all day; yet I cant dwell on it <ᴧby reflection.>—   M.ʳ Boyd said in his letter yesterday that he "cannot help indulging the idea of everything ending happily".   I have prayed that it may end *happily*, not that ≪it≫ may end in a particular

---

1. "Successors."
2. For her letter, see Appendix I, p. 284.

Diary by E.B.B.

way, by our leaving Hope End or retaining Hope End; but that we may be led to do <∧or suffer> what is best for us. Lord Jesus hear this prayer!——

5 *Since M.ʳ Boyd expressed his hope to me, mine has risen up in a presentimental form; but whether it be a spirit of health or Goblin damned,[1] there is no saying, or thinking! Well: ≪all≫ <∧things> will be wisely ordered—if not happily for the very present moment.*

I have dogged myself on in study today, that I ≪might≫ not be dogged by less pleasant thoughts than studious ones. I have finished
10 *Theophrastus, who is a spirited amusing writer. Something in his manner, might catch the popular ear, at least as well as the tinkling of certain fools' bells! Shall I try? There is time enough to think of it.*

I have read also Callimachus's Hymn to Jupiter. Is there any-
15 *thing fine in this hymn? Nothing, that I can discover; & ≪it does≫ not bribe my ear high enough <∧for it> to render up the key of my judgment. No harmony. <Too> many pauses & breaks in the lines!—— The Greek is not very easy. Such is my sentence on Callimachus's first hymn. Si sic omnia, I shall have to wear a black*
20 *cap all my life, as far as he is concerned.*

I have read too a part of the panegyric of Isocrates. The rhythm is very flowing & harmonious, fuller to the ear than Plato's: but I have, as yet, met with nothing in the matter particularly striking or beautiful.

25 *Friday. August 26.*

Read some passages from Shelley's Revolt of Islam[2] before I was up. He is a great poet; but we acknowledge him to be a great poet as we ≪acknowledge≫ Spenser[3] <∧to be so,> & do not love him for it. He resembles Spenser in one thing, & one thing only, that his
30 *poetry it too immaterial for our sympathies to enclasp it firmly. ≪It≫ reverses the lot of human plants: its roots are in the air, not earth!—— But as I read him on, I may reverse this opinion.*

Will there be a letter today? If there is, it ≪will≫ be a decisive

---

1. *Hamlet* I.iv.39-40.
2. Percy Bysshe Shelley, *The Revolt of Islam* (London, 1817).
3. Edmund Spenser, author of *The Faerie Queene*.

[102]

one. *God give us strength!—— I am afraid that dear Henrietta clings
too strongly to hope, & that when it give way altogether, she may fall
low!—— God give her strength———*

*<Let me consider> circumstances, while I am calm, in a degree.
I may have to leave this place where I have walked & talked & dreamt* 5
*in much joy; & where I have heard most beloved voices which I can
no more hear, & clasped beloved hands which I ≪can≫ no more clasp:
where I have smiled with the living & wept above the dead ≪&≫ where
I have read immortal books, & written pleasant thoughts, & known
at least one very dear friend—— I may have to do this; & it will be* 10
*sorrow to me!—— But let me think of it calmly. I can take with me
the dear members of my own family,—& my recollections which, in
some cases, were all that was left to me here: I ≪can≫ take with me
my books & my studious tastes,—and above all, the knowledge that
"all things" whether sorrowful or joyous, "work together for good to* 15
*those who love God".[1] And my dear Papa's mind,—(should he not
be dearest to me?;) will be more tranquil perhaps when he is away
from a place so productive of anxieties. There is one person, whom
it will indeed pain me to leave. But he may follow us,—& in the
meantime he will write to me & not forget me. Oh I hope ≪not≫!* 20
*To whatever place ≪we≫ go, I will seclude myself there, & try to
know & like nobody,—but live with my books & writings & dear
family. With them, can I be altogether unhappy? I am unhappy
now. There is no use in disguising it from myself!—— I will wait
for the letters, & in the meantime, get on with Isocrates.* 25

*Thank God! Hope End, dear Hope End, is not sold. <It> was
bought in by our antagonists themselves; ≪&≫ may yet go by private contract: but still, thank God for this reprieve. A letter from
Papa!—*

I was in the dining room. Bummy ≪came≫ in to me with over- 30
*flowing eyes, & an exclamation of "Good news!" The good news
≪were≫ too much for me, prepared as I was for the worst news: and
I should have sunk to the floor, if she had not caught me. Thank
God ≪for this≫ blessed good news! Many tears were shed, & all for
joy, at Hope End today* 35

---

1. Rom. viii.28: "And we know that all things work together for good to them that
love God, to them who are called according to his purpose."

Diary by E.B.B.

Saturday. August 27.

I determined yesterday to be the bearer of certain news to M.ʳ
Boyd today: and the news of my having proposed to do so, appeared
to have excited a tumult down stairs. According to Henrietta's report,
5 Bummy exclaimed "What has M.ʳ Boyd to do with it?" What has M.ʳ
Boyd to do with it? Why if he has <u>nothing</u> to do with it, ≪ . . . ≫
what must be the sincerity of his professed regard for me? H & B
had sent to the Martins; and is <u>my</u> friend to be treated with less
consideration than theirs? I said so to H, who irritated me by her
10 reply about the cases being different, & about ≪the≫ impropriety
of ≪my≫ feeling <u>more friendship for M.ʳ Boyd than for the Martins!</u>—
It is extraordinary that ≪ . . . ≫ more than one person in this house,
≪should entertain≫ such dispositions towards ≪a≫ person whom
everybody knows, ≪ . . . ≫ I, justly or injustly, consider as my dear
15 & intimate friend. I believe the fact to be this. They have, as most
people have, clearer ideas of the aristocracy of rank & wealth, than
of the aristocracy of mind. Therefore it appears singular to them,
≪& not≫ very ≪reasonable≫, that I sh.ᵈ so obviously prefer M.ʳ Boyd's
society to that of some other individuals. I love dearest B & H ≪to≫
20 the bottom of my heart; and they deserve my love, to the bottom of
theirs: but without my pursuits they cannot have my tastes, & without ≪having≫ my tastes, they cannot be expected to understand them.
It w.ᵈ be <wrong> in me to blame, a miscomprehension—≪or≫ to
go on scribbling speculatively in this way, when ≪there≫ are facts to
25 <ₐbe> stated <u>memorabilialy.</u>

The poney ≪wd'nt≫ be caught, so I could'nt get away from this
place until 9. N. B. Bummy thought me "quite right" in going, when
I proposed it <u>to</u> her—& made no shade of objection <ₐopenly,>
whatever the darkness might have been in the private committee. Got
30 to Ruby Cottage, just as M.ʳˢ B's breakfast was in an incipient state.
Told her the good news! She had the tears in her eyes, & kissed me
again & again! & I c.ᵈ not help being affected by this kindness of manner. Uncomfortable account of Annie, upon w.ʰch my annotations &
<reflections> assume the brun foncè. I wish she were, or c.ᵈ be made,
35 unlike herself in <u>some</u> respects. Not in all. There is much good in
her,—& more might be elicited. If she c.ᵈ be married to a sensible
man whom she entirely loved, she might be happy & make him so.
But the love <u>must</u> be strong enough to place her altogether under his

[104]

influence!—or the <happiness> w.ᵈ be beyond both his & her's—
M.ʳ Boyd sent for me; & his first words were "Have you heard?" A
smile was his answer after hearing mine, & I ≪am sure≫, a pleased
smile: but no enthusiastic pleasure was expressed!— We talked until
shaving time, & then I was exiled for ≪half≫ an hour; & then re- 5
admitted. Read two poems of Gregorys, "I ≪would≫ I were a dove."
& "Where are my winged words".¹ They have both great merit, but
the last is too much drawn out—too much Procrustianized.² The
Ηθελον³ &c <is> really fine; very fine. I read besides, but did not
translate, the last ten lines of the <poem> De vita suâ,⁴ & admired 10
them very much indeed. Gregory is not a great poet, scarcely a real
poet: ≪ . . . ≫ in general, Gods men & columns w.ᵈ have nothing to
do with him:⁵ but there is, sometimes, much <in> his poetry, which
is <ₐeven> admirable.

After dinner, while we were at desert, a voice at the door, said, 15
"Porsonia, are you ready to come?" Yes she was ready & willing to
come.

Read a little more Gregory, & talked about Burgess the Bishop of
Salisbury,⁶ (who must be a benevolent man by what I heard of him),
—≪& on≫ several other subjects. At last I thought & asked about 20
the Greek epigram on the Tories, which I was to have procured from
M.ʳ Spowers. M.ʳ Boyd let me write it down from his dictation, &
then manumitted me, to send it to the Times,—but without his ini-
tials.⁷ On the whole, I had another happy day today.

---

1. Carmen VI, "De Vitæ Huius Vanitate atque Incertitudine" and Carmen VIII, "Ad Seipsum per Interrogationem & Responsionem" (*GNO*, II, 75-76 and 77-78). A partial translation of the former was included in H.S.B.'s *Select Poems, of Synesius and Gregory Nazianzen* (London, 1814), pp. 59-62. His translation of the latter appeared in *The Fathers Not Papists, or, Six Discourses by the Most Eloquent Fathers of the Church*, new edn. (London, 1834), pp. 405-406. E.B.B.'s translation of the second poem was contained in part II of "Some Account of the Greek Christian Poets" (*The Athenæum*, 5 March 1842, pp. 210-212).

2. In the manner of the famous robber Procrustes, who stretched or mutilated his victims to make them fit his bed.

3. The initial word of the poem "I would I were a dove."

4. *GNO*, II, 1-31.

5. Cf. Horace, *Ars Poetica*, lines 372-373: "mediocribus esse poetis | non homines, non di, non concessere columnæ." ("But that poets be of middling rank, neither men nor gods nor booksellers ever brooked," *LCL-HO/S*, pp. 480-481.)

6. Thomas Burgess (1756-1837), theological author, elected Bishop of St. David's 1803, translated to Salisbury 1825.

7. The epigram appeared in *The Times*, 30 August (see fn. 2, p. 111).

[105]

Diary by E.B.B.

*Agreed with Miss Gibbons, who wishes to hear M.ʳ Curzon—that
<she> sh.ᵈ go to Hope End tomorrow & dine with us.   Got home
late, (at half past eight) & got a scold, both for my lateness & the
Gibbons business.   If she were to come from any house but M.ʳ Boyd's,*
5   *it w.ᵈ not be so.   I was excited into complaining that no objection
was ever made to the visitors of other people; but that whatever person I invited, ≪on≫ him or her, every objection was concentrated.
Sorry I sh.ᵈ have said so, tho' ≪there's≫ some truth in it.   Long
pauses, & sharp words down stairs tonight.   None of them mine how-*
10 *ever, after that one ebullition.*
     Wrote to the Editor of the Times about M.ʳ Boyd's Greek epigram.

Sunday August 28.
     *Did not go to church.   Miss Gibbons arrived at one o'clock, &
≪M.ʳˢ≫ Boyd with her; ≪. . . Some≫ playing at cross purposes; M.ʳˢ*
15   *B having walked down the road to meet me as I came from Church,
while I was sitting with Miss G in the <morning> room.   ≪. . .≫ She
seems to be a feeling kind hearted woman, tho' not a faultless <one>.
Looking at me, she observed that I did not appear able to bear much
fatigue; & when I said "I am ≪stronger≫ than, I was some months*
20 *ago, & very much wonder at it", the tears <overflowed> her eyes
≪. . .≫ in a moment, & she told me to trust that ≪Friend≫ who is
more than father or mother, & "sticketh closer than a brother"—¹*
     *A note from Eliza Cliffe.   The Cliffes are not coming today, at
which I <am> not exactly sorry.   Dined, & went down to chapel—*
25   *M.ʳ Curzon preached very well; & our visitors were delighted.*
     *Miss Gibbons inclined to returning to Hope End,—so there she
did return,—& she & M.ʳˢ Boyd climbed our ≪mushroomed≫ hills.
Collision with the Martin party; & fire struck between Miss G & M.ʳ M
in consequence of my report to her of his report to me of her con-*
30 *troversial conversations at Eastnor.   The Martin party came down the
hill & into the house with us; & then there was an exposè of Eliza's
representation of me.   Abused, nem: con: M.ʳ Martin proposes that
as Eliza has not & never can attain to my mouth, she should paint a
book before it.   I vote for a black crape—which w.ᵈ add a good*

---

1. Proverbs xviii.24: "A man that hath friends must show himself friendly: and there
is a friend that sticketh closer than a brother."

[106]

<deal> to my sublimity, according to Burke.[1]   ≪Not Burke of Edinburgh!—[2]≫

Miss Gibbons glued herself to me all day, & we talked eternally. She praised Miss Bordman, & told me <how> much M.ʳ Boyd enjoyed her society.   Well!—I ought to be glad of this.

She asked me when I was going again to Malvern.   "Whenever I can", I <said>, "for my Malvern days are my happy days—they are my holidays.≪...≫   But I must not go too often."   "You cannot go too often. M.ʳ Boyd does so thoroughly enjoy the days which you spend with him! they are his holidays!"   "I did not exactly mean that—I meant that I must not leave home & occupy the carriage too often. I like to dream that M.ʳ Boyd has pleasure in seeing me, tho' I know that whatever pleasure his is, mine must double it."   "Indeed! I dont think it does! and how can you know ≪this≫?"   "By certain inward oracles".   "But tho' you understand your own oracles, you cant understand M.ʳ Boyd's".

I am half sorry that this conversation sh.ᵈ have ≪passed≫: but ≪passed≫ it has.

≪Miss≫ Gibbons considers that learning is standing between M.ʳ Boyd & God.   I defended his religious state with my best powers. May God increase the grace, which I am certain ≪He≫ has bestowed. M.ʳˢ B & Miss G went away at 8 oclock, & then we had prayers,— & then Bummy went up stairs & did not come down again.

No letters.

August 29.   Monday.

I have been reading Dawes's Miscellanea Critica <ₐall the morning,> & writing some of his emendations in the margin of my Callimachus.   They seem to me ingenious & satisfactory.

Not in the humour ≪for≫ trying to make the darkness of the digamma at all visible ≪& I≫ stumbled & grumbled over Kidd's

1. [Edmund Burke], A Philosophical Enquiry into the Origin of our Ideas of the Sublime and Beautiful (London, 1757), pp. 64-65: ". . . when the highest degree of the sublime is intended, the materials and ornaments ought neither to be white, nor green, nor yellow, nor blue, nor of a pale red, nor violet, nor spotted, but of sad and fuscous colours, as black, or brown, or deep purple, and the like. . . ."

2. William Burke (1792-1829), executed on 28 January 1829 for multiple murders, committed in order that he might sell his victims' bodies. The Times, 2 February 1829, in the course of an account of the execution, said: ". . . the actual number of murders in which Burke acknowledged himself to be concerned was 16. . . ."

notes & Dawes's text on that subject, ≪nearly≫ vainly <ᴧ& quite stupidly!—> N B. Try it tomorrow.

Henrietta to the heath: & B & A in the carriage to the Bartons. <My> company was asked for in a dispensable manner,—of which I
5 eagerly took advantage by staying at home. Read a few pages of Isocrates. I wish I had a more readable copy than mine, which is dark & squeezy,—& printed in columns.[1] My wishes are so miscellaneous, that I ≪might≫ as well be comprehensive, & wish for ≪Aladdin's≫ lamp at once.

10 Mushroom hunting. Bro was pick ≪nicing≫ today on <the> Malvern hills, with twenty eight other persons, besides Sam. It was proposed that they sh.^{d} meet "on the top of the <monument>".[2] In that case they might have <ᴧalso> met at the bottom of a monument.

15 Tuesday August 30.

Mr Curzon is to be at Mr Boyd's today. I hope he will be satisfied with regard to his spiritual state,—& that Miss Gibbons may not intrude her commentary on <character>. Will there be a letter today. Bummy hopes yes. I fear yes; & hope no. The next news is not likely
20 to be good news.

I have been exploring Dawes this morning, & writing his critical emendations on Euripides & Sophocles in the margins of my books. Have'nt tried the digamma yet. Kidds notes upon it, are not put in an interesting form.

25 <A> little of Isocrates—, & then Eliza Cliffe came. Went down stairs, & found her & Bummy discussing cum furore, the Walls. I said little, & meant to have said nothing. Poor Eliza sh.^{d} not suffer by hearing her friend spoken harshly of; when ≪she has to suffer by knowing≫ that ≪this≫ friend deserves it. She dined with us—
30 and just before dinner, the letters came. One from my dear Papa, to me—& dated the isle of Wight— He seems pleased with it— delighted with the scenery & Mr Sipthorpe.[3] Oh if he sh.^{d} intend to

1. H. Wolf's 1613 edition, which formed Lot 785 of the 1913 Browning Sale.

2. A 90-foot high obelisk erected in Eastnor Park by Earl Somers in 1812, and inscribed to the memory of three members of his family.

3. The Rev. Richard Waldo Sibthorp (1792-1879), incumbent of St. James's Church, Ryde, I.o.W.

settle there—if we sh.^d be ≪separated≫ from England by the sea!—
Mr Boyd will not follow us <u>there</u>—   I hope, I hope, this dungeon in
the air, will fall into ruins.   Hastings, Eastbourne, Brighton—Ports-
mouth—any place but the isle of Wight!—

Dont let me fall into a Pythian fury, yet, at any rate.¹   ≪. . . I   5
thank God that my dearest Papa is better!—≫

B A & I went in the carriage to the Wyche, & Eliza was our cavalry
≪escort≫. Bummy was heroic enough to walk along the whole length
of the terrace as far as the great elm, without her head having any
extra motion, circularly.   I rode Eliza's horse wh^{ch} Eliza <led>.   10
Proposed—that I sh.^d run down to see Mr Boyd.   Down I went, &
Eliza with me,—and yet not <u>with</u> me, for I was before her.   I ran,
slipped, rolled, presto prestissimo, to the bottom.   Got into Mr Boyd's
room, & got scolded for being out of breath—the necessary result
of such <u>a descensus averni.</u>   Told him of Papa's letter.   He hoped that   15
we sh.^d not go to the isle of Wight, & ≪recommended≫ me to write
tomorrow a petition that in the case of our leaving Hope End, ≪Papa≫
w.^d settle at Hastings or Eastbourne.   Now he certainly w.^d not care
where we settled, if he had no idea of following us.   It is clear to my
mind that he has that idea, & I have been made very happy by it.   20

Mr Curzon was at dinner with the rest of the party.   Mr Boyd
smiled when I said "I never thought until <this> moment, of his
meaning to be here today".

Eliza came into the room—& immediately Mr Boyd began with
"I have to congratulate you Miss Cliffe, on the late amiable conduct   25
of y.^r friend ≪Miss≫ Wall."   I interposed, but Mrs Boyd's calling me
out of the room, made void my interposition.   An explanation of
Annie's doings at Stanwell.   She is <u>not</u> coming home.   Back again to
Mr Boyd.   I upbraided him for his attack on Eliza, & wished him
good bye.   He told me that he ≪disliked≫ my ≪coming≫ for so   30
short a time; & hoped that I w.^d visit him meo more "long measure",
before long.   <Promised>!— Miss Gibbons came into the room for
a moment, & <u>embraced</u> me, & begged that of the two minutes I was
going to spend at Ruby Cottage, I w.^d spare a quarter of ≪one≫ to
Mr Curzon & herself!—after all I forgot it, & went out of the house   35

---

1. Described in a letter to H.S.B. as "Pythian contortions & agitations of her body, which always precede an oracle" (letter of [10 December 1831]; see Appendix I, p. 294).

Diary by E.B.B.

*without seeing him, or re-seeing her. A happy little visit. Ascended
the hill capitally.   If Horace had been there, nil admirari ≪w.ᵈ≫
never have been written;—so I am rather glad he was not. Bummy
said "I will trust you again["]: & towards home we went. Met the*

5   *Martins by the rocky seat—≪ . . . ≫   M.ʳ M in trepidation & consternation at my determination of riding by the horse which M.ʳ de
Marizet¹ was leading.   He begged me to ≪get≫ off in vain; & at
length <decided> that "temerity & timidity were the characteristics
of my sex".   They wanted us to ≪drink≫ tea at Colwall & to wait*

10   *for them at the turnpike, neither of wh.ᶜʰ we did. Got home in the
dark.   So ends this chapter of my life, which is a kind of chapter of
hats—& walking shoes!—*

Wednesday August 31.ˢᵗ
   A note from Eliza, while we were at breakfast, speaking of our

15   *going, <ₐ&> of Miss Wall's <u>not</u> going, to dine at Mathon on Friday.
<u>I</u> w.ᵈ rather <u>not</u>.   A discussion about it after breakfast—, & the nos
had it.   Bummy Arabel & I drove off with our refusal & my picture,
to call on M.ʳˢ Cliffe.   Called in viâ on the Martins—& I had a french
conversation with M.ʳ de Marizet.   He seems to me—nay, he certain-*

20   *ly is, an agreable & clever man!—   An emphatic discription of his
<u>horreur</u> yesterday in witnessing my <u>temeritè</u>.*
   *<Off> to the Cliffes;—& got <u>off</u> the invitation.   Rummaged
Eliza's room, & read some verses <u>of</u> Miss Walls, & some letters of
<her's> relating to us, & took a fancy to Goldoni's back. Miss Wall's*

25   *letters are impertinent & ≪heartless≫. Eliza ought not, strictly speaking, to have shown them to us,—but Arabel over-insisted.*
   *Went down stairs.   It was necessary as to courtesy to mention
M.ʳˢ Bests book to her:² it was necessary as to conscience, not to
praise it warmly.   I managed the "betwixt & between" very dexter-*

30   *ously—I flatter myself.   "M.ʳˢ Best I was pleased both to procure y.ʳ
book & to read it"; which was the absolute fact, & civil besides.   But
M.ʳˢ Best required no one to talk about her book except herself.   She
is evidently extremely satisfied with both parties.   "I consult Lowth
<Horseley> Scott & Whitby; but they always leave me wherever*

1. A French guest of the Martins.
2. Mary Catherine Best, *An Illustration of the Prophecy of Hosea* (London, 1831).

[110]

there is a difficulty, & then I ≪have recourse≫ to my studyings &
references".[1]   So ≪those great≫ commentators (vulgarly called great)
can be ≪nobody≫ to Mrs Best!!—   This degoutè—d me.

Got home at three.   No letters.   But Mr Boyd's Greek epigram in
the paper.[2]   Very glad of it.   I am tired, & have been resting my
body in my arm chair, & my mind in Goldoni.   Read his Pamela, &
Pamela Maritata.[3]   The merit of the first, is Richardson's,[4] & there
is not much in the second, for anybody to claim!—

Tomorrow being the 1.st of September & a holiday, I ≪will≫ go
to Malvern.

Thursday.   Sept. 1.

Th'o today is the 1.st of September & a holiday,[5] I ≪do≫ not go
to Malvern, for it ≪rains≫ most past-bearingly.   If I had my own way
quite, I w.^d go, rain or shine: but, as it is, . . I will comfort myself with
Goldoni & Greek.   Will there be a letter today?   There may—& with
an account of my dear Sam,—for the arrival of the packet was in
yesterday's paper.[6]   I am uncomfortably presentimental about the
letters today: & feel the more angry with the rain, as something may
prevent my visiting my dear friend tomorrow.   I feel as if it may.

I dreamt last night that I was married, just married; & in an agony
to ＜procure＞ a dissolution of the engagement.   Scarcely ever considered my single state with more satisfaction than when I awoke!—
I never will marry: but if I ever were to do ≪such≫ a foolish thing, I

5

10

15

20

---

1. William Lowth (1660-1732), Samuel Horsley (1733-1806), Thomas Scott (1747-1821)
and Daniel Whitby (1638-1726) were all eminent theological writers and commentators.

2. The epigram appeared in *The Times*, 30 August 1831; we are indebted to the Rt.
Hon. Quintin Hogg, Q.C., M.P., for the translation given below.

EPIGRAMMA IN —

Αι, αι, των αχεων, Τοριες γε τορως τορεουσιν.
῾Ως πηλος, Πηλος τριβεται ιλυοεις.

Woe, woe, for grief, the Tories pierce like a bore.
Filthy Peel is threshed about like mud.

3. Carlo Goldoni, *Pamela*, a comedy in three acts, first performed in 1750, and later re-
titled *Pamela Nubile*. *Pamela Maritata*, also a three-act comedy, was first performed in 1760.

4. [Samuel Richardson], *Pamela: or, Virtue Rewarded*, 2 vols. (London, 1741).   This
inspired many derivative works, including Goldoni's *Pamela*.

5. As this was not a family birthday, the holiday was presumably owing to 1 September
being the opening of the partridge shooting season.

6. *The Times*, 30 August 1831, announced the arrival at Falmouth, on 26 August, of
the packet *Cygnet* with mails; she had sailed from Jamaica on 21 July.

[111]

Diary by E.B.B.

hope I may not feel as I did last night!—≪"Of such stuff
My dreams are made!—"≫[1]
Oh! I hope there may be ≪no≫ letters today!!——

No letters: & no paper also.   What can be the cause of that?
5 I am in a μαντι κακων[2] humour.   In an idle one besides: for I
have been lounging over Goldoni half the day—   ≪I≫ looked
over ≪l'avventuriere≫ onorato, & il vero amico, & la vedova scaltra.[3]
They are all very artificial, & defective in interest & unity: & ≪˄do
not show≫ much digging in the Attic salt mines.[4]   ≪I have≫ been,
10 besides, ≪...≫ wearing "my brains upon my sleeve
For Dawes to peck at."[5]
& transcribing some of his emendations into my Homer, not my Homer
the great, but Heyne's Homer, which I value so much because M:ʳ Boyd
gave it to me on his birthday.   Kidd has certainly managed his notes
15 very badly, in a straggling Barker-like ≪way,[6] ...≫ and Dawes does
not write in ≪an ...≫ interesting manner on the digamma subject.
Therefore I wont teaze myself anymore with it.   I will take the book
back to M:ʳ Boyd tomorrow, & say my say, & beg him to say his.   By
the bye, shall I go tomorrow?   Will it rain or not?—   Oh I hope
20 not!——

I wrote to Papa this morning before breakfast; & my letter was
an accompaniment to two ≪brace≫ of partridges.
Hœc hactenus!——[7]
By the bye I hate those words.   I quoted them once before———.

25 Friday. Sept. 2:ᵈ

Aspettare e non venire being one of the tre cose a far morire,[8] I
was in an expiring state until ≪9≫ oclock this morning.   Ordered
the carriage at a quarter to 8: & past 9 when I sate [sic] off!!   If I

1. *Tempest* IV.i.156-158.

2. "Prophesying ill."

3. Three of Goldoni's comedies, first performed in 1751, 1750, and 1748 respectively.

4. Attic salt: elegant and delicate wit (*RE*).

5. Following her struggles with Dawes's *Miscellanea Critica*, a play on: "But I will wear
my heart upon my sleeve | For daws to peck at" (*Othello* I.i.65-66).

6. i.e., in the manner of Boyd's friend, Edmund Henry Barker.

7. "Enough of this." (Cicero, "Epistularum ad Atticum," XVI, 6, *LCL-C*, III, 390-391.)

8. Perhaps a slight misquotation of "Aspettare e non venire è cosa da morire" (" 'Tis
death to wait for that which never comes")—Giordano Bruno, *Candelaio*, IV.i.1.

[112]

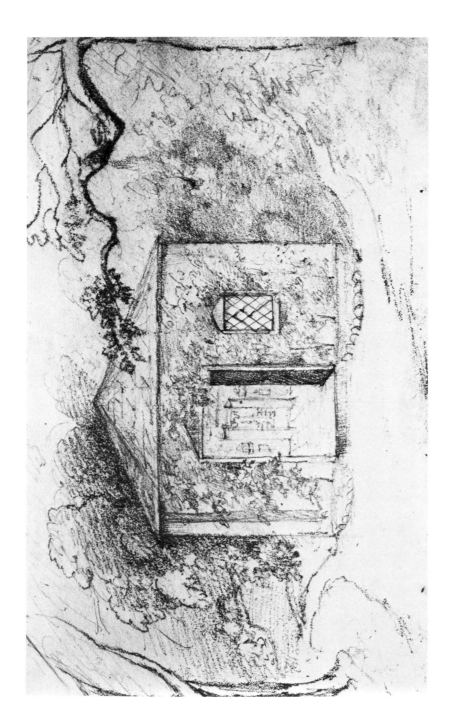

SUMMER COTTAGE, 1831

Pencil sketch by Henrietta Barrett

FROM THE SCHOOL ROOM WINDOW, 1831

Pencil sketch by Henrietta Barrett

had been Jupiter, Billy w.^d have been thunderstruck, as sure as I _was_
Jupiter!—

    Got to Malvern at breakfast time meo more.　The feminine gender
observed that they, in their joy to see me, buzzed about me like bees.
I hope there was no _humming_ as well as buzzing!—　But never mind,   5
if there ≪were≫! Mr Boyd came to the breakfast room door, to call
≪Miss≫ Boyd, & Mrs Boyd cried out "You dont know who is here!!"
After he had known it, he walked up & down in front of the house:
but I was not angry at that!　No indeed I was not,—tho' I have
memorabiliazed it!—　He knew that I always stayed & must stay for   10
a few minutes with the majority, before the minority had me all to
himself.　I went up stairs very soon to his room, & we talked on
religious subjects & several others, & I had scold the second, for running down the hill: and then we sate down to Gregory.　I read two
very long passages out of the hexameter & pentameter poem, beginning   15
Δυσμορος.¹　How happy, how _very_ happy I was, when I was reading
it! ≪†≫ A thunderstorm came, & in the midst of it, Miss Bordman.
She came to beg me to go into the drawing room that I might be protected by numbers: good generalship, Mr Boyd said, to get me away.
She w.^d have gone out of the room, but he called her back to say   20
something about the Socinians, & there she remained for a full half
hour . . I abdicated my chair <in> her favour, <ʌ& sate vis a vis to
her & the lightening!—> Now did Mr Boyd _wish_ her to stay or not?
—or was it ≪good≫ nature in the abstract, on his part?　I am a goose.

    After dinner, before desert was finaled, a message came ≪for≫   25
me from him.　I was very glad to obey the summons, & did so immediately.　He showed me over again, some of his antiquities in the
form of Editions of the Fathers.　A Gregory wh^ch will be ≪300≫
years old in 19 years—　≪A Basil≫ wh^ch will be 300 years old in
18 years.　≪Another≫ Basil edited by Erasmus—but <ʌwith> his   30
preface torn out.　A Gregory Nyssen which will be 300 y.^rs old, in
one year! I offered <ʌhim> my Rivinus (the anthologia)—² <Re-
jected>.　Carriage came at 7; & as I went away I was thanked for
≪coming≫ so often.　"I am very much obliged to you", Mr Boyd
said.　Very much obliged to _me_!!—   35

    1. "Ill-fated"; the initial word of the poem "De Animæ Suæ Calamitatibus Carmen
Lugubre" (_GNO_, II, 68-69).
    2. Andreas Rivinus, _Anthologia_ (Gotha, 1650).

[113]

Diary by E.B.B.

That Dawes was certainly born to torment me, as well as to eluci-
date the classics.   In the midst of my ≪good≫ intentions of conveying
him back to Ruby Cottage, I let him slip out of the carriage.   Ecce the
effect of reverie-ing, which I was doing all the way from home to
5   *Malvern!—   I am <₍ₐ₎a> goose—for the second time of affirming!—*
Enquired at Benbow's[1] & both the turnpikes, in vain.   Now what
am I to do?   Send to Worcester or to Papa for another copy?

    Got home at 5 ≪minutes≫ to 8.   Capital time—& good humoured
reception.

10   *Played on the guitar to please the people who asked me, till my*
voice was worn out.

    I wish I ≪were≫ going to Malvern tomorrow!———

    No letters today———

    I forget the first two lines of M.ʳ Boyd's epigram on Miss Wall,
15   *repeated to me today.   (N.B. She & M.ʳ ≪Coventry≫[2] were going*
to be married.)   Did they run this way?   (I dont mean Miss W &
≪M.ʳ≫ C)

          ≪Since of≫ all women, I aver,
          ≪None can more heartless soulless≫ be!
20   *If Coventry wont go to her,*
          ≪Why≫ let her go to Coventry!—

another—

          "Coventry weds, to please the eye"
          Her vulgar mother's heard to bawl!
25   *≪Then who can doubt the reason why≫*
          He thus delays to wed Miss Wall.

Saturday.   Sept.ʳ 3.ᵈ

    I wish I were going to Malvern again today!—   Well!   Henrietta
came up stairs to propose it,—<to propose> that we sh.ᵈ have our
30   *dinner on the hills.   But when <Bummy> was consulted, I suppose*
a veto or at least a nolo was given.   I w.ᵈ willingly go down ≪to≫
ask Bummy over again: but my motives will be ≪apprehended≫—

---

1. "The Admiral Benbow," an inn close to Ruby Cottage, (now "The Hornyold Arms";
(map ref. D8).

2. Not positively identified, but probably the Hon. and Rev. Thomas Henry Coventry
(1792-1869), 3rd son of the 7th Earl of Coventry, at this time Rector of Croome D'Abitot,
about 6½ miles east of Great Malvern, and a bachelor.

I shall be <accused> *of thinking twice of M.ʳ Boyd & once of the hills.   Guilty!*

    It is provoking of Arabel, to refuse to say one word on the subject to Bummy.   ≪She≫ might have done it.   If we go or not, I ≪will≫ at any rate, send Eaton's <catalogue> *to M.ʳ Boyd: because I promised it.   There is the dinner bell—   I hope something favorable may be said at dinner, for I sh.ᵈ certainly like to lay claim to scold the third.*

    Will there be any letters?   I hope not!—   No letters.

    I wrote to Eaton today to sacrifice my Origen[1] which I had ordered there, & to beg him to send Dawes instead, & immediately.

    Pro & conning about going to the Wyche.   My opinion of course ≪pro≫.   At last Henrietta A & I agreed to go, that I might run down with the catalogue to M.ʳ Boyd's, whereupon Bummy changed her mind & agreed to go too.   But the sight of my parcel did no good— "She w.ᵈ not have gone with us, had she for a moment thought that I meant to visit M.ʳ Boyd; & that I seemed never to go to the Whyche, without meaning to visit him".   So I acted ≪Serena≫ on the occasion,[2] & promised not to mean to visit him, but to send down my parcel instead of taking it.   It was tantalizing to see him in the road, & to remain on the walk, which I did & was good humoured besides. We walked past Essington's, & then I grew tired & ≪proposed≫ making a <session> *of it until they were tired.   They walked on to the well house, while I amused myself by vanishing.   Vanished into the fern, just above the ash seat, & was discovered by my pocket handkerchief only.   I wish Desdemona & I ≪had≫ kept our handkerchiefs in our pockets.*

    Got home at eight in the starlight, after spending a most lovely ≪evening amidst≫ most exquisite scenery.   But I was tired, wretchedly tired, & had to go to bed prematurely to save myself from being ill.   Slept uncomfortably.   Dreamt of M.ʳ Boyd, & that he was going to have the walls of his room painted after the manner of a cathedral window.

1. One of the most prolific writers and distinguished theologians of the ancient church (*c.* 185-*c.* 254).

2. In his poem "Laus Serenae," Claudian (*c.* 370-*c.* 410) tells how Serena, the wife of Stilicho, warns him from afar of a conspiracy against him, by sending letters and messages (*LCL-CL*; II, 256-257, lines 232-236).

Diary by E.B.B.

Sunday Sept. 4th*.*

Went to Church,—& neither Arabel nor I particularly well. Mr Deane's sermon was *issimo*, but not *benissimo*. Mrs Griffith invited us, & me especially, to meet Mr Corry[1] tomorrow evening, at the
5 Bartons. Refused!— Mrs Cliffe gave me the seat of her footman (thank her) behind her carriage: & she & Eliza dined here. An exposè of Miss Wall's letter. Most abusive insolent & unfeminine. I am glad I never knew her intimately.

Found Mrs Boyd Miss Gibbons & Miss Bordman at the chapel.
10 M.^{rs} B came an [sic] avant to beg me not to invite any of them to the house. Out of some hesitation, I extracted or think I extracted that Mr Boyd was ≪afraid lest≫ any superabundant attention sh.^{d} be shown by me to Miss Gibbons. Before we parted, I said to Mrs Boyd, —"Tell Mr Boyd that I am surprised at his being so *vindictive*". Per-
15 haps he may be surprised at my being so impudent. His precaution arose from a feeling which is consistent enough with human nature; but not consistent with his nature. And yet, he is mint ≪sauce≫ after all, as I told him once.

I have just heard that poor Minny's father is removed from the
20 reach of her affection & anxiety. ≪May≫ God support her! I have not seen her yet.

I have been down to see dear Minny. She <is> lying on the bed, crying bitterly. Oh! our very grief sh.^{d} console us for the loss of those for whom we grieve; seeing that while we feel its acuteness we
25 may remember "such, *they* can feel no more". And yet how hard, how impossible, to remember or to reason when the heart is break-ing!——

Monday Sept ≪*5*≫*.*th

Eliza Cliffe came here to breakfast according to the arrangement
30 yesterday; & the morning was bright for our expedition to the hills. Before breakfast, I went in to see dear Minny, whom I found much more composed & comfortable. For this, I thank God!—

Clouds coming over—a few drops of rain; but the rain ceased,— & then we set off. Bummy <Arabel> & I in the carriage; Henrietta

---

1. James Corry (1772-1848) of Cheltenham, a close friend of Thomas Moore since childhood.

& Eliza on horseback.   Before we had past Mrs Brown's,[1] on the rain came again,—& we paused under a tree, a semi-colon pause.   I was dreadfully afraid of a full stop.   But we were eloquent & Bummy persuadible; & we made our way en «avant» to the wyche; while "The rain «it» rainëd all the way".[2]   But at the «whyche», the clouds brightened up, & so did our faces: & after sending «the» horses down to Barnets,[3] we proceeded with our veal pye, much faster than ministers are doing with the reform bill.   Encamped a few yards above the ash,—

& laughed & ate, laughed & ate,
Laughed & ate & laughed again—

As the silver «knives» & forks could not be left without protection, I took them under mine, in my slipping down to Ruby Cottage. Turned to the left hand side instead of to the right, as soon as I had past the Ruby gate, & elicited notes of admiration from Mr Boyd & Miss Boyd who were walking in front of the house.   Miss Boyd could not imagine to whom my black figure belonged, & had some doubts as to my being "a spirit."   A black spirit!   How infernal I must have looked!   Mr Boyd w.^d go into the house, tho' I was hypocritical enough to remonstrate a little.   A very little,—for I felt in my secret soul that if my remonstrance had had any effect on him, all my philosophy w.^d have had no effect upon me.   But I went in to the breakfast room for a moment or two, before I was summoned to his room.   It was about three I suppose when I arrived at Ruby Cottage, —& I stayed until six.   Mr Boyd had his dinner at his usual hour— Until then we talked; & after then we read.   Read a <poem> of Gregory's which has been translated by Mr Boyd, beginning πολλακι;[4] & began another, beginning Γαια φιλη.[5]   The former is fine.   I was very very happy as I was reading both of them! † <An> explanation of his vindictiveness on Sunday.   No vindictiveness in the case.

5

10

15

20

25

30

1. Mrs. Brown was the tenant of Cummins Farm, a little more than a mile east of Hope End, on the road to Barton Court and Malvern (map ref. E6).

2. Cf. the Clown's song, *Twelfth Night* V.i.375ff: "For the rain it raineth every day."

3. Joseph Barnett was the tenant of Winnings Farm, about ¾ mile from the Wyche, on the Ledbury side (map ref. D7).

4. "Often"; the opening word of Carmen V, "Conqueritur de Suis Calamitatibus" (*GNO*, II, 73-75).

5. "Beloved land"; the opening words of the poem, "Ærumnas, Suas Luget, Christumq: Obsecrat" (*GNO*, II, 76-77).

Diary by E.B.B.

I thought it <u>could not</u> be! But Mrs Boyd's manner being a mystery, was a raiser of doubts. He objected to their going to Hope End, <u>only</u> on account of the intrusive appearance such a visit might have.

Mrs Boyd came into the room, to tell me that she meant to search
5 *over the hills for my party, and ask them to drink tea ≪ ₐwith her!—≫ "Why sh.^d you ask them?" said Mr Boyd. "I hope they wont come". After ≪she had≫ gone, there was some kindness of manner thrown away, in the ≪fear≫ that he had "hurt or offended me, by what he had just said with so little premeditation." I assured him ≪of≫ my*
10 *being in no degree hurt or offended. Began an elaborate apology for Arabel, who has not once called on Mrs Boyd since they settled at Ruby Cottage—but it w.^d'nt do: I saw that plainly. I was telling him about Miss Wall's Bacchanalian letter, when Arabel & Eliza came for me. He shook hands with Arabel, at "their exits & their entrances"[1]*
15 *—& did no more. Not one word, did he speak to her. We stayed only a few <minutes>—& then our good bye was said. "Must you go so soon?" he asked me!— I promised to go again <u>so soon</u>!*

I forgot to mention that Miss Bordman came previously, to say that as Miss Gibbons was <u>not</u> going to drink tea with Mr Wood, M.^{rs}
20 *Boyd w.^d <u>not</u> send to my party. She fancies or rather penetrates Bummy's dislike to Miss G. Mr Boyd asked what Miss Bordman said to me. My answer was, "Something that will relieve <u>you</u>". "<Re- lieve> <u>me</u>! what is it? are you going to sleep here tonight?" I <liked> to hear him say <u>that</u>. Indeed <u>all</u> his manner ≪ . . . ≫ was <u>all</u>*
25 *kindness ≪ . . . ≫ today: & I felt convinced from the beginning to the end of it, that my absurdities towards him, & his regard for me, were very great. Not that his regard & friendship are equal to mine. But as long as there <u>is</u> a reciprocity, I have no right to expect an equality, —and that he really has a real regard & friendship for me, I feel sure*
30 *—at least today!———*

Arabel is angry at his silence to her; but I persuaded her not to <u>speak</u> her anger at home. Foolish, that silence was! I ≪will≫ speak to him about it, whenever I see him next. He & I feel very differently upon some points, & this is one; that when people about whom I dont

---

1. *As You Like It* II.vii.139-141:

> All the world's a stage,
> And all the men and women merely players;
> They have their exits and their entrances.

[118]

care, neglect me, I never <u>*think*</u> *about their neglect.   Now* <u>*he*</u> *certainly does not care much whether he sees Arabel or not; and yet he not only thinks about her neglect, but takes the trouble of avenging it. Besides she never intended any degree of neglect or incivility, to any person at Ruby Cottage.* 5

≪*Miss Bordman goes to M.ʳ Davidson's tomorrow, for ten days!—*≫

We got home at eight, & sent an escort to Mathon with Eliza.   A delightful day.   ≪ . . . Food≫ for dreams!—

Tuesday, Sept.ʳ 6.

≪*Dear Minny is much better.*≫ 10

I have been unwell all the morning.   Nota bene, never eat <u>*new*</u> *honey.   Lay in bed nearly all day, in consequence of that nota bene not having been noted yesterday.*

A letter from Papa to Henrietta: and—thank God for it,—a happy satisfactory letter.   He is perfectly recovered from the effects 15 *of his late attack, & is in good spirits, & does not talk of returning. Bummy is in hopes that he may be "doing something"; indeed she feels "sure that he* <u>*must*</u> *be doing something."   I wont—≪I≫ dare not trust myself to, hope for* <u>*more*</u> *than a respite!—*

Perdidi diem[1] ≪*—*≫ *if reading Goldoni's Il cavaliere e la Dama*[2] 20 *does not redeem it, which I <suspect> it does not!—   ≪*<u>*Mind!*</u>*≫ The honey is to have the blame of ≪my≫ doing what Titus did!—*

Wednesday Sept. 7.

Wrote a note to M.ʳ Boyd about the direction to M.ʳ Bohn, & about Papa's letter—[3] *No letters from anybody.* 25

I began to consider Romans, as M.ʳ Boyd desired me to do.   I ≪ . . . ≫ read <ₐalso> a little of Isocrates.   ≪ . . . ≫ An invitation from the Martins to Bro & Henrietta, to go with them down the Wye.[4] *Henrietta was heroic enough to resist; & was* <u>*good humoured besides,*</u> *as I say of myself sometimes.* 30

1. See fn. 2, p. 74.   2. Comedy first performed in 1749.

3. For the letter, see Appendix I, p. 285. Henry G. Bohn, a London bookseller, had advertised (in *The Times*, 2 September 1831 and other issues) a catalogue of "above 4,000 articles of the first quality, in every department of literature, . . . Among the black letter and Aldine editions are many that have never before been heard of, . . ."

4. A river that rises in Wales, and flows west of Hereford, to join the Severn near Chepstow. Large stretches of it are renowned for scenic beauty.

Diary by E.B.B.

Thursday. Sept 8.

Bro left home at 7 this morning, for the purpose of going down the Wye; but we hear that the rain has kept him shooting at Mr Biddulphs— I dare say he will go tomorrow. I hope so, if it will give
5 *him pleasure. For my part, I should like to go down the Wye, but I w.^d choose my company, & not choose the cold formal ≪commonplace≫ Miss Biddulphs, who have no sympathy in their voice countenance or conversation, with the wild graceful varrying excellences of nature. Mr Martin is a clever man naturally; but ≪I w^{dnt}≫ go with*
10 *him; he is rugged & unpoetical. Mrs Martin has some sensitiveness as well as sense; but I w^{dnt} go with her—because . . . because, we dont amalgammate. Mr de Marizet is a clever agreable man,—&, I hear, admires me, which is a sign of abundant judgment—but he is French, & essentially unpoetical I dare say. At least as I know nothing to the*
15 *contrary, I am reasonable in believing so—so I w^{dnt} go with him. Mr Boyd!— <Yes. I> sh.^d like that very very much—if he c.^d see!!—*

I think I sh.^d like to go down the Wye with that fair Damsel who accompanied Thalaba on his last voyage—and then as
20 ≪*Our*≫ *little boat fell rapidly*

Adown the river-stream,
if she said to me with her "melancholy smile"

"Wilt thou go on with me?"
my answer sh.^d still be "I will go on with thee"—[1]

25 *What dreaming all this is!— Well! after all, I am as likely to go down the Wye with Thalaba's Damsel, as to go down the Wye at all!———*

<Poor> Bro & the King! How it does rain!—[2] *Was it a fine day on the last corronation?*[3] *If it were, I wish Fate had changed*
30 *the days. Never mind! Our patriotic monarch has sunshine within;*

1. Robert Southey, *Thalaba the Destroyer*, 2 vols. (London, 1801), II, 290-292.

2. This was the day appointed for the coronation of King William IV. *The Literary Beacon,* 17 September 1831, pp. 44-46, in an eye-witness account, said of the weather: "Bless my heart! what a shower! what a soaker for the thousands of jackets, exposed at this moment, to its pitiless pelting! . . . I wonder what part of the ceremony is going forward, the national anthem I should think, and the people must be shouting 'On us be pleased to pour—long may *it reign.*'..."

3. That of King George IV on 19 July 1821. *The Times,* 20 July 1821: ". . . add to all this, that the weather had become settled, the sun rose in unclouded majesty, nor was it possible to select any day more favourable for any national commemoration or rejoicing. . . ."

which the "other <sceptered> thing" could *not* have had!— ≪A letter from M*rs* Boyd to answer mine to M*r* Boyd, & desire me to write to Bohn.≫

Dawes was born to plague me, as well as Bentley.[1] He has just arrived from Eaton, & may go back again if Eaton will take him; for Dominic announces that the lost book is found!— Eighteen shillings for nothing—except for the consciousness of having deserved to lose ≪them≫!

I have been hard at work all day, reading & meditating on the first eleven chapters of Romans. D*r* Adam Clarke is wrong, I ≪think≫, about "the whole creation", & wrong about "who shall separate us from the love of Christ."[2]

The close of the 5*th* chapter, strikes me strongly as it has done before, as favoring the doctrine of general redemption. Why should any body of Christians struggle to deny it? Is it not enough, that redemption is by *free grace*,—& *only* of God who showeth mercy? <I> cannot believe that the christian church will ever have a united opinion on some passages of Romans; and if my opinion of those passages sh*d* ever become clearer & more decided than it now is, I could not look upon ≪Christians≫ who differed from me, less as brethren than I now do.

Guitaring <in> the evening, for Bummy. I have <sighed> to go to Malvern tomorrow. It wont do!—Lane wants the carriage, that he may consult D*r* Garlick![3]—and the clouds besides!!— ≪I wrote to M*r* Bohn.≫

Friday. Sep*t* 9.

Lane has gone—so I shall not go! That is quite clear!—

Bro did not return last night. We therefore conclude that the

1. Presumably the Bentley of Worcester who conducted the auction of the Hope End crops, and who provided the ticket of admission for the Walls' party, whose visit so much angered E.B.B.

2. In *The Holy Bible, . . . with a Commentary and Critical Notes, Designed as a Help to a Better Understanding of the Sacred Writings*, by Adam Clarke, LL.D., 8 vols. (London, 1810-25). His commentary on the interpretation of Romans viii.19-25 and 35 was very lengthy. In brief, he held that the restoration of creation to a state of happiness, the subject of verses 19-25, related only to the Gentiles, rather than to a general redemption. Verse 35 he interpreted as relating to the severance of Man's love of Christ, rather than vice versa.

3. Dr. William Bennett Garlike (1756?-1841), of Melton House, Great Malvern, described as "a physician of great eminence" in *A Description of Malvern* [by Mary Southall], (Malvern, 1822), p. 10.

Diary by E.B.B.

Wye party proceeds this morning; & as the wind has changed, & the clouds are more scattered, the probability is greater «than» it w^d. otherwise be.

    I have been thinking over Mrs Boyd's letter yesterday. It certain-
5 *ly does strike at the most sensitive part of me <$_\wedge$(wherever that is)>, that M^r. Boyd sh^d. write to me only <u>when</u> he is obliged, & only <u>what</u> he is obliged—that he sh^d. not even answer my letters, but commission another person to do it!—and yet when I am with him, how can I doubt his regard for me? Sometimes <$_\wedge$it> is actually & altogether*
10 *impossible to do so: and if it is so sometimes, why not always? Can «a» person's feelings ebb & flow in the course of two or three days? It seems evident to me <u>sometimes</u>, that to have me with him is «his greatest» happiness—or at least a very great one: and yet he grudges to write the few lines which he <u>knows</u> will give <u>me</u> happiness!—*
15 *Well!—I cant understand it!—*

    I have been considering the Romans again today. I think that the 8th chapter <u>must</u> be <u>spiritually</u> understood—& that the 9th does not necessarily convey any doctrine of particular election. May God grant me more light & «clearer» knowledge. «. . .»
20   *I have made up my mind to go to Malvern tomorrow—if I can by any means. I want to talk to M^r. Boyd about Romans—, & a hundred other subjects!—& I want to <u>see</u> him besides!— I made a motion to the effect that there sh^d. be a party on the hills tomorrow, while we were gathering mushrooms on Coome hill. The ayes had*
25 *it——*

    Think of Bro coming home, without going down the Wye. Adjourned sine die, because the clouds looked glum!— And now they are looking as bright with sunshine, as summer ever saw them looking. Stupid people!—

30 *Saturday Sept. 10th. †*

    We did not get away from Hope End until nearly half past ten, which provoked me: but, oh shade of Marcus Antoninus, be it known to thee, that it did not put me out of humour. Henrietta was on the high horse <u>literally</u>; & Arabel & Bummy & I in the wheelbarrow,
35 *having a basket of sandwiches & puffs under our immediate chaperoneship— Sent the horses down to Barnets,—& walked along the «right» side terrace. As soon as we arrived at the spot above M^r.*

[122]

*Boyd's house, I & a little basket of grapes & geranium cuttings began
our descent, by slipping.   I got safely thro the first gate, when two
little black & white dogs with open mouths, began to chase me,—&
I, ≪tho' I≫ had never seen Diana, fell into a fright.   I trembled from
head to foot, when I got into M.ʳ Boyd's house.   Was soon sent for by*　5
*M.ʳ Boyd, who told me that he had fancied the probability of my
arrival today.   I always like to hear that.*

*I had scarcely begun to finish Γαια φιλη¹ when M.ʳ Addison²
arrived, & Miss Boyd, as a consequence, came into M.ʳ Boyd's room.
So then we were interrupted; & M.ʳ Boyd asked her to read the news-*　10
paper to him, during which time, I sate dumbie.

*She need not have stayed so long in the room as she did; but that
was not M.ʳ Boyd's fault—nor mine.   Finished the γαια φιλη.   Nothing said about my reading any more—which disappointed me!—
M.ʳˢ Boyd came in to the room to give the weather a good character,*　15
*& to propose M.ʳ Boyd's going out.   I <seconded> her proposition.
No!—he w.ᵈ not go out until after dinner.   After dinner—before
after dinner, a message came to me—"As soon as I had dined, M.ʳ
Boyd wished me to go to his room".   Dined as soon as I could, à
fortissimâ.   Talked about the Romans,—& agreed about the close of*　20
*the 5ᵗʰ chapter seeming to lean to the general redemption doctrine—
& agreed & disagreed on some other points.   He asked me to read with
attention the 17ᵗʰ of John, & the ≪commentary≫ of Chrysostom on
some verses in Romans, & to beat Gregory's cover a little, on the
subject of election.*　25

*To be sincere with myself, today was not so pleasant & happy a
day, as many, I have spent with M.ʳ Boyd.   He does not——but I
will not!——   I forgot to say that I observed to him—"So you
were determined to be vindictive after all"—   "What do you mean?"
"[sic] I soon told him what I meant—that I alluded to his reception*　30
*of Arabel the other day!—   She did not, when she came for me, go
into his room,—for which she is not to blame, in my opinion.   M.ʳˢ
Boyd & Miss Boyd walked up the hill with us, & accompanied us
even to the Wyche.   Got home at ten minutes past seven.   I am*

---

1. The poem she began reading with H.S.B. on 5 September.
2. Believed to be William Addison, surgeon, of Great Malvern, author of *A Dissertation
on the Nature and Properties of the Malvern Water* (London, 1828).

Diary by E.B.B.

*tired, & not in very good spirits.   I <am> very extravagant both in
my expectations & feelings!——*

Sunday.   Sept. 11th.

A controversy between Bummy & me, on the subject of my go-
5   *ing to church.   Feeling convinced as I do, that the gospel is not
consistently preached there, & that my time can be more usefully
& scripturally occupied at home, am I right in going?   I think not;
but there was so much thunder & lightening about it that I yielded
the point.   "Very goodnatured & amiable of me," perhaps Bummy*
10 *thought; for she kissed me with a smile: "Very weak & wrong of
me" I doubted,—≪for her≫ kiss & smile did not give me as much
pleasure as usual.*

*Met at church, the usual concourse, the Miss Biddulphs & M^{r.} de
Marizet among them.   He spoke to me of Lamartine.   Mrs Martin*
15 *held my hand in her's in an affectionate manner, which I liked.   An
affectionate manner certainly does go to my heart which is itself far
too affectionate!—   Far too affectionate! Oh I feel <u>that</u> whenever
I feel pain; & almost <u>ever</u> when I feel pleasure.*

Mrs Cliffe Mrs Best & Eliza & <u>Eliza's niece</u> dined with us, & went
20 *afterwards to chapel: Eliza drove me down in the wheelbarrow, &
gave me in the way, Miss Wall's last letter to read.   There is something
in Miss Wall's impetuosity, which I like, because (what a very bad
reason:) ≪it≫ resembles my own: and if she had less coarseness of
mind, I could even like <u>her</u>.   She is very angry with my expression*
25 *regarding her own conduct here—"I w^d. rather that it were done <u>to</u>
me than <u>by</u> me"; & thinks that ≪there≫ was a want of delicacy in
my making use of such an expression to her friend.   Well! the subject was not introduced by <u>me</u>; ≪&≫ when it was introduced before
<ₐme,> tho' I said those words, I said no others.   My own heart*
30 *knows that I w^d. not stand between friend & friend; <ₐor wound
the ear of one by the accusation of another,> for the gain of a great
good—, far less for the gratification of a petty malice! ≪ . . . ≫ I am
sorry that I said even those words; tho' Eliza had previously spoken
with more severity of the person they referred to, than was conveyed*
35 *by them—I am very sorry!*

*We met Miss Gibbons at the chapel, & ≪after≫ the service was
over, she & I talked together a little.   She spoke to me really with*

kindness. Mr Boyd on one side, & Bummy on the other, <restrained>
me; or I w.^d have asked her to go to the house. Now I almost wish
I had done so, in spite of everybody.   I hope she did not think me
unkind for _not_ doing so: because her manner to _me_ is far from being
undeserving of a kind return.   5

Mr Curzon's sermon was shorter than usual.   He grew very pale &
could scarcely terminate it: but we c.^d not persuade him to allow himself to be taken to Ledbury in either our carriage or Miss Gibbons's,
notwithstanding his indisposition.

Read Chrysostom, & extracted from him—for Mr Boyd!   The   10
bible besides, ≪as≫ usual!—

No letter today.

Monday Sept. 12.

Mr Jefferson[1] came to breakfast that he might shoot afterwards.
It is very extraordinary: but I never was acquainted with a _young_   15
man of any mind or imagination—except Mr Knowles. I do _except_
him.   They went out to shoot afterwards: & B, H A & I had the
honor of their company at dinner—that is to say they talked while
we ate. A disagreable kind of non-sympathy. We went to the Cliffes,
nearly as soon as they went to the cricket match.   Found the Cliffes   20
gathering mushrooms.   Mrs Best & I with linked arms, not souls,
talked about her future & ≪past≫ publications. An amiable, not an
interesting, not a very superior woman.   I asked her opinion of the
general redemption doctrines.   She seemed to ≪me≫ <to> have
undecided & indistinct opinions on this subject.   She <ᴧseems to>   25
≪believe≫ that all _may_ be saved; but that the blood of Christ was shed
only for those who _are_ saved.   Her little girl is a delicate intelligent
little thing which I could love.   She ≪wishes≫ to die, as Alfieri did
at her age!—[2]   Got home in the dark, at least with no more than

---

1. Not positively identified, but from other references apparently a friend of Allen Cliffe.

2. Count Vittorio Alfieri (1749-1803), Italian dramatist, recorded in _Memoirs of the_
Life and Writings of Victor Alfieri, 2 vols. (London, 1810), I, 11: "When about five years
of age, I was reduced to the last extremity by a violent dysentery.... I knew not then what
death was, yet I anxiously looked forward to it as the termination of my sufferings. I had
heard it said, when my youngest brother died, that he would become a little angel." E.B.B.
enlarged upon his death-wish in her "Poets' Record":

> Only five suns had met Alfieri's sight,
> What time, with shrinking soul, he loathed the light—

Diary by E.B.B.

a quarter of a moon,—but such a soft ≪moonlighty≫ air!   You know—, I mean, I know—, it is possible to feel, as well as to see the moon.

The Greek testament was all the Greek which I read today.

5   *Tuesday.   Sept 13.*

So Sam came home in an irrational unchristian state, from the Cricket match last night!   Henrietta heard him carried up stairs, & was very much frightened.   Neither he nor Bro appeared at break-
10 *fast; for Bro went out to shoot, & he went to Mathon—& the farther he goes the better.   Henrietta is very very angry, & threatens not to speak to him for a fortnight, which w^d. be, in my opinion, both wrong abstractedly speaking, & impolitic.   ≪Nobody is immaculate; &≫ young men are more inclined to a fault of this kind, than to many others: & our <sulleness> w^d do no more good in ≪such a≫ case,*
15 *than Xerxes's whipping did to the ≪ . . . ≫ sea.¹   I hate sullenness, whether it be the quality of the offended or offender.*

I read parts of scripture with reference to the Calvinistic contro-versy, & little else today.   I am going thro' all the epistles, marking with my pencil every expression that seems to glance at or against
20 *the doctrine of ≪particular≫ exclusive election.*

Five feeble steps, his tender feet had taen
On earthly paths—he sighed to turn again!
Sad child! no toy, no boon, his prayer would crave,
But one—to slumber in his brother's grave,—
Down in the silence & the dust to lay
His rosy brows, & let them fade away—
And while, thro' life, for life, the croud is sighing,
To learn the best that Life can give— —by dying!
For oft his brother's angel seemed to spread
Celestial ringlets on his midnight bed,
Leaning, with smile as soft as moonshine, o'er
Those folded eyes which viewed the earth no more,—
And beckoning light from glory left behind,
And murmuring words like music, but more kind—
"Thy world is dark & cold! Oh come & be
A playmate in our happy Heav'n with me!
Our land of wings & song,—where they who sighed,
Sigh not, and tears, except of joy, are dried!
With *thee* I cannot linger. While I speak
The air of sin & sorrow pales my cheek—
Fast comes my breath, & stiff my pinions lie—
Another hour—this heart may learn to sigh!
Oh brother, leave thy dark cold world, & be
A playmate in our happy Heav'n with me! ["]

(From one of two autograph manuscripts at Wellesley; this version not previously published.)

1. See fn. 1, p. 38.

Wednesday Sept 14.

Agreed—that we are to drink tea with the Peyton's this evening. A bore; but more tolerable than if we were to drink tea with them tomorrow, when my dreams lead me to Malvern.

Comparing scripture with scripture. <Reading> besides Self con- 5
trol[1] which Henrietta has borrowed from M.ʳˢ Martin. It is formed on the model of Clarissa Harlowe;[2] but the heroine is more immaculate than even Clarissa, & more happy finally!— The book is well-written & interesting. ≪A≫ combination of fortitude & delicacy always interests me in a <particular> manner. 10

B H A & I to the Bartons! Met there M.ʳ Allen Cliffe & M.ʳ Jefferson . . again!! I wished to hear M.ʳ Allen Cliffe dissert on the Dublin university that I might report him to M.ʳ Boyd. No! he w.ᵈ abuse my picture, until my hopes of his entering on another subject, were gasping! They were rediviva! After a little while, I had an 15
account of the Bishop's examination, prior to his ordination. "What is the meaning of the word catholic?" "What is the meaning of the word paraclete?" "I have heard a high character of the Dublin Uni-sity with regard to Divinity: and you justify it".

Flagrant!—— Abominable! If any ≪thing is≫ "justified", it 20
is M.ʳ Beverley's opinion![3]

Well! M.ʳ Cliffe talked on—& called Homer "rigmarole"& "stupid stuff",—& expressed an opinion, that "any stupid fool c.ᵈ be an elegant classical scholar" while a degree of "ability" was requisite for the mathematics. <ₐI have heard a low opinion of the D university 25
with regard to the classics; & he justifies it!—> I observed (how c.ᵈ I do otherwise?) that "as M.ʳ Cliffe ≪must≫ speak from observation & experience, ≪I≫ was quite convinced & ready to admit ≪the≫ <ₐfact of> all the classical scholars of Dublin University ≪being≫ stupid fools" 30

M.ʳ Cliffe is no exception to my general observation on young men. Vide September the 12. He rode with us to our gate. Half past ten, when we got home: & I employed the last moment of my

---

1. [Mary Brunton], *Self-Control: A Novel*, 2 vols. (Edinburgh, 1811).

2. The heroine of [Samuel Richardson's] *Clarissa; or, the History of a Young Lady*, 7 vols. (London, 1748).

3. Robert Mackenzie Beverley (1796?-1868), who had published several pamphlets attacking the corrupt state of the Church of England (see fn. 3, p. 133).

Diary by E.B.B.

*sitting up to speak of going to Malvern tomorrow.   Well received by
everybody.*

Thursday Sept. 15th. †

  I had a note on Tuesday from Mrs Boyd, to desire me, from M^r
5   *Boyd, to take with me on my next visit, Chrysostom's commentary
on the Romans.   Chrysostom Ann & I set off at about half past
eight, & arrived at Ruby Cottage before their breakfast time.   Miss
Bordman did not go yesterday.   I sate & talked with her & Mrs Boyd,
& Miss Boyd on her appearing, until Mr Boyd's message summoned*
10   *me.   "Why how did he know of her being here," said Mrs Boyd.
"I told him",—answered Miss Bordman.   "And why did you tell
him? You who pretend to wish to have Ba with you?"   "I did not
think he w^d send so soon for her."   "Why you know that he was sure
to send immediately, when he knew of her being here."*

15   *Now I was pleased to hear this: and yet why sh^d I be?   He sent
for me, because he thought that I should be <u>annoyed</u>, if he did <u>not</u>
sent [sic]. Perhaps <u>that</u> was the reason!——*

  *I wonder why they all like me so much at Ruby Cottage—I mean,
why Miss Boyd & Miss Gibbons & Miss Bordman like me ≪so much.≫*
20   *It is always so!——   I am liked most by those whom —— —— but such
reflections are "vainest of all vain things".   Went up to Mr Boyd.   "Is
that <u>you</u>, Porsonia?"   I read to him out of Chrysostom's commentary, & we agreed in ≪the saint's≫ heterodoxy about original sin.
Then I read a passage from the poem beginning δυσμορος; a passage*
25   *<relating> the vision of Holiness & Temperance.¹   It has beautiful
lines,—but is not a beautiful passage—at least not particularly so.*

  *Miss Bordman came into the room, to say good bye.   Mr Boyd
seemed sorry to say it to her.   Well! if he likes her, that is natural; &
it is natural that he sh^d like her.*

30   *He went to his bedroom, & when he came back, observed to me
—"I was thinking in the other room ≪how fortunate≫ it is ≪ . . . ≫
(I am afraid only <u>fortunate</u> was the word, or perhaps <u>happy</u>) that I am
able to bear your voice.   For if your voice had been in that particular
key which I cannot bear, I never c^d have associated with you."   "I*

---

1. Δυσμορος: "ill-fated"; the initial word of the poem she began to read on 2 September.
The passage of which she speaks occurs at lines 277 ff.

[128]

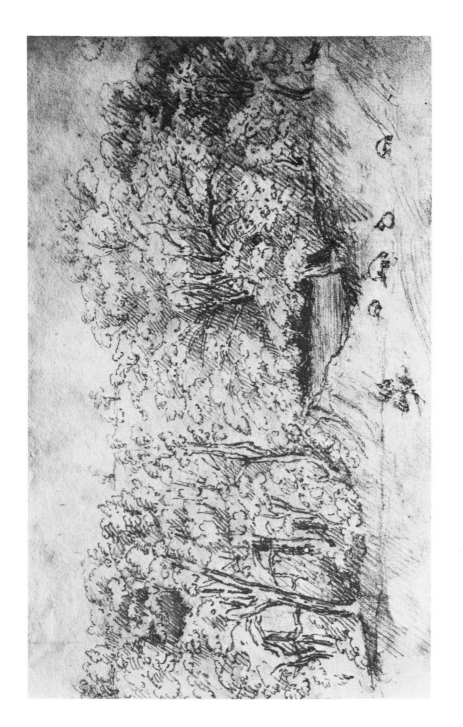

VIEW OF THE UPPER POND, 1831

Pencil sketch by Henrietta Barrett

HOPE END: VIEW FROM THE DEER PARK

Water-colour by Philip Ballard

HOPE END: VIEW FROM THE LOWER POND

Water-colour by Philip Ballard

am very glad it is not. I certainly sh^d not have liked to have been told on my _∧first> visit to you, that you did not wish me to visit you again." "Oh I ≪w^d≫ not have done it then. I ≪w^d≫ have tried two or three times, ≪if I≫ could bear your voice,—& if I could not have borne it, I ≪w^d≫ have told Mrs Boyd to tell you about it." Just as he told Mrs Boyd to tell Miss Gibbons about not coming into his room!! Oh! if I had thought—if I could have thought ≪at that time≫— Am I another Leila? Am I destined to associate with snow?————¹

That is too strong. I did not feel ≪so strongly while≫ he said it; & I ought to consider now that Mr Boyd's organs are in a very excitable state, & that it ≪does≫ not _∧lie> in his inclination, to controul & calm them. But still, when he was aware of the possibility —nay, of the probability, of not being able to endure my voice, he sh^d not have urged me to go to see him in <the> manner he did, four years ago. And above all, to speak of making Mrs Boyd the instrument of turning me away!————

I was kept down stairs at dawdling dinner, for more than an hour & a half—& sate with Mr Boyd only half an hour afterwards.

I called at Mrs Trant's for a few minutes, which were Procrustianized into twenty by Dominic's nonsense. Because I asked him the cause of his high spirits—, he <accused> me of "fishing for a compliment"; & I had to assure him that I was neither accustomed nor necessitated to earn compliments by the sweat of my brow. Then he began to insist upon my lending him Mr Boyd's Chrysostom for two or three days. I yielded like a saviour of the capitol.²

Got home in time for tea, & found Mr Bohn's catalogue, directed to E B Barrett Esqr, waiting for me!—³ No letters. ≪Bro was at the Hereford M M today, by the help of dear Bummy's ticket.⁴≫

1. Taken to be a reference to her own lines in *Leila: a Tale* (London, 1913), p. 15:

> He only shook his silv'ry locks of snow
> With smile that half reproach half kindness meant,
> Gazed on her laughing brow, and blessed her as he went.

2. i.e., like a goose—the legend being that the sacred geese saved the Capitol by cackling when the invading Gauls reached the ramparts (*RE*).

3. *Catalogue of a Very Select Collection of Books English and Foreign Offered . . . by Henry G. Bohn* (London, 1831).

4. The Hereford Music Meeting: the third and last day of the 108th Meeting of the Three Choirs of Hereford, Gloucester and Worcester, held under the patronage of the King to benefit the widows and orphans of the clergy of the three dioceses.

Diary by E.B.B.

Friday—Sept 16.

I wrote a letter to Papa,—& a note to Mʳ Boyd ≪containing the≫ *palinodia* of my folly in lending Chrysostom to Dominick.¹   He may be angry with me; for I am sure that he *can* be angry with me, if I give him cause.   I forgot to <memorabilize> his idea of sending to the Times newspaper, a letter upon 'οι πολλοι;² & his having written to Mʳ Davidson on the subject.   He can write to Mʳ Davidson!   But with regard to sending a letter to the Times Newspaper, he thought of what I had once said, & that I might not like it.   I said—"never mind *me*".   No! if *he* does not mind, the probable consequences of publishing ≪such≫ <∧a> letter in the Times—never mind *me*!!

As we were going out to drive today, Mʳ Martin intercepted us with an invitation to drink tea at Colwall.   So we drove round by Mʳ Deane's, down the rough road, where we found a pure cool look-ing stream & washed our hands in it,—& arrived at Colwall before six.   <∧I wish I cᵈ have washed my hands of *that*!—>   Mʳ de Marizet left it today.   ≪A≫ <still> life evening, which ended by Mʳ Martin walking home with our carriage.   ≪No letters≫

Saturday.   Sept 17

Today's account, will not end as yesterday's did.   And yet, it is possible that ≪there≫ *may* be no letters.   No letters.   I have been reading the new Testament with its comparative evidences, today, all day.   I cannot—the word is correctly said—I *cannot* make up my mind from Scripture, to do otherwise than embrace the ≪doctrine≫ of general redemption.   Perhaps the *cannot* may be reversed some day; and yet how is it possible to understand otherwise than I do at present, the latter verses of the 5ᵗʰ chapter of Romans; <tho'> Mʳ Boyd's argument on the 'οι πολλοι, is ≪certainly≫ rendered null & void by the occurence of that expression in the last verse of the second of the Second Epis: to the Corinthians.³

Maddox came, which is the beginning of a pleasant dream; namely that I ≪shall≫ go to Malvern with her on Monday.   Shall I?   *Can I?*

---

1. For the letter to H.S.B. see Appendix I, p. 286.

2. "The many."

3. II Cor. ii.17: "For we are not as many [οἱ πολλοί], which corrupt the word of God: but as of sincerity, but as of God, in the sight of God speak we in Christ."

Sunday.   Sept. 18.

Went to church with B & A in the wheelbarrow.   If this were likely <u>to last</u>, I w.^d not go; and as it is, I am not clear—indeed I am afraid I <u>am</u> clear, that I am not doing right.   But my disposition is a yielding one.   I have a constitutional dislike of all contention; & therefore I suppose I prefer contending with myself, to contending with other people . . because I am weaker than they are.

On the road, Bummy observed, "Most likely, you are preparing for your journey on Monday."   She had penetrated, not heard of, my dream about Maddox.   Yes! I see that I <u>can</u> go.

A better sermon from Mr Dean, than any I had ever before listened to, from <u>him</u>.   Mrs Cliffe & Eliza accompanied us home, because Mr Allen Cliffe excommunicated them from his congregation.   Bro & Sam <u>w</u>.^d belong to it, & heard a very decent discourse on <u>responsibilities</u>.

<u>We</u> went down to our gate, where Mr Moens[1] was Mr Curzon's substitute.   "The Lord is my salvation."[2]   He is a converted Jew; & his sermon was most touching & interesting—& made the tears come into my eyes more than once.   The simplicity which is in Christ, is in this disciple of Christ.   There is something irresistibly winning in his very manner.   Dear old man!—   He met Papa in London, two months _∧ago,> on the <morning> on which he heard of the death of dear Mary; ≪ . . .≫ & walked with him for more than two miles. "Blessed are the dead", he exclaimed when telling us of this meeting, "who die in the Lord; for <u>they</u> rest from their labours."[3]

≪This evening≫, Henrietta proposed inviting Mrs Griffith to drink tea here tomorrow,—upon which, Bummy insisted on my returning from Malvern sooner than I sh.^d otherwise do!!   I was annoyed & said so—& even refused going at all, in the case of my being obliged to come back, by anything else than darkness.   Henrietta need not have asked M.^{rs} G tomorrow,—nor, if she had asked her, need <u>I</u> have been forced to receive her company.   But the point was yielded at last—of course by <u>me</u>!—   Not much to yield, after all.   No letters.

5
10
15
20
25
30

1. Not identified.

2. Psalms xxvii.1: "The Lord is my light and my salvation; whom shall I fear? the Lord is the strength of my life; of whom shall I be afraid?"

3. Rev. xiv.13: "And I heard a voice from heaven saying unto me, Write, Blessed are the dead which die in the Lord from henceforth: Yea, saith the Spirit, that they may rest from their labours; and their works do follow them."

Diary by E.B.B.

Monday. Sept. 19. †

Off at 8 in the morning, with <Maddox>—after have [sic] tea'd
& bread & buttered with her & Minny.   Intercepted by Dominic &
Henry, who wanted me to breakfast at Mrs Trant's, & talked a great
deal of <u>native</u> nonsense—Dominick especially.   He accused Henry of
making use of his ideas in conversation,—which, thinks I to myself,
≪accounts≫ for Henry's nonsense.   Breakfast at Ruby Cottage not
begun; but Miss <u>Boyd</u> met me at the door,—& Mrs Boyd ran down
stairs in a flannel dressing-gown & nightcap, to hold communion with
me on the subject of Mr Biscoe's distresses.   Annie does <u>not</u> love him,
& <u>therefore</u> is not worthy of his love.   If I were a man, & had a
heart, I w.^d not covet the possession of her's—Oh! <u>no</u> <u>no</u>! Mr Boyd
≪sent for me≫ twice, before Mrs Boyd released me from letter read-
ing & her bedroom.   When I went to him, & explained <my> deten-
tion, he regretted . . not that it <u>had happened</u> at all, but that it had
not happened later in the day; <u>because</u>—no very flattering reason,—
the earlier he heard Greek reading, the better ≪he≫ liked it.   I am
making an anachronism.   ≪This≫ observation was not made until
<after> he was shaved, during which operation, I was of course ex-
iled!—

He showed me his Benedictine edition of Gregory.[1]   It is in high
preservation, & very beautiful.   I will get one like it, whenever I have
next the use of Fortunatus's purse[2]—or any purse, heavy enough.
He allowed me to read a part of the Apologetic, out of it <_∧(from
τουτοις εγω συνειμι[3])>; a high privilege, granted on solemnly enforced
conditions of not leaning my arm on any part of <_∧any> page.   I
liked & admired much of what I read.   I do like & admire Gregory's
prose!!—& I <u>enjoy</u> reading a beautiful style so much the more, when
I can read it <u>with</u> one who enjoys it too—when I <_∧can> read it
with Mr Boyd.

1. Subsequently given to E.B.B., it appeared as Lot 717 in the 1913 Browning Sale;
(*Sancti Patris Nostri Gregorii . . . Nazianzeni . . . Opera Omnia, Quæ Extant . . .* Vol. I,
Parisiis, 1778).

2. Fortunatus possessed an inexhaustible purse and a wishing cap; both he and his sons
were eventually ruined by these magic gifts (*RE*).

3. Τούτοις ἐγὼ σύνειμι: "With these [thoughts] I am occupied." A marginal note by
E.B.B. in *WG*, p. 30, records: "I read from this place with Mr Boyd. Sept. 19th 1831." and
indicates that the reading continued to the foot of p. 32 (112 lines). Another note in *WG*,
at the commencement of the "Apologeticus," records this as being "a very fine passage."

Because he went out of the room for a moment, Miss Boyd came in,—& when <u>he</u> came in, he hinted rather broadly I thought, that she sh.^d go out. "Sister". "What?" "Oh I only wanted to know if you were in the room <u>still</u>".

When her exit had taken place—,"What was my sister talking to you about?" ≪ . . . ≫ "She was praising the old fashion of cutting trees into peacocks & towers,—& <she> was abusing Samson Agonistes".[1] "Abusing Sampson Agonistes!! But did she not notice my Gregory?" "No! she did not". He was <u>not</u> angry with me for ≪the rape≫ of his Chrysostom, by D[ominick] T[rant].

5

10

We talked & discussed a good deal about the Romans,—& he agreed with me, not altogether I think, about <u>them</u>; but that the 'οι πολλοι must be yielded ≪up.≫ I <u>think</u> that he likes to agree with <u>me</u>. I am <u>sure</u> that I like to agree with <u>him</u>—particularly on religious subjects!— And yet the desire of agreeing with him, <u>never</u>, as far as I know myself, <u>never</u> <u>did</u> or <u>could</u> occasion any change or modification of those opinions of my understanding which are independant of my inclination,—least of all on religious subjects! We were only an hour at dinner!! How prestissimo. Milo c^d not have been longer dining, than Mrs Boyd ≪is≫![2] Mr Boyd sent for me before we had quite had our deserts. Glad of it. He lent me Beverley's pamphlets,[3] which I took away with me at six—intended to be a quarter past five. Billy's <u>apologia</u> was, that clocks are different. So are tempers. I may get a <u>scold</u> when I get home. Called for a moment at Mrs Trants, to ≪take≫ Chrysostom. Interrupted the finale of their dinner, & was importunated to stay. Dominick & the Grand Duchess Helena![4] He is growing very forward; & gliding into a taste which is most unmanly & ungentlemanly—that of ≪exciting≫ confusion of countenance, in

15

20

25

1. John Milton, *Paradise Regained. A Poem. In IV Books. To which is added Samson Agonistes* (London, 1671).

2. Milo, an athlete of Crotona, who is said to have eaten the whole of a four-year-old heifer (*RE*).

3. The entry of 21 September makes it clear that these were *A Letter to His Grace the Archbishop of York, on the Present Corrupt State of the Church of England* (Beverley, 1831) and *The Tombs of the Prophets, a Lay Sermon on the Corruption of the Church of Christ* (Beverley, 1831), by Robert Mackenzie Beverley (1796?-1868).

4. The Grand Duchess Helena (1807-73), daughter of Prince Paul of Württemberg and sister-in-law of Czar Nicholas I of Russia, had been staying with a numerous suite at Cheltenham. The *Gloucester Journal*, 3 September 1831, recorded that she had made an excursion to Malvern Wells and Little Malvern on 29 August. Unfortunately, we do not know the no doubt scurrilous story that caused so much mirth when relayed to Arabel later in the day.

order to enjoy it. *There was an impertinence in his manner today,*
which was quite intolerable,—& which my want of presence of mind
made me suffer from, more than I sh.ᵈ have otherwise done. *It is*
provoking ≪. . .≫, that such a fool as Dominick, should have made
5 *me feel confused even for one moment: want of presence of mind*
is my comet "which from its horrid hair, shakes" (& has shaken)
<several> annoyances.¹

Found M.ʳˢ Griffith & Charlotte Peyton,² among the arrivals—
and only half past six—& tea only just gone in—& everybody in
10 *good humour.* *My hair was wet, & M.ʳˢ G. pigtailed it with my*
pocket handkerchief. *Very fine effect, I have no doubt!*

Told Arabel about the Grand Duchess & D T,—& made her
laugh until there was a bedquake.

Tuesday. *Sept. 20.ᵗʰ*
15 *So Bummy has agreed to join M.ʳˢ Cliffe's pic nic today; & so I*
am to go!— Heigho!—

B A & I set off in the wheelbarrow; H & Sam on horseback, &
arrived safely at the wind's point.³ M.ʳˢ Cliffe & Co had begun their
ascent, but Eliza returned to be our co. *I mounted Henrietta's "high*
20 *horse", & Sam took the bridle,—& when we had overtaken the other*
squadron, M.ʳ Allen Cliffe took the bridle, & talked very . . uninterest-
ingly, until we had topped the hill. *Glorious hills! How finely they*
seemed to overlook the great expanse, as if they exulted in their own
beauty. *But the wind blew away all reverieing! I got off the horse,*
25 *& ran about a little in my allegro style, until dinner was ready.* *The*
exposè of Henrietta's lamb & tarts, threw her into an embarras! *The*
union between England & Ireland w.ᵈ affect her much less!— Si sic
omnia, I sh.ᵈ have been sick, instead of eating my dinner.

---

1. John Milton, *Paradise Lost* (London, 1667), Bk. II, lines 706-711:

> . . . on th' other side
> Incenc't with indignation Satan stood
> Unterrifi'd, and like a Comet burn'd,
> That fires the length of Ophiucus huge
> In th' Arctick Sky, and from his horrid hair
> Shakes Pestilence and Warr.

2. Mrs. Griffith's granddaughter, Charlotte Lea Peyton (1813-1842), the eldest of the nine Peyton children.

3. Wynds Point, on the northern slope of the Herefordshire Beacon, about 2½ miles E.S.E. of Hope End (map ref. E7).

[134]

M.ʳ Davis[1] who with M.ʳ C & Sam, made our trium*virate*, may be in love with Eliza Cliffe, as she seems to wish—, but I hope he will never be in love with me.   They say he is clever.   He may know something of antiquities, & something of many things besides; but as to his being a clever man, I cry you mercy!———

After dinner my high horse, & Eliza my leader, took me up to the summit of the Herefordshire beacon.   Nota bene.   The Worcestershire side is finest!!   What with the rain & wind & height & sight, I grew altogether inebriated,—& after leaving the "high horse"; to Sam's guidance, began to run & slip down to the bottom.   Quoth M.ʳ Davis to Sam, "What immense spirits your sister has."!—

≪Ah≫ if he knew!—   But I felt then, as if I were ten years old, & as if that were my birthday!

We were rained upon until we took refuge in M.ʳˢ Clarke's cottage[2] —& there we remained until our hair & stockings were dry.   The excitement had gone off, & I felt quite exhausted!—   Got home, where we found M.ʳ Jefferson who had breakfasted with us & shot with Bro.   After tea, music began.   I glided off to bed <ₐat eight,> ≪. . .≫ unwell with overfatigue.   These kind of things do not agree with me.

I read only until twelve today.   I wish I had stayed at home, tho' I did enjoy about ≪. . .≫ an hour of the time, when we were on the H beacon.   With a few abstractions, the party w.ᵈ have been pleasanter. As parties go, it was very well.

Wednesday Sept. 21ˢᵗ.

Very unwell—could scarcely get down stairs, my legs trembled so much.   On going into the dining room, a ≪note≫ was given to me from M.ʳˢ Martin, praying me to meet her at the gate, & accompany her, together with Bummy, to Bromesberrow.[3]   I felt so unwell, that I negatived the proposal,—& this set B's combustible particles on fire.   ≪. . .≫ She spoke crossly to me,—& I who was on the very verge of hysterics, & required only a finger touch to ≪impel≫ me

1. Not positively identified; possibly the clergyman at Cradley, a story about whom E.B.B. recounted to H.S.B. (letter of [30 May 1831], *EBB/HSB*, pp. 138-139).

2. Not identified.

3. A village about 5 miles S.S.E. of Hope End.   Mrs. Martin's friend Mrs. Hill, wife of the Rev. Charles Hill, lived there (map ref. J6).

Diary by E.B.B.

*forwards, burst into tears, & had that horrible dead precursive feeling
all thro' my hands & feet.   But I made an effort—a great effort was
really necessary—& got <over> it.   I dare say Bummy thought it
was all humbug.   Indeed from her cool manner to me from morning
to night, I have no doubt that she actually thought so.   But what c.^d
I do!?   I lay down on my bed after breakfast, because I c.^d scarcely
sit up—<and> yet when time drew near for us to meet Mrs Martin,
I sent Henrietta in to Bummy to carry my palinodia.   I w.^d go, if she
wished it.   No!—it w.^d not do.   If I did not feel equal to it, she
wished nothing of the kind—, so she & Henrietta went instead of
me.   In the meantime, I read Mr Beverley's pamphlets which Mr Boyd
had lent to me; the letter to the Archbishop of York, & the Tombs
of the prophets.—   They are clever & forcible; coarse enough, &
in some places too highly colored.   For instance, I do <u>not</u> believe
that the body of the established clergy are as much opposed to the
reading of the scriptures, as the papistical clergy are; and I <u>do</u> know
instances of members of that body, refusing the sacrament to persons
of immoral character.*

*I read besides a good deal of ≪Lamartines≫,—second volume
of Meditations poetiques et religieuses.[1]   Inferior to the first.   He
certainly Procrustianizes.   ≪ . . . ≫*

No letter today again.   How very extraordinary it is.

Thursday.   Sept. 22.^d

*The Jackdaw has torn one of the leaves of my Heynes Homer, the
Homer which Mr Boyd gave to me on his birthday.   And why did he
tear it?   Because Georgie ventured to take the book into the schoolroom, & without asking my leave.   Georgie <∧was> scolded of
course.   I had the philosophy not to cry.*

*Well!   I have tried with gum & Ann & philosophy to make the
best of the torn leaf.   If it had but been a book which Mr Boyd did
not give me!——*

*I heard Storm & Georgie double reading lessons of fifty lines
each, out of Homer & ≪Euripides≫, on account of their idleness*

1. E.B.B. has confused titles. The quotation given on 23 July comes from Lamartine's
Méditations Poétiques, but the poems named in the entry of 23 September prove that she
was now reading volume two of *Harmonies Poétiques et Religieuses*, 2 vols. (Paris, 1830).

yesterday: and for my own study, I have been reading Isocrates—
his panegyricus still!—

    A letter from Papa to me!   Very kind & very cheerful—but he
has not heard yet from Sam!   I wish he had heard, or could hear!—
Not a word of the Hope End business; & Bummy & Henrietta augur   5
most favorably from this silence.   I am a μαντις κακων.[1]   *At least I*
think that if any happy change of circumstance had taken place, Papa
w^d. have told us of it; and I think it is foolish to look so exclusively at
the bright side ≪that our≫ eyes are blinded to the darker side where
our way may lead!   May lead!   That is putting it in the softest   10
language.   Probability says, will lead.

    M^r. & Mrs Martin called here today—& I was called down to
them.   Mrs M. said, she hoped that I was recovered from my real
and imaginary fatigue.   I answered that there was nothing imaginary
in my fatigue, but I was recovered.   15

    This has been Bummy's report.   Not kind in her; but I will take
no notice of it.   It is not worth either irritating or being irritated
about.   ≪Sam H & A rode to Gt Malvern in the evening.≫

Friday.   Sept 23.

    I mean to go to Malvern tomorrow, if I can peaceably, & obliging-   20
ly.   Finished the ≪Panegyricus≫, at last.   What is the reason that I
have been able to dawdle over it?   There must be some reason.   A
long passage near the end, has a great deal of eloquence, & vivida vis
besides: and the general style is very flowing & beautiful.   In general,
perhaps, more flowing than glowing—which may account for my   25
"reluctant indolent delay".[2]   *Another thing which <∧materially>*
≪blunted≫ the edge of my interest, is, ≪ . . . ≫ my deficiency in
historical information.   This I really must correct.

    Read some more of Lamartine.   He is certainly verbose, & apt to
mistake "≪words≫ that burn" for "thoughts that breathe".[3]   *There*   30

---

    1. "Prophet of ill."

    2. This quotation has not been traced. E.B.B. may be misquoting Milton's "Yielded
with coy submission, modest pride, | And sweet reluctant amorous delay" (*Paradise Lost*,
ed. cit., Bk. IV, lines 310-311).

    3. *Odes by Mr. Gray* (Strawberry Hill, 1757), Ode I, III, 3, p. 11:

        Bright-eyed Fancy hovering o'er
        Scatters from her pictur'd urn
        Thoughts, that breathe, and words, that burn.

*is much lengthiness together with much picturesqueness & <u>Goldsmith</u>,
in his mille, ou la terre natale; but le tombeau d'une mere, is perfectly
exquisite.*[1]   *I read also some of Shelley—the whole of his Queen
Mab as extant "free from the objectionable passages."*[2]   *It is not in*

5   *my opinion, written in the highest vein of poetry; & it is dull & heavy.*

<So> *Bummy has agreed (for me & herself) to drink tea with
the Martins tonight, that we may escort Henrietta home, who after
driving out with Mrs Martin is to dine with her.   I made no objections,
tho' I had several, ready made.   Mushroom hunting; & hair curling*

10   *preparatives.*

*Dull evening at the Martins; & for a fitting peroration, Henrietta
asked Mrs Martin to dine here tomorrow at five oclock, after having
driven her out at twelve.   All over, then, with my drive to Malvern.
I am better than c^d be expected.*

15   *Saturday Sept 4 [sic, for 24].*

*Henrietta went out to drive at twelve oclock with Mrs Martin.   I
heard the boys read Greek—& Latin on account of Bro being at
Worcester.   By the bye, I hope he may bring home my shoes & combs
& Theophylact.*[3]

20   *I wonder if Mr Boyd is expecting me; & if he will be disappointed
at my not coming!——*

Shelleys <u>Adonais</u> (the Elegy on Keats) is perfectly exquisite.[4]
Oh! it is <u>so</u> beautiful!   He walks in Bion's footsteps,[5] *& thinks about
Adonis, evidently; but who would quarrel with ≪an≫ earthly piper*

25   *for imitating the music of the spheres?   Shelley was one of the Θεοι
παρεδροι,*[6] *without any doubt.   Finished Lamartine who is a poet
too—tho' he is a frenchman.   <u>Can any good poetry come out of</u>*

1. Lamartine's *Harmonies*, ed. cit., "Milly, ou la Terre Natale," II, 19-38; "Le Tombeau d'une Mère," II, 101-106.

2. The poem was originally published in 1813, but E.B.B.'s reference is to *Queen Mab, or the Destiny of Man*, Revised Edition. Free from all the Objectionable Passages (London, 1830).

3. Eleventh century Archbishop of Achrida, known for his theological commentaries, modelled on those of St. John Chrysostom.

4. *Adonais: an Elegy on the Death of John Keats* (Pisa, 1821).

5. Bion of Smyrna (*fl. c.* 100 B.C.), best known for his *Lament for Adonis*, which E.B.B. translated and published in her *Poems* (London, 1850), I, 191-198.

6. "Those sitting near the gods."

Paris?— My answer today is quite a different one from what it w.^d
<have> been a year ago.[1]

Mrs Martin—yes! & Mr Martin,—came to dinner; & afterwards
I talked to the latter, about the pleasure of writing letters.   It _was_ a
pleasure to me! And indeed, while my dear Papa is away, it _is_.   What   5
is the quia of Mrs Martin icing me all over, as she undeniably does?

She & Henrietta were at the Moneys[2] today.   They say that
Eugenia is almost pretty, & quite agreable.   Mr Martin went away
sooner than he liked, on account of M.^rs M's influencing influenza.
I forgot to speak of my having been attrappèed today by ≪Messrs.≫   10
Davis & Allen Cliffe, who were deputed by Eliza to search our books,
for the model of a triumphal chariot.   It wd.^nt do; but to make them
amends for their walk, I showed them my Homer the Great.   I almost
admired _them_, for their admiration of it.

Sunday.   Sept 25th.   15

Went to Church, & took the sacrament.   I wish the sacramental
service were shortened, & weeded of its expressions "holy mysteries"
&c.   What mystery is there, can there be, in this simple rite?   Are
there not many <ʌweak brethren> who shrink back from ≪holy≫
mysteries, ≪and≫ <ʌwho> w.^d hurry on with a trembling joy to "do   20
this in remembrance" of their Lord?[3]   Blessed Lord Jesus!   Thou
who art the strength of the weak, strengthen _my_ heart—& let the
remembrance of ≪Thee≫, outlast, within it, ≪the affecting≫ rite
which I, in my unworthiness, performed this morning.

The Cliffes dined here as usual.   Afterwards we waited more than   25
half an hour at the chapel where no Mr Moens appeared.   Returned
disappointed, & _not_ wet; tho' the wetness seemed the more natural
& probable consequence of our expedition.   I hope it ≪may≫ be
fine tomorrow, at least until I get to Malvern.   When I do get there,
it may rain newfoundland dogs & Tom Cats,—≪& be≫ welcome—   30
if ≪any≫ rain ≪c.^d≫ keep me there.

1. In her letter to H.S.B. of 8 August [1829?] she had said: "The French have no part
or lot in poetry. I am more and more convinced that they have _none_" (Weaver, p. 400).

2. The Rev. Kyrle Ernle Money and his family. He was Prelector and Prebendary of
Hereford Cathedral, and Vicar of Much Marcle, about 8 miles S.W. of Hope End.

3. Luke xxii.19.

Diary by E.B.B.

So Bro met Mrs Boyd yesterday, & she complained of my not going to Malvern!

No letters. How it is raining!—

Monday Sept 26th.

5   A splendid day; as if earth as well as Heaven were all sunshine.
Breakfasted in the nursery; & off to Malvern before ≪eight≫ oclock.
Called at Miss Steers's, with Shelley's poems. Could'nt get in on
account of her being unwell, & not up. Mrs Boyd, whom the sound
of my chariot wheels, disturbed, emerged in her flannel robes to the
10 top of the stairs, & ≪received≫ me very graciously indeed. But after
talking with me a little, in her bedroom, she dismissed me into the
drawing room, not into Mr Boyd's room—because, she said, he was
breakfasting!— In a few minutes however, I was permitted, to try
to be admitted. "How do you do, Mr Boyd". "Why Porsonia! can
15 that be you?" "Did you not know of my being here?["] "No! to
be sure I did not. Have you been here long?" And when I explained
about the breakfast, he remonstrated with me for delaying going in to
him on ≪$_\wedge$such an≫ account. I was glad to hear that remonstrance.
Well! we talked a great deal, principally on religious subjects—, &
20 I read to him some passages from St John's gospel referring to the
doctrine of Election & perseverance. He told me of D^r A Clarke's
remark, in a sermon of his, on one of those passages. "Yes!—No
man can pluck ≪His sheep≫ out of ≪His≫ hand—but they may slip
≪thro' His≫ fingers". Very unscriptural—& not very ≪reverent≫.
25 We read another passage from Gregory's Apologia—not a very
fine one. Then we read the exordium of The Orations against Julian.
It is majestic—μεγαλοφωνοτατος.[1]

Mr Boyd walked out a little with Miss Boyd; but when Miss Boyd
returned into the drawing room, I did not immediately return into his
30 sitting room, because she brought me no message from him. There I
sate for a quarter of an hour—twenty minutes—& no message came.
I was beginning to be offended, when Mrs Boyd proposed my going
to him. "W^d he not send for me, if he wished me to go?" "No! it
is disinterestedness that prevents him from sending". So I went, &
35 found Mr Boyd beginning to be offended too. "He had shortened

1. "Grandiloquent."

[140]

*his walk on purpose that he might hear me read on: he thought that
I liked reading.   I knew that he had gone out only for exercise,—&
therefore it seemed unnecessary to him that he sh.ᵈ send a message
to me, when I c.ᵈ not be ignorant of his having returned".[1]   Then I
was "sorry that he had shortened his walk on my account." ≪Then≫
He "certainly liked walking; but he liked hearing me read too".   Not
very flattering—<I> was obliged to be satisfied.   "Since my return,
I have been amusing myself in making observations on you,—on the
manner in which you have arranged my books.   You certainly are
the most careless creature about books, that is possible."[2]*

*† After our long Milonian dinner, he went out again.   M.ʳˢ Boyd
walked out with him then.   What can be the reason that I am never
asked to walk out with him?—   I should like very much to know;
and yet perhaps it is as well that I do not know it.   Ah! It is that,
that I fear!——*

*We talked till the carriage came which it did at half past five; &
M.ʳˢ Boyd drove with me to nearly the bottom of the great hill.   The
last time I was there with her, was the first time I met M.ʳ Boyd!—
So Miss Bordman returns on Wednesday!—& has sent her "very very
best love" to me.   It must be a mere orientalism,—& I do not like
orientalisms.   I have heard too many of them.*

*At the chances pitch turnpike, I met the three youngest little Pey-
tons, & took them up in the carriage, & put them down at ≪Barton≫
Court door.[3]   Berry Peyton is a dear interesting little child,—but
woe unto me for making her my company; inasmuch as M.ʳˢ Griffith
came to the door & sent by me to Bummy a message about our drinking tea with her & meeting the Biddulphs there on Friday.*

*Commended generally, on my arrival at home, for coming home
in such good time.   Too good time—if I am commended for it!—
The last occasion in the world, on which I would practise works of
supererogation.*

1. In the manuscript, opening quotation marks are repeated at the commencement of each new line of this passage; we give only the initial and final quotation marks.

2. We also omit the lineal repetition of opening quotation marks in this passage.

3. Returning to Hope End from Ruby Cottage by the southern route (i.e., by way of Little Malvern, avoiding the Wyche) one left the Chances Pitch Turnpike some six hundred yards south of Barton Court. Excepting the newly-born baby, the three youngest Peytons were Charles William (b. 1823), Elizabeth Rosetta (b. 1825) and Eliza Berry (b. 1827).

Diary by E.B.B.

Henrietta has been to the Commelines[1] with Mrs Martin, during my absence; & Bro, shooting partridges with Mr Martin. We compared notes of happiness—& each of us contended for the prize. Surely <u>I</u> was happiest!—

5 *Tuesday Sept 27th*

I wrote this morning to my dear Papa; that my letter might go with 2 brace & ½ of partridges. No letters in return. Composing a Greek song, for an air to the guitar. I rather like the <u>ideas</u>; but the <u>harmony</u> has been torn to pieces, by ≪my≫ looking first to the
10 <u>musical measure</u>, & next to the poetical measure. "How <u>happy</u> could I be with <u>either</u>"!²—and how unsuccessful with both. <u>Reading</u> besides. Mr Boyd lent me Dr Clarke's Sermon "What shall I do to be <u>saved?</u>"³ which I <u>began</u>. By the bye, I <u>thought</u> yesterday that I had let it fall out of the <u>carriage</u>. If I had, I ≪would≫ have taken Sappho's
15 leap of forgetfulness.⁴ ≪Perhaps I sh.^{d} have taken it, <u>before the loss!</u>—≫ Singing on the guitar, in the evening.

Wednesday. Sept 28th.

Wrote to Miss Price, because Bummy wanted me to write to Sir Robert⁵ & enclose a letter for her. Hearing the boys—and now; it is
20 agreed that we shall go to the Wyche!— Shall I go anywhere <u>below</u> the Wyche!— How happy I should be if I could! But no—I must not mention it; & if Bummy mentions it, she will be very good natured, & I — — very glad!—

---

1. The Rev. James Commeline, his wife, son and two daughters had been on friendly terms with the Barretts from their earliest days at Hope End. He was Vicar of Redmarley D'Abitot, 6 miles S.E. of Ledbury (map ref. K6). He later "unhappily fell asleep while reading Horace in bed & was burnt to death" (unpublished letter dated 8 March 1889, from George Moulton-Barrett to Robert Browning: Collection of Edward R. Moulton-Barrett, Esq.).

2. John Gay, *The Beggar's Opera* (London, 1728), p. 35, Air XVII, sung by Macheath:

How happy could I be with either,
Were t'other dear Charmer away!
But while you thus teaze me together,
To neither a Word will I say.

3. Adam Clarke, *The Doctrine of Salvation by Faith Proved; or, an Answer to the Important Question, What Must I do to be Saved?* (London, 1816).

4. Her supposed jump into the sea from the Leucadian cliff, in consequence of her advances having been rejected.

5. Miss Price's brother, Sir Robert Price (1786-1857), Member of Parliament for the County of Hereford 1818-41, and for the City of Hereford 1845-56. He succeeded to the baronetcy upon the death of their father, Sir Uvedale Price, in 1829.

*Rain came on—& thunder & lightening besides,—so there is no
going. I read some of Dionysius Tractatus de priscis scriptoribus.
Not Dionysius's really, I suppose—& not very interesting.*

Thursday Sept 29th

No letter again. I have been reading, Iphigenia in Aulide, for the 5
*first time. The opening is very un-Euripidœan—which I think Porson
observes in his ≪Prœlectio≫, but I forget his observations upon it.[1] A
cloudy sunny looking day—like my disposition. Bummy A & I set
off in the wheelbarrow, to go somewhere—perhaps, to the Wyche;
but the rain began at the Barton corner, & we were obliged to turn our* 10
*backs on the hills. Found Mrs Cliffe & Eliza & Mr Allen Cliffe at
home, when we arrived there. They did not stay ≪long≫.*

Friday Sept 30th

*Oh that party at the Bartons. "Ahi dolente parti— ... ta!"[2]
I must go to it, so I may as well make up my mind gracefully <as>* 15
ungracefully. The Peytons! The Biddulphs!!—

*I wont go out of the house before six, at any rate. The drive
there, & the talking there, will be exercise enough for one day—so
let me get on with Iphigenia.*

No! I did not get on much with her. I read a great deal of St 20
*Luke instead, & examined the 53^d of Isaiah ≪for≫ πολλοι[3] according
to Mr Boyd's desire expressed in a note from Mrs Boyd. I wrote to
her, with her & Miss Gibbons's bonnets which I thought it best to
send: and she, in her reply, speaks of Miss Bordman's return, & of her
own agitation in consequence of ≪a≫ letter received from Mr Biscoe.* 25
What can that letter say? She does not say.

*The carriage went backwards & forwards with our party to the
Bartons; therefore I of course made a point of going in the last carriage-
full. Arabel & Sam & I, were lightened upon in the hollow way—
which frightened me nearly as much as the sight of the tremendous* 30
assembly in the Barton Court drawing room, of Biddulphs, Brights,[4]

---

1. Richard Porson, *Prœlectio in Euripidem Recitata in Scholis Publicis Cantabrigiœ
MDCCXCII* (Cambridge, 1828). On p. 9 he observed that the opening of *Iphigenia in
Aulide* is in the manner of Sophocles.

2. "Oh rueful party!"   3. The word occurs in Is. lii.14, but not in Is. liii.

4. The Bright family from Brand Lodge.

Diary by E.B.B.

*Cliffes[,] Peytons! I talked a little to two or three people, ≪of≫
whom little Fanny Peyton[1] ≪was≫ by <far> the most agreable. I
wish Berry had not gone to bed——or I wish I had gone there with
her!—— What a pity it is ≪that some people≫ sh^d take more pains*

5 *about covering their intellects than their shoulders!—— Got home
tired, & unanimous in every part of me, body mind & heart, that
what is called "going out" should be called "the greatest bore in the
world".*

There was a letter from my dearest Papa today! & to me! He

10 *speaks of having heard of, not from, poor Sam, who describes himself in a letter to some Captain as being "low in body & mind". Somebody however, who has seen him, assures Papa that he is looking,
tho' thin, better than c^d be expected. He ought to have written
to Papa!— Papa, dear Papa, <u>seems</u> in good spirits, & writes most*

15 *affectionately— May God bless him.*

<Saturday> Oct. 1st

*Pheasant shooting of course,[2] —& two brace & a half, & a hare,
sent down to be packed up for London: & that is not of course; but
very "good sport". I hope Bro will give me a brace for Mr Boyd.*

20 *By the bye, I had dreamt of going to see <u>him</u> today; but Mrs Biddulph
woke me, by asking Henrietta to dine with her,—& Henrietta will
want the carriage.*

*After all Henrietta wants no such thing. She is to go in the
other, with Bro & Sam—& Bummy A & I, I believe, are going out*

25 *to drive. B proposed it herself. Perhaps we shall go to the Wyche;
perhaps I shall go . . but I wont go to sleep again. Bummy wrote a
note to Papa today, & she has been telling me its object—namely to
enquire about Papa's plans & circumstances, in order to ascertain
whether or not she ≪may≫ be free to return to the north & receive*

30 *Charlotte [Butler]. She says that if Papa's circumstances remain <u>as</u>
<u>they were</u>, she will not on any account ≪leave≫ us, even to receive
Charlotte. Dearest Bummy!— I told her that Charlotte has the
first claim upon her—but I could not say it without tears in my eyes.
I do not wish her to sacrifice any pleasure, <much> less so great a*

1. Frances Maria (1820-1900), the 2nd daughter and 4th child of the Peytons.
2. This was the opening day of the season.

one, to our comfort—but I could not relinquish that comfort, the comfort of her society—, without pain.

What will Papa's answer be?— My hope of any change of circumstance, is very very faint indeed!— Bummy's seems to be strong!—

I have finished Dr Clarke's Discourse. It is very clever: but as all metaphysical discourses on scriptural subjects, must be,—seeking only to convince <ʌthe human reason,> it is unconvincing. At least this is true of one or two material parts, where even I have detected fallacies. Dr Card's sermon on the Athanasian creed,¹ is bound up <in> the same volume; & I have read it. How could Mr Boyd praise it, as he has done!— "Impressive eloquence"! unimpressive verbosity!— "Convincing reasoning"! No reasoning at all! "An ardent zeal for truth"!—An excessive dogmatism in prejudice!— There is my commentary, on Mr Boyd's!— I shall tell Mr Boyd that the only passage which I like very much, is the one which speaks in his praise!—² And that is the truth!——

Well: we have been to Malvern—& I have seen Mr Boyd!— It was a most lovely evening. The air was too good for mere human beings to breathe!— We left our carriage at the Wyche, & walked along that lovely walk to the ash: and then Bummy said "Let us turn down this way", turning down my way. We walked & walked nearer & nearer Ruby Cottage, until I began to suspect something. Thro' the gate!— ≪The≫ something was developped! How pleased I was! Bummy told me that I might stay with Mr Boyd, half an hour. How pleased I was!— Stayed for a few moments with Miss Bordman & Mrs Boyd: & then up to Mr Boyd! The room so dark, ≪that≫ I could scarcely see him: & I so unexpected, that I had to speak twice before he recognized me. He reproached me for coming for so short a time. "I w.^d rather that you did not come at all than come so late; if this visit is to stand for a longer one". But he seemed satisfied when I promised to visit him again, long measure, on Monday. He gave me something to do, in hunting the Septuagint, by the help of Cruden, for the words election foreknowledge &c: and I am to take

---

1. Dr. Henry Card, *The Uses of the Athanasian Creed Explained and Vindicated* (Worcester, 1825).

2. H.S.B. was nowhere mentioned by name in Dr. Card's Sermon, but presumably was the "learned friend" referred to in Note F on p. 41, in connection with a Greek manuscript in the Vatican.

my Septuagint & notes on white paper, to him.[1] *Suppose he were to ask me to leave the former at Ruby Cottage—with all my marginal annotations! I hope not! M.rs Boyd told me that she was to have written to me tonight, if I had not gone: (Quære—was M.r Boyd to*

5 *dictate?): and M.r Boyd told me that he wished me to spend two or three days with him. I told him that it all depended on Papa's answer to Bummy's application, which answer might arrive on Tuesday or Wednesday. I am pleased at his inviting me; & wish—how I wish —that I could go to him!— But as a presentiment once said to me,*

10 *no more! I soon said good bye, & went back to meet my party. M.rs Boyd gave me M.r Biscoe's letter, to read: to be sent back tomorrow.* †

Nearly dark when we got home. B, <A>, & I, three'd it, very comfortably. I lay on the sofa, tired; ≪&≫ B read Lord Brougham[2] *& L.d Londonderry's war & treaty of peace.*[3] *Sorry they made the*

15 *latter. The flashing of swords is sometimes agreable, . . . to lookers-on.*

Sunday. Oct 2.d

I dont think Henrietta enjoyed herself or her party last night. What was the reason? She generally does enjoy everything of that kind.

20 *I wrote a letter to M.rs Boyd: a commentary on M.r Biscoe's letter —& advice! Advice from me, who never know what is best to be done for myself!—who generally advise myself to walk into water or fire: I advised M.rs Boyd not to write to M.r Biscoe until she had ascertained <ₐthe state of > Annie's feelings respecting him: (they*

25 *will not be regarding him—) & in <the case> of their being as I suspect . . untouched,—to break off the business at once & alto- gether. ≪Sent the letter, with a brace of pheasants for M.r Boyd.≫*

No Church at Colwall. Uninteresting sermon at M.r Curzon's. He is going to lend me a book—letters on particular redemption—

---

1. Alexander Cruden, *A Complete Concordance to the Holy Scriptures of the Old and New Testament* (London, 1738). The several references given under "Election," "Fore-know," and "Foreknowledge" are all in the New Testament, not the Septuagint.

2. Henry Brougham (1778-1868), 1st Baron Brougham and Vaux, was Lord Chancellor 1830-34. Although he was a prolific political writer, it seems likely that Bummy was read-ing from *The Times* of 30 September, which summarized his speeches in the House of Lords the previous day (on Reform, *inter alia*).

3. Charles William Vane, 3rd Marquess of Londonderry, *Narrative of the War in Germany and France, in 1813 and 1814* (London, 1830).

which is "to do me a great deal of good".[1] I asked to lend it to Mr Boyd. "Yes. I am going to write to M.^{r} — —" What was the ≪name≫? "and I sh.^{d} like to have your & Mr Boyd's ≪annotations≫". "My annotations", I answered "w.^{d} be valueless." So they w.^{d}

I enquired Mr Curzon's opinion of Miss Gibbons. He enquired mine: And I said something of her vanity & selfishness, (tho' at the same time, I "liked her in several respects",—) which I have reproached myself ever since for saying. "Did Mr Boyd observe it to you: or did you observe it?" "I observed it; & it does not render her Christian character attractive." Now what business had I to say anything of the kind? If I were a Roman catholic, I w.^{d} whip myself for it. I dare say I am quite as vain as Miss Gibbons,—used to be at any rate,—& sh.^{d} still be, if ≪I≫ had had my own way. Miss Gibbons was very kind & feeling to me, in her manner at least: & I ought at least to have been silent before Mr Curzon, whose good opinion she was anxious, I know, to obtain. ＜Agreed＞ with Mrs Cliffe—I am to go to the wyche early tomorrow, & walk to Ruby Cottage; & she is to call for me at four. This will save ＜$_\wedge$me＞ ≪half≫ a crown. Not that I ＜grudge＞ half a crown: but I am obliged to ask Bro for all my turnpike money—& Papa may not like the bill. We caught a squirrel; & I claimed it.

Monday Oct 3.^{d}

† Meant to have been off at seven. Off at a quarter past 8—& B & A my convoy. A lovely morning, which I hoped w.^{d} turn into rain that nobody might be able to come for me. Found the majority at breakfast. The minority looked into the room in a few minutes, to ask "Is Miss Barrett here?" I shook hands with him. "I am going to walk up & down in front of the house for a little while". He walked there, a very little while. Went up to him, & he inspected, ≪ . . . ≫ or rather felt my Greek Bible which I had brought with me —& I read the title pages, & preface—loud out. Then we talked about election; & "Oh wretched man that I am."[2] On the latter

1. [William Rushton], *A Defence of Particular Redemption, Wherein the Doctrine of the late Mr. Fuller, Relative to the Atonement of Christ, is Tried by the Word of God. In Four Letters to a Baptist Minister* (London, 1831).

2. Rom. vii.24: "O wretched man that I am! who shall deliver me from the body of this death?"

point, he made me change my opinion. Certainly when you read the 6th chapter [of Romans], & _then_ the 7—the close of the 7th, appears to be a description of Paul in his unregenerate state, under the law. Mr Wood came in—& I went out. "I believe you are Miss Barrett".

5 ⟨"Yes"⟩ "How is Mr Barrett"? ⟨He⟩ has a more gentlemanly appearance than I had expected,—& an agreable countenance. Stayed half an hour—or nearly so— Then Mr Boyd went out to walk with Miss Boyd— Then it was nearly three, ≪at≫ which time, dinner was ordered. Then, the Cliffe's came!! Very soon Eliza interrupted

10 us. I said a few words to her, & sate down again, intending to remain in the room. But Mr Boyd did not speak—w.^d not speak. ≪It was≫ evident from his manner, that he w.^d prefer my being out of the room. So I went—of course!— Went—of course!——

Mrs Boyd & co dined, while I sate with Mrs Cliffe. They were

15 obliged to dine, on account of Annie, whom Mrs Boyd is going to bring home. ⟨M.^{rs}⟩ Cliffe & I talked of Annie. B has been saying of her, what it is unpardonable to say. I defended her with vehemence, & tears in my eyes. No use in writing down here either attack or defence—but . . I wish she were married. Married, she soon will be,

20 _I believe_: if there is faith in man—(which by the bye there isnt) for Mrs Boyd means to _permit_ Mr Biscoe to take her to India—has written to him, _almost_ to say so—& showed me the letter.

Called Eliza away from Mr Boyd, & took leave of him—rather cooly. I could not help it. He said "are you obliged to go?" or

25 "cant you stay?" or something of that kind. After all, I cannot doubt his preferring my society to Eliza's—but he does not value it as I value his.

He said to me today, "It is quite enough to satisy me if you come here yourself, without ⟨∧your⟩ sending me any pheasants." Never-

30 theless I will send them, whenever I can get them. He intends to lend me Ignatius.[1] Glad of it. I wish I had gone to Malvern today in my own carriage. For _then_, this rain w.^d have ⟨excused⟩ my staying there, for ≪a≫ night at least. One thing has very much pleased me in ≪one way—Mrs Boyd≫ consents to Annie's going to India. Now

35 if she does go, she will go in March; & there will then be no obstacle

---

1. Saint Ignatius Theophorus (_fl._ A.D. 110), Bishop of Antioch, one of the Fathers of the Church, martyred under the Emperor Trajan. Some of the _Epistles_ written during his final journey from Antioch to Rome are extant.

to Mr Boyd's staying at Malvern if we stay here, or going where we go—if we go from ≪hence≫.   At any rate the obstacles will be diminished in number.

May Annie be happy!— I am not . . & yet I _am_ . . _quite selfish._

Tuesday Oct: 4.

5

Will there be a letter from Papa today? If there is . . , what will it be—rainy or sunshiney?

I have been reading again the 6th. & 7th. of Romans. Mr Boyd is certainly right.

We are going today to Mathon.   I w^d. rather stay at Hope End. 10
And yet it is not kind to Eliza to think so; & after all I sh^d. like to see her drawing, before it is exhibited.   One oclock—we sh^d. go now if we are to go at all.

How provoked I am. Henrietta has determined not to go, because Sam will want the horse at four—or rather (the only sufficient reason) 15
because she dislikes it.   She says that Eliza Cliffe is _my_ friend. My friend!!!   As if I ever did, or c^d., or w^d., apply that word so lightly!! I never applied it to any person but one; & that person is not Eliza Cliffe.   I like her on many accounts; I am grateful to her on many accounts;—but she is not, & never c^d. be my friend!— 20

No poney caught—because either H or I was careless. B says I: I say H—of course.   Both <of us, perhaps>. So we did not arrive at Mrs Cliffe's until nearly three, too late for the drive to Colonel West's.[1]   Glad of it.   Eliza's drawing for the Worcester Exhibition, is perfectly beautiful.[2] 25

Got home at 6, or past six; & had tea.   From what Bummy said afterwards, we discovered that she had heard from Papa.   No good, from her manner. ≪My squirrel very well.≫

Wednesday. Oct. 5.

The bible meeting at Ledbury today.   Sorry for it.   It is our duty 30
to go; and some allusion _may_ be made to Papa's absence & the cause

1. The visit was postponed until 24 November.

2. The exhibition of the Worcester Society of Artists, held 19 October-26 November 1831. The _Worcester Herald_, 22 October 1831, noting the opening of the exhibition, said: "There are altogether 164 pictures, and we find amongst the exhibitors most of the principal professional artists of this city and county, as well as some talented amateurs. . . ."

of it; & this, I cannot always bear.

No painful allusion, in a very uninteresting meeting: but M.ʳ Curzon startled me by asking me to go down to his house before I left Led-bury that he might have ten minutes conversation with me. What c.ᵈ

5 *he mean to say? Papa—M.ʳ Boyd, glanced across my mind! I am so used to hear what is distressing. I went with M.ʳ Curzon. He offered me his arm, & we walked very <fast> before everybody; & when we were safe & silent in his drawing room, he showed me both Miss Gibbons's letter & his own reply to it. She wishes to be baptized—*

10 *& to come for that purpose to his house in ten or twelve days.*

His object in speaking to me <ₐon the subject>, which ≪he≫ did with every recommendation to secrecy,—seems to ≪be≫, that he is doubtful about her state—not from his own observations, but from M.ʳ Boyd's. I recanted my inconsiderate words of last Sunday—

15 *but I sh.ᵈ be sorry if any recantation of mine, sh.ᵈ seem to expose M.ʳ Boyd to any accusation of malice prepense in his charges against her. I am more interested about him, than about Miss Gibbons. There-fore I will write, I think, to M.ʳ Curzon, to explain my explanation.*

A note from M.ʳ Boyd, to desire me to consult Cruden from [sic]

20 *him, on justification, & glorification. A note indeed! Down one page; & beginning "my dear Porsonia"!— I shall be convinced at last.*

Shall we go to Malvern tomorrow. Henrietta says "Yes"; but she has agreed to dine at the Watts's, & there is sure to be a difficulty

25 *of some kind.*

Began a letter to M.ʳ Curzon.

When will M.ʳ Boyd begin & finish a letter to me?— Not until he changes, again.

≪Thursday≫ Oct 6.ᵗʰ 1831.

30 *I finished my letter to M.ʳ Curzon today, & Henrietta took it to Ledbury where she went to dine with the Watts's. My letter speaks a part of my heart with regard to my dear friend—, & the whole of my heart with regard to myself. It is not <ₐan> uncandid letter. If Miss Gibbons herself were to read it, she c.ᵈ scarcely, I think, be*

35 *very severe on me.*

M.ʳˢ Cliffe here until after one o'clock—therefore no doing any-thing meo more—except talking nonsense—≪& except≫ (the more

[150]

*agreable exception) arranging a plan for Malvern tomorrow. She is to
be with us at ten; & Miss Peyton one of our "≪pleasaunt≫ companie".
They will be my "pleasaunt companie" only as far as Ruby Cottage!—*

*Bummy read the debates to Arabel & me[1]—after I had told a
story, which Occyta did not seem to like as much as he generally
does my stories, about the sea of honey & milk & wine—, & the
prince ≪who≫ was born in the straights of Gibralter & was consequently half black & half white. That was "all out of my own head"
as Occyta says! I have a great mind to write an opposition budget
to mother goose's—<Seriously>, I may be goose enough to do it.*

*An answer from M͞r͟ Curzon to my letter. His begins "my very
dear friend". Lights make shades seem darker!——*

*<There was> a reform meeting at Ledbury today, to which all
the boys down to Henry, went. Dearest Bro spoke, I hear, very well,
& for ten minutes.[2] How I sh͟d͟ have liked to have heard him!— M͞r͟
Curzon sent the Letters on particular redemption, with his letter.*

Friday Oct 7͟th͟

*Well! It is a fine, windy day—& M͞rs͟ Cliffe not come! She thinks
I suppose all of the wind, & nothing of the fineness! Provoking!—
A message is sent to Charlotte Peyton!— It may rain tomorrow!
Provoking!— But she may come after all, for it is only just eleven.*

*M͞rs͟ Cliffe came, & then the rain came. I put on my hat, but every-
body else was reasonable enough to be prepared for a disappointment.*

*We did not go. M͞rs͟ Cliffe stayed until three or four—longer
than my patience did. Eliza at least will come tomorrow, in the case
of sunshine.*

I read on with M͞r͟ Curzon's book.

*The reform bill is sure to be thrown out ≪of≫ the House of
Lords—, & then what will be the consequences? More fatal ones,
than those of today's rain.*

*A great deal of music mending & binding, down stairs tonight,
which occasioned a most sublime confusion. My head ached with it.*

---

1. The debates in the House of Lords on 4 October, on the question of Reform. The
report of the discussion occupied 14 columns in *The Times*, 5 October 1831.

2. The *Hereford Journal*, 12 October 1831, in its report of the meeting in the Town
Hall, mentioned Edward Moulton-Barrett Jr. twice, once as the proposer of a motion, once
as the seconder.

Diary by E.B.B.

Saturday Oct: ≪8≫.ᵗʰ

    A cloudy day again. Nobody <u>will</u> go, except me; & I <u>cant</u> go. But I can & will go on Monday, that is, if I am <well>—et cœtera!——

    Mᵣˢ Martin called here with Mᵣˢ Hill;¹ a lady who seems to have
5 *too many teeth, & <ʌquite enough> ideas. ≪ . . . ≫*

    Rain again!— No going to Malvern.

    Finished Mᵣ Curzon's book, which disappoints me by not exactly suiting my case. It suits Mᵣ Curzon's better—for it is directed against Fuller's Doctrine of ≪indefinite≫ redemption² —i.e. the doctrine of
10 *atonement for <u>sin</u>, not <u>sinners</u>. The book appears to me to want compression & arrangement, & some other things besides. But I like much of it.*

    Mᵣ Hinton is not spared; nor does he deserve it.³

    No letters. Bro & Sam at Worcester.

15 *Sunday Oct: ≪9≫.ᵗʰ*

    To church, & heard a bad sermon of Mᵣ Deane's for the <u>second</u> time. Persuaded Mᵣˢ Martin to try Mᵣ Curzon again. When I had heard his text "God commended his love for us &c"⁴ I thought that all her trials were over! But she liked him <u>moderately better</u>. The
20 *Cliffe's dined with us of course!—*

    The bill thrown out! majority 41!!! What will the people do!— What will the king do? What will Lord Grey do? Resign—or make the Lords resign. ≪ . . . ≫ I am <u>afraid</u> that there will be a change of ministry—in spite of the sentence in italics in the Times newspaper.⁵

---

1. Wife of the Rev. Charles Hill, of Bromesberrow.

2. Andrew Fuller, *Dialogues, Letters and Essays, on Various Subjects* (London, 1806), pp. 233-251: "Conversation the Third: On Particular Redemption."

3. In Rushton's *Defence*, ed. cit., a note on Letter II, pp. 52-62, was severely critical of Hinton's treatise on the Holy Spirit "not long since published," i.e., *The Work of the Holy Spirit in Conversion Considered in its Relation to the Condition of Man and the Ways of God* (London, 1830), by John Howard Hinton (1791-1873).

4. Rom. v.8: "But God commendeth his love toward us, in that, while we were yet sinners, Christ died for us."

5. The vote was 199 to 158 against. *The Times*, 8 October 1831, devoted the entire issue to the previous day's proceedings in the House of Lords (23 columns to a summary of the debate; 1 column to the editorial). E.B.B.'s reference was to a sentence in the editorial on p. 4: "*There will be no change of Ministry*—the rats may assure themselves of that." The editorial also contained the sombre query: "Is any man on earth prepared to conjecture what will take place in England before this day week?"

    Charles Grey (1764-1845), 2nd Earl Grey, became Prime Minister in 1830, after the defeat of Wellington's Administration in the Commons. He had long championed the issue

But on the other hand, what Tory administration <u>can</u> carry on the government against such an House of Commons? Well!—nous verrons.

I sh^d have liked to have sent the news to Mr Boyd as he desired, & as I ≪_∧intended to≫ have done, if it had arrived on any day but Sunday. As it is, he shall <hear> everything tomorrow from <u>me</u>!— I <u>will</u> go to Malvern tomorrow. Arabel <u>wishes</u> & <u>ought</u> to go too: but her proposing such <_∧a> thing will occasion an earthquake at least, down stairs. I hope, I hope, it may not ≪do so;≫ for my sake, as well as <_∧her's &> Annie's!— Bro never wrote to Papa today!— I am fidgetted about it. Papa is sure to be uneasy & angry.

I believe, when I examine myself, that I am more than half sorry for Annie's return! When she was last at home, she made me feel <u>so</u> much pain!!— But I ought to forget <u>that</u>!— It is not remembering <u>that</u>, but <fearing> something similar to it; which makes me feel as "half sorry" as I do.

Arabel's going to Malvern proposed! Controversy on the subject —& Bummy <u>contra</u>. It wont do! It is more prudent for A to give it up, particularly as in the case of her going, B w^d be left alone.

Monday. Oct 10th

Arabel is very amiable & goodtempered. She gave up the point of going, earnest as she was about it, & not <u>sullenly</u>—for she wrote a note which I took to Annie. I did not leave home until 20 minutes past 8, intended to be 20 minutes past 7. Went by the Wyche, & found Mrs Boyd at the exordium of breakfast. Annie was out— calling on Miss Steers. In a few minutes, I was allowed to go up stairs. Mr Boyd & I talked about the Bill, until he appeared disinclined for reading. "The worst of it is, it disturbs one's mind". However we read afterwards a passage from the orations against Julian, & the one on Paschal Sunday. †

I read a passage or two to him from Rushton's book; one in particular which I thought <_∧a> satisfactory commentary on a difficult text in the 5th of Romans "For as by one man's disobedience &c."[1]

5

10

15

20

25

30

of reform, having introduced a Bill on the subject as far back as 1797. Following the Lords' vote, Parliament was prorogued, and a general election confirmed Grey's position, so there was no change of Ministry despite E.B.B.'s fears.

1. Rom. v.19: "For as by one man's disobedience many were made sinners; so by the obedience of one shall many be made righteous." Rushton's arguments on the text were developed in his *Defence*, ed. cit., pp. 94 ff.

Diary by E.B.B.

*M.ʳ Boyd said to me one or two things, which gave me pain—≪&≫
not for ≪myself≫ individually.   I cannot bear to hear him say anything which even <u>sounds</u> anti scriptural!   The tears were in my eyes
today: I could not help it—   There never was a truer friendship than
mine for him!——   Do I not pray for his spiritual welfare! Lord
Thou knowest!—   And only Thou canst know whether his heart is
right in thy sight!—*

*The opinion which he <u>tolerated</u> today, & gave me so much pain
by tolerating, was Wesley's opinion; & that Wesley was a spiritual
Christian, no Christian can doubt.   And yet, I wish he had <u>not</u> toler-
ated it!—*

*Altogether, today I had not quite a happy visit.   My doubts on
the subject of his regard for me, rose more than once into a painful
certainty.   <Others> may be more <u>worthy</u> of his regard in all ways
but <u>one!</u> <u>Not in that one</u>!!!———*

*He asked me if I had heard the result of Bummy's thoughts about
going away—& if I w.ᵈ go to see him for a few days. He seemed to
wish me to go.   But ≪the≫ "seeming" might proceed from ≪a≫
general spirit of benevolence—<u>inclusive of me.</u> Oh how I hate that
idea!!   I submitted if it were not the best course to wait & see how
matters were settled, without running the risks of displeasing Papa or
acting unkindly to Bummy!—and he yielded, after observing that by
delay, I ran the risk of the occurrence of circumstances which w.ᵈ
prevent my ever visiting him at Malvern.   He recommended to me
the policy of <u>having attention paid to Annie</u>—lest in the case of our
remaining at <u>Hope End</u>, she sh.ᵈ make M.ʳˢ B <leave> Malvern at the
end of the twelve month.   "I suppose—≪or I hope≫—that <ₐin
that case> you w.ᵈ still wish us to stay here"!—*

*Annie & Miss Boyd are two.   From what I can understand &
observe, there is some fault on both sides.   One is provoking—&
the other sensitive.*

*But I cant help blaming <u>Annie</u>!—   As she was with me in the
carriage,—for I took her in it, a little way,—I recommended a concileating manner to her! No! She w.ᵈ <u>not</u> conciliate!— She w.ᵈ
<u>not</u> speak to Miss B any more!——*

*The carriage came at <a> quarter to 5.   At 5 I went.   Nota
bene—never go the wyche road again!—   I thought that I never
should go the whole of it, last night! Such a hill!——*

[154]

≪*Annie is indifferent to poor M.ʳ Biscoe!!*—≫

M.ʳ Boyd <told> me,—when I had told <u>him</u> about Arabel's intending to visit Annie this week,—that ≪her≫ coming w.ᵈ be an excuse for me to pay him another visit in a day or two!— I wish that "universal benevolence" were out of my head.— There was a letter today from Miss Gibbons to M.ʳˢ Boyd. Her "very best love to me"—, & she wished very much "to hear from me". Now I do <u>not</u> like writing to her—& I do <u>not</u> like being unkind. What can I do!— She leaves M.ʳˢ Yorke's[1] on Thursday. Then she will be at M.ʳ Curzon's on Thursday. By the bye M.ʳˢ Boyd asked me, if she was going to be baptized, & if she had called on M.ʳ Curzon in her way thro' Ledbury. I answered evasively, "I believe she did <u>not</u> call"——

Got home in the dark. Guitaring in the evening.

Tuesday. Oct. 11ᵗʰ

Gent has gone for the letters: what will be in them? <If> Papa writes, we shall all be scolded I know, for our silence. Bro's letter to him, sh.ᵈ have gone on Friday instead of yesterday.

Today we are to dine at the ≪Martins≫. A bore!— And yet M.ʳˢ Martin lent me D.ʳ Channing's <treatise> "On the importance & means of a national Literature",[2] & I ought to be grateful to her. I have been reading it this morning. It is a very admirable, & lucidly & energetically written production. The style is less graceful than powerful. Indeed it has so much strength, that the <u>muscles</u> are by necessity, ≪rather≫ too obvious & prominent. But its writer is obviously & prominently an extraordinary man—& if <u>he</u> were to dine at Colwall today, I w.ᵈ go to meet him, without sighing . . . much!—

My love of solitude is growing with my growth. I am inclined to shun the acquaintance of those whom I do not like <ᴧ& love;> on account of the <u>ennui</u>: & the acquaintance of those whom I might like & love,—on account of the <u>pain</u>!—— Oh the pain attendant on liking & loving, ≪may≫ <ᴧseem> a little cloud,—but it blots from us all the light of the sun!!—

B H & I went to Colwall in B's carriage. The Commelines there—

1. The Hon. Mrs. Yorke, of Newland, some 4 miles N.N.W. of Malvern Wells (map ref. A9).

2. William Ellery Channing, *The Importance and Means of a National Literature* (London, 1830).

Diary by E.B.B.

Miss C Miss L C & M. *C Senior. Miss Commeline decides that half of me has vanished away in my thinness! Who can wonder at it? M.* *Hill seems to ≪me≫ an amiable woman. She is said to have the talent of making friends. I do not envy her that. Has she the talent of*
5 *keeping them?*

Besides; the meaning which she attaches to the word friend, is probably not my meaning. M. *Webb who sate next me at dinner, sang very well after dinner—with expression & spirit,—better than he talked. M.* *& Miss Peyton,*[1] *M.* *Deane, H, & I have settled the English*
10 *form of government <for> next year. It is to be a <parthenocracy>. For Universal suffrage will include our sex,—the married people will neutralize each others votes by voting pro & con; & then how can the young ≪men≫ be uninfluenced by the young ladies? Impossible!— "What a happy people, you will be," was my exclamation. M.* *D.*
15 *asked me how M.* *Boyd was. Hearing his name in the midst of a crowd of people whom I cared nothing for, was like ≪Robinson≫ Crusoe's ≪detection≫ of ≪a≫ man's footprint in his desert!—*

"He is ≪as≫ well as can be expected, considering the distress which he is now suffering in common with all good patriots".
20 *"But he sh.* *be consoled by reflecting, that tho' the <decision> of the H of Lords has displeased him, it has pleased others".*

"Not at all! That reflection increases his suffering. He has to bewail not only his own want of felicity, but the want of wisdom in his fellowcreatures". M. *D is a goodnatured man.*
25 *Glad to get home!—*

Wednesday Oct. 12.

Eliza Cliffe came to help Henrietta to bind music. I w. *not be bound to help her. <An> unsatisfactory day: my politeness drawing me one way & my studiousness another.*
30 *After consecrating about ≪12≫ hours to the binding ≪business≫, H's music book is bound almost as well as if she had paid 6.* *for it. How much is time worth? Sixpence an hour?———*

The rain came on, & arrested Eliza in her way home. If M. *Cliffe is angry, <she> deserves to be drowned!— Music in the*

---

1. Nicholson Peyton (1783-1841), the son-in-law of Mrs. Griffith of Barton Court, and his sister.

evening. Guitar, <at least>, & singing,—which ought to have been music.

Thursday, Oct. 13.

Eliza went away soon after breakfast; & Bummy & Henrietta went away soon after _her_, to call at the Bartons. I begged Henrietta to close with any proposition made by Mrs Griffith on the subject of taking me in her carriage tomorrow as far as Mr Boyd's. Eliza promised to try to persuade Mrs Cliffe to call here in _her_ carriage at ten. So there are <two> chances for me!—

Mr Curzon arrived at two; & he & I were tête à tête until five or near five, when H & B arrived. They have been to Colwall Green to invite M.^{r} & Mrs Deane to dine here on Saturday; & to Colwall, where Mr Martin has warned them off his premises by frigidity & rigidity. Bummy is clear on the point of his disliking _her_.

_I_ am neither frigid nor rigid; it w.^{d} be an improvement, were I a little of both; and Mr Curzon may wish me to be _much_ of both, rather than inconsiderate enough to forget his luncheon. How careless I was! And how hungry he must have been!—

Miss Gibbons is to be at his house tomorrow, & baptized on Monday! And on Sunday, I am permitted to divulge!——

A great deal of talking between M.^{r} C & me about election. I wish my mind were more settled on that subject.

Friday. Oct 14.

M.^{r} C stayed all night. Before breakfast this morning, I was writing a letter to my dear Papa, which _must_ go today. At breakfast, Miss Peyton's poney arrived ≪ . . . ≫ to enable Arabel to ride to Malvern. Very goodnatured ≪in≫ Miss Peyton!— Altho' Mrs Griffith did not actually offer _me_ a seat in her carriage, I might have had it: nay, I might have squezzed [sic] my little body into ≪our≫ wheelbarrow, if Bummy had not been alone & Mr Curzon here!— As it ≪was≫, I was obliged to stay behind!—

Mr Curzon remained here until nearly three. He is an excellent Christian & most amiable man: but in conversation, he is . . heavy. There is no denying _that_! Besides I c.^{d} not help thinking now & then, of Mr Boyd!——

B & I went out to walk; & into the garden, for the first time since

[157]

that loss which must be a loss for ever.[1] *I mean, Bummy's first time—not mine. I have been there very often. Dearest B's eyes had tears in them I am sure, tho' they were turned away from me!—*

They came home at 5, or past 5. Sette was quite heroic about his teeth, as he is about everything; & Henry rather cowardly, as he is about everything. Arabel called at Ruby Cottage, while Miss Peyton & <Henrietta> went on to Miss Steers's. Very unkind of Henrietta not to call for one moment to see Annie after her four months' absence! But I will say nothing. Arabel did not see M^{r}. Boyd. I wonder if he was disappointed at my not having gone. Henrietta says that he was not, & that I overrate his regard to me. No! I do not do that!— M^{rs}. Boyd has sent me a note by Arabel, to communicate Annie's return of love for M^{r}. Biscoe. "Oh! that prophaned word."!![2]

They are all to be here tomorrow, in the case of Miss Bordman being able to come. I hope she may; <because> if they do not come tomorrow, they are to do so on Monday—in which case I must stay at home to receive them, instead of visiting M^{r}. B.

Saturday. Oct 15th.

They did not come. Provoking! Now I shall not be able to go to Malvern on Monday. I had made up my mind to write, & had even sealed my letter to M^{rs}. Boyd, praying her to remember that ≪by≫ not coming or writing, she was keeping me at home. But Henrietta wished to send Billy to the Bartons instead of to the post: & besides she complained of my always taking the poney away on Monday—& besides—I thought it best not to send my letter. M^{rs}. Boyd may write herself to me <tomorrow>.

By the way of distracting Georgie & myself from Homer, I let out my squirrel. He leapt up into the air, & climbed ≪my≫ bookcase, & performed so many tight rope maneuvres, that I was inclined to wish him to be tight again. Particularly in the evening, when Atalanta herself <$_{\wedge}$seemed to> ≪have≫ no chance of catching him. Arabel & Bummy & Ann & I, were about an hour at it. At last, he wisely ran into his cage, when he c^{d}. run no where else; & thus he was caught, as the anti-reformers will be. M^{r}. Deane & a goose for dinner. No

1. The death of E.B.B.'s mother, Bummy's sister, on 7 October 1828.

2. Possibly a reference to Shelley's "One word is too often profaned | For me to profane it" *(Posthumous Poems of Percy Bysshe Shelley,* London, 1824, p. 200).

identity hinted at!—[1]   He is a good natured man, & not without sense; & he has lent me the _London Encyclopædia_.[2]   I played on the guitar; but my voice had gone away with my breath, in the squirrel chase.   He & Bro & H sang—or tried at it.

Sunday Oct 16.

    At breakfast Arabel called upon me to divulge the secret.   How angry Bummy was!—   I "ought not to have received such a confidence!"—   Now how could I help it?   I am <u>not</u> to blame.   I never solicited, but c.^d not reject, much less c.^d I abuse Mr Curzon's confidence.   I ≪can≫ only <u>regret</u> its being extended to me.

    It has been on my mind from the first, that Miss Gibbons sh.^d have communicated her intention to her parents; ≪sh^d≫ have acted firmly on it, but still have communicated it.   Upon this point, however I was not <consulted>; &, as Mr Curzon <approves> of the concealment, I sh.^d not <ˌhave> ≪been≫ justified in giving an opinion.   He said to me today at the school, "Somebody sends her love to you"—& he <announced> the celebration of the ordinance of baptism at four, tomorrow afternoon.   May God bless & sanctify it to her soul.

    Mr Curzon's text was "knowing the terrors of the Lord, we persuade men".[3]   An impressive discourse.

    I had today a letter from my dear dear Papa—dearer to me than he ever was!—very kind & satisfactory, but silent on <u>the</u> subject.   I am sure there is no hope!—   Minny thinks the same; & she is more likely to be right than I am.   Kenrick, she says, had a letter a fortnight ago, desiring him to purchase horses for ploughing, & announcing that everything w.^d soon be finally settled!   Well! however it may be settled, <u>God</u> will abide with <u>us!</u>—

    All this makes me more anxious than usual to be with my dear friend Mr Boyd, as much as I can.   Tomorrow my usual expedition is cancelled!   But I am thinking that I may be well dedommagèe[4] by

5

10

15

20

25

30

1. So much for Mrs. Dean!

2. _The London Encyclopædia, or Universal Dictionary of Science, Art, Literature, and Practical Mechanics_ [ed. Thomas Curtis], 22 vols. (London, 1829).

3. II Corin. v.11: "Knowing therefore the terror of the Lord, we persuade men; but we are made manifest unto God; and I trust also are made manifest in your consciences."

4. "Compensated."

[159]

Diary by E.B.B.

going back with Mrs *Boyd, sleeping at Ruby Cottage, & returning here on Tuesday. To come however to this happy conclusion, certain premises are necessary. Will she ask me? If she does not, I must stay on my own. If she does, my "yes" is ready; & how happy shall I be in saying it!—*

Bummy has scarcely spoken to me all day. How can I possibly help Miss Gibbons's being baptized?——

Monday Oct 17.

Arabel says that Mrs *Boyd is sure not to ask me to do what I want to do: If she does not, I must call up my philosophy from the shades. It is five minutes to eleven, & she has not arrived. Perhaps there may be no room for me in the carriage. Perhaps Miss Bordman may not come, & then there will be room. I wish—I scarcely know what, exactly. I think, I almost certainly think that I sh*^d *write a little note to poor Miss Gibbons today. And yet if I do, Bummy will be so angry!— And I dont like to write incog.!— I will write the note, & see how it looks!———*

Wrote the note. It looks well enough to send, but I wont send it.[1]

Mrs *Boyd did not come at all. Resolved—that I will go to Ruby Cottage tomorrow.*

Tuesday Oct. 18. †

Went to Malvern with Ann, & Billy as an <u>Automaedon</u>,[2] *according to M*^r *Boyd. Everybody in bed. M*^{rs} *Boyd "motioned" me into her room, & there we discussed M*^r *Biscoe, the probability, of ≪a≫ letter arriving from him that day, & the possible nature of its contents. M*^{rs} *B doubted his faith. I did not. An embassy from Annie took me up into her room, where I found herself & Miss Bordman in bed together. From thence I went in to M*^r *Boyd who had breakfasted. I spent a happy day with him, hearing him repeat passages from the Prometheus, & conversing. Miss Hurd was in the house; ≪for≫ he had sent for her, supposing that everybody was going to Hope End & that he w*^d *be left alone. She came into his room only for ≪a short time≫—&*

---

1. She must have changed her mind, because the entry of 20 October speaks of a reply.
2. The mythological charioteer of Achilles.

*the paper was read to him only a little. Altogether I had nothing to
complain of.*

*A letter from Mr Biscoe! Mrs Boyd <u>is</u> right. A cold letter! a
resolved letter! He relinquishes for ever, Annie's love!— This—
this is the love of Man! We were much afraid, even I was, of the
effect of this letter upon her; but she bore it as calmly as I should
bear my squirrel's running away. That ≪such≫ a conclusion should
take place, is happiest for <u>both of them</u>!—*

*Well! I had wished Mr Boyd good bye,—& had put on my hat, &
was tying on my cloak, when Annie proposed my staying all night. I
resisted—She insisted—And my heart let go its hold in a moment!—
The temptation was too great!— Wrote a note to Bummy, & sent
away the carriage. The plan is, to go <ˌhome> with Mrs Boyd tomorrow; but in the case of her not going, I begged Bummy to drive
for me to the Wyche.*

*≪ . . . ≫ A letter from Mr Barker. Miss Bordman took it in to M.^r
Boyd & read it to him. I am afraid—— Mr Barker speaks a good
deal about me & my letters, & his pressure of business, & intention of
writing to me. I thought I was disfranchised from his correspondence
—put into schedule A.¹ <Sh.^d> not be distressed about it, if I
were——*

*Mr Boyd seemed pleased at my staying. He did not seem so
much pleased just at first. He <said>, "Ah! <u>Ann</u> had to say only
a word to induce you to remain." My answer was—"But if I had
thought only of <Ann>, perhaps I w.^d not have remained." And
then I explained the broad line of difference between staying from
home, <u>one</u> night, & many nights. Miss Steers came immediately
after tea, & I was obliged to <play> a game at chess with Annie.
Afterwards Mrs Boyd dismissed me to Mr Boyd. Sate with him until
past eleven!— †*

Wednesday Oct 19.th

*Annie & I slept together last night, & she described to me enough
of the state of her mind while she was at Stanwell, for me to feel
confirmed in my opinion about the happiness of certain chains being*

---

1. Schedule A of the Reform Bill listed the 57 boroughs that would no longer return
Members to Parliament.

broken. *She exacted my secresy* ≪*towards*≫ *M*^*rs* *Boyd,* ≪—≫ *there-fore I c*^*d* *console her only generally.* *I did not sleep well last night, & am not well this morning.* *Was in M*^*r* *Boyd's room a little after nine.* *Nervous & out of spirits; so that during several hours of the day, I c*^*d*

5 *scarcely keep my eyes clear from tears!—* *Read some of Gregory to M*^*r* *Boyd.* *He was fancied to be cool in his manner to me; & there were other things which made me uncomfortable.*

Miss Bordman gave him a Septuagint, which I think she received from her Father for the purpose. *Miss Boyd said something about it*

10 *when I was in the room,—& he seemed uncomfortable & observed "we will talk of that another time".* *He evidently did not wish me to know of it Why?——* *M*^*rs* *Boyd told me of it afterwards.* *Why did Miss Bordman give it to him?* *I wish she had not done so.* *I had intended to do it: & besides———*

15 *Perhaps it is wrong in me to feel as much annoyed as I really do.* *I am of an intolerably exclusive disposition; & yet I wish some other people were like me!———*

M^*r* *Boyd went out to walk twice today.* *That annoyed me too a little, tho' he did not stay long.* *Afterwards my spirits* <*came*> *back*

20 *again while I was sitting with him;—& when it grew darker & darker, they were still more reinforced.* *"Do you think they will not come for you?"* *He seemed anxious that they sh*^*d* *not!—*

At last the darkness grew so palpable, that we had a candle & opened Gregory again—when, lo!—a note from Bummy dated from

25 *the Wyche!* *They were afraid of coming down to me; but I might either go to them, or they w*^*d* *come again for me tomorrow.* *"To-morrow" M*^*r* *Boyd urged* <*eagerly*>, *if not anxiously.* *"Tomorrow," said my inclinations.* *"Tomorrow" said my pen.* † *M*^*r* *Boyd & I had a happy evening again.* *A good deal of proing & contraing about*

30 *whether I sh*^*d* *wait until he went to bed before hearing Miss Boyd's story.* *She is like the Princess Scheherazade, but were she the Princess herself, I w*^*d* *not leave M*^*r* *Boyd to go to her.* *So he yielded, and after all Her Royal Highness told no story, even after he had gone to bed.*

Thursday Oct 20^*th*

35 *Was in M*^*r* *Boyd's room before nine.* *Heard him say over the passages in the Prometheus, & read Gregory.* *He told me that he had a great mind to buy a book mentioned in Bohn's catalogue, a very*

ancient edition of Gregory's orations, price £2—12^{s}—6^{d}—^{1} & that in
that case he w^{d}. ask me to make Papa get it for him. He might receive
the book from me, & pay <for> it from his private purse,—& so
escape ≪a≫ reproach ≪of≫ extravagance from M^{rs}. Boyd. I had made
up my mind that if _I_ procured it for him thro' Papa, he sh^{d}. never pay   5
for it from his private or public purse. But he decided at last not to
have it. It was an extravagant thing to do,—& besides, by taking the
book, another copy of which he had, he w^{d}. prevent some other person
from having it. I smiled at this disinterested benevolence & resolved
that the book sh^{d}. be his. ≪ . . . ≫ Writing out treasonable epigrams   10
for M^{r}. Boyd, M^{r}. Curzon interrupted us!—But I was allowed to be
present at the audience. A great deal of talking about the compatability ≪or≫ incompatibility of intellectual & religious ≪pleasures≫.
<Of> course M^{r}. Boyd & I took the right side of the question.
Dinner!— In the midst of it, the carriage came. I saw M^{r}. Boyd   15
for a few minutes before I went away,—& then the good bye came.
<An> effort was necessary to steady my voice & say it,—≪but≫
the tears would crowd into my eyes in spite of every effort. He did
not seem to care . . _much_ about parting with me— †

≪Henrietta≫ & Arabel were my escort home, & we called for a   20
moment at M^{rs}. Trant's. She was at dinner, & evidently w^{d}. have
preferred our being there too. Not that she wished us to dine with
her.—

Dear Bummy not at all angry at my having stayed. I had fancied
her note cool, & M^{r}. Boyd had recommended me to put it into the fire   25
& warm it,—but I dont <think> now that she meant to write cooly.

My spirits are rather depressed tonight!— _Rather!!_—

≪I found here a note from Miss Gibbons, in answer to mine.≫

Friday Oct 21.

I was cudgelling my brains last night, to find out how I could get   30
money to buy that book for M^{r}. Boyd. At last I decided; & this morning executed my design. I wrote to Eliza who is at Worcester, & sent
to her my editions of Bolingbroke's & Harris's works^{2} to be disposed

---

1. Bohn's _Catalogue_, ed. cit., Item 433, an Aldine edition of 1536.

2. _The Works of the Right Hon. Henry St. John, Lord Viscount Bolingbroke_, 7 vols.
(London, 1754-98); _The Works of James Harris, Esq._, ed. James Harris, 1st Earl of Malmes-
bury, 2 vols. (London, 1801).

Diary by E.B.B.

of at Eaton's, desiring her to make him write immediately to Bohn for the Gregory. My books I w.^d rather have not parted with; but my heart & soul ≪are≫ fixed on this new purchase. <I> did not look very regrettingly on them, while Ann was packing them up!— Sent

5 *the sheet of epigrams to the Times newspaper.[1] How happy I was yesterday, when my dear friend was dictating them,—& when <u>we</u> were consulting <ʌ about> & reforming some of them!— ≪He told me to put the bishops into verse for him, as puzzling about them, made his head heavy.≫*

10 *Read!—& heard the boys read!—*

Saturday. Oct. 22.

I <have> written a brief account of my visit my happy visit, my last visit—perhaps! to Malvern, because not having my Diary with me, I was obliged to trust my memory. I have been writing to Mr Boyd

15 *this morning.[2] My note to him may be too expressive of regard!! <As> his letters to me express actually <u>none</u>, I have often resolved to ice mine over also; but I dont know how it ≪is≫—the frost scarcely begins, when a ray of sunshine melts it all away!— I wish I had told him of my having written for the Gregory. They hurried me so*

20 *while I wrote, that I had no time to consider anything; & now there is no ≪use in reconsidering anything≫! I addressed two lines to Mrs Boyd in the envelope. I hope she wont think it is too little. My letter to Mr Boyd began "my dearest friend". How will his begin to me? Lord Byron used to make "much ado about nothing" when*

25 *≪ . . . ≫ his ≪friends addressed≫ him as only "my dear Byron".[3] Lord Byron was at school then,—& I am not at school!— Well! I cannot help it! The probability, after all, is that ≪a certain≫ person will write <u>no</u> kind of letter to me!—*

I am reading Amadis of Gaul. The conceit of the old knight's

30 *garland half fresh & half withered, is a very pretty one—& may be put to use.[4]*

1. They were not printed—perhaps E.B.B.'s epithet "treasonable" (20 October) supplies the explanation.

2. For the letter, see Appendix I, p. 287.

3. Moore's *Letters and Journals*, ed. cit., I, 50: "There are . . . some curious proofs of the passionate and jealous sensibility of Byron. . . . We collect that he had taken offence at his young friend's addressing him 'my dear Byron,' instead of 'my dearest;' . . ."

4. In Robert Southey's version of Vasco Lobeira's epic (4 vols., London, 1803); the

Sunday Oct. 23.

"*Heigho the wind & the rain!*"[1] *I wish they had come last Thursday instead of this morning!— No going to church. My squirrel has eaten three chesnuts out of my hand, & has tried to eat my hand besides. It did not bite much. I should grow very fond of it, if it w:ᵈ* 5 *but grow fond of me, & if I c:ᵈ but persuade it to «become» more odoriferous. We have brought a myrtle tree up into the room, for it to have leaping room upon. Arabel's proposition.*

A long conversation down stairs this morning about our leaving Hope End. Bummy seems to have very very little hope . . I have 10 *none. Charlotte* [Butler], *if she comes to England at all, must come «. . .» the last week of this month— And where is she to go? Dear Bummy is anxious & embarassed between the desire of receiving her, & the dislike of parting with us!—and no letter from Papa. There is one from M:ʳˢ Boyd, who says, "M:ʳ B sends his kind love: he is going* 15 *to send you two or three epigrams; but as he does not like to be the cause of your reading such things on Sunday, you may expect to receive them by Monday's post." So I suppose he will write with them,—or «. . .» I shall be as burning hot as ever Amreeta cup made Kehama!—[2] Annie is not well,—& M:ʳˢ Boyd attributes her* 20 *indisposition to distress of mind «at» M:ʳ Biscoe's secession. How distress of mind can be the consequence of the secession of a man whom she does not, did not, cannot love, I do not understand. That is one of the things which are "not dreamt of in my philosophy".[3] Annie & Miss Boyd are to be sent here on the first fine day. Annie* 25

garland was "of flowers, the half whereof were as beautiful and fresh as though they had just been cut from the living stem; the other half so withered and dry, that it seemed they would crumble at a touch. . . . When this garland of flowers shall be set upon the head of that Lady or Damsel, that with the same surpassing love doth love her husband or friend, the dry flowers shall again become fresh and green" (II, 216).

1. The Clown's song, *Twelfth Night* V.i.375 ff.

2. Southey's poem, *The Curse of Kehama* (London, 1810), pp. 263-264, tells how, after Kehama had drunk from the cup:

> . . . through his veins
> Torture at once, and immortality,
> A stream of poison doth the Amreeta run,
>   Infinite everlasting agony.
> And while within the burning anguish flows,
>   His outward body glows
> Like molten ore, beneath the avenging eye,
> Doom'd thus to live and burn eternally.

3. Cf. *Hamlet* I.v.166-167.

said something when I was at Malvern about bringing her nightcap some day, & sleeping here.   I could not object; but there <u>will</u> be objectors.   At any rate, if she comes with only Miss Boyd, she will not like Miss Boyd to return alone.

5   *Bummy & I walked to the gate, because there was an interregnum in the rain.   No preacher there!—*

Monday Oct 24.

      Bro, dear Bro, is gone to some place near Overbury, to the Miss Martins I think, to shoot with M.ʳ Martin.[1]   *<He> does not come*
10 *back to us until tomorrow night or the next day morning.   I hope that he may miss us, less than we must miss him.   Bummy has sent Gent to Ledbury.   So I shall have my letter!—   What kind of letter is it likely to be?—*

      My squirrel was found this morning, asleep under the ≪cushion≫
15 *of my chair.   Suppose I had sate down upon ≪him≫!—   ≪He≫ is growing more & more civilized, ≪& has eaten≫ out of my hand several times.   ≪ . . . ≫ I told Annie that she might have ≪him≫, if she liked it.   Now that ≪he≫ has become so tame, I hope she wont like it.*

20   *Gent has returned from Ledbury: & no letter for me!—   What can be the meaning of that?*

      <Miss Boyd> & Annie have arrived!—   Perhaps Annie will propose staying.   What shall I do?——

      She has proposed it—she is going to stay.   I drew Bummy into
25 *my room & told her how it was; & she was not argumentative about it.   Henrietta was quite angry!!.   I cannot help it.   ≪Annie has brought a letter for me from M.ʳ Boyd—beginning "dearest Porsonia"—≫*

      Miss Boyd & I walked round the park, & into the garden, until
30 *I, for one, was completely tired—& into every corner of the house besides.   She took off her gloves, that <she> might feel with <ₐher> hands, my staff of Marathon.   I liked her all the better for that bubbling up of enthusiasm—   After she had tired me, she said that my recompense should be in the manner of a Troubadour; & she let me*

---

1. James Martin had three unmarried sisters living near Overbury Court, his father's home, about 15 miles east of Hope End.

lead her into the library where she told me a story yclepped "The mountain & the lovers," from the lais of Marie.[1] *Her voice & manner are unpleasing & ungraceful: but her language is* ≪ . . . ≫ *so accurate & ready, that anyone with his eyes shut, w*ᵈ *suspect a book of being before hers. She dined with us at two; & went away at five. Annie, I am to* take *to Ruby Cottage tomorrow morning. Hurrah!——*   5

Guitar playing & book binding in the evening; the whole to conclude by Arabel & Annie sleeping together in the Turkish room.

*Tuesday. Oct 25*ᵗʰ*.*

Annie & ≪*Arabel*≫ *& I were off at eleven. We were very nearly*   10 *off in a less satisfactory manner; inasmuch as we discovered the insecurity of the iron rim round one of the wheels. Stopped at the Bartons, to save our lives. Miss Glasco superintended, very kindly. I like her. She called me her pet today, & "could not help treating me still as a child". I like her: but I am not sure that I could* love   15 *her—even if I were* <ₐto> *try!—which I dont mean to do.*

*Another interruption was a note from M*ʳˢ *Martin, received just as I was getting into the carriage, & saying that she w*ᵈ. *dine with us. So we must be back before six!——*

*Arrived at Malvern at nearly one—& soon went into M*ʳ *Boyd's*   20 *room. Miss Boyd was sitting with him,* <reading> *the paper,—& held up her hands in an interjectional manner on seeing me. "Who is that?" asked M*ʳ *Boyd. "Whom do you think?" And then I spoke!— He seemed very very glad to see me, &* <ₐwas> *very very kind in his manner, & reproached me for not "making Ann come before". What*   25 *did he mean by saying in his letter yesterday that he did not deserve my regard—that he was not sufficiently kind & attentive to me?* <There> *is only one way in which he* can *be unworthy of it—by its' not being reciprocal; & if I c*ᵈ *get general benevolence out of my head, I w*ᵈ *not believe in that species of unworthiness. With regard*   30 *to his being inattentive & unkind to me, I w*ᵈ *not hear his enemy say so; & why sh*ᵈ. *I hear him?— If he w*ᵈ *but write to me oftener & more at length!!—— I did not comment upon his letter before him. I could not do that.* †

1. Marie de France, 13th century Anglo-Norman poetess. This particular Lay, entitled "Les Deux Amants," appeared in an English translation by Mary Mathilda Betham, *The Lay of Marie* (London, 1816).

Diary by E.B.B.

We read Gregory—a part of the funeral oration on his father:[1]
and we talked about what is called the ≪times≫ for the maturity &
the decay of the intellectual faculties. I denied the whole hypothesis.
As if man's mind were man's body, & had its three warnings!!—
Sir Uvedale Price[2] was as eloquent ≪and≫ imaginative at eighty—
more so, in every probality [sic]—than he was at eighteen. And at
sixty he first became an author.

It is very dangerous to hold such a doctrine; for to despond about
the strength of one's mind, is to diminish its strength. <Such> a
doctrine w^d do more actual harm at fifty, than the ≪weight≫ of
ninety years c^d do, without it!—

Mr Boyd confessed to me that he thought his translation of a
part of the oration which we read today, translated at the age of 22,
was well done.[3] "He might say so to me"!!—

I do not infer ≪ . . . ≫ from that little circumstance, but from
many, that his confidence in me is really the confidence of a friend.
He evidently _thinks_ loud out before me!——

I went out of the room for a few minutes while he went to dinner;
but I was recalled before his dinner came to a conclusion. He w^d not
mind dining before me!—And we talked until past 5. Then over the
hill & far away!— I do hate saying good bye . . . to some people!—

I did not feel very well today, & could scarcely help bursting into
tears while I was reading Gregory. One passage in it made me think
of the beloved & gone!—

Mr Curzon is to be at Ruby Cottage again on Thursday.

≪Arabel≫ & I had a ≪pleasant≫ drive home, <only> half in the
dark. Mrs Martin ready for us. Guitaring in the evening,—& no
other memorabilia. M^{rs} M slept here.

Wednesday Oct. 26.

Well!—I had a very happy visit yesterday, & am happy today in
thinking of it. How c^d I forget to say that Mr Boyd told me "to
≪ . . . ≫ come again as soon as I could". Shall I not do it?—

---

1. Oration 19 (*GNO*, I, 286-316).

2. Sir Uvedale Price, Bt. (1747-1829), who sought E.B.B.'s opinion and advice regarding
his Greek writings.

3. The exordium and the peroration of Gregory's "Funeral Oration in Praise of His Dead
Father" appeared in H.S.B.'s *Select Passages*, 2nd. edn. (London, 1810), pp. 156-173.

Bummy proposes my driving to Eastnor tomorrow to see Lady Margaret. I will do it.

Thursday, Oct 27th.

The wheel of the carriage is gone to Ledbury; therefore going to Eastnor is out of the question. A battle of the frogs & mice[1] about 5 dining at Mrs Martin's. She sent a note of invitation yesterday. I wish she w^d send no note of the kind to me. Bummy wont go,—but she wishes <Henrietta> & me to go. Now Henrietta always wishes to go everywhere,—so there is no veto from her. But I wish to go nowhere,—& it seems hard that my inclination should be forced 10 whenever an opportunity is <offered>. I grew out of humour—& complained of it!— It was very wrong of me to be out of humour, particularly on such an <ʌun>important occasion. I gave up at last —& wrote an assent to Mrs Martin—, & then I made friends with dear Bummy. I cannot—I ought not ≪ . . . ≫ to, bear, "displeasing 15 her!—["]

After all, there need not have been such a fuss; for the rain settled the question finally. We c^d not go thro' it.

Dear Bummy is uncomfortable about Charlotte, who, if she does not come to England at the end of this month or at the beginning of 20 november, will not be able to come at all. Dear kind Bummy has written to Papa to tell him so—but to say also that she will not leave us even to receive Charlotte, in the case of our being obliged to leave Hope End immediately. When will his answer come?— I feel, I feel, that not for our sakes, is dear Bummy so kind—but for the sake 25 of one more beloved than the living can be!— That feeling makes me prize the kindness more. May God bless her for it!—— Surely we ought to try to do everything most likely to please her. I was very wrong this morning. Sent a brace of pheasants to Mr Boyd.

Friday Oct. ≪28≫th. 30

Drove with Henrietta to Eastnor. I think I would upon the whole have preferred going by myself; because I want to say to Lady Margaret what I sh^d not like to say before a third person—for fear of

---

1. A reference to Homer's mock-heroic *Batrachomyomachia*. An early English version of this appeared as *The Strange, wonderfull and bloudy Battell betweene Frogs and Mise*, trans. W. F[owldes]., (London, 1603).

Diary by E.B.B.

<rejected> addresses.   But Lady Margaret was not alone—& therefore no harm was done by my not being so.

    A great deal con poor Miss Gibbons.   Lady Margaret "had a regard for her".   Ah! that had!—   It was not meant for the affections!!——

5   I knew that Lady Margaret would be angry; because I knew her papistical attachment to the Church of England.   It is exactly that. She considers the church as an interpreter of scripture,—& in a maternal point of view!—   Mʳ James Cocks the red & talkative made an amusing enough contrast to Mʳ James Cocks the white & silent.   But

10 they agreed in shaking their heads over their ≪defected≫ cousin.[1] Old Lady Somers was there also.[2]   Beauty in the past tense,—& agreableness (as people go) in the present!—   Poor Mʳˢ Selwyn called in the course of our visit.   She is about to set off for Brighton where she will remain two or three months with Mʳ & Mʳˢ Blizzard[3] —to

15 meet, as Mʳ Selwyn suggests, the cholera morbus.   She is less disfigured than, I imagined—and yet I could not judge thro' her cloak.[4] I wish she had not talked & laughed so much!—   There was something out of keeping in it!—

    We called for a moment at Mʳˢ Watson's,[5] who was out.   Good-

20 natured Fates!—

    Lady Margaret said with a smiling face that she had been glad to hear of ≪there≫ being more probability of our not being lost to the neighbourhood—at least not so soon!   The smile vanished when she heard my answer.   I could say only, that I believed things remained

25 as they were.

    1. James Somers Cocks (1790-1856), Prebendary of Hereford and Worcester, brother of Lady Margaret, and their father's cousin James Cocks, M.P. for Reigate; it seems likely that the epithet "red and talkative" applied to the politician rather than the priest, but we have no proof of this. No relationship has been traced between the Cocks and Gibbons families that would explain the use of "defected cousin."

    2. Anne, née Pole-Carew (? -1833), widow of Charles Cocks, Lord Somers, and stepmother of the 1st Earl.

    3. Thomas Blizard and his wife left Donnington Hall, near Ledbury, in 1829, to live in Brighton, and were presented with a piece of plate as a mark of esteem (Mr. Biddulph's Diary, 6 April 1829). "No medical man ever gave more time and attention to the Sick & infirm even when paid for their Services" (op. cit., 22 July 1832).

    4. This reference cannot be explained; we trust it has no connection with the rather chilling entry in Mr. Biddulph's Diary for 12 July 1829: "Mrs Selwyn at Dinner—poor woman she is grieving at parting with her Husband who hates her very undeservedly, & will probably do her some bodily harm if she returns to him which she is resolved to do." Her husband, Congreve Selwyn, was one of the medical men of Ledbury.

    5. Wife of G. Watson, Esq., of Bronsil, quite near Eastnor Castle (map ref. G6).

We got home at about four.   A letter from Papa to Henrietta—&
not a word in it!—   How extraordinary! Poor Bummy does not know
what to do.   A parcel too from Ruby Cottage, conveyed to Ledbury
by Mʳ Curzon, & containing North's Plato,[1] *& a note from Mʳˢ Boyd*
—but with no message about the book. Mʳ Boyd <ₐwhen I saw him   5
last,> wondered at my having only Foster's Selections from Plato,[2] *&*
at my not applying to Papa about procuring another edition of him.
Now is it possible, that he means to give me this little book? I hope
—I hope not!—   It contains besides what I have read before, only the
X book De legibus, & the 2ᵈ of Alcibiades. I began to read De legibus.   10

Mʳˢ Boyd gives a bad account of Miss Bordman's <ₐfather:> a
better one of Annie.   I cant say that I am uneasy about Annie. No
letter from Alençon! Mʳ Biscoe's evergreen love has withered—&
like all earthly eternal things, is at an end. Is not that ≪ . . .≫ Annie's
own fault?—   Mʳˢ Boyd <speaks> of having heard ≪from≫ Miss   15
Cockburn,[3] *& of one of the Cheltenham houses which were desiderata*
last May, ≪ . . .≫ not being taken.   I suppose Mʳˢ Boyd is very
anxious indeed, to make me so,—but she shall not succeed.

Saturday Oct. ≪29≫.
Finished the 5ᵗʰ chapter De legibus—but very unwell all day.   20
Wrote to Mʳˢ Boyd,—& told her what I thought wᵈ have been the
consequence, had she gone to "that ≪desirable≫ Cheltenham"—
namely that by this time she wᵈ have deeply lamented it. I hope the
consequence of my saying so, may not be a repetition of Annie's
vote of censure!—[4] *H & Daisy rode to Marcle*[5] *with the Martins.*   25
<How> very unwell I have been today!—— ≪Told the stories of
Sindbad the sailor <ₐ& Baron Munchhausen,>[6] *to the children this*
evening≫

---

1. [Hon. John North, ed.], *Platonis de Rebus Divinis Dialogi Selecti* (Cambridge, 1673).

2. Lot 990 of the 1913 Browning Sale was her copy of *Platonis Dialogi V*, ed. Nathaniel Forster (Oxford, 1752).

3. A friend of Mrs. Boyd, who ran a small boarding school at Charlton Villa, Cheltenham.

4. For E.B.B.'s interference in H.S.B.'s plans (see fn. 2, p. 2).

5. Little Marcle was a village about 5 miles S.W. of Hope End; Much Marcle about 7 miles S.W. (map refs. H1 and J1). It is likely that they rode to the latter, as this was where the Martins' friends, the Moneys, lived.

6. [Rudolf Erich Raspe], *Baron Munchausen's Narrative of his Marvellous Travels and Campaigns in Russia* (Oxford, 1786).

Diary by E.B.B.

Sunday. Oct ≪30≫.

 We cannot persuade Bummy to write to Papa to urge his decision. After all, I believe that she is right.   He is in possession of every circumstance relating to her embarassment, & is not likely to allow her to remain in it, if he is able to do otherwise.   Poor dear dear Papa!—may God support him, & bless him!—— I feel as if I loved him more than I ever did before!—

 I hear that Eliza Cliffe <u>was</u> to have returned last Thursday.   Has she brought my book?   Shall I have it today?   I am in fidgets about it!—   And if it does come, how shall ⟨I give⟩ it to M.ʳ Boyd?   Take it?—or send it?—   Will he be pleased?—   He must be pleased with <u>it</u>: but will he be pleased with <u>me</u>?—

 There <u>may</u> be a letter from Papa to Bummy, today.

 No letter—& no book!—   This is <u>borribile dictu</u>!—

Monday.   ≪Oct 31ˢᵗ≫

  ≪a mistake.≫[1]

 The first of November!—   How & where will this month end to us?   Shall we have moral joys as well as physical ones?   Now I w.ᵈ not be a prophet, & be able to answer my own questions for the world.

 Tho' I said "no letter", yesterday, there was a letter from M.ʳˢ Boyd to me.   She speaks of St ≪Lennard's≫,[2] & of the advantage of our going there & her settling close to us!   Well!   that <u>w.ᵈ</u> make me very happy indeed!—   I see how inclined she is to draw me again into a Malvern controversy—, but it wont do—I had enough of it last spring!—   Henrietta went out to drive with M.ʳˢ Martin: & all the boys ran with the hounds!—

 Finished the 9ᵗʰ chapter De legibus.   Plato's circles have made me giddy!—   I cant make them out; but I must try at them again. I wish he were not ≪quite≫ so meta-meta-metaphysical!———

Tuesday.   Nov: ≪1ˢ.ᵗ≫

 Intended to be off to Malvern at seven.   On being <u>awakened</u> at seven, "Ye Gods & <u>little fishes</u>" w.ᵈ ⟨ₐhave⟩ ≪been≫ an appropriate

---

 1. This entry was originally dated 1 November, and the next eight entries were correspondingly misdated before E.B.B. became aware of the mistake.

 2. Sic, for St. Leonard's, a resort near Hastings on the S.E. coast.

[172]

enough interjection—for the sky was full of clouds, & the clouds letting down rain "sans intermission"!— Ann & Arabel questioned or seemed to question the integrity of my brains, in still thinking of going to Malvern. Out & in bed ≪I≫ jumped, in my O'connellization about it! I must go, if I can—so I will dress!— Dressed, break-fasted. It only sprinkled: ≪&≫ I set out!—sprinkled all the way to the wells, where it stopped—, & *I* soon stopped. Everybody in bed, except M.ʳ Boyd who had done breakfast, & to whom I went.— He seemed—oh he *was*—glad to see me! How could I ever doubt his regard for me! We read 158 lines from the 2.ᵈ ≪oration≫ against Julian.¹ Very very very happy today!— †

We were smoked out of M.ʳ Boyd's room two or three times, & were both of us, glad to get in again everytime!— Annie's fondness for me has quite returned! It stopped raining too—but began again before night. De te (Annie!) fabula narratur!² —≪tho'≫ the weather is rather steadier—of the ⟨two⟩!!— She proposed a subscription for a scrap book,—& I was desired to take the paper home.

Dined at four. I was supplicated by Annie & M.ʳˢ Boyd & every-body to stay. What was harder to resist, was M.ʳ Boyd's request on the same subject! But I did ≪resist≫—to the eternal praise of my philosophy, be it spoken!—& came away after promising to sleep there another night. Dear M.ʳ Boyd asked me again & again: is it not wonderful that he sh.ᵈ have ⟨asked⟩ *once* in vain?— But I thought it was better not to run the risk of making Bummy displeased—& so soon after my last aberration!——— Went away at five—& got home in the dark. Nobody was angry. Bummy only said that I required more looking after than my squirrel, & that I ought to have a cage made for me!— What a happy day I have had today!— No letter from Papa. A note of invitation from M.ʳˢ Peyton for Thursday, which was agreed to in my absence—*bore-ibile* dictu, again!— By the bye, I was determined that M.ʳ Boyd sh.ᵈ know that ⟨the book⟩ which he wished for, did not remain in M.ʳ Bohn's shop when I *had*

5

10

15

20

25

30

---

1. This exposes an error in the marginalia in *WG*, where she recorded on p. 126: "Read with M.ʳ Boyd Nov.ʳ 2.ᵈ 1831 158 lines". Presumably when she discovered that she had mis-dated several entries in the Diary, through thinking October had only 30 days, she forgot to alter the note in her Gregory.

2. "The tale is told of you." (Horace, "Satires," I.i, lines 69-70, *LCL-HO/S*, pp. 8-11: "why laugh? Change but the name, and the tale is told of you.")

Diary by E.B.B.

it in my power to ≪buy≫ it.   I told him that it was bought.   Therefore he must know about my having enquired—at least!—   He asked
no questions.   That he might ask none, I put off my information till
the last moment!—

5   Wednesday ≪Nov 2.ᵈ≫
My cold is better, in spite of my wet drive yesterday.   Reading
Plato De Legibus—but read nothing very fine.
No letter.   I hear that the fields;—all the fields, & grounds, are
on the verge of being let, & that the taker & his wife are going to
10   live at the farm!!   May God bless my dear dear Papa!   That is all my
commentary.   If resignation is possible to him, it sh.ᵈ be easy to us!—
Went out in the cold & against my will!—   Arabel & I have agreed
to say nothing about the subscription plan—but to buy a scrap book
for Annie!—   The difficulty is only one—we have no money—
15   <which> is a less difficulty than the subscription plan threatens.
How c.ᵈ Annie be so inconsiderate.   I am inconsiderate enough: but
I never c.ᵈ have thought of doing such a thing!—

Thursday Nov.ʳ ≪3.ᵈ≫
Going to the Peytons today!—   Henrietta & I are north & south
20   about it.   I ≪would≫ cry; if crying ≪would≫ keep me at home.—
They have arranged some plan about going in the close carriage,
with carthorses.   If we are to be upset, I hope it may be in going,—
as by those means, the dinner may be averted.   Six of us going!!—
I am sure they might have left ≪unus≫ multorum at home—una it
25   sh.ᵈ be!¹—
Reading Plato.   Some kind of philosophy certainly necessary.
Carthorses wᵈnt do: so we are to go in the wheelbarrow—two
wheelbarrows full.
Went—nobody there except ourselves.   My cough was the pleas-
30   antest part of the evening; & that was very bad & disagreable.   I am
going to have a "prodigious" cold.   Nem. con:
Miss Glasco gave me a comico-botanico-poetico-kind of composition to read, by Baron Smith.²   There are some clever things in it.

1. Unus multorum (masc.), una multorum (fem.): "one of the many."
2. We cannot trace a peer styling himself Baron Smith at this time. In view of E.B.B.'s
habitual carelessness with names, it seems likely that she meant Percy Clinton Sidney Smythe

But why sh.^d people who can think, write in a hurry. Why cant they understand that there is no merit in being in a hurry?

They wanted me to sleep at the Bartons tonight. If I had known, what I knew afterwards,—that the people there mean to go to Malvern tomorrow, & thought of taking me with them, I w.^d have dared it all!— All means the bed & the breakfast & the company. How ungrateful!—   5

≪*Friday Novr 4th*≫

My cold has increased, is increasing, & ought to be diminished. I could scarcely speak this morng.   10

No letter. I went to bed ≪at≫ nine, & read till half past ten— read Greek!— Finished Plato de legibus; that is his X^{th} book. The passage like one in the Psalms, which Mr Boyd repeated to me, about δικη,[1] *is the finest thing in it. I do not think that it can boast of many ≪very≫ fine things.*   15

<*Saturday*> *Nov* ≪5≫^{th}.

Reform meetings at Worcester & Hereford:[2] *& Sam to the former, & Bro to the latter. I think too that my cough is reforming: but it is not "the whole bill": only a "bit by bit" reform.*

I wrote my little poem called "the weakest thing"[3] *—with a view*   20 *to Miss Bordman's album. She asked me to give her something, & the idea of this poem struck me. It is not "the weakest thing" I ever wrote—but I dont know whether it is suited to an album.*

Sky rocketting among the boys.[4] *We went to the window, & "laid*

(1780-1855), 6th Viscount Strangford and 1st Baron Penshurst. His *Poems, from the Portuguese of Luis de Camoëns* (London, 1803) were well received, but we cannot identify any published work meriting the description "comico-botanico-poetico." As he was a close friend of Thomas Moore, it is possible to hypothesize that this was a manuscript composition, given to Moore, who in turn lent it to his friend James Corry, who was on visiting terms at Barton Court, and so might have shown it there.

1. "Cause." The word appears 6 times in Bk. X of *De Legibus*, and 5 times in Psalms; we cannot identify the particular passage E.B.B. had in mind.

2. Both reported in the *Worcester Herald*, 12 November 1831. The Hereford meeting was attended by ". . . an assemblage of freeholders, and others, to the number of nearly 3000 . . . the address . . . avowed, in addition, the disappointment of the meeting at the rejection of the Reform Bill, . . . [and] was carried with the strongest symptoms of approbation."

3. Included in *The Seraphim and Other Poems* (London, 1838), pp. 354-355 (see Appendix II, p. 315).

4. To celebrate Guy Fawkes' Day.

our golden cushions down". [1]   *Afterwards I was faint & hystericky.*
Why, nobody can say.

   Read two chapter [sic] *from the 2ᵈ Alcibiades.*

   Sam brings back the news of the cholera having appeared in Sunder-
5 *land. May God shield our country, & dear friends—& dear selves!—*

Sunday Nov ≪6≫ᵗʰ

   Sam gave me at breakfast, a note from Mʳˢ Boyd, which he called
for yesterday.   Condolences about my cold!   So Mʳ Biscoe's last
letter does not contain even the "affectation of feeling"!   "Oh this
10 *—love! this love!"   A cold thing at the warmest!—   But Annie*
certainly must bear her part of the blame.

   Bummy & Henrietta to <church> in the rain! Mʳ Deane's fare-
well sermon, as Mʳ Wynn is to preach there next Sunday, [2] *& call upon*
us in the interim.   Mʳ Deane versus Gregory.   I will back Gregory.
15 *Nevertheless I am sorry for Mʳ Deane who is an amiable unpresuming*
man.

   The <Papers> come—& the cholera actually in Sunderland—15
miles from Newcastle! [3] *I am glad, very glad that dear Bummy did*
not go there, & carry Charlotte there.   Surely surely God orders all
20 *things wisely!   Let not ≪ . . . ≫ the pestilence come nigh us, oh God*
our shield!—   With such a shield we need not fear—& yet I am
human & did fear in reading the paper today.

   No letter from Papa.   It is wonderful.

   Bro & A & I wasted ≪some≫ yards of time today, in watching my
25 *squirrel who <ate> two or three chesnuts on my knee, & ran up Bro's*
shoulder.   I intended to go to Malvern tomorrow—cold serving—
but an invitation has come from Colwall, & our carriage must take B

   1. This quotation has not been traced.

   2. The *Worcester Herald*, 26 November 1831, announced the collation of the Rev.
Thomas Wynn to the Rectory of Colwall. Mr. Dean, the Curate, had been the preacher by
necessity, as the previous Rector, the recently-deceased James Charles Clarke, had not visited
the parish for 20 years. This neglect, and the overlooking of Mr. Dean's strong claim to the
vacant living, prompted Mr. Martin to write a savagely critical open letter to the Bishop of
Hereford (see Appendix I, p. 288). Mr. Biddulph was another of the local gentry who favoured
Mr. Dean's appointment; on 26 October he recorded in his diary that he had applied to the
Bishop for the living on Mr. Dean's behalf.

   3. *The Times*, 5 November 1831: "We regret to be under the necessity of announcing
that the cholera has at length really reached the shores of Great Britain . . . Advices received
this day from Sunderland, both by authority and by private hands, convey the melancholy
fact. . . ."

& H & Bro & Sam there, at half past four. What a bore!— Rhyme
& Reason! But I am resigned to one misfortune, by escaping another.
I am <u>not</u> to dine there!— Huzza!

    Read Hooker's Discourse on Justification.[1] Admirable & amiable.
It not only bears but <u>dares</u>, being read a hundred times. Read also 5
or 6 chapters of the Galatians,—& some of St Mathew's Gospel in
Greek.

Monday ≪7≫^{th} Nov^r
    A fine day. How provoking, when I cant go to Malvern!— Bro
to Worcester
    Finished the 2^d Alcibiades, & liked it—

Tuesday ≪8≫^{th} Nov.

— — — —

— — —

— — — —

Tuesday Nov: 15.
    I have not written a word in my diary for this week,—& why?
Because this day week I went to Malvern—& now I must go on in a
diary-cal way.

    On Tuesday, Gent drove me there, & after a long happy day, when
at half past three he appeared with the carriage Mr Boyd had begged
me so much about staying, that I sent him home with a note instead
of me. †† On ≪Wednesday≫ Henry brought the carriage for me,
—& in spite of everybody's entreaties I had wished everybody good-
bye, when he ≪observed≫ "Well!—it is sure to break down!—&
Saunders[2] says so too." And then I was informed of a breakage in
the seat which w.^d make my <u>situation</u> on it very precarious indeed.
Therefore it was agreed that Henry sh.^d ride home the poney & leave
the vehicle with Mr Saunders. How happy I felt!—— † †
    I walked out with Mr Boyd today, in front of the house!—

1. Richard Hooker, *A Learned Discourse of Justification, Workes, and How the Founda-*
tion of Faith is Overthrowne (Oxford, 1612).
  2. Not identified, but from the context probably the local blacksmith.

Diary by E.B.B.

On ≪Thursday≫, no poney was sent, & no carriage done! † On Friday Sam arrived with a kind note from Bummy—but at the same time came a letter to M.ʳˢ Boyd announcing the death of poor Miss Bordman's father,¹ & I could not think of the joy of staying another day.   Poor poor Miss Bordman!—   I went in to the room where she lay on the sofa, the tears rolling down her cheeks.   She threw her arms round my neck & kissed me, & I talked to her as well as I could, of the love of Him who afflicteth not willingly!—²   She bore it ≪strongly≫ in His strength!

I returned to M.ʳ Boyd, & walked out with him, & then we went on reading! †

≪ . . . ≫

Read the ≪letter≫ from Papa which Sam had brought me, & which I could not read at first, on account of being a good deal agitated by the bad news.   <∧Read it to M.ʳ Boyd.>   ≪Bummy≫ came to see me in M.ʳˢ Cliffe's carriage.   Very very kind of her!—

I am surprised at Miss Bordman's equanimity.   She is amiable & has feeling, but not impassioned ≪feeling≫!—

On Saturday, nothing came for me!—   ≪But M.ʳ Curzon most kindly, to see Miss Bordman.≫

On Sunday, there was a letter from Henrietta & Arabel: I was annoyed today by M.ʳ Boyd having Miss Boyd in his room so much longer than usual.   For annoyed, read pained.   I think I am never annoyed simply!—   Miss Bordman's spirits quite astonish me!— Well! we should thank God for it!—   M.ʳ Boyd asked me last night to propose going to the chapel today.   It w.ᵈ be a kindness to M.ʳˢ Boyd who seemed to have given up going to church or chapel, ≪&≫ who would sooner do it to please me than to please him!!   Well! I hinted my wish as broadly as was civil!   But she w.ᵈ not go—not even to please me!—   And there was no appearance of reading the bible, or passing the sabbath according to the bible!—   How much happier M.ʳˢ Boyd & Annie w.ᵈ be, could they be enabled to draw nearer the only source of real happiness!—

1. The *Kentish Gazette*, 11 November 1831, under DEATHS: "Nov. 9, at Preston next Wingham, the Rev. James Bordman, M.A. late of Oriel College, Oxford, and Curate of Ickham, in this county."

2. Lam. iii.33: "For he doth not afflict willingly nor grieve the children of men."

*On Monday I read to M.ʳ Boyd; & wrote a letter for him besides,
to M.ʳ Barker.   He <seemed> at a loss for something to say; & I
suggested sending the political epigrams.   "Oh yes" said M.ʳ Boyd
—"they will fill up."   "I suppose that is your motive for sending
them to me!"   ["]No! I do assure you! No, Indeed! My motive*   5
*for sending them to you, was the mere wish of amusing you a little.
You have not much judgment in every thing".   ["] I suppose in nothing
—but in thinking that you are not cross!—"   "You have not—
certainly—, in that."   We had been talking about the crossness which
he persevered in attributing to himself.   M.ʳˢ Boyd attributed <ₐit>*   10
*to him—& he for his own part, was quite conscious that he had
sometimes spoken crossly to me.   Never in his life!—*

*He does not like Miss Bordman as much as he used to do.   He
says that he does not like her much.   The reason is that she evidently
does not value his society.   Now if she had valued ≪it≫, the reason*   15
*w.ᵈ have weighed the other way—& she might have been preferred to
me. He does not like my quick way of talking—"But if you had not
that, you w.ᵈ be too fascinating — — & agreable"—   Nonsense—
We argued about his absence of mind.   I think he has at least as much
as I have!—*   20

*≪M.ʳˢ≫ Boyd came to tell me that the carriage was come!   I had
hoped, & M.ʳ Boyd's smile had seemed to hope, that the rain w.ᵈ have
prevented its coming.   I could not help shedding tears, as I said good
bye!——*

I think it was on Friday night, when I spoke to M.ʳ Boyd of the   25
*business of ≪1829's≫ spring.¹   A defence! but not such a one as I
can think of with much satisfaction.   We read a great deal of Gregory
Nazianzen, during the course of my visit.   I have marked the passages
in my Gregory.²   He proposed to me to translate the two orations*

---

1. This is taken to refer to her repeated refusal to visit H.S.B. for more than six months
after the death of her mother, despite his entreaties (*EBB/HSB*, xxiii).

2. The marginalia in *WG* indicate that their readings covered:

   a) Orat. 3, "Adversus Julianum, I." On p. 76: "Read for the third time with M.ʳ
   Boyd. Nov.ʳ 1831." (2½ cols.); b) Orat. 4, "Adversus Julianum, II." On p. 129:
   "Read with M.ʳ Boyd Nov. 1831." (Amount read is not clear.); c) Orat. 20, "In
   Laudem Basilii." On p. 371: "Read with M.ʳ Boyd. Nov.ʳ 1831." (2½ cols.); d) Orat.
   35, "De Filio, I." On p. 574: "Read with M.ʳ Boyd twice. I did not finish the passage
   the first time at Malvern in 1830, but at Malvern Wells, Nov.ʳ 1831." (Nearly 2 cols.);
   e) Orat. 43, "In Novam Dominicam." On p. 703: "Read with M.ʳ Boyd Nov.ʳ 12 &
   13ᵗʰ 1831, at Malvern Wells." (Nearly 2 cols.)

against Julian—& to translate the Prometheus into blank verse.   I
begged him to do it, instead of me; & there the entreaties dropped!—
On my arrival at home on Monday, Occyta came running down
stairs to meet me as if he were delighted.   Dearest little thing!—
5 *Afterwards he sate on my knee, & I told him stories.—*
M.ʳˢ Boyd proposed Annie's returning with me,—& I was obliged
after a good deal of consideration & embarassment, to tell her why
we were unwilling to have her with us. ≪In my absence, off ran my
squirrel.   How provoking!—≫
10 _____

Tuesday.   15 Nov.
By the newspapers, cholera seems to be retreating.[1]   No letter
from Papa!   I hear that he has been written to about withdrawing
his cattle from the park which is taken together with the rest of the
15 *land, by Ward.   I began a letter to M.ʳ Boyd, which I shall not be able*
to send, on account of the snow.

Wednesday Nov 16.
Off to M.ʳˢ Cliffe's with Bummy & Arabel.   W.ᵈ rather have stayed
at home.   At number one I sh.ᵈ think, in the thermometer.   Eliza
20 *showed us her preparations for lithography—& they gave us luncheon,*
& wanted us to stay all night—& gave me a history of a disputation
of theirs about me in which Eliza had stated that I w.ᵈ not marry an
angel from Heaven.   Certainly if ever I were ≪to≫ <ₐmake up my
mind> to marry, I w.ᵈ fancy my selection to be an angel, at the very
25 *least.   But I never never will marry!——   ≪ . . . ≫*
I sent off a parcel to M.ʳˢ Boyd this morning, containing books—
a note from me to her—a note from Arabel to Annie—& a letter
from me to M.ʳ Boyd.[2]   In it I said that I missed both him & the
squirrel very much indeed,—tho' I was modest enough to believe
30 *in the possibility of its being best for both of them, that I sh.ᵈ.   I*

1. *The Times,* 14 November 1831: "Lieutenant-Colonel Creagh, in his despatches from
Sunderland of the 10th of November, states that he has pleasure in reporting, for the information of the Lords of the Privy Council, that only one slight case of cholera has occurred in
that town since his communication of the 9th." This "retreat" was only temporary; by the
end of the year 525 cases had been reported in Sunderland, 196 of them fatal (*The Times,*
29 December 1831).

2. For the letter, see Appendix I, p. 290.

wonder if he will answer my letter.   I told him that he need not do so, if he felt disinclined; ≪& he≫ does not care enough for me, to obviate the probability of his feeling disinclined.   And yet I shall be certainly pained if he does not write.   My letter was written rather in a playful than professing manner.   I will write no more professing   5 letters . . till the next time.——

Henrietta went away on Monday with Mrs Martin & the Miss Biddulphs, to ≪pay a visit≫ to Mrs Jones.   She is now at Ledbury where she will sleep tonight.   Bro went with her;——   He came here for a few minutes this evening——   Back again to the Biddulphs.   10

A reading evening down stairs!——<Bummy> over the Quarterly,[1] & I over Camoens, & Moliére!——

Thursday Novr 17.

Reading Camoens last night, suggested what I have been writing this morning——"Catarina to Camoens".[2]   I do not dislike it.   ≪A   15 letter from Papa, speaking of his return!——≫

Henrietta returned, <&> delighted with her visit.   But she always is delighted with anything like a visit——except where the Boyds are either active or passive.   She brought——what delighted me in no degree——an invitation from the Biddulphs to Bummy & me for next   20 Tuesday, to dine & sleep there.   Botherissimè——I dare say Bummy will go.

Friday Nov. 18.

No!——Bummy wont——she followed me up stairs after breakfast to say so.   I was determined not to oppose any wish of hers——&   25 luckily no wish of her's ran counter to mine.   Henrietta quite angry with me, because Bummy w^{dnt} go.   It was all my fault——my fault!!!! and I ought to be ashamed of myself!——   A note of invitation from Mrs Martin addressed to us all four, about dining & sleeping at Colwall. Now if we all four had been judged necessary to go, I w^d ≪have≫   30 gone par necessitè.   But what w^d have been the use of my going with Bummy when I hated it superlatively & Henrietta liked it superlatively. Henrietta out of humour with me.   To Mr Boyd's I can go at any time ——to Mrs Martin's never!——   Comparing for a moment Mr Boyd &

1. *The Quarterly Review*, November 1831.   2. For the poem, see Appendix II, p. 316.

Diary by E.B.B.

Mrs Martin!! I never cultivate the acquaintance of any one who can
be of use to me!— Translate _that_ by — — any one who has a large
establishment, & gives gay parties.

I wish Henrietta would estimate people more by their <u>minds</u> than
she actually does—, & that she were not so fond of visiting for
visiting's sake. At any rate, as I do not attempt to oppress her with
my influence on that or any other subject, I have a right to be myself unoppressed by her's. I told Bummy that if <u>she</u> wished me to
go to Colwall, I w.^d go. Bummy evidently did not care about it.

Reading Iphigenia in Aulis. I will go thro' it now.

Telling stories to Occyta & Sette, in the evening. Cinderella &
Blue Beard!—

Saturday. Nov. 19.

Getting on with Iphigenia . . I am very much interested in it—
particularly in the scene between Iphigenia & her father.[1] How much
simple affectionate nature there is in her character! The opposition
between her's, & Clytemnestra's stately dignity, is skilfully conceived.

Miss Glasco & Miss Peyton called—& Miss G talked to me about
Moore. His friend Mr Corry could not find out what article in the
<Edinburgh> was his;[2] & Moore figures himself in consequence, on
being masqueraded. I wonder if I shall pull off the mask, or leave it
on.

Bummy & Henrietta are not come & not coming home today.
Henrietta called for a few minutes to say so. She must be quite happy
between the Miss Biddulphs & Mrs Martin— How <u>unhappy</u> could
<u>I</u> be with either?[3] not that I mean to under-estimate Mrs Martin, who
deserves better of me & everybody. A letter from <u>Mrs Boyd</u>. She
reports that Mr Boyd has a "pretty message" to send to me, but that

5

10

15

20

25

1. _LCL-E_, I, 58-65, lines 631-685.

2. James Corry (1772-1848), at this time living in Cheltenham, had been a close friend
of Thomas Moore (1779-1852) since childhood, and they had both belonged to the Kilkenny
amateur theatrical company. In his diary for 13 September 1831, Moore recorded the des-
patch to _The Edinburgh Review_ of an article that he had been writing in collaboration with
his neighbour, Dr. Brabant. He described the subject as "German Rationalism in consequence
of Dr. Brabant having pointed out to me some errors in a late work on that topic" (_Memoirs,
Journal, and Correspondence of Thomas Moore_, ed. Lord John Russell, 8 vols., London,
1853-56, VI, 219). The article appeared in the issue of September 1831, pp. 238-255, but
without any indication of authorship.

3. Cf. fn 2, p. 142.

she cant tell him of her being in the act of writing. Therefore he had no means of sending it. I certainly think that he might have written himself. But never mind!——

Bro "cut Miss Wall dead" at Worcester today. Sorry for it!——

Sunday. Nov. 20   5

I wrote last night & sent my letter this morng to Mrs Boyd, enclosing Mr Martin's circular.¹ In my letter I told her, & begged her to tell Mr Boyd, about Papa's return, & about the apprehended consequences.

The Cliffes came to dinner. Not so Bummy & Henrietta, who are not coming home again today. ≪As I≫ understood that they,   10 *Biddulphs & all, were to be at the gate this evening, I hesitated about going, for fear of an invitation. It was wrong to hesitate. I went, & then a little plot of Bummy's was blown up. She had excused herself & me from dining at the Biddulphs <on> Tuesday, because I had a swelled face!—— Behold me at the gate with cheeks as thin as*   15 *usual!——*

I have had a pain in my face for the last two or three days—but the swelling is among things invisible.

Mr Curzon hinted at my taking him either to or fro' Malvern in our carriage,—≪tomorrow,——≫ & Arabel & I promised the fro', &   20 *settled to set off early tomorrow morning. How pleased we were! And now comes an embarrassment!—Bummy has desired Bro to take the carriage to Colwall tomorrow morng, for them to come away in— What in the world shall I do!——*

Monday Novr 21.st   25

Arabel & I got over the "triste embarras" by writing to Bummy, & begging her to "walk" home. Agreed to,—& we set off at about eight. Found Annie half dressed & Mrs Boyd quite undressed. Nearly ten before I was admitted into Mr Boyd's room. He spoke to me very kindly—& we read the exordium & peroration of Gregory's 2.^d   30 *oration on the paschal.² †*

1. His open letter to the Bishop of Hereford (see fn. 2, p. 176 and Appendix I, p. 288). Apart from appearing in the papers, Mr. Martin's letter was privately printed and circulated in the area.

2. Oration 42, (*GNO*, I, 676-697). A marginal note in *WG*, p. 676, recorded: "Read with Mr Boyd. Nov. 21. 1831." (61 lines.) Another, on p. 696: "Read with Mr Boyd. Nov 21 1831. Malvern Wells." (2 columns.)

Diary by E.B.B.

M.ʳ Curzon talked for about one half hour to M.ʳ Boyd while I was in the room. He & we did not go away until five. Dark all the way. Talked about M.ʳ Boyd whom M.ʳ Curzon "cant understand," & about our Hope End business which I cant understand. Let down M.ʳ C at
5 *our gate. Rather a happy day. For the very happy ones . . Eheu fugaces!———¹*

Tuesday. Nov 22.ᵈ

So I hear Bummy was very angry at Arabel's going with me yesterday. What she said before the <boys> about Annie, was enough
10 *to make me so, & did. It is not kind.*

Wednesday Nov.ʳ 23

Very unwell indeed all day—& lazy besides. ≪A note of invitation from Lady Margaret. Battle of the frogs & mice with Henrietta, about it.≫

15 *Thursday. Nov. 24.*

Obliged to go to Mathon with Bummy & Arabel. The latter slept at the Bartons last night. I hope she had enough of it.

Went with the Cliffe's to see poor Col. West's house:² Cards lying on the table,—Bro's among them! I could not bear looking at any-
20 *thing. So soon passeth it away, & we are gone!— M.ʳ Cliffe sulky.³ Only saw him at dinner and at tea. Never heard him—& none the worse for it. M.ʳ Allen Cliffe goodnatured, & nothing beside. Had guitaring & fortune telling & "all that" in the evening. And reading M.ʳˢ Sherwood's Roxabel.⁴ Bad & vulgar.*

25 *Friday. Nov. 25.*

The Cliffes wanted us to stay, but we "must go". I have to answer

---

1. "Alas, they glide swiftly by." (Horace, "Odes," II.xiv, lines 1-4, *LCL-HO/O*, pp. 142-143: "Alas, O Postumus, Postumus, the years glide swiftly by, nor will righteousness give pause to wrinkles, to advancing age, or Death invincible.")

2. Mathon Lodge, the home of the late Col. James Dawson West, who had died on 2 August (map ref. C7). The *Worcester Herald*, 22 October, announced its sale by auction on 14 December, and the issue of 19 November, the sale of the contents.

3. William Bateson Cliffe (1803-85), the elder brother of Eliza and Allen.

4. Mary Martha Sherwood, *Roxobel*, 3 vols. (London, 1830). Mrs. Sherwood was a friend of the Cliffes, and was one of the witnesses at the marriage of Mary Catherine Cliffe to Thomas Best in 1827.

Lady Margaret's note, & must say yes—or I dont know what Bummy w^d. say. Reading poor M^r. Hockin's epitaph[1]—& M^r. Reece's pseudo-Latin one.[2] ≪M^{essrs}≫ Dean & Sill[3] came, & worked at a translation verbatim. Mrs Cliffe prayed me for a "new version". Granted—& praised. Got home— Wrote yea to Lady Madge. Bothered about it.

Saturday. Nov. 26.

    Wrote to Mrs Boyd to beg her to write & let me know whether I should be acceptable to her party on Monday—to write to Eastnor. Lady Margaret asked me to stay with her two or three days; but I wont stay a day later than Monday morng. And late enough,— by the presiding Goddess of Ennui. Ann & I set off in the wheelbarrow. Dinner & tea & supper very solemn. The Dowager Lady Somers, & Miss Baker constituting the <u>omnes</u>.

Sunday. Nov 27.

    Heard M^r. Higgins twice at church, & once in the Eastnor dining room.[4] Dont like him—or rather, cant tolerate him! Walked on the terrace with Miss Baker & Lady Margaret, et cum silentio.[5] Lord Somers c^d. not help admiring the manner in which my hair was dressed—!! at dinner today—just like Vandyke's pictures—<u>or</u> Sir Peter Lelys.[6] Mem. to repeat that compliment wherever my long locks make themselves unpopular. Looked into Phillips's Sacred

5

10

15

20

---

    1. The Rev. John Pearce Hockin, Rector of Coddington since 1810, had died on 26 October. The epitaph E.B.B. read was presumably the following, used on the memorial tablet erected in All Saints' Church, Coddington, where he was buried:

> Heavily my years have rolled along
> Nor mirth nor joy inspire my song
> Heavily my years have rolled away
> And now behold a lump of clay
> My mind was vexed by anxious grief
> Firm trust in God brought kind relief.

    2. The Rev. George Reece (1768-1847), at this time Curate of Mathon, was an old friend of the Cliffe family, and had baptized Eliza. It is not possible to say whether the "pseudo-Latin" epitaph was for his late confrère, Mr. Hockin (who had been his contemporary at Cambridge), or for his brother, Dr. Richard Reece, the author of *The Domestic Medical Guide* and other works, who had died in London in July.

    3. The Rev. John Parkinson Sill (1803?-83), Curate of Bosbury.

    4. The Rev. Joseph Higgins (1771?-1847), Rector of Eastnor since 1795.

    5. "And in silence."

    6. Sir Anthony Van Dyck (1599-1641) and Sir Peter Lely (1618-80)

Diary by E.B.B.

Literature, where Gregory's orations against Julian, are called "pointed thunder".[1]

How stupid we are!!—And how wise I am! to have brought my desk, & left my key!———

5 ≪Monday≫. Nov. 28.

Read when I was in bed last night, Marmontel's Sheperdess of the Alps.[2] Very pretty; but the heroine never never shd have married again. Well! that cant be helped now. Talked to Miss Baker, about . . love!— She told me some passages in her life, which might have 10 been <ʌleft> dark passages, without injury to her or me—or at least, lit by only a sky light!—after all she is a sensible woman.—

Nota bene—her prophecy, that Lord Somers will marry again.[3] If <he> does, he should marry <some> great great great great do do do do granddaughter of Stentor, or the <courtship> will never get on 15 with his deafness. Nota bene—my prophecy, that he will vote for reform, tho' he thinks against it.[4] Glad to get away from Eastnor. A letter from Papa to me. An expression in it about "the happy results" of our long separation, seemed to me at first, to glance at a particular subject. Other people consider it a general expression; & 20 so it may be. What can the report be to which Mrs Boyd alludes? I am not very uneasy.

Poor Mr Pindar died this morning.[5]

It has been arranged απανευθε[6] from me, that Misses Glasco & Peyton dine with us today.

25 Evening past away in a more lively manner than my two last evenings did. Miss Glasco is going to exhibit her puppet show, & has engaged Bro & Henrietta as performers in it. Wont do with Papa.

1. T[homas] P[hillips], *The Study of Sacred Literature Fully Stated and Considered* (London, 1756), p. 35: "The Invectives of the Former [St. Gregory the Divine] against the Apostate Emperor Julian, carry with them a Thunder as pointed as that of the Philippics; . . ."

2. Jean François Marmontel, *La Bergère des Alpes* (Paris, 1766), a verse pastorale in three acts.

3. He did, on 3 June 1834, when he married his cousin Jane Waddington (*née* Cocks), a widow.

4. He did, in the decisive division of 14 April 1832 (*Dod's Parliamentary Companion*, 3rd. edn., London, 1833).

5. The *Worcester Herald*, 3 December 1831, under DIED: "Nov. 28th, at his residence, the Upper Hall, near Ledbury, in the 77th year of his age, deeply regretted by his family and friends, the Rev. Reginald Pyndar, A.M. rector of Madresfield, in this county . . ."

6. "Remote."

Tuesday Nov. 29.

   Today Miss Boyd & Miss Bordman leave Malvern.   Had a letter from Mrs Boyd which I ought to have had last Sunday; & then I might have gone to say good bye on Monday.   But it is as well.   I cant bear saying good bye.——   And I shall see more of Mr Boyd, who always   5 must & will stand first in the canvass, by going on Wednesday.   Mrs Boyd says that she has ["]invited Miss <H M>.!!"——^1   I annoyed. I wont go to Ruby Cottage as long as she is there—shant be wanted: & wont be wanted.   Sent two little poems & a letter to the editor of the N M M—Bulwer, I think his name is.^2   If he does not pay me for   10 my contributions, what in the world am I to do with all my debts?——

   Papa is coming this week.   Dear dear Papa!——   Pro & conning about Bummy ≪Henrietta≫ & Bro dining at Eastnor on Thursday, according to invitation.   Conned out of the question.   ≪Wrote to Papa!——≫   15

Wednesday Nov 30.

   Off to Malvern, by favour of Mr Lane's driving, at eight in the morning.   Slipped gently into the house, & presently into the kitchen, to find out whether Mr Boyd had had his breakfast.   Jane^3 just going to take it up to him.   So I ventured to precede it.   20

   He seemed pleased to see me, & I had a happy day with him.   †   ≪He "assured me"≫ <that> Miss H M's coming was by no means his wish—but Mrs Boyd's & Annie's.   The annoyance is wearing off—& perhaps I may go to Ruby Cottage while she is there—after all.   We read passages from Gregory's apologetick,^4—comparing his   25

   1. Henrietta Mushet (1802-65), who later married the Rev. George Roberts, Curate of Coleford, was the second child of David Mushet, the metallurgist. She was an old friend of H.S.B., and sometimes acted as his amanuensis; that they had a serious disagreement in 1832 is clear from E.B.B.'s letters, but the references are too oblique to reveal the cause of the upset (*EBB/HSB*, pp. 178 ff.).

   2. Edward George Lytton Bulwer (1803-73), later (1843) Bulwer-Lytton and (1866) 1st Baron Lytton. He was editor 1831-33 of *The New Monthly Magazine and Literary Journal*. E.B.B.'s poems were not published.

   3. The Boyds' maid.

   4. There are two marginal notes in *WG* dated 30 November; one on p. 3 refers to a passage of 50 lines, the other on p. 6, 23 lines. In a long note at the commencement of this Oration, E.B.B. said that the passage on p. 3 "has great dignity & harmony;" and that the second passage contained "a series of similes in the Homeric manner: (how novel & beautiful Gregory's similes usually are!)"

Diary by E.B.B.

marks with mine, in different copies,—& came to the conclusion, that our tastes certainly do agree!! And so they do.

I began to write my Caterina in Annie's album. Got home at a little after five—& too lazy to write further particulars.

5   *Thursday. Dec. 1ˢᵗ*

Wrote a letter to Mʳ Boyd,—but not a very long one, about some things which he enquired about, in Isocrates & Zenophon.¹ Did not send it!— No letter—& no Papa. Dealing with Gregory!—

Friday. Dec. 2ᵈ

10   *Sent my letter to Mʳ Boyd. Dealing with Euripides. The Iphigenia in Tauris. Very inferior to the Iph: in Aulide, as far as I <u>can read</u>.*

Saturday Dec 3ᵈ

A letter from Mʳ Boyd—a very short one—but kind, & in his own manner. Pleased to receive it. If he cared <u>very</u> much about

15   *pleasing me, he wᵈ write <u>very</u> much oftener. Mʳˢ Cliffe & Eliza called, & spirited away Henrietta & Arabel to sleep at Mathon!— Suppose Papa were to come home in the meantime!*

Sunday. Decʳ 4ᵗʰ

A few lines from Papa in a fish. We are not to write,—& he is

20   *to come home "early in the week.["] Arabel went back to Mathon, with the intention of riding with Eliza & Mʳˢ Cliffe to Malvern next day. If <little> Billy cᵈ be ridden & driven at once, I wᵈ be driven to Malvern to-morrow. As it was, I was in an <agitation> about going, & at last by Bummy's inspiration, called up my impudence &*

25   *wrote a note to Mʳˢ C, begging her to drive me there.*

≪Monday≫. Dec 5ᵗʰ

Sent my note, had an <ₐaffirmative> answer, & walked down to the gate with Bummy to meet the carriage. The worst of it was, that Mʳˢ C & Eliza made another proposition to meet mine, namely

---

1. For the letter, see Appendix I, p. 292.

that they w^d sleep here—because otherwise they might have been benighted in going round & round on my account. Agreed to, of course: but, thinks I to myself, if Papa were to arrive on Tuesday Morning & find them here!——

Well! but I had a pleasant three hour visit at my dear friend's house. I was in his room before he was; & when he heard my voice, he smiled as if in pleased surprise. † He wished that I ≪could≫ have come in our own carriage, & have stayed later!—— ≪We talked a≫ good deal—yet not a word about —— what I dont want to hear. I wonder ≪whether≫ some people are penetrating.

Tuesday Dec 6th.

We spirited away M^{rs} C & Eliza & Mr Allen C who made one of our party by an <u>un</u>happy accident,—for fear Papa sh^d come. But he did not—& not a letter!—

Wednesday Dec 7th.

No letter—no Papa.

Thursday Dec 8th.

A letter to me: and papa is to be with us tomorrow. My dear dear Papa! His coming is a thing feared & wished for! For what feelings must, & what circumstances may, attend it.

Phillips's sacred literature which I had sent for to Eastnor, by Mr Boyd's request, arrived. Now, thinks I to myself if I c^d get to Malvern after dinner today, how pleasant it w^d be. By these means I could deliver the book immediately & have an interview with my dear friend before Papa's arrival. Je propose. Ran down stairs to Bummy, & had the game in my own hands. She w^d go with me. Very kind of her. She & Arabel & I set off accordingly at <past> two;—& what with the rain, & what with the fog, which imitated rain most successfully in the distance, I c^d scarcely get Bummy on. Contrived it however .. I was ≪set≫ down at Ruby Cottage, & they, after offering to take Annie with them, drove on to Gt Malvern. Annie was at Miss Steers's!—

Mr Boyd certainly pleased to see me. I read what he wanted to

[189]

Diary by E.B.B.

hear out of Phillips—& something from the apologetick besides. †
A happy visit of nearly an hour & a half.   He gave me <Wesleys>
treatise on Predestination.¹   On our way home <ᴧover the hills>
Bro & Sam frightened us with their gallopade in the dark.   My hands
5   & feet went to sleep meo more.

Friday Dec 9ᵗʰ.
     Our beloved Papa arrived ≪ . . . ≫ between 11 & 12.   Tho' the
thoughts of seeing him made me sick & trembling hours before, yet
when I saw his dear face, my fear of distressing him outgrew other
10   fears.   I did not faint; or cry . . much.   Henrietta & Arabel cried
too! Our dear dear Papa.
     He is apparently well, & in good spirits.   He talked to us all day,
in his animated agreable manner; & I could almost believe him to be
happy.
15   Only once his eyes wandered to the window.   There were those
horrible cows of Capᵗ. Johnson's in the park.²   His countenance
changed; & his eyes were turned away.

Saturday.   Decʳ. 10ᵗʰ
     Wrote to Mʳ. Boyd a long letter, to give him an account of the
20   tongues & politics.³   I told him not to answer it, unless he felt inclined to do so—*will* he feel inclined?
     Bummy has been speaking to Papa.   She will not tell me exactly
what was said—but two things are clear—that we shall go—& that
we shall *not* go immediately.

25   *Sunday Deᶜ 11ᵗʰ.*
     Read Wesley's treatise.   It is clear & powerful; but not by any
means satisfactory to me everywhere.   Papa & we walked down to

---

1. John Wesley, *Predestination Calmly Considered* (London, 1752).
2. Capt. John Johnstone (1784- ?), of Mainstone Court, near Ledbury (map ref. F1),
brother of Lady Knowles, and lessee of part of the Hope End land.
3. For the letter, see Appendix I, p. 293. "The tongues" refer to the much-discussed
occurrences in October at the Regent's Square church, London, during sermons by the Rev.
Edward Irving (1792-1834). Sundry members of the congregation purported to have been
inspired to speak in an unknown tongue by the Holy Spirit, and this sparked off a storm of
theological argument. These two lines, taken from a "magnificent burst" quoted in the
Kentish Gazette, 1 November 1831, illustrate the "gift" claimed by 15 of Irving's flock:
"Hippo—gerosto—hippo—booros—senoote | Foorime Oorin Hoopo Tanto Noostin—"

the gate, to hear — — nobody.   The Bristol students were minus:
on account of the rain perhaps.

Monday Dec 12.
    Rain by buckets.   Finished the Iphigenia in Tauris—not worth
re-reading!—and began the Hippolytus.   5

Tuesday Dec.ʳ 13ᵗʰ.
    Reading Greek—Hippolytus.   ≪A letter from Fanny to Bummy,
about engaging Miss Steers.[1]≫

Wednesday, Dec.ʳ 14ᵗʰ.
    Bummy wrote a note of propositions to Miss Steers: and Arabel   10
sent Annie's newly painted basket by the same conveyance.
    I wish for Fanny's sake, that Miss Steers may consent to her
proposal; & for Annie's sake, that it may be rejected.
    A note from Miss Steers, who says neither ≪yea≫ nor nay,—but
desires to see Bummy tomorrow.   Hurrah!—I hope B may go.   15
    Reading the Hippolytus.

Thurday [sic] Dec.ʳ 15ᵗʰ

Friday Dec.ʳ 16ᵗʰ
    Bummy wᵈnt go at first—settled that she wᵈnt: and I ran up
stairs in an in-disposition.   Presently up into my room came Bummy.   20
She wᵈ. go.   I had been walking up & down, in my dungeon building
mood, half resolving not to go with <ₐher> on Monday for fear of
— ——?—— My resolution is not to be tried.   We went.   The
rain & mist did <all> they cᵈ. to drive us back, when we had trav-
elled half way; but they missed their object.   I argued so logically   25
& entreated so persuasively that we went en avant!—   Bummy was
supererogatorily civil to Mʳˢ. Trant, & wᵈ. call on her.   Half an hour's
boring.   And then on to Miss Steers where Bummy wished me to go
in & hear the preliminaries.   Went in.   Miss S disinclined for Ireland.

---

1. Bummy's younger sister Frances (1790-1868), wife of Sir Thomas Butler, Bt. (1783-1861), was looking for a governess for her four sons, and Miss Steers had been suggested for the post.

Diary by E.B.B.

On Annie's account I am glad: on no other.   She would be an excel-
lent governess.   She unites a very active & cultivated mind, to agre-
able ladylike manners, & many accomplishments.   Arabel drove me to
Ruby Cottage, & returned to Bummy after a few minutes warming.
5   *≪M.ʳ≫ Boyd pleased to see me. A very happy two hours visit! † I*
read to myself some extracts from his translations & letters against
Exley, in the Methodist magazine; and begged him to let me take the
book home.[1]   Granted—tho' I am so careless!— He does not like
the idea of our going to the isle of Wight; because he does not like the
10   *idea of crossing the sea.   "Unless you wish to go there yourself, do*
try & prevent such a plan."   "I assure you I do not wish to go there.
I w.ᵈ rather go anywhere where you w.ᵈ go!—"   He certainly means
to be with us wherever we go!—

   Got home thro' wind & rain & darkness. Papa not angry. Miss
15   *— — —.   What was I going to say? They called me down to tea,*
& I forgot!——

Saturday.   Dec ≪17≫.ᵗʰ

   Arabel told me last night that Miss H M was expected at R C at
three.   <We> did not leave it until four.   What an escape!

20   *A letter or rather note waiting at home for me, from M.ʳˢ Boyd,—*
conveying a message from M.ʳ Boyd.   His love, & he hoped that I w.ᵈ
soon be able to go & see him.   He said much the same thing to me
yesterday.   Could I not spend a whole day with him as usual, & soon?
I suppose he must really wish it.

25   *Sunday Dec ≪18≫.ᵗʰ*

   I read Wesley's pamphlet thro' a second time; and I read near-
ly three chapters of Baxter's Saint's rest, & Erskine's prolegomena.

---

1. *The Methodist Magazine for the Year 1818* (London, 1818). H.S.B.'s translation of
St. Basil's Homily "On the Faith," with a covering letter, appeared on pp. 248-253. A letter
from H.S.B. on the Creed of St. Gregory Thaumaturgus appeared on pp. 434-436. Further
letters from him, on the subject of the Eternal Sonship, occurred on pp. 196-202; 254-256;
257-260; 333-335; 335-338; and 338-340. This last group of letters expressed criticism of
the views propounded by Thomas Exley in his pamphlet *A Vindication of Dr. Adam Clarke,
in Answer to Mr. Moore's Thoughts on the Eternal Sonship of the Second Person of the
Holy Trinity* (Bristol, [1817]). Exley dealt with H.S.B.'s letters on pp. 67 ff. of a further
pamphlet, *Reply to Mr. Watson's Remarks on the Eternal Sonship of Christ; and the Use of
Reason in Matters of Revelation. . . . To which are Added Remarks on Mr. Boyd's Letters
on the Same Subject in the Methodist Magazine*, (London, 1818).

Baxter is exquisite. He sings with the spirit, & he sings with the understanding also—[1]

A tame but inoffensive preacher at the gate. I was not at church.

Monday. Dec. ≪*19*≫*th.*

*Annie is to go to Mathon to day. M*rs *Cliffe's carriage is the medium; & I have been dreaming that M*rs *Cliffe's goodnature might* mediate *for me, & suggest calling for me at our gate at least. All a dream. The waking was not agreable. But I read myself into a good humour. Hippolytus is not one of Euripides's best plays, tho' it is very superior to the Ipheginia in* ≪*Tauris*≫.

5

10

Tuesday. Dec ≪*20*≫*th.*

The Cliffes & Annie came. Annie says that Miss Mushet is a phrenologist, as well as being wonderful in other things. I am indisposed towards Miss Mushet. Not that I am "jealous" as Annie suggested, of her knowledge of Greek. If her knowledge ≪*were*≫ *double what it is, I sh*d *not be jealous of that; & if it were none at all, I should feel equally* indisposèe— *I shall not like going to R C while she is there—I wonder how long she will stay.*

15

Wednesday. Dec ≪*21*st*≫*

What did I do today. Greek of course. But I was idle, as I have been lately, about my diary; & kept no account. We drove to Eastnor.

20

Thursday. Dec ≪*22*d*≫*

A note from Eliza <*enforcing*> *a proposition which she made to Bro yesterday, about their (Annie & all) sleeping here, on the night of the puppet show. I wrote an assent. A note enclosed from M*rs *Boyd. In it she says that Miss Mushet is plainer than she was, but "just as amiable as ever". If she was & is amiable, how did M*r *Boyd's coolness towards her, arise? and why should it not be thawed away*

25

1. Richard Baxter (1615-91) first published *The Saints Everlasting Rest; or, a Treatise of the Blessed State of the Saints in their Enjoyment of God in Glory* in 1650 (London). It was subsequently abridged by Benjamin Fawcett (1715-80), and the 16th edn. of this shortened version (London, 1824) contained an Introductory Essay by Thomas Erskine (1788-1870).

Diary by E.B.B.

≪now?≫   I shall _not_ like going to R C—But I said that before.

Finished the Hippolytus,—& began the Supplices of Æschylus.
I read a part of it before; but I have left off now my _partial_ habits of
reading.

5   My dear Papa in good spirits.

Friday Dec ≪23≫.ᵈ

No memorabilia—Attributable in part to my idleness.   I wrote
to Mʳˢ Boyd, & did not say a word about going to R C.; but sent my
note there by Henry.   She ≪wᵈ not≫ keep Henry—She will write
10   tomorrow.   My reason for sending him, was that Mʳ Boyd might have
≪the≫ Methodist Magazine which he wished to have in a week!   A
week today since I saw him!—

Saturday Dec ≪24ᵗʰ.≫

It was determined last night, by Papa & the rest of the senators,
15   that the boys shᵈ have a holiday today, Christmas eve.   A relief to
me.   Miss Glasco is to exhibit her puppet show next Friday, & she
wants my prologue.   I hate that kind of composition—am not in a
humour for it—but I suppose she must have what she wants.

A note from Mʳˢ Boyd.   I am "very naughty but very kind" for
20   sending the turkey.   Mʳ Boyd she "dares say," "will write to me next
time".   Never! when he can help it.   He is "quite reconciled to H M
≪notwithstanding≫ all his fears".

I knew it wᵈ be so.   If he does write to me, his writing will be no
proof of his having thought of me,—but only of his having received
25   a turkey!   Low spirited this evening.   Wrote to Mʳˢ Boyd three
times—before I cᵈ write what pleased me.   I said ≪at last≫ "I have
thought that Mʳ B wᵈ like Miss H M ≪as≫ much as ever; so you see
your information was anticipated".   Not a word about ≪his writing≫
to me, or my going there.   If I were to go there, & to perceive that
30   he wᵈ have preferred my having stayed away,—Oh I cannot get over
the reluctance.

Sunday Dec. ≪25≫.ᵗʰ

My letter went—

We went to church; & as B H & I took the sacrament there, we
35   went to chapel also before we returned home.   A nothing-particular

[194]

*preacher at the latter place.   No letter!   Christmas day—& I am out
of spirits.*

Monday.   Dec. ≪26≫th.

*   A continuation of the Christmas holidays.   A pain in my face &
head kept me awake all last night,—& I am not at all well this morng.   5
A note from Miss Glasco.   She wants to know what her rascally poet
is doing about the prologue.   Promised to let her have it tomorrow.
And yet how <u>can</u> I write when I am so unwell?*

*   The Cliffes & Mrs Best & Annie called.   They wont sleep here on
Sunday,—≪ . . . ≫ <u>because</u> M^{rs} C does not esteem my note as being   10
sufficiently pressing; and thinks that I was quite in earnest in recom-
mending her to sleep at the Horse & Jockey¹ instead of here!!!!—
Maddox came.*

Tuesday.   Dec ≪27≫th.

*   Unwell still.   I could not do more than write a few lines—no!   15
more than few! of the prologue.   Miss Glasco must wait for tomorrow.
No letter!*

Wednesday.   Dec ≪28≫th.

*   Finished the prologue.²   Read it to Bummy & Papa—& both of
them pleased.   Sent it off by Bro to Miss G—& both of <u>them</u> pleased.   20
<u>I</u> am pleased besides: and am a great deal better.*

*   A note from Mrs Boyd, to tell me of Annie & Eliza & M^r A Cliffe
having been <_∧at> ≪R C≫, & of all she has heard about my horribly
rude note to Mrs Cliffe!!   Wrote a few lines to M^{rs} B, offering ≪a≫ bed
to Jane for Friday night—& one line of astonishment at M^{rs} C's ob-   25
tuseness.   Sent it by Maddox whom we took to the Ledbury Turnpike.
Taken in to call on the Pindars.   I <u>meant</u> to enquire after them,—&
they <u>wished</u> to see us.   <u>Us</u> means H A & me.   Dear Stormy's birthday.³*

Thursday Dec ≪29≫.

*   Gent took Bummy's <u>final</u> to Miss Steers today; & a note full of   30
addenda to my note yesterday, to Mrs Boyd.   He has come back.   As*

1. A Public House in Colwall (map ref. E6).
2. We do not know of any extant copy of this.   3. His 17th.

she was not at home, there is of course, no answer.   And no letter for
me by the post!!   It is clear that M.ʳ Boyd did not, & does not, intend
to write to me, notwithstanding what M.ʳˢ Boyd said.   Is it kind?—
Perhaps it is better.   I am not sure whether I ought or ought not to
5 *go to R C without waiting much longer for an intimation from him*
on the subject.   After all, I can only be pained; & to that I am accus-
tomed.   So perhaps I had better go.   If I do not, my staying away
may be made an excuse for his quarrelling with me,—& to that I am
not accustomed.   I c.ᵈ not bear <that> kind of pain.   I wonder what
10 *book Miss H M is reading with him.   There is no use in wondering——*

H & A have ridden to Mathon, to combat M.ʳˢ Cliffes estravaganzas.
Do I wish them all to sleep here tomorrow—really wish it?—   I wish
dear Annie to do as she wishes; & I wish M.ʳˢ Boyd not to be displeased
with me or any of us.   But I am not, I believe, in a humour for a
15 *crowd of people.   May I escape the Barton crowd tomorrow!   Ora*
pro nobis—

I knew from the beginning, how it w.ᵈ be ≪about≫ Miss H M.
Well!   The last time I was at R C, I was very happy.   The last time!——

H & A come back.   M.ʳˢ C intractable!—   A brought a note for
20 *me from M.ʳˢ Boyd.   M.ʳ Boyd ≪sends≫ me a message! of thanks for*
the turkey, and expresses himself "sorry at my not having come over,
yet, as" (What force there is in some words!) "he ≪wishes the≫ two
rival <Queens> to meet".   And so I am to go to R C to be shown
off & with Miss H M!!—   ≪The≫ coolness of M.ʳ Boyd's expressions,
25 *& the indifference he shows about writing to me, ≪went≫ to my*
heart; & when I was in the room by myself, I could not help shedding
actual tears.   He ≪did≫ not deserve one of them—and yet they
were shed!——

Wrote a note to M.ʳˢ B, in which I told her the real reason of my
30 *not having been to R C before.   "I remembered that M.ʳ Boyd might*
have reading to do with Miss Mushet at the time of my arrival; & that
such an interruption w.ᵈ be <neither> pleasant for him nor me.   Cer-
tainly not for me"—   Then I said—"With regard to the question of
regality, tell M.ʳ Boyd that
35   *A breath unmakes me, as a breath has made:* [1]

---

1. This implies that E.B.B. had studied Isaac Disraeli's *Curiosities of Literature*. In the
7th edn. (5 vols., London, 1823), IV, 147-148, Disraeli quoted the following couplet from

and that I willingly & properly yield all my pseudo, Princess-Olive ≪pretensions≫, to the legal claimant.''

My spirits were so depressed <this> evening, that it was an effort to me to talk even as little as I usually do.   Write myself down an ass!— 5

Friday Dec 30.

Sent my note to M*rs* Boyd.   What will be thought of it?— Not, I hope, that I ≪was≫ out of humour when I wrote it.   I am more, much more angry with myself than with M*r* Boyd.   He has professed too much—& I have expected too much.   We are both in fault: but 10 my fault is the worst, because it has been persevered in, longest—& against clear evidences.   I said in my note that I w*d* try to go to Malvern tomorrow, for an hour; but that if I did not go, I was not to be expected next week, on account of the boys who have had their christmas holidays & sh*d* have no others immediately.   I almost hope 15 that I may not go.

Eheu![1]—Papa has sent me word that I must not stay at home tonight!—

Curling hair & dressing to meet a crowd of people whom I know nothing of, & care for less than I know.   Off at half past six: And 20 saw Ionson Bluebeard & my prologue enacted at eight.   The puppets are admirable; very very ingenious—& put to shame many whom they counterfeit.   Bro spoke my prologue, & spoke it very well indeed. Applauded; & Miss Glasco presented me afterwards with a wreath of bay!   If M*r* Biddulph had been there, he was to have placed it on my 25 head, with an oration to boot.   An escape!—

Fifty people we were, in all; or perhaps rather more.   The outside of M*rs* Watsons head, larger a very great deal, than the inside.   Does she plume herself upon that?   Annie kind in her manner to me.   I

Oliver Goldsmith's *The Deserted Village* (London, 1770), p. 4:

> Princes and lords may flourish, or may fade;
> A breath can make them, as a breath has made.

Disraeli then suggested that Goldsmith had drawn inspiration from a poem ["L'Horloge de Sable"] by [Gilles] de Caux, containing these lines:

> C'est un verre qui luit
> Qu'un souffle peut detruire, et qu'un souffle a produit

and felt that Goldsmith's couplet should perhaps have ended "A breath unmakes them, as a breath has made.''

1. "Alas!"

[197]

think I feel kindness more & more susceptibly.   Eliza sate next me some time; & I told her some of my thoughts about my want of etiquette, & M^{rs} C's want of ≪judgment≫.   She told me that Mr Boyd had wondered before her, at my not having been to visit him as

5 *usual.   I have determined to go tomorrow.*

    Got home at half past one: & Occyta pretended not to be sleepy.

Saturday.   ≪Dec^r≫ 31st

    I have been to R C.   The fog made Bummy protest at first against my going; & then the rain made me resign myself to its effects.   But

10 *the rain cleared away,——& the clearing away of the fog seemed to be ≪the≫ future in rus: so Arabel & I set off to the Wyche.   She drove of course,——& we left the carriage, & the poney rugged close to the turnpike.   I nervous & fidgetty about R C.   Down the rocky path— Arabel's short way—not mine!!   Went into the house!   Nobody in*

15 *the dining room, or drawing room!   Into Mr Boyd's room!   A made me go!   M^r B & Miss M reading together.   She is five feet ten & plain; with an agreable voice,——but rather an independance & unshrinking-ness of manners.   Very unaffected tho', & sensible.   She did not seem to think of leaving the room.   M^r B said that he was sorry to hear of*

20 *my having been unwell——& that he had not expected me today on account of the rain!——   Mrs Boyd came in,——& A & I went out with her.   Had luncheon & talked as lingeringly as I c^d   I did not like the idea of going back to Miss M.   Presently she came down, & then I went up.   Mrs Boyd had proposed my going up, before.*

25   *He began to talk to me about my letter.   There were two things in it.   About the prologue: it c^d not require his revision,——but reading it, w^d not have been troublesome to him.   And then, about my going to see him.   ["]There was plenty of time for him to read with Miss Mushet——   Did I forget that she was staying in the house &c?"   I*

30 *answered, I recollected when I was staying there that he did not like Miss Cliffe or anybody to interrupt him.   "Did I really conceive the cases to be parallel?   Miss Cliffe & I!   If I thought that he c^d compare ≪me≫ with any other person, he c^d only say that he was sorry for it."   And yet his manner was not the manner I liked.   And when he asked*

35 *me to go soon & early as usual—to go next week—or if I c^d not do that, early in the following week, his manner was not the manner I liked.*

[198]

[The remainder of this day's entry is cross-written.]

*Does he not evidently wish me to go then, for <u>my</u> sake,—not <u>his?</u>
My spirits were gone!—   A & I were at home at 20 minutes to five.
Miss M walked with us to the Wyche, much to my annoyance.*

*The last day of the old year!—   What will next year see?   A great
deal of sorrow perhaps,—& perhaps my grave.—   Oh Thou in whose*   5
*hands are the forces of life & death,—& whose will is wisdom & love
—Thy will be done.*

[This entry concludes the first portion of the Diary.]

NEW YEAR CARD, 1827

Ink sketch by Eliza Cliffe

ENTRY OF 8 JANUARY 1832

Jany 1ˢ.ᵗ 1832 Hope End.

Sunday.   I suppose I must go on here with my diary,—as I cant get another book.[1]

This is the first day of a new year; and I am not in the humour for being wished a happy one.   Into thy hands oh God of all consolation, into thy merciful hands which chastise not willingly I commit the remains of my earthly happiness: and Thou mayest will that from these few barley loaves & small fishes, twelve basketfuls may be gathered.

My heart sinks within me—but not when I think of Thee!— Lord gracious & merciful, teach me to think of thee more often, & with more love——

No church.   Examination day ≪on≫ the heath;[2] & almost everybody, except Papa & Bummy & me, went there.   We down to the gate.   A good sermon from M.ʳ Curzon's vice.   In the evening Papa read to us M.ʳ MacGhee's letter to D.ʳ Whately Archbishop of Dublin, on the subject of Irish education.[3]   An admirable letter.   I abused D.ʳ W. as I <always> have & will do.   He wrote against evangelical religion, & clinched his arguments by a translation of Plutarch's treatise on superstition.[4]   An intimation that Plutarch knew more of christianity than he did?—

Monday Jan.ʸ 2.

Bummy has proposed calling at the Bartons, & going early that we may be able to drive somewhere else afterwards.   Where will the somewhere else be?   I would like to go to the Wyche,—& not for the sake of the Wyche.

Packed up M.ʳ Boyd's Gregory (Gregory's poems) & Mess[rs]. Pilkington & Beverley on the unknown tongues,[5] which I put within

---

1. The second half of the Diary is written in a separate book (see p. xxxiii).

2. i.e., of Wesleyan-Methodist candidates.

3. The letter, dated Dublin 15 December 1831, appeared in *The Dublin Evening Mail*, 23 December 1831.   It was subsequently printed and sold as a pamphlet, *Education in Ireland. A Letter to the Most Reverend Doctor Whately, Archbishop of Dublin*, by Robert James M'Ghee (Aberdeen, 1832).

4. E.B.B. refers to his book, *The Errors of Romanism Traced to their Origin in Human Nature* (London, 1830), pp. 1-76 of which dealt with superstition.

5. George Pilkington, *The Unknown Tongues Discovered to be English, Spanish, and Latin; and the Rev. Edw. Irving Proved to be Erroneous in Attributing their Utterance to the Influence of the Holy Spirit* (London, 1831); Robert Mackenzie Beverley, *A Sermon*

Diary by E.B.B.

Mr Boyd's parcel, for Miss H M. I hope she (yet not exactly _she_)
may think me attentive in doing so. I cant bear anyone to think
me .. what I am!— Last night I read some of my diary to Arabel in
bed! My diary is not meant to be read by any person except myself:
5   but _she_ deserves to be ≪let behind≫ the scenes. Mine are very ill
painted.

⟨ . . . ⟩¹

Friday. Jany 6.
    I fancied last night that I heard Papa whisper to Occyta a proposal
10   about taking <or> sending him & everybody to Worcester. All
fancy!—

          Where was Fancy bred
          In the heart or in the head?—²

Not in the _head_ I think, on this occasion. M^{dme} de Sevignè says that
15   the thoughts early in a morning, are couleur de rose. Mine were so
much the contrary, before I got up this morning, that they made me
cry—
    Wrote to Mrs Boyd. It is better to do so. Told her how jet black
my spirits were, but did not mention Mr Clarke Jarvis,³ _nor nothing._
20   Desired _to be remembered_ to Miss Mushet. My best regards are kept
for better occasions. Finished the Choephori, & began the Eumenides.
Read more than 500 lines of Greek, & was more tired by them than by
the 800 the other day, because I met with more difficulties. Enervated
& inclined to go to sleep.
25   This is the twelfth day. How many happy twelfth days I have
spent!—— If it is fine tomorrow, I must make a proposition about
R C. But it wont be fine. _Fogissimo all today!_—— The choruses
both in the Supplices & Choephori are the finest parts≪;≫ and yet
the conclusion of the latter, is very fine. Æschylus, & worthy of
30   Æschylus.

Preached at Hull, on the XIII. of November, MDCCCXXXI, on the Unknown Tongues (London, 1831).

  1. Two leaves, i.e., 4 pages, excised.

  2. _Merchant of Venice_, III.ii.63-64.

  3. Not identified.

Saturday. Jany 7th

I have been to R C. Bummy & Henrietta almost disinclined me
from thinking of it; <but> at last I put on all my brass, & went into
the dining room to ask Papa for some silver. No objection from him!
Henry drove, & Sette & I were driven. Got to R C at about half past   5
twelve, or a little before: & talked to Mrs Boyd as long as I could in
the dining room— Quantum mutata!— No not mutata!— I may
as well have quoted it literally!—[1] *Miss H M came into the room, &*
after a minute or two, I went up into Mr Boyd's. He showed me his
three new books, his Dion Chrysostom, & Gregory, & Heliodorus: 10
and I read one or two short passages out of each. He told me that he
had written to ask me to spend a day or two with him! Would I do
such a thing? No indeed— There was a passage in Gregory's funeral
oration on his father, of which he c.^d not make out the meaning. I
was made to try at it. It did not appear to me quite incomprehensible,   15
—but then, I am not infallible. At a quarter past three I went away.
Not a happy day: I <w.^d> not mind sharing or yielding ≪my≫ laurels,
if I had any, with or to anybody: but in the regard of those whom I
regard, I must be aut Cæsar aut [nihil] [2]

⟨. . .⟩[3]   20

≪. . .≫

Dearest Occyta playing with me all the evening. I do love him.
Began a note to Mr Boyd <tonight>.

≪. . .≫

Sunday. Jany 8th   25

Finished & sent my note to Mr Boyd.[4] *It thanked him for his*
invitation,—& spoke of his letter being "a black swan"[5] *—& spoke*
of Mr Bulteel[6] *& Mr Irving, & the epigram on Lady M*[argaret]
C[ocks]. ≪. . .≫

1. See fn. 1, p. 31. Quoting literally would have involved the use of the masculine
rather than feminine gender, emphasizing that the change was really in H.S.B.
2. "Either Cæsar or nothing," the motto of Cesare Borgia.   3. Half a page excised.
4. For the letter, see Appendix I, p. 295.   5. i.e., *rara avis.*
6. Henry Bullenden Bulteel (1800-66), who left the Anglican church in 1831, and em-
braced some of Irving's ideas in 1832.

[203]

Diary by E.B.B.

⟨ . . . ⟩[1]

*After dinner, Arabel told me about ＜something＞ which Bummy
had heard from Mrs Best & seemed pleased at repeating, respecting
the Boyds going away next May.   Altho' we shall probably be gone
before then, the very idea of their going possibly before we do, made
me feel quite unhappy.*

≪ . . . ≫

*Papa & I talked about predestination this evening.   The first time
I have ventured on the subject these two years—I mean with* him.
*Dreamt about Adolphe & Endymion, & a lady who was by turns
Emily & Amalthœa, & of her murdering Endymion whose soul was
infused into Adolphe.   Papa reproached her.   But she held up her
beautiful face, & said, "I am yet very fair".   "Clay Walls" said
Papa!——*[2]

A funny dream!——

Monday. Jany 9th
*Papa has made today another holiday.   Out of spirits this morning
—& feeling disinclined to read ＜_ΛÆschylus＞ or ≪do≫ anything in
the way of Greek.   Prayed for help from God: and He in answer to
prayer, has often made me happy when all other resources seemed
shut against me.   Surely I sh^d trust Him.*
*Wrote my poem on the cholera.   I think I like it, & shall send it
to the Times tomorrow.   I wonder if, tomorrow, I shall hear from or
about Mr Boyd, or about* us. * I wish I were more comfortable.*

Tuesday Jany 10th
Sent away my poem to the Times, this morning.[3]
Out of spirits all the morning, & unwell & thinking about the

1. Half a page excised.

2. In this context, identification must necessarily be tentative. It seems reasonable to
suppose, in view of E.B.B.'s reading habits, that Adolphe was the hero of Benjamin Constant
de Rebecque's celebrated novel of that name (Paris, 1816), and that Emily was Emily St.
Aubert, the heroine of *The Mysteries of Udolpho*, read by E.B.B. the previous July. Endymion was the beautiful youth of Greek mythology; Amalthæa, daughter of Melisseus, king
of Crete, fed the infant Zeus with goat's milk.

3. "The Pestilence," printed in *The Times*, 13 January 1832 (see Appendix II, p. 319).

[204]

post, the Malvern post & the London post. Will *Papa hear anything*

⟨ . . . ⟩¹

[Thursday, 12 January.] *wonder if I shall have a pleasant—a happy visit. Better not to hope it—*

H & A rode home with Eliza, & heard Mrs Cliffe ≪discursive≫ 5
about Annie—in her praise, & in the dispraise of her calumniators, Candlers² & Walls. How long ago was it, that I was discursive on the same subject, against Mrs Cliffe? Never mind!—I like Mrs Cliffe the better, much *the better, for what I have heard today!— How it is raining! Suppose I sh^d not be able to go tomorrow!— Then I must* 10
stay.

I sent a note today, to ask little Curzon³ to come here tomorrow, & dine, & sleep. The boys are in a phrenzy with me for it; & Sette came up to <ask> me if the report were really true*. Poor little fellows! I am sorry I have asked him for tomorrow, as it is Sam's* 15
birthday⁴ & their holiday: but what can a ≪body≫ do more than make an apology?—

Arabel wishes to go with me to ≪Malvern≫. I wish she may be able; but there is sure to be a "factious opposition."

She is to go!— Hurrah!— 20

Friday. Jany 13.
Arabel & I off at half past eight or before. A clear cold morning. It is clear that it was cold!— We drove along the upper road by Steers's Hotel.   Splendid view; but I doubt whether the poney ap-proved of it as much as we did. 25

Nobody down stairs at R C: & Mrs Boyd sent down to desire me not to go in to Mr Boyd's room until she had seen me—so there I sate, & had to write out my poem about Camoens in Annie's album, & have breakfast the second, before Mr Boyd sent for me. Went up stairs. He would not have taken the liberty!! of sending for me if he 30

1. Two leaves, i.e., four pages, excised.

2. This family has not been identified.

3. Mr. Curzon's nine-year-old only child, Henry George Roper-Curzon (1822-92), who became 17th Baron Teynham on his father's death in 1889.

4. His 20th.

Diary by E.B.B.

had not soon expected his barber!!   He asked

⟨ . . . ⟩[1]

[Thursday, 19 January.] *see my mouth—(Quære ≪were≫ there gass*
lights round my mouth?—) & she told M.ʳ Boyd, it was painful to
5   *look at it.   It indicated intense feeling, & deep suffering!—   A great*
deal of feeling is expressed also in Arabel's countenance.   M.ʳ Boyd's
head is "very intellectual".[2]

He asked me to "come again soon."   So I will, if I can!—   Got
home before five.   Bro at the Onslows,[3] *Arabel & Sam at the Peytons,*
10   *—B H & I at dinner at Hope End.   B thought me quite mad for going*
this morning.

≪ . . . ≫

No letter from London.
Read some of the Eumenides, but c.ᵈ not finish it.   That enchant-
15   *ing little beast Occyta w.ᵈ not let me go up stairs in time.*

Friday.   Jan.ʸ 20
Finished the Eumenides.   The choruses are in Æschylus's best
manner: but the conception of Orestes' trial, is more Lucianic than
sublime.[4]   *So Arabel is not coming home.   A bore.   I dont know*
20   *what in the world to do without her,—& the most provoking part*
of the business is, that I dare say she w.ᵈ at least as soon be here as
there.   Daisy & Sette to the Bartons, for pigeon shooting.   The most
cowardly mean-spirited, no-spirited amusement possible.   If it had
been a tiger hunt!——
25   *Henry dined there, & rode back by himself at twelve o clock at*
night.   Minny in a flustration, which was a frustration.   Nonsense.

1. Five leaves, i.e., ten pages, excised. See Appendix I, p. 295, for letter written by E.B.B.
to H.S.B. on 14 January 1832.

2. "She" is Miss Henrietta Mushet. One of her interests was phrenology (see p. 193),
and it seems probable that she had been persuaded to give a "reading."

3. The Ven. Richard Francis Onslow (1775?-1849), Archdeacon of Worcester, lived at
Court House, Newent. He had three sons and four daughters.

4. Lucian (*c.* A.D. 120-200), Greek satirist and humorist. Orestes was acquitted of
murder by the deciding vote of Athena, as the jury of ten cast equal votes for and against
him (*LCL-A*, II, 322-347, lines 566-777).

[206]

No letter from Papa!—

I have now read thro', regularly thro', every play of Æschylus. He is a wonderful writer; & no one ever thought like him, or expressed his thoughts like him, from the beginning of the creation until this 1832— 5

By the bye, Papa's not writing is almost as wonderful, as Æschylus. Read two Olympic odes,—& one, not a short one.

Saturday. Jany 21.

Read the 7th Olympic ode—about Agesias, & Rhodes.[1] There are very fine things in it, & it deserves to be written in gold, as it once 10 *was. Bro & Arabel came home. Very glad of it. B & H walked to the B[artons] for A. I walked by myself, & reveried.*

No letter from Papa!—

It is doubtful whether or not the cholera is in London: ≪If it≫ is, & if Papa remains there, I shall be miserable. My misery depends on 15 *two ifs, & one ≪might≫ keep me from it. Sent my prologue & a few lines to Annie; ≪& my books & a few lines to Eliza Cliffe—≫ Bro dined yesterday at the Archdeacon's—& hunted today with the two Archdeacons Onslow & <Probyn>.[2] The very venerables!—*

Sunday. Jany. ≪22≫^d 20

Will there be a letter today?—

<There> was one for Henrietta, but nothing in it satisfactory,— except that Papa cannot leave London ≪∧before≫ Tuesday, which seems to indicate that on Tuesday, he may be able to leave it. He is delighted with my verses on the cholera, & considers them "beautiful, 25 *most beautiful."[3] He has sent them to Mrs Bayford, & given them to the Editor of the Pulpit in which they will soon appear.[4]*

1. She is confusing this with her reading of the day before. The 6th Ode is to Agesias of Syracuse; the 7th to Diagoras of Rhodes.

2. The Ven. John Probyn (1761?-1843), Dean and Archdeacon of Llandaff. E.B.B. told an amusing story about him, in relation to the "unknown tongues," in her letter to H.S.B. of 1 December 1831 (see Appendix I, p. 292).

3. For the letter, see Appendix I, p. 297.

4. Mrs. Bayford, who lived in London, had been very friendly with E.B.B.'s paternal grandmother. Some degree of consanguinity existed between the two families, and E.B.B. spoke of Mrs. Bayford's daughters as "cousins," but the blood relationship was certainly not a close one. (In an undated letter to Miss Mitford, at Wellesley, E.B.B. said: "We, you know, number our cousins after the tribes of Israel. . . .") Her verses were not printed in *The Pulpit,* probably because two poems dealing with pestilence had appeared in recent issues.

Diary by E.B.B.

Now as Papa wont be at home until Wednesday at any rate, I certainly might go to Malvern tomorrow, sleep there, & return on Tuesday. Henrietta & Arabel <see> no "just cause or impediment"[1] —but Bummy can see thro' a post where poor M. Boyd is concerned.

5   *The Peytons are asked to dine here tomorrow,—so I must prorogue until Tuesday.*

    The Peytons wont come, so I need not prorogue at all.

    How surprised I was to hear M. Curzon's voice at the gate today —& pleased too. We thought he was in Ireland, or on the sea!—

10   *An interesting sermon on that <interesting> text "confident rather & willing to be absent from the body & present with the Lord".[2] He enforced the distinction between our willingness to be absent from the body—from pain & sorrow & disappointment,—& «our» willingness to be present with the Lord!— I felt the distinction. It is easy to*

15   *consent to part with this sorrowful life. Lord make me confident & willing <ₐalso> to be present with Thee.*

    Now about Malvern. After we came up stairs stairs [sic] to bed, Arabel advised me to have an interview with B on the subject. No!— I could not do it! I went to speak to Henrietta, & she promised me

20   *to feel B's pulsations. «...»*

Monday. Jan.ʸ 23.ᵈ

    How disappointed I am. H has been into my room to say that B is very adverse, & thinks me very unreasonable. I think her very unkind!— Well!—I wont go; & how much disappointed I am, I

25   *cant say, «...»: and yet perhaps after all, if I had gone, I might have been pained by something: «...» Finished Baxter's Saints Rest. Quite exquisite!—— After finishing it, nothing ought to distress or disappoint me. I will read it again before I die,—that is, if I do not die before the expiration of "the years of man",—which in all*

30   *probability, I shall do. I am "not (I think) built for posterity"—as M. Martin says of Colwall.*

    Now I write down my palinodia. Dear Bummy has been here to speak of my going to Malvern, & has proposed my staying until

---

1. *Book of Common Prayer*, "Solemnization of Matrimony" ("cause, or just impediment").

2. II Corinth. v.8: "We are confident, I say, and willing rather to be absent from the body, and to be present with the Lord."

*Wednesday!!   Hurrah!—I am going.   She & A will convoy me to
the wyche.*

*They did,—& walked down with me & my bundle.   Mrs Boyd
at dinner.   My companions stayed only a few minutes; & then I
dined, & then I went in to Mr Boyd.   I really believe he was pleased.*   5
*A smile lasted on his face for several minutes!—& he told me not to
go into the drawing room for the snuffers which we wanted, for fear
they sh.^d keep me there.   It w.^d be better to ring the bell.*

*We went on with Gregory's oration on Christmas day;[1] & <after
tea> went on with the going on.   Half past eleven before we went*   10
to bed!— †

Tuesday.   Jany 24th

*In Mr Boyd's room before breakfast, & reading.   Read until twelve;
& then he proposed walking out.   It was a surprise to me when he
asked me to walk with him,—and a pleasure!   Up & down the garden*   15
for half an hour!—

⋘ . . . ⋙

*He speaks of her, not in a very cordial manner.[2]   He speaks of her
being uncandid in argument: and "she w.^d rather never see a book
again than never see a dog. ⋘ . . . ⋙   There's mind for you!—" and she*   20
*irritated him & made his head heavy on Sunday evening!—   Perhaps
he spoke as he did, only because he was temporarily irritated: &*

⋘ . . . ⋙

*She has a sensible unaffected manner as I said before, & she appears
to be particularly goodnatured & obliging; but she is not an interesting*   25
person to me.   †

Wednesday.   Jany 25th

*I lay awake last night listening to the rain, & hoping that it w.^d
rain on.   But it did not!—a fine morning.*

In Mr Boyd's room only a few minutes before breakfast today,—   30

1. Oration 38 (*GNO*, I, 613-624). Following the final line of the text in *WG*, p. 624, is
the note: "Read the 7 preceding columns with Mr Boyd. Jany. 23 24 25. Ruby Cottage."

2. Miss Henrietta Mushet was the subject of their conversation.

Diary by E.B.B.

& M.ʳ Rickards[1] came afterwards, so that I <was> not settled there until later than usual.

Finished the oration. It is very fine <&> M.ʳ Boyd has determined on translating it. I begged him to do so. Miss H M will be his secre-
5 tary. I protested against his sending it to the Methodists' Magazine, few of whose readers could estimate a line of it.[2]

He wished _me to_ translate it while he was translating it, & at the end make what "is odious." I w.ᵈ not do such a thing for πασαν την οικουμενην,[3] & all the seas & deserts thrown in!— Besides, (I know
10 him,) the very act of seeming to compete with him, tho' suggested by himself, w.ᵈ diminish his regard for me. And really there is none to spare.

≪ . . . ≫

M.ʳ Boyd asked me to visit him again next week— That I cant
15 do!—except by a morning visit.

I see plainly that M.ʳˢ Boyd & Annie have determined on leaving Malvern next May!—

≪ . . . ≫

Annie asked me at breakfast where I had advised M.ʳ Boyd to settle?—
20 What a question!— I c.ᵈ not help the tears <coming> into my eyes.

All well at home. Sam with H[enry] T[rant] somewhere!— I wish they had not come for me until tomorrow.

Thursday. Jan.ʸ 26ᵗʰ
Wrote a very kind letter to M.ʳ Boyd, expressive of my regard for
25 him, & the happiness I had in being with him.[4]

≪ . . . ≫

1. Not positively identified; possibly Thomas Rickards of Preston Court, 3 miles S.W. of Ledbury (map ref. I2).

2. Despite her objection, H.S.B.'s translation was published in *The Methodist Magazine*, December 1832, pp. 848-861. Writing to Mrs. Martin on 14 December 1832, she said: "Mr. Boyd has made me quite angry by publishing his translations by rotation in numbers of the 'Wesleyan Magazine,' instead of making them up into a separate publication, as I had persuaded him to do. There is the effect, you see, of going, even for a time, out of my reach! The readers . . . are pious people, but not cultivated, nor, for the most part, capable of estimating either the talents of Gregory or his translator's" (Kenyon, I, 17).

3. "All the inhabited world."

4. For the letter, see Appendix I, p. 298.

[210]

Began to read over again Gregory's oration,—& even to translate it: not with the intention of showing my translation to M.ʳ Boyd or any body else, not with the wish of competing with him; but that by translating the whole I might have a clearer idea of parts, & might save him the trouble of ≪thinking≫ on some points which appeared to both of us, obscure. I shall not even tell him of my having translated it. ≪M.ʳ Curzon came at 3 & stayed till 10— Kind of him.≫

Friday. Jan.ʸ 27ᵗʰ

Going on with my translation which I have just finished. I have written ≪as≫ hard & fast as I cᵈ write,—& therefore had no time for sentencerounding & polishing. In two days more I cᵈ accomplish that: & <then> my version wᵈ not be a very bad one—tho' I says it as should'nt. M.ʳ Boyd meant to be a fortnight about it. I shᵈ be four days. Write me down a dray horse.

One puzzling passage about the χρονικον κινημα[1] I have a very clear idea of,—& have written down my interpretation in as humble & submissive <ᴧa> way as I could, & sent it in another letter to M.ʳ Boyd.[2] A few lines to M.ʳˢ Boyd in the envelope, to say that I cant see why she shᵈ not come to see us with Annie & Miss Mushet. <The first> fruits of my controversy with Arabel this morning. Arabel need not have been so impatient about it.

Saturday Jan.ʸ 28ᵗʰ

Finished my translation quite, & sent off my letter to M.ʳ Boyd. I think that the late puzzling passages now puzzle me no more— except the μικρον μεν 'υστερον οψει[3]—& just as I was going to con- sider that, a letter from Malvern came which deranged me altogether. ≪The≫ greater part ≪of≫ it, was from M.ʳˢ Boyd & kind enough— but there were a few lines from M.ʳ Boyd, ≪ . . . ≫. He ≪asks≫ me to spend two days with him next week—

≪ . . . ≫

---

1. "Temporal movement." In *WG*, p. 616, E.B.B. has underscored this passage with a series of short dashes. In the margin, a note: "why χρονικόν?" has been deleted and she has written "I understand."

2. For the letter, see Appendix I, p. 300.

3. "A little later you will see." This phrase occurs in the Oration "In Christi Nativitatem" (*GNO*, I, 622).

Diary by E.B.B.

And he does not mean to translate the oration. It is too much labour!— He <u>has</u> translated the passage at the close of the oration on the son, which I <admire> so much, & which he wishes me to "come & see".

≪ . . . ≫

⟨ . . . ⟩[1]

[Thursday, 2 February.] a very beautiful & powerful one: & afterwards communicated them to Mrs Boyd. He agreed to by far the greater number; & asked me to visit him again next Thursday or Friday or Saturday, to finish my criticisms. But I am not to mention at home ≪his≫ reason for wishing to see me then: for fear he might be under rated by ≪a≫ <_∧misapprehension of it.> That is a feeling which I do not understand. Sir Uvedale Price had no personal regard for me, & yet he used to speak openly of sending me his mss 26 miles, to be criticised previous to their publication!——

M^r. B had thought of writing to ask me to pass two more days with him in the capacity of his secretary; as Miss H M found the fatigue too much for her. I told M^r. Boyd immediately that in the case of my coming, being a convenience to him, I was ready to come. He answered in a quick way—"Oh it was only in case of Miss H M being unwell!— She is quite well now"— I said nothing.

He speaks of Miss H M as if he did not like her. He says that she takes no interest in what he is writing, <is> of an uncandid mind, & very different from what she was formerly.

≪ . . . ≫

Miss Heard has told him that I am the most engaging person she ever knew, & that she quite adores me!—— I heard this a little bitterly. People like me better at first than they do afterwards. I wish they w^d. not like me at all. I dont mean to imply that Miss H.'s language was not exaggerated.

Took courage & told <M^r.> B of my ≪translation≫ of the Prometheus. He seemed pleased, & surprised at my having done so much, & so unparaphrastically. I asked him inconsiderately, if he w^d. read

1. Two leaves, i.e., four pages, excised.

*it, if he w^d read some part of it!— His answer did not please me:
and yet he ≪did≫ not say "I will not"— M^rs B*

⟨. . .⟩¹

*I w^d have done, if it had not been for one reason. An express sent off
to Bro who is dining & sleeping at the Commelines. A little of the
Prometheus tonight.*

Friday Feb 3^d.

 *Bro returned before breakfast: & our dearest Papa ⟨before⟩
twelve. I thought his face was grave when ≪he≫ kissed me—but
fatigue & a bad cold may <ʌ have> been the reasons of his gravity—*

⟨. . .⟩¹

*persuaded him to go to bed; & he slept for three hours. In the
evening he was quite cheerful. While he was asleep, I went on with
my Prometheus.*

Saturday Feb 4th

 *Mrs Martin called & saw Papa & all of us. Papa talked in a fast
feverish manner, as if he were determined to be considered "himself".
<He> told Bummy that he w^d be happy to see James!— But James
wont come, I am certain!—*

 *B A I (Henrietta riding punch) drove as far as Barnets. A lovely
day!— Busy with my Prometheus. I have finished the 370th. line.
Reading what I have written to Bro who approves very much indeed.
If I publish it, I will also publish a preliminary essay which might be
made very critical & interesting.*

Sunday. Feb 5th

 *Everybody gone to church save me. Yesterday I sent a note to
Mrs Boyd with a message to Mr Boyd, explaining why, i.e. on account
of Papa's return, I cant write to him about Nisbet.² A message to
Mr Boyd!*

5

10

15

20

25

---

1. Half a page excised.
2. James Nisbet, bookseller and publisher, of 21 Berners Street, London.

Diary by E.B.B.

≪ . . . ≫

M.ʳ Curzon preached beautifully.
Not in a humour for writing in a diary.

Monday Feb 6ᵗʰ
5   *Hard at work at the Prometheus.   Finished the translation of*
≪130≫ lines.   Who c.ᵈ write in a diary after that?—   ≪Tired; &
walked up & down, to make my self more physically so than men-
tally≫ Papa at the Ledbury Committee,—& presented every member
of it with a bible.

10   *Tuesday Feb 7.ᵗʰ*
Translated a hundred lines of Æschylus.   Up & at work both
today & yesterday before breakfast.
≪A letter from≫ Malvern.   A few lines from M.ʳ Boyd, ≪ . . . ≫
begging me to go to him on Thursday.   I did not think he w.ᵈ write,
15   *& am rather pleased.   Rather!—   ≪ . . . ≫*

Wednesday Feb 8.ᵗʰ
Up before breakfast, at <work>—   Finished another hundred,
in spite of M.ʳˢ Trant & M.ʳ Curzon.   The latter dined here, & I must
go down now & drink tea with him.   Going to Malvern tomorrow!——

20   *Thursday. Feb. 9.ᵗʰ*
Bummy & Arabel went in the carriage to Malvern with me: & H
& Stormy were outriders.   We went after breakfast, at eleven o'clock.
M.ʳˢ Trant carried my party to Gt Malvern in a fly, & I pursued my
course to R C in ≪my≫ wheelbarrow.
25   *M.ʳˢ B Annie & Miss H M in the dining room.   I soon went up*
to M.ʳ Boyd.   He received me as Leila's friends w.ᵈ have done:[1] &
immediately talked of going out to walk with Miss H M—   But I
ought not to blame him.   He assured me again & again that if he had
not had a heaviness in his head he w.ᵈ not have thought of it—that he
30   *preferred staying with me.   I urged him to go.   After all he did not!—*

1. E.B.B.'s poem (*Leila*, ed. cit., pp. 32-35) told how Leila from motives of sympathy
released a captive, who then killed her father, so that Leila was indirectly responsible for his
death.

[214]

He found that I c.^d make my criticisms as I was reading,—& therefore he w.^d stay to ≪hear≫ them: & they lasted until half past three. <He adopted> nearly every one of them, & my construction of the passage πως ου κατηγορεις εκεινο;¹ besides. We had Gregory out, & it was pronounced to be certainly right in defiance of the Latin version which was in my critical teeth. †

Before I went away, I asked if M.^rs B had mentioned going away in May. Not lately. "But why sh.^d you be anxious for us to stay when you think there is no chance of staying yourself <ₐaltogether> at Hope End?" Because <ₐthe period of> our staying is ≪uncertain≫.

Left Mr Boyd at four. He asked me to go again next week to examine some observations of Billius on the oration which he has translated—² By the way it is really a beautiful translation.

Friday Feb 10.th
    Writing—but not in my diary.

Saturday Feb 11.th
    Intended to have finished the Prometheus today. Not possible.

Sunday Feb 12
    At church; & found the Cliffes there— They had luncheon here; & upon Papa's invitation agreed to dine here on Wednesday. They sleep here besides. I hope Annie wont hear of it, & be on the Trojan horse i.e. a very high one.

Monday Feb 13
    Writing hard.

Tuesday Feb 14
    Oh ye Athenians how hard do I work to obtain your praise. The Prometheus not finished after all.

---

1. Gregory's phrase was: "ἐκεῖνο δὲ πῶς οὐ κατηγορεῖς" ("How then do you not make that accusation?": *GNO*, I, 621, "In Christi Nativitatem"). E.B.B. has omitted the particle "then" and has changed the word order.

2. Jacques de Billy (1535-81), Latinized as Jacobus Billius, was the editor and principal commentator of E.B.B.'s 1690 edition of Gregory.

Diary by E.B.B.

Wednesday Feb 15

I have finished my translation. ≪1075≫ lines of Æschylus translated in a fortnight. ⟨And⟩ I think I am satisfied—tolerably satisfied. But the original is too magnificent for translation.

5   Mrs Cliffe & Eliza came. Nota bene Mr Davis's coming too. It was odd & cool. Nothing in <this> world can be at the same time, odd & <u>cold.</u> I dont admire Mr Davis as much as either Mrs Cliffe or Eliza does. He does not suit <u>me</u>. He is talkative & forward & pedantic & self complacent. He does not suit <u>me</u>. Slept here,—& kept us up
10   previously in an awful suspence, until nearly two— Too bad!— Intensely stupid evening. Eliza was at Malvern on Tuesday. Miss H M is to stay until April & take Annie with her. ≪ . . . ≫

Thursday Feb 16

After M.^{rs} C & E had gone away, I wrote to Miss Bordman. I
15   asked her to dissuade M.^{rs} B from leaving Malvern. Will she try, or not?— I wrote a long & kind letter. Then I began to copy out my Prometheus. I must endeavour to finish by tomorrow, as I must positively go to R C next day.

≪ . . . ≫

20   *Friday Feb 17.*

Bummy has proposed of her own accord, to go with me to Malvern, tomorrow, if I like. My yea is soon said. Could not quite finish the copying out on account of a perforce walk. Papa finished Mr Beverley's second letter to the Archbishop of York tonight[1] —finished
25   reading it out loud. It is very <clever>—

⟨ . . . ⟩[2]

[Saturday, 18 February] -ment, considering that the county is Herefordshire. But I am much pleased that he was pleased at all. After tea, he suggested ≪my≫ writing to Mr Barker & enquiring whether
30   Valpy w.^d publish my work in the Classical Library. Wont do ≪it≫

---

1. Robert Mackenzie Beverley, *A Second Letter to His Grace the Archbishop of York, on the Present Corrupt State of the Church of England* (Beverley, 1832).

2. Two leaves, i.e., four pages, excised.

without consulting M.ʳ Boyd. Wrote to him tonight, a short letter—[1]

≪ . . . ≫

I told him not to write himself, but to send some short message to me,
which M.ʳˢ B or Annie might be kind enough to convey.

Sunday Feb 18.ᵗʰ [sic, for 19th]   5
   Not ≪at≫ church.   At the gate M.ʳ Curzon preached beautifully.
He is to dine here,—he & M.ʳˢ Curzon;[2] *on Wednesday—& to sleep.*

Monday Feb 19.ᵗʰ [sic, for 20th]
   A letter from M.ʳ Boyd!   How it surprised me.   He does not like
the Valpy plan.[3]   *If the translation is good enough to be creditable*   10
to me, it sh.ᵈ be published separately; besides he has made a confusion
between the Family & Classical library!—   ≪His≫ letter is cool
enough.   I answered it by a note of explanation on Valpy's work;
≪ . . . ≫ by rating very humbly my translation—& by telling him how
little inclined I feel to publishing, & how I ≪have≫ wished that I had   15
never done so.   The real truth!—   If I never had, I never sh.ᵈ have
been exposed to the pain which has < ₍ₐ₎been > & is oppressing me.

Tuesday Feb 20.ᵗʰ [sic, for 21st]
   H ≪Bro≫ & Sam to M.ʳˢ Trants.
   I could not write today.   20

Wednesday.   Feb 21.ˢᵗ [sic, for 22nd]
   Another letter from M.ʳ Boyd.   "My dear M.ʳ Boyd" seems to agree
with him.   He enclosed a letter from ≪M.ʳˢ≫ Smith D.ʳ A Clarke's
youngest daughter.[4]   *≪ . . . ≫ M.ʳ Boyd's letter ≪was≫ written by*

   1. Abraham John Valpy (1787-1854), London editor and publisher, one of whose assist-
ants was H.S.B.'s friend, E. H. Barker. For E.B.B.'s letter, see Appendix I, p. 301.
   2. Eliza, *née* Joynes (? -1871), who married Mr. Curzon on 10 February 1822.
   3. Despite this, the translation was published by Valpy. (*Prometheus Bound. Translated
from the Greek of Æschylus. And Miscellaneous Poems*, London, 1833.)
   4. Mary Ann Smith, a close friend of H.S.B., who was with him when he died. It was to
Mrs. Smith that E.B.B. then addressed a request for the return of her letters to H.S.B. Mrs.
Smith declined to conform to this convention, and it was some forty years before Robert
Browning secured possession of them. In an unpublished letter to her sister Arabel, dated
6-7 June [1849], E.B.B. wrote that Mrs. Smith "is, we must all confess, a vulgar, coarse
woman, . . only I know her to be excellent in her peculiar way, & respect & am grateful to her

[217]

Diary by E.B.B.

Miss H M,—& cool enough still.   I wonder he sh.^d have thought it
worth while to write it at all.   He "cannot see" why I should regret
having ever published.   I wish ≪I≫ could not.   He does not "dis-
approve of Valpy."   He is ≪translating≫ the exordium of Greg.^s 2
5   *Paschal oration.*[1]   *I read it with him last november.   He desires me*
to send him the ⟨beginning⟩ of my translation, & 30 or 40 lines of
one of the ⟨choral odes.   What⟩ is his motive?   Not, I am afraid,
a wish of seeing ≪my≫ work.   Perhaps he perceives that ≪my≫
manner of writing is not what it was.   I sent the extracts, & wrote in
10   *my "new style",—begging him not to read what I sent.   ≪ . . . ≫*

⟨ . . . ⟩[2]

Would I not a thousand & a thousand times <u>rather</u> have <u>his</u> work
attended to than mine?—
   M.^r & Mrs Curzon came.   A discussion about M.^r B in the evening.
15   *M.^r C evidently does not think well of his religious state.   I was writing*
some of my preface this morng.

Thursday Feb 22.^d [sic, for 23rd]
   The Curzons did not go away until nearly three.   M.^rs C is cer-
tainly improved.   Mr Curzon is what he always was—a follower of
20   *Christ in spirit & conduct—kind & feeling.   ≪ . . . ≫*

Friday Feb 23.^d [sic, for 24th]

≪ . . . ≫

⟨ . . . ⟩[3]

Saturday Feb 24. [sic, for 25th]
25   *What did I do today?—   Not write in my diary.   ≪Bro Stormy*

---

for her faithful affection to my dear friend, Mr. Boyd. Robert only sees the indelicacy of
keeping my letters . . ." (Collection of Miss Myrtle and Col. R. A. Moulton-Barrett).

   1. Published in H.S.B.'s *The Fathers Not Papists: or, Six Discourses by the Most Eloquent
Fathers of the Church*, a new edition, considerably enlarged (London, 1834).

   2. Three lines excised.

   3. Four lines excised at foot of page, together with the following two leaves, i.e., four
pages.

Henry & Sette to Worcester. 5 tugs & Sette's tooth,—& he did not cry!≫

Sunday. Feb 25ᵗʰ. [sic, for 26ᵗʰ]

Confined in the house all day with one of my violent colds. Did not even go down to chapel. Finished Mʳ. Gipps's book[1] which pleased me, but not ⟨altogether⟩. No letter. ≪Yes≫!—there was one from Eliza Cliffe, speaking of Annie's album, & the present which I mean to give Mʳ. Boyd on his birthday. I have determined upon Scholefield's Æschylus,[2]—& shall write to Eliza to say so.

5

Monday Feb 26ᵗʰ. [sic, for 27th]

Wrote to Eliza,—but cᵈ not send my letter. Wrote also two or three lines to Mʳˢ Boyd, to enclose Mʳ. Hockin's catalogue[3] for Mʳ. Boyd,—& to say that we hoped Annie might receive her scrapbook this week. Mʳˢ. Trant came here to

10

⟨. . .⟩[4]

15

ness. In the evening I wrote out A thought on thoughts[5] *by Bummy's desire, for Papa to read. He read & liked it extremely, & asked me to give the copy right to him.*

Tuesday. Feb 27ᵗʰ. [sic, for 28th]

Finished the preface to my Prometheus,—& delivered it to Papa in the evening. I read it or rather spelt it aloud,—& in my opinion, [he] did not very much ≪. . . like≫ it,—tho' I am assured otherwise by other observers. He has heard from Mʳ. Curzon who means to dine with us tomorrow. Papa says that he had told him how unwilling he was to pass a week without seeing him. Does that unwillingness arise

20

25

1. The Rev. Henry Gipps was Rector of St. Owen's and Vicar of St. Peter's, Hereford. He had written several books, but E.B.B. probably was referring to the most-recently published, *A Treatise on "The First Resurrection" and "The Thousand Years" Foretold in the Twentieth Chapter of the Book of Revelations* (London, 1831).

2. James Scholefield, ed. *Æschylus* (Cambridge, 1828).

3. The Catalogue of the library of the late Rev. J. P. Hockin, which was to be dispersed by auction in Ledbury on 7 March 1832 (*Hereford Journal*, 29 February 1832).

4. Two lines excised.

5. See Appendix I, p. 275.

Diary by E.B.B.

from increased regard to M. Curzon,—or from a belief that*

⟨ . . . ⟩[1]

[? Thursday, 1 March] *enough.*
    *In the evening I read a part of Pindar's 8.*th *olympic. And* <M*dme*>
5 *de Genlis's story of Delphine in the Tales of the castle,*[2] *which I like,*
because it puts me in mind of being as happy as I was when I read it
first.

⟨ . . . ⟩[3]

[Friday, 2 March] *Arrived there at about two & stayed until three.*
10 *We were shown into the* ≪dining≫ *room where Miss Baker & Miss*
*Pindar were at luncheon with M.*rs *Ricardo.*[4]   *Surprised to see Miss*
*Baker. After they were gone, we talked; until M.*rs *Webb came, &*
then until all the Onslows &

⟨ . . . ⟩[5]

15 *to call upon me tomorrow.*   *I could not go to Malvern at any rate,*
on account of the poney.

Saturday. ≪March≫ *3.*d
    Preliminaries of a sore throat,—but tamarinds ≪cured me≫. *Miss*
Baker came at half past two, & spent an hour with me. *She objects to*
20 *such books as Corinne*[6] *& Mathilde,*[7] *because they lead the mind to*
expect more in life than can be met in life. *Well!—allow that they*

---

    1. Excision of one and a third pages.
    2. Stéphanie Félicité, Comtesse de Genlis, *Tales of the Castle: or, Stories of Instruction and Delight*, trans. Thomas Holcroft, 4 vols. (Dublin, 1785). "Delphine: or, The Fortunate Cure" appears in I, 12-62.
    3. Excision of two-thirds of a page.
    4. Harriet (*née* Mallory), wife of Osman Ricardo, High Sheriff of Worcester, of Bromesberrow Place, 5 miles from Ledbury. The luncheon was at Eastnor Castle.
    5. Excision of one-third of a page.
    6. [Anne Louise, Comtesse de Staël-Holstein], *Corinne, ou l'Italie*, 3 vols. (Paris, 1807). In her letter to H.S.B. of 9 June 1832 E.B.B. said: "I have read Corinne for the third time, and admired it more than ever. It is an immortal book . . ." (*EBB/HSB*, p. 176).
    7. From the context it seems probable that E.B.B. meant *Matilda; A Tale of the Day* (London, 1825), [by Constantine Henry Phipps, Lord Normanby].

do!— The expectation brings more happiness than any reality,— as realities go,—c^d do. Romance of spirit is a far rarer fault than worldliness of spirit. I wish I knew a few people who had been "spoilt" by reading Corinne. I know nobody. Could not quite finish the Supplices. It is an interesting, & in some parts, an affecting play. ≪Evadne≫ is very striking & affecting. [1]

Miss Baker has a melancholy opinion of the West Indies. It w^d be agreable to know that Papa's estates are not burnt up [2] *—& still more agreable to know where we are going! ≪Fear≫ ＜ₐas well as＞ Hope ≪ . . . ≫ deferred, maketh the heart sick.* [3]

≪ . . . ≫

Sunday. March 4th.

Dearest Henrietta's birthday. [4] *May God bless & preserve her & make her happy!— Did I write down in my diary last Tuesday that Bummy wrote to Miss Battie to ＜ask＞ Mr Battie to enquire of Hatchard* [5] *whether he w^d read my ms of Prometheus, & consent to publish it together with about 30 original poems, in the case of his approving it? ＜I＞ think—indeed I see—that I did not. ≪An≫ answer may arrive today. Nay or yea? Nay!—in my opinion; tho' B says differently.*

No answer.

Instead of preaching at the gate today, Mr Curzon sent us word that he was not quite well.

Monday March 5

Dear H's birthday kept; & I took advantage of the holiday by going

1. Evadne, the wife of Capaneus, one of the Seven Against Thebes, threw herself on his funeral pyre (Euripides, "Supplices," lines 990-1071, *LCL-E*, III, 578-587).

2. *The Times*, 20 February 1832, reported a partial insurrection of the slaves in Jamaica, mainly in the parishes of St. James's, Portland and Trelawney (the Barretts had land in St. James's and Trelawney, although their principal estate was in the parish of Cambridge): "Shortly after the 20th of December the slaves on several estates refused to go to their work, and large bodies of them met together and set fire to many plantation buildings. On the 30th of December martial law was proclaimed . . ." As far as can be ascertained from the family papers, the Barrett estates were not injured at this time.

3. Cf. Proverbs xiii.12: "Hope deferred maketh the heart sick: But when the desire cometh, it is a tree of life."

4. Her 23rd.

5. John Hatchard (1769-1849), the publisher, of Piccadilly, London. The Batties have not been identified.

Diary by E.B.B.

to Malvern with Arabel.   As we went into Ruby Cottage, there were
so many packages in the breakfast room the door of which was half
open,

≪ . . . ≫

5 *Annie lying on the sofa in the drawing room with a pain in her face,*
—& Mrs Boyd with symptoms of a cough.   As soon as I c^d get into
Mr Boyd's room, I went there.   He made me read his preface & some
additional translations.

≪ . . . ≫

10 *He had had my extracts read to him.   After some verbal criticisms, he*
observed with regard to the blank verses that some of the lines were
beautiful, some poor: a circumstance for which he did not so much
blame me, as Æschylus.   It could not be otherwise in any literal trans-
lation of the Prometheus.   With regard to the lyrical portion of the
15 *extracts, they seemed to him "rather poor", considering they were*
my writing—but then "the short time you were in writing them"!—
He asked me to let him have some other extracts—the speech about
Typhon,[1] *& another choral ode,—but he did not press me, so I need*
not presser.   "<Has> anything [been] fixed about your going away?"
20 *No indeed!—nothing!—*
    ≪*He lent me Blomfield's Æschylus,*[2] *at my request.*≫

Tuesday.   March 6th
    My birthday!—[3]*   My thoughts will go to the past—the past*
—to the ever ever beloved!—   My happy days went away with
25 *her!—   If I were to count up every happy hour since, how few they*
w^d be!—   But there is no use in all this!   The tears which I am
shedding at this moment are as vain,— — —as if they were smiles!—
In another year, where shall I be,—& what shall I have suffered?—
A great deal I dare say—and my heart <appears to> be giving way
30 *even now.*

1. *Prometheus Bound*, ed. cit., pp. 22-24.
2. Charles James Blomfield (1786-1857), Bishop of London, edited five plays of Æschylus. The entry of 8 March indicates that E.B.B. borrowed *Æschyli Prometheus Vinctus*
(Cambridge, 1810).
3. Her 26th.

[222]

Wednesday. March 7th

A letter from London to Bummy from the Batties. A note from Mr Battie informs her that ≪Hatchard≫ is ready to ≪publish≫ my book; but not a word about the copyright. He seems to have mis-understood her,—or else M^r H will have nothing to do with it. B & I have determined on writing to explain. I have written a very explanatory note to M^r H, & she has enclosed it to Mr B. I know perfectly well, that H will turn his back on me!— Well! I dont much mind.

5

Thursday March 8

10

Answers went to the post.

I forgot to say yesterday that I finished early in the morning, conferring Bothe[1] & Blomfield. I do wish I had translated from Blomfield.[2]

Getting on with my notes—for the sake of killing time & some thoughts I believe. And yet, I "give myself unto prayer",[3]—& why should I fear?—

15

Friday March 9th

The Cliffes came,—& Eliza brought the Album for Annie. It is a beautiful green one. I hope she may think the first epithet. Schole-field for Mr Boyd's birthday is to come soon.

20

Getting on with notes.

Saturday March 10th

Notes again. Out walking. I dont feel quite well,—& no wonder —for my spirits are quite worn threadbare.

25

Sunday March 11th

I was not at church,—& B H & A only half way there. A letter from Mr Boyd brief enough, but to ask me to ask Papa to allow me

---

1. Friedrich Heinrich Bothe, ed. *Aeschyli Dramata quae Supersunt* (Leipzig, 1805).

2. That she used Bothe's edition is surprising, because H.S.B. apparently did not esteem him, and as far back as 3 March 1828 E.B.B. had promised to settle him "in the dustiest corner of my bookcase" at the earliest opportunity (*EBB/HSB*, p. 21). Her copy of the 1805 edition formed Lot 309 of the 1913 Browning Sale.

3. Psalms cix.4: "For my love they are my adversaries: But I give myself unto prayer."

to go to R C on Monday & stay until ≪Thursday≫; for the sake of
writing his digamma essay for him.   Miss H M has an inflammation
in one of her eyes!——   Now I wish very very much to go; but am
very very much afraid of asking.

5   I asked Papa in the evening.   He will not allow it.   He says that
I am turning into a shadow, & looking worse & worse,——& that he
will not be a party to giving me any fatigue.   I assured him that
writing for M.ʳ Boyd c.ᵈ not fatigue me so much as what I do every
day at home.   He told me that if I liked to hold a pistol to my head
10   —ainsi soit il—but that he w.ᵈ not have anything to do with it.

≪ . . . ≫

I dont exactly know why.   Only it would have been a pleasure to me
to have gone there, ≪ . . . knowing≫ that I was not in the way.

Monday. March 12.
15   Wrote a letter to M.ʳ Boyd[1]——≪ . . . ≫   I never will be too kind
again to anybody, in the way of writing or speaking.   Told him what
Papa said!——   Told him that I was far far more disappointed than he
c.ᵈ be; for that Miss H M's eyes w.ᵈ probably soon be well, & that then
he w.ᵈ have "a more agreable & satisfactory, tho' not a more willing &
20   anxious secretary, than I could be".   After I had sent away the letter,
I regretted that expression.   I think he will take some notice of it.
Out of spirits all day.

Tuesday: March 13.ᵗʰ
      Not daring to say a word about going to Malvern, & yet wishing
25   ≪to go≫.   At last I sent Henry down to Papa at eleven, to ask if
Papa had any objection to my going.   ≪ . . . ≫   None!!   A went
with me.   Arrived there at half past one, & met Annie at the door.
Into the drawing room,——& after a proper pause, into M.ʳ Boyd's
room.   He had written to me!—and my last letters to him were
30   lying on the table.   So was the commencement of his essay on the
digamma, which Miss H M, whose eyes were convalescent, had been
writing for him that day.   Miss Hurd was to be sent for the next day,
to <proceed>.   I read the essay—so far,—and liked it very much.

1. For the letter, see Appendix I, p. 301.

[224]

He asked me why I had not sent my extracts from Prometheus, to
him? I told him that I w.^d really prefer his giving an undivided atten-
tion to his own work. He told me that ≪ . . . ≫ in fact he thought it
better <for> me not to send them for a few days: until he had finished
his essay. Ainsi soit il—. Not a word was said about my observation   5
in my yesterday's letter: therefore it was certainly an accurate one.
And yet Mr Boyd's manner to me, was kind today: like ≪his≫ own
old manner. He gave me a lecture about the poney being thin. I will
take care that it shall have more corn.

≪ . . . ≫   10

Before I went away, I asked him, if anything was settled about
their going. Nothing about the <u>place</u>. He told me that <u>he thought</u>
<u>they w.^d go.</u>

≪ . . . ≫

Went home, ≪ . . . ≫. Miss H M   15

⟨ . . . ⟩[1]

Sunday March 18.
    Did not go to church: but B H & A did—besides all the boys
except Bro—poor Bro—who is rather rheumatic. I read Bunyan
& the Greek testament, instead. Rain came, & Mrs Cliffe did not.   20
<Rain off>,—and we off to the school. Mr Curzon preached beau-
tifully. Afterwards he asked me when I was going to Malvern. I
answered, "some time this week": and he desired me to herald him
on Thursday.

⟨ . . . ⟩[2]   25

. . much.

Monday March 19.
    Finished my writing out: but I am not sure about the first choral

---

1. Excision of one and a third pages.
2. Excision of one-third of a page.

ode after all.   That <ξυμπιπνων>, *& the extra* βυθος *which both Scholefield & Blomfield introduce.*[1]

*Tuesday.   March 20*th

Went to Malvern in Bummy's suite, & Arabel's.   Called in passing
5   *at M*rs *Trant's, & had to listen to some exquisite selections from her own & Miss Harriet Berrington's*[2] *album—"accursed were she who first cried hold enough",*[3] *by the laws of politeness,—*

⟨ . . . ⟩[4]

to oppose her wish of leaving Malvern; & that, altho' it was wrong
10   *in him, he c*d *not help feeling pleased on hearing about the cholera, because that appeared to him a likely means of frightening M*rs *Boyd into staying.   Certainly he said, it might do him good, to* ≪change the air;≫ *but still, he w*d *rather not go.   When I told him of what I had said to Bummy, his exclamation was, "Why you complained of my*
15   *wishing to go: and now you wish to go y*r*self".   My answer to that was succeeded by an enquiry about the state of the fire.* ≪ . . . ≫
Annie gave me "National Ballads,[5]

*Wednesday March 21*st

*M*r *Boyd gave me Nonnus's paraphrase of St John's Gospel—*lent
20   *it to me—yesterday; that I might hunt for hiatus[e]s for him.   I was reading some of it today, which is the day of the general fast.*[6]   *Whenever he says exactly what is in Scripture, he does not say it as well as*

---

1. ξυμπιπνων is a misspelling of ξυμπιτνων, "dashing together"; βυθος: "the deep." Bothe's edition of *Prometheus Vinctus*, which E.B.B. was using as the basis for her translation, differs slightly in this passage (p. 33) from the other versions she cited.

2. The Berringtons were a prominent Catholic family, living near Little Malvern Church.

3. *Macbeth* V.viii.33-34: "Lay on, Macduff; | And damn'd be him that first cries 'Hold, enough!' "

4. Two leaves, i.e., four pages, excised.

5. Not identified. Possibly one of the series by Thomas Moore published under the title *National Airs*.

6. *The Times*, 21 March 1832, carried a Form of Prayer "To be used in all Churches and Chapels . . . on Wednesday, the Twenty-first day of March, 1832, being the day appointed by Proclamation for a General Fast and Humiliation before Almighty God, . . . For obtaining pardon of our sins, and averting the heavy judgments which our manifold provocations have most justly deserved; and particularly for beseeching God to remove from us that grievous disease with which several places in this kingdom are at this time visited."

*Scripture says it: and whenever he introduces more than is scriptural,
he does it ill.   Jesus wept is "done into" Jesus shed "unaccustomed
tears from eyes unused to weep"* ομμασιν ακλαυτοισιν αηθεα δακρυα
λειβων.[1] *The whole of the passage, that exquisite narration, respecting the woman taken in adultery, is omitted.*   5

*I was quite exhausted with fasting today.   My head was dizzy, &
my limbs languid, & my ≪mind≫ incapable of applying ≪itself≫ to
any subject.   This was not I believe altogether as it sh*ᵈ *be.   I wont
fast again without being more sure of Scriptural premises than I can
feel just now.   At church.*   10

*Thursday March 22*ᵈ

*Not reading Nonnus,—but correcting my press instead.   My
translation does not please me altogether.   No letter from Hatchard,
again!—*

*Friday March 23*ᵈ   15

My dear friend's birthday.[2] *May God bless him.   I said so when
I prayed.*

*Sent my Scholefield, with this line from the Chœphorœ written
on the first leaf—*

εωθ' εωχε φωνην ἐυφρον' αγγελου δωκην.[3]   20

That did. *Wrote a note besides,—*

⟨ . . . ⟩[4]

[? Saturday 24 March] *chairs; for when I went down to ask her to
walk out, & the rain came on, she asked me to stay & talk to her
instead.*   25

≪ . . . ≫

1. *Nonni Panopolitani Paraphrasis Evangelii S. Johannis*, Cap. XI, 124. E.B.B. quoted
Nonnus in the second part of her article, "Some Account of the Greek Christian Poets,"
in *The Athenœum*, 5 March 1842, pp. 210-212: "The two well-known words, bearing on
their brief vibration the whole passion of a world saved through pain from pain, are thus
traduced . . ."

2. H.S.B.'s 51st.

3. "If only, like a messenger, it had a kindly voice" (*LCL-A*, II, 178-179, line 195).

4. Excision of two-thirds of a page.

Diary by E.B.B.

⟨ . . . ⟩[1]

Monday. March 26.

*After M͟r͟s Trant had been here 10 minutes, & had gone,—B made
me go with her to Colwal, where she & A & I sate with M͟r͟s Martin a*
5 *tremendous time. M͟r͟s M. is a superior woman in feeling & good sense,*

⟨ . . . ⟩[2]

≪ . . . ≫

*I ≪ . . . ≫ began today, the Andromache, the only one of Euripides'
plays, which I never read. Next ≪Sunday≫ is the 1͟s͟t of April. Most*
10 *likely there will be more rain than sunshine in it, for me!—*

Tuesday March 27͟t͟h

*Went to Malvern with B & A. So much pro & conning about who
should go, that we were not off until past eleven. Provoking. Left B
at M͟r͟s Trant's,—& A drove me on. Into the dining room at R C,*
15 *where I waited half an hour at the very least, before M͟r Boyd let me
go into his room. Scholefield was lying before him, covered with
white paper. He said a great deal about it—, after he had said a little
about my coming so late. He is certainly pleased with my present to
him, binding & all. I ≪looked≫ at different readings in it for him,—*
20 *& read to him nearly two whole odes from the Supplices. We thought
the short passage ending κερσειεν αωτον, exquisite,[3] but indeed there
is a great deal of beauty all the way thro'. He said today that it was
one of the unpleasant circumstances attending his blindness, that he
was forced to have recourse to the services of those whom he did not*
25 *like! "Now when Miss Mushet is kind enough to offer to read anything for me, I cannot help taking advantage of her doing so: and I
dont like Miss Mushet." I observed, "I thought you did like her very
much." "I did for the first four or five days—but not since,—not*

---

1. Excision of one and a third pages. See Appendix I, p. 302, for a letter from E.B.B. to
H.S.B. written on this day.

2. Excision of two-thirds of a page.

3. These words conclude line 666: E.B.B.'s "short passage" was probably lines 656-666,
ending: "But may the flower of its youth be uncalled, and may Ares, the partner of Aphro-
dite's bed, he who maketh havoc of men, not shear off their bloom" (*LCL-A*, I, 68-69).

[228]

since I have discovered what kind of mind she has". ≪...≫

Nothing more, he says, is settled,—<since> I was last at R C. What will be settled at <u>last</u>?— I hear from Arabel, that Mrs Boyd <u>may</u> go to Frome on Monday. I am sure <u>that</u> is, ≪to≫ make enquiries about houses,—tho' Arabel says it is not. ≪...≫

Annie & Miss H M talk of coming here on Thursday,—on Annie's way to Mathon where she will sleep. She <u>ought</u> to be asked to sleep here—and yet I am not anxious about it <u>certainly</u>.

≪...≫

⟨...⟩[1]

[Thursday 29 March] *in her power, tho' in vain, to induce them to go to Clifton!!! My presentiments were prophecies. Henrietta says that she* [Miss H. Mushet] *evidently does not like Mr Boyd very much!!! She told Henrietta how very extraordinary he ≪is≫,—& how nervous —& how he encourages his nervousness by giving up to it!!— She spoke highly of Mrs Boyd for whom she professed to <entertain> the "greatest regard:" tho' she blamed her for being too <u>submissive</u> to Mr Boyd!!!!!! It is settled now. I do <u>not</u> like Miss H Mushet. Before I knew all this, she asked me to show her my room,—& I showed it. Here she told me that Mr Boyd rejected all associations, & considered everything abstractedly. Not true.*

M^{rs} B brought a note for me from Mr Boyd. Cool enough—but he wishes me to write my name in Scholefield,—& to send him some more extracts from my translation. He likes the last better. Prometheus's speech is reported, "extremely good." This morning, I wrote two or three lines, about hiatuses,—& sent them to him by Mrs Boyd. [2] *≪After they were≫ gone, I walked out with Bummy. Felt tired,— & was very unwell afterwards. How weak & thin I am growing.*

Friday <March> 30th 1832.

Better today. Wrote out some lyrical extracts for Mr Boyd,—& sent them to him.

Finished the Andromache. I have now read every play of Æschylus Sophocles & Euripides. I must go quite thro' with Pindar next.

---

1. One leaf, i.e., two pages, excised.   2. For her letter, see Appendix I, p. 303.

Diary by E.B.B.

*A letter from M.ʳ Battye to Bummy. Hatchard wont buy the copy-
right—tho he will publish—that is, if I please—which I dont.*

Saturday. March 31.ˢᵗ[1]
     Dearest Sam's birthday.[2] God bless him!— Henrietta & Arabel
5 *went out to ride with Eliza Cliffe, thro' Cradley woods,[3] & I dont
know where.   H has made an engagement with E to ride there again
on the 28ᵗʰ of next July. Will that engagement be kept?— Sent to
M.ʳ Deane's for any edition of Æschylus, which is not Blomfield's
Scholefield's or Bothe's. He has sent me Schutz's—but without notes*
10 *which ≪are≫ the most valuable part of Schutz.[4] While H & A were
away, I was very very unwell. Fainting & hysterics—but they went
off at last. Maddox came.*

<Sunday> April 1.ˢᵗ
     The 1.ˢᵗ of April!—   How time does pass away,—& joy with
15 *it!—   But the beginning of next month will be more painful to me
—perhaps it will—than the beginning of this. They went to church,
—but I did not.   I do not feel at all well, tho' better than I felt yesterday. Reading S.ᵗ John's Gospel,—& Nonnus's paraphrase upon it.
I do not like Nonnus.*
20   *Went down in the carriage to hear M.ʳ Curzon. He preached a
good sermon; & Miss Glasco had the advantage of it. He is to come
here on Wednesday.*

Monday. April 2—
     M.ʳ Curzon asked me yesterday before Papa, when I was going to
25 *Malvern.   Answer—some time this week. Out walking with B &
Arabel. B out of spirits, & not in a talking mood by any means. I
out of spirits too.*

Tuesday. April 3.ᵈ
     To Malvern with Henrietta & Maddox.   Met M.ʳ Boyd walking
30 *with Miss H M, a little past the turnpike. Not very far from the*

---

1. See Appendix I, p. 304, for letter conjecturally dated this day.
2. Her uncle's 45th.   3. About 4 miles N.E. of Hope End (map ref. B6).
4. This edition would have been *Aeschyli Tragoediae Septem*, ed. Christian Godofr.
Schütz, 2 vols. (Halle, 1800).

place where I met him first. How much has been felt & unfelt since
then!   He did not ask me to get out of the carriage & ≪walk≫ with
him, or I would have done so; but he turned back immediately, & was
at R C ≪nearly≫ as soon as we were.   We called for one moment at
Mrs Trant's; & she was out.   H drove Maddox on nearly to the Great 5
M turnpike, & I was left at R C.   Mrs Boyd talked to me, but about
nothing interesting, either to me or her,—except that Mr Andrè[1] *was*
expected in England!—   Annie will at last marry some one whom she
cannot love, & who cannot make her happy.   In to Mr Boyd's room.
He asked me if we had not met today where we met first.   His Schole- 10
field was lying before him,—& he made me read some passages for
him in the Agamemnon, & the first chorus of the Supplices, nearly
from the beginning to the end.   He did not, from some reason, ask
me to write my name in it.   He has either forgotten it, or changed
his mind. 15

I told him of my having now read every play of Euripides; & he
seemed very much surprised, & called me "a funny girl",—& observed,
that very few men had done as much.

A return to the subject of Annie's invention respecting Mr Boyd's
"wish of leaving Malvern."   It appears that he has mentioned it ≪to≫ 20
her, & that she denies having even named his name!—   The result
of which denial, is, that he doubts the veracity of the other party:
suggesting that B & A may have made up the story from an amiable
motive as far as I am concerned—to diminish my regret in the case
of Mr Boyd's going,—by diminishing my regard for him now!—   He 25
made me promise to propose a confrontation to Arabel.   I promised:
but I am annoyed at his having made a fuss about such nonsense; &
told him so.   When I was going away, he asked me to forgive him; &
observed that he had something to forgive me, on account of my
having believed the possibility of his being guilty of any conduct so 30
"base & deceitful."   I told him that I never accused him of a long
process of dessimulation,—but supposed on the contrary that he had
lately changed ≪his≫ mind on the point in question.

He said, it w^d be only kind in Papa if he w^d consent to my spend-
ing a few days with him.   There is no use in proposing such a thing. 35

1. Not identified, but from the context another of Annie Boyd's suitors; he was no
more successful than Mr. Biscoe.

Diary by E.B.B.

Miss Mushet[1] ≪goes≫ to R C on Saturday, & leaves it on Monday with Miss H M & Annie. Annie came back from Mathon with Eliza, while I was there. Took Clarke's commentary for Papa.[2]

In consequence of M.ʳˢ Trant having gone to Eastnor, Henrietta
5 *was by herself & walked all over the hills in the same company. Miss H M told M.ʳ Boyd that she ≪was very≫ pretty; & that in the case of Miss H M having been a man, she w.ᵈ have ≪fallen≫ in love with her. She is certainly,—very pretty. Got home in good time. I thought as I drove away from the door where Miss H M & Annie were standing . .*
10 *"Shall I ever see Annie standing at that door again"? Why did the thought come to me?— I half promised to go to Malvern again next Saturday,—but Miss Mushet will be there. I dont like to meet strangers. And besides, M.ʳˢ Trant is to be here—which I dont like either.*

15 *Wednesday April 4.*

I read yesterday in M.ʳ Joseph Clarke's Sacred Literature, that Nonnus is an author whom few can read, & fewer admire.[3] So that my opinion is nothing outrageous. I do not feel well; & look like a ghost. M.ʳˢ Martin called, & thought so too!—
20 *Henrietta & Arabel are both of opinion that B is trying this morning to speak to Papa. They are right. She has spoken. She has been here to tell me that she is going to Kinnersley[4] tomorrow to stay away until Tuesday!!! only Tuesday!! & wishes me to go with her. Now that I hate—& I have made over the <pleasure>, such as it may*
25 *be, to Henrietta!— B tells me of having proposed to Papa, her going on Friday,—& of his objecting on account of his being unwilling for her to pass thro' Ledbury on the day of the church missionary meeting without attending it. Something is certainly the matter,—or B w.ᵈ not go ≪to Kinnersley≫ for so very short a time,—or so suddenly*

---

1. Henrietta Mushet's elder sister Margaret (1799-1885).

2. His *Commentary* on the Bible. See fn. 2, p. 121.

3. Adam Clarke and Joseph Clarke, *A Concise View of the Succession of Sacred Literature*, 2 vols. (London, 1830-32), II, 124-125: "*Paraphrase of St. John.*—Here the beautifully simple and sublime Gospel of St. John is converted into an inflated Greek hexameter Poem: few have or ever will read it, and those who have taken this trouble have met with nothing to please the taste or gratify curiosity."

4. Kinnersley Castle, some 12 miles N.W. of Hereford, was the home of Bummy's elder brother, John Altham Graham-Clarke (1782-1862).

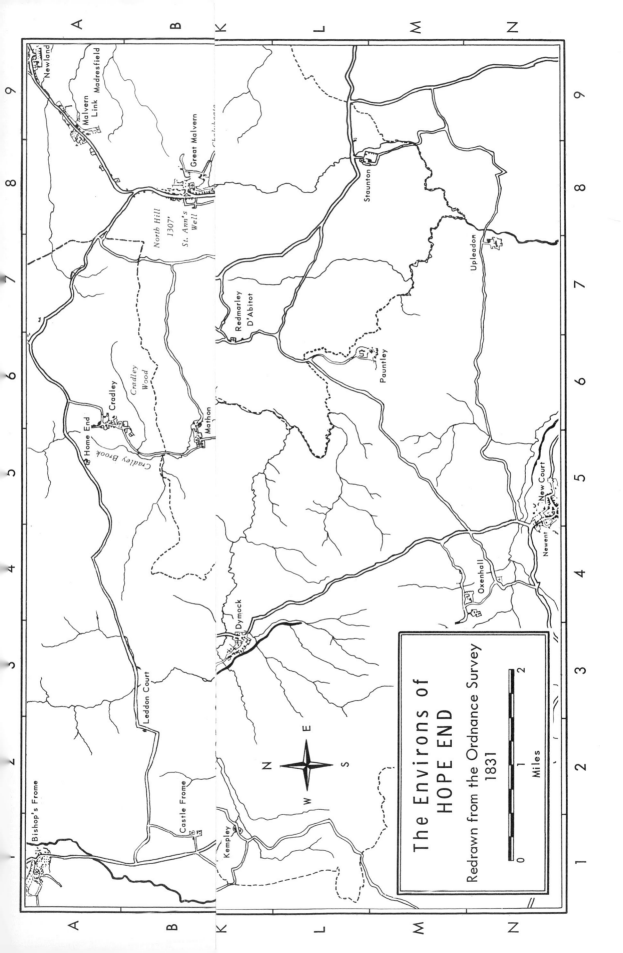

The Environs of
HOPE END

Redrawn from the Ordnance Survey
1831

Miles
0   1   2

as not even to let them know of her intention. *Either* we *are going,*
—or Papa is going to London. Oh I hope—I do hope he *is not going*
away from us again.

After dinner, B & I lay down on the bed in her room; & talked.
I said something about the probability of Papa's going away, & her   5
answer was—"I sh.^d not be surprised— I think, Ba, you are anxious
to leave this place altogether." I acknowledged I was—considering
everything. Mr Curzon came today with his little boy, & is to sleep
here. While he was coming, B H A & I were sitting on the grassy
green hill above the rock, basking in the lovely sun.   10
He was agreable this evening.

Thursday, April 5.
Dear B & H off at 20 minutes to twelve. They mean to spend
one day with Miss Price,[1] & to return here on Tuesday certainly. M.^r
Curzon left us between two & three. Not at all well, is the descrip-   15
tion of me today. In the evening I lost a game at chess to Papa.

Friday April 6.
How extraordinary it is, that Papa sh.^d take no part in the Church
missionary society today. But I am glad of it; for last year, what a
scene there was in consequence of his doing otherwise. I believe he   20
has sent his subscription. His not going, & Bummy's going, make me
feel confident that something is coming. Bummy told me with tears
—"nothing shall induce me to remain away from you ≪longer≫ than
Tuesday". Dear dear Bummy.
They have been dragging the pond—Sam & Stormy in the water.   25
I have been reading Pindar's 9th Olympiad, & must go back to it.
Pindar's subjects are of little interest to my mind. Arabel has written
to Annie, observing upon her want of memory in the late affair. That
is certainly the mildest construction; & is perhaps, the true <one>.

Saturday April 7th   30
What did I do today? Not write in my diary.[2]

---

1. At Foxley, the seat of Sir Robert Price, 8 miles W.N.W. of Hereford, and about 4
miles from Kinnersley Castle.
2. She wrote to H.S.B. (see Appendix I, p. 305).

Diary by E.B.B.

Sunday. April 8—

*A & I did not go to church. I finished St John's Gospel in Greek:
not in Nonnus's Greek. ≪E Cliffe came.≫*

Went down to the gate. Miss H M was there, & brought me
5 *Synesius's hymns¹ from Mr Boyd. He was sorry that he had not
≪lent≫ them to me before! Miss H M & Annie do not go tomorrow.
I cant help feeling something like being sorry. They may not go
until next week.*

Read two hymns of Synesius this evening. I think I like him.

10 *Monday April 9.*

*Finished not only the whole of Synesius's poems, but four odes
of Gregory, contained in the same little volume.² And yet I really
read nothing superficially. There is a great deal in Synesius which
is very fine. He stands on a much higher step than Gregory does, as*
15 *a poet; tho' <ₐoccasional> diffuseness is the fault of each. I like
the 7th <hymn> extremely. A slip of paper in the first leaf, tells
me that in Mr Boyd's opinion the 1.st 5.th & 6.th are <ₐperhaps> the
finest, next to the 9th I w.^d lay a very strong emphasis on perhaps.
The 9th is, I agree with him, decidedly the finest.*

20 *A & I walked out on the terrace opposite the drawing room windows. Oh I do wish, fervently wish, that something were settled.
I c.^d be happy—at least, happier, if it were.*

My eyes ached <tonight> with reading today.

Tuesday. April 10.

25 *How the days are wearing away. I translated some passages from
Synesius,³ which Mr Boyd had translated before me—pour m'amuser,
—& try a variety of versification. I was in the midst of the*

1. Synesius of Cyrene (*c.* 370-413), Bishop of Ptolemaïs, whose extant works include
twelve Hymns.

2. It is clear from E.B.B.'s letter to H.S.B. [16 April 1832] that she was reading an
edition by Franciscus Portus (1511-81). This might have been *Synesii Cyrenæi, Episcopi
Ptolemaïdis, Hymni vario* (Paris, 1618), which included Gregory Nazianzen's odes commencing "Te immortalem monarcham," "Quid tibi vis fieri," "Te etiam nunc laudamus" and
"Dubio procul quamplurima contingunt."

3. Her translation of the 9th Hymn appeared in the third part of "Some Account of the
Greek Christian Poets," in *The Athenæum*, 12 March 1842, pp. 229-231. H.S.B.'s transla-
tion of the same Hymn appeared in his *Select Poems of Synesius and Gregory Nazianzen*
(London, 1814), which also contained portions of the first three Hymns.

⟨ . . . ⟩[1]

Daisy. Hood[2] is very clever.

Wednesday April 11.
    Dearest Occyta's birthday,[3] & I have not kissed

⟨ . . . ⟩[4]   5

*[Sunday, 15 April] past the 2^d reading which it did yesterday morn^g
by a majority of nine,[5] she delivered to me Mr Boyd's message on the
same subject.*
    Mr Curzon preached, what I thought a good sermon.
    ≪Much out of spirits.≫   10

Monday April 16.
    *Rain!! and no going to Malvern. I am very sorry. But we might
have gone on the clearing-up, if Mrs Cliffe had not been afraid of
trusting her horse on the heavy roads. So Eliza explained in a note,
which prorogued our journey until Wednesday. I am not half inclined*   15
*to go on Wednesday.   Began to write to Mr Boyd about Synesius—
but I wont send my letter until tomorrow.   Mrs Hanford & Miss
Martin called here.*
    *I wish I could get at some Greek books which I cant get at!—the
Alexandrian writers for instance, & Plato whole—& Athenæus—&*   20
Aristophanes.

Tuesday April 17th
    *I always think on Tuesday—"there may be some letter, some
decisive letter to Papa". But none comes—nothing comes!——*
    ≪Sent≫ my letter to Mr Boyd:[6] a short one, & free from any   25

1. Excision of seven-eighths of a page.
2. Thomas Hood (1799-1845), poet and humorist.   3. His 8th.
4. Excision of seven-eighths of a page, together with the following leaf, i.e., two and seven-eighths pages altogether.
5. The House of Lords voted 184-175 in favour of the 2nd Reading of the Reform Bill. *The Times,* 14 April 1832, in a report of the proceedings, noted that the debate began on the afternoon of 13 April, but that Their Lordships did not adjourn until 7.15 a.m. on 14 April.
6. For her letter, see Appendix I, p. 306.

Diary by E.B.B.

allusion to the first subject in my fears.   Arabel enclosed a note to
Annie.   Bummy says nothing, will say nothing; & I sink into bad
spirits very very often every day.   What will be the end of it.   Nothing
quite exhilarates me but prayer.

5   *B had a letter from Selina[1] today, from which it is sufficiently*
apparent, that James does not mean to come here.   At least they
are expecting him at Bradly.[2]   Not sorry for it, on one account.   I
scarcely slept all ≪ . . . ≫ last night.   What shall I do tonight?   Read
the two last Olympic odes today,—except a few lines of the last but
10   *one.   The very last, to the Graces, is most harmonious & beautiful.[3]*
I <recollect> Mr. Boyd's repeating it to me at Great Malvern in 1830,
when I was paying him a long & happy visit.   νυν δ᾽ ολωλε!!—[4]   Not
the ode—which is deathless.

    Bro fishing at Mathon,—and now at 8 oclock, he has not returned.
15   *We dine almost every day, at seven or near seven.   What can Papa be*
doing, in the small portion of ground in which he can do anything, so
long & late?   Oh I do wish—what is vain.

<Wednesday>.   April 18.
    Mrs Cliffe & Eliza took Arabel & me to Malvern; & it began to rain
20   *before we arrived at our gate, & rained all the way.   Annie met us at*
the door of Ruby Cottage.   She is going tomorrow, if Mr Roberts[5]
comes tonight—which he wont do—or on Saturday.   Went into the
dining room.   I felt so depressed, that I should have been merciful,
in letting myself cry.   But I would not permit that.   Soon into M^r
25   *Boyd's room.   He received me kindly, & asked if I had heard any*
≪more harm of him.≫   I said, no.   And then he told <∧me> of M^{rs}
Boyd having repeated to him an "extraordinary" expression which
she had made use of, in her letter to Arabel—that he had ≪only≫
<∧one> objection to quitting Malvern; namely his dislike of travel-
30   *ling!!   I [H.S.B.] said to Mrs Boyd—"That was a a [sic] very extra-*
ordinary observation ≪for≫ you to make.   Miss ≪Barrett≫ will

1. Selina Graham, a distant cousin of Bummy.

2. Bradley, in Co. Durham, the temporary residence of Bummy's youngest sister, Mrs. Jane Hedley (1796-1877).

3. No. 13, to Xenophon of Corinth, and no. 14, to Asopichus of Orchomenus.   The reference to the Graces is in strophe 1 of no. 14.

4. "Now perished."

5. Possibly the Rev. George Roberts, who later married Miss Henrietta Mushet.

suppose that I have no objection to leaving her. M.ʳˢ Boyd's answer was, "Ba knows she is going away herself". I observed she seems to have doubts of it sometimes. "Then," replied M.ʳˢ Boyd, "she is very foolish." Besides, he said, M.ʳˢ Boyd's expression was incorrect in every way. I have an objection to leaving Malvern on account of 5
my health, which has been better here than any where else."[1] He asked me, why I had not written to him as usual, about Synesius; & had not received my letter. Talked about Synesius. I told him, that I preferred the 3.ᵈ & 7.ᵗʰ, to the 5 & 6.ᵗʰ hymns which he & M.ʳ Joseph Clarke selected for admiration. M.ʳ Clarke's observation, with regard 10
to the 3.ᵈ hymn being a mere string of epithetical appellations, is decidedly incorrect.[2] † Miss H M had asked M.ʳˢ Boyd, if Miss Mushet might come into the room for a little while; ≪because≫ she wished to talk to me. M.ʳ Boyd was obliged to agree. So she came in & sate working a provokingly long time, while M.ʳ Boyd & I disputed 15
about Calvinism, & the claims of metaphysical & physical science. He told me afterwards that I was very cunning; that I did not argue so well when he & I were together, as when other persons were present —that he never heard me so powerful in argument as today. I could not forbear smiling. That was <u>not</u> a compliment. He asked me if I 20
observed any similarity between Synesius & Pindar. Surely not.

He let me stay in the room while he dined; but by <u>my</u> request. We did not go away until five. They all came to the door, & I proposed going to the Wyche tomorrow or next day, & running down to see them. 25

M.ʳ Boyd spoke to me about Arabel,—& sent me a long message to be delivered gravely, tho' meant jokingly, to convince her of his little degree of respect for her <veracity>. He assured me, that if the question of an untruth having been told by either, was between Annie, & me—he w.ᵈ acquit me at once. 30

---

1. Although slightly confusing at first reading, we decided to leave the quotation marks in this passage exactly as E.B.B. wrote them.

2. Clarke's *Concise View*, ed. cit., II, 131-132: "Hymns.—These are by far the most elegant of Synesius' productions; still however, though hymns, they are very defective in theology, a science in which this Bishop by no means excelled; . . . the *third* is little else than periphrastic names for God, with a few beautiful lines here and there, such as 380-400; the *fifth* and *sixth* are highly poetic, however defective in doctrine; the *seventh* represents Christ as going down into hell to recover (βoηθooς) the damned; (l.37); and the same doctrine is more full in the *ninth*, (1.9-20), which is far, very far, superior as a Poem to all the rest; . . . the language is exalted, the thoughts sublime, and the composition inimitable.—"

Diary by E.B.B.

≪ . . . ≫

*Pouring all the way home. M*ʳˢ *Cliffe afraid to face Papa, put Arabel*
& me out of her carriage,—below the first gate,—& home we had to
wade in mud & thin shoes. They were in the middle of dinner!!! B
5   *came out, to ask me to go to bed! We went up stairs to dress & have*
dinner in my room,—& were not scolded after all. Little Fanny
Hanford here.[1]   *She too, was caught in the rain. An intelligent*
little girl.

Thursday April 19ᵗʰ
10   *Wrote to M*ʳ *Boyd about the parallel passage in Synesius & Ana-*
creon,[2] *—& nearly went thro' the whole of the first & Second pythian*
odes.[3] *The first is very very fine,—& there are splendid things too in*
the second. B ≪spoke≫ rather not very harshly today; & I could not
help crying for nearly an hour afterwards. My spirits are quite beaten
15   *down on all sides. How shall I go thro' next month?— B H & A*
*went to Colwall & the Bartons. M*ʳˢ *Martin set off three quarters of*
an hour after receiving the letters, to Ireland. Her mother is very ill.
    <I went> out by myself, thro' the garden to the hill above it,
where I walked up & down, & thought of one who liked to walk there.
20   *Nothing has happened.*

Friday April 20.
      ≪*Good Friday.*≫
      How time is going. Made this list of days & cried over it after-
wards. B H & A to church. No—A did not go—, as I found out
25   *afterwards. Read 8 Greek chapters from St Luke's gospel. A letter*
*from Annie, & a note from M*ʳˢ *Boyd to Arabel: the latter begging her*
*to return <no> answer to any message M*ʳ *Boyd might have sent by*
me, as she might be provoked to resent what his love of argument
induced him to say. Better not to tell <u>*me*</u> *about it, M*ʳˢ *Boyd says,*
30   *because "poor dear Ba is sure to tell M*ʳ *Boyd". She wishes that I*
*did not tell M*ʳ *Boyd everything he asked me! Annie among other*
*things, asks if Arabel thinks that M*ʳ *Barrett w*ᵈ *like them to live near*

---

1. The daughter of Mrs. Martin's friend, Mrs. Hanford, of Woolashill Hall.
2. For the letter, see Appendix I, p. 307.
3. Of Pindar; both to Hiero the Ætnæan.

us—   In M^{rs} B's opinion he w^{d} not."

≪ . . . ≫

Arabel wrote both to Annie & M^{rs} <Boyd> immediately, & she means to send it before breakfast tomorrow, that Annie may have it before she goes.   Arabel w^{d} not say much.   She did maintain the   5 point of Papa's inclination, and the probability of his being very sorry, if they were to leave Malvern while our plans were unsettled.   She said besides, I dont know what Ba will do if you dont settle near us.

The Peytons have invited me to go in the Car to Malvern on Mon- day, when they promise to set me down at R C.   10

Saturday April 21.
    I am <u>not</u> well . .

≪ . . . ≫

Read the 2^{d} Pythian—& walked out a little.   In the evening Papa read us Mr Curzon's prospectus of the Echo, the new periodical   15 he wishes to edit & print in Ledbury.^{1}   It wont answer.   His letter to Papa, engages Papa's "dear daughter" as a poetical contributer.

I heard tonight, that when B & Mrs Hanford & A were walking this morning, M^{rs} H asked B if there was any chance of my paying her a visit.   B said in a peculiar manner, "it quite depends upon cir-   20 cumstances."   Then M^{rs} H asked B how long she was likely to remain at Hope End.   "My plans are not at all fixed".   "Shall you go to Ireland"?   "No! when I leave <u>them</u>, I shall return immediately home."   I do wish—I do wish—, things c^{d} be settled before May.

Sunday.   April 22.   25
    All at church except me.   I am not at all well, tho' better since the morning.   B made me promise to sit down stairs while they were absent, on account of my room being voted close.   The closeness of my room, never never injured me.   Mrs C. & Eliza came,—& we walked down to the gate.   I fancied that the lady who sate near   30 Arabel was Miss Mushet.   No!—after service Mr Curzon gave a note to her from Annie.   So they are gone.

1. As far as can be established, nothing came of this project.

[239]

Diary by E.B.B.

Monday April 23.

    Walked down to the gate with B H & A to meet the Peytons'
carriage. The sky looked lowering & B portended a rainy day. Never
mind!—we got off. The rain came on as portended; & they left me
5   *in a cataract at R C. M.ʳˢ Boyd sate with me for a moment in the*
drawing room & then I was dismissed to M.ʳ Boyd, with a pen & ink.
He wanted me to make a memorandum of the additional number of
Greek lines he has learnt, & also to write my name in Scholefield—
to put "To" before Hugh Stuart Boyd, & "from his friend E B Barrett"
10 *afterwards. I wrote "from his attached friend". He has learnt 8000*
Greek lines, except 80,—& this 80 he wishes for my aid to acquire.
I shall like it!— I heard him repeat a good part of ≪ . . . ≫ Gregory's
ode to his soul.[1] *Indeed, he ≪learnt≫ some more of it, while I was*
with him.

15   *Afterwards we doubted how to select the 80 lines. The rest of*
Gregory's ode?— The fine passage in the 1ˢᵗ orat: against Julian,
beginning ω ευηθεστατε?—[2] *I read a great part of it: but that*
w.ᵈ not do. He has nearly decided on some of the geographical des-
criptions in the Prometheus,—& we are to begin upon them next
20 *time. With regard to my Prometheus, he told me how much he sh.ᵈ*
like to hear it read—that M.ʳˢ Boyd said she had no time—but that
even if she had time, he knew perfectly well, she w.ᵈ not like to do it.
She w.ᵈ not read a page of his own translation. She has no taste for
anything of that kind—

25   *If she has no taste, she might have kindness. But I answered truly*
that I never expected him to read the whole, & was much obliged by
the degree of trouble he had already given himself. M.ʳˢ Boyd ≪is≫
certainly an extraordinary woman, to be M.ʳˢ Boyd.

    He asked me about Arabel; & I told him only that she doubted his
30 *being in earnest. A great deal said about ≪my≫ not having invited*
Annie this winter—& M.ʳˢ ≪ . . . [Cliffe]≫ opposed. So M.ʳˢ ≪ . . .

    1. "Ad suam Animam Anacreonticum Carmen" (*GNO*, II, 182-185). A translation by
E.B.B. appeared in the second part of her article "Some Account of the Greek Christian
Poets" (*The Athenæum*, 5 March 1842, p. 211).

    2. "O most stupid." A marginal note against this passage in *WG*, p. 76, recorded: "read
for the second time, with M.ʳ Boyd. October 23.ᵈ 1830. Read for the third time with M.ʳ
Boyd. Nov.ʳ 1831. Read a part of this column for the fourth time with M.ʳ Boyd, April
1832." In her notes on the flyleaf, E.B.B. called this the "most splendid passage in the two
orations!—"

[Cliffe]≫ *has had the ostentation & want of delicacy & want of truth*
to have maintained not only at R C but to Miss Steers that in conse-
quence of certain reports, she had invited Annie to Mathon & taken
her to Worcester. It is not true!!!— Witness all that is past—witness
*all that has been said by M.*ʳˢ ≪ . . . [Cliffe]≫ *to me—by me to M.*ʳˢ   5
≪ . . . [Cliffe]≫ *Witness all that is written in this diary* <on> *the*
*subject. M.*ʳˢ ≪ . . . [Cliffe]≫ *w.*ᵈ *not put her little finger in danger to*
save——but there is no use in writing. The world is the world. I
*cannot make it Heaven. Only it is hard that I who w.*ᵈ *have done*
≪*everything*≫, *sh.*ᵈ *be directed by those for whom I w.*ᵈ *have done it,*   10
*to the example of those who w.*ᵈ *have done nothing.*

*M.*ʳ *Boyd pressed me earnestly to go to see him for two or three*
days—"There is no harm in asking!— Do ask your Papa." I was
obliged to say "I will think of it": tho' thinking is vain!   †

Went away in the pouring rain. Left   15

⟨ . . . ⟩¹

1. Nine leaves, i.e., eighteen pages, excised. See Appendix I, p. 308, for a letter from
E.B.B. to H.S.B. written on 25 April.

TEXTUAL NOTES

MANUSCRIPT ALTERATIONS

Any reader studying these textual notes may find it helpful to have an amplification of the verbal usage, as follows:

altered from: denotes that E.B.B. changed an existing word or phrase, incorporating some letters or parts of letters of the original word(s).

superimposed on: denotes that E.B.B. wrote the new word or phrase on top of the original word(s), without deleting the original, or incorporating any part of it in the new construction.

effaced: denotes that E.B.B. used some form of bleaching agent to remove all but a faint trace of the original word(s).

deleted: denotes that E.B.B. made a normal deletion, by scoring through the word(s).

obliterated: denotes that a heavy deletion was made, with the apparent intention of preventing the original word(s) from being capable of decipherment.

added above/below line: denotes interlineation.

As in the text of the Diary, E.B.B.'s hand is represented by italics, and editorial conjectures by Roman type.

PAGE 1

line 2 *4* superimposed on *5,* then deleted, and re-written below line
line 3 *like* superimposed on *as*
line 4 *begun* altered from *began*
line 6 *my* deleted
line 8 *then* altered from *how*
line 12 *know* superimposed on *sh*[all]
line 19 *bodies* altered from *body*
line 20 *for* superimposed on *&;* new ampersand inserted
line 22 *I* superimposed on effaced *m*[e]
line 24 *received* altered from *arrived*
line 25 originally *prophet about; ess* added to *prophet,* and *about* rewritten
line 26 *on* altered from *a*[bout]

PAGE 2

line 6 *Macbeth's* deleted
line 10 Closing double quotation marks deleted
line 18 originally *with cold; your* superimposed on *with; cold* altered to *love,* then deleted, and *love* added above line with caret
line 29 *sends* altered from *says*

PAGE 3

line 5 *help* altered from *hep*
line 6 At this point, a line was drawn across the page to end the day's entry; having second thoughts, the first phrase of E.B.B.'s addendum was superimposed on the line

[243]

Diary by E.B.B.

PAGE 3 (continued)

line 13   *& perhaps* et seq.: post-entry between lines. Originally *we shall feel* but inserted between the wrong lines, and then effaced, the longer phrase being added in the correct sequence

line 17   *repeated* superimposed on effaced *said*

line 18   *5* altered from *6*

line 21   *in* superimposed on effaced *after*

PAGE 4

line 4   *him* superimposed on effaced <u>*my*</u>

PAGE 5

line 6   *6* superimposed on *7*

line 25   *or fancied* superimposed on effaced *to read*

PAGE 6

line 5   *7* superimposed on *8*

line 8   *in writing* altered from *to write*

line 9   <u>*goose*</u> altered from *gooo*[se]

line 15   *loves* altered from *loved*

line 16   *Papa* altered from *B*[ro]

line 17   *fishing* superimposed on effaced *brook*

line 23   *travel* superimposed on effaced *go*

PAGE 7

line 6   *a* superimposed on *its*

line 7   *to* superimposed on *in*

line 8   *attracting* altered from *attracts*

line 12   *shed* superimposed on *cried*

line 14   originally *But as*; *But* deleted and *as* capitalized

line 15   originally *with my; still* altered from *with; with* superimposed on effaced *my*

line 19   *inserted* superimposed on *wrote*

line 20   *Fame* altered from *Faith*

line 22   *king* altered from *kind*

line 23   *Papa walked* et seq.: post-entry between lines

line 24   *8* superimposed on *9*

line 27   *for writing* superimposed on *for say*[ing]

line 27   *the* altered from *her*

PAGE 8

line 7   caret superimposed on *?*

line 11   *the* superimposed on *his*

line 13   *I said as little as I could; thro'* altered from *I say as little as I can; but*

line 17   *9* superimposed on *10*

line 19   *about* altered from *h*[alf]

line 22   *me* altered from *ne*[arly]

line 23   *turning* altered from *turned*

line 24   *walked* superimposed on effaced *ran*

PAGE 9

line 18   *He hoped* et seq.: post-entry between lines; *seemed* altered from *been*

line 22   *was a mere copyist* altered from *is a mere copyer*

line 23   *should* altered from *stood; stand* squeezed in margin

PAGE 10

line 6   *detained* superimposed on effaced *kept*

line 7   *Blomfield's*: *B* superimposed on *the*

line 10   *at about 6 o'cl*[ock] inserted above line with caret then deleted; *She* superimposed on *M^r*[s]

line 11   *go* altered from *come*

line 12   *I* altered from *A*

line 16   *We talked* et seq.: post-entry between lines

line 18   *10* altered from *11*

line 22   *text* superimposed on effaced *hand*

line 22   *them* superimposed on *it*

line 26   *& singing,* inserted above deleted *cheerfully*

line 30   *had arrived* superimposed on *were come*

line 34   *our* superimposed on effaced *God*

PAGE 11

line 2   *at* superimposed on *now*

line 7   *have* originally written twice; the first deleted

line 13   *exclaim* superimposed on *say*

line 13   *did* altered from *do*

line 14   double underscore deleted

line 14 *how* superimposed on effaced *that*

line 17 beginning of word effaced; indecipherable

line 17 *If they dont go* et seq.: post-entry between lines

line 19 *11* altered from *12*

line 21 *He* superimposed on effaced *They*

line 22 *tell nobody* superimposed on effaced *mention it to*

PAGE 12

line 4 *known* altered from *know*

line 5 *bank* superimposed on *hill*

line 8 *not* superimposed on effaced *less*

line 12 *but not unhappy* reinstated above the same phrase deleted; remainder of phrase post-entry between lines

line 14 *12* altered from *13*

line 19 *Over* altered from *over*

PAGE 13

line 5 *thought* altered from *pr*[oposed]

line 5 *Tuesday* altered from *Monday*

line 17 *for* altered from *to*

line 17 *live* altered from *leave*

line 18 *certainty, by* altered from *certainly in*

line 19 *Fear* altered from *fear*

line 21 *!!* superimposed on *?*

line 23 *my* superimposed on *this*

line 24 *Miss* altered from *M*ᵗˢ

line 27 *I hope this is a wrong thought* deleted

PAGE 14

line 1 *13* altered from *14*

line 4 *sleep* altered from *slep*

line 13 *14* altered from *15*

line 24 *show* deleted

line 25 *there* deleted

PAGE 15

line 1 *absent* altered from *away*

line 8 *with* altered from *to*

line 16 *to*: post-entry, squeezed in margin

line 20 *talking* altered from *talk*

line 22 *talking* altered from *talk*

line 28 *shed* altered from *cried*

PAGE 16

line 8 *Only that more people* et seq.: post-entry between lines

line 12 *15* altered from *16*

PAGE 17

line 14 *his* altered from *a*

line 16 *Barrett* altered from *Barrette*; *never* superimposed on effaced *expected*

line 19 *does* altered from *did*

line 21 *vulgarissimus* altered from *vulgarissimo*

PAGE 18

line 2 *good* superimposed on effaced *bad*

line 5 *likely* altered from *to s*[trike]

line 12 *also* deleted

line 13 *After* altered from *after*

line 18 *what I have to bear* inserted above deleted *all that I can feel*

PAGE 19

line 3 *was* altered from *were*

line 6 *I* deleted

line 8 *used not to be* altered from *had not been*

line 13 *are* altered from *is*

line 13 *by* altered from *a*[s]

line 15 *annihilate* superimposed on effaced *erase*

line 17 *Friendship* altered from *friendship*

line 20 *is* altered from *are*

line 24 *was* superimposed on *in*

line 24 *good* altered from *god*

line 28 *to* deleted

PAGE 20

line 5 *The* altered from *the*

line 14 *Almost* superimposed on *Be*[fore]

line 14 *tail* superimposed on *d*[ream]

PAGE 21

line 17 *mention* superimposed on *say*

line 17 *M*ᵗˢ altered from *Miss*

line 20 *us* superimposed on *me*

line 21 *for* deleted

line 30 *today* deleted

PAGE 22

line 1 *he* altered from *if*; *would* super-

Diary by E.B.B.

PAGE 22 (continued)

                imposed on effaced *he*

line 6   *Wrote to Knibb* et seq.: post-entry between lines

line 12 *If it comes* et seq.: post-entry in top margin

line 23 *he* superimposed on *in*

line 24 *& sh.ᵈ be made!*—: post-entry between lines; *& sh.ᵈ* superimposed on indecipherable effaced word

line 25 *for* superimposed on effaced *of*

line 27 *hs* altered from *Hs*, then deleted and re-written above line

line 31 *can* superimposed on *am*

PAGE 23

line 2   *benefit* altered from *benefits*

line 4   *Him* altered from *him*

line 5   *this* altered from *the*

line 6   *some who seem* altered from *those who are*

line 7   *Thou* altered from *thou*

line 8   *Thou* altered from *thou*

line 9   *Thee* altered from *thee*

line 20 *Shoes* altered from *shoes*

PAGE 24

line 3   *have* superimposed on *be* and efface *ju*[dged]

line 12 *blessing* altered from *blessings*

line 21 *to* deleted

line 34 *Two of my wishes were* altered from *One of my wishes was*

PAGE 25

line 11 *a* altered from *an*

line 14 *Huzza* altered from *hurrah*

line 18 *We* altered from *I*

line 27 *Of* altered from *of*

line 28 *Miss* altered from *M.ʳ*

PAGE 26

line 2   *Soon* altered from *I*

line 3   *other* superimposed on effaced *p*[erson's]

line 5   *standing* superimposed on *being*

line 11 *Steers* altered from *Stears*

line 11 *go* superimposed on *de*[part]

line 15 *longer* superimposed on *more*

line 22 *reading* superimposed on effaced *saying*

PAGE 27

line 2   *we* altered from *I*

line 17 *As he was hearing* altered from *When he heard*

line 20 *mentioned* superimposed on *asked him*

line 22 *would* altered from *should*

line 25 *for me* inserted with caret, then effaced

line 30 *Eliza did not come* et seq.: post-entry between lines

PAGE 28

line 3   *Oh* superimposed on closing double quotation marks

line 18 *drank* altered from *drunk*

line 19 *at* superimposed on *&*

PAGE 29

line 13 *This* altered from *That*

line 14 *responded* superimposed on *exclaimed*

line 20 redundant *a* deleted; *walk* altered from *walke*

line 21 *summit* altered from *submit*

line 22 *by* altered from *on*

line 23 *there* altered from *There*; *And* squeezed in

PAGE 30

line 4   *irrepressibly* altered from *inexpressibly*

line 24 *the* superimposed on effaced *at the*

PAGE 31

line 3   *moment* superimposed on *time*

line 17 *what* altered from *as*

line 20 *he* altered from *his*

line 20 originally *distant*; *in* post-entry

line 21 *had* superimposed on *&*

line 21 *but* superimposed on *&*

PAGE 32

line 4   *having* superimposed on *be*[ing]

line 7   *continued* inserted above deleted *observed*

line 9   *right*: *r* superimposed on *w*

line 12 *his* superimposed on *a*

line 15 *I wonder where* et seq.: post-entry between lines

line 26 *the* superimposed on *any*

line 27   *them*: t superimposed on *o*[r]

line 29   *on account of* et seq.: post-entry between lines

line 30   *25* altered from *26*

line 31   *seems* altered from *seemed*

PAGE 33

line 3   *my* altered from *their*

line 12   *myself unallegorically* superimposed on *EBB to HSB*

line 14   *he* altered from *I*

line 17   *A note* et seq.: post-entry between lines

line 21   *Bro read prayers.*: post-entry between lines

line 25   *brought* superimposed on effaced *gave*

PAGE 34

line 3   *he* altered from *He*

line 12   *we* superimposed on *I*

line 17   *that* altered from *than*

line 17   *Has she any?* superimposed on effaced *Henrietta walked*

line 23   *sent* altered from *send*

line 30   Two letters or figures effaced

PAGE 35

line 1   *into my room* deleted

line 6   *with* superimposed on *to*

line 10   *bed.*; post-entry, superimposed on period

line 10   *Thought* superimposed on effaced *throughout*

line 12   *even* deleted

line 16   *His birthday* et seq.: post-entry between lines

line 17   *Pindar's*: P superimposed on *X*

line 19   *Will it not,* et seq.: post-entry between lines

line 21   *Bro rode* et seq.: post-entry between lines

line 30   *had* altered from *has*

PAGE 36

line 3   *cause* superimposed on *reason*

line 9   *historical*: hi altered from *hy*

line 12   *2* effaced

line 15   *When* superimposed on *No*

line 22   *feel* altered from *feee*[l]

line 27   *half* altered from *all*

line 29   *M^{rs}* superimposed on effaced *Yes!*

line 30   *object &* deleted

line 31   *it—* superimposed on effaced *doing*

PAGE 37

line 3   *away* superimposed on —

line 6   *that* altered from *the*

line 10   *write* deleted

line 10   *to* deleted

line 13   *Selecting* altered from *selecting*

line 22   *fright* altered from *run*

line 30   *Thee* altered from *thee*

PAGE 38

line 1   *ocean* altered from *sea*

line 2   originally *at*; *to* superimposed first, and then *in*

line 5   *H* deleted

line 5   *&* altered from *I*

line 10   *in the case* deleted

line 25   *the* superimposed on effaced *ditto*

line 25   *our* superimposed on *the*

PAGE 39

line 2   *near* superimposed on effaced *at*

line 16   *putting* altered from *not*

PAGE 40

line 9   *Saturday* superimposed on effaced *July*

line 32   *Maddox came.*: post-entry between lines

PAGE 41

line 5   *there* deleted

PAGE 42

line 13   *lock* altered from *be locked aga*[inst]

line 18   *bed* altered from *bel*

line 20   *was* superimposed on effaced *had been*

line 28   *boil* altered from *boyl*[e]

line 30   indecipherable word of three or four letters effaced

PAGE 43

line 2   *and* altered from *but*

line 8   *like* altered from *as*

line 14   *to* altered from *a*; *a* squeezed in margin

PAGE 43 (continued)

line 20 *Agamemnon* altered from *Agam-memnon*

line 24 *amanuensis* altered from *amman-uensis*

PAGE 44

line 3 *longed to beg him to trust* me superimposed on effaced *I begged him to employ me, & to*

line 4 *too* altered from *so*

line 8 *the* superimposed on *my*

line 13 *you* superimposed on *no body*

line 14 *should* altered from *would*

line 17 *whether* superimposed on *if*

line 18 *whether* superimposed on *if*

line 22 *I wish* superimposed on *would*; *that* deleted

line 23 *be* deleted; *devolve* altered from *devolved*

line 23 *It* altered from *If*

line 26 *&* superimposed on effaced *for*

line 29 *But*: post-entry, squeezed in

line 38 *away* altered from *aware*

PAGE 45

line 15 *were* altered from *was*

line 16 *&* superimposed on *so*; *that* deleted

PAGE 46

line 4 *I* superimposed on effaced *there*

line 9 *nearest* superimposed on effaced *first gate*

line 18 *less* superimposed on *not*

line 28 *came* inserted above deleted *walked*

PAGE 47

line 2 *it* superimposed on *us*; interpolated *to do so* deleted

line 3 *Brighton's* inserted above deleted *its*

line 4 *in* superimposed on effaced *dur[-ing]*

line 4 *would* altered from *should*

line 5 *That* superimposed on *I*

line 7 *of* deleted

line 14 *&* altered from *to*

line 15 *I* superimposed on effaced *M.ͬ*

line 16 *got* superimposed on *fl*[ew]

line 16 *Three* superimposed on effaced *Dinner*

line 22 *July* altered from *June*

line 25 *he* altered from *I*

line 28 *ergo* superimposed on *also*

PAGE 48

line 1 ⟨inte⟩*resting*: restored reading; ink blot obscures first four letters

line 6 *to* superimposed on *at*

line 19 *Miss* superimposed on *They*

line 27 originally *afterw*[ards]; *w* effaced

line 33 *a* superimposed on effaced *the*

PAGE 49

line 1 *prefers* superimposed on effaced *like*[s]

line 3 *July* altered from *June*

line 7 *over* superimposed on effaced *for*

line 15 *Bummy wrote* et seq.: post-entry between lines

line 27 *been* superimposed on *in*

PAGE 50

line 4 *odours* altered from *smells*

line 9 *July* altered from *June*

line 20 *&* post-entry, squeezed in

line 31 *A* effaced

line 32 *while* superimposed on effaced *Miss*

PAGE 51

line 3 *lend* altered from *lent*

line 8 *so* superimposed on effaced *she*

line 14 *but* *did* *expect* superimposed on effaced *& yet almost*

line 16 *that* superimposed on *it*; *had* altered from *has*

line 21 *But I could* *not* deleted

line 31 *the* superimposed on *it*

line 33 *Time* altered from *time*

PAGE 52

line 1 *did* deleted

line 7 *said* altered from *says*

line 11 *by* superimposed on *at*

line 14 *could* altered from *can*

line 21 *w.ͩ* superimposed on *sh.ͩ*

line 23 *But* altered from *but*

line 26 *punctually* inserted above deleted *properly*

line 32 *of* effaced

PAGE 53

line 3   *Wednesday*: *W* superimposed on effaced *Th*[ursday]

line 11   *the* inserted above deleted *yesterday's*

line 24   *this* superimposed on *it*

line 28   *an idea* altered from *a mistake*

line 30   *going* altered from *coming*

PAGE 54

line 1   *be* superimposed on *to*

line 8   *our* superimposed on *the*

line 11   *this* altered from *the*

line 12   *here* superimposed on *!*

line 15   *into* superimposed on *to*

line 21   *Le* superimposed on *The*

line 23   *even* superimposed on *to*; *to* squeezed in margin

line 26   *teeth* superimposed on *&*

line 28   *teeth* altered from *to*[ngue]

PAGE 55

line 9   *with* superimposed on *in*

line 9   *wild* inserted above deleted *Exeter Change*

line 11   *himself*: *self* post-entry, squeezed in

line 15   *confessed*: *c* superimposed on *s*[aid]

PAGE 56

line 8   *so* superimposed on *it*

line 9   *No letter!* et seq.: post-entry between lines

line 13   *He* superimposed on effaced *In*

line 13   *type* deleted

line 14   *there* altered from *their*

line 16   *on account* superimposed on effaced *for the*

line 17   *I shall appear to go* altered from *it will appear to be*

line 25   *B H* superimposed on effaced *H A*

PAGE 57

line 4   *woman* altered from *women*

line 4   *amalgamate* altered from *amalgammate*

line 12   *Dreamt last night* superimposed on effaced *Read a little of the*

line 19   *meant* superimposed on effaced *was*

line 23   *to* superimposed on *for*

line 25   *Well!* et seq.: post-entry between lines

line 26   *the* superimposed on *my*

PAGE 58

line 6   *&* deleted

line 11   *His* superimposed on effaced *Miss*

line 13   *Her father* superimposed on effaced *She could*

line 21   *said* superimposed on effaced *told*

line 28   *Joanna Baillie* superimposed on effaced *Miss Joanna*

line 29   *when* superimposed on *his*

line 33   *that* superimposed on *&*

PAGE 59

line 4   *him* superimposed on *M.ʳ Boyd*

line 11   *asked* superimposed on effaced *begged*

line 15   *nobody* superimposed on effaced *Bro*

PAGE 60

line 1   *in* superimposed on effaced *to*

line 21   *walked* superimposed on effaced *ran*

line 25   *is it* altered from *it is*

line 26   *the* altered from *that*

line 27   *not* deleted

line 28   *confirmed* altered from *affirmed*

line 29   *know* superimposed on *see*

line 29   *which he has* altered from *where he is*; *taken—* added above line without caret

line 33   *steeper* altered from *steepest*

PAGE 61

line 12   *donkey* altered from *donky*; *had* deleted

line 26   *thought* superimposed on effaced *knew*

PAGE 62

line 21   *He* superimposed on effaced *When*

line 23   *whom* altered from *who*

line 26   *knowing of* deleted

line 26   *offering* superimposed on effaced *hand*

line 28   *—* superimposed on effaced *the*

Diary by E.B.B.

PAGE 62 (continued)
line 29 *the* altered from *that*
line 33 *It* <u>*shall*</u> *be* altered from *I will*
         have it
line 34 *The follow*[ing] deleted
line 35 ɛκ deleted
PAGE 63
line 2   *about* superimposed on *with*
line 6   *oblige* altered from *obliges*
line 12 *home* superimposed on *away*
line 14 *Bad* effaced
line 22 *Next* altered from *New*
line 26 *Nearly* superimposed on effaced
         And
PAGE 64
line 9   *He* altered from *he*
line 10 *on* altered from *in*
line 11 *or* altered from *&*; both super-
         imposed on effaced *of*
line 12 *myself* altered from *me*
line 16 *here* superimposed on *to*
line 26 *that* superimposed on effaced
         wh[ich]
PAGE 65
line 4   *thou* superimposed on *you*
line 4   *human,* inserted above deleted
         mortal
line 12 *so* superimposed on *it*
line 23 *that* deleted
PAGE 66
line 3   *will* altered from *can*
line 6   *Christ* altered from *Cri*[st]; <u>*can*</u>
         superimposed on effaced *m*[ay]
line 13 *at the* superimposed on effaced
         & make
line 13 *& she p* inserted with caret, then
         effaced
line 18 *answered* superimposed on
         effaced *most*
line 21 *entreating* superimposed on
         effaced *arguing*
line 25 *even* deleted
PAGE 67
line 3   *not* superimposed on effaced *to*
line 6   *I had* et seq.: post-entry, squeez-
         ed in
line 13 *cried* superimposed on *said*

line 17 *w*^d altered from *sh*^d
line 24 *Out of spirits* altered from *Low*
         spirited
PAGE 68
line 6   *by* deleted
line 6   *those* altered from *the*
line 7   *Lord's*: *L* superimposed on *w* [ill]
line 11 *a very* superimposed on *in a*
line 13 *Heard from M*^{rs} *Boyd* et seq.:
         post-entry between lines
line 17 *which* superimposed on effaced
         qu[oted]
PAGE 69
line 8   *some* superimposed on effaced
         my
line 9   *dumb Greeks* superimposed on
         Greek books
line 21 *a unicorn* superimposed on *an*
         Arab & a
line 24 *him*⟨se⟩*lf*: restored reading; word
         partially obscured by ink blot
line 25 *an elevation* inserted above delet-
         ed *a force*
PAGE 70
line 5   *they* superimposed on *it*
line 10 *for* altered from *to*
line 17 *in* effaced
line 21 *him* superimposed on *me*
line 26 *no* altered from *not*
PAGE 71
line 1   *S* altered from *B*[ible]
line 9   *do so* superimposed on effaced
         walk
line 10 *Now his*: *Now* inserted with caret
         above deleted *No,*; *his* altered
         from *His*
line 10 *being his* superimposed on
         effaced *walking in*
line 11 *the* superimposed on effaced
         front
line 11 *carriages or* superimposed on
         effaced *coaches &*
line 16 *& deleted*
line 18 *answered* superimposed on
         effaced *said*
line 26 *& deleted*
line 30 *restrain* superimposed on

[250]

con[trol]

line 30 *&* superimposed on effaced opening double quotation marks

PAGE 72

line 1 *with* altered from *will*; *You* deleted

line 9 *care* superimposed on effaced *do*

line 21 *But I never* et seq.: post-entry between lines

line 26 *in return* inserted above deleted *about*

PAGE 73

line 1 *of* superimposed on effaced *off*

line 4 *I* altered from *He*

line 4 *literally* altered from *literary*

line 12 *&* superimposed on effaced *will*

line 20 indecipherable word of about 5 letters deleted

line 22 *at* inserted above deleted *of*

line 23 *I* superimposed on effaced *for*

line 24 *may* altered from *my*

line 31 *M*^*rs* *C* et seq.: post-entry between lines; *came* altered from *call*

PAGE 74

line 5 *Jumped* superimposed on effaced *En*[tered]

line 6 *Tuesday* superimposed on effaced *M*^*rs* *Cliffe*

line 8 *Moor* inserted above line then effaced; *Moore's* superimposed on effaced *Lord*

line 14 *of* deleted

line 25 *I read half the* superimposed on effaced *Wednesday. Aug*

line 30 *Yes* superimposed on *No*

LINE 75

line 9 *storytelling* superimposed on effaced *tale of*

line 22 *M*^*r* *Martin* superimposed on *they had*

PAGE 76

line 8 *bedroom* altered from *dressing-room*

line 16 *is* deleted

line 17 *which is* deleted

line 17 *utmost* altered from *utter*

line 20 *or* superimposed on effaced *but*

line 28 *breakfast* superimposed on effaced *dining*

line 33 *as* inserted above deleted *that*

line 34 *which* inserted above deleted *and that*

line 34 *it* deleted

PAGE 77

line 5 *to this* deleted

line 9 *originating* altered from *originated*

line 15 *was so* superimposed on effaced *came down*

line 21 *oftener* superimposed on effaced *more*

line 25 *enough* deleted

line 32 *And yet* deleted; *He* altered from *he*

line 34 *seemed* altered from *resem*[bled]

PAGE 78

line 2 *!* superimposed on effaced closing double quotation marks

line 6 *one of* superimposed on effaced *Miss Board*[man]

line 7 *he* altered from *his*

line 9 *Dust* altered from *dust*

line 17 *evening* superimposed on effaced *day*

PAGE 79

line 11 *&* deleted

line 13 *Except that Eliza* inserted above deleted *Saturday. August 6.*

line 18 *?* deleted

line 20 *this* altered from *these*

line 21 *irrepressibly:* first *e* altered from *r*

PAGE 80

line 6 *first* deleted

line 15 *were* altered from *weir*

line 18 *27* altered from *23*

line 20 *M*^*r*. altered from *M*^*rs*

line 22 *said* superimposed on effaced *smiled*

PAGE 81

line 14 *the* deleted

line 14 *affidavit* altered from *affidavite*

line 34 *once* altered from *one*

Diary by E.B.B.

PAGE 82

line 4   indecipherable phrase of about three words obliterated

line 12 *my* superimposed on *it*

line 27 *Arabel* altered from *Arabel's*

line 28 *Sam* altered from *Sam's*

PAGE 83

line 5 *him* superimposed on effaced *me*

line 5 *becoming by* superimposed on *doing in*

line 23 *the* altered from *The*; *&* inserted in margin

line 29 *breakfast* superimposed on effaced *dining*

PAGE 84

line 25 *If* superimposed on effaced *No*

line 30 *did* altered from *do*

PAGE 85

line 3 *have* superimposed on *en*[joy]

line 5 *w*^{d}. altered from *sh*^{d}.

line 6 *had been* superimposed on *were*

line 7 *Shelley, &* altered from *Shelley's A*

line 9 *Did she ever possess* superimposed on effaced *Had she ever any?*

line 9 *his* superimposed on effaced *their*

line 14 *object* superimposed on *do*

line 25 *The* superimposed on effaced *Why*

PAGE 86

line 10 *her* superimposed on *a*

PAGE 87

line 2 originally *a s*[pot]; *the* superimposed on *a*; *g* superimposed on *s*

line 8 *Papa* superimposed on *Bro*

line 9 *read* superimposed on effaced *open*

line 11 *on* superimposed on effaced *to*

line 11 *pic nic* altered from *pick nick*

line 13 *this* altered from *the*

line 15 *an order* altered from *a dis-ch*[arge]

line 22 *among* superimposed on effaced *hi*[m]

line 26 *13* altered from *12*

PAGE 88

line 12 *the* superimposed on *her*

line 14 *this* superimposed on *it*

line 14 *this* superimposed on *it*

line 14 *this* superimposed on *it*

line 16 originally *let it b*[e]; *let* deleted; *be* superimposed on *it*; *p* superimposed on *b*

line 17 *my* superimposed on *this*

line 18 *Thine* altered from *thine*

line 19 *Thy* altered from *thy*

PAGE 89

line 1 indecipherable obliteration of three or four letters

line 8 *the* superimposed on *Je*[wel's]

line 11 *vinegar* altered from *vinigar*

line 12 *vinegar* altered from *vinigar*

line 16 *some* superimposed on a

line 18 *Jewel* altered from *Jewell*

line 21 *&* superimposed on effaced *who*

line 25 *feel* superimposed on *me*

line 26 *made* superimposed on *had*

line 31 *will* superimposed on effaced *sh*[all]

PAGE 90

line 8 originally *I wonder if I had*; *I wonder if I* deleted; *had* altered to *Had*

line 18 originally *—the nearly*; *—the* deleted; *nearly* altered to *Nearly*

line 30 *if* altered from *it*

PAGE 91

line 3 *I* superimposed on effaced *It*

line 16 *idiom* altered from *idioms*

line 16 *I want* superimposed on effaced *Will*

line 25 *I took* et seq.: post-entry between lines

line 28 *trickery* superimposed on effaced *note*

line 31 *it* superimposed on *to*

PAGE 92

line 5 *When I go, I shall not be missed!—* deleted

line 23 *sent* altered from *send*

line 24 *Italian* deleted

line 26 *Finished Cebes* et seq.: post-entry between lines

line 27 *yesterday's* superimposed on

effaced *a thunder*

line 28   *at* superimposed on *&*

line 32   *rather icy* superimposed on *icy to*

PAGE 93

line 6   *my* superimposed on effaced *the*

line 7   *Poets* altered from *poetry*

line 14   *were* superimposed on *a*[re]

line 18   *Poets* altered from *poets*

line 19   originally *that throne he*; *that* altered to *the*; *throne he* deleted and *seat* inserted above

line 20   *radiance* inserted above deleted *light*

line 27   *the* superimposed on *a*

line 29   two indecipherable words obliterated

PAGE 94

line 1   *Dionysius* altered from *Dionysius's*

line 8   *up* superimposed on *to*

line 12   *had to* superimposed on effaced *were a*[ll]

line 20   *again* superimposed on *more*

line 27   *unwieldy* altered from *unwieldly*

PAGE 95

line 1   *uplifts* altered from *undoes*

line 2   *which* deleted; *veiling* altered from *veils*

line 2   *such sublime* inserted above deleted *the*

line 4   *comme* altered from *come*

line 4   *a* inserted above deleted *their*

line 7   *& as* added above the line without caret

line 12   *carry* superimposed on effaced *bring*

line 15   *& does* superimposed on effaced *not*

line 21   *Eliza* altered from *Eliza's*

line 26   *The white* altered from *She has*

line 27   opening double quotation marks deleted

PAGE 96

line 6   *without* altered from *wh*

line 12   *Discourses* superimposed on effaced *Lectures*

line 21   *text* inserted above deleted

sermon

line 24   *that* altered from *than*

line 27   *this* altered from *the*

PAGE 97

line 6   *dare* superimposed on *must*

line 15   *will* superimposed on effaced *sha*[ll]

line 17   *are* altered from *were*

line 23   *exclaimed* superimposed on *said*

line 32   *next* deleted

PAGE 98

line 3   *tho'* superimposed on *but*

line 7   *abide* superimposed on effaced *bear*

line 9   *&* superimposed on *in*

line 10   *is* deleted

line 13   *opinion* altered from *mind*

line 15   *sang* superimposed on effaced *played*

line 16   originally *had heard all*; *had* altered to *thought*; *heard* deleted; *that* superimposed on *all*

PAGE 99

line 11   *a shame* superimposed on effaced *too bad*

line 13   *that I might* inserted above deleted *for me to*

line 17   opening parenthesis deleted

line 19   *that* altered from *which*

line 21   *must* superimposed on effaced *wh*[ich]

line 25   *has* superimposed on *is*

line 28   *I called* et seq.: post-entry between lines

PAGE 100

line 6   *him* superimposed on *me*

line 6   *upon* inserted above deleted *about*

line 11   *Bro's* superimposed on *his*

line 22   *affixed* altered from *applied*

line 22   *gained* altered from *reached*

line 28   *his* superimposed on *the*

line 28   *his* deleted

PAGE 101

line 1   *bed* inserted with caret, then effaced

line 2   *yet*: post-entry, squeezed in; *we*

Diary by E.B.B.

PAGE 101 (continued)
  altered from *We*
line 5 *was* altered from *were*
line 20 *I* superimposed on effaced *he*
line 22 *him*[self] inserted above line then effaced
line 33 *it* altered from *in*

PAGE 102
line 6 *all* superimposed on *it*
line 8 *might* altered from *may*
line 15 *it does* superimposed on effaced *there is*
line 28 *acknowledge* altered from *know*
line 30 *It* inserted above deleted *His genius*
line 33 *will* superimposed on *may*

PAGE 103
line 7 *can* superimposed on *m*[ay]
line 8 *&* superimposed on *;*
line 13 *can* altered from *shall*
line 20 *not* superimposed on *so*
line 21 *we* superimposed on *I*
line 27 *&* superimposed on *it*
line 30 *came* superimposed on *ran*
line 32 *were* altered from *was*
line 34 *for this* superimposed on *!——*

PAGE 104
line 6 *I must be heartless & thoughtless: for* deleted
line 10 *the* superimposed on *my*
line 11 *my* superimposed on *in*
line 12 *there sh.^d be in* deleted
line 13 *should entertain* inserted above deleted *with*
line 13 *a* inserted above deleted *the*
line 14 *that* deleted
line 18 *& not* superimposed on effaced *that I*
line 18 *reasonable* inserted above deleted *high thinking*
line 19 *to* superimposed on *at*
line 22 *having* superimposed on effaced *my t*[astes]
line 23 *or* altered from *&*
line 24 *there* altered from *they*
line 26 *wd'nt* altered from *wdn't*

PAGE 105
line 3 *am sure* inserted above deleted *think*
line 5 *half* altered from *a time*
line 6 *would* altered from *wish*
line 12 *&* deleted
line 20 *& on: on* superimposed on *&; &* post-entry squeezed in

PAGE 106
line 7 *on* superimposed on *to*
line 8 *there's* altered from *there is*
line 14 *M.^rs* altered from *Miss*
line 14 originally *& some; &* deleted; *some* altered to *Some*
line 16 *Talked of* deleted
line 19 *stronger* superimposed on effaced *better*
line 20 *overflowed* inserted above deleted *came into*
line 21 *& overflowed them* deleted
line 21 *Friend* altered from *friend*
line 27 *mushroomed* altered from *mushroom*

PAGE 107
line 1 *Not Burke* et seq.: post-entry between lines
line 8 closing double quotation marks deleted
line 14 *this* superimposed on *it*
line 17 *passed* altered from *past*
line 18 *passed* altered from *past*
line 19 *Miss* superimposed on effaced *M.^rs B*
line 21 *He* altered from *he*
line 29 *for* superimposed on *of*
line 30 *&* superimposed on *,*; *I* superimposed on *&*

PAGE 108
line 1 *nearly* superimposed on *quite*
line 8 *might* altered from *must*
line 8 *Aladdin's* altered from *Alladdin's*
line 10 *nicing* altered from *nicking*
line 28 *she has to suffer by* inserted above deleted *it is bad enough to*; *knowing* altered from *know*
line 29 *this* superimposed on *her*

PAGE 109
line 1 *separated* altered from *seperated*
line 5 *. . . I thank God* et seq.: post-entry between lines; *A* effaced
line 8 *escort* superimposed on *attendent*
line 16 *recommended* superimposed on effaced *begged*
line 17 *Papa* superimposed on *he*
line 26 *Miss* altered from *M^{rs}.*
line 30 *disliked: dis* post-entry, squeezed in
line 30 *coming* altered from *going*
line 34 *one* superimposed on effaced *a one*

PAGE 110
line 2 *w^d.* superimposed on effaced *had*
line 5 *&* deleted
line 7 *get* altered from *dr*
line 9 *drink* superimposed on effaced *wait*
line 25 *heartless* altered from *harsh*

PAGE 111
line 1 *have recourse* inserted above deleted *am left*
line 2 *those great* superimposed on effaced *Lowth &*
line 3 *nobody* altered from *nothing*
line 9 *will* altered from *shall*
line 12 *do* altered from *did*
line 13 *rains* altered from *rained*
line 23 *such* altered from *so*

PAGE 112
line 1 *Of such* et seq.: post-entry between lines
line 3 *no* altered from *not*
line 6 *I* superimposed on *&*
line 7 *l'avventuriere* superimposed on *the a*[dventurer]
line 8 *do not show* inserted above deleted *not*
line 9 *I have* superimposed on effaced *Yes! I*
line 10 opening double quotation marks deleted
line 15 *way* altered from *manner; and what he thinks about the digamma* deleted

line 16 *an* altered from *a; clear* deleted
line 22 *brace* altered from *braces*
line 27 *9* superimposed on *6*

PAGE 113
line 6 *were* altered from *was*
line 7 *Miss* altered from *M^{rs}.*
line 17 *†* superimposed on effaced *Eheu*
line 24 *good* superimposed on effaced *more*
line 25 *for* altered from *from*
line 28 *300* altered from *3000*
line 29 *A Basil* inserted above deleted *Another*
line 30 *Another* altered from *A*
line 34 *coming* superimposed on *going*

PAGE 114
line 2 *good* superimposed on *in*[tentions]
line 8 *minutes* altered from *mintes*
line 12 *were* altered from *was*
line 15 *Coventry* altered from *Conventry*
line 17 *M^r.* altered from *Miss*
line 18 *Since of* inserted above deleted *Among*
line 19 *None can more heartless soulless* inserted above deleted *Not one more cold & false can*
line 21 *Why* superimposed on *Then*
line 25 *Then who can doubt the reason why* inserted below deleted line, which had been changed as follows: 1) originally *And hence the reason I espy*; 2) altered to *And hence proceeds the reason why*; 3) line deleted and replaced by *Then can one longer wonder why*; 4) altered to *Then who can longer wonder why*; 5) altered to *Then who again can wonder why*; 6) line deleted
line 31 *to* superimposed on *&*
line 32 *apprehended* altered from *misapprehended*

PAGE 115
line 4 *She* superimposed on effaced *At*
line 4 *will* altered from *shall*
line 13 *pro* superimposed on *con*

[255]

Diary by E.B.B.

PAGE 115 (continued)

line 18   *Serena*: *S* altered from *L*

line 22   *proposed* altered from *promised*

line 26   *had* altered from *have*

line 29   *evening amidst* superimposed on *scenery in*

PAGE 116

line 12   *afraid lest* superimposed on effaced *unwilling*

line 17   *sauce* altered from *sause*

line 20   *May* superimposed on *I*

line 28   *5* altered from *6*

PAGE 117

line 4   *avant* altered from repetitive *en*

line 5   *it* altered from *in*

line 5   *whyche* altered from *wyche*

line 6   *the* altered from *our*

line 12   *knives* altered from *knifes*

PAGE 118

line 5   *with* superimposed on effaced *at*

line 7   *she had* superimposed on *he said*

line 8   *fear* superimposed on effaced *assurance*

line 9   *of* superimposed on effaced *that*

line 24   *to me* deleted

line 25   *to me* deleted

line 32   *will* superimposed on effaced *sha*[ll]

PAGE 119

line 6   *Miss Bordman* et seq.: post-entry between lines; *goes* superimposed on effaced *went*

line 8   *Some* deleted; *Food* altered from *food*

line 10   *Dear Minny* et seq.: post-entry between lines

line 18   *I* superimposed on *&*

line 20   — superimposed on effaced *like*

line 21   *Mind!*: post-entry, squeezed in

line 22   *my* superimposed on *it*

line 27   caret deleted

line 27   *besides* deleted

PAGE 120

line 6   *commonplace* superimposed on effaced *Miss B*[iddulphs]

line 9   *I w*<u>dnt</u> superimposed on effaced *he is*

line 20   *Our* superimposed on *The*

PAGE 121

line 1   *A letter* et seq.: post-entry between lines

line 8   *them* superimposed on *it*

line 10   *think* altered from *thing*

line 20   *Christians* superimposed on effaced *those*

line 24   *I wrote* et seq.: post-entry between lines

PAGE 122

line 2   *than* superimposed on —

line 11   *a* superimposed on effaced *feel*[ings]

line 12   *his greatest* superimposed on effaced *a very great*

line 19   *clearer* superimposed on effaced *kn*[owledge]

line 19   *I am tired* deleted

line 37   *right* superimposed on *l*[eft]

PAGE 123

line 4   *tho' I* altered from *who*

line 23   *commentary* altered from *commentaring*

PAGE 124

line 11   *for* superimposed on *and*; *her* inserted above deleted *that*

line 23   *it* altered from *in*

line 26   *there* superimposed on effaced *such*

line 28   *&* superimposed on *I*

line 32   *& ho*[w] deleted

line 36   *after* altered from *afterw*[ards]

PAGE 125

line 11   *as* superimposed on *!*—

line 22   *past* altered from *present*

line 24   *me* superimposed on *be*

line 26   *believe* altered from *believes*

line 28   *wishes* altered from *is*

PAGE 126

line 1   *moonlighty* altered from *moony*

line 12   *Nobody is immaculate; &* superimposed on effaced *Young men are not imma*[culate]

line 14   *such a* inserted above deleted *this*

line 15   indecipherable word deleted

line 20   *particular* inserted above *exclusive*

PAGE 127

line 9   *A* superimposed on *The*

line 20   *thing is* altered from *one is jus*[tified]

line 27   *must* superimposed on effaced *spoke*

line 28   *I* superimposed on effaced *it*

line 28   *the* altered from *that*

line 29   *being* superimposed on *were*

PAGE 128

line 19   *so much* superimposed on *!——*

line 23   *the saint's* inserted above deleted *his*

line 31   *how fortunate* inserted above deleted *what a blessing*

line 31   *(I think he said blessing!)* deleted

PAGE 129

line 3   *w^{d}.* altered from *sh^{d}.*

line 3   *w^{d}.* altered from *sh^{d}.*

line 4   *if I* superimposed on effaced *before*

line 5   *w^{d}.* altered from *sh^{d}.*

line 7   *at that time* superimposed on ——

line 10   *so strongly while* altered from *too strongly as*

line 12   *does* superimposed on *is*

line 28   *Bro was at* et seq.: post-entry between lines

PAGE 130

line 2   *containing the* superimposed on effaced *making a*

line 11   *such* superimposed on *his*

line 17   *A* altered from *An*

line 18   *No letters*: post-entry between lines

line 21   *there* altered from *they*

line 24   *doctrine* altered from *doctrines*

line 28   *certainly* inserted above obliterated word

line 32   *shall* altered from *sh^{d}.*

PAGE 131

line 22   four or five words obliterated

line 25   *This evening* superimposed on effaced *Monday, Sept. 19.*

PAGE 132

line 7   *accounts* superimposed on *is*

line 13   *sent for me* superimposed on effaced *had not been*

line 17   *he* altered from *her*

line 18   *This* altered from *The*

PAGE 133

line 6   indecipherable word obliterated

line 10   *the rape* superimposed on effaced *letting*

line 13   *up.* inserted above deleted *yielded*

line 20   *is* superimposed on *!*

line 25   *take* superimposed on effaced *get*

line 28   *exciting* altered from *excited*

PAGE 134

line 4   *to me* deleted

PAGE 135

line 12   *Ah* altered from *Oh*

line 19   *quite* deleted

line 22   *half* deleted

line 27   *note* superimposed on effaced *letter*

line 31   *What c^{d}. I do?* deleted

line 32   *impel* superimposed on *dr*[ive]

PAGE 136

line 19   *Lamartines* altered from *Lammartines*

line 21   one or two words obliterated

line 33   *Euripides* superimposed on effaced *Xenophon*

PAGE 137

line 9   *that our* altered from *than see*

line 18   *Sam H & A* et seq.: post-entry between lines

line 21   *Panegyricus* altered from *panegyricus*

line 27   *blunted* altered from *blunts*

line 27   *a good deal, is* deleted

line 30   *words* superimposed on effaced *tho*[ughts]

PAGE 138

line 24   *an* altered from *any*

PAGE 139

line 10   *Messrs.* altered from *M^{rs}.*

line 19   *holy* inserted above deleted *these*

line 20   *and* superimposed on *who*

line 23   *Thee* altered from *thee*

Diary by E.B.B.

PAGE 139 (continued)

line 23 *the affecting*: *the* altered from *that*; *affecting* superimposed on effaced *rite*

line 28 *may* altered from *my*

line 30 *& be*: *be* superimposed on *&*; another ampersand then squeezed in

line 31 *any* superimposed on *the*

line 31 *c*^{d} altered from *w*^{d}

PAGE 140

line 6 *eight* superimposed on effaced *breakfast*

line 10 *received* altered from *recieved*

line 18 *such an* inserted above deleted *that*

line 23 *His sheep* inserted above deleted *them*

line 23 *His* altered from *his*

line 24 *thro' His*: *thro'* superimposed on *out*; *His* altered from *his*

line 24 *reverent* altered from *reverend*

PAGE 141

line 5 *Then*: post-entry, squeezed in before *He*

line 23 *Barton* superimposed on effaced *the*

PAGE 142

line 9 *my* superimposed on effaced *loo*[king]

line 14 *would* altered from *should*

line 15 *Perhaps I sh*^{d}. et seq.: post-entry between lines

PAGE 143

line 7 *Prælectio* altered from *Prælectia*

line 12 *long* altered from *longer*

line 21 *for* superimposed on *a*[ccording]

line 25 *a* superimposed on effaced *her*

PAGE 144

line 1 *of* superimposed on effaced *but*

line 2 *was* altered from *way*

line 4 *that some people* superimposed on effaced *Thursday Sept 29*th.

line 29 *may* superimposed on effaced *sha*[ll]

line 31 *leave* altered from *leaves*

PAGE 145

line 23 *The* altered from *She*

line 26 *that*: post-entry, squeezed in margin

PAGE 146

line 13 *&* superimposed on effaced *as*

line 27 *Sent the letter* et seq.: post-entry between lines

PAGE 147

line 3 *name* altered from *man*

line 3 *annotations* superimposed on effaced *opinion*

line 13 *I* superimposed on *it*

line 18 *half* superimposed on *m*[oney]

line 30 *my* deleted

PAGE 148

line 8 *at* superimposed on effaced *whe*[n]

line 11 *It was* superimposed on effaced *—& it*

line 33 *a* superimposed on *one*

line 34 *one way—M*^{rs} *Boyd* superimposed on effaced *Tuesday Oct. 4*

PAGE 149

line 2 *hence* altered from *here*

line 28 *My squirrel* et seq.: post-entry between lines

PAGE 150

line 11 *he* altered from *hed*

line 12 *be* superimposed on *me*

line 29 *Thursday* superimposed on effaced *Wednesday*

line 37 *& except* superimposed on effaced *agreed that we*

PAGE 151

line 2 *pleasaunt* altered from *pleasant*

line 7 *who* superimposed on effaced *bo*[rn]

line 28 *of* superimposed on *in*

PAGE 152

line 1 *8* altered from *9*

line 5 *enough* deleted

line 9 *indefinite* superimposed on effaced *particular*

line 15 *9* altered from *10*

line 23 *Oh* deleted

PAGE 153

line 4   *intended to* inserted above deleted *w^d.*

line 8   *do so;* superimposed on —

PAGE 154

line 1   *&* superimposed on —

line 2   *myself* altered from *me*

line 18   *the* superimposed on *his*

line 18   *a* superimposed on *the*

line 27   *or I hope* superimposed on effaced *(& I hope*

PAGE 155

line 1   *Annie is indifferent* et seq.: post-entry between lines

line 3   *her* superimposed on *I*

line 18   *Martins* superimposed on effaced *Barton*[s]

line 24   *rather:* post-entry, in margin

line 31   *may* superimposed on *is*

PAGE 156

line 3   *me* superimposed on *be*

line 13   *men* altered from *man*

line 16   *Robinson* altered from *Robinson's*

line 17   *detection* altered from *detections*

line 17   *a* superimposed on *the*

line 18   *as* altered from *is*

line 30   *12* altered from *16*

line 30   *business* superimposed on *m*[usic]

PAGE 157

line 26   *as a* [indecipherable word] deleted

line 27   *in* superimposed on *of*

line 29   *our* superimposed on *the*

line 30   *was* superimposed on *is*

PAGE 158

line 21   *by* altered from *my*

line 28   *my* superimposed on *the*

line 31   *have* altered from *had*

PAGE 159

line 10   *can* altered from *cannot*

line 12   *sh^d* superimposed on *;*

line 15   *been* altered from *be*

PAGE 160

line 25   *a* superimposed on effaced *his*

line 31   *for* superimposed on effaced *but*

line 33   *a short time* superimposed on effaced *a few minutes*

PAGE 161

line 7   *such* superimposed on *it*

line 16   *A parcel for Miss Bordman from her father I suspect* deleted

PAGE 162

line 1   *towards* altered from *to*

line 1   — superimposed on *&*

PAGE 163

line 4   *a* superimposed on *the*

line 4   *of* superimposed on *for*

line 10   *How provoking!* deleted

line 13   *or* superimposed on *of*

line 13   *pleasures* altered from *pleasure*

line 17   *but* superimposed on *and*

line 20   *Henrietta* superimposed on effaced *We called for*

line 28   *I found* et seq.: post-entry between lines

PAGE 164

line 3   *are* superimposed on *is*

line 7   *He told me* et seq.: post-entry between lines

line 17   *is* superimposed on *was*

line 21   *use in reconsidering anything* altered from *time to reconsider it.*

line 25   *any of* deleted

line 25   *friends addressed* superimposed on effaced *dear friends*

line 27   *a certain* superimposed on effaced *Mr Boyd*

PAGE 165

line 6   *become* superimposed on effaced *grow*

line 12   *in* deleted

line 19   redundant *or* deleted

line 21   *at* altered from *on*

PAGE 166

line 14   *cushion* superimposed on *seat*

line 15   *him* superimposed on *it*

line 15   *He* superimposed on *It*

line 16   *& has eaten: has* superimposed on *&; eaten* altered from *our;* new ampersand squeezed in

line 17   two or three indecipherable

Diary by E.B.B.

PAGE 166 (continued)
       words obliterated
line 17   *him* superimposed on *it*
line 18   *he* superimposed on *it*
line 26   *Annie has brought* et seq.: post-entry between lines
PAGE 167
line 3   *so* deleted
line 10   *Arabel* altered from *A &*
PAGE 168
line 2   *times* altered from *time*
line 5   *and* altered from *as*
line 10   *weight* altered from *weighty*
line 15   *it* deleted
line 26   *Arabel* superimposed on *We*
line 26   *pleasant* altered from *pleasand*
line 32   opening double quotation marks deleted
PAGE 169
line 11   *offered* altered from *afforded*
line 15   comma deleted
line 30   *28* altered from *29*
PAGE 170
line 10   *defected* altered from *dejected*
line 22   *there* altered from *their*
PAGE 171
line 14   *in the* [?] inserted with caret, then effaced
line 15   *from* altered from *of*
line 17   *as* deleted
line 19   *29* altered from *30*
line 22   *desirable* altered from *detestable*
line 26   *Told the stories* et seq.: post-entry between lines; *stories* altered from *story*
PAGE 172
line 1   *30* altered from *31*
line 15   *Oct 31st* inserted above deleted *November 1st*
line 16   *a mistake.*: post-entry, written above *first of November*
line 22   *Lennard's* altered from *Lennord's*
line 30   *quite* superimposed on *so*
line 31   *1st* superimposed on *2^{d}*
line 33   *been* altered from *be*
PAGE 173
line 4   *I* superimposed on *&*

line 6   *&* superimposed on *so*
line 10   *oration* altered from *orations*
line 15   *tho'* superimposed on *only*
line 20   *resist* altered from *resit*
PAGE 174
line 1   *buy*: *b* superimposed on *p*
line 5   *Nov 2^{d}* altered from *Oct 3^{d}*
line 18   *3^{d}* superimposed on *4th*
line 20   *would* altered from *could*
line 20   *would* altered from *could*
line 24   *unus* altered from *una*
PAGE 175
line 8   *Friday Novr 4th* altered from *Thursday Novr 5th*
line 11   *at* altered from *&*
line 15   *very* superimposed on effaced *f*[ine]
line 16   *5* superimposed on *6*
PAGE 176
line 6   *6* superimposed on *7*
line 20   opening double quotation marks effaced
line 24   *some*: *s* superimposed on *y*[ards]
PAGE 177
line 8   *7* superimposed on *8*
line 12   *8* superimposed on *9*
line 24   *Wednesday* altered from *Tuesday*
line 26   *observed* superimposed on effaced *said*
PAGE 178
line 1   *Thursday* altered from *Wednesday*
line 9   *strongly* superimposed on effaced *well*
line 12   *On Saturday, Bummy came to see me, in Mrs Cliffe's carriage—very very kind of her! I really think that this was the day instead of yesterday, on which Miss Bordman had the bad news!* deleted
line 13   *letter* altered from *Letter*
line 15   *Bummy* superimposed on effaced *Miss Bord*[man]
line 18   *feeling* altered from *feelings*
line 19   *But Mr Curzon* et seq.: post-entry between lines
line 27   *&* superimposed on *or*

PAGE 179
line 15   *it* superimposed on *the*
line 21   *M.^{rs}* superimposed on effaced *They*
line 26   *1829's* superimposed on effaced *last*

PAGE 180
line 8   *In my absence,* et seq.: post-entry between lines
line 23   *to*: post-entry, squeezed in margin
line 25   *Even if I could love* effaced

PAGE 181
line 2   *& he*: *&* squeezed in; *he* altered from *He*
line 8   *pay a visit* superimposed on *call upon*
line 15   *A letter* et seq.: post-entry between lines
line 30   *have* superimposed on *of*

PAGE 183
line 10   *As I* superimposed on effaced *I was*
line 20   *tomorrow,—* inserted above *carriage,* without caret

PAGE 184
line 12   *A note* et seq.: post-entry between lines

PAGE 185
line 3   *M^{essrs}* altered from *M.^{rs}*

PAGE 186
line 5   *Monday* altered from *Tuesday*

PAGE 187
line 13   *Henrietta* superimposed on *Bro*
line 14   *Wrote to Papa!*—: post-entry between lines
line 22   *He "assured me"* altered from *I "assured" him*

PAGE 188
line 26   *Monday* altered from *Tuesday*

PAGE 189
line 7   *could* superimposed on *had*
line 8   *We talked a* superimposed on effaced *Not a mention*
line 10   *whether* superimposed on effaced *if*
line 30   *set* altered from *let*

PAGE 190
line 7   *at* deleted

PAGE 191
line 7   *A letter* et seq.: post-entry between lines
line 14   *yea* altered from *yeas*

PAGE 192
line 5   *M.^r* superimposed on effaced *Annie*
line 17   *17* altered from *16*
line 25   *18* altered from *17*

PAGE 193
line 4   *19* altered from *18*
line 10   *Tauris* superimposed on *A* [ulide]
line 11   *20* inserted above deleted *19*
line 15   *were* altered from *was*
line 19   *21.st* altered from *20th*
line 23   *22.^d* altered from *21.st*

PAGE 194
line 6   *23* altered from *22*
line 9   *w.^d not* superimposed on effaced *wrote a*
line 11   *the* superimposed on effaced *my*
line 13   *24th.* altered from *23^d*
line 22   *notwithstanding* superimposed on *in* [spite of]
line 26   *at last*: post-entry in margin
line 32   *25* altered from *24*

PAGE 195
line 3   *26* altered from *25*
line 10   *&* deleted
line 14   *27* altered from *26*
line 18   *28* altered from *27*
line 23   *R C* superimposed on *there*
line 24   *a* superimposed on *to*
line 29   *29* altered from *28*

PAGE 196
line 17   *about* superimposed on *with*
line 20   *sends* superimposed on *desires*
line 22   *wishes the* altered from *wished Miss*
line 24   *The* superimposed on *M.^r*
line 25   *went* superimposed on *go*
line 27   *did* altered from *does*

PAGE 197
line 2   *pretensions* altered from *pretentions*

Diary by E.B.B.

PAGE 197 (continued)

line 8   *was* superimposed on *am*

PAGE 198

line 3   *judgment* superimposed on *penetration*

line 7   *Dec.ʳ* superimposed on *Jan.*

line 11   *the* superimposed on effaced *in*

line 33   *me* superimposed on *us*

PAGE 201

line 13   *on* superimposed on *at*

PAGE 202

line 5   *let behind* superimposed on effaced *treated as if*

line 28   *;* superimposed on effaced *of*

PAGE 203

line 17   *my* superimposed on *any*

line 21   two lines obliterated; the passage includes the phrase: *nothing which alluded to my being first* which suggests that the subject of this deletion was E.B.B.'s fear that H.S.B. held Miss Mushet in higher esteem than her.

line 24   *I did not begin* [my dearest friend ?]; *& never signed it.* deleted

line 29   *& ended—"May God bless* deleted

PAGE 204

line 7   two and a half lines obliterated; the passage commences: *I had a good cry* and is obviously a continuation of the previous remarks concerning the Boyds' possible removal.

line 18   *do* altered from *doing*

PAGE 205

line 5   *discursive* altered from *discourse*

line 16   *body*: *b* superimposed on effaced *p*[erson]

line 18   *Malvern* superimposed on *tomorrow*

PAGE 206

line 3   *were* altered from *was*

line 12   one and a half lines obliterated; the passage includes the words: *I said that . . . by my visit he was pleased!—* and appears to defend her going to Ruby Cottage that day.

PAGE 207

line 14   *If it* altered from *I shall*

line 16   *might* altered from *me*

line 17   *& my books* et seq.: post-entry between lines

line 20   *22* altered from *23*

line 23   *before* inserted above deleted *on*

PAGE 208

line 13   *our* altered from *of*

line 20   *on the su*[bject] deleted

line 25   one line obliterated; it includes the words: [no use?] *crying about it*

line 26   one line obliterated

PAGE 209

line 17   E.B.B. has deleted the following passage: *Why did'nt he ask Miss M to walk with him? Because he liked walking with me better? Better not learn the reason.*

line 20   closing double inverted quotation marks deleted

line 23   three lines obliterated

PAGE 210

line 13   four lines obliterated; the passage includes the words: *Very warmest of visits today.* and: *In hopes that H & A w.ᵈ not come for me. They did come & I went with them.*

line 18   *& Miss H M with them!!— I can't bear to think of it.* deleted

line 26   eight lines obliterated

PAGE 211

line 5   *thinking* superimposed on effaced *puzzling*

line 7   *M.ʳ Curzon* et seq.: post-entry between lines; *at* superimposed on *&*

line 10   *as* superimposed on *har*[d]

line 27   *The* superimposed on *A*

line 27   *of* superimposed on *wa*[s]

line 28   five or six words obliterated

line 28   *asks* altered from *asked*

line 30   three lines obliterated; the passage includes the phrase: *I will never write again as I have* and appears to spring from her annoyance at H.S.B.'s writing so little to her in his own hand.

PAGE 212

line 5   two and a half lines obliterated; the passage commences: *If he had sent for me in the way he sent before, I*

line 11   *his* superimposed on *any*

line 12   *a* superimposed on *it*

line 25   three lines obliterated; the passage includes the words: *since she has been at R C, his manner to me is changed;* "she" is obviously Miss Mushet.

line 31   *translation* altered from *translating*

PAGE 213

line 2   *did* superimposed on effaced *said*

line 9   *he* superimposed on *I*

PAGE 214

line 1   two lines obliterated

line 6   *130* altered from *500* [?]

line 6   *Tired;* et seq.: post-entry between lines

line 13   *A letter from* superimposed on *Wednesday Feb 8.*

line 13   line obliterated

line 15   four or five words obliterated

line 24   *my* superimposed on *the*

PAGE 215

line 2   *hear* altered in pencil from *here*

line 10   *uncertain* superimposed on *an uncert*[ainty]

PAGE 216

line 2   *1075* altered from *1065*

line 3   *And:* conjectural reading—manuscript obscured by ink-blot

line 12   two or three words obliterated

line 19   one and a half lines obliterated

line 29   *my* superimposed on *that I sh*[$\overset{d}{\cdot}$]

line 30   *it* superimposed on *so*

PAGE 217

line 2   three lines obliterated; the passage commences: *beginning "my*

dear Mr *Boyd,"* & ending "yours affec^{tely}" and appears to summarize the contents of the letter

line 6   *at* altered from *to*

line 12   *His* superimposed on *I wrote*

line 14   *&* deleted

line 15   *have* underscored in pencil

line 19   *Bro* superimposed on *&*

line 23   *M^{rs}* altered from *Miss*

line 24   four or five words obliterated

line 24   *was* altered from *is*

PAGE 218

line 3   *I* underscored in pencil

line 4   *translating* inserted above deleted *beginning*

line 8   *my* superimposed on *the*

line 8   *my* superimposed on *I*

line 10   *Oh I do not* deleted

line 20   four words obliterated

line 22   four lines obliterated; the passage commences: *Nothing written today. No letter. I sick in heart*

line 25   *Bro* et seq.: post-entry between lines

PAGE 219

line 6   *Yes* superimposed on effaced *Monda*[y]

line 22   *. . . like: I* deleted; *like* altered from *liked*

PAGE 220

line 10   *dining* superimposed on *luncheon*

line 17   *March* superimposed on *Feb*

line 18   *cured me* inserted above deleted *remedied them*

PAGE 221

line 9   *Fear:* post-entry, squeezed in

line 10   *(or fear)* deleted

line 11   one and a half lines obliterated

line 18   *An* altered from *And*

PAGE 222

line 4   *my heart seemed to be unable to bear it!—but able it was!* deleted

line 9   four lines obliterated; the passage includes the phrase: *as to his manner to me, there was not much warmth in that.*

line 21   *He lent me* et seq.: post-entry.

Diary by E.B.B.

PAGE 223

line 3   *Hatchard* superimposed on *he is*

line 3   *publish* superimposed on *acc*[ept]

PAGE 224

line 1   *Thursday* altered from *Tuesday*

line 11 three lines obliterated; the passage commences: *Dreadfully disappointed—& could not help crying. Tears came hard &* [fast?]

line 13 . . . *knowing*: *&* deleted; *knowing* altered from *known*

line 15 five or six words obliterated

line 25 *to go* superimposed on *for it*

line 26 *to Malvern* deleted

PAGE 225

line 3   *he w.ᵈ* deleted

line 7   *his* altered from *him*

line 10 two lines obliterated

line 14 two lines obliterated

line 15 *not very happy* deleted

PAGE 226

line 12 *change the air;* inserted above deleted *leave Malvern*

line 16 six or seven words obliterated

PAGE 227

line 7   *mind* inserted above deleted *self*

line 7   *itself* inserted above deleted *my thoughts*

line 26 six lines obliterated

PAGE 228

line 7   two lines obliterated

line 8   *have* deleted

line 9   *Sunday* altered from *Saturday*

line 19 *looked* superimposed on effaced *read*

PAGE 229

line 1   four or five words obliterated

line 4   *to* superimposed on *in*

line 5   one line, ending *I have prayed.* deleted

line 9   three lines obliterated

line 14 *is* inserted above deleted *was*

line 27 *After they were* superimposed on effaced *Friday, March 30.*

PAGE 230

line 10 *are* superimposed on *is*

PAGE 231

line 2   *walk* altered from *walke*

line 4   *nearly* superimposed on *as*

line 20 *to* superimposed on effaced *at*

line 33 *his* altered from *in*

PAGE 232

line 1   *goes* altered from *comes*

line 6   *was very* altered from *is so*

line 7   *fallen* altered from *have*

line 29 *to Kinnersley* superimposed on effaced *away*

PAGE 233

line 23 *longer* superimposed on *past*

PAGE 234

line 3   *E Cliffe came.*: post-entry between lines

line 6   *lent* altered from *sent*

PAGE 235

line 10 *Much out of spirits.*: post-entry between lines

line 25 *Sent* altered from *Send*

PAGE 236

line 8   *night* deleted

line 26 *more harm of him.* inserted above deleted *thing else bad about*

line 28 *only* altered from *one*

line 31 *for* altered from *to*

line 31 *Barrett* altered from *Barretted*

PAGE 237

line 13 *because* superimposed on effaced *wh*[ile]

PAGE 238

line 1   Seven lines obliterated

line 13 *spoke* superimposed on *asked m*[e]

line 22 *Good Friday.*: post-entry between lines

PAGE 239

line 2   *That sentence has opened out a flood of unhappiness upon me. But God sees it.* deleted

line 13 *I feel that if I c.ᵈ be less anxious, I sh.ᵈ be better. It is wrong to be anxious. Sh.ᵈ not I trust God?—* deleted

PAGE 240

line 12 *Synesius* deleted

line 13	*learnt* altered from *he*	**PAGE 241**	
line 27	*is* superimposed on *was*	line 5	*C* deleted
line 30	*my* superimposed on *our*	line 6	*C* deleted
line 31	*Cliffe* deleted	line 7	*C* deleted
line 31	*Cliffe* deleted	line 10	*everything* altered from *anything*

IRREGULAR SPELLINGS

It is emphasized that the primary purpose of this list is to provide the reader with a means of verifying that variant spellings are correct transcriptions of E.B.B.'s text. Although many of her usages are recognized by the *Oxford English Dictionary*, in cases where that usage is not the current, preferred, English usage, the word is included in this check-list.

The variants "sate," "agreable," "disagreable," "poney" and "lightening" are used frequently and consistently; the individual instances of their use are not, therefore, detailed below.

PAGE 3
line 11 *dependant*, for dependent
PAGE 4
line 3 *Barnaby*, for Barneby
PAGE 5
line 7 *Kenrick*, for Kendrick
line 14 *sory*, for sorry
line 20 *Kenrick*, for Kendrick
PAGE 6
line 15 *shew*, for show
PAGE 8
line 7 *embarassed*, for embarrassed
line 25 *shewn*, for shown
PAGE 9
line 6 *apprize*, for apprise
PAGE 12
line 16 *Deane*, for Dean
PAGE 13
line 24 *alledged*, for alleged
PAGE 14
line 24 *Hurd*, for Heard
line 29 *Hurd*, for Heard
PAGE 16
line 10 *Mericks*, for Meyricks
line 14 *Kenrick*, for Kendrick
line 16 *Kenrick*, for Kendrick
PAGE 17
line 9 *Cheifs*, for Chiefs

line 21 *Biddulp*, for Biddulph
PAGE 18
line 14 *cooly*, for coolly
line 20 *Hurd*, for Heard
PAGE 19
line 5 *Hurd*, for Heard
PAGE 20
line 1 *Jaques*, for Jacques
line 11 *Anne*, for Ann
PAGE 21
line 2 *past*, for passed
PAGE 23
line 5 *thankgiving*, for thanksgiving
PAGE 24
line 28 *Hurd*, for Heard
PAGE 25
line 14 *servent*, for servant
line 19 *Hurd*, for Heard
PAGE 29
line 7 *teazing*, for teasing
line 21 *coome*, for Coombe
PAGE 31
line 13 *Haldon*, for Halden
line 21 *it's*, for its
PAGE 35
line 13 *servent*, for servant
PAGE 36
line 3 *favorable*, for favourable

Diary by E.B.B.

line 3   *unfavorable*, for unfavourable
PAGE 37
line 17   *Kenrick's*, for Kendrick's
line 22   *Trehern*, for Treherne
line 29   *suspence*, for suspense
PAGE 38
line 11   *pummel*, for pommel
line 22   *Allan's*, for Allen's
PAGE 39
line 21   *past*, for passed
PAGE 41
line 2   *Deane*, for Dean
PAGE 42
line 28   *Bently*, for Bentley
PAGE 43
line 20   *Casandra's*, for Cassandra's
PAGE 45
line 10   *Pindars*, for Pyndars
line 12   *Pindars*, for Pyndars
PAGE 46
line 23   *shewn*, for shown
line 29   *chearful*, for cheerful
PAGE 47
line 12   *Pindars*, for Pyndar's
line 14   *Pindar*, for Pyndar
line 30   *interupted*, for interrupted
PAGE 49
line 12   *asside*, for aside
PAGE 50
line 11   *Zenophon*, for Xenophon
PAGE 52
line 19   *unfavorable*, for unfavourable
line 22   *staid*, for stayed
PAGE 53
line 3   *dispairing*, for despairing
PAGE 54
line 18   *Zenophon*, for Xenophon
PAGE 55
line 4   *Drumond*, for Drummond
PAGE 60
line 15   *favorable*, for favourable
PAGE 65
line 19   *Wheatley's* for Whately's
line 20   *Wheatly*, for Whately
line 25   *Wheatly*, for Whately
PAGE 67
line 29   *disagreably*, for disagreeably

PAGE 70
line 15   *Boadman*, for Bordman
line 17   *Boadman*, for Bordman
line 24   *Boadman*, for Bordman
line 30   *Boadman*, for Bordman
line 31   *Boadman*, for Bordman
PAGE 71
line 10   *effect*, for affect
line 14   *Boadman*, for Bordman
line 29   *Boadman*, for Bordman
PAGE 72
line 16   *Boadman*, for Bordman
line 20   *Boadman*, for Bordman
PAGE 73
line 2   *dependant*, for dependent
PAGE 74
line 15   *Colwal*, for Colwall
PAGE 75
line 1   *extrame*, for extreme
line 2   *extrame*, for extreme
PAGE 76
line 28   *Boadman*, for Bordman
line 31   *Boadman*, for Bordman
PAGE 77
line 16   *sallts*, for salts
line 33   *Boadman*, for Bordman
PAGE 80
line 8   *inclosure*, for enclosure
line 13   *'oclock*, for o'clock
line 21   *past*, for passed
line 28   *Boadman*, for Bordman
PAGE 81
line 9   *Jaques*, for Jacques
line 13   *occurences*, for occurrences
PAGE 82
line 22   *Zenophon*, for Xenophon
PAGE 83
line 1   *honor*, for honour
line 11   *dessolated*, for desolated
PAGE 84
line 12   *Amphiarus*, for Amphiaraüs
PAGE 85
line 7   *Colleridge's*, for Coleridge's
line 23   *chearfully*, for cheerfully
line 30   *favorite*, for favourite
PAGE 86
line 20   *Shelly*, for Shelley

PAGE 88

line 15   *dessolately*, for desolately

line 23   *canvass*, for canvas

line 30   *Warm's*, for Walm's

PAGE 90

line 11   *Ossuna*, for Osuna

PAGE 91

line 28   *embassador*, for ambassador

PAGE 92

line 19   *favor*, for favour

PAGE 93

line 3   *Colossions*, for Colossians

line 13   *disapointed*, for disappointed

PAGE 94

line 11   *past*, for passed

PAGE 95

line 22   *route*, for rout

PAGE 96

line 32   *extroardinary*, for extra-ordinary

PAGE 97

line 10   *controul*, for control

line 26   *shewn*, for shown

PAGE 98

line 1   *favorite*, for favourite

line 7   *Colossions*, for Colossians

PAGE 99

line 13   *ferrett*, for ferret

PAGE 100

line 19   *Deane's*, for Dean's

line 21   *Deane's*, for Dean's

PAGE 104

line 14   *injustly*, for unjustly

line 25   *memorabilialy*, for memorabilial-ly

PAGE 105

line 15   *desert*, for dessert

PAGE 108

line 32   *Sipthorpe*, for Sibthorp

PAGE 110

line 20   *discription*, for description

line 34   *Horseley*, for Horsley

PAGE 111

line 12   *Th'o* for Tho'

PAGE 112

line 17   *teaze*, for tease

line 28   *sate*, for set

PAGE 113

line 25   *desert*, for dessert

PAGE 115

line 6   *favorable*, for favourable

PAGE 116

line 3   *Deane's*, for Dean's

line 10   *an*, for en

PAGE 117

line 1   *past*, for passed

line 7   *Barnets*, for Barnett's

line 7   *pye*, for pie

line 15   *past*, for passed

PAGE 120

line 8   *varrying*, for varying

line 12   *amalgammate*, for amalga-mate

line 29   *corronation*, for coronation

PAGE 121

line 6   *Dominic*, for Dominick

line 14   *favoring*, for favouring

line 24   *Garlick*, for Garlike

PAGE 122

line 24   *Coome*, for Coombe

line 36   *Barnets*, for Barnett's

PAGE 125

line 18   *honor*, for honour

PAGE 126

line 14   *sulleness*, for sullenness

PAGE 128

line 17   *sent*, for send

PAGE 129

line 13   *controul*, for control

line 21   *Dominic's*, for Dominick's

PAGE 130

line 14   *Deane's*, for Dean's

line 29   *occurence*, for occurrence

PAGE 132

line 2   *have*, for having

line 3   *Dominic*, for Dominick

PAGE 133

line 8   *Sampson*, for Samson

line 17   *independant*, for independent

line 21   *deserts*, for desserts

PAGE 134

line 18   *wind's*, for Wynds

PAGE 136

line 14   *colored*, for coloured

Diary by E.B.B.

PAGE 137
line 6   *favorably*, for favourably
PAGE 138
line 2   *mille*, for Milly
PAGE 145
line 23   *developped*, for developed
PAGE 148
line 24   *cooly*, for coolly
PAGE 149
line 7   *sunshiney*, for sunshiny
PAGE 150
line 12   *secresy*, for secrecy
PAGE 151
line 7   *straights*, for straits
line 7   *Gibralter*, for Gibraltar
PAGE 152
line 16   *Deane's*, for Dean's
PAGE 154
line 33   *concileating*, for conciliating
PAGE 156
line 9   *Deane*, for Dean
PAGE 157
line 12   *Deane*, for Dean
line 29   *squezzed*, for squeezed
PAGE 158
line 13   *prophaned*, for profaned
line 29   *maneuvres*, for manœuvres
line 34   *Deane*, for Dean
PAGE 159
line 25   *Kenrick*, for Kendrick
PAGE 160
line 31   *Hurd*, for Heard
PAGE 162
line 1   *secresy*, for secrecy
PAGE 163
line 12   *compatability*, for compatibility
line 26   *cooly*, for coolly
PAGE 165
line 4   *chesnuts*, for chestnuts
line 13   *embarassed*, for embarrassed
PAGE 168
line 6   *probality*, for probability
PAGE 170
line 12   *agreableness*, for agreeableness
line 14   *Blizzard*, for Blizard
PAGE 171
line 6   *Foster*, for Forster

line 27   *Sindbad*, for Sinbad
line 27   *Munchhausen*, for Munchausen
PAGE 172
line 4   *embarassment*, for embarrassment
line 22   *Lennard's* for Leonard's
PAGE 176
line 3   *chapter*, for chapters
line 12   *Deane's*, for Dean's
line 14   *Deane*, for Dean
line 15   *Deane*, for Dean
line 25   *chesnuts*, for chestnuts
PAGE 177
line 6   *Mathew's*, for Matthew's
PAGE 180
line 7   *embarassment*, for embarrassment
PAGE 184
line 24   *Roxabel*, for Roxobel
PAGE 185
line 20   *Vandyke's*, for Van Dyck's
PAGE 186
line 6   *Sheperdess*, for Shepherdess
line 22   *Pindar*, for Pyndar
line 25   *past*, for passed
PAGE 187
line 25   *apologetick*, for Apologetic
PAGE 188
line 7   *Zenophon*, for Xenophon
PAGE 190
line 1   *apologetick*, for Apologetic
line 16   *Johnson's*, for Johnstone's
PAGE 191
line 17   *Thurday*, for Thursday
PAGE 192
line 27   *Saint's*, for Saints'
PAGE 193
line 10   *Ipheginia*, for Iphigenia
PAGE 195
line 27   *Pindars*, for Pyndars
PAGE 198
line 17   *independance*, for independence
PAGE 205
line 13   *phrenzy*, for frenzy
PAGE 206
line 3   *gass*, for gas

PAGE 212
line 15   *criticised*, for
           criticized
PAGE 213
line 20   *Barnets*, for Barnett's
PAGE 216
line 10   *suspence*, for suspense
PAGE 220
line 11   *Pindar*, for Pyndar
PAGE 224
line 32   *Hurd*, for Heard
PAGE 227
line 18   *Chœphorœ*, for Chœphori

PAGE 228
line 4   *Colwal*, for Colwall
PAGE 230
line 1   *Battye*, for Battie
line 8   *Deane's*, for Dean's
PAGE 231
line 32   *dessimulation*, for dissimulation
PAGE 235
line 6   *past*, for passed
PAGE 236
line 7   *Bradly*, for Bradley
PAGE 239
line 17   *contributer*, for contributor

APPENDIX I

LETTERS

I: E.B.B. TO H.S.B., [22 JUNE 1831]¹

Previous Publication: Weaver, p. 407 (without enclosure).
Manuscript Location: Huntington.

My dearest friend,

I send you a long description of Paganini & his performances, to help your imagination in his apotheosis.   After reading it, of course the whole scale of immortalized intellect,—from the *lowest* step, on which poor Homer happened to set his foot, up to the *highest,* where Sir Humphrey Davy has placed his safety lamp,—will be thrown to the ground, & Paganini, like another Marius, established on the ruins.   I hope I shall soon see you again.

Ever affectionately yours
E B Barrett.

Hope End
Wednesday.

[Enclosure]²

PAGANINI'S CONCERT.

This performance, respecting which public curiosity has been so highly excited, took place yesterday evening at the King's Theatre. The chief, or rather the sole, interest of the concert centred in Paganini himself; the artists engaged, and the music selected, with the exception of his compositions and performance, comprising no novelty, nor any thing beyond the attraction of an ordinary concert. Paganini executed three pieces. The first was a concerto of three movements, described in his own programme—an *Allegro Maestoso*, an *Adagio Appassionato*, and a *Rondo brillante*. The second piece was a *Sonata militaire*, performed wholly on the first string. These two pieces had the accompaniment of the orchestra. The third piece was a solo, an air with variations on the theme of "Non piu Andrai," from Mozart's Figaro.

Nothing can be more difficult than to describe Paganini's performance on the violin, so as to make the effect of it intelligible to those who have never heard him. Hence, and it is but justice to say so much of this extraordinary man, all the anticipations formed of him, however highly coloured, have fallen short of the reality. He is not only the finest player perhaps that has ever existed on that instrument, but he forms a class by himself, and produces effects which he has been the first to discover, and in which few, if any, imitators will be able to follow him. The difficulty and complexity of the passages played by Paganini are truly wonderful, and the ease with which he conquers them is perfect. They do not, however, form that which is most to be admired in him. His genius is displayed in a far greater degree in his slow movements, in which

---

1. The Diary entry for 22 June makes it possible to supply this dating.

2. E.B.B.'s enclosure has not been preserved with the letter, but in view of her daily reading of *The Times* it seems reasonable to infer that she sent H.S.B. the critique which appeared in the issue of 4 June 1831; it is this that is here reprinted.

he develops, as it may without exaggeration be said, every shade and gradation of feeling. His violin in such passages seems to be a part of himself, and to become that medium in which he can best portray the workings of his mind. If the instrument could be said to speak and to feel, it does so in his hands. The delicacy and truth of his intonation are in all cases conspicuous. The note, attenuated almost to a thread, is still heard as distinctly as when he draws forth the whole power of the instrument.

The most remarkable parts of Paganini's mechanism are, his use of notes produced by the fingers of the left hand, simultaneously with those produced by the bow; and his harmonic notes, which are made by the slightest possible pressure of the string, and resemble, from their clearness and sweetness, the very high notes of the flute. The formation of these latter is familiar to a certain extent to all musicians, but they seldom or ever travel out of the common chord. Paganini, however, gives long and difficult passages, double notes, and even shakes, in this medium. He changes also with rapidity from the harmonic to the common passages, without any sensible break in the rythm [sic]. By the use of the pizzicato at the same time with the bowed notes, he may be said to combine the violin and the guitar in the same instrument. There is more of trick and mere dexterity in this than in any other part of his performance, and it is that on which we should be disposed to place the least value, though it appears to have excited the most wonder. His *arpaggios* [sic] are given with a neatness and precision which is altogether without parallel. His execution of double shakes and octave passages is highly beautiful. The latter are given with such perfect intonation, that they appear, unless one listens with extreme attention, to be the same note. Paganini does the *staccato* in a manner quite different from all other performers. He strikes his bow once on the string, and it seems to run by a tremulous motion over as many notes as he chooses to include in the *staccato* passage. This, too, he does with the quickness almost of thought itself. His manner of striking chords was quite peculiar. He always used either end of the bow for that purpose, and in such a way, that before it touched the strings, one might have thought that the effect must be decidedly bad, instead of being, as it was, perfect. The personal appearance of Paganini is remarkable. He is a tall thin man, with features rather emaciated, pale complexion, a sharp aquiline nose, and a keen eye, the expression of which is greatly heightened when he is animated by his performance. His hair, which is dark, is worn long behind, and combed off his forehead and temples in a manner that gives an air of great simplicity to his countenance. He seems to be about 50 years of age. There is a singularity in his manner, which, though partaking of the grotesque, denotes a man of no ordinary stamp, and rivets attention in a very extraordinary degree. This interest which he excited was a good deal increased by his appearing to be in a very weak state of health. Indeed, up to a late hour in the day, it was doubtful, we understand, whether he would be able to perform; and his appearance altogether is said to have been contrary to the judgment of his medical advisers.

The enthusiasm which his performances excited last night among the audience, certainly surpassed any thing of the kind within these walls. Every *tour de force* and striking passage was not only applauded but cheered by the whole audience, and some of the variations were encored. At the end of every performance, and especially after the last, the applause, cheers, and waving of handkerchiefs and hats, altogether presented a most extraordinary scene.

On the whole, the reception experienced by Paganini last night must have convinced him that the opposition encountered to the scandalous attempt to double the prices, in which it is very probable he himself had no share, did not arise from any prejudice against this distinguished artist, or the ability to appreciate his performance as it deserves. Foreigners who have been present at his concerts in several other parts of Europe, remarked that the applause bestowed and the enthusiasm excited last night, was greater than they had ever witnessed before.

The grouping on the stage when Paganini played his concluding piece was extremely striking. All the veterans of the orchestra, Spagnoletti, Dragonetti, Lindley, and others, had placed themselves so as to watch his performance to the best advantage, and they marked strongly by their countenances the lively impression it made upon them. They were not the least fervent in their applause of what they of course were the best able to form a judgment.

There were some vocal performances during the intervals of Paganini's playing, by Madame Lalande, Mademoiselle Beck, Curioni, Lablache, and Santini.

The pit and gallery were crowded at an early hour. The boxes were not well filled.

II: E.B.B. TO H.S.B., [25] JUNE 1831[1]
           Previous Publication: *EBB/HSB*, pp. 141-142 (in part).
           Manuscript Location: Wellesley.

Sir,

When I announce myself as about to give you a brief account of the much abused & misrepresented race of the Thoughts, too well am I aware that my doing so might require an apology,—were I not addressing myself to *you*. Too well am I aware that upon such an announcement, some young readers might immediately begin to yawn soporifically, some old readers, to sigh dolorifically, and many would-be young & must-be old female ones, to steal a frightened glance at their mirror—, with a "Dear me!—I have been avoiding these people all my life!—and now that they should thurst [sic] themselves upon me in this manner! How very impertinent & provoking!—" But *your* nature & habits are well known to me. I cannot doubt *your* willingness to hear, & hear leniently, a Thought upon Thoughts.[2]

Before you can understand one sentence of my epistle, it is necessary for me to introduce to your attention certain ancient acquaintances of my family. I allude to the respectable house of the Words, lenial descendants from the Alphabet, & near connections of the Syllables. There is often much harmony & sweetness of disposition among the persons in

1. Although E.B.B. dated this letter 24 June 1831, the Diary entry for 25 June makes it clear that the letter should have borne that date.

2. This essay was subsequently revised and submitted to *The New Monthly Magazine*, but was not printed; the manuscript of this version is in the Miriam Lutcher Stark Library of the University of Texas. After further revision, the essay was published in *The Athenæum*, 23 July 1836, pp. 522-523; this last version was reprinted in *HUP*, II, 157-165.

question, (as none can prove better than yourself) and yet they are of so pugnacious a nature, that the "war of words" is considered the most interminable war. Words could not pass between you & your best friend without your quarrelling,—and Gray seals the opinion of their fiery temperament by his expression "words that burn." Indeed notwithstanding great obligations to this hapless race, the poets seem to regard it with abhorrence,—of which, among a thousand other proofs, I may mention Virgil's "non innoxia verba", & Lord Byron's "Away with words",—& Shakespeare's more serious libel on their reputation when he asserts "Words pay no debts". This *must* be a calumny, for we all know that *words cost nothing,*—and besides, even if they do not pay their own debts, they are very often employed to pay other people's.

In former times, the Words were intimate with the Thoughts,—and, to speak justly, were extremely kind in introducing them into the best society. It is moreover just to acknowledge that when several of the Thoughts were falling fast into poverty, the Words most benevolently came to their assistance, and fed & clothed them. Horace says

Verbaque provisam rem, non invita sequentur,

but upon many occasions the Words, tho' the Thoughts had *provided nothing* for their entertainment [sic], paid them every attention, & attendance. In return however for this charity, they exacted so much,—insisting upon so servile an obsequiousness, and general a precedence, that the Thoughts, who are of noble blood, would bear it no longer. And thus, a coldness arising between the two families, it is now considered the height of ill-breeding to invite them to the same party in the fashionable world.

The first member of the Thought family, of whom I will make mention, is Philosophical Thought, a personnage of retired habits & eccentric disposition. He knew Plato & Socrates & Cicero & Bacon very well,—and was intimate enough with Sir Isaac Newton to hold him down in a frolic before a blazing fire, until the distinguished victim's proper person was converted into a *centre of gravity.* But I heard this story from the Words, & they are far from being always accurate. And certain it is, that between them & Philosophical Thought there has been much dissention. Dugald Stewart a friend of the latter, has brought his wrongs before the public, & warmly inveighed against the treachery used towards him by that branch of the Words called Synonymes: and the dissention is so generally known, that when he sits in his usual solitary silent way, people allude at once to his separation from the Words & his contempt for them, by saying "He has not a Word to throw to a dog". Philosophical Thought has done a great deal of good in his time,—and he takes a great deal of time to do good. He has meddled with all the wheel & steam & wind & water engines which man ever travelled by, *in* the air & *by* the air, and *in* the water & *over* the water & *under* the water,—and with all the printing machines & thrashing machines & thinking machines—& with all the mathematical instruments & astronomical instruments & surgical instruments & musical instruments—with all the wind instruments, from St Cecilia's to a pair of bellows,—& with all the stringed instruments, from Paganini's to a horsewhip—and with all the staring at the stars,—and with all the ordering of legislatures, & with all the arranging of ordinances,— & with all the dying of Tyrian purple & printing of English calicos—in short with all that we comprehend, touch, smell, taste, hear, & see,—besides a great deal that we do not see, hear, taste, smell, touch,—or by any means comprehend. Notwithstanding this, he is generally considered as rather a useful than a pleasant person. He is too wise & too grave & too self important & too pedigree-able to be agreable. He will talk an infinite deal of nothing; and nothing can be more learnedly dull than what he will talk. A silly report was once spread about his children the Ideas having had the use of their eyesight from the moment of their entrance into the world. He had no idea of such a report being spread. He made friends with the Words (M.ʳ Locke was the go-between) merely that they might maintain a contrary assertion,—& convince the public of the Ideas having seen neither sun moon nor stars nor his own parental face, until some time after their birth.

Poetical Thought is a venerable old lady with all the fire of youth about her,—& boasts of having led Homer about in leading strings, & whipped many a poet with his own bay. She is still a great dresser, & flirts away most vigorously with the Words, who continue her humble servants tho' at variance with the rest of the family. Indeed in order to pay her attention they sacrifice their own dignity & decorum, & submit to all her caprices, even to allowing themselves to be *cut & slurred over,* —and HER reputation has in some degree suffered by her intimacy with them. I except from these observations one branch of the Words, yclepped Technical Terms, who are a stiff necked set of people, & never approached her in their lives without giving her reason to be sorry for it, —and now they are upon no kind of *terms* with her. *They* are intimate with Philosophical Thought. Philosophical Thought & Poetical Thought used to be good friends,—but lately whenever they meet in Paternoster Row where they both like walking, Poetical Thought looks another way. From the beginning there have been temporary coldnesses between them, —and they had one serious quarrel about Plato, whom Poetical Thought never names without shaking her head & letting the tears come into her eyes.

[277]

But the other members of our family must not be so long dwelt upon. I will mention them briefly. There are Thoughts of the present, who will make you both smile & sigh,—and Thoughts of the future, who are far too flighty,—& Thoughts of the past, who are very bad company. There are merry Thoughts, who will almost kill you with laughing,—and sad Thoughts, who will go to your heart,—& provoking Thoughts, who are sure to come in with your most frequent morning visitors. There are hacknied Thoughts, who have patronized Murray since L<u>d</u> Byron's death, —and new Thoughts, who take a great deal upon themselves, and will introduce you into a very mixed society. There are witty Thoughts, who are very amusing but hard to be met with,—and foolish Thoughts, who are more sociable, & according to the general opinion, quite as agreable. There are aspiring Thoughts, who wear their beavers up,—and humble Thoughts, who are quite out of fashion. *They* associate with Religious Thoughts: and *they*—oh nobody thinks of *them!*— There are besides free Thoughts, who go to a Unitarian Chapel; and vain Thoughts, who often talk of human goodness & happiness,—and idle Thought, who is — —myself.

Now with regard to myself, the Words abuse me cruelly,—but Lord Byron says "All words are *idle*",—so that they should keep their abuse *to themselves*. Does anyone enquire about my capabilities,—I will answer him thus. I can make time pass as pleasantly as most of my relatives. I will sit with you while you are fishing, for hours together,—and watch the clouds for you, out of the window,—& draw portraits for you, in the fire, —and build castles for you, in the air,—and write dissertations for you, like *these presents*. You will commend me I am sure,—but if you do or do not, you will make use of me.

Before I conclude, let me entreat you to consider the wrongs of our family. Are we to be chained & imprisoned by that branch of the Words, called epithets? Are we to be thrown into the shade by the vile conduct of Words who appear incognito? Are we to be absolutely knocked down by Words of six syllables? Are we to be subject to the aspersions of the world,—such as "A Thought strikes me"—and to its contempt—such as, "A penny for your Thoughts"? Let me entreat you to assist us: and I am ready to assure you, in behalf of all our illustrious house, that as we have ever been so we shall ever be

Yours to command.

I had just thrown down my pen, when turning I beheld Condensed Thought an eccentric cousin of ours, so close in his economy as to be considered the Hume of our household. His dwarfish form is contracted by tight stays,—his tiny feet, by Chinese shoes,—for as to be great, is the common ambition of mankind, so, to be little, is the ambition of our cousin. Now as Condensed Thought utterly detests the Words, I expected nothing less than a compliment upon my performance. Imagine my consternation at hearing the following harangue. "Nobody", said my cousin (with an epigrammatic turn of the hand) "except *idle* Thought, would have thought of doing such a thing. Assist our family by such a letter! How! Have you not the wit to observe that in every line of it, you have submitted to the power of those very words whose tyranny you deprecate?"

Was my cousin right? Farewell! lest you should think he was!—

My dearest friend,

You know you need not read this long letter from your allegorical correspondent, *thro'*, if you should feel any disinclinations upon the subject. Pray *dont*, if you *do*. I shall not be in the very least degree offended by such omission,—nor, if you put it into the fire,—by such a *commission*. As I conclude that Mrs Boyd has returned, I will send my love to her.

Yours affectionately
E B Barrett.

Hope End.   I got home yesterday *before eight*; & Bro observed
June 24.th 1831.   that the poney looked as "fresh" as when he went out of the stable.

III: **E.B.B. TO H.S.B., [17 JULY 1831]**[1]

          Previous Publication: *EBB/HSB*, pp. 142-143.
          Manuscript Location: Wellesley.

Were you very angry with me for forgetting to tell Mr Spowers about the newspaper? If you were, you have your revenge: for I was very angry with myself, & would have turned back as soon as I thought of my forgetfulness, if I had not also thought that by the time I had driven two miles, you would most probably have employed somebody else to deliver the message. It is not a usual fault in me, to forget anything you tell me.

I have both written & spoken to Eliza Cliffe about the chapel, & she & Mrs Cliffe will go. As for ourselves, we are all going, if it should be fine externally & internally. There was no letter yesterday, & is none today: and no advertisement. Now if you were a professor of Lagoda [sic], how many "sunbeams" could you extract from these "cucumbers"?

---

1. The Diary entry for 17 July makes it possible to supply this dating.

Diary by E.B.B.

I *thunderstruck* Bro & all of them with the Homer; and I am thinking of raising a supply for the Greeks by making a show of it—admittance half a crown. Dont you think that I should soon have the Græcian boundaries extended & fixed,—and make Prince Leopold wish in his heart that he had taken the first crown offered to him, instead of the second?

I know I did not say half I ought to have said to you yesterday,—I mean, not half I felt. I will not try to say it now. But even at the risk of appearing ungrateful, I must say one thing—that I am *sorry* you should have thought of making me so costly a present. Was it not quite uncalled for, & unnecessary? Was it likely that I should require a present of any kind from you,—particularly after you had made me so many? And even if it were, do you not know that if you had given me something not valuable in itself, it would have been AT LEAST as valuable to *me*, as Wolf's Homer,—had Wolf's Homer been given to me by some other person?—Therefore you would have acted more politicly & prudently if you had kept your costly presents for people, to whom your presents are not valuable *unless* they are costly.

After all these wise reflections, you must know very well how proud I am about the cause of them,—& how much I shall value it, both per *se* and pro *te*. And after all my "sorrow," I am *pleased*,—in associating the most beautiful book I ever saw, with the kindest & most valued friend I ever had.

Yours affectionately
E B Barrett.

Give my love to Mrs Boyd.
Sunday Evening.
Hope End.

IV: EDWARD MOULTON-BARRETT TO HENRIETTA
        MOULTON-BARRETT, 18 JULY 1831

Previous Publication: None.
Manuscript Location: Collection of Mrs. V. M. Altham.

London July 18. 1831

My beloved Daddles

I was detained so long in the city on Saturday that I was unable to write, & tho' I have but a few minutes to do so this morning, fearful you may be disappointed or may suspect that I am ill or what is worse forgetfulness of you all, I shall employ the minutes in writing to you. Thank you for your letters & all your affectionate expressions contained therein;

also tell Ba with what real delight I read her note with the exception of that part announcing the melancholy death of poor Jack-old Boy; Poor Stormy, I deeply sympathise with him in his loss, but I am glad to find that he is likely still to have been in possession free from the possibility of his escape from him. I went yesterday Evening for the first time since I have been here, to hear Irving. He is certainly at best on that occasion, to wit; He told us a curious thing of the casting out of a Devil, which I will keep for you when we meet. They are looking for plague, pestilence & famine, & consider the gifts conferred on various persons as conveying evidences that the same proofs, which accompanied the Apostles that their power was from on high, are still in the Church & were always but from want of faith & honoring the saved held back for ages; but more of this when I see you. I have been several times in the House of Commons, & must confess that the opposition to the Great Bill is worthy of a better excuse; never did men die harder than they do; I find the fatigue severe, but having not much to do, I am upon the whole interested & amused with the debates. I hope you will exercise your discretion in calling upon Bro for means to contribute to the necessities of our neighbours, when you see occasion. I am realy [sic] very unwilling to send this scrawl, but as 10d will not be indifferently spent in telling you I am well, I shall let it go, with all its imperfections in its hand. Remember me to all my beloved ones, & tell them I am fairly miserable in the deprivation of not seeing them daily, a blessing I trust that will soon be offered to me. God bless you,

Yrs most attached & affectionate

E M Barrett

Tell our dear Bell that I have her note to James by me which I have not forwarded supposing it of no great consequence; but that if she wants it to be sent to the north I will hasten to do so upon receiving her word.

V: EDWARD MOULTON-BARRETT TO SAMUEL
       MOULTON-BARRETT, 4 AUGUST 1831

Previous Publication: None.
Manuscript Location: Wellesley.

London, August 4 1831

My beloved Sam

Where can I find words to communicate to you the shock, which the Letter of your dear Christian friend M.ʳ Waddell gave me & the affliction that it afforded to us in informing us of a loss we can never cease to be sensible of & as regards myself & Children to lament over; but if I am in want

Diary by E.B.B.

of language to depict the state of my feelings on this distressing event, what can I say when I consider it with reference to yourself, verily as regards human comfort, nothing, for I know full well from my own personal experience under a similar deprivation that of all earthly consolations, it may well be said "miserable Comforters are ye all" and hence I would only have recourse to the means by which I was enabled to sustain the burden laid upon me & by the grace of God comfort you by the same comfort wherewith I myself was comforted of God in my tribulation— I found that reading & meditating & praying over the Scriptures were precious vehicles by bringing me to him who is alone the manifestation of God's love to his people & who is present in all the afflictions of his Believers to bear them up, pouring into their broken hearts that Unction from above which binds, heals & comforts them, realising the promise that "according to your day so shall your strength be." As means let me refer you to the 1 Thess: 4c. 13v to the end, and particularly, as regards the blessed deceased to the 14v. for indeed we cannot doubt that she sleeps in Jesus, as hers was not a name to live only, but there existed in her the power of Godliness, & here I cannot help remarking that two Missionaries now in England from Jamaica, Birchall & Cantilow, bear ample testimony to her anxiety & labor of love in behalf of the poor Negroes & the loss, humanly speaking, that the cause has sustained in her departure; & surely this is having obtained a good report through faith: If then she has entered into her rest & who can doubt it, as all Scripture is true, we cannot, we dare not, as we love, disturb that rest by even a wish to bring such a Spirit back to a world of Sin, Sorrow, disease & trouble in order only to gratify our selfish, for we cannot give it a better epithet, desires— I am sure my dear Sam has been better instructed than to entertain such a wish— I am satisfied that your Mary with my Mary, like the Mary of old, did choose that better part which shall not be taken from them & hence that they are now in the joy of their Lord; that they were the Children whom the Father gave him with whom He travails on the Cross & is satisfied & they I am convinced are satisfied, therefore let us in faith be satisfied & joy in our tribulation. Now read the 12 Heb: to the end of the 13v. & know who has done this & the end He had in view in doing it, to alienate us from the Creature in order to fix our whole Soul on the Creator, to take us from time to eternity, to prove to us He chastens only as a Father of infinite wisdom, mercy & love for our own good, & therefore let us bless him in the midst of our sufferings, kiss every twig of the Rod, & say Father it was well done, for Thou didst it— Oh my Brother I cannot doubt that our beloved ones are now singing the song of Moses & the song of the Lamb, & are waiting in bliss for the adoption, to wit, the redemption of the body.

[282]

Oh may we by the Grace of our God, be alike partakers with them & be made, the short time we are permitted to linger here daily more & more meet for the Kingdom of Heaven & fit companions of them, who have gone before us in the faith of the Gospel; Let us not then quench the Spirit neither hide the talent we each have committed to us for our Lord's service, but let us be more Zealous, more faithful & rejoice the more on our dependance on him who having proved his infinite love in giving his Son to die for us, cannot withhold any good thing from those who love him—— My paper will not let me add any more, than to pray, which is my morning & evening exercise, that the God of all comfort & consolation will support, guide & bless you in time & eternity——

Yr very affectionate Brother E M Barrett

Tell dear Mr Waddell, I will write to him when I can do so without a charge to him—— The Lord bless him & give him to rejoice over much fruit of the Seed he is enabled to save——

VI: **E.B.B. TO H.S.B., 23 AUGUST 1831**

Previous Publication: *EBB/HSB*, pp. 143-144.
Manuscript Location: Wellesley.

Tuesday morn^g August 23^d 1831.

My dearest friend,

I send Keats's poems for Miss Boyd,——& will at the same time tell you, that if Dominick goes to see you, which he certainly will do, you must not blame me. I did not say one word about you to him, on my way home yesterday,——but his first words to me were "I had intended to do myself the pleasure of calling upon Mr Boyd today, if——" I forget what subject the "if" introduced. He is "*anxious to consult you about the Greek historians*". I took your part so far as to observe that you had not paid much attention to historical subjects: but nothing will save you—depend upon it!—— So I advise you to be as philosophical, if not as historical,——& certainly as *grave*, as you can!——

D^r & Mrs Card, M^{rs} & Miss Wall & Miss Wall's uncle, provided with a ticket of admission from Bentley of Worcester, made a *party of pleasure* to this place yesterday. As the ticket was not a proper one, they were not allowed to go farther than the dining room,——& Bro who was a good deal excited, said to Lane in a voice, meant to be audible, that if Lane did not instantly see them out of the house, he himself would do so. Accordingly they went out of the house,——& had the moderation to be satisfied by walking along the walks, & looking in at the windows of the tent-room &

[283]

Diary by E.B.B.

drawing room where my aunt was sitting. I conclude that they *were* satisfied & pleased, as there was a good deal of very loud laughing & talking, —Miss Wall the coryphœus!— Not long ago I saw a letter from her to Eliza Cliffe in which she professed a strong feeling of "compassion" for "those poor girls". She is happy in her manner of illustrating it,—& of acting, at the same time, consistently with the delicacy & good feeling & womanly kindness which I ever attributed to her!— Her acquaintance with us, slight as it has been, places all this in a stronger & more creditable point of view.

You know how little I care about the conduct of people for *whom* I dont care,—but still it is very painful to be exposed to such intrusions— to live as we have lived lately & have never been used to live: so *very* painful, that I should long ago have wished myself away, even from Hope End, —if it were not for *you*!— Well! I suppose both the pain & consolation will soon be over. I mean, this particular kind of pain—& every kind of consolation.

Ever affectionately yours
E B Barrett.

Since coming to an end of this note, Bro has received one from our dear Papa, who, in addition to his other troubles, has had a violent attack of cholera. He is weak & low in consequence of it—, & is going out of London for two days, to regain his strength by changing the air. Oh if it had been the will of God to have taken *him* from us! What should we have done *then*? It is certainly wrong & sinful to repine, when there might be so much greater reason for sorrow: and as long as he is left to us, I should not have talked of losing every kind of consolation—*earthly* consolation, of course I meant!—

May God bless you with joy as long as joy will last,—and with *all* consolation afterwards!—

Papa says nothing about Hope End—

VII: **E.B.B. TO H.S.B., 24 AUGUST [1831]**

Previous Publication: *EBB/HSB*, p. 145.
Manuscript Location: Wellesley.

My dearest friend,

Tho' you entirely "acquit Dr Card", I am very sure that what *he* did, you are the very last person in the world to have done. Recollect the circumstances, well known to everybody, under which Hope End is advertised,—& the other circumstance of Papa's daughters being there. Now

[284]

would any *very* considerate & feeling person have taken advantage of the advertisement & joined a party of pleasure,—remember, a *mere* party of pleasure,—to go there & remind them of their distresses? Oh no!—

I never supposed otherwise than that the Walls were the sole movers & instigators of the measure. Everything you know "after its kind",—— which is true of creeping things as well as of leviathans!— It is amusing that Mrs Cliffe should have told me only last Sunday a long story about "dear Millicent" who when her uncle asked her to ride over to Hope End on account of its being advertised, refused at once. "She would not do such a thing on any account",—and Mrs Cliffe estimated her amiability accordingly. I wonder what the estimation will be now!

I did not understand until today that this estate is valued at £32,000, *without* the timber which is considerable,—so that altogether the sum is nearly £50,000. It is not probable—is it?—that any man would purchase to such an amount without examining his purchase,—& only one gentleman has been here with that apparent object. *He* seemed to think more of disturbing us than of examining the premises, & would look only into the lower rooms, tho' Lane asked him to go up stairs. By the way, his conduct was a contrast to that of some other people. He walked as lightly as he could that his footsteps might not be heard by us, & seemed unwilling to see even as many rooms as he did see, for fear of "disturbing or distressing Mr Barrett's family".

I have found—ferretted out, Mr Kidd for you. Thank you for your letter. You cannot think how pleased I was to see the signature—which does not mean that I was pleased to get to the end of the letter,—because I saw the signature first.

Yours affectionately
E B Barrett.

August 24th.

VIII: E.B.B. TO H.S.B., [7] SEPTEMBER [1831]¹
          Previous Publication: *EBB/HSB*, p. 146.
          Manuscript Location: Wellesley.

I am going to write one line, *upon business*. I quite forgot to give you on Monday, the direction of Mr Henry Bohn, 4 York St. Covent Garden, London, which you may perhaps like to have, & which, if you do not have

---

1. Although E.B.B. dated this letter Wednesday, 6 September, Wednesday fell on 7 September; the Diary entry for 7 September makes it clear that the letter should have borne that date.

it now, will be of the less use to you.　He has advertised in the Times, a catalogue, just published, of very rare & valuable books, Aldine editions, &c, & states in the advertisement that he will send it gratis to any gentleman who will give his name & pay the postage.　Now I meant on Monday to ask you whether I should write for you or not: & I wont mean to put off asking you, because this weather is so very rainy-looking, & *may* be very obstinate.

　We had a satisfactory letter from our dear Papa yesterday.　He has recovered from all the effects of his late attack, & writes in better spirits than usual,—& without making any direct reference to *the* business, or saying one word about his return.　On the contrary, he speaks of intending to write to *me*.　Therefore he cant be coming, & we cant be going, *immediately!*——　My aunt thinks decidedly that he is making some new exertion —but I will not trust myself with hoping for anything beyond a respite.

　Tell M[rs] Boyd with my love, that I had intended to send her some partridges today, & that on another day, I shall be more successful.　You know your pheasants cannot have the honour of being shot at, until the first of October.

Ever yours affectionately
E B Barrett.

Wednesday
Sept. 6th

IX:　　　E.B.B. TO H.S.B., [16 SEPTEMBER 1831][1]
> Previous Publication:　　Weaver, p. 403.
> Manuscript Location:　　Huntington.

My dearest friend,

　I found M[r] Bohn's parcel directed to *E B Barrett Esq[r]* on my return home yesterday.　I cannot get anyone to take it to Ruby Cottage today, & perhaps you would rather have it by the post as soon as you can, than wait until another day.　M[r] Bohn seems to have some valuable books: but you beat his whole catalogue in the antiquity of your Gregories.

　Will you ever forgive me for trusting Chrysostom in profane hands? Dominick Trant siezed upon the book yesterday, & began to wish more sensibly than usual, that he had all the contents in his head.　I observed that in that case, he would have to read his recantation instead of his mass book next Sunday: upon which he began to beg & entreat & make such a

---

1. The Diary entry for 16 September makes it possible to supply this dating.

bustle in the middle of the road about my lending him what I had no right to lend, that I gave up the point. Now I have been as angry with myself as you can be, ever since; tho' he faithfully promised to take as much care of the book as I could do, & to return it to me, the next time I drove by. He wishes to "consult somebody about it"! Nonsense! I do believe, now that I can think cooly, that he made the fuss merely for the sake of making a fuss; & from a spirit of opposition, because he saw how unwilling I was to do what he asked. He does not know which comes first, alpha or omega, and therefore — — but I am as great a goose as he is—and if *you* are not in a passion, you are canonizable.

No letters again today. I have delayed writing this, until the last moment, because until then, I had not decided on sending the catalogue.

Ever affectionately yours
E B Barrett.

Hope End
Friday.

X: **E.B.B. TO H.S.B., [22 OCTOBER 1831]**[1]

Previous Publication: *EBB/HSB*, pp. 147-148.
Manuscript Location: Wellesley.

Hope End.
Saturday.

My dearest friend,

I got home very well, & had no trouble in being absolved from all my sins of the last few days. So, you see, I stole "the sheep" without "being hanged"!!— I sent away the letter with a seal large enough to be taken for the Lord Chancellor's,—& do not doubt about its striking the Editor with sufficient awe & admiration, for you to have every chance of being prosecuted for libel. I have just heard from Sam, who has seen an evening paper, that Parliament is prorogued, & by the King in person, & until the 22ᵈ of November. This is quite satisfactory,—is it not? & calculated to make the anti-reformers *almost* as uncomfortable as if they were in the neighbourhood of rope & lamp post, & out of sight of the police!—

Such an account as I have heard of Mʳ Knowles!— He is branded for ever in my opinion,—& will be in yours, when what has reached me reaches you. Can you believe that the whole weight of the Shaftesbury expenses falls upon poor Dominic,—& that it should fall entirely upon

---

1. The Diary entry for 22 October makes it possible to supply this dating.

him, was the evident & only cause of Mr Knowles' forcing him into the business?   Mr Knowles will not, or cannot, pay *his own part* of those expenses!!   Dominic acknowledges that Mr Knowles completely deceived & cheated him,—but does not wish people to know, to what extent.   Well! not satisfied with being sleight of hand, & slight of conscience with respect to Dominic, he went down to Poole a short time ago & offered himself as a reform candidate: when finding that the interests of the place were in the power of two anti-reformers, in order to get in, he prefixed *anti* to his old political disignation, & had the assurance to write to Dominic to tell him that he had become a *moderate* reformer.   The newspapers wondered what could be the politics of Mr Knowles who stood now on one side, & now on another,—& the people of Poole had good sense enough to turn him out.   But is not this even more intolerable in the eyes of Heaven & Earth, than could be dreamt of from his philosophy?—

I was very happy in being with you last Monday & Tuesday & Wednesday,—& the more so, as it was a happiness which my Fancy had half resigned for ever!—   There has been no letter from Papa since I left home. It is supposed here, that the next will be final!—   Whatever it may be, & whatever may be its consequences, neither it nor they nor any other thing can make me less than I have been & am,

Your attached friend

E B Barrett.

I forgot to ask you to speak to Miss Boyd about my Battle of Marathon.   If she is kind enough to think it worth her acceptance, I certainly will not receive it back again.

Do my dear Mrs Boyd let me hear everything about everybody, & when I may hope to see you.   As the boy is going I cant write a word more. Have you *heard*?—

Y^{rs} affec^{tely}

E B B

XI: JAMES MARTIN TO THE RIGHT REV. THE BISHOP
        OF HEREFORD, 11 NOVEMBER 1831

Previous Publication: *The Times*, 17 November 1831; *Hereford Journal*,
                        23 November 1831; also issued as a circular.
Manuscript Location: Unknown.

MY LORD,

Your constant residence in a distant part of the kingdom, and your occupations as Warden of Winchester College, have probably rendered you less attentive to your duties here as Bishop of Hereford, than you otherwise would and ought to be; I therefore shall take the liberty of drawing your attention to the following statement of facts.

Your Lordship is no doubt well aware of the large church preferment attached to the see of Hereford; and, amongst others, the rectory of this and the four surrounding parishes, namely—Colwall, Cradley, Bosbury, Little Marcle, and Coddington.

Cradley, with a population of 1500 souls, is possessed by a rich pluralist, the son of the late bishop, who never resides.

Bosbury, with a population of 1100 souls, your Lordship has lately given to a young man who never resides, or even keeps a resident curate; the church being served by a tutor in a gentleman's family, who lives in a distant parish.

Little Marcle, with 200 parishioners, is held by a pluralist, and has neither resident rector nor curate.

The parish of Coddington was presented to another relative of the late bishop, many years since, and has been, during the greater part of that period, sequestered for the payment of his debts,—he living in a state of beggary, drunkenness, and infamy that is scarcely credible by any but the two hundred unfortunate parishioners intrusted to his care.

This same divine was also for many years the only officiating minister of this parish (Colwall), and, when sufficiently sober, performed the church service in both parishes; our rector, never having been amongst us for twenty years, intrusted a population of 1100 persons to the entire management of this non-resident curate!

About three years since, we, the parishioners of Colwall, with great difficulty obtained the removal of this person from this curacy, and a resident clergyman of great respectability was appointed in his place. From that period this gentleman has diligently fulfilled all the duties of a parish priest, divine service has been performed twice instead of once on Sundays, the sick have been visited at their own homes, the needy have been constantly relieved out of his small salary, and in short I can attest, as a resident and a magistrate in the parish, that the conduct of this gentleman has visibly improved the morals and ameliorated the condition of the poor; and consequently that he has made himself beloved by his flock, and respected by his neighbours.

Upon the recent death of our long absent rector, a petition was immediately forwarded to your Lordship, from the inhabitants and landowners of this parish, requesting you to appoint our curate to the living. This petition was backed by the recommendation of several of the most respectable individuals in the neighbourhood. The only result of these urgent applications has been the appointment of a stranger, who, we understand, is a pluralist, has no intention of residing, and is about to remove our worthy curate to make way for a young relative preparing for orders.

I trust, my Lord, the foregoing statement will justify me in calling your immediate attention to the circumstances related by

Your Lordship's obedient servant,
JAMES MARTIN.

Old Colwall, Nov. 11th, 1831.[1]

XII: E.B.B. TO H.S.B., 15 NOVEMBER [1831]

Previous Publication: *EBB/HSB*, pp. 148-150.
Manuscript Location: Wellesley.

Hope End. Novr 15th.
Tuesday.

As you have such a regard for the bishops, you will be glad to hear that Mr Martin has written a letter to the Bishop of Hereford, severe enough, & containing a *charge* about the state of the surrounding parishes with regard to clergymen.   A copy is sent to the Times—therefore dont forget to have his signature ferretted for!   No anonymousness! no initials! but *James Martin* at full length.   He will have the whole church militant in this part of the world upon him, Mrs Cliffe as well as his correspondent,—& will be more unpopular than even *you* were, in your imaginary zenith.   You know I have not seen the letter—only heard of it.   The spirit of it is likely to be far from the right spirit, & rather *magistraterial* than theologian,—and yet I am sure you will be more glad than otherwise at its having been written.   So much for the mint sauce!—   You are exactly in Mr Tone's humour just now,—who used to bless everybody generally, & . . do the contrary . . to the bishops particularly!—

I got home very well yesterday, in spite of the wind which blew my bonnet into an *hexagonal* shape—is not that the word? Occyta ran down stairs with a face much brighter than the daylight was *then,* & gave me such a flattering reception that I forgot all about you for three or four minutes.   Afterwards he sate on my knee until *one* of us was tired,—my gratitude wont let me say which,—& began to tell me all about my squirrel running away, & how he could not stand at my door all day as its guard, because Minny *would* make him do his lessons.   In short he is the

---

1. Reprinted from the *Hereford Journal*, 23 November 1831. This letter provoked a spirited correspondence, printed in the following issues of the paper.

dearest thing of the kind that ever was or will be.

No letter from Papa by today's post!— I hear that he has been written to about his sheep & cows which have hitherto remained in the park & are now to be turned out. He must send some answer: and *what* answer? Well!—there is no use in thinking of it.

A better account of the cholera than of the reform bill in today's paper. Suppose it should be thrown out again!— Would not the Marquis of Londonderry have reason to rejoice if he were only thrown *at*, as a consequence? If such a catastrophe were to occur, nolo episcopari would be more sincerely said than it ever was before. But surely Ministers cannot be quite so linially descended from the saviours of the capitol, for us to be justified in *supposing* any such thing. I have been reading an article in the Quarterly Review this morning *about* the administration, where of course bill the second, is prophetically considered as dead & buried, & Lord Grey turned out. Nothing beats the insolence of the writer except his own folly!— All the excitement of the people attributed not to the rejection of the reform bill by the Lords, but to the stirring up, with a long pole, of those "BEASTISES" vulgarly called the people, by the king's government! If nothing had been said about a second reform bill, we should have been perfectly quiet by this time,—& now we are only waiting for its rejection, in order to become so. Therefore you see you may keep up your spirits!—

Did you know that D.ʳ Wheatly is the new archbishop of Dublin? *I* did not until this morning, & am most particularly particularly sorry for it, as I am sure you will be. You will recollect that he wrote against evangelical religion, & clenched his arguments by translating Plutarch's treatise on superstition,—implying of course that Plutarch knew more about christianity than he did!!—— And yet this man is now the archbishop of Dublin!— And he means too to be an active archbishop; & has told his friend D.ʳ Willis (M.ʳˢ Martin's brother in law) that whatever may be the archbishop of Canterbury's intentions, *he* will instantly commence a reform of the church in Ireland!—— What kind of reform will it be? An ejection of evangelical preachers,—& persecution of dissenting ministers?——

I have written more than I quite intended,—NOT that I intend now to make you answer what you may be disinclined to answer—so do'nt think of *that!*— I miss the squirrel & you very much indeed; but I am modest enough to believe in the possibility of it's being better for both of you that I should.

May God bless you my dearest friend—

Ever yours affectionately
E B Barrett.

Diary by E.B.B.

XIII: E.B.B. TO H.S.B., 1 DECEMBER 1831

Previous Publication: *EBB/HSB*, pp. 150-151 (in part).
Manuscript Location: Wellesley.

Hope End.
December 1.   1831.

My dearest friend,

I think I had better tell you about the t s and s s, without waiting for the *opportunity* of forgetting them again.   You know my Isocrates is a bad edition.   In it, there is sometimes a double tau & sometimes a double sigma quite ad libitum.   For instance, there is *thalatta* on one part of a page, & *thalassa* on another—"how happy could I be with either".   The *sun* seems to be undeviatingly preferred to the *ksun*.

In both Simpson's & Hutchinson's editions of Zenophon, the double tau takes the place of the double sigma,—and *sun* of *ksun*.

I have found that passage in the Apologetick, which I hunted for in vain yesterday,—at least I think I have found it.   You will be able to decide whether it is the right one or not, when I see you next.   *To'd eu nikato.*   I hope the seeing next, may be seeing soon.   No letter today, and no Papa!—and we thought that one of them was certain to arrive!   But I dare say you will excuse my sending you all the groans of Testy & Sensitive; and will prefer a very good & true story about the unknown tongues. Now listen.   Archdeacon Probin or Probbin (I am not sure of the spelling) is the father of those inspired twins, respecting whom, you will recollect, Papa wrote to me.   The Archdeacon has been lately in some little difficulty as to his temporal affairs,—and in the midst of it, up came the two children.   "Papa!—never mind about your business—dont think about it!   The Spirit says that the world is coming to an end".   Therefore the archdeacon, being a believer in their inspiration, did'nt mind about his business—did'nt think about his business—& . . lost his estate!!— As soon as he had heard of the loss, up came the children again—"Papa! we have made a mistake.   The Spirit says that the world is NOT coming to an end"!—   If I had been the archdeacon, I would have requested them to deliver their future prophecies in the unknown tongue.   Would not *you*?

Ever yours affectionately
E B Barrett.

Best love to Mrs Boyd & Annie.

[292]

XIV: E.B.B. TO H.S.B., [10 DECEMBER 1831]¹
         Previous Publication: *EBB/HSB*, pp. 151-154.
         Manuscript Location: Wellesley.

Hope End Saturday

I am going to tell you what you wished to hear about the reform bill
& the unknown tongues,—at least all that Papa has told me about either
of them.   He thinks that the King & his ministers are certainly honest
men,—that the next bill will be equally efficient with the last—that it
will pass—and that, in the improbable case of its being rejected, a revolu-
tion must ensue.   The bishop of Bath & Wells has come over to the right
side of the question;—and Lord Harrowby is coming.   M.^r O'Connell &
Mr Hunt have shown no principle, on this, as on other subjects,—& Lord
London-don-don-derry (as Occyta calls him) is mad.   The bishops, as a
body, are supposed to be less mad than they were,—& the *compos mentis*
may be proved by their next vote.   Altogether, Papa's view of politics,
walks on the sunshiney side of the street.   I advise your's to cross over.
   Now with regard to the unknown tongues.   Four thousand persons are
assembled every Sunday at Mr Irving's chapel,—two thousand sitting, and
two thousand standing; and after his fervent extempore prayer, he folds
his arms in his black gown, & exclaims in his majestic manner, & deep sol-
emn voice, "I wait, until it please the Holy Ghost to speak unto us by the
mouth of his servants".   Then comes the unknown tongue: the most terrif-
ic sound, Papa says, that he ever heard or expects to hear.   "Believe it, or
do not believe it—you must be awed by it."   He was present at the first
exhibition,—women shrieked & fainted, & there was a general rush towards the doors.   Papa jumped upon a bench, & shouted to everyone who
would hear him, that the danger of the pressure in rushing out, was greater
than any danger they could meet with in remaining"; and while he spoke,
he thought that there was real danger: he mistook the voice of the exhib-
itor for the roar of flames.   You may imagine what a voice it was.   All
London was & is, in a state of excitement.   Everybody acquits Mr Irving
of being intentionally deceptive,—and some people acquit the exhibitors
—but there is not so much unanimity in the latter decision.   Mr Nisbet
the bookseller, an intelligent & pious man & one who *used* to be a thick &
thin follower of Irving, said to Papa—"I would not be too confident in
them.   I call Miss Emma Cardale *a light character*."   Papa recollecting
that Mr Nisbet was a starch stiff presbyterian, & that "a light character"
with him, might be a heavy character with anybody else, begged for an

1. The Diary entry of 10 December makes it possible to supply this dating.

[293]

explanation.   Mr Nisbet told him that Miss Emma & another inspireè, had been heard talking & laughing very loud just before service, and arranging how they would disobey their husbands, whenever they happened to marry, by speaking in the unknown tongue, whether the aforesaid husbands liked it or not.   Miss Emma is not however, on all occasions, so selfwilled.   She dined at Albury's, Mr Drummond's, in company with Mr MacNeil,—who is not a believer in spite of all that I told you,—& several of the faithful.   On a sudden, symptoms of the tongues came on, Pythian contortions & agitations of her body, which always precede an oracle.   But Mr MacNeil would not stand this.   He fixed his eyes upon hers, exclaiming in the most imperious tone "I command you to be silent.   Speak if you dare."   The young lady was quiet in a moment.

Papa heard "a very fine sermon" from him, on the subject of the tongues.   Mr Irving was alluded to in it, in an affecting manner—as "one whom he loved with the love of a brother".   Did you ever hear, or are you hearing now for the first time, that Mrs Irving dreams dreams, & sees visions?   Visions are all the fashion in Mr Irving's chapel,—where one man has seen a "handwriting on the wall", and another, the "ghost of a skull". I have not read Wesley's Treatise, because I talked to Papa, or rather heard him talk, the whole of yesterday.   He is looking quite well,—a little thin, *I* fancy—but everybody else calls that, fancy indeed.   It is clear enough that nothing has been done.   Nothing has been said to me—except an inference of Miss Clarke's, about the non probability of our moving immediately.   Of our moving sooner or later, there can be no doubt whatever. Papa enquired after you, even before he enquired after Mr Curzon,—& indeed made a great many minute interrogations about you.   He wore a thick mask of high spirits yesterday.   He must feel bitterly—and when I think ONLY of him,—and I certainly OUGHT to do so always,—I cannot wish his time of trial here to be much prolonged.

Is Mrs Boyd's headache gone?   I hope so.   Give my love to her & Annie —and tell yourself that whenever I write a long letter or any kind of letter to you, I dont mean to saddle you with the *necessity* of answering it.   Whenever I take it into my wise head, that you write to me because you cant help yourself . . then all my pleasure in reading what you write, comes to an end.   This scribble must come to an end at any rate.   In a great hurry,

Ever yours affectionately
E B B.

Think of my forgetting to tell you, that Papa certainly does *NOT* believe in the tongues.

XV: E.B.B. TO H.S.B., [7-8 JANUARY 1832][1]

Previous Publication: *EBB/HSB*, pp. 157-158.
Manuscript Location: Wellesley.

Hope End.   Saturday night.

I was very glad to find that black swan, a letter from *you*, ready to meet me here, tho' I had learnt the table of contents at Ruby Cottage.   I believe I did not thank you for asking me again to your house, when I said that I could not go.   If I did not thank you then, I must do so now instead.

You desired me some time ago to look at Chrysostom's commentary on the latter part of the chapter of Romans.   I did not forget to look at it, but I have had no opportunity of telling you what I saw.   Chrysostom as far as I can understand him, seems to be perfectly orthodox in his exposition of the texts in question.

Papa says that M.ʳ Irving did lately in his presence, address the whole of his congregation of four thousand, in this manner—"You are saved!— I do not say that you are in a salvable state, but that you are saved."   In a few minutes afterwards, he exclaimed with all the inconsistency which must always characterize error—"Repent, and turn unto the Lord, or you will be damned."!—   "Follow the leader" is a hard game to play at, with M.ʳ Irving,—and I think & hope that M.ʳ Bulteel will be tired, before it is half over.   Do you recollect the little Calvinistic book which M.ʳ Curzon lent to you & me?   He sent that very book to M.ʳ Bulteel, as a book he was likely to be particularly pleased with.

I do not object to the *RHYME*, in your epigram.

May God bless you!—
Ever yours affectionately
E B Barrett.

XVI: E.B.B. TO H.S.B., [14 JANUARY 1832][2]

Previous Publication: *EBB/HSB*, pp. 154-155 (in part).
Manuscript Location: Wellesley.

Saturday night.
Hope End.

I send you a list of those letters of Gregory which you have marked.

1. To Seleusius.   Did you think it witty?   I suppose so,—but the wit |

---

1. The Diary entries of 7 and 8 January make it possible to supply this dating.

2. The reference to E.B.B.'s "The Pestilence", published 13 January, makes it possible to supply this dating.

seems to *me* rather rigid & wire drawn.

7. To Basil.

9 To Basil. An affectionate & beautiful letter.

10. To Basil.

15 To the Bishop of Colonne. There is a striking & simple dignity in this letter.

18. To Sophronius on the death of Cæsarius. Pathetic & beautiful.

34. To Gregory Nyssen. I admire it *very* much.

37 To Greg: Nyss: Very pathetic.

50 To Olympius.

95. To Greg: Nyss:

112 To Pansophius

201– To Thecla—

202. To the same. It is certainly beautiful.

You have also marked the 39th. & 40th, which you know, you translated.

Now I will mention some letters which are unmarked, & undeservedly so,—and after all, I am sure that some letters will be unmentioned, & undeservedly so.

25th To Basil.

26– On meeting with an accuser of Basil. The opening is beautiful, but you will be tired before you get to the end.

27– To Basil who seems to have taken offence at some advice of Gregory's. The first part is extremely touching.

29. To Eusebius. Rather a panegyric than a letter: but an eloquent panegyric.

The last sentence of the 31st. very pathetic—

48th. to Asterius— Elegant, animated, & ingenious.

49th To Olympius. More oratorical than epistolary—but very fine.

The 59th. (To Sophronius) is a touching & affectionate letter,—and the 73d (to Amazonius) an interesting one.

I admire every letter which you have marked,—and I hope you will return my compliment. I have done as you desired, as well as I could,—but your ferret was in a hurry today: and (to vary the metaphor) my sieve has holes in it, & has let through several letters, I dare say, which dont deserve to lie among the chaff. But the ennumeration of those with your mark attached to them, is certainly accurate,—& *that* is the point of consequence.

I had a letter from our dear dear Papa yesterday, beginning "My be-loved Ba, cum multis aliis"—written as if he were *determined* to be in good spirits. He says that he has "tasted so much happiness" with us lately, that it is but fair for him to feel a little of its contrary now. We are to hear tomorrow on what day he returns. Now if he does not return on Tuesday, I think I will not go to you on Monday when Henrietta may want the poney, but on another day when I can have it without inconveniencing anybody. Therefore dont expect me. You cant think how much I was pleased by your seeming to wish me to go to see you again before Papa's return.

Did I tell you, or not,—for your cholera panic interrupted me,—that I had sent the verses I spoke of, to the Times? They were in today's paper, —with a motto from Lucretius, which I assure you is enough in itself to give anybody an attack of the *real Asiatic*. Dont be afraid,—the paper is not going your way!——

I had intended to answer Mrs Boyd's & Annie's *very* kind letters,—but you & Papa have taken to yourselves all my time today. Good bye must be said now,—as it is nearly twelve—so good bye, my dearest friend!—

Yours affectionately
E B Barrett.

XVII: EDWARD MOULTON-BARRETT TO HENRIETTA MOULTON-BARRETT, 21 JANUARY 1832

Previous Publication: None.
Manuscript Location: Collection of Mrs. V. M. Altham

Jany. 21. 1832.

My dearest Daddles

I had been in hopes that I should have been [able to] write you before this & I suspect such must have been your opinion or I should have heard from some one this morning but here I am & must be here until Tuesday next in any event, however favorable things may progress, as the Yankees say, towards my departure. I doubt not that you are well and flatter my-self that you are all miserable without me as I truely am without you & our joyous Evengs. I should have written to Ba on the subject of her Lines on the Pestilence but that I may not give umbrage to her modesty or rath-er increase her self-complacency I will say my say to you. I think them beautiful, most beautiful & there is a spirit in them like Milton's South West Wind on a bank of Violets, breathing & giving odours; the effect of the repetitions à la gifted Persons at Tronis, is very good and when read over often so as to feel them produce something of the same awe upon the Mind—and now as to my dislikes, the last verse but one is too tame for what precedes and as ushering it [sic] what succeeds; in the last stanza there is a mistake namely the "Serpent's brass" for it was not a brass of a Serpent that Moses made, but a serpent of brass, therefore in all humility I submit, it should be written "The Serpent brass"— I met a friend of Mrs Bafford's & sent her the number of the Times which contained it. I have given it to the Publisher of the Pulpit who will insert it soon. There is no truth in Miss Gibbons holding forth at Irvines, the only addition to the former number being a Gentleman from Doncaster of the name of Baxter. I have been twice to Irvine, but was disappointed both times in hearing the gifted Persons, the last Time which was last Wednesday Evening I heard such doctrine & such opinions that I shall keep out of the way of being offended in like manner again—the man is clearly in great darkness, I pray God to give him light that he may escape for his life. The weather here is miserable, cold, dirty & foggy; I find the Cold must have been more severe here about Christmas than it was with us, as the [ice] was strong enough to afford two days skaiting. I hope that you are all good & gentle and require but very little correction but which whenever necessary I hereby empower Seppy & Occyta to inflict with a bundle of Nettles.

You my beloved ones most attached

E M Barrett

I sent you all the other day some fish.   I hope it was good.

Let me hear from some of you on Tuesday.   The *Lord bless you all*.

XVIII: E.B.B. TO H.S.B., [26 JANUARY 1832][1]

Previous Publication: *EBB/HSB*, pp. 155-156 (in part).
Manuscript Location: Wellesley.

Hope End.   Thursday.

My dearest friend,

Altho' I have begun to write upon this *halo polleen*, I am not going to write a long letter which would exact (or seem to do so) a long reading, & take you away from Gregory.   Either a long or a short letter, however, I must write to you today: and that is the *long & the short of it*.   If you were as cold as I was yesterday on our way home, you would take away the towel & the coat & even the skreen, & enter upon a *holy* alliance

---

1. The Diary entry of 26 January, taken together with the reference the previous day to *The Methodist Magazine*, makes it possible to supply this dating.

with the fire, as you know, my shoes do sometimes. We met the Miss Berringtons,—& one of them told me that she had heard of your being "metal most attractive" & wondered why she had never seen you. "Does he never walk out? I have seen *Miss* Boyd, but I never saw *him*." Now your principle of general benevolence will certainly make you 'lift up' or 'elevate' that green curtain of yours, & come more in front of the stage, & gratify people who are moderately curious.

I have been thinking that when you have finished your translation, there could be no harm in *trying* whether Mr Nisbet would or would not buy the copyright. If he will, you are saved trouble & anxiety in both maximum & minimum,—& if he wont, you are right & I am wrong,—which will be another kind of satisfaction to you. In this way you will have two anchors to depend upon—as Pindar said once,—or two strings to your bow,—as our great great great grandpapas used to say. Besides if Nisbet objects, from some Goth & Vandal reason, to publishing, Hatchard will publish, I dare say,—& if Hatchard wont, there are other booksellers in London. I protest against the Methodists' Magazine, again & again & again & again,—& never shall be consoled if you are obstinate about it. In the case of Nisbets accepting you, could not you go on publishing a few of the finest of Gregory's orations, in the same—i.e. the pamphlet form? The labour to you would be very trifling,—& their being bought by the booksellers, would be a security, almost, for their being bought by the public. But we can talk about this. In the meantime, do think about it.

I hope there is not a very great deal of harm in my envying Miss Mushet for her occupation,—because if there is, I have "sinned damnably", as a clergyman told Papa, *he* had done, in holding an opinion favorable to Catholic emmancipation. I dont mean to imply — — "equal the fault"! I cant help mine,—nor could I help being very very sorry indeed at going away from Ruby Cottage yesterday. It seems to me likely enough that by force of feeling so much pain of different kinds, my nature will become more capable of feeling it acutely than of feeling pleasure acutely. But perhaps it may seem otherwise to me, when I see you again!— There was a letter today from Papa to Bro who would not read the whole to us,—& the part which he did read, mentioned his return as remaining an uncertainty;—& not a word of business! My love to Mrs Boyd & Annie—& my regards to Miss Mushet. May God bless you my dearest friend! Can I ever cease to be

Your affectionate E B Barrett.

Mr Curzon has not come yet. I dont think I ever told you Mr Martin's high compliment to the Commelines— But I cant now—for Bro is waiting!—

Diary by E.B.B.

XIX: E.B.B. TO H.S.B., [27 JANUARY 1832][1]

Previous Publication: *EBB/HSB*, pp. 156-157 (in part).
Manuscript Location: Wellesley.

Friday night.

My dearest friend,

I have been reading thro' your oration again,—and something has come into my head about that *chronicon* business which puzzled me so much the other day.   You know Gregory says that what we call *time*, is eternity with the invisibles, eternity co-extensive with their existences. Now do look at the passage & see whether the whole mystery does not lie in that word *sumparekteinomenon*,—& whether the next clause of the sentence is not a mere illustration of the meaning contained in it.   Is not the word to be translated *"extended in a parallel manner"*?   And then comes the illustration—"as it were, according to some temporal movement, or parallelism": that is, Eternity is extended in a parallel manner with the angelic or invisible existences, just as in our present state of being, one thing can be moved & extended in a parallel line with another.   *Diasteema* seems to involve the idea of parallelism,—and the general idea seems to me tolerably obvious.   Yet it may be *"but* seeming," like many things of more consequence to me,—and in that case you will set me right some time before I have lived all the days of man,—& I will kiss the rod as in allegiance bound to do.   Mind! not your walking club!

M.r Curzon very kindly walked here yesterday at three o'clock, & back again in the dark at ten.   He told me to tell you that his long absence had much increased his business & engagements here,—otherwise he would have gone to see you immediately.   He intends to do so as soon as time will let him.   I wish you could have heard him talk about Miss Gibbons whom he "admires more than ever", & acquits of even *believing* in the tongues.

Now I am going to tell you M.r Martin's compliment to the Commelines, —but first of all, I must tell you something about *them*.   Some of them are very amusing sensible sharp-minded people,—and as they dont spare their pricks in making remarks on their neighbours, they are considered not altogether as good-natured as they might be.   A short time ago, at a very large & formal dinner-party at Eastnor castle, M.r Martin said, "I cant help liking those Commelines, tho' I know I shall be damned for it".   The compliment was of course repeated to Miss Commeline who told Bro that

---

1. The Diary entry of 27 January makes it possible to supply this dating.

her family considered it the very highest they could under any circumstances receive.

Well!—I suppose I must not waste your time any more—or I "shall be d——d for it." If you had M.ʳ Martin's good habit, I am sure I should!—

Yours affectionately
E B Barrett.

XX: **E.B.B. TO H.S.B., [18 FEBRUARY 1832]**[1]

     Previous Publication: *EBB/HSB*, pp. 158-159.
     Manuscript Location: Wellesley.

My dear M.ʳ Boyd,

I am going to ask only one question. While I was with you this morning, Papa was taking a great fancy to my translation,—& this evening he wishes me to write to M.ʳ Barker to enquire from him whether his friend M.ʳ Valpy will publish it in a future number of the *Classical library*,—where, consistently with the plan of the work, a translation of Æschylus will of course appear. I want to know what you think about it. I do not ask *you* to write to me; but M.ʳˢ Boyd or Annie might be so kind as to write down some short message from you.

I forgot to tell you one thing today. Papa, who knows M.ʳ Nisbet & the character of his publications, thinks that he wont do for your publisher.

Yours affec.ᵗᵉˡʸ
E B Barrett.

Hope End
Saturday night.
Of course I will not write until I hear your advice.

XXI: **E.B.B. TO H.S.B., [12 MARCH 1832]**[2]

     Previous Publication: *EBB/HSB*, p. 165.
     Manuscript Location: Wellesley.

My dear M.ʳ Boyd,

I need not tell you how much I have wished & wish to go to you today, & to do everything you require. I told Papa last night of my wish & yours, & begged him & argued with him as long as I had any chance of being

1. The Diary entry of 18 February makes it possible to supply this dating.
2. The Diary entry of 12 March makes it possible to supply this dating.

heard. It was all in vain! He said—I will tell you exactly, that you may not be *more* angry than you are sure to be at any rate,—that he would willingly oblige you, but that he could not be a party to anything likely to fatigue me in any way just now—that I was turning into a shadow, thinner & thinner every day, & that he knew perfectly well what would be the end of it—meaning, I suppose, the end of *me*. I assured him of the fact of my doing much less with you than by myself,—& of there being no mental exertion necessary on my part to write what you dictated. But he was sure of my being fatigued, in the case of my going to you,—and as to my fatiguing myself at home, I might commit suicide if I pleased, but he would not be party to it, by consenting to your proposal. I am disappointed—far far more disappointed than YOU are,—for I dare say Miss H Mushet's eyes will soon be better,—& then you will have a more agreable & satisfactory secretary, tho' not a more willing & anxious one than I could be. You know how much pleasure it gives me to write to your dictation,—to write even a letter,—besides the pleasure of doing what you wish. Perhaps Papa MAY relent,—but he seems to be in a panic about me all at once, because he thinks or fancies that I am looking thinner & worse than usual. If I am, it is not wonderful,—& certainly not attributable to mental exertion.

Whenever I can go to you, I am ready to write all the time I stay,—if you will let me,—and a good deal can be done you know, in five hours.

Yours affectionately
E B Barrett—

Hope End
Monday.

XXII: E.B.B. TO H.S.B., [24 MARCH 1832][1]

Previous Publication: *EBB/HSB*, pp. 162-163.
Manuscript Location: Wellesley.

Saturday night

If I do not write tonight, I may have no means of sending a letter on Monday, & you may not hear about the preface until you hear *me*—which may be on Tuesday or Wednesday. This is a list of *may bes,* & now I come to the *must bes*. I am very glad to receive your letter, & to understand from it that you forgive Scholefield & me for our impertinence in reminding you of your birthday. If you had been a woman, we would not have

---

1. The reference to the gift of Scholefield's *Æschylus* on H.S.B.'s birthday makes it possible to supply this dating.

[302]

done such a thing for the world,—but you know you are not as bad as *that!!*—and indeed notwithstanding your dislike to birthdays, you must excuse my saying that I hope you will see a great many of them.

I have gone thro' Wolf's prefaces with your object in view. Another time, instead of beginning at the beginning of any business, I will try how beginning at the end answers: for just at, or just before, the very last page of the very last preface, there is the remark about brackets. He says that in this business of including passages supposed spurious, within brackets, he has followed in every particular the judgment of the ancients,—and has affixed the *atrocem notam* (quite the right expression) to no verse which has not been remarked upon, or entirely rejected by the best Greek critics.

In page 60 there is a little, but nothing that you would consider valuable, about the hiatus; and an acknowledgement of the authority of the digamma—, as "a doctissimis Britannis repertum".

If I were you, I would not mind this general reference to the judgment of the ancients, by Wolf. Aristarchus was an ancient. The system of mutilating Homer, whether it was introduced by ancients or moderns, is quite monstrous,—and cries out, like a naughty child, for a little of your flogging. When Coriolanus said that he "would rather be a dog & bay the moon," he did not mean Homer's moon.

I will take the extracts to you, & you may read them whenever you like,—but I must say over again that *I* should like you not to do it, until you have quite done with every line of your own work.

Ever yours affectionately
E B Barrett.

When I had Payne Knight here, I took the trouble of counting the number of lines he has thought proper to leave out of *his* Homer. If I made no mistake, about 2500 lines are left out of his Iliad, and 1926, out of his Odyssey. Is not this *atrox*?

XXIII: E.B.B. TO H.S.B., [29 MARCH 1832]¹

       Previous Publication: None.
       Manuscript Location: Wellesley.

Nonnus appears to have few instances of hiatus. I have observed— αυτοθι εμπεδα—ὁ εν—χαρμα οπως—γλυκυ ὑμετερον—

1. Although this letter was not dated by E.B.B., it seems to match the entry of 29 March 1832, particularly as she mentioned on 21 March that H.S.B. had lent her his copy of Nonnus for the purpose of finding examples of hiatus; we therefore conjecturally give it the former date.

Diary by E.B.B.

In the Iliad, δε ανηρ!! δε ἑ—μεγα ιαχουσα απο ἑο—Ουλυμποιο απο —τα ἀ—φοιτα ανα—δε ἑκας—τε ενθα—ενθα ἁλις—συ εσσι—τι ετι —φωτα εκαστον—μηδε εα—δε ιδων—τε ετας—μετα εθνος—ενι οικω —δωκα εκων—διακρι[ν]θεντε ὁ—ανδρι ικελη—εγχεϊ οξυοεντι—αορι ιφι—ουλε ονειρε—ηϋτε εθνεα—τα εκηλοι—αξετο ιετο—προτι αστυ— διαμονι ισος—Ζεφυροιο εχευατο—αποθυμια ερδοι—σειετο ὑλη—ωκυ ετωσιον—μαλιστα Αλεξανδρω—ποτνια Ἡρη—ωκεα Ιρις—

I have tried in vain to find εγω in hiatus, and another instance of ανηρ being so.

E B B.

XXIV: E.B.B. TO H.S.B., [?31 MARCH 1832]¹

Previous Publication: *EBB/HSB*, pp. 163-164 (in part).
Manuscript Location: Wellesley.

My dear M.ʳ Boyd,

I think it may be better to write directly to yourself, on the subject you enquire about.

In Theocritus—καλα εργα—ὁσσα ισατι—χαιρε Αδωὶ αγαπατε —Idyll:15.   κατατριψοντι, ακρεσπερον—Idyll:24.   in Hesiod— κλυθι ιδων—εις ωπα εϊσκειν—Κρονιωνι ανακτι—Works & days. ὑιε αναξ—ἀμα εργον—ανεφαινετο εργον—ἠμερα ασσον—ωκεα Ιρις— Theogony.

I have not any complete edition of either Hesiod or Theocritus; and would not write to you by today's post, that I might have time to borrow them. M.ʳ Deane however, to whom I sent, is without either. Dalzel gives very copious extracts,—& these I have examined,—but I cannot find in them, ανηρ in the right position.   I will try to procure the books some-where else,—and if I succeed, you shall hear again from me.

Yours affec^{tely}
EBB

Saturday evening
Hope End.

---

1. The reference in the entry of 31 March to sending to Mr. Dean's to borrow books, and the indication the previous Thursday that E.B.B. was gathering examples of the use of the hiatus, make it possible to conjecture that this letter was written on 31 March.

XXV: E.B.B. TO H.S.B., [7 APRIL 1832]¹

Previous Publication: *EBB/HSB*, pp. 159-160.
Manuscript Location: Wellesley.

Saturday night.

I like your blank verse translation very much indeed,—but after all, I am quite obstinate in thinking that what is lyrical in Greek should be lyrical in English—& that in losing the sudden transition from one measure to another, you lose a great deal of what is animated expressive & beautiful. That is my creed,—& one not founded, I do assure you, upon any prejudice in favour of my own translation which I have sent to the tomb of the Capulets, & without a *resurgam* by way of epitaph.

I was pleased to receive your letter,—as, you know, I am apt to be on such occasions. What made you expect to hear from me this week?— Your letter is dated Thursday, & I was with you on Tuesday,—and you did not ask me to write immediately. The other thing which you did ask me to do, I have done. I leave Arabel to speak for herself. Both you & I appear to *me* to have acted wrong, or at least with what the Westminster Review elegantly terms, *unwisdom*. When *you* mean to repent I dont know,—but *I* began to do so last Tuesday.

Yes! I liked the article in the Times which you like,—at least if you like the one in which poor Lord Grey is looked upon with a prophetic eye as an "archangel ruined". Papa thought is was extravagant,—but I thought nothing of the kind. After all the bill will pass—

Whigs or no Whigs, their votes will turn to Grey—

See if it will not be so. If it will not, I would as soon be in the cholera hospital as in Downing street. The king will make new peers, or the people will unmake old ones: and either way, our end will be answered.

I am in hopes that our affairs must come to a crisis before very long. My aunt's going away to Kinnersley in such a very sudden manner, without giving herself time even to write & tell them of her intention,—& her deciding upon returning in four days, prove to me that something is impending. She said to me with tears in her eyes, that nothing should induce her to remain a day longer away from us,—& that if I would consent to go with her, she would remain away only two days. But *that*, I could not & would not do. I dread one thing—the probability of Papa going to London again—& when the cholera is there. And yet there may be no cause for this dread. If he goes, it may not be to London,—& he may not go alone. My aunt left us, out of spirits & unwilling to leave us, even

---

1. The reference to her aunt's visit to Kinnersley makes it possible to supply this dating.

for so short a time.   She had *intended* to spend some *weeks* with her brother,—& there certainly must be a reason for this sudden movement of hers.

The poney's feet are not very well, & I have been warned not to make any use of him for a week,—which week will not be at an end until Wednesday.   The Miss Mushets will be disappointed in hearing Mr Curzon tomorrow,—but Mr Preace is to be the substitute, & is reported "a good preacher".   I did not receive your letter until today—!

Ever yours affectionately
E B Barrett.

XXVI: E.B.B. TO H.S.B., [16 APRIL 1832]¹

Previous Publication: *EBB/HSB*, pp. 160-161.
Manuscript Location: Wellesley.

I believe I ought to have written to you before to thank you for lending Synesius to me,—but I thought I should have seen you long before now, & did not think that you would expect to hear from me.   The rain prevented Mrs Cliffe from taking me with her to Malvern this morning. Tomorrow she is engaged at home,—but on Wednesday she has promised to call for me.   In the meantime I will write.

I have gone thro' the whole of Synesius,—and notwithstanding his occasional diffuseness & self-repetition,—which seem to be haunting faults among writers of the first centuries;—he does *make you feel* that he is a poet.   Your Gregory is not as despotic: *he* will *let* you *think* so of him,— but he does not *make* you *feel* it.   Synesius is certainly a better poet & Platonist than a christian,—& deserves the warning prologue of Franciscus Portus.   But I cant write any more about him or anybody else.   Only, for fear of forgetting to mention it to you when I see you again, I will observe here, that the finest part of the 9th hymn is a mere paraphrase of the fine passage in Gregory's oration on the nativity, which relates to the gifts of the magi.   You will recollect what I mean,—& Synesius's verses form so beautiful & striking an illustration of it, that I think you should, either in your preface or in a note, refer to them.

I was planning to send a messenger over to you with the reform news, if I had not seen Miss Henrietta Mushet,—and it appeared from her account that you knew it before I did.   They will be obliged to make peers after all.

1. The Diary entry of 16 April makes it possible to supply this dating.

I hear nothing which I can tell you—& feel nothing pleasant which I can tell you—therefore it is surely better that I should come to an end.

Ever yours affectionately
E B Barrett.

Hope End.
Monday.

XXVII: E.B.B. TO H.S.B., [19 APRIL 1832][1]

Previous Publication: *EBB/HSB*, pp. 161-162.
Manuscript Location: Wellesley.

Hope End.   Thursday.

My dearest friend,

After all we have found it impossible to do as we intended & wished, about going to Malvern today or tomorrow.   The Wyche is a steep fatiguing road, & the poney is considered not quite well enough to attempt it. Therefore it must be given up—& we must send our kind love to Annie & our kind remembrances to the Miss Mushets—instead of ourselves.   I hope & think that dear Annie will have a pleasant visit—but not *too* pleasant.

These are the lines from Anacreon,

Makarizomen se tettix,

Hote dendreoon ep' akroon

Oligeen droson pepookoos,

Basileus hopoos, aeideis—

and there is a lightness & delicacy in them, which Synesius does not preserve in his copy.   When I was turning over Anacreon's leaves, I came to that pretty ingenious ode, beginning

Ee Tantalou pot' estee.

Did I ever observe to you, or did you ever observe to me, that it is a dilation of Romeo's idea, "Would that I were a glove upon that hand,"?

I have looked over the first Pythian again.   The finest passage in it, is LONGER than Synesius's ninth hymn.

I gave your message to Arabel almost immediately,—& of course she thinks you more "impudent" than ever.

Ever yours affectionately
E B Barrett.

It seems to me that I have said nothing to you today—   My love to Mrs Boyd.

---

1. The Diary entry of 19 April makes it possible to supply this dating.

Diary by E.B.B.

XXVIII: E.B.B. TO H.S.B., [25 APRIL 1832][1]

Previous Publication: *EBB/HSB*, pp. 164-165.
Manuscript Location: Wellesley.

Hope End.
Wednesday—

I enclose a note directed to you.   It was in the parcel containing Dr Clarke's commentary,—and as you never opened the parcel last year, you did not, of course, find the note.   I forgot to give it to you until now—a forgetfulness you will readily forgive, as by this time it is likely to contain as little news as this letter of mine.

Do not be angry with me.   I have not asked Papa.   I have thought about it, & spoken about it, & Henrietta & Arabel think with me that it would be quite a vain attempt.   Suppose Papa were to be displeased at my teazing him so much on the same subject.   In that case, it might be *worse* than vain.   He was not pleased on Monday at my having left home on such a day, & told me that I would certainly kill myself—& *then* I might be satisfied.   That was not a good time to ask the question—was it?—and indeed there seems to be little chance of a good time coming. I would not mind running the risk of being scolded,—but the risk of being prevented from passing some hours with you very soon again, I do not like to run.   The poney's feet are a great deal better,—and I hope you will make up your mind about the additional Greek lines, that we may begin as soon as ever I get into your room—when the air of your head is most rarified.   I shall like to be able to say, "Mr Boyd can repeat eight thousand Greek lines"!!—

There is another thing which I should like to be able to say—how much your seeming to wish me to spend two or three days at Ruby Cottage, gratified me—   It gave me as much pleasure as any thing could give me NOW,—or is likely to give me,—& for this I ought to thank you, & do thank you.   May God bless you.   It is not injurious to everybody, *to be happy*!   To *me*, it must be so,—or my spirits would not have been permitted to be so broken down & rooted up on every side.

Your ever affectionate friend
E B Barrett

My love to Mrs Boyd.

---

1.   The Diary entry of 23 April makes it possible to supply this dating.

APPENDIX II

POEMS

I

KINGS[1]

One stood on England's sea-girt plain:
　　One who was strange before—
And the clanking of a nation's chain
　　Proclaimed him conqueror!
In Freedom's heart was the Norman's sting—
　　And *he*—he was a king.

One stood on England's plain, contending
　　With a priest for England's throne;
And when the rebel perished, bending
　　In false wail o'er the stone,
These, baser clay than death's, did fling—
　　And *he*—he was a king.

One stood on England's plain, whose crown
　　Hid not the stain of strife—
The sceptre which he trusted on
　　Was an assassin's knife;
His people's homage, shuddering;
　　And *he*—he was a king.

One stood on England's plain—the sound
　　Of battle o'er him swept.
Was the battle-shout the sweetest found,
　　When his people loudest wept?
Did his victor hands their withers wring?
　　Yet *he*—he was a king.

One stood on England's plain, with thirst
　　Of gold upon his soul.
Blood—tears, from English eyes that burst,
　　Did, his Pactolus, roll;
Vilely he stooped to quaff that spring—
　　And *he*—he was a king.

---

1. Reprinted from *The Times*, 31 May 1831, p. 2. The poem was subsequently republished (with the omission of v. 3, and with minor textual deviations) in an article by Barbara P. McCarthy in *Notes & Queries*, 15 September 1951, CXCVI, 410. A manuscript version, corresponding to *The Times* text, but with minor differences of punctuation and capitalization, is at Huntington.

Diary by E.B.B.

One stood on England's plain—a book
    In his scholastic hand.
How could he turn therefrom to look
    Upon a mourning land?
Yet heard he Spain one mandate bring;
    And *that*—he was a *king*.

One stands on England's sea-girt plain—
    The pomp of courts forsaking—
And if before him clanks the chain,
    It is alone in breaking;
Its links to captive hearts shall cling—
    And *he*—he is a king.

Blest land! when "Live the Monarch" goes
    Forth, as the patriot's cry—
Blest king! when "Live the people" shows
    That people's loyalty.
Others may wear a jewelled thing—
    But HE—he is a KING.

May 28.   E.B.B.

II

SONG[1]

Is't loving to list to the night guitar,
    And praise the serenading;
Yet think of naught, when the minstrel's far,
    But of beauty & of braiding?
Is't loving to bask 'neath tender eyes,
    'Neath others on their removing,
And join new vows to old perjuries?
    Ah no! this is not loving!

Unless you can think, when the song is done,—
    No other's worth the pondering!
Unless you can feel, when the minstrel's gone—
    Mine heart with him is wandering!
Unless you can dream that his faith is fast
    Thro' months & years of roving—
Unless you can DIE when the dream is past—
    Ah no! this is not loving!

1. Text taken from an undated manuscript in E.B.B.'s autograph, now in the Berg Collection, that was found in the same trunk as the Diary. A copy of this version (with minor differences of punctuation), in an unidentified hand, is in the British Museum, and was used by Wise in *A Bibliography of the Writings of Elizabeth Barrett Browning* (London, 1918), p. 140. Another copy, in Henrietta's hand, dated 28 April 1838 (having minor deviations from the Berg ms.) is at Huntington. The poem was altered and expanded to five verses, and printed in *Blackwood's Edinburgh Magazine*, October 1846, pp. 488-489, under the title "A Woman's Shortcomings," and was later included in *Poems* (London, 1850), II, 398-399. This version retained only two of the four lines quoted by E.B.B. in the entry of 4 August 1831.

    Yale has two manuscripts of the poem, in E.B.B.'s autograph: one is a two-verse text, and the other a heavily-altered five-verse version; both differ considerably from the published texts.

Diary by E.B.B.

III

TO E.W.C. PAINTING MY PICTURE[1]

Ah Painter! wherefore wouldst thou trace
With cunning hand my form & face?
Albeit the canvass wierdly taught,
Assume the looks thine own have caught—
The lips that breathe thy name—the brow
Hope-lighted in thy presence now—
Albeit each line & hue agree—
It will not long resemble me—

For when mine eyes have wept away
In human tears their latest ray—
And when my lips are mute & faded—
And when my brows are cold & shaded—
These pictured brows, & lips & eyes
Will keep their gaudy mockeries!—
Ah painter! thou wilt sighing see,
They cannot long resemble me—

Too soon, all human as thou art,
Some natural woe may touch thine heart!
The first words of the changed may grieve thee—
The last words of the true, bereave thee!—
Then, when thy weeping eyes behold
Her picture, not unloved of old:—
How calm & bright it yet will be!—
Think not 'twill then resemble me!—

No! not on canvass gentle friend,
With artful hues, mine image blend
But on thy heart, to pencil try,
What moves my lip, & lights mine eye!
And when an image thou hast made,
Of love & truth that cannot fade,
Tho' woe & death before us be,
Ah! *that* will aye resemble me!—

1. Text taken from a manuscript in the hand of Henrietta, dated 28 April 1838, now at Huntington. This was the source of the version published in *HUP* (II, 179-180), but minor differences of spelling and punctuation exist between the two texts.

IV

THE WEAKEST THING[1]

Weaker I am, woe's me!—
                    DONNE.

WHICH is the weakest thing of all
        Mine heart can ponder?
The sun, a little cloud can pall
        With darkness yonder?
The cloud, a little wind can move
        Where'er it listeth?
The wind, a leaf which hangs above,
        Though sere, resisteth?

What time that yellow leaf was green,
        My days were gladder—
Now on its branch each summer-sheen
        May find me sadder!
Ah me! a *leaf* with sighs can wring
        My lips asunder—
Then is mine heart the weakest thing
        Itself can ponder!

Yet, Heart, when sun and cloud are pined,
        And drop together;
And at a blast which is not wind,
        The forests wither;
Thou, from the darkening deathly curse,
        To glory breakest—
The Strongest of the universe
        Guarding the weakest!

1. Reprinted from *The Seraphim and Other Poems* (London, 1838), pp. 354-355. We have not traced any manuscript version of this poem.

V

CATERINA TO CAMOENS[1]

Rose o' the cheek it drops away
Smile o' the lips it flowers no more . .
Were you near me, would you say
'Love, I love you' as before?
    When death lies
    On the eyes
Which you called once I ween
'Sweetest eyes, were ever seen'.

When I heard you hymn them so
In my courtly days & bowers,
Others' praise I let it go,
Only hearing that of yours
    Only saying
    In heart-playing
'Eyes the happiest mine have been
Since the sweetest His have seen'.

Now you wander far, oh farther,
Little guessing of my pain!
Now you see me smiling rather
In your reverie again,
    Ay and oft
    Murmur soft
To yourself with lips serene—
"Sweetest eyes, were ever seen".

1. Text taken from a hitherto unpublished manuscript in PML, believed to be the earliest version of this poem. After extensive revision and expansion, the poem was printed in *Graham's Magazine*, October 1843, pp. 208-209, and with further changes was included in the 1844 edition of *Poems*, II, 229-236. A fourth version, in the hand of Henrietta and dated 28 April 1838, is at Huntington; this text was published (with minor deviations) in *The Poets' Enchiridion* (Boston, 1914), pp. 47-49.

And I think were you beside
The low bed I die upon,
Tho' you missed their light & pride
As you stood there looking down
      But would still
      Say at will
For the love's sake found therein,
[']Sweetest eyes, were ever seen.'

Nay! if you looked down upon them
And if they looked up to you
All the light which had forgone them
Would be gathered back anew—
      They would be
      Verily
Love-transformed to beauty's sheen
Sweetest eyes were ever seen.

Will you come? When I am gone
Where all sweetnesses are hid—
Where thy voice beside the stone
Will not lift up either lid
      Cry & call
      At the low wall
'Farewell Love'—& with Catrine
Sweetest eyes, were ever seen.

Will you come? Yes!—come & keep
This the poor band which bound my hair,
Clasp it—feeling if you weep
Not alone in y^r despair
      You, with saintly
      Watch unfaintly
Out of Heaven shall overlean
Sweetest eyes were ever seen.

But . . but now . . they are not yet
Up in Heaven, & glisten fast!
Ah beloved! you may forget
In the future all the past—
     That old phrase
     May be praise
For another bosom-queen
Sweetest eyed of ladies seen.

Eyes of mine! what do ye here?
Faithless, faithless! praised amiss!
Close in death before that tear
Fall for any hope of His!—
     Sunshine gild you
     Angels shield you
Whatsoever eyes terrene
Shall be sweetest His have seen!

VI

THE PESTILENCE[1]

Nec requies erat ulla mali.—LUCRETIUS.

The Pestilence is breathing
    The Gangean stream beside;
The yellow sunshine wreathing
    With death mists o'er its tide.

"Thou canst not live among us,
    "Oh plague of icy breath,—
"Our torrid sun hath flung us
    "Shields from the cold blue death."

They are shiv'ring—they are shiv'ring—
    Beneath their torrid sun—
Their lips are blue and quiv'ring,
    Their life is chilled and done.

The Pestilence is riding
    On Russia's icy wold;
The snow-plumed blast bestriding,
    With more unearthly cold.

"Thou canst not live among us,
    "Plague of the fierce sunshine!
"Our native snows have strung us
    "To fear no cold of thine."

They are lying—they are lying—
    On the snows they used to tread—
Their strength is sunk and dying—
    Their hearts are still and dead.

The Pestilence is nearing
    To England's merry shore:
A million ghosts appearing,
    Beckon a thousand more.

1. Reprinted from *The Times*, 13 January 1832. A manuscript copy of *The Times* text has not been traced. A version in the hand of Henrietta, dated 28 April 1838, is at Huntington, and this was the basis of the text published in *HUP*, II, 176-178. Another copy, in E.B.B.'s autograph, but not dated, is in the Berg Collection. These two manuscripts vary in minor detail, both from each other, and from the two published versions.

Diary by E.B.B.

"Thou canst not live among us,
    "Plague of the sun and snow!
"Our healthful gales have sung us
    "A charm from deathly woe."

They are wailing—they are wailing—
    Where healthful gales had sung—
There, iron hearts are failing—
    There, fun'ral shrouds are flung.

Alas! in healthful breezes,
    My brothers, hope not ye!
Nor yet in spots where ceases
    The hum of men to be—

Nor yet in hills where sweepeth
    The fresh and pleasant sward—
Nor yet in hearths where keepeth
    Vain Love his frantic guard.

Hope ye in God! and viewing
    The Serpent's brass displayed—
Believing, mourning, suing,
    His "plague" may yet be "stayed."

E.B.B.

APPENDIX III

HOPE END SALE CATALOGUE

HOPE END SALE CATALOGUE

The following Catalogue, with its detailed map, is the most precise description of the Hope End Estate known. The copy reproduced here (reduced to 62 per cent of original size) was once owned by the solicitor James Holbrook, of Ledbury, who acted as local agent for the mortgagees. The notes and interleavings are either his or those of his office staff. It is now in the possession of Stephen Ballard, Esq., by whose permission it is reprinted.

A protective wrapper with the Catalogue (not reproduced here) provides confirmation that Edward Moulton-Barrett himself finally left Hope End on 22 September 1832.

The estate was offered for sale by auction on 25 August 1831, as stated in the Catalogue, but was withdrawn when bidding fell short of the reserve price. The sale was eventually concluded by private treaty, and it has always been assumed that Edward Moulton-Barrett then sold the entire estate. It is, therefore, of interest to record that he did not do so; a list of his personal property made after his death in 1857, by his son George, proves that he had retained ownership of a considerable acreage of the estate, principally of woodland.

HEREFORDSHIRE,
ON THE BORDERS OF WORCESTERSHIRE.

IMPORTANT FREEHOLD & COPYHOLD ESTATE,
A desirable Property for Residence and Investment,

CAPITAL MANSION, WITH OFFICES,
Pleasure Grounds, extensive Garden and Grapery, Farm Buildings, upon a superior principle,
AND UPWARDS OF

FOUR HUNDRED AND SEVENTY-TWO ACRES
OF EXCELLENT MEADOW, PASTURE, ARABLE, & WOOD LAND, & HOP GARDEN.

Particulars and Conditions of Sale,
OF THE VERY IMPORTANT

FREEHOLD ESTATE,
With a small Part Copyhold,
CALLED

HOPE END,
SITUATE

In the Parishes of LEDBURY, COLWALL, and CODDINGTON, in the COUNTY OF HEREFORD,
On the Borders of Worcestershire,

About Two Miles from LEDBURY, commanding the Romantic Scenery of the MALVERN and ADJACENT HILLS, with Views from various parts of the Property, highly interesting, and of great extent.

THE HOPE END MANSION
IS ADAPTED FOR THE ACCOMMODATION OF

A NOBLEMAN, OR FAMILY OF THE FIRST DISTINCTION,
Is Pleasantly seated in its own Grounds, having an extensive Lawn in front,
WITH A FINE SHEET OF WATER, FED BY SPRINGS, CASCADE, &c.
And well Stocked with Fish,
AND IS APPROACHED BY AN EXTENSIVE CARRIAGE DRIVE, LEADING THROUGH THE GROUNDS, WHICH ARE LAID OUT IN A PARK-LIKE STYLE, AND WITH ACKNOWLEDGED TASTE.

The Residence is Erected in the Eastern Style of Architecture,
AND MAY JUSTLY BE ESTEEMED
A CHEF-D'ŒUVRE, UNRIVALLED IN THIS KINGDOM.
The Domestic Offices
Are well arranged, and amply supplied with excellent Water;
COMPRISING
COMMODIOUS STABLING & COACH HOUSES, and various other OUT-OFFICES;
THE BEAUTIFUL PLEASURE GROUNDS,
Intersected by extensive Gravelled Walks, include a SHRUBBERY, ornamented with magnificent Timber Trees, thriving Evergreens, Parterres of Flowers, &c.
AN ALCOVE; PRODUCTIVE WALLED GARDEN, CLOTHED WITH CHOICE FRUIT TREES,
And containing a GRAPERY, &c.
ATTACHED TO THE PROPERTY THERE IS
A WELL-CONSTRUCTED FARM YARD,
With BAILIFF'S HOUSE, and substantial AGRICULTURAL BUILDINGS, planned in a superior style,
AND THE WHOLE ESTATE COMPRISING
SUNDRY COTTAGES, WITH GARDENS,
CONTAINS UPWARDS OF
FOUR HUNDRED AND SEVENTY-TWO ACRES
OF
Excellent Grass and Meadow, Arable, and Wood Land, Hop Garden, and Plantation,
In a fine thriving State, the Soil of a very excellent Quality, producing fine Grain, Hay, &c.
AND FORMS A MOST ELIGIBLE PROPERTY FOR RESIDENCE AND INVESTMENT,
In an excellent Neighbourhood, the Country abounding with Game, and enjoying the Beauties of the EASTNOR WOODS, with its Fertile Scenery.

HOPE END has been justly considered to vie with EASTNOR CASTLE,
AND MAY BE PRONOUNCED THE CHIEF ORNAMENT OF THE SURROUNDING COUNTRY:

To be Sold by Auction,
By Order of the Mortgagees under a Power of Sale,

BY MR. REID,
Son-in-Law and Successor to the late

MR. JOHN ROBINS,
OF WARWICK HOUSE, REGENT STREET,
AT GARRAWAY'S COFFEE HOUSE, 'CHANGE ALLEY, CORNHILL,
On THURSDAY, 25th of AUGUST, 1831, at Twelve o'Clock.

The Estate is distant from MALVERN about Four Miles, and the Canal from LEDBURY to GLOUCESTER affords every facility for the Conveyance of Produce to that City and the neighbouring Towns; and this will be considerably extended by the intended Continuation of the Canal to HEREFORD. There are Coaches daily to and from the Metropolis.

The Mansion to be viewed by Tickets. Particulars may be had of JAMES HOLBROOK, Esq. Solicitor (who will grant Tickets), and at the Feathers Inn, Ledbury; Swan, Ross; City Hotel, Hereford; the Foley Arms, and Belle Vue, Great Malvern; of Mr. BENTLEY, and at the Star and Hop Pole Inns, Worcester; Plough, Cheltenham; Angel, Oxford; and in London, of Messrs. FRESHFIELD, New Bank Buildings; at GARRAWAY'S; and of Mr. REID, No. 170, Regent Street, where a Plan of the Estate may be seen, and Tickets for viewing may be had.

CONDITIONS OF SALE.

I. THAT the highest Bidder shall be declared the Purchaser; and if any Dispute shall arise between two or more Bidders, the Estate shall be immediately put up again.

II. That no Person advance less than Fifty Pounds at each Bidding.

III. The Purchaser shall pay down immediately, into the Hands of Mr. REID, a Deposit of Fifteen Pounds per Cent. in Part of the Purchase-Money, and sign an Agreement for Payment of the Remainder, and of the Amount of the Valuations mentioned in the Sixth Condition, on or before the 21st of December next; and on Payment thereof he shall have a proper Conveyance of the Freehold, and Surrenders of the Copyhold, Parts of the Estate, such Conveyance and Surrenders to be prepared at his Expense. All Out-goings will be cleared by the Vendors up to the 21st of December next; and from that Day the Purchaser shall be entitled to Possession of the Mansion and such other Parts of the Estate as are in hand, and to the Rents and Profits of the other Parts; and if the Completion of the Purchase shall be delayed after the 21st of December next, from any Cause whatever, the Vendors shall be entitled to Interest on the Amount of the Purchase-Money, and the Valuations, after deducting the Deposit, at the Rate of Four Pounds per Cent. per Annum, from that Day to the Time of completing of the Purchase.

IV. The Vendors will deliver an Abstract of their Title (at their own Expense) within One Month from the Day of Sale; but they shall not be required to produce any Title to the three small Pieces of Land in Roadgate Common Field, Nos. 8, 9, 10, containing together 1A. 0R. 5P.; or No. 45, containing 0A. 8R. 28P. prior to the Year 1791; or, to a small Piece of Land, containing about Three Acres, Part of No. 6, and lying at the extremity thereof, prior to a Conveyance thereof to a late Proprietor of this Estate in 1799; or to No. 16, or any other Lands, which formerly belonged to the Rectory of Colwall, and which were sold under the Provisions of the Acts of Parliament for Redemption of the Land Tax, prior to the Conveyance of the same to the same Gentleman, in the Year 1804; or to the small Piece of Land No. 13, containing 4A. 0R. 26P. prior to the Conveyance thereof in the Year 1809; nor shall any Objection be taken to the Title to the Freehold Interest in a Messuage called the Swallow, and about Four Acres of Land, Part of No. 28, which were formerly Copyhold of the Manor of Ledbury Forren, and which were enfranchised in the Year 1816, by the Commissioner for inclosing Lands within the Parish of Ledbury, under the Authority of the Act of Parliament for inclosing those Lands, on account of one of the Parties whose Consent was required not having executed the Commissioner's Award; nor shall the Vendors be required to procure any other Evidence of such Consent having been obtained. And all Attested and other Copies of Deeds, Wills, and Documents, and Deeds of Covenant for the Production of Deeds and Documents, which the Purchaser may require for the purpose of verifying the Abstract, or otherwise, shall be procured by him at his Expense.

V. As a recent Survey has been made of this Estate, by which the present Descriptions and Quantities of the Land have been ascertained, and various Alterations have taken place on this Estate, by the Removal of Fences and laying various Fields together, the Vendors are not to be required to give further Proof of the Identity, or Quantities of the Parcels, or to procure any other Evidence for identifying the Copyhold Parts of the Estate than such as is afforded by the above Survey, together with the Descriptions in the Documents of Title and the old Maps in their Possession. But if any such further or other Proof or Evidence shall be required by or on behalf of the Purchaser, the same shall be procured by him at his own Expense, and the Completion of the Purchase shall not be delayed on Account thereof.

VI. *The Timber, Timber-like Trees, Tellers, Pollards, Saplings, and other Trees, down to One Shilling per Stick, inclusive; and also the Coppice and Underwood; and all Ploughings, Seedings, Dressings, Half-Dressings, Fallows, and Manure, and all other Things in or upon the Lands, for which, by the Custom of the Country, a Tenant quitting Lands is entitled to be paid, shall be taken at a Valuation by the Purchaser, and paid for at the Time of completing the Purchase, in addition to the Residue of the Purchase-Money, agreed to be paid at this Sale; such Valuation to be made by two indifferent Persons (one to be appointed by the Vendors, and the other by the Purchaser), and in Case they cannot agree in their Valuation, on or before the 1st Day of October next, the same shall be referred to a third Person, to be chosen by the former two before they enter upon such Valuation, and the Decision of such two Persons, or such one Person, as the Case may happen, shall be final.*

VII. The Auction-Duty of Seven Pence in the Pound to be borne in equal Moieties by the Vendors and Purchaser, and the Amount paid at the Time of Sale.

VIII. If any Mistake shall be discovered in the Quantity or Description of the Property, or any Error whatever shall appear in the Particulars of the Estate, or the Tenure or Out-goings thereof, such Mistake or Error shall not annul the Sale; but a Compensation or Equivalent shall be given or taken, as the Case may require, such Compensation or Equivalent to be settled by two Referees, or their Umpire; each Party, within Three Weeks after the Discovery of such Mistake or Error, and Notice thereof given by one to the other, to appoint a Referee, by writing; the two Referees to appoint an Umpire before they proceed to Business; and the Decision of such Referees or Umpire, as the Case may happen, to be final.

Lastly, If the Purchaser shall neglect or refuse to comply with these Conditions, the Deposit-Money shall be actually forfeited to the Vendors, who shall then be at full Liberty to re-sell the Estate, either by Public Auction or Private Contract, the Expenses of which, Interest of Money, and the Deficiency in the Produce of such second Sale, shall immediately after such second Sale be made good by the Defaulter at this present Sale; and in Case of Non-Payment thereof, the whole shall be recoverable by the Vendors as and for liquidated Damages, and it shall not be necessary previously to tender a Conveyance to the Purchaser.

Printed by T. Brettell, Rupert Street, Haymarket, London.

[326]

HEREFORDSHIRE,
On the Borders of Worcestershire.

IMPORTANT

FREEHOLD AND COPYHOLD ESTATE,

CAPITAL FAMILY MANSION,

WITH OFFICES, PLEASURE GROUNDS, GARDEN,

Capital Farm Buildings on a superior Principle,

AND UPWARDS OF

FOUR HUNDRED AND SEVENTY-TWO ACRES

OF

Excellent Meadow, Pasture, Arable, and Wood Land, and Hop Garden.

PARTICULARS.

THE VERY IMPORTANT

FREEHOLD ESTATE,

AND SMALL PART COPYHOLD,

CALLED

HOPE END,

SITUATE IN THE

PARISHES OF LEDBURY, COLWALL, AND CODDINGTON,

IN THE

County of Hereford, on the Borders of Worcestershire,

ABOUT TWO MILES FROM LEDBURY.

THE HOPE END MANSION

IS ADAPTED FOR THE ACCOMMODATION OF

A NOBLEMAN OR FAMILY OF THE FIRST DISTINCTION;

Is pleasantly seated in its own Grounds, with Lawn in Front,

A FINE SHEET OF WATER,

FED BY SPRINGS, CASCADE, &c. AND WELL STORED WITH FISH,

ERECTED IN THE EASTERN STYLE OF ARCHITECTURE,

AND MAY JUSTLY BE CONSIDERED

A CHEF-D'ŒUVRE, UNRIVALLED IN THIS KINGDOM;

AN EXTENSIVE CARRIAGE DRIVE

LEADS THROUGH THE GROUNDS, WHICH ARE LAID OUT IN A PARK-LIKE STYLE,

TO

AN ENCLOSED PORTICO, WITH VAULTED ROOF,

FOLDING DOORS, FILLED WITH STAINED GLASS;

A NOBLE VESTIBULE SUPPORTED BY COLUMNS,

A CAPITAL DINING PARLOUR,

Walls hung with Crimson Flock Paper, and bordered, handsome Cornice, Verd Antique Chimney-Piece with Columns;

An Excellent Library,

WALLS STUCCOED AND PAINTED; FRENCH WINDOW, WITH PAINTED HEAD;

A MORNING ROOM, WITH BOWED END,

Walls handsomely Papered and Bordered, neat Cornice, Fire-Place under Window, with Marble Chimney-Piece;

GOTHIC WINDOWS LOOKING TO THE LAWN AND WATER,

Large Folding Doors, painted Amboyna and Satin Wood, communicating with

A SALOON,

FRENCH GLAZED DOORS, OPENING TO THE LAWN, AND FOLDING DOORS

TO

A MAGNIFICENT DRAWING ROOM,

About 36 Feet by 21 Feet, with Circular End,

Walls handsomely papered, elegant Cornice, Doors and Windows painted white, and finished with gilt Mouldings, beautiful marble Chimney-piece, richly ornamented with Or-molu.

The above Three Rooms form a splendid Suite of spacious lofty Apartments, with a Grand Scenery in Front.

PASSAGE AND WATER CLOSET.

A NOBLE PRINCIPAL STONE STAIRCASE,

LIGHTED BY A DOME,

With centre Stair and Landing, branching right and left, Brass Balustre and Mahogany Hand-rail, Walls Stuccoed and Painted, leading to

A GALLERY,

A BILLIARD ROOM, WITH VAULTED CEILING,

Walls ornamented with Turkish Views;

CLOSET,

A CAPITAL PRINCIPAL BED CHAMBER, CLOSET, AND DRESSING ROOM ADJOINING,

Neat Cornice, Marble Chimneypiece, Doors ornamented in the Chinese style;

Over the Portico,

A Capital Bed Chamber,

Vaulted Ceiling, Walls Painted, Marble Chimney-piece, Gothic Windows filled with Stained Glass, commanding a View of

EASTNOR CASTLE,

A BOUDOIR AND DRESSING ROOM ADJOINING,

A BED CHAMBER,

With Bowed End, over the Drawing Room,

Walls papered and bordered, Black Marble Chimney-piece, French Sashes, opening to Balconies, Closet, &c.;

A BED CHAMBER ADJOINING,

With Oval Sash, Walls papered, Marble Chimney-piece.

THE DOORS ON THIS FLOOR ARE ALL OF THE FINEST MAHOGANY.

A WATER CLOSET,

A PRINCIPAL AND SECONDARY BED CHAMBER,

With Bowed End, Windows looking to the Lawn and Water;

NURSERY, SITTING ROOM, TWO SLEEPING ROOMS, WATER CLOSET, AND HOUSEMAID'S CLOSET, SLEEPING ROOM, BATH ROOM, AND ROOM FOR SHOWER BATH;

A SECONDARY STAIRCASE,

Communicating with the Landing on the Principal Floor,

TO

A BOUDOIR, TWO STORE CLOSETS, TWO BED ROOMS, AND DRESSING ROOM;

TWO BED ROOMS ADJOINING

LARGE GALLERY;

SCHOOL ROOM, commanding a View of EASTNOR; TWO ROOMS for Maid Servants.

THE DOMESTIC OFFICES

COMPRISE

BUTLER'S PANTRY, with Dresser, Sink, and Water Laid on ; PLATE CLOSET ; HOUSEMAID'S CLOSET ;

HOUSEKEEPER'S ROOM ; STORE CLOSET ; TWO STORE ROOMS ; SERVANTS' HALL ;

Two Rooms for Men Servants, Floors Tarrassed ;

A CAPITAL KITCHEN, fitted up with Dresser and Shelves, Scullery, Larder, and Meat Larder.

Detached,

DAIRY, Fitted with Poole Tiles and Marble Dressers ; SCULLERY ; COOL LARDER ; BAKEHOUSE ;
A Servants' WATER CLOSET ;

The upper Part of the House well supplied with Water ;

SERVANTS' ENTRANCE ; PAVED YARD, ENCLOSED BY IRON RAILING ;

EXCELLENT DRY CELLARING IN THE BASEMENT, FOR WINE, ALE, BEER, &c.

A COURT YARD,

Enclosed by Gates, with an Archway, and Turret for Clock ;

TWO FOUR-STALL STABLES,

Harness Room, and Lofts over ;

TWO COACH HOUSES, with MEN'S ROOMS over ;

WASH HOUSE ; BREW HOUSE ; LAUNDRY ; AND CELLARS ;

Outer Yard ;

CIDER HOUSE ; SHED ; TWO LOOSE BOXES ; CINDER SHED ; KNIFE AND SHOE HOLE, &c.

A SUBTERRANEOUS PASSAGE

Leads from the Mansion to Extensive Gravelled Walks through a Shrubbery, Ornamented with Magnificent
Timber Trees, thriving Evergreens, and Parterres of Flowers ;

AN ALCOVE,

Fitted with Poole Tiles, Paved ; KITCHEN adjoining ;

A CAPITAL PRODUCTIVE WALLED GARDEN,

Clothed with choice Fruit Trees, fully Stocked and Cropped ;

AN ERECTION AT THE BACK, WITH FLUES FOR HEATING THE GRAPERY, AND SMALL GREEN HOUSE ;

Gardener's Tool House ; Well of Water ; and an Outer Garden ;

AT A CONVENIENT DISTANCE

A WELL-CONSTRUCTED FARM YARD ;

BAILIFF'S HOUSE ; OAST HOUSE, WITH KILNS ; HOP ROOM, AND BAGGING ROOM ;

Store Room, &c. ; underneath are Lodges, Piggeries, &c. ;

A BARN ; STABLES ; RANGE OF CART LODGES ; AND STRAW SHEDS, WITH LOFTS OVER ;

CATTLE SHEDS, WITH FATTING STALLS ;

All very substantially Built upon a superior Principle ;

B

AND SUNDRY ENCLOSURES OF EXCELLENT

Grass and Meadow, Arable and Wood Land, Hop Ground, and Plantation,

IN A FINE THRIVING STATE,

CONTAINING

A.	R.	P.

468 : 3 : 26,

(IN HAND,)

VIZ.

Woods & Plantations not available as yearly A R P Take

	Reference to Plan.			A.	R.	P.	Meadow & pasture arable A. R. P.			Arable available A. R. P.		
8 3 20	No. 1.	The Mansion House, Offices, Lawn, and Plantation		8	3	20						
6 3 4	2.	Kitchen Garden, and Plantation		6	3	4						
1 1 9	3.	The Home Park	pasture	60	0	20	60	0	20			
	4.	The Grove	plantation	1	1	9						
8 0 2	5.	Dumbleton Plantation	wood	8	0	2						
	6.	The South Park	pasture	90	3	13	90	3	13			
2 1 0	6a.	Lanterns Wood	wood	2	1	0						
12 1 2	7.	Hope End Plantation	ditto	12	1	2						
	8.	Roadgate Common Field	arable	0	1	12				0	1	12
	9.	Ditto	ditto	0	1	11				0	1	11
	10.	Ditto	ditto	0	1	22				0	1	22
	11.	The Birches	pasture	5	3	13	5	3	13			
	12.	Great Roadgate Field	ditto	7	2	24	7	2	24			
	13.	Gay Piece	ditto	4	0	26	4	0	26			
	14.	Laffinger Field	ditto	6	1	25	6	1	25			
	16.	Colwall Glebe Land	ditto	1	1	28	1	1	28			
	17. Prices	arable	11	1	26				11	1	26
5 2 10	18.	The Freiths	wood	5	2	10						
	19. Great Cavington	arable	16	2	34				16	2	34
	20. Sideing and Linder	ditto	15	1	1				15	1	1
	21.	Sideing Croft	pasture	8	0	28	8	0	28			
5 1 1	23.	Sideing Wood	wood	5	1	1						
	24.	Owls Meadow	meadow	4	3	6	4	3	6			
	25.	Veldgate Meadow	ditto	4	3	28	4	3	28			
1 2 22	26.	Dogberry Pond	water	1	2	22						
	27. Old Dogberry and Andole	arable	15	3	1				15	3	1
	28.	Comlow	pasture	25	1	25	25	1	25			
	30.	Bailiff's House and Homestead		1	1	4	1	1	4			
0 2 18	30a.	Lane		0	2	18						
	32.	Loxter Fields	pasture	29	2	17	29	2	17			
11 0 38	33.	Raccum Wood	wood	11	0	38						
0 1 0	34.	Adjoining Long Orchard		0	1	0						
	35.	Long Orchard	pasture	2	0	19	2	0	19			
25 2 11	36.	Ravenhall Wood	wood	25	2	11						
	37. The Callow	arable	8	3	34				8	3	34
	38. The Breaches	hop ground	11	1	12				11	1	12
19 3 29	39.	Cannon Heathwood	wood	19	3	29						
	40. Shop Field	arable	5	3	9				5	3	9
	42.	Calves Meadow	meadow	15	3	14	15	3	14			
	43.	Cockpit Pleck	ditto	2	2	31	2	2	31	87	2	6
0 3 29	44.	Sallee Bed	wood	0	3	29						
	45.	Dunkirk Pleck	meadow	0	3	28	0	3	28			
110 1 35		Carried forward					270	3	25			
							468	3	26			

Meadow & Pasture a r p 270 . 3 . 25   270 . 3 25
Woods & Plantation 110 : 1 : 35
arable 87 : 2 : 6   87 . 2 . 6
468 : 3 : 26   358 . 1 . 31
124 . 1 . 2 In Mr Barrett's possession
234 . 0 . 29 To be let at Michs 1831

For Wheat Mich. 1831.	a	r	p
No. 17	11	1	26
19	16	2	34
20	15	1	1
27	5	~	~
37	8	3	34
40	5	3	9
	63	0	24
	15	1	1

For Lent Corn Spring 1832.			
No. 27	10	0	0

29 Nov. 1831. Hammond to survey the Park wood fences at Hope End. found wanting about 12 Rails 10 foot long —
40 Good Spurs.
4 Doz of Hurdles.

Gates 1 at Top of Hopyard next Common
1 Next Poddington woods in the Upper Park
The one at Lochsters field wants a place. the Top bar being broke

Post at Common Heath wood Gate & Gate wants repairing —

Gate 1 at Old Coach Road & one Posts. at Plantation
1 Lochsters field near the Farm
1 Top of Clarenton. Bars wanting
1 In Pieces. In a tree split
1 opposite leading to lower park wants repairing —

Mr Wm Kendrick began 31 March 1831 at 10/ per Week & look over the Woods. if he had to superintend the farming it was to be more — He attended to the planting of the peas. the ploughing of the fallows Weeding & Mowing the Wheat & Beans & Pease — The Lawn Mowed & make & Hay & taken to the Farm where it is now in thatched — The Trees in the Garden should be cut. They are loose from the walls. now will bring them down — John Nekyron's house

Mr Barrett has Sowed in the following pieces.			
Homepark	8	—	—
Inlong or	—	2	—
In fallow	—	—	—
In Breaches	2	—	—
& Calves mead			

Hopyard

Hope End fallows measured by Wm Jones 15 Sep. 1831

5	0	18	Part of Old Dogberry & Middle
10	1	4	Prices
8	0	31	The Callow —
5	1	27	Shop field
29	0	0	Measured no further than ploughed

[331]

Cottages.

John Fisherman Rent.   wants the Carpenter for
                                         2 or 3 Days.

Thomas Cook.   near the Farm House must be
                    Thatched.

John Leisure.   at Sidlings — Windows almost out.

Bryant.   The weather. The upper House

1 Post and 3 Rails at the Old Coach Road
3 Strips 3 feet long at the gate at Prices
4 Rails 10 feet long between the Wood and the House Park in
the place of a Gate
1 New Gate at the top of the Hop Yard 9 feet long
1 New Post at the Lenham Heath Wood and the Gate mended
12 New Rails from 9 to 12 feet long
4 Dozen of Hurdles
3 Rails at the Upper House 13. 14. and 15 feet long

The Ledbury assessment upon Mr Barretts Land
is as follows:

E M Barrett Esq. — Upper House Ld and 181. 1. 1. 20/. a 9d

d°. ————————— Woods ————— 53. 3. 27 - 10/

d°. ————————— Tillage ————— 12. 0. 0. — 16 Gas

d°. ————————— New Plantations of 1. 1. 0. — 5 £

assignees or Mortgagees Ledbury 6th Rate 1. 4. 3 ⎫ Woods and
                                  11. d° 2. 0. 6 ⎭ New plantations

Colwall
  Rates.   Poor —

Mr Ward to pay — 1.. 16. 0 ——— 3d Rate Road — 0. 10. 0

Capt Johnstone — 3. 4. 6 —————————— 1. 12. 3

Mortgagees ——— 0. 9. 1½ —————————— 0. 4. 7

E M Barrett ? 1. 4. 6 ————————————— 0. 12. 3

And of one 6 Rate. 6. 14. 1½ ————————— 3. 7. 1

The Composition for Highways on the whole Estate 200£ ⎫
    or four Teams duty ——————————————— ⎭

|1832 June 22. agreed with Ebbon to pay composⁿ on 6 days
    at 6/ per day — 1:16:0

Lambert of Wellington Heath says he helped to take up greater
part of the fence between Mr Rayers Land and Mr Barretts
in the park. and the greater part belongs to the park if
any of Mr Rayers 'tis at the farther end —

      460
       27
      —————
      3276
       836
      —————
     11,636

May 1824

By an Extract or Copy made from an old Terrier then in the possession of Mr Hockin the Rector of Coddington it appeared the Glebe of Coddington including the Homestead consisted of 26 pieces. of which at that time 21 could be distinctly made out. neither of which could are in the Hopeland Estate

THREE of the five were <u>supposed</u> to be in the Hopeland Estate.

		a. r. p
Viz	Part of Raccum Wood . .	1. 3. 4
	a small parcel of grass Land adjoining it . }	0. 1. 13
"In Coly Cott (lotty Meadow.	0. 2. 31 " — 0 2. 31

556

Old Lands supposed to be in old Colwall Estate ———] 0. 2. 12   0. 2. 0   pieces
In Pieces pieces

+Saberdine Hopp and supposed to be in old Colwall Estate] 0. 2. 14 —   Mr Smyth pays. Mr B. rent for this

4. Petty France which belonged to old Colwall.

3: 1st Garden Hedge

Mr 38 Land purchased of Bellers.

37 The Garden Fence.

34 Land purchased of Solloway who purchased of Gwatkin

28 for All old Lane purchased of Lome who purchased under Ledbury Inclosure —

Quarry Hole from which Stone was laid out adjoins to Richard Daniels Land

17 Supposed to be Colwall Glebe lying in Saberdine

Cloyty or Clotty Meadow is supposed to be holding ten for

Hon the Bishops rec. for Glebe purchase Lane purchased of Parish Officers — 80£ —

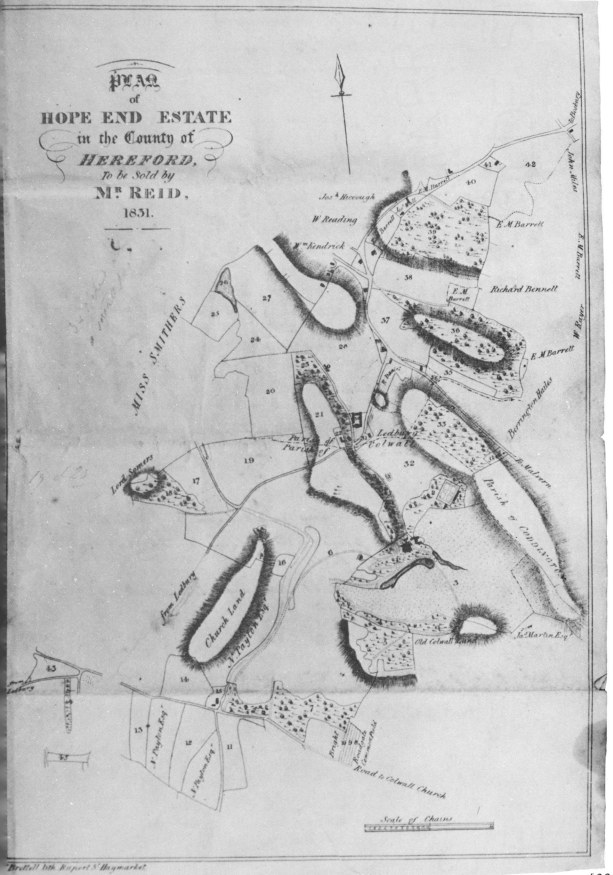

PLAN
of
HOPE END ESTATE
in the County of
HEREFORD,
To be Sold by
Mr. REID,
1831.

Scale of Chains

			A. R. P.			A. R. P.

Brought forward 468 3 26

Cottages, Gardens, &c.

CONTAINING

A.	R.	P.

3 : 3 : 18,

VIZ.

Reference to Plan.						A	R	P
No. 15.	Cottage and Garden	......	Mrs. Barker	}	1	0	22
	Chapel, or School House	......	In Hand				
22.	Cottage and Garden	......	J. Lane		0	1	34
29.	Ditto	......	— Treherne		0	3	4
31.	Ditto	......	Thomas Cook		0	2	28
41.	Ditto	......	C. Bryan		0	3	10

3 3 18

TOTAL 472 3 4

472,, 3,, 4

OUT-GOINGS.

	£.	s.	d.
Land Tax, per Annum, on Colwall Parish	0	4	2
Ditto on Ledbury Ditto	0	3	4
	0	7	6

THE ESTATE IS FREEHOLD,

EXCEPT

No. 33, containing 11A. 0R. 38P., which is Copyhold of the Manor of
Copyhold. 47,, 0,,38

BOSBURY, CODDINGTON, AND COLWALL,
Freehold 425,,2,,6

And about 36A., which are also Copyhold of the same Manor, or of the Manor of BARTON COLWALL, and the Quit Rents payable in respect of the Copyhold Parts of the Estate are supposed to amount to about £.2 per Annum.

There is a Right of Road over Nos. 36, 38, and 39, to BELLIS's Farm, and other Lands.

THE HOPE END MANSION

Has been justly considered to vie with EASTNOR CASTLE, and may be pronounced the chief Ornament of the surrounding Country.

The Estate

Is situate in an excellent Neighbourhood, enlivened by the Scenery of

THE EASTNOR WOODS,

ITS RICH FERTILE LANDS, AND MAGNIFICENT TIMBER,

WITH

The Malvern and adjacent Hills,

And other highly Interesting and Romantic Views of great Extent and Beauty;

THE SOIL

Is of a very excellent Quality, producing fine Grain, Hay, &c.

THE PROPERTY

PRESENTS A MOST ELIGIBLE OPPORTUNITY FOR

RESIDENCE OR INVESTMENT;

The Country abounds with Game.

MALVERN

Is only about four miles distant, and the Canal from

LEDBURY TO GLOUCESTER

Affords great facility for the Conveyance of Produce to that City and the neighbouring Towns, and this will be considerably extended by the intended Continuation of the Canal to HEREFORD.

COACHES DAILY TO AND FROM THE METROPOLIS.

HEREFORDSHIRE,

On the Borders of Worcestershire.

PARTICULARS AND CONDITIONS OF SALE,

Of a very Important

FREEHOLD ESTATE,

SMALL PART COPYHOLD,

HOPE END,

Situate in the Parishes of LEDBURY, COLWALL, & CODDINGTON,

IN THE COUNTY OF HEREFORD,

On the Borders of Worcestershire, about Two Miles from Ledbury,
commanding the Romantic Scenery of the Malvern
and adjacent Hills.

HOPE END MANSION

IS ADAPTED FOR

The Accommodation of a Nobleman, or Family of the First
Distinction,

*Pleasantly erected in its own Grounds, a Lawn in front, with a fine
Sheet of Water, stored with Fish, Cascade, &c.*

THE RESIDENCE IS ERECTED IN THE EASTERN STYLE OF
ARCHITECTURE, AND MAY JUSTLY BE ESTEEMED

A Chef-d'Œuvre, unrivalled in this Kingdom,

With all requisite Attached and Detached Offices;

COMMODIOUS STABLING, COACH HOUSES, AND VARIOUS OUT-
OFFICES;

BEAUTIFUL PLEASURE GROUNDS,

Shrubbery, as Above, Productive Walled Garden, Grapery, &c.

SUNDRY COTTAGES, WITH GARDENS,
AND UPWARDS OF

FOUR HUNDRED & SEVENTY-TWO ACRES

OF EXCELLENT

Grass and Meadow, Arable, Wood Land, Hop Garden and
Plantation,

AN ELIGIBLE PROPERTY FOR RESIDENCE & INVESTMENT :

By Order of the Mortgagees, under a Power of Sale,

To be Sold by Auction,

BY MR. REID,

Son-in-Law and Successor to the late

MR. JOHN ROBINS,

At Garraway's Coffee House, 'Change Alley, Cornhill,

On *THURSDAY, 25th of AUGUST,* 1831,

At Twelve o'Clock.

170, Regent Street.

INDEX

INDEX

Adam, 1

Addison, William, 123

Adolphe, 204

Adonis, 55, 138

Æschylus, 16, 20, 30, 31, 32, 43, 77, 80 f., 202, 204, 206, 207, 229, 230, 301

  Aeschyli Dramata quae Supersunt (ed. Bothe), 223, 226, 230

  Æschyli Prometheus Vinctus (ed. Blomfield), 222, 223, 226, 230

  Aeschyli Tragoediae Septem (ed. C. G. Schütz), 230

  Æschylus (ed. Capps), xlvi, 31 n., 43 n., 84 n., 206 n., 227 n., 228 n.

  Æschylus (ed. Scholefield), 219, 223, 226, 227, 228, 229, 230, 231, 240, 302

  Agamemnon, 16, 43, 52 n., 231

  Choephori, 202, 227

  Eumenides, 202, 206

  Persæ, 43

  Prometheus Vinctus, 43, 53, 59, 91, 160, 162, 180, 212, 213, 214, 215, 216, 217, 222, 240

  Septem Contra Thebas, 10, 15 f., 17, 18, 25, 31, 47, 53, 58, 59, 70, 82, 84, 87, 90, 91, 92, 93, 97

  Supplices, 194, 202, 228, 231

Agamemnon, xviii

Agamemnon, 16, 43, 52 n., 231

Aladdin, 108

Alcestis, 56, 57, 62, 63

Alcibiades, 171, 176, 177

Aldine editions, 119 n., 163 n., 286

Alfieri, Count Vittorio, 125 f.

Allen (the Overseer), 38

Altham, Harry S., xiii, 45 n., 65 n.

Altham, Mary, xiii

Altham, Richard J. L., xiv

Altham, Mrs. Violet M., viii, xiii f., 280, 297

Amalthæa, 204

Amos, Book of, 96

Amphiaraüs, 84

Amreeta, 165

Anacreon, xvii, 238, 307

André, Mr., 231

Andromache, 228, 229

Ann (E.B.B.'s maid), xxxvii, 20, 69, 70, 128, 136, 158, 160, 164, 173, 185

Annie. *See* Boyd, Ann Henrietta

Antoninus, Marcus Aurelius, Emperor, v, 67, 68, 79, 84, 87, 88, 90 n., 99, 122

  Communings with Himself (tr. Haines), xlvii, 67 n., 84 n.

  De Rebus Suis (ed. Gataker), 55, 66, 67, 68, 69, 70, 73, 74, 79, 80, 82, 83, 86

Apologeticus, 132, 140, 187 f., 190, 292

Aristarchus, 303

Aristophanes, 235

Arminianism, 99

Armstrong Browning Library, xiii, xx n.

Armstrong, Mrs. Mary M., xii

As You Like It, 118 n.

Ash, The Great, 47 f.

Atalanta, 158

Athenæum, The, 105 n., 227 n., 234 n., 240 n., 275 n.

Athenæus, 235

Atossa, 43

Attic Salt Mines, 112

Aulnoy, Marie Catherine, Comtesse d', "La Chatte Blanche," 75 n.

Automaedon, 160

Avernus, 38 n., 109

Bacon, Roger, 276

Baillie, Joanna, 58

Baker, Harriet, 45, 47, 185, 186, 220, 221

Ballard, Stephen, viii, ix, xiv, 323

Bamboo Room, 14

Baptist Magazine, The, 41 n.

Barker, Mrs., 49, 60, 61, 337

Barker, Edmund Henry, 15, 17, 112, 161, 179, 216, 217 n., 301

  A Greek and English Lexicon, 25

Barneby, Rev. Thomas, 4

Barnes, Joshua, *Euripidis Tragoediæ XX*, 55

Barnett, Joseph, **117**, 122, 213

Barrett, Alfred Price Moulton-, ("Daisy"), xvi, xxxv, xxxvii, 14, 16, 24, 25, 171, 206, 235

Barrett, Arabella Barrett Moulton-, viii, xx, xxv, xxxiv, xxxvi, xxxvii, xliii, 1, *et passim*
   dreams H.S.B. dead, 1
   E.B.B.'s character sketch of, 42
   angry at H.S.B.'s silence, 118
   E.B.B. reads Diary to, 202

Barrett, Charles John Barrett Moulton-, ("Stormie"), xvi, xxiii, xxxvi, 6, 18, 40, 47, 74, 82, 136, 195, 214, 218, 233, 281

Barrett, Edward (of Cinnamon Hill), xxi, xxxv, 11 n.

Barrett, Edward Barrett Moulton-, (Papa), xv ff., xxxv, xli, *et passim*
   missing letters from E.B.B., xi
   purchase of Hope End, xv
   rebuilding Hope End, xv f.
   religious views, xvii
   financial difficulties, xxi
   forced to sell Hope End, xxii
   leaves Hope End, xxiv, 323
   E.B.B.'s attachment to, xl, xlii
   attack of cholera, 100, 119, 284
   delighted with E.B.B.'s poem, 207, 297
   Mrs. Cliffe afraid to face, 238

Barrett, Edward Barrett Moulton-, ("Bro"), xv, xvi, xvii, xxiv, xxxvi, 1, 3, 6, 8, 10, 11, 16, 18, 30, 33, 34, 35, 36, 38, 39, 44, 49, 50, 55, 56, 57, 59, 60, 66 n., 67, 75, 79, 80, 81, 82, 87, 92, 94, 95, 96, 100, 108, 119, 120, 121, 122, 126, 129, 131, 135, 138, 140, 142, 144, 147, 151, 152, 153, 155, 159, 166, 175, 176, 177, 181, 183, 184, 186, 187, 190, 193, 195, 197, 206, 207, 213, 217, 218, 225, 236, 279, 280, 281, 283, 284, 299, 300

Barrett, Lt.-Col. Edward F. Moulton-, xiii

Barrett, Edward R. Moulton-, xiii, xiv, xv n., xvi n., 4 n., 18 n., 142 n.

Barrett, Gp.-Capt. Edward S. Moulton-, viii, xiii, xxxiv

Barrett, Mrs. Edward S. Moulton-, viii, xiii

Barrett, Elizabeth Barrett Moulton-, xxxv f.
   discovery of Diary, xi
   missing letters to Papa, xi
   nickname "Ba", xvi
   early interest in writing, xvii
   lessons in Greek and Latin, xvii
   first published works, xviii
   start of friendship with H.S.B., xx f.
   concern over sale of Hope End, xxii
   reason for discontinuing Diary, xxiii
   leaves Hope End, xxiv
   with H.S.B. at Sidmouth, xxiv
   last meeting with H.S.B., xxv
   writing mannerisms, xxvi ff.
   attachment to her father, xl, xlii
   "Electra complex," xlii
   H.S.B. a substitute father, xliii
   vows to seclude herself, 103
   has only one friend, 149
   love of solitude growing, 155
   CONTRIBUTIONS TO PERIODICALS, ETC.
     Athenæum, The, 105 n., 227 n., 234 n., 240 n., 275 n.
     Blackwood's Edinburgh Magazine, 313 n.
     Graham's Magazine, 316 n.
     Jewish Expositor, xx
     New Monthly Magazine, The, xviii, 187, 275 n.
     Times, The, 204, 297, 311 f., 319 f.
   DREAMS: xviii, 7, 20, 40, 54, 57, 63, 69, 111, 115, 204
   HEALTH: 54, 59, 63, 67, 68, 69, 82, 87, 89, 97, 119, 135 f., 162, 171, 174, 175, 183, 184, 195, 204, 219, 220, 223, 224, 229, 230, 232, 233, 239, 302
   first serious illness, xviii f.
   LETTERS RECEIVED FROM:
   Barrett, Arabella & Henrietta Moulton-, 178
   Barrett, Edward Moulton-, xv, xvii, 66, 108 f., 137, 144, 159, 178, 181, 186, 188, 189, 297
   Boyd/Mrs. Boyd, xx, xxiii, 1, 34, 36, 52, 56, 65, 68, 93, 96, 101, 121, 128, 143, 150, 158, 165, 166, 171, 172, 176, 182, 187, 188, 192, 193, 194, 195, 196, 211, 214, 217, 223, 229
   Boyd, Annie, 34, 68, 101
   Clarke, Arabella Graham-, 162, 178
   Cliffe, Eliza, 5, 81, 106, 110, 193, 219, 235
   Cocks, Lady Margaret, 184
   Curzon, G. H. Roper-, 89, 151
   Gibbons, Eliza, 163
   Glasco, Miss, 195
   Martin, Mrs. Julia, 33, 74, 135, 167, 181
   Price, Caroline, 82, 100

Price, Sir Uvedale, xix
Steers, Frances, 93
LETTERS WRITTEN TO:
Barker, E. H., 179
Barrett, Arabella Moulton-, xxv, xxxiv
Barrett, Edward Moulton- (Papa), 29, 55 f., 60, 64, 82, 94, 112, 130, 142, 157, 187
Barrett, Edward Moulton- ("Bro"), 100
Barrett, Samuel Moulton-, 78
Best, Mrs. Mary, 28
Bohn, H. G., 121
Bordman, Eleanor, 216
Boyd, Mrs., 4, 35, 37, 47, 65, 67, 101, 143, 146, 158, 164, 171, 180, 183, 185, 194, 195, 196, 197, 202, 211, 213, 219
Boyd, Annie, 2, 37, 90, 207
Boyd, H. S., xx, xxii, xxiv, xxv, 1 n., 10, 28, 33, 47, 48, 56, 59, 60, 100, 101, 119, 130, 164, 180, 188, 190, 203, 210, 211, 217, 218, 224, 229, 233 n., 235, 238, 241 n., 273-280, 283-288, 290-308
Browning, Robert, xxv n.
Clarke, Arabella Graham-, 162, 177, 183
Cliffe, Eliza, 163, 193, 207, 219, 279
Cliffe, Mrs. Elizabeth, 188, 195
Cocks, Lady Margaret, 185
Curzon, G. H. Roper-, 90, 150, 205
Eaton, T., 47, 115
Editor, New Monthly Magazine, 187
Editor, The Times, 106, 287
Gibbons, Eliza, 160
Hatchard, John, 223
Horne, R. H., xviii n., xix n., xxiii
Knowles, Charlotte, 5
Martin, Mrs. J., xxiv, 33, 73, 86, 169, 210 n.
Moulton, Mrs. Elizabeth, xxi
Price, Caroline, 90, 142
Price, Sir Uvedale, xx n.
LITERARY OPINIONS: 4, 31, 43, 50, 56, 64, 65, 69, 83, 84, 86, 87, 89, 90, 91, 93, 94 f., 97, 98, 102, 105, 107, 112, 117, 121, 127, 128, 132, 136, 137, 138, 140, 145, 152, 155, 164, 172, 175, 177, 182, 184, 186, 187 n., 188, 190, 191, 193, 202, 206, 207, 208, 215, 216, 217, 220, 221, 226, 228, 233, 234, 236, 237, 238
POLITICAL OPINIONS: 34, 152, 156
READING BY:
Æschylus, 15 f., 17, 18, 20, 25, 30, 31, 32, 43, 47, 53, 58, 59, 70, 80 f., 82, 84, 87, 90, 91, 194, 202, 206, 228, 231
Antoninus, Marcus Aurelius, 66, 67, 68, 69, 70, 73, 74, 79, 80, 82, 83, 86, 87
Bible, The Holy, 13, 19, 22, 41, 53, 64, 74, 119, 121, 122, 125, 126, 127, 130, 140, 143, 147, 149, 177, 225, 230, 234, 238
Bunyan, 225
Callimachus, 102
Cebes, 90, 92
Chrysostom, St. John, 4, 26, 125, 128
Dion Chrysostom, 203
Dionysius, 94, 143
Epictetus, 64, 66
Euripides, 56, 57, 63, 143, 182, 188, 191, 193, 194, 221, 228, 229
Goldoni, 111, 112, 119
Heliodorus, 203
Homer, xviii
Isocrates, 95, 102, 103, 108, 119, 137
Keats, 93, 94
Lamartine, 35, 54, 136, 137, 138
Misc. poetry, 14, 50, 54, 87, 98, 181, 186
Misc. theology, 22, 65, 89, 96, 97, 136, 142, 145, 151, 152, 153, 177, 185 f., 189 f., 192, 208, 219, 232
Molière, 181
Nazianzen, St. Gregory, 97 f., 105, 113, 117, 123, 128, 132, 140, 153, 162, 168, 173, 179 f., 183, 187 f., 190, 203, 209 f., 211, 234
Nonnus, 226 f., 230
Novels, etc., 51, 54, 56, 82, 83, 86, 107 f., 112, 127, 155, 184, 220
Periodicals, 50, 192, 291
Pindar, 35, 36, 37, 38, 50, 207, 220, 233, 236, 238, 239
Plato, 171, 172, 174, 175, 176, 177
Shelley, 102, 138
Southey, 164 f.
Synesius, 234, 306
Theophrastus, 92, 94 f., 96, 101, 102
Wesley, 190, 192
RELIGIOUS OPINIONS: 71, 121, 122, 124, 130, 136, 139, 154, 201
VISITS TO H.S.B.: xxi, 8 ff., 14 ff., 25 ff., 30 ff., 42 ff., 45 f., 53, 57 ff., 61, 62 f., 70 ff., 76 ff., 80 f., 83 ff., 90 ff., 97 ff., 104 f., 109, 112 f., 117 f., 123, 128 f.,

Barrett, Elizabeth Barrett Moulton- (cont.)
140 f., 145 f., 147 f., 153 f., 160 ff.,
167 f., 173, 177 ff., 183 f., 187 f.,
189 f., 192, 198, 203, 205 f., 209 f.,
214 f., 222, 224 f., 226, 228 f.,
231 f., 236 f., 240 f.
WORKS BY AND ABOUT:
"Adventures of our Journey . . . to
Worthing," 49 n.
Battle of Marathon, The, xviii, xxxv,
xlii, 288
Bibliography (ed. Wise), 313 n.
Bion (trans. of), 138 n.
"Catarina to Camoens," 181, 188,
205, 316-318
"Elizabeth Barrett and Hope End,"
xv n.
Elizabeth Barrett to Mr. Boyd, xx n.,
xxii n., xxiv n., xlvi, 1 n., 2 n.,
14 n., 15 n., 26 n., 53 n., 78 n.,
92 n., 135 n., 179 n., 187 n., 220 n.,
223 n., 275, 279, 283, 284, 285,
287, 290, 292, 293, 295, 298, 300,
301, 302, 304, 305, 306, 307, 308
Elizabeth Barrett to Miss Mitford,
xxii n., xlvi
Essay on Mind, An, xix f., xxi n., 22,
25 f., 32
"Glimpses into My Own Life," xvii
"Hark What Deep Tone," 18 n.
Hitherto Unpublished Poems, xvii n.,
xxi n., xlvi, 5 n., 18 n., 40 n., 275 n.,
314 n., 319 n.
"Kings," 1, 2 f., 7, 9, 311 f.
"Lament for Adonis, A," 138 n.
Leila, 129 n., 214 n.
Letters (ed. Kenyon), xxiv n., xlvi,
210 n.
Letters (the love letters), xxv, xlvi
Letters . . . to George Barrett, xiv,
xviii n., xix n., xlvi
Letters . . . to . . . Horne, xviii n.,
xix n., xxiii n., xlvi
Nazianzen, St. Gregory (trans. of),
105 n., 211, 240 n.
"Pestilence, The," 204, 207, 295 n.,
297 f., 319 f.
Plato, Disquisitions on, 97
Poems (1844), 316 n.
Poems (1850), xxv n., 138 n., 313 n.
Poet's Enchiridion, The, 316 n.
"Poets' Record," 93, 125 n.

Prologue for Puppet Show, 194, 195,
197, 198, 207
Prometheus Bound, 212, 213, 214,
215, 216, 217, 218, 219, 221, 222,
223, 225 f., 229, 240, 301
Seraphim, The, 88 n., 175 n., 315 n.
"Sleep, The," 88 n.
"Some Account of the Greek Christian
Poets," 105 n., 227 n., 234 n., 240 n.
"Some Unpublished Papers" (ed. Hell-
man), xxi n.
Sonnets on the Death of H.S.B., xxv
Synesius (trans. of), 234
"A Thought on Thoughts," 33, 36,
219, 275-279
"To E.W.C. Painting my Picture," 95 n.,
314
"Twenty Unpublished Letters" (ed.
Weaver), xlvii, 139 n., 273, 286
"Weakest Thing, The," 175, 315
"Woman's Shortcomings, A," 76, 313
Barrett, Rev. Frank M. Moulton-, xxxiv
Barrett, George Goodin Barrett Moulton-,
xvi, xxiii, xxxiv, xxxvii, 4 n., 6, 18,
23, 36, 40, 47, 82, 100, 136, 142 n.,
158, 323
*Letters of the Brownings to George Bar-
rett*, xiv, xviii n., xix n., xlvi
Barrett, Lt.-Col. Harry P. Moulton-, xi f.,
xxxiv
Barrett, Henrietta Barrett Moulton-, viii,
xv, xvi, xx, xxxv, xxxvi, xxxvii, *et
passim*
thinks E.B.B. overrates H.S.B.'s regard,
158
thought very pretty, 232
Barrett, Henry Barrett Moulton-, xxxiv,
xxxvii, 6, 12, 14, 16, 24, 25, 27, 36, 40,
53, 68, 151, 158, 177, 194, 203, 206,
219, 224
Barrett, Kenneth A. Moulton-, xi, xiii,
xxxiv
Barrett, Mrs. Kenneth A. Moulton-, xi, xiii
Barrett, Mary Barrett Moulton-, xvi
Barrett, Mrs. Mary Clementina Moulton-
(*née* Clay-Addams), 64, 131, 281 f.
Barrett, Mrs. Mary Moulton- (*née* Graham-
Clarke), xv, xvi, xx, xxi, xxiv, xxxv,
xxxvii, 54, 64, 88, 158 n., 179 n., 222,
238, 282
Barrett, Myrtle Moulton-, xiii, xiv, 1 n.,
218 n.

Barrett, Octavius Butler Barrett Moulton-, ("Occyta"), xxxvii, 33, 151, 180, 182, 198, 202, 203, 206, 235, 290, 293, 298

Barrett, Col. Ronald A. Moulton-, xiii, xiv, 1 n., 218 n.

Barrett, Mrs. Ronald A. Moulton-, xiii

Barrett, Samuel Barrett Moulton-, (uncle), xxii, xxxv, 11 f., 21, 64, 78, 100 n., 111, 137, 144, 230, 281-283

Barrett, Samuel Barrett Moulton-, (brother), xxxvi, 6, 11, 16, 24, 32, 38, 39, 49, 50, 53, 56, 59, 75, 80, 81, 82, 100, 108, 126, 131, 134, 135, 137, 143, 144, 149, 152, 175, 176, 177, 178, 190, 205, 206, 210, 217, 233, 287

Barrett, Septimus James Barrett Moulton-, ("Sette"), xxxvii, 24, 25, 33, 158, 182, 203, 205, 206, 219, 298

Barton Court (otherwise The Bartons), xiii, xix, 3 n., 8, 20 n., 29, 35, 48, 50, 52, 54, 57, 66, 67, 83, 108, 116, 117 n., 127, 141, 143, 156 n., 157, 158, 167, 175, 184, 196, 201, 206, 207, 238

Basil, St., 91, 113, 296
    "In Laudem Basilii," 43, 179
    "On the Faith," 192 n.
    Select Passages of the Writings . . . of St. Basil, 26 n., 43 f., 168 n.

Bath and Wells, Bishop of, 293

Bathampton, xxiii, xxiv

Bathurst, Hon. Mrs. Elizabeth Hervey-, xiii

Battie, Miss, 221

Battie, Mr., 221, 223, 230

Batties, The, 221 n., 223

Battye, Mr. See Battie, Mr.

Baxter, Richard, 193
    The Saints Everlasting Rest, 192 f., 208

Bayford, Mrs., 207, 298

Baylor University, xiii, xx n.

Bee, The, 20 n.

Belgium, Invasion of, 95

Benbow, Admiral John, 7 n.

"Benbow, The Admiral," 114

Bentley (of Worcester), 121, 283, 325

Bentley, Richard, 42

Beresford, James, The Miseries of Human Life, 20 n.

Berg Collection, Henry W. and Albert A., viii, xii n., xiv, xxv n., xxxiv, xlvi, 313 n., 319 n.

Berrington, Harriet, 226

Berringtons, The, 226 n., 299

Berrow's Worcester Journal, 40 n., 59 n., 64 n., 75 n.

Besier, Rudolf, The Barretts of Wimpole Street, xii n.

Best, Fanny, 39, 47 f., 124, 125

Best, Mrs. Mary Catherine (née Cliffe), 13, 15 n., 16, 17, 23, 28, 33, 39, 47 f., 110 f., 124, 125, 184 n., 195, 204
    An Illustration of the Prophecy of Hosea, 110
    "The Garden of Eden," 16, 23, 28

Best, Thomas, 13 n., 184 n.

Betham, Mary M., The Lay of Marie, 167 n.

Beverley, Robert Mackenzie, 127, 133
    A Letter to His Grace the Archbishop of York, 133 n., 136
    A Second Letter to His Grace the Archbishop of York, 216
    A Sermon Preached on the Unknown Tongues, 201 f.
    The Tombs of the Prophets, 133 n., 136

Bible, The Holy. See E.B.B., Reading by

Bible Society, The, 71

Biblical Texts, 12, 45, 65, 73, 88, 96, 103, 106, 121, 130, 131, 139, 147, 152, 153, 159, 178, 208, 221, 223, 282

Biddulph, Lord, xiv

Biddulph, Miss, 55, 57

Biddulph, Mrs. Augusta, 19 n., 57, 144

Biddulph, John, xiv, 17 n., 19 n., 55 n., 120, 170 n., 176 n., 197

Biddulph, Penelope, 17

Biddulphs, The, xix, 17 n., 19, 39, 49, 51, 120, 124, 141, 143, 181, 182, 183

Billius, Jacobus, xlvi, 215

Billy. See Treherne, William

Billy, Jacques de, xlvi, 215

Bion, xvii, 98, 138
    A Lament for Adonis, 138 n.

Birthdays, 33, 35, 42, 68, 195, 205, 221, 222, 223, 227, 230, 235, 302

Biscoe, Mr., 53, 76, 84, 132, 143, 146, 148, 155, 158, 160, 161, 165, 171, 176, 231 n.

Biscoe, Joseph, 53 n.

Biscoe, Rev. William, 53 n.

Blackwood's Edinburgh Magazine, 313 n.

Blaize, Mrs. Mary, 20

Blizard, Mr. and Mrs. Thomas, 170

Blomfield, Charles James:
    Æschyli Prometheus Vinctus, 222, 223, 226

Blomfield, Charles James (cont.)
Æschyli Septem Contra Thebas, 10, 17, 25
Bluebeard, 182
Boadman, Miss. *See* Bordman, Eleanor
Bohn, Henry G., **119**, 121, 164, 173, 285 f.
Catalogue of a Very Select Collection of Books, **129**, 162 f., 286
Boiardo, Count Matteo Maria, *Orlando Innamorato*, 73, 74
Bolidori, 86
Bolingbroke, Viscount, *Works*, 163
Bordman, Eleanor Page (later Jago), 58, 70, 71, 72, 76, 77, 80, 91, 92, 99, 107, 113, 116, 118, 119, 128, 141, 143, 145, 158, 160, 161, 162, 171, 175, 178, 179, 187, 216
Bordman, Rev. James, 58 n., 162, 171, 178
Bosbury, 6, 7, 185 n., 289, 337
Bothe, Friedrich H., *Aeschyli Dramata quae Supersunt*, 223, 226
Bowers, Capt., 17
Boyd, Miss, 44, 58, 65, 68, 70, 71, 73, 76, 77, 78, 84 f., 86, 91, 92, 96, 101, 113, 117, 123, 128, 132, 133, 140, 148, 154, 162, 165, 166 f., 178, 187, 283, 288, 299
Boyd, Mrs. Ann (*née* Lowry), xx, 1, *et passim*
    trying person to spend day with, 48
    has lost taste for poetry, 85
    has given up church-going, 178
    H. Mushet's opinion of, 229
    no time to read to H.S.B., 240
    strange woman to be H.S.B.'s wife, 240
Boyd, Ann Henrietta (later Hayes), 2, *et passim*
    comments on "Kings," 2 f.
    E.B.B. apprehensive about, 6, 8
    cool reception of E.B.B., 9
    thought jealous of Eliza Cliffe, 15, 45
    Æ.B.B. writes poem in album, 188, 205
Boyd, Hugh Stuart, xx, *et passim*
    first letter to E.B.B., xx
    E.B.B.'s first visit, xxi, 6 n., 7 n.
    E.B.B.'s description of, xxi
    disappearance of letters to E.B.B., xxiii
    moves to Bathampton, xxiii
    moves to Sidmouth, xxiv
    living in London, xxiv
    death of, xxv
    substitute father to E.B.B., xliii
    dislike of "Kings," 1, 3, 9

cannot bear noise, 25
    doubted authorship of *Essay on Mind*, 32
    E.B.B. not witty in conversation, 32
    preserves E.B.B.'s letters, 32
    E.B.B. sends ms. of "Thoughts versus Words," 33, 275-279
    his constitution, 42 f.
    regrets E.B.B.'s intimacy with E. Cliffe, 77
    not aware of faults in E.B.B., 77
    opinion of E.B.B.'s singing, 98
    unworthy of E.B.B.'s regard, 101, 167
    his religious state, 107, 218
    anti-scriptural views pain E.B.B., 154
    his head very intellectual, 206
    unpleasant effects of blindness, 228
    calls E.B.B. "a funny girl," 231
    knows nearly 8000 lines of Greek, 240
    WORKS BY AND ABOUT:
        Agamemnon of Æschylus, The, 52 n.
        Elizabeth Barrett to Mr. Boyd. See E.B.B., Works by and about
        Epigrams, 105, 106, 111, 114, 163, 164, 165, 179, 203, 295
        Essay on the Digamma, 224
        Essay on the Greek Article, An, 43 n.
        Fathers Not Papists, The, 105 n., 218 n.
        Methodist Magazine, The (contrib. to), 192, 210
        Nazianzen, St. Gregory (trans. of), 212, 215, 218, *et infra*
        Select Passages of . . . St. Chrysostom, St. Gregory Nazianzen, and St. Basil, 26 n., 43 f., 168 n.
        Select Poems, of Synesius and Gregory Nazianzen, 105 n., 234 n.
Boyle, Charles, 42
Brackets, Editorial use of, xxxi f.
Bradley, 236
Brand Lodge, 69, 143 n.
Brighton, 19, 47, 109, 170
Brights, The, xiii, 143
British Museum, The, xiv, 65 n., 313 n.
Bromesberrow, 135, 152 n.
Bromesberrow Place, 220 n.
Bronsil, 170 n.
Brougham, Henry, Lord, 146
Brown, Mrs., 117
Browning, Mrs. Fannie (*née* Coddington), xi n.
Browning, Robert, xi, xvi, xxv n., xxxiii, xxxiv, xxxvi, xxxvii, xlii, 4 n., 18 n.,

142 n., 217 n.

Letters (the love letters), xxv, xlvi

Browning, Robert Wiedemann Barrett, ("Pen"), xi n., xxxiv, xxxvi, xxxvii

Browning Collections: Catalogue of Messrs. Sotheby, Wilkinson & Hodge, The (1913 Sale Catalogue), xlvii, 67 n.

Browning Sale, 1913, xxiii, xxxiv, xlvii, 17 n., 33 n., 55 n., 57 n., 79 n., 85 n., 89 n., 92 n., 94 n., 108 n., 132 n., 171 n., 223 n.

Bruno, Giordano, *Candelaio*, 112 n.

Brunton, Mrs. Mary, *Self-Control*, 127

Bruyère, Jean de La, 63

Brydges, The, 11, 21

Bulteel, Rev. Henry Bullenden, 203, 295

Bulwer, Edward George Lytton (later 1st Baron Lytton), 187

Bunyan, John, 225

Burchell, Mr. (*alias* Sir Wm. Thornhill), 4, 15, 45

Burgess, Thomas, Bishop of Salisbury, 105

Burke, Edmund, 107

Burke, William, 107

Burns, Robert, 43 n., 50 n.

Butler, Lady (*née* Frances Graham-Clarke), 191

Butler, Mrs. Charlotte (*née* Graham-Clarke), 13, 144, 165, 169, 176

Butler, Richard Pierce, 13 n.

Butler, Sir Thomas, 191 n.

Byron, George Gordon, Lord, xix, 39, 54, 58, 164, 276, 278
Letters and Journals (ed. Moore), 74, 85, 164 n.

Cæsar, Julius, 20, 27 n., 203

Cæsarius, Oration on, 43

Callimachus, 90
Hymni et Epigrammata, 55, 90 n., 102, 107

Calvinism, 15, 99, 126, 237

Camoëns, Luis de, 175 n., 181
"Caterina to Camoens," 181, 188, 205, 316-318

Candlers, The, 205

Canon Frome, 11

Canterbury, Archbishop of, 291

Card, Mrs., 283

Card, Dr. Henry, 99, 101, 283, 284 f.
The Uses of the Athanasian Creed Explained, 145

Carden, Dr. John, xviii

Cards, The, 99

Carrubba, Robert W., xiv

Cassandra, 43

Catholicism, Roman, xvii, 15

Cebes, 90
Tabula, 90 n., 92

Cecilia, St., 277

Channing, William Ellery, *The Importance and Means of a National Literature*, 155

Charlotte. *See* Butler, Mrs. Charlotte

Cheltenham, xxxvii, 2 n., 13, 27, 77, 87, 116 n., 133 n., 171, 182 n.

Choephori, 202, 227

Cholera, 100, 170, 176, 180, 204, 207, 226, 284, 291, 297, 305
General Fast Day on account of, 226
"The Pestilence," 204, 207, 297 f., 319 f.

Chrysostom, St. John, 4, 129, 130, 133, 138 n., 286
Homily on Ephesians, 4
Homily on Eutropius, 26
Homily on Romans, 123, 125, 128, 295
Select Passages of the Writings of St. Chrysostom . . . , 26 n., 43 f., 168 n.

Cicero, 276
De Officiis, 8 n.
Letters to Atticus, xlvi, 112 n.

Cinderella, 182

Clarke, Mrs., 135

Clarke, Dr. Adam, xxv, 9, 10, 121, 140, 192 n., 217
Concise View of the Succession of Sacred Literature, 232, 237
Doctrine of Salvation by Faith Proved, 142, 145
Holy Bible . . . With a Commentary, The, 121 n., 232, 308

Clarke, Arabella Graham- (*née* Altham), xv, xvi, xxxvii

Clarke, Arabella Sarah Graham-, ("Bummy"), xvi, xxiv, xxxvii, xliv, *et passim*
arrival at Hope End, xxii
criticizes H.S.B.'s conduct, 92
speaks harshly of Annie Boyd, 148, 184
angry with E.B.B. over Miss Gibbons, 159
goes to Kinnersley Castle, 232, 233, 305

Clarke, James Altham Graham-, 21, 213, 236, 281

Clarke, Rev. James Charles, 176 n., 289

Clarke, John Altham Graham-, 232 n.

Clarke, John Graham-, xxxvii

Clarke, Joseph, *A Concise View of the Succession of Sacred Literature*, 232, 237

Claudian, xvii, 115

Claudian, xlvi, 115

Cliffe, Rev. Allen, Sr., 15 n., 29 n.

Cliffe, Rev. Allen, Jr., 1 n., 80, 125 n., 127, 131, 134, 135, 139, 143, 184, 189, 195

Cliffe, Eliza Wilhelmina (later Giles), viii, xix, xliv, 1, *et passim*

  Annie Boyd thought jealous of, 15, 45

  her portrait of E.B.B., viii, 21, 28, 47, 74, 88, 89, 95 f., 106, 110

  H.S.B. regrets E.B.B.'s intimacy with, 77

  E.B.B.'s opinion of, 79, 149

  "To E.W.C. Painting my Picture," 95 n., 314

  drawing for Worcester Exhibition, 149

  not regarded as friend by E.B.B., 149

  says E.B.B. would not marry angel, 180

Cliffe, Mrs. Elizabeth (née Deane), 13, 21, 22, 28, 29, 31, 35, 39, 41, 47, 50, 51, 56, 59, 61, 62, 63, 73, 89, 96, 110, 116, 124, 131, 134, 143, 147, 148, 149, 150, 151, 156, 157, 178, 180, 185, 188, 189, 193, 195, 196, 198, 205, 216, 225, 235, 236, 238, 239, 240 f., 279, 285, 290, 306

Cliffe, Mary C. *See* Best, Mrs. Mary C.

Cliffe, William Bateson, 184

Cliffes, The, 4, 16, 17, 29 n., 59, 66, 81, 106, 110, 125, 139, 144, 148, 152, 183, 184, 185 n., 193, 195, 215, 223

Clifton, 229

Clytemnestra, 182

Cockburn, Miss, 171

Cocks, Charles, Lord Somers, 170 n.

Cocks, James, 170

Cocks, Rev. James Somers, 170

Cocks, Jane (later Waddington, later Lady Somers), 186 n.

Cocks, John Somers, 1st Earl Somers, xvi, xix, 41 n., 47, 55, 108 n., 170 n., 185, 186, 335

Cocks, Lady Margaret Maria, 41, 45 n., 46 f., 55, 169, 170, 184, 185, 203

Coddington, 80 n., 185 n., 289, 325, 327, 334, 335, 337, 338

Coker, Dr. William, xviii

Coleridge, Samuel Taylor, xix, 85

Coles, Dr. Robert, "Psychoanalytical Observations," xxxix-xlv

Collyer, Rev. William Bengo, 61

Colossians, Epistle to the, 91, 92, 93, 98

Colwall, 12 n., 96, 146, 176 n., 289, 325, 326, 327, 335, 337, 338

Colwall Green, 38, 69 n., 157

Colwall, Old. *See* Old Colwall

Commeline, Miss, 156, 300

Commeline, Laura H., 156

Commeline, Rev. James, 142, 156

Commelines, The, xvi, xix, 142, 155 f., 213, 299, 300

Commons, House of, 9 n., 34 n., 75, 82 n., 142 n., 153, 161 n., 281, 287

Conjectural readings, xxxi

Conway, Eustace, *Anthony Munday and Other Essays*, 93 n.

Cook, Jack, xxxviii, 16

Cook, Thomas, xxxviii, 332, 337

Cook, William Surtees, xxxvi

Coombe Hill, 29, 122

Corinthians, Second Epistle to the, 130, 159 n., 208 n.

Coriolanus, 303

Corry, James, 116, 175 n., 182

Court House, 206 n.

Coventry, Hon. & Rev. Thomas Henry, 114

Cowper, William, 63

Cradley, 99 n., 135 n., 230, 289

Crane, Mary Brilliana (later Cliffe), 1 n.

Crane, Samuel, 1 n.

Cranes, The, 4

Cranes, The Miss, 1

Cruden, Alexander, 145, 150

  A Complete Concordance to the Holy Scriptures, 146 n.

Crusoe, Robinson, xxix, 156

Cue Titles, xlvi f.

Cummings Farm, 117 n.

Curiosities of Literature, 196 n.

Curzon, Mrs. Eliza (née Joynes), 217, 218

Curzon, Hon. & Rev. George Henry Roper- (later 16th Baron Teynham), 4, 5, 13, 15, 22, 33 f., 41 n., 72 n., 81 n., 89, 90, 92 f., 96, 98, 106, 108, 109, 125, 131, 146, 147, 150, 151, 152, 155, 157, 159, 163, 168, 171, 178, 183, 184, 201, 205 n., 208, 211, 214, 217, 218, 219 f., 221, 225, 230, 233, 235, 239, 294, 295, 299, 300, 306

Curzon, Henry George Roper- (later 17th Baron Teynham), 205, 233

Dagger, E.B.B.'s use of, 99 n.

Daily Gleaner, The, xxii n.
Daly, xxxviii, 16
Davidson, Mr., 97, 119, 130
Da Vinci, Leonardo:
  A Treatise on Painting, 55, 60
Davis, Mr., 72 n., 81, 135, 139, 216
Davison, Rev. John, 97 n.
Davy, Sir Humphry, 273
Dawes, Richard, *Miscellanea Critica*, 99, 107 f., 112, 114, 115, 121
Dean, Mrs. Thomas, 157, 159
Dean, Rev. Thomas, 12, 41, 65, 81, 100, 116, 130, 131, 152, 156, 157, 158, 176, 185, 230, 289, 304
Deane, Mr. *See* Dean, Rev. Thomas
Deaths, xi, xvi, xxi, xxiv, xxv, xxxiv-xxxvii *passim*, 41 n., 54 n., 64, 116, 131, 158, 176 n., 178, 179 n., 184 n., 185 n., 186
Deathwatch beetle, 54
Deighton, Henry, 28
Delavigne, Casimir J. F., *Trois Messéniennes*, 87
"Delphine, or, The Fortunate Cure," 220
Demonicus, 95
Description of Diary manuscript, xxxiii
Desdemona, 115
Destiny, 56, 57
Diana, 123
Diary, Description and provenance of ms., xxxiii f.
Diary, Psychoanalytical Observations on, xxxix-xlv
Dickens, Charles, 3 n.
Dion Chrysostom, 203
Dionysius, 94, 143
Disraeli, Isaac, *Curiosities of Literature*, 196 f.
Dominick. *See* Trant, Dominick
Don Quixote, 90
Donnington, 53 n.
Donnington Court, 87 n.
Donnington Hall, 170 n.
Drummond, Col. and Mrs., 55
Drummond, Henry, 294
Dublin, Archbishop of, 65 n., 201, 291
Dublin, 80 n., 127, 201 n.
Dublin Evening Mail, The, 201 n.

Eastbourne, 34, 35, 109
Eastnor, 100, 185 n., 232, 328
Eastnor Castle, xiii, xix, 41, 45, 46 f., 106, 169, 170 n., 185, 186, 187, 189, 193,
300, 325, 328, 337
Eastnor Park, 108 n.
Eaton, T., 32, 36, 40, 46, 47, 55, 115, 121, 164
  Catalogue, 36, 37, 115
Echo, The, 239
Edinburgh Review, The, 35, 182
Editorial apparatus, xxx-xxxii
Editorial approach, xxvi-xxx
Electra complex ascribed to E.B.B., xlii
Eliza. *See* Cliffe, Eliza Wilhelmina
Elliott, Rev. E., 41
Ely, The, 10
Emily, 204
Endymion, 204
England, Church of, xvii, 127 n., 133 n., 170, 216 n.
  Apologia Ecclesiæ Anglicanæ, 89, 96, 97
Ephesians, Epistle to the, 4, 91
Epictetus, 66
  Enchiridion, 64 f.
  Epicteti Manuale (ed. Simpson), 55
  Epictetus: The Discourses ... (trans. Oldfather), xlvi, 65
Erasmus, Desiderius, 113
Erskine, Thomas, 192 f.
Essington's Hotel, 61, 115
Eumenides, 202, 206
Euripides, 43, 136, 229, 231
  Alcestis, 56, 57, 62, 63
  Andromache, 228, 229
  Euripides (trans. Way), xlvi, 43 n., 62 n., 182 n., 221 n.
  Euripidis Tragoediæ XX (ed. Barnes), 55, 108
  Hecuba, 58
  Hippolytus, 191, 193, 194
  Iphigenia in Aulide, 143, 182, 188
  Iphigenia in Tauris, 188, 191, 193
  Medea, 43
  Prælectio in Euripidem, 143
  Supplices, 221
Eutropius, 26
Evadne, 221
Evangelical Magazine & Missionary Chronicle, The, 71 n.
Evangelical Register, The, 59 n.
Exchange, The Royal, 23
Exeter 'Change, 55
Exley, Thomas, 192

Fast and Humiliation, General, 226

Fawkes, Guy, 175 n.
Ferrier, Susan Edmondstone:
  Destiny, 56, 57
  The Inheritance, 56
Fielding, Henry, *Tom Jones*, 31
Footnotes, Use of, xxviii
Foreign words and phrases, Translation of, xxviii
Forster, Nathaniel, *Platonis Dialogi V*, 171
Fortunatus, 132
Foxley, xix, 82 n., 233 n.
French, Hannah D., xiv
Frogs and Mice, Battle of the, 169, 184
Frome, 229
Fuller, Andrew, 147 n., 152

Galatians, Epistle to the, 177
Garlike, Dr. William Bennett, 121
Gataker, Thomas, 69
  De Novi Instrumenti Stylo Dissertatio, 69 n.
  Marci Antonini . . . De Rebus Suis, 55, 67
Gay, John, *The Beggar's Opera*, 142 n.
General Fast and Humiliation, Day of, 226
Genlis, Stéphanie Félicité, Comtesse de, *Tales of the Castle*, 220
Gent, xxxviii, 30, 46, 155, 166, 177, 195
George IV, King, 120 n.
Gibbons, Lady, 96 n., 159
Gibbons, Charlotte, 34
Gibbons, Eliza, **65**, 70, 71, 80, 84, 91, 92, 98, 106, 107, 108, 109, 116, 118, 124 f., 128, 129, 143, 147, 150, 155, 157, 159, 160, 163, 170, 298, 300
Gibbons, Emily, 34
Gibbons, Sir John, 2, 9, 34 n., 65 n., 96 n., 159
Gibbons, Joseph, 96 n.
Gibbons, Richard, 96 n.
Gibraltar, Straits of, 151
Giles, Mrs. Eliza. *See* Cliffe, Eliza Wilhelmina (later Giles)
Gipps, Rev. Henry, 219
Glasco, Miss, **66**, 74, 75, 83, 87, 167, 174, 182, 186, 194, 195, 197, 230
Gloucester, xix, 34, 41 n., 129 n., 325, 337
Gloucester Journal, 75 n., 133 n.
Goethe, Johann Wolfgang von, *Die Leiden des jungen Werthers*, 55
Goldoni, Carlo, 110, 111, 112, 119
Goldsmith, Oliver, 138
  "Elegy on . . . Mary Blaize, An," 20 n.

Deserted Village, The, 197 n.
Vicar of Wakefield, The, 4 n.
Goodrich Court, 16 n.
Gordan, John D., xiii
Graham, Selina, 236
Graham-Clarke. *See* Clarke, Graham-
Graham's Magazine, 316 n.
Gray, Thomas, 78, 276
  Ode on a Distant Prospect of Eton College, 79 n.
  Odes by Mr. Gray, 91 n., 137 n.
Gregory. *See* Nazianzen, St. Gregory
Gregory of Nyssa, St., 113, 296
Grey, Charles, 2nd Earl Grey, 9 n., 34 n., 152 f., 291, 305
Griffith, Mrs. Charlotte, 3 n., 8, **20**, 35, 50, 66, 67, 74, 116, 131, 134, 141, 156 n., 157
Griffith, Thomas, 20 n.
Guggenheim Memorial Foundation, John Simon, xiii

Hailes, Berrington, 95, 335
Hamilton, Mrs. Elizabeth, *Memoirs of Modern Philosophers*, 31
Hamlet, 102, 165 n.
Hampstead, 52 n., 58 n.
Hanford, Mrs. C., **57**, 235, 238 n., 239
Hanford, Fanny, 238
Harlowe, Clarissa, 127
Harper's Monthly Magazine, xxi n.
Harris, Mr. and Mrs. Godfrey, xiii
Harris, James, *Works*, 163
Harrowby, Lord, 293
Hastings, 34, 109, 172 n.
Hatchard, John, **221**, 223, 227, 230, 299
Heard, Miss, **14**, 18, 19, 24, 25, 30, 160, 212, 224
  The Shipwreck of the Dryad, 14
Hebrews, Epistle to the, 282
Hecuba, 58
Helena, Grand Duchess, 133, 134
Helicon, 87
Heliodorus, 203
Hellman, George S., "Some Unpublished Papers of Robert and Elizabeth Barrett Browning," xxi n.
Henry V, 18 n., 89 n.
Hereford, 119 n., 139 n., 142 n., 170 n., 175, 219 n., 233 n., 325, 327, 337, 338
Hereford, Bishop of, 176 n., 183 n., 288-290

Hereford Assizes, 75
Hereford City Library, xiv, 19 n.
Hereford Music Meeting, 129
Hereford Journal, 3 n., 11 n., 12 n., 17, 40 n., 75 n., 151 n., 219 n., 288, 290 n.
Herefordshire Beacon, 134 n., 135
Herodotus (trans. Godley), xlvi, 38 n.
Hesiod, 304
Hewlett, Dorothy, xiv
Heyne, Christian Gottlob:
  Homeri Carmina, 112, 136
  Pindari Carmina, 28, 33
Higgins, Rev. Joseph, xvi, 185
Hill, Mrs. Charles, 135 n., 152, 156
Hill, Rev. Charles, 135 n., 152 n.
Hinton, John Howard, 152
Hippolytus, 191, 193, 194
H. M., Miss. *See* Mushet, Henrietta
Hockin, Rev. John Pearce, 185, 219, 334
Hogg, Rt. Hon. Quintin, xiv, 111 n.
Holbrook, James, 323, 325
Holstein, Anne Louise, Comtesse de Staël-, *Corinne*, 220 f.
Holwell, William, *Selecti Dionysii*, 94
Homer, xvii, xviii, 18, 43, 50, 54, 61, 82, 92, 127, 136, 158, 187 n., 273, 277, 303
  Batrachomyomachia, 169 n.
  Homeri Carmina (ed. Heyne), 112, 136
  Homeri . . . Opera (ed. Wolf), 53, 56, 57 f., 59 f., 62, 78, 112, 139, 280, 303
  Iliad, 303, 304
  Odyssey, 303
Honan, Park, xiii
Hood, Thomas, 235
Hooker, Richard, *A Learned Discourse of Justification*, 177
Hope End:
  present owner, xiv
  Moulton-Barrett purchase of, xv, xxxv
  rebuilding of, xv f.
  mortgagees foreclose on, xxii
  Moulton-Barretts leave, xxiv, xli, 323
  inspected by possible purchasers, 10, 16, 21, 94, 100 f., 285
  advertised for sale, 11, 16, 17, 35, 60, 75
  auction of crops, 40, 44, 121 n.
  auction of estate, 90, 101, 103, 323
  the Walls visit, 99, 121 n., 283 f.
  value of estate, 285
  Moulton-Barretts retain woodland, 323
  description of house, 327-329
  rates levied on, 333

Hope End Household, xxxv-xxxviii
Hope End Sale Catalogue, xvi, xxx, 323-338
Horace, xvii, 110, 142 n., 276
  First Satire . . . Imitated, The, 100 n.
  Horace: Satires, Epistles and Ars Poetica (trans. Fairclough), xlvi, 14 n., 72 n., 79 n., 105 n., 173 n.
  Horace: The Odes and Epodes (trans. Bennett), xlvi, 184 n.
Horne, Richard Hengist, xxiii
  Letters of Elizabeth Barrett Browning Addressed to . . . Horne, xviii n., xix n., xxiii n., xlvi
Horne, Thomas Hartwell, *An Introduction to . . . the Holy Scriptures*, 22
"Hornyold Arms, The," 114 n.
"Horse and Jockey, The," 195
Horsley, Dr. Samuel, 110 f.
Horton, Clifford E., xiv
Houghton, Arthur A., Jr., xv n.
Hugo, Victor, 54
Hume, David, 278
Hunt, Henry, 293
Huntington Library, The Henry E., xiv, xx n., xlvi, 273, 286, 311 n., 313 n., 314 n., 316 n., 319 n.
Hurd, Miss. *See* Heard, Miss
Hyperion, 93

Ignatius, St., 148
Illinois, University of, xiv
Iphigenia in Aulide, 143, 182, 188
Iphigenia in Tauris, 188, 191, 193
Ireland, 13 n., 208, 238
Irving, Mrs. Edward, 294
Irving, Rev. Edward, 190 n., 201 n., 203, 281, 293, 294, 295, 298
Isaiah, Book of, 143
Isocrates, 119, 188, 292
  "Ad Demonicum," 95
  Orationes et Epistolæ (ed. Wolf), 55, 108
  "Panegyricus," 94, 95, 102, 103, 137

Jackson, Richard, 8
Jago, Mrs. *See* Bordman, Eleanor Page
Jamaica, xxii, xxxv, xxxvi, xxxvii, 12, 18 n., 64, 111 n., 221, 282
James. *See* Clarke, James Altham Graham-
James, Rev. John Angell, 59, 61, 63
Jane (the Boyds' maid), 187, 195
Jarvis, Clarke, 202
Jean-Jacques. *See* Rousseau, Jean-Jacques

Jefferson, Mr., 125, 127, 135

Jewel, John, Bp. of Salisbury, *Apologia Ecclesiæ Anglicanæ*, 89, 96, 97

Jewish Expositor, xx

John, Gospel According to St., 88 n., 123, 140, 230, 234
   Nonnus's *Paraphrase*, 226 f., 230, 232 n.

Johnstone, Capt. John, 3 n., 32 n., 190, 333

Jones, Mrs. Augusta E. (*née* Biddulph), 55 n., 181

Jones, Mrs. G., 55

Judges, Book of, 12 n.

Julianus, Flavius Claudius, Emperor, 140, 153, 173, 179 f., 186, 240

Jupiter, 102, 113

Kearneys, The, xvi

Keats, John, 85, 93, 101, 283
   Adonais, 138
   Endymion, 94
   "Hyperion," 93
   Lamia . . . and Other Poems, 93

Kehama, 165

Kelley, Mrs. Marjorie M., xiii

Kelley, Mrs. Velma Prince, xiii

Kelley, Dr. Warren R., xiii

Kelley, Dr. William D., xiii

Kendrick, William, 5, 16, 37, 159, 331, 335

Kenrick. *See* Kendrick, William

Kentish Gazette, 178 n., 190 n.

Kenyon, Frederic G., *Letters of Elizabeth Barrett Browning*, xxiv n., xlvi, 210 n.

Kidd, Thomas, 99, 107 f., 112, 285

Kinnersley Castle, 232, 233 n., 305

Klopstock, Gottlieb F., *Der Messias*, 55

Knibb, James, 22, 23, 28

Knight, Payne, 68, 303

Knowles, The, 32

Knowles, Lady (*née* Charlotte Johnstone), xx, 5 n., 32, 190 n.

Knowles, Adm. Sir Charles, xx, 5 n., 32 n.

Knowles, Charlotte Laura, 5

Knowles, Francis C., 5, 80, 125, 287 f.

Lafontaine, August H. J., *Die Familie von Halden*, 31

Lagado, 279

Lamartine, Alphonse M. L. de, 48, 124
   Dernier Chant . . . d'Harold, Le, 54
   Harmonies, 136, 137, 138

Méditations, 35, 64, 136 n.
   "Milly, ou la Terre Natale," 138
   "Tombeau d'une Mère, Le," 138

Lamb, Charles, *Prince Dorus*, 75 n.

Lambert, Henry, xv n., 8 n., 20 n.

Lamentations, Book of, 178 n.

Landis, Paul, *Letters of the Brownings to George Barrett. See* E.B.B., Works by and about

Landon, Letitia E. (later Maclean), 50

Lane, John, xxxviii, 10, 11, 21 f., 60, 87, 94, 121, 187, 283, 285, 332, 337

Lang, Cecil Y., xiii

Last, G. H., xxiii

Last Man, The, 79, 81, 82, 83, 86

Latin, E.B.B.'s use of pseudo-, xxviii

Ledbury, xv, *et passim*

Ledbury, Hints of, 100 n.

Leila, 129, 214

Lely, Sir Peter, 185

Leopold, Prince, 280

Literary Beacon, The, 120 n.

Literary Souvenir, The, 50

Lloyd, Mrs. Elizabeth, xiii

Lobeira, Vasco, 164 n.

Locke, John, 277

London, xi, xxii, xxiv, *et passim*

London, Old and New, 55 n.

London Encyclopædia, The, 159

Londonderry, 3rd Marquess of, 291, 293
   Narrative of the War in Germany and France, 146

Lords, House of, 30, 47, 146 n., 151, 152, 156, 235 n., 287, 291

Loudon, John Claudius, xvi

Lowry, Wilson, 1 n.

Lowth, Rev. William, 110 f.

Lucan (Marcus Annaeus Lucanus), 27

Lucian, 206

Lucretius, 297, 319

Luke, Gospel According to St., 139, 143, 238

Lytton, Edward George Bulwer-, 187 n.

Macbeth, 2, 226 n.

Macbeth, Lady, 63

McCarthy, Barbara P., 311 n.
   Elizabeth Barrett to Mr. Boyd. See E.B.B., Works by and about

M'Ghee, Robert James, 201

McNeile, Hugh, 294

McSwiney, Daniel, xvii

Maddox, Mary, 40, 41, 42, 79, 81, 82, 130, 131, 132, 195, 230, 231
Mainstone Court, 32 n., 190 n.
Malvern, xvi, *et passim*
Malvern Public Library, viii, xiv, 62
Malvern, A Description of, 47 n., 121 n.
Malvern, A Guide to, 61 n.
Malvern Descriptive and Historical, Letters on, 88 n.
Mann, Phyllis G., xiii
Marathon, Staff of, 166
Marcle, Little, 171 n., 289
Marcle, Much, 139 n., 171 n.
Margaret, Lady. *See* Cocks, Lady Margaret
Marginal line, Use of, xxx
Marie de France, 167
Marius, Caius, 273
Marizet, Mr. de, **110**, 120, 124, 130
Marmontel, J. F., *Bergère des Alpes*, 186
Marriages, 1 n., 5, 80, 217 n.
Marshall, Miss, 53
Martin, Miss, 235
Martin, The Misses, 166
Martin, Lady Anne Holland-, xiii
Martin, James, 35, 39, 41, 49, 51, 56, 60, 74, 75, 78, 92, 106, 110, 120, 130, 137, 139, 142, 157, 166, 208, 299, 300 f., 335
  Letter to the Bp. of Hereford, 176 n., 183, 288-290
Martin, Mrs. Julia (*née* Vignoles), xxiv, 32, 33, 35, 37, 39, 41, 45, 46, 49, 51, 57, 60, 63, 65, 73, 74, 78, 79, 81, 82, 85, 86, 92, 96, 120, 124, 127, 135, 136, 137, 138, 139, 142, 152, 155, 167, 168, 169, 172, 181, 182, 210 n., 213, 228, 232, 238, 291
Martins, The, xiii, xix, 39, 51, 82, 100, 104, 106, 110, 119, 138, 155, 171
Mathon, xix, 29, 32, 50, 51, 110, 119, 126, 149, 184, 185 n., 188, 193, 196, 229, 232, 236, 241
Mathon House, 29 n.
Mathon Lodge, 184
Matthew, Gospel According to, 45 n., 177
Mayer, S. R. Townshend, *Letters of Elizabeth Barrett Browning Addressed to . . . Horne. See* E.B.B., Works by and about
Meleager, 98
Melindore, 77
Melton House, 121 n.
Merchant of Venice, 202 n.

Mericks, The. *See* Meyricks, The
Methodist Magazine, The, 192, 194, 210, 298 n., 299
Methodists, 6 n., 8, 73 n., 201 n.
Meyrick, Dr. Samuel Rush, 16 n.
Meyricks, The, 16, 21
Migne, J. P., *Patrologiæ Cursus Completus*, xlvii, 4 n., 26 n.
Miller, Betty, *Elizabeth Barrett to Miss Mitford*, xxii n., xlvi
Milo, **133**, 141
Milton, John, 297
  Comus, 17 n.
  "L'Allegro," 56 n.
  Paradise Lost, 134 n., 137 n.
  Samson Agonistes, 133
Minny. *See* Robinson, Mrs. Mary
Mitford, Mary Russell, 207 n.
  Elizabeth Barrett to Miss Mitford, xxii n.
Moens, Mr., 131, 139
Mogg, Edward, *Paterson's Roads*, 6 n.
Molière, 181
Money, Eugenia, 139
Money, Col. James, 3 n.
Money, Rev. Kyrle Ernle, 139 n.
Moneys, The, 139, 171 n.
Montagu, Lady Anne, xiii
Moore, Thomas, 116 n., 175 n., 182
  Letters and Journals of Lord Byron, 74, 85, 164 n.
  Memoirs, Journal, and Correspondence, 182 n.
  National Airs, 226 n.
Moschus, 98
Moses, 282, 298
Mother Goose, 151
Moulton, Mrs. Elizabeth Barrett, xxi, 5 n., 16 n., 48 n., 100, 207 n.
Moulton, Sarah Goodin Barrett ("Pinkie"), xxxv
Moulton-Barrett. *See* Barrett, Moulton-
Munchausen, Baron, xxix, 171
Murray, Sir John, xiii
Murray, John Grey, xiv
Mushet, David, 187 n.
Mushet, Henrietta (later Roberts), xxx, 187, 192, 193, 194, 196, 198, 199, 202, 203, 206 n., 209, 210, 211, 212, 214, 216, 218, 224, 225, 228, 229, 230, 232, 234, 236 n., 237, 299, 302, 306, 307
Mushet, Margaret, 232, 237, 239, 306, 307

Nazianzen, St. Gregory, 91, 123, 132, 162, 164, 176, 188, 201, 203, 210 n., 234, 286, 295 f., 298, 299, 300, 306
  "Adversus Julianum Imperatorem," 140, 153, 173, 179 f., 186, 240
  "Apologeticus," 132, 140, 187 f., 190, 292
  "De Filio," 179 n., 212
  "In Christi Nativitatem," 209 f., 211, 215, 306
  "In Laudem Basilii Magni," 43, 179 n.
  "In Laudem Cæsarii," 43
  "In Laudem Patris Sui Mortui," 168, 203
  "In Novam Dominicam," 179 n.
  "In Sanctum Pascha," 153, 183, 218
  Opera Omnia (Benedictine edn.), 132 f.
  Opera Omnia (ed. de Billy), xlvi, xlvii, 43 n., 97 n., 99 n., 105 n., 113 n., 117 n., 132 n., 168 n., 183 n., 209 n., 211 n., 215 n., 240 n.
  Poems, 97, 105, 113, 117, 123, 128, 234 n., 240
  Select Passages, 26 n., 43 f., 168 n.
  Select Poems, 105 n., 234 n.
New Monthly Magazine, The, xviii, 187, 275 n.
New York Public Library, xiv, xxxiv
Newcastle, 176
Newent, 6, 206 n.
Newland, 155 n.
Newton, Sir Isaac, 276
Nisbet, James, 213, 293 f., 299, 301
Nonnus, 303
  Paraphrasis Evangelii S. Johannis, 226 f., 230, 232, 234
Normanby, Lord, *Matilda*, 220 n.
North, John, *Platonis . . . Dialogi Selecti*, 171
Notes & Queries, 311 n.
Nyssa, St. Gregory of, 113, 296

Obliterations, Treatment of, xxix
O'Connell, Daniel, 82, 173, 293
Œdipus Colonœus, 43
Old Colwall, xiii, xix, 39 n., 49, 51, 55, 69, 74, 83, 110, 130, 155, 157, 176, 181, 182, 183, 208, 228, 238, 290, 334, 335
"Olympic Odes." *See* Pindar
Onslow, Ven. Richard Francis, 206 n., 207
Onslows, The, 206, 220
Orestes, 206

Origen, 115
Osuna, 90
Othello, 112 n.
Overbury, 166
Ovid, xvii
Oxford English Dictionary, xxvii, 30 n., 38 n.

Paganini, Nicolo, 28, 30, 79, 273-275, 277
Paris, 139
Parker, N. H., xiv
Parliament. *See* Commons, House of Lords, House of Reform, Parliamentary
Parliamentary Companion, Dod's, 186 n.
Paschal Sunday, Oration on. *See* Nazianzen, St. Gregory, "In Sanctum Pascha"
Paul, St., 65, 148
Peel, Sir Robert, 111 n.
Pegasus, xvii
Penshurst, 1st Baron, 175 n.
Persœ, 43
Petrarch (Francesco Petrarca), 86
Petty France, 96, 334
Peyton, Charles William, 141
Peyton, Charlotte (?), **20**, 50, 56, 63, 74, 151, 156, 157, 158, 182, 186
Peyton, Charlotte Lea, 134
Peyton, Mrs. Eliza (*née* Griffith), **3**, 28, 29, 35, 66, 173
Peyton, Eliza Berry, 141, 144
Peyton, Elizabeth Rosetta, 141
Peyton, Frances Maria, 144
Peyton, Nicholson, 3 n., 20 n., 156, 334, 335
Peyton, Nicholson Julius, 74
Peyton, Reynolds, 56
Peyton, Thomas Griffith, 56
Peytons, The, xiii, xix, 8 n., 74 n., 127, 143, 144, 174, 206, 208, 239, 240
Phillips, Mrs., 57
Phillips, Thomas, *The Study of Sacred Literature*, 185 f., 189 f.
Philosophical Society of America, xiii
Pierpont Morgan Library, xiv, xviii n., xlvii, 316 n.
Pilkington, George, 201
Pindar (Pindaros), 35, 36, 37, 38, 40, 50, 207, 220, 229, 233, 236, 237, 238, 239, 299, 307
  Pindari Carmina (ed. Heyne), 28, 33
Pindar, Miss. *See* Pyndar, Mary (?)

Pindar, Mr. *See* Pyndar, Rev. Reginald
Pindar, Mrs. *See* Pyndar, Mrs.
Pindars, The. *See* Pyndars, The
Plato, xvii, xix, 94, 97, 102, 235, 276, 277
  "Alcibiades Secundus," 171, 176, 177
  "De Legibus," 171, 172, 174, 175
  Dialogi Selecti (ed. North), 171
  Dialogi V (ed. Forster), 171
Plutarch, 16, 201, 291
  Moralia (trans. Babbitt), xlvii, 41 n.
PMLA. *See* Weaver, Bennett
Pocock, Emma, 5 n., 80
Pocock, Sir George, 5 n.
Poole, 288
Pope, Alexander, xviii, xix, 100 n.
Popular Superstitions, 54 n.
Porson, Richard, 70
  Æschyli Tragœdiæ Septem, 15 f.
  Prælectio in Euripidem, 143
Porsonia, 70, 71, 105, 128, 140, 150, 166
Portsmouth, 109
Portus, Franciscus, *Synesii . . . Hymni*,
  234 n., 306
Potter, John Philips, *Essays*, 65
Prayer, Book of Common, 208 n.
Preace, Mr., 306
Preston Court, 210 n.
Price, Caroline, 82, 90, 100, 142, 233
Price, Sir Robert, 142, 233 n.
Price, Sir Uvedale, xix, 82 n., 142 n., 168,
  212
  Dialogue on . . . the Picturesque, 68
  *Essay on the Modern Pronunciation of
    the Greek and Latin Languages*, xx
Priory, The, 47 n.
Probyn, Ven. John, 207, 292
Procrustes, 105, 129, 136
Prometheus Bound. See E.B.B., Works by
Prometheus Vinctus. See Æschylus
Provenance of Diary, xxxiii
Proverbs, Book of, 106 n., 221 n.
Psalms, Book of, 12 n., 88 n., 131 n., 175,
  223 n.
"Psychoanalytical Observations," xxxix ff.
Pulpit, The, 207, 298
Punctuation, E.B.B.'s use of, xxvii
Pyndar, Mrs., 47
Pyndar, Mary (?), 220
Pyndar, Rev. Reginald, **45 n.**, 47, 186
Pyndars, The, 45, 195
Pythian fury, 109, 294
"Pythian Odes." *See* Pindar

Quarterly Review, The, 181, 291

Radcliffe, Mrs. Ann, 51, 54
  The Mysteries of Udolpho, 51, 54, 56,
  204 n.
Raspe, Rudolf Erich, *Baron Munchausen's
  Narrative*, 171 n.
Ray, Gordon N., xiii
Reader's Encyclopedia, The, xlvii, 112 n.,
  132 n., 133 n.
Rebecque, Benjamin C. de, *Adolphe*, 204
Redemption, A Defence of Particular,
  146 f., 151, 152, 153
Redmarley D'Abitot, xix, 8, 142 n.
Reece, Rev. George, 185
Reece, Dr. Richard, 185 n.
Reform, Parliamentary, 3, 9, 30, 34, 47,
  117, 146 n., 151, 152 f., 156, 161 n.,
  175, 186, 235, 281, 287 f., 291, 293, 305
Reid, Mr., 5, 11, 60, 325, 335, 338
Reigate, 47, 170 n.
Revelations, Book of, 131 n., 219 n.
Reynolds, Sir Joshua, *Seven Discourses*,
  60, 93, 96
Ricardo, Mrs. Harriet (*née* Mallory), 220
Ricardo, Osman, 220 n.
Richardson, Samuel:
  Clarissa, 127 n.
  Pamela, 111
Rickards, Thomas, 210
Rivinus, Andreas, *Anthologia*, 55, 113
Roberts, Mr., 236
Roberts, Rev. George, 187 n., 236 n.
Robinson, Mrs. Mary, ("Minny"), xxxvii,
  1, 28, 33, 35, 52, 54, 60, 69, 74, 116,
  119, 132, 159, 206, 290
Rogers, Neville, xiv
Romans, Epistle to the, 98 f., 103 n., 119,
  121, 122, 123, 125, 128, 130, 133, 147,
  148, 149, 152 n., 153
Romeo, 307
Roper-Curzon. *See* Curzon, Roper-
Ross-on-Wye, 16
Rousseau, Jean-Jacques, 20, 81
Ruby Cottage (The Ruby), xiii, xxi, xxii,
  xxiii, xxx, **7**, *et passim*
Rushton, William, *A Defence of Particular
  Redemption*, **146 f.**, 151, 152, 153
Russell, Lord John, 34
  *Memoirs, Journal, and Correspondence
    of Thomas Moore*, 182 n.
Ryde, I. o. W., 108 n.

St. Aubert, Emily, 204
St. Leonard's, 172
St. Marylebone Public Library, xiv
Salamanca, 90
Sappho, 142
Saturn, 93
Saunders, Mr., 177
Saunders, Mrs. Ann, xiv
Schedule A, 161
Scheherazade, Princess, xxix, 162
Scholefield, James, *Æschylus*, **219**, 223, 226, 227, 228, 229, 231, 240, 302
Schütz, Christian G., *Aeschyli Tragoediae Septem*, 230
Scott, Rev. Thomas, 110 f.
Selwyn, Congreve, 28 n., 170
Selwyn, Mrs. Congreve, 28, 170
Septuagint, The, 145 f., 162
Serena, 115
Severus, Lucius Septimus, 67
Sévigné, Mme. de, 202
Shaftesbury, 80 n., 287
Shakespeare, William, 43, 276. *See also play titles*
Shelley, Mrs. Mary Wollstonecraft:
    Frankenstein, 83
    The Last Man, 79, 81, 82, 83, 86
Shelley, Percy Bysshe, 85, 93, 138, 140
    Adonais, 138
    Posthumous Poems, 158 n.
    Queen Mab, 138
    The Revolt of Islam, 102
Sherwood, J. F. W., xiv
Sherwood, Mrs. Mary M., *Roxobel*, 184
Shipend House, 29 n.
Sibthorp, Rev. Richard Waldo, 108
Sidmouth, xxiv, xxxv
Sill, Rev. John Parkinson, 185
Simpson, J., *Epicteti Manuale*, 55
Sinbad, 171
Sisera, 12
Smith, Baron, 174
Smith, Mrs. Charlotte, *The Young Philosopher*, 31
Smith, Mrs. Mary A. (*née* Clarke), xxv, 217
Smith, Elder & Co., xxxiv n.
Smythe, Percy Clinton Sidney, Viscount Strangford and Baron Penshurst, 174 f.
Socinians, The, 71, 113
Socrates, 276
Somers, Anne, Lady (*née* Pole-Carew), 170, 185

Somers, Earl. *See* Cocks, John Somers, 1st Earl Somers
Somers, Lord (Charles Cocks), 170 n.
Somers, Margaret, Countess, 41 n.
Sophocles, 43, 108, 143 n., 229
    Œdipus Colonœus, 43
Sotheby, Wilkinson & Hodge, xxiii, xxxiv n., xlvii. *See also Browning Collections*
South Lodge, 11 n., 16, 59
Southall, Mary, *A Description of Malvern*, 47 n., 121 n.
Southey, Robert:
    Amadis of Gaul, 164 f.
    Thalaba the Destroyer, 120
    The Curse of Kehama, 165
Spelling irregularities, xxvi f., 265-269
Spenser, Edmund, 102
Spowers, G., 52, 58, 59, 61, 62, 105, 279
Stanwell Place, 2 n., 65 n., 96 n., 109, 161
Stark Library, Miriam Lutcher, 275 n.
Steers, Frances, xiv, 4, 7, 10, 13, 14, 21, 23, 25 f., 39, 44, 47, 48, 54, 85, 92, 93, 140, 153, 158, 161, 189, 191 f., 195, 241
Steers's Hotel, 205
Stentor, 186
Stewart, Dugald, 276
Stewart, John, *The Resurrection*, 14
Stonebridge, A. J. D., xiv
Strangford, 6th Viscount, 175 n.
Sun, The, 11, 75 n.
Sunderland, 176, 180 n.
Supplices (Æschylus), 194, 202, 228, 231
Supplices (Euripides), 221
Synesius, 234, 235, 237, 238, 306, 307
    Hymni vario, 234
    Select Poems, 105 n., 234 n.
Szladits, Dr. Lola L., xiv

Taylor, Luke, 3
Tempest, Sir Henry Vane, 8 n.
Tempest, The, 112 n.
Tent Room, 283
Terence (Publius Terentius Afer), 78
Testy and Sensitive, 20, 292
Texas, University of, 275 n.
Textual notes, xxix, 243-265
Teynham, 16th Baron, 4 n.
Teynham, 17th Baron, 205 n.
Thalaba, 120
Thaumaturgus, St. Gregory, 192 n.
Theocritus, 304
Theophorus, St. Ignatius, 148

Theophrastus, *Ethical Characters*, 92, 94, 95, 96, 101, 102
Theophylact, 138
Thessalonians, Epistle to the, 73 n., 282
Times, The, 1 n., 9, 22 n., 30 n., 34 n., 36, 95 n., 105, 106, 107 n., 111, 119 n., 120 n., 130, 146 n., 151 n., 152, 164, 176 n., 180 n., 204, 221 n., 226 n., 235 n., 273 n., 286, 288, 290, 297, 298, 305, 311 n., 319 n.
Timothy, Epistle to, 65 n.
Titus, Flavius Sabinus Vespasianus, 74 n., 119
Tongues, The unknown, **190**, 201, 207 n., 292, 293 f., 300
Tories, Epigram on the, 105, 106, 111
Torquay, xxiv, xxxvi
Trajan (Marcus Ulpius Trajanus), 148 n.
Trant, Dominick, 80 f., 82 f., 100, 121, 129, 130, 132, 133 f., 283, 286 f., 288
Trant, Henry, **11**, 80, 132, 210
Trant, James, 16 n.
Trant, Mrs. Mary (*née* Barrett), xx, 11 n., **16**, 25, 27, 36, 37, 53, 57, 80, 83, 99, 129, 132, 133, 163, 191, 214, 217, 219, 226, 228, 231, 232
Trants, The, 82
Treherne, John, xxxviii, 332, 337
Treherne, William ("Billy"), xxxviii, 37, 70, 113, 133, 158, 160
Turkish Room, 167
Twelfth Night, 117 n., 165 n.
Typhon, 222

Udolpho, Mysteries of, 51, 54, 56, 204 n.
Underdown, 55 n.
Underscoring, E.B.B.'s use of, xxviii
Uniack, Miss, 13
Unknown Tongues, The, **190**, 201, 207 n., 292, 293 f., 300
Upper Hall, 45 n., 186 n.

Valpy, Abraham John, **216** f., 218, 301
Van Dyck, Sir Anthony, 185
Vane, Charles William, 3rd Marquess of Londonderry, 291, 293
  Narrative of the War in Germany and France, 146
Victoria, Queen, xvi
Virgil, xvii, 61, 92, 276
  Aeneid, 31 n., 38 n.
  Georgics, 29 n.

Virgil (trans. Fairclough), xlvii, 31 n.
Vocabolario Italiano-Latina . . . , 92

Waddington, Mrs. Jane (*née* Cocks, later Countess Somers), 186 n.
Wakefield, Gilbert, Βιωνος και Μοσχου, 98
Walker, Mr., 31
Wall, Millicent, **15**, 59, 99, 100, 109, 110, 114, 116, 118, 124, 183, 283, 284, 285
Walls, The, 99, 101, 108, 205, 283, 285
Walm's Well, 88
Ward, Mr., 180, 333
Warren, Robert, xliii, 3, 7, 9
Watkins, Alfred, "Elizabeth Barrett and Hope End," xv n.
Watson, Mr. G., 170 n.
Watson, Mrs. G., 170, 197
Watts, Rev. James, 33
Watts, The, 150
Weaver, Bennett, "Twenty Unpublished Letters . . . ," xlvii, 139 n., 273, 286
Webb, Mr., 156
Webb, Mrs., 220
Webb, Richard, 87 n.
Webb, Thomas, 87 n.
Webbs, The, 87
Well House, 4 n., 115
Wellesley College Library, xiv, xx n., xxi n., xxii n., xlvii, 49 n., 93 n., 100 n., 126 n., 207 n., 275, 279, 281, 283, 284, 285, 287, 290, 292, 293, 295, 298, 300, 301, 302, 303, 304, 305, 306, 307, 308
  The Wellesley *Gregory*, xlvii, 43 n., 99 n., 132 n., 173 n., 179 n., 183 n., 187 n., 209 n., 211 n., 240 n.
Wellington Heath, 73, 108, 201, 333
Wesley, John, 154
  Predestination Calmly Considered, 190, 192, 294
Wesleyan-Methodist Magazine, 8 n.
Wesleyans, The, 6 n., 8, 9 n., 10, 73 n., 201 n.
West, Col. James Dawson, 149, 184
Westminster Review, The, 305
Whately, Dr. Richard, 65, 291
  Education in Ireland . . . , 201
  The Errors of Romanism, 201 n.
Wheatley, Dr. *See* Whately, Dr. Richard
Wheatly, Dr. *See* Whately, Dr. Richard
Whitby, Dr. Daniel, 110 f.
Whyche, The. *See* Wyche, The
Wight, Isle of, 108 f., 192

Diary by E.B.B.

William IV, King, 30 n., 120, 129 n., 152, 287, 293, 305
Willis, Dr., 291
Winnings Farm, 117 n.
Wise, Thomas J., xi n., 313 n.
Wither, George, *Fair Virtue*, 79 n.
Wolf, Friedrich A., *Homeri . . . Opera*, 53, 56, 57 f., 59 f., 62, 78, 112, 139, 280 303
Wolf, H., *Isocrates Orationes*, 55, 108
Wood, Rev. John, 59, 98, 118, 148
Woodland Lodge, xxi, 2 n., 15
Woolashill Hall, 57 n., 238 n.
Worcester, xviii, 10, 17, 22 n., 23, 27, 28, 32 n., 35, 36, 45 n., 60, 75, 93, 97 n., 114, 121 n., 129, 138, 149, 152, 163, 170 n., 175, 177, 183, 202, 206 n., 219, 220 n., 241, 283
Worcester Herald, 3 n., 16, 17 n., 35 n., 36 n., 75 n., 149 n., 175 n., 176 n., 184 n., 186 n.

Worcestershire Beacon, The, 6 n.
Wyatt, Thomas, xvi
Wyche, The, 6, *et passim*
Wye, River, **119**, 120, 122
Wynds Point, 134
Wynn, Rev. Thomas, 176, 290

Xenophon, xvii, 18, 50, 54, 82, 100, 188, 292
Xerxes, 37 f., 126

Yale University Library, 313 n.
York, A Letter to His Grace the Archbishop of, 133 n., 136
York, A Second Letter to His Grace the Archbishop of, 216
Yorke, Hon. Mrs., 155
Young, Edward, *The Complaint*, 17 n.

Zenophon. *See* Xenophon
Zeus, 204 n.

DATE DUE

MAY 22 1997			